CAVOUR AND GARIBALDI
1860

CAVOUR

CAVOUR AND GARIBALDI 1860

A STUDY IN POLITICAL CONFLICT

BY

D. MACK SMITH

FELLOW OF PETERHOUSE

CAMBRIDGE

AT THE UNIVERSITY PRESS

1954

KRAUS REPRINT CO.
New York
1968

PUBLISHED BY
THE SYNDICS OF THE CAMBRIDGE UNIVERSITY PRESS
London Office: Bentley House, N.W. I
American Branch: New York
Agents for Canada, India, and Pakistan: Macmillan

L.C. Catalog Card Number 54-3061

First published 1954
Reprinted by permission of the Cambridge University Press
· KRAUS REPRINT CO.
A U.S. Division of Kraus-Thomson Organization Limited

Printed in Germany

To
G. M. *and* JANET TREVELYAN

CONTENTS

Contents

PLATES

END-PAPER

ITALY IN THE SUMMER OF 1860

PREFACE

Among the many people who helped to make this book possible, there are some who should be mentioned by name. Professor Ghisalberti, the president of the Risorgimento Institute at Rome, is the benevolent patron of all who work in this field. Dr Mordini very kindly let an unknown foreign student have the free run of his family papers at Barga. Dr Camerani lent the proofs of his edition of Ricasoli's letters, and Professor Avetta made available the proofs and typescript of the latest volumes prepared by the National Commission on Cavour's correspondence. Without the expert assistance of many librarians and archivists all over Italy, some of the technical difficulties of this particular subject might have been insoluble; and without the kind encouragement and hospitality of many other Italians, the work involved would have been much less enjoyable than it proved to be. I hope these people will recognize themselves, and accept my thanks. I should also like to record my gratitude to the Master and Fellows of Peterhouse for their generosity and forbearance over a number of years; and in particular to Professor Butterfield and Professor Postan, from whom I have learnt, to the best of my ability, all I know about the study and the writing of history. For the skilled and exacting labour of compiling the index, I am greatly indebted to Mr G. V. Carey. And lastly, it was from Dr G. M. Trevelyan that, with so many others, I caught my first enthusiasm for Italy and the *risorgimento*. To him and Mrs Trevelyan this volume is dedicated in admiration and gratitude.

By way of foreword, it may be useful to have a brief statement of what the book is about and why this particular subject was chosen for such detailed treatment. The intention has been to analyse a striking conflict of personalities and principles which arose in 1860 against a background of revolution in Sicily and Naples. At the root of that conflict was the problem of what political system would best suit a liberated Italy, and how to set about achieving it. This problem, in all its various aspects, raised what now seem to have been perhaps the most interesting and important questions in the whole of nineteenth-century Italian history. It was during these decisive months of 1860 in Sicily that the conflict over ends and means entered its sharpest phase, and became most dramatic and most complete.

In its original form this volume was composed five years ago, as the Thirlwall prize essay. It suffered from the grave disability that private citizens have never been allowed free access to the Cavour archives. The greatest of all Cavourian scholars, Adolfo Omodeo, was the latest to fight against this crippling inhibition on scholarship, but he fought in vain. What it meant in practice can best be described by saying that over a quarter of the published documents were known to have been falsified or mutilated by earlier editors, and the suspicion was not wanting that there might sometimes have been an intention to conceal important truths. It therefore seemed undesirable to publish the book in its original form, because an unorthodox interpretation of events would have been insecurely grounded without confirmation from a more reliable text. It was thought better to wait until the reconstituted National Editorial Commission could publish the letters which Cavour wrote about his annexation of southern Italy in 1860. Probably the most important documents relevant to his views on the south are now at last included in the eight or nine volumes covering this period which are already published or ready for publication. It has thus become possible, after an interval, to rewrite the first essay round this new and invaluable source. Although the general conclusions have not had to be modified in the interval, they can now be stated with greater assurance and argued in more detail, and a different emphasis can be placed on the contribution made by Cavour.

The other main sources used may be briefly summarized here. Published diaries for the year 1860 include those of Crispi, Persano and Pallavicino; and published letters for the same year include those of

Mazzini, La Farina, Amari, Nigra, Bargoni and Castelli. The most important collections of unpublished material which have been examined are the private papers of Crispi, Mordini, Depretis, Bertani, Ricasoli, Farini, Cattaneo and Cordova; and also of minor figures in the story like d'Azeglio, Minghetti, Torrearsa, Massari, Sirtori and Visconti-Venosta. The consular and ambassadorial reports of the British and United States representatives in Italy have been used, as have the debates in the Turin parliament, and the official documents still surviving of Garibaldi's government at Palermo and Naples. The files of above three dozen newspapers had to be read. Some miscellaneous information was also found in the more untrustworthy source of personal memoirs, of which there are a great number covering one part or other of the events of this year.

I should not like to close this preface without expressing my thanks to the Syndics and staff of the Cambridge University Press for much valuable help and advice.

D. M. S.

CAMBRIDGE
January 1953

ABBREVIATIONS

For convenience of printing, some abbreviations have been used in footnotes:

ASR	Archivio di Stato, Rome.
AME	Archivio del Ministero degli Esteri, Rome.
MRR	Museo del Risorgimento, Rome.
MRM	Museo del Risorgimento, Milan.
ACM	Archivio Curàtulo.
ABCM	Archivio Bertani-Crispi.
ABM	Archivio Bertani.
AMB	Archivio Mordini, Barga.
ASF	Archivio di Stato, Florence.
BR	Carte Bianchi-Ricasoli.
CF	Carte Farini, Biblioteca Classense, Ravenna.
ASP	Archivio di Stato, Palermo.
ACP	Archivio Crispi.
FT	Biblioteca Fardelliana, Trapani.
PRO	Public Record Office, London.
F.O.	Foreign Office papers.
RP	Russell papers.
CC	*Carteggi di Camillo Cavour* (published).
Lib. del Mezz.	*La liberazione del Mezzogiorno.*
Cavour–Nigra	*Il carteggio Cavour-Nigra.*
Ing.	*Cavour e l' Inghilterra.*

INTRODUCTION

The year 1860 was the *annus mirabilis* of the Italian *risorgimento*. In the space of a few months, Piedmont-Sardinia more than doubled its size, and combined most of central and all of southern Italy. The formerly independent states of Tuscany, Modena and Parma, with the Papal provinces of the Romagna, Umbria and the Marches, and the far larger area covered by the Two Sicilies, all these invoked the sovereignty of the House of Savoy; and early in 1861 the existence of a new kingdom of Italy was officially proclaimed. Few people were more surprised at the success and speed of this achievement than Cavour, its chief architect; and few more disappointed than Mazzini and Garibaldi, the two men who had looked forward to this moment most keenly and who had sacrificed most for its attainment. Here is a paradox which will serve to indicate at the outset that this was a complicated and controversial passage of history.

The complications and controversies are worth examining for their own sake. They are also important for their influence on the type of state Italy became after 1861, and for the fact that they make a small but interesting chapter in the larger history of nationalism. The subject is more accurately studied in particular than in general. In recent years there have been a number of broad surveys written about the national movement in Italy; the need now is not so much for outline histories, as for detailed monographs to test the generally accepted canons of interpretation. There are still too many gaps in our knowledge of what went on underneath the main episodes of this national revolution. Even for the critical conquest of the south in 1860, much is unknown or known only in part. On the straightforward narrative of Garibaldi's victories in Sicily there may be very little to add to what G. M. Trevelyan wrote half a century ago. On the other hand, the internal politics of this civil war in southern Italy have not received nearly as much attention as their interest and importance would warrant.

The following chapters are designed as a study in revolutionary politics during a civil war. They are not concerned with military or diplomatic history except by the way. They leave out of consideration the Bourbons of Naples who lost, and deal only with the nationalists who won. They do not even try to give any detailed chronology of the sequence of events, except where this may seem necessary to explain particular states of mind. The intention is to discover more about some of the main impulses which helped to make events take the course they did; in particular to distinguish the aims of the several revolutionary parties, and the contribution which each made to success. Without interruption during this period there was serious internal conflict among the patriots, and that conflict was even at some periods in the year a necessary constituent in the making of Italy. On occasion, only clashes inside the nationalist camp (principally between the 'party of order' and the 'party of action') can explain the course taken by the revolution. The chief interest therefore reposes, not just in the conscious policy of the various liberal and radical groups, but in the struggle which grew up between them; not that is to say only in pure, but also in applied politics.

The simplest thread running through the political tangle attaches itself to the guerrilla leader Giuseppe Garibaldi. A second thread, far more difficult to follow, will be found in the policy of Count Camillo di Cavour, the Piedmontese prime minister at Turin. These two men represent the two poles of opinion inside the nationalist party. Behind Cavour there was the miscellaneous variety of liberal politicians in Piedmont; behind Garibaldi, the radical democrats who enthusiastically followed him to Palermo and Naples. These radicals must not be confused with the relatively insignificant extreme Left of republicans and socialists; just as Cavour's following of liberal-conservatives must likewise be distinguished from the equally inconsiderable extreme Right of reactionary conservatives and clericals. Neither Cavour nor Garibaldi was, strictly speaking, an extremist, although both could be relentlessly uncompromising or wildly unrealistic on occasion. As a background to the struggle between them, there is the indigenous population of Sicily. This was the raw material on which Cavour and Garibaldi had to work in the decisive phase of this revolution. Sicilian public opinion never spoke with a single voice. Nor, it must be remembered, did either of those two main sections of the patriotic party which, for convenience, are called radical and liberal. Generally, however, the broader trends of opinion can be identified, and their interaction upon each other observed.

To concentrate on Sicily and Naples alone, during the short period from April to December 1860, and even then with only a restricted field of vision, might be thought unnecessarily finical. But such a limitation of time and place is designed to make these political conflicts a coherent subject of study. By observing these conflicts as they developed day by day, and going for this purpose to the most detailed sources of evidence, it may be possible to throw some light upon the whole movement for national unification. The invasion of Sicily was Garibaldi's finest and most typical achievement, as that of Umbria was probably Cavour's. This period is thus the most interesting of all for such a study, and the wealth of documentary evidence makes it also the most feasible.

One special interest of these particular months in the south is that, for almost the only time in these formative years, men of distinctly unorthodox political principles held great authority and power. For a short while the radical 'party of action' controlled a dictatorial government, possessed a large army, and enjoyed the prestige of having conquered half the peninsula. This was probably the time when Cavour's genius was most severely taxed; for though foreign politics were less exacting than he had known them before, inside Italy the liberals and radicals were openly attacking each other. Very little has been written about the opposition groups to the Left of Cavour, for there is a tendency to justify the victors and forget the defeated. The radicals themselves were too busy making history to write it; and if they did write, were either too bitter for sound judgement, or else too illiterate to write convincingly and for posterity. This makes it the more instructive to be able to follow some of Cavour's opponents in detail, especially as this was one of the few periods when they were strong, and when there was play for rival theories about the conduct of Italian affairs. One conclusion which emerges upon close examination is that the radical opposition was more moderate, more realistic, and more intelligent than the liberal politicians and historians used to allow.

A further interest is added by the fact that at no other single moment during the *risorgimento* were so many national leaders of every type and hue personally involved in what was happening. Quite apart from Cavour and d'Azeglio, there were as many as ten future prime ministers of Italy who had some part to play in this particular revolution. Seven of them were in southern Italy for some of the time: Crispi and Cairoli in Garibaldi's retinue; Farini, Lanza and Zanardelli in that of Cavour; Depretis and Di Rudinì contriving, or rather attempting with indifferent success, to serve both masters at once. In addition to these, there were Ricasoli and Minghetti who had an important share in the shaping of Cavour's policy as ministers in the north. Finally, there was Rattazzi, a dim figure spinning a tenuous web of conspiracy, who tried to form an alliance between the revolutionary radicals, the 'parliamentary Left' and the court party, to accomplish the defeat of Cavour. The leaders of the various radical groups of course travelled south to be at the scene of action. There was Mazzini himself, with Bertani, Nicotera and Mario who were not far removed from him in their political ideas. There were Cattaneo and Ferrari, the two leading Italian federalists; and Sineo, Asproni and Pallavicino who belonged rather to the 'constitutional opposition'. Other distinguished future ministers of Italy who were more or less actively engaged, either in Palermo or Naples, included Amari, Cordova, Ferrara, De Sanctis, Visconti-Venosta, Mancini, Scialoia and Spaventa. These names by themselves tell in part why the duel between the two principals, Cavour and Garibaldi, was fought on such an elevated plane.

Very briefly, the central theme is as follows. In April 1860 a revolt broke out among Sicilians against the Bourbon government at Naples. This was in the main a local movement against administrative oppression; but incidentally it became tinged with politics, for it had been actively encouraged by the radicals, and was accepted only with some reluctance by the moderate liberals. Then in May the arrival of Garibaldi with his Thousand from the north confirmed and continued this radical inspiration of the revolt. The name of Garibaldi was a guarantee that the battle would be fought for Italy and not just for the local needs of Sicily, but it also represented political ideals very different from those of Cavour. Garibaldi was a great soldier, and the revolution developed with unexpected success beneath his protection and encouragement. In July he marched through to the eastern seaboard of Sicily. In August he crossed over to Calabria. On 7 September he entered Naples, and soon the whole of southern Italy up to the River Volturno was under his radical dictatorship. Later in September he felt strong enough to begin his march on Rome, and even to ask that Cavour be dismissed from the post of prime minister. But then, suddenly, the political direction of the movement changed, and Garibaldi was manoeuvred into a position where he had to surrender. Cavour's troops invaded Naples before the revolt could spread to Rome. On 21 October, Sicily and Naples elected by plebiscite for the merger of all the south into the kingdom governed from Turin by Victor Emanuel. This vote brought the revolution to a close. It represented a notable victory for Cavour, who had dramatically captured the political and military initiative.

As a result the radicals had to wait many years for the partial attainment of their various desires: until 1870 for the realization of Garibaldi's designs on Rome; until 1876 for the victory of Depretis and the Left in parliament; until the turn of the century for recognition of the special economic and social needs of the south; and until after 1946 for the achievement of Mazzini's republican dream and Cattaneo's cherished ideal of regional autonomy. And yet a false picture will be given if it is assumed in advance that, in the year 1860, a monarchic and unitary state was the only conclusion which had any chance of emerging from the revolution. For in fact, although the method of a plebiscite seemed to lead easily enough to the creation of a united kingdom, many people had feared until the last moment that a constituent assembly might meet instead, and that a federalist or a republican solution would be considered.

This alternative of plebiscite or constituent assembly became the issue round which the various political programmes took shape in southern Italy. The victory of the plebiscite marked the success of one set of ideas and one set of men over another. The limitations and incompleteness of this victory, as well as the manner of its achievement, were to be of great importance for the future history of Italy. Not only did they bear directly on the emergence of a 'southern question' in Italian politics, but neither the radicals nor the regionalists were ever quite reconciled to finding the fruit of their labours plucked by other people. The tensions set up between the various regions and political parties were never to be properly resolved. Some of the ablest of Italian politicians were kept for decades in unproductive opposition, and, when at last they were accepted into the ruling élite, were too old to learn the delicate art of responsible government. The southern provinces were also taught by this victory and its aftermath to resent the domination of the 'Piedmontese'—as their new governors from the north were generically termed. Political opposition thus became identified in part with regional opposition, and this in turn with social and religious opposition; for little effort was made to reconcile either the southern peasants or the Church to this sudden triumph of a secular, middle-class state.

Cavour has his place secure among the greatest statesmen and the greatest liberals of any nation. Few historical characters have had such a consistently 'good press' since their death. And yet, as with all historical figures, his true stature will be understood only if he is looked at with a critical eye. Wherever historians can spend longer studying a statesman's reaction to a problem than that statesman once spent on the problem itself, it often occurs that events appear to have happened more unpredictably and with less conscious purpose behind them than had formerly been thought. It also becomes possible to question some of the legends left behind by historical recollection. It will be seen that Cavour was by no means infallible; and his chosen colleagues often fell far short of what the moment required. The kingdom of Italy, which they did so much to create, was one of the most notable achievements of the age, and this gives to these critical months of its formation a particular interest. Nevertheless, in some important respects it was to prove highly unstable; and many Italians agreed that this was due to flaws in its original creation.

For these various reasons it is specially interesting to observe Cavour's political theory and method in response to—and as an initiating force upon—the development of Garibaldi's revolution. And Sicily, which was the centre of that revolution and where the radicals were strongest and most successful, inevitably becomes the centre of attention. It was to public opinion in Sicily that both Cavour and Garibaldi appealed, and a detailed study of this one area may help incidentally to clarify that elusive concept, public opinion, upon which liberals and nationalists so freely (and often illegitimately) relied. In following the course of events in Sicily one is never far from the larger problem of how and why Italy became a united nation.

CHAPTER I

POLITICAL OPINIONS IN SICILY: APRIL–JUNE 1860

The most convenient point to begin a study of the Sicilian revolution is the Palermo rising of 4 April 1860; and the first question which presents itself is, what was in the mind of those Sicilians who then rose and for a full month kept alive a flickering rebellion on their own.

It may be assumed from the start that most thinking people in the island were at one in their dislike of being ruled by the Neapolitan Bourbons. Foreign observers in Palermo were generally agreed that the revolution 'had not its origin in any sudden fit of anger or disappointment, but in a long and deep-rooted animosity on the part of the entire people of Sicily'.[1] Such a situation gave plenty of scope to the active revolutionaries. Any organization there was behind the movement had largely been the work of Mazzini's disciples. For some years now, Giuseppe Mazzini had been looking towards southern Italy as the probable scene of his next revolution, since his influence in the north had been growing ever smaller since Cavour's rival and more moderate programme had won its first great success in 1856. In March 1860 Mazzini's friends, Pilo and Corrao, had therefore set out from Genoa to stir up an insurrection in Sicily. Here they found an excellent field for their activity. The Bourbon government had already had cause to note with dismay how all classes there were becoming familiar with 'popular sovereignty, universal suffrage and other extravagant notions'.[2] Even some of the more conservative Sicilians had lately been asking Cavour how much he would concede to their desire for local autonomy if they managed to revolt and invoke Piedmontese sovereignty; but Cavour gave them little encouragement, and the conservatives proved to be by nature too timid to make good revolutionaries. In general,

[1] 11 May, a note from five British commercial firms addressed to consul Goodwin in Palermo (F.O. 165/134).
[2] 8 March, Castelcicala the governor of Sicily to the minister for Sicilian affairs at Naples (ACP, fasc. 138).

motives were very mixed, and those few people who really knew their minds wanted very different things. One British witness of what was happening remarked on the 'amazing development which the notion of annexation and a single Italian kingdom has acquired within the last six months both in Naples and Sicily'.[1] Another, describing what he had himself seen of the Palermo revolt, wrote as follows:

the letter of the *Times* Correspondent of April 10th contains some errors. No cries were heard in Palermo of 'long live Victoria and Annexation to England'. The cries were 'Victor Emanuel and annexation to Piedmont' everywhere....

The movement was indeed premature and urged on by the police, while the best friends of the country tried to keep it down...from the conviction it would fail....The outbreak was not known to the Liberals until 24 hours before it took place....Not one of the Liberals had anything to do with it. Riso [its leader] belongs to the Mazzinians.[2]

Apparently most Sicilians, whether liberals, conservatives, autonomists, or without positive views on politics, were sufficiently agreed in their dislike of the Bourbons to accept in principle the extreme means of revolution; but it is equally obvious that the lack of organization, the fear and suspicion among different groups of people, and the unwillingness of the 'liberals' to design and lead an actual insurrection, all contributed to inhibit action and leave the field open to the extremists. In the eyes of most Sicilians the rising in Palermo came prematurely, and respectable people looked askance at it. But the radicals, both inside Sicily and outside, were prepared to exploit whatever happened for political ends of their own.

If the initiative chiefly lay with a few Mazzinian intellectuals, who wanted unification of Italy and if possible a republic, the immediate driving force behind the movement came from the uneducated people to whom 'United Italy' must have been a meaningless phrase. This is one of those moments when we catch a glimpse of the *bassa gente*, the *plebaglia*, the masses as distinct from the classes. Sicilians at this level were always verging on starvation, and had little to lose if they took any chance to rebel for a better means of livelihood. They knew nothing of Italy or of republicanism, but they disliked all government on

[1] 30 April, Elliot the British minister in Naples to Lord John Russell (F.O. 70/315/153).   [2] 2 May, Goodwin to Elliot (F.O. 165/134).

principle, and had an especial hatred for government by Neapolitan functionaries who were at once inefficient, cruel, unjust and extortionate. This was why a few political leaders could rouse the common citizens of Palermo in another Sicilian Vespers, and so begin an upsurge which soon became unexpectedly large and complicated. The national movement was not strong, but for a brief while it coincided with a social movement of great strength. As the government was paralysed by the non-cooperation of the leading families in each village, political rebellion joined hands with social revolution and spread from Palermo into the countryside. This in turn brought about the collapse of local authorities all through the island; the police fled for their lives; family feuds and social grievances came out into the open, and society was soon in a state of more or less complete dissolution.

One incidental result of this was to confirm the middle and upper classes in their initial doubts about the desirability of this premature revolution. However much they too had political grievances against the Bourbons, their primary instinct was to restore social order and end the contagious epidemic of land-occupation. Even many of those who called themselves liberals, when faced by a peasants' revolt acted to damp it down rather than fan it further into flame.[1] They also had clearly in their minds the menace of a Bourbon counter-revolution. Several times earlier in the century a popular insurrection had reached this point, but each time the dynasty had won back the ground lost; and this had invariably meant not only political proscription of the liberals, but a 'white terror' against men of property, as the *lazzaroni* and *contadini* were incited by both Church and State to take a bloody revenge. Mindful of what had happened to their ancestors, some even among the more enlightened in 1860 were unwilling to commit themselves until the upshot was clear, until the peasants' revolt had been tamed and the threatening counter-revolution defeated. At the end of April this irresolute attitude aided the Bourbons, just as earlier in the month it had aided the outbreak of insurrection. Passively, and often actively as members of the national guard, many of the liberals assisted the gradual restoration of law and order.

At the beginning of May, when the revolt in Sicily was on the point

[1] D. Mack Smith, 'The Peasants' Revolt of Sicily in 1860', *Studi in onore di Gino Luzzatto*, vol. III, 1950, pp. 208–15.

of being brought under control by the authorities, Garibaldi and his Thousand set out from a point near Genoa on their quixotic journey to aid the rebels. They landed in Sicily on 11 May. Occasionally they met an understandable perplexity on the part of the local peasants, but Garibaldi was able to report on the second day that 'the people have welcomed us with enthusiasm and are joining up in crowds...I hope we shall become an avalanche...I have found the people better even than you said they would be'.[1] On the 'invitation' of one village after another, he proclaimed himself dictator, and then handed over to Francesco Crispi the task of organizing government and countersigning dictatorial decrees. Whenever the country districts had fallen back into a state of apathy and resignation, the news of his coming sufficed almost by itself to rouse them once more.[2] Only in three or four of the bigger towns did people deliberately wait until the volunteers first encountered a regular army in pitched battle.[3] On 27 May Garibaldi convinced most of the waverers when he successfully attacked Palermo. By the end of the month, after astonishing adventures, he thus found himself nominally ruler of all Sicily except the eastern seaboard. By this time Crispi had already appointed governors to all the twenty-four districts of the island; and out of many spontaneously formed local committees and private armies, an improvised system of centralized administration had begun to grow.

Such an extraordinary success with the slenderest of resources is a clear indication that public opinion had little sympathy with the old regime. No doubt many proprietors would have continued to support the Neapolitan government if by so doing they could have been certain of avoiding the devastation brought by social and civil war; but once there was no further possibility of restraining the revolt, Garibaldi became their best hope of law and order. The consensus of feeling against the Bourbons in all social classes and political camps gave to his advance a powerful momentum. Some of the volunteers wrote home that the city of Palermo had given no help to the attackers;[4] but this

---

[1] 13 May, Garibaldi to Bertani (ABM).

[2] 27 May, the intendant of Messina to the minister for Sicilian affairs (ASP, Affari Esteri, busta 1239).   [3] 19 June, *Gazzetta di Catania.*

[4] 29 May, S. Calvino to A. Bargoni (*Memorie di Angelo Bargoni 1829–1901*, ed. Attilio Bargoni, 1911, p. 101).

kind of lament is common among invading armies, and Garibaldi's success is only explicable on the assumption that, in countless unspectacular ways, his advance against the Neapolitans was generally favoured.

People were far less certain when it came to positive wishes for the future. So deep-rooted were the ancient traditions of insular independence that no one dared to advocate publicly a resumption of Bourbon absolutism. What still found some encouragement was the proposal for a mitigation of Bourbon rule through something like a dual monarchy of Naples and Sicily, or an independent Sicily ruled by a Bourbon cadet. But for this to become practicable, King Francesco would probably have had to offer Sicilians their old 1812 constitution at once, and he was not intelligent enough to consider such an escape while there was yet time. 'The people seem to be divided into two primary parties', said a British naval officer in Sicily, 'the larger one having the annexation to Piedmont in view, the smaller and more enlightened party desiring the constitution of 1812 under the present ruler. Since the appearance of Garibaldi on the scene, the hopes of the latter party have evidently diminished.'[1] There were some Sicilians, especially among the aristocracy, who were never very happy at the thought that this dictator from the north, by right of conquest, might claim to impose on them a system alien to their native traditions. But for the moment Garibaldi's provisional government was one 'which the people all acknowledge and obey with pleasure'.[2] It was long since anyone had been able to say so much of any government in Sicily.

United against Naples and temporarily in favour of Garibaldi, Sicilians found it a little harder to agree over a long-term alternative to Neapolitan rule. One can affirm at once—and this is important in view of the accusations upon which Cavour later built his policy—that there was hardly the least glimmer of a republican party in the south:[3] even that arch-republican Mazzini was now working alongside the monarchists towards the common goal of a national state, and had

[1] 18 May, Captain Cochran to Admiral Fanshawe (F.O. 70/325).
[2] 21 May, Commander Marryat to Admiral Mundy (F.O. 70/326).
[3] 8 August, M. Amari to G. P. Vieusseux: 'I have not been able to discover any republican party, even searching for it with a microscope' (*Carteggio di Michele Amari*, ed. A. d'Ancona, vol. III, 1907, p. 205).

declared himself ready to accept the popular wish for a king so long as that king believed in a united nation. There still could be found some Sicilian separatists, but usually their object was only to find a practical method of splitting off from Naples, and most of them were to champion union with Piedmont as soon as Garibaldi's unexpected success made this a more feasible means to their end. If divorce from Naples could be bought only at the price of marriage with Piedmont, some people who would have preferred complete independence were yet prepared to pay that price.[1] The names of the duke of Genoa, the duke of Parma, the count of Syracuse and even of Prince Napoleon were discussed as possible kings of Sicily. But this was idle speculation for Sicily would hardly have been viable as an independent state. Nor did any European state except Piedmont have designs upon her. Reputable Italian scholars still repeat that Great Britain had ambitions to include Sicily in her Empire, but they are careful not to indicate when such an idea entered the head of any British statesman as a practical proposition.

All the obvious facts pointed to Sicily forming some sort of union with Piedmont-Sardinia. Such a union had already existed for a short while after 1713, and had again been canvassed in 1848. If in 1860 it seemed still more of a possibility, this was partly because the northern kingdom in the interim had become more Italian and less French, especially by her recent exchange of Nice and Savoy for Lombardy and Tuscany. Many schemes were now propounded for incorporating Sicily in the old kingdom of Sardinia, and they were to cover everything from unqualified annexation to the grant of more or less complete home rule. Round the alternative of 'annexation' or 'autonomy' there was to grow up an important controversy among those who favoured this Piedmontese connexion.

Cavour's aim soon became that of getting as near to outright annexation of Sicily as he could. At first he had not hoped for anything at all, and he was surprised when Garibaldi's victories suggested that another move towards national unification might at last be practical politics; but he gradually allowed himself to be converted, and ended with the peremptory demand for unqualified surrender by the south. Giuseppe

[1] E.g. Count Amari, cousin of Michele Amari the historian. See his letter of 13 February to Marchese di Torrearsa (FT, Trapani).

La Farina, a Sicilian long exiled at Turin, had encouraged Cavour to
believe that Mazzini's concept of national unity was not so utopian as
had been thought: the idea only needed to be taken over from its
prophet, detached from his republicanism, watered down from his
notion of catastrophic creation, and changed into the conception of
a gradual absorption of successive provinces by Piedmont. This was
the attitude of the so-called 'annexationists', who wanted the gradual
annexation of Italy region by region. Cavour soon found a strong
party in Sicily which for various reasons agreed with him on this.

Quite distinct were the views of the unqualified champions of unity,
whose most notable representative was Francesco Crispi. Crispi stood
in something of the same relation to Garibaldi as did his enemy La
Farina to Cavour. He was a leader of the quasi-Mazzinian opposition,
in revolt against those whom he thought wanted the mere aggrandizement of Piedmont. While quite ready to accept the dynasty of Savoy,
his first object was to unify the whole nation, and this could best be
achieved not by piecemeal annexation, but by letting Garibaldi's
revolutionary forces sweep up in one move to Rome. The acquisition
of Rome would make Italy an altogether new kingdom with a new
character and emphasis, and would prevent the nation becoming merely
that enlargement of Piedmont which was as anathema to all radical
democrats as it was dear to the court aristocracy of Turin. To reach
Rome would also be a victory for the democratic 'party of action',
such as would place the radicals in a very strong political position. Best
of all from Crispi's point of view, it would involve the conquest of the
Papal States, and so would mean the final consummation of the
national movement. For such a purpose it was important to keep
Garibaldi's army alive and its enthusiasm hot; whereas annexation to
Piedmont would cut short the revolution, and would mean breaking
up the volunteer army and halting the process of unification half-way.

The division of patriotic Italians into liberal and radical thus more or
less corresponded with a further division into what with some over-
simplification can be called 'annexationist' and 'unitarian'. In this year
1860 they were to fight out their differences in Sicily. The decision
eventually went against Crispi and in favour of La Farina and Cavour.
One result was to be that Rome remained for ten years outside the new
state; another that the south was in the long run goaded into rebellion

against these northern 'conquerors' with their centralized government on a French or Piedmontese pattern. It was in apprehension of this prosaic and disappointing conclusion to the revolution that many of the intellectuals and politically-minded Sicilians in 1860 took up a position distinct from that of both La Farina and Crispi: they would gladly join a united kingdom of Italy, but only if union were mitigated by a measure of local autonomy. In the opinion of these autonomists, Sicily was a nation, or at least it was as much an indefeasible unit as was Italy itself. For some of them, indeed, conditional annexation to Piedmont was a sacrifice they would make merely to find a safe harbour against a resumption of Neapolitan tyranny.

It is impossible to discover with any precision the degree of popular support behind these various opinions at any one time. After the first outburst of spontaneous rebellion, popular opinion became less ascertainable than that of particular groups or individuals. Although every party claimed to stand for the people, *vox populi* was never clearly heard: indeed, it was to be heard but imperfectly even in the plebiscite of 21 October. Goodwin, the British consul at Palermo, although he lived too much in the past to make completely reliable political judgements, thought that intelligent Sicilians would have preferred just a reconcession of the 1812 constitution under the Bourbons,[1] and that the invocation of Piedmont was rather a pretext than a positive desire.[2] A study of contemporary newspapers in Palermo confirms what one might have expected, that opinions were too complicated and varied for useful analysis. Most people do seem to have been conscious of Sicily's peculiar interests, and of her need for special regional concessions whatever king might reign. The annexationist school was split between those who wanted administrative centralization on the French model, and those who took at more than their face value Cavour's deceptive hints on the future development of Sicily as an autonomous region. A similar division existed among the radicals, separating the unconditional supporters of unity from those desirous of administrative or even

[1] 15 May, Goodwin to Elliot: 'this morning a leading liberal has told me that the party for Annexation is the most numerous, but the party for the Constitution embraces all men of weight and intelligence' (F.O. 70/316).

[2] These were his words as reported by the Bourbonist General Lanza on 25 May to the minister for Sicilian affairs (ASP, Affari Siciliani, polizia, b. 1239).

political self-government in Sicily. But in general the autonomists appear to have been more vocal, if not also more numerous. A number of pamphlets pointed out how badly placed in the world were outlying dependencies like India, the island of Sardinia, Malta and especially Ireland; and then tried to contrast with this the benefits which they thought Scotland had secured from a union limited by enlightened legal and fiscal exemptions. An audible party stood for autonomy inside an Italian federation, but would have preferred complete independence if the alternative were not a federal but a unitary state. The following letter written from Catania in June may be quoted to show the strength of insular traditions and housepride:

is it not enough for our poor Sicily to have had forty years of Neapolitan tyranny to endure that we must now listen to the voice of another master from Turin? Must we be slaves to one still further away?...Not even Garibaldi can venerate Victor Emanuel as I do, and yet I think Sicily will be deserted if chained to his chariot....

Be sure of one thing: that the desire for annexation has arisen out of the desperation of slaves in a moment of enthusiasm, and will only implant the seeds of civil war to come....It is a disservice to our country to wish it a province of Turin. If such a disaster is by now inescapable, let the devil's will be done, and let us prepare to fight and free ourselves from our new masters....

Our real wishes are two: first the unification of Italy, and secondly the retention of our autonomy. The most conciliatory course would just be to form a defensive and offensive league between the Italian regions. But if you persist in your present plan you will open the way for a return of the Bourbons.[1]

This letter is the more convincing for being written by a man of moderate views, who believed both in a united Italy and in the northern dynasty of Savoy.

Whatever were the merits or popularity of these ideas, one must acknowledge that Garibaldi acquired a completely deciding voice in Sicilian politics whenever he could spare the time to make up his mind and interfere. During his six months' dictatorship, whenever he overcame his natural hesitancy and decided firmly upon any line of policy, his will was law almost automatically, and this because of the amazing

[1] 5 June, Vigo to Crispi (ACP, f. 135).

trust and almost worship with which people regarded him. Whatever his enemies might say, there was little of the police state about his rule. It was spontaneous affection and confidence, not terror, which led even the newspaper-reading public to accept statements such as that, 'every action of the great man cannot but be just and magnanimous, and we must blindly obey'.[1] For all that he could be vulgar, irreverent, head-strong and blustering, he was a great man in his own way, and instinctively recognized to be such by the common people. In courage and capacity for energetic action he was second to none; but he combined with this an earnestness of purpose, a disinterested love of his country, a zeal for social reform, and a simplicity of character and absence of ostentation or personal ambition, all of which endeared him to the multitude. It is therefore the more important to note that, in the various political crises which preceded the final plebiscite, his wishes were sometimes not known; and this rendered ineffective that decisive body of people who took their views from what he was supposed to want. For most of the time his thoughts were concentrated on winning the war, and his political views, whenever they were translated into practical statements of policy, often seemed second-hand, vague and changeable. Only dimly could people trace any linear development in his opinions, and his frequent changes of tack were evidently dictated less by mind than by instinct or emotion. What was even more confusing, he allowed his subordinates to make the most contradictory pronouncements in his name.

Garibaldi was no thinker, and indeed could not be called very intelligent; but still he was a man of principle, and instinctively held fast to certain general criteria of action which had their importance for the history of Sicily in 1860. A man who had seen a good deal of him the previous year wrote that 'his views though broad and honest hardly ever rise above the level of trite and popular generalities'; adding, however, that 'for this very reason perhaps he exercises an influence on his hearers which a more cultivated intelligence might fail to produce'.[2] He was seen to possess almost childish illusions about human nature, and he believed excessively in the good sense and resilience of the common people; but even illusions can sometimes be a powerful stimulus to right

[1] 22 August, *La Cicala Italiana* (Palermo).
[2] 31 October 1859, Colonel Cadogan to Russell (RP G.D. 22/73).

GARIBALDI

conduct and effective action. He had learnt from Mazzini to set his heart on the unification of Italy, and accordingly had no truck with the Sicilian separatists. It was his intention to carry through his campaign if possible to the walls of Rome, there on the Capitoline hill to proclaim Victor Emanuel as king of Italy. He was and remained, that is to say, a loyal and enthusiastic monarchist, and indeed he had broken with Mazzini on this precise point. Ever since 1856 he had been advocating that all Italian patriots should override their private convictions and rally to the strongest force existing inside the country, namely to the liberal-conservative kingdom of Piedmont-Sardinia. Garibaldi thus stood some way between the two main factions of the nationalist party. Nevertheless, he leant well towards the Left in most matters of internal politics. He was generally on amicable terms with Mazzini, and continued to revere him as the prophet and standard-bearer of the Italian movement. Like Mazzini, and unlike the liberal-conservatives who looked for their inspiration to Cavour, he believed that Italians should at all costs redeem themselves by their own initiative, and should not have to rely on French soldiers and diplomatic bargaining to win their battles for them. One aspect of this same belief was his fervent confidence in the effectiveness of a volunteer force; and he rejoiced to show off the mettle of his irregulars, especially in front of those Piedmontese generals who had purposely and contemptuously given him so small a part to play in earlier wars.

Garibaldi was always possessed by a basic distrust of Cavour, and this distrust was never sharper than in the summer months of 1860, just after Cavour had bartered away to France Garibaldi's homeland of Nice. The government of Turin had been trying hard to make nationalism respectable by transferring it from the field of revolution to that of diplomacy, and this had led to the formation of an alliance with Louis Napoleon, and so to the subsequent bargaining of Nice for Tuscany. Such a process was taken to illustrate the point that, instead of accepting national unification as an axiom, Cavour seemed to prefer the less immediately attractive but apparently more realistic idea of a gradually expanding Piedmont—if necessary, sacrificing 'national territory' in the process. Garibaldi resented this. He knew as well that in Farini and Fanti the cabinet at Turin contained two of his bitter enemies, the two men with whom he had clashed in 1859 when on a former occasion he had tried to march on Rome. He also knew how hard this same cabinet had tried in May 1860 to stop him setting out for Sicily. Much of Cavour's conduct gave good grounds for supposing that at Turin they still wanted to divide Italy in half, merely allying with Bourbon Naples in order to conquer Venice from Austria, and then perhaps returning Sicily to Francesco II as compensation. Even when Cavour in June began a campaign for annexing Sicily to Piedmont, his motives were still suspect. In the first place, possession of Sicily might have been in his eyes just a bargaining counter to obtain this Neapolitan alliance; and in the second place, annexation might well have been designed simply to prevent Garibaldi leading another expedition from Sicily to win Naples and Rome. This was why Cavour's proposal to hold a plebiscite in the island was so fiercely contested. No stroke of Machiavellism was now thought to be beyond him. Quite apart from these considerations, Garibaldi felt that to allow a plebiscite in Sicily would amount to giving tacit sanction to the loss of Nice, since this had also been ceded by means of a similar vote. His intention was therefore to postpone any popular vote, and to defer surrendering his conquest at least until the revolution was well established; and postponement began to appear all the more desirable when he discovered Cavour secretly working to end the revolution and force his surrender in a way that profoundly exacerbated his instinctive distrust. He by no means excluded helping the Piedmontese, but he insisted on having evidence that they meant to make Italy a nation, and were not just out to push the selfish interests of their province. He firmly believed in Sicily submitting to the dynasty of Savoy; but only when this would be a contribution and not an obstacle to national unity.

That Garibaldi held these general opinions will give some idea of the political significance of his success in Sicily. He had saved the revolution from petering out, but he had also captured it for a political programme. In practice we shall see that his views and his actions were more moderate and even more statesmanlike than is often said; and yet they were bound to give Cavour as well as the Bourbons some cause for worry. This was almost the only time during the whole *risorgimento* that the radical democrats had a *pied à terre*, and not only that but also an army, a momentum, and something of a practical programme. There was the further possibility to be feared that they might receive some support in parliament. Rattazzi, Brofferio and the opposition deputies did indeed make some attempt to keep in touch with Garibaldi in Sicily and use him to overturn Cavour. Brofferio, for instance, wrote in June to express the wish that his southern army 'would liberate Italy not only from Palermo to Rome, but from Rome to Turin', and upset 'our anti-national parliament'.[1] But the dictator had other things to think about, and apparently did not answer their letters. He had as little confidence in Cavour as they had, but he was more of a patriot than they ever were, and for him the making of Italy came first, with or without his political opponents. In this respect Garibaldi differed strikingly from both of the main parliamentary groups.

Mazzini was present at Palermo only in spirit. He had long been excommunicated from the company of almost all the deputies in parliament whether of the Left or Right, and had been living exiled in England under sentence of death from the government of Piedmont. But the news from southern Italy had been too exciting: it seemed to prove at long last the correctness of his political analysis and of his technique of revolution. As he wrote, 'the Sicilians, God bless them for always, have for the second time given a glorious example of popular initiative. If only our country knows how to profit from this, they will have saved Italy.'[2] Although the London police thought they still had him under observation, on 8 May Mazzini was back at Genoa in hiding. Since the Thousand had already sailed, his first plan was to build up another expedition which he could launch in June through the Papal States to link up with Garibaldi in the south.[3] In this he was prevented, because most people preferred to concentrate all available resources upon Sicily. He therefore had to rest content with advising from a distance, trying to encourage Garibaldi to stand fast upon the radical-democratic programme, and to resist the machinations of the Cavourians and the Sicilian 'independentists'. He was delighted to find

[1] 25 June, Angelo Brofferio to Agostino Bertani (ABM). The letter added that he had just written 'again' to Garibaldi. Altogether in this collection there are eleven letters addressed to Bertani by Brofferio between June and December 1860.

[2] 9 June, Mazzini to Crispi (*Epistolario di Giuseppe Mazzini*, ed. naz., vol. XL, 1934, pp. 30–3).

[3] May, letter from Mazzini to Libertini (quoted by Emilia Morelli, 'Mazzini e la polizia Napoletana', *Rassegna Storica del Risorgimento*, Anno XXVIII, 1941, p. 504).

that, after all his years of persecution, public opinion in Italy was enthusiastic for the radical-democratic programme; and he was equally delighted that Cavour had put himself in the wrong, both over the question of Nice, and over the government's initial distrust of the Sicilian revolution. Accordingly he counselled Garibaldi to use his strong position to wean the king from reliance on Cavour, as this would be the simplest and most effective way to make political follow military victory.[1] Bertani now wrote to Crispi: 'be careful the General is not prevailed upon to leave Sicily and resign his command before having firmly established our political future there'. 'Thank God the power is in your hands—hold on to it!...Between us we will turn Italy upside down.'[2] For Mazzini this was a moment of great elation, a moment for which he had toiled thirty years in poverty and exile. 'My Italians will astonish the world', he said; and he prayed that the revolutionary momentum would not slacken until Cavour and the other respectable conservatives were either dragged into it, or else were forced to make way for his own more radical solution to the Italian question.

Mazzini, however, was far from the scene of action, and the new dictator of Sicily, although his friend, was a radical with a difference. Garibaldi was justifiably suspicious of Cavour, and yet combined this suspicion with a sensible and realistic appreciation that Piedmont and the liberal-conservatives were necessary for success. At no moment during successive triumph and defeat did he waver in his adherence to the monarchy and the programme of ultimate union with Piedmont. Before landing at Marsala he announced his programme as 'Italy and Victor Emanuel'. He then declared the flag of Sicily to be that of the 'kingdom of Italy'. The Sicilian army was to be organized on Piedmontese lines, with the same rations and payments as in the north, and its navy was to have Piedmontese laws and uniforms. Customs barriers were removed between Sicily and the other provinces of northern Italy, even though Victor Emanuel could offer no formal reciprocity.[3] Garibaldi also showed his good intentions by appointing moderate

---

[1] 28 June, Mazzini to Garibaldi (*Epistolario*, vol. XL, p. 110).

[2] 9 and 16 June, Bertani to Crispi (*The Memoirs of Francesco Crispi*, ed. Palamenghi-Crispi, vol. I, 1912, pp. 260–1).

[3] Decrees dated 13, 16 June and 5 July, *Raccolta degli atti del governo dittatoriale e prodittatoriale in Sicilia* (Palermo, 1861).

conservatives to ministerial position in Palermo, just as he did later again at Naples. Although the radical Crispi remained the chief minister except for two three-week intervals, the government was to be a coalition, in which the radicals were and always remained a minority. Garibaldi wanted to postpone any vote or act of union until he was certain that it would not bring his movement to a premature halt, because he meant to continue as far as Naples, and then to Rome if fortune should permit. Apart from this, however, he had no dubious political objective, and Cavour was certainly wrong to think he took advice from Mazzini. True enough, even though an elected deputy, Garibaldi was no conventional parliamentary democrat; but neither had he the ambition or wit to play the Cromwell or the Napoleon. The acquisition of maximum liberty for the greatest number was a basic dogma in his political system, and if he turned naturally to dictatorship, this was so that he might fight tyranny the more effectively and then force people to be free. In everything he proved to be honest, simple and single-minded. He lived as a warrior, yet he probably spoke at least a half-truth when he said that he did not like war.[1] Unlike Mazzini, he had no subtle mental reservations; and unlike Cavour, he always meant what he said. Hence it was that the people of the south loved him as perhaps they have loved no previous or subsequent ruler. Commander Forbes was deeply impressed to find that 'there is a sort of intimate communion of mind between Garibaldi and the masses which is perfectly electrifying'.[2] The political events of these months in Sicily were inevitably coloured by this fact.

[1] 4 March 1861, Garibaldi to Lord John Russell (RP G.D. 22/68).

[2] 28 July, Commander C. S. Forbes, *The Campaign of Garibaldi in the Two Sicilies*, 1861, p. 118. 'Garibaldianism is with them as completely a religion as was Mohammedanism with the fanatical followers of the prophet', pp. 340–1.

CHAPTER II

CAVOUR AND THE DIPLOMATS: APRIL–JUNE

The outbreak of revolution in the south found Cavour unusually confused and uncertain in his movements. His political life in ten years of office had mainly been devoted to the development of constitutional government and economic prosperity in the small subalpine state which comprised the provinces of Savoy, Piedmont, Liguria and Sardinia. Latterly he had turned his attention to other regions in the northern half of the peninsula, and in 1859–60 with French help he had partially displaced Austria and obtained for his king the additional provinces of Lombardy and the duchies. He still did not concern himself very much with the centre and south. Unquestionably he wanted to establish the independence of Italy from Austrian influence, but he had no idea how near this was to achievement. He had privately expressed the hope that Naples and Sicily would remain quiet for several years, and it was in keeping with this thought that his official representative at the Bourbon court was a man whom he himself recognized as second rate. In his plans for Italy he leant rather to an alliance or a confederation of states than to centralized unity. The idea of national independence by no means implied for him a united nation.[1] He had shown signs of resting content with Victor Emanuel as king of the north, and the Bourbon Francesco as king of the south. He himself knew no other part of Italy except the north-western corner, and he continued to look on Rome as a mysterious and not altogether pleasant city. Unification as a doctrine, so far as he was concerned, carried some of the taint of Mazzini about it. There was always the suspicion that in practice it might mean a republic; and the conversion of Italy into a republic was something he would not have at any price. What he hoped at this stage was to keep Italy out of trouble for a few years while he consolidated his regime in the north. It might then be possible to see more clearly if the balance of power in Europe would permit any further expansion against Venice or the Papal States.

[1] Cf. Salmour's comment (CC Carteggio Cavour-Salmour, 1936, p. 99).

In the spring of 1860 Cavour was in a particularly weak situation. He had just been forced into the surrender of Nice and Savoy to France despite strong opposition at home and abroad. It was not only that in this he had broken his promise, nor merely that he had proceeded 'unconstitutionally'; but the act also made Turin into a frontier city, militarily untenable, and his alienation of national territory was something which the *italianissimi* could by no means forgive him. The chief opposition paper at Turin, *Il Diritto*, commented that 'the treaty of 24 March mutilated and decapitated the nation, and ceded one of the choicest regions of Italy to a foreign government'.[1] On 12 April Garibaldi himself had arrived in parliament to denounce this ignoble traffic in peoples, and to protest that the conduct of the plebiscite in his home town of Nice had been farcically improper. Before long it was an issue on which even members of Cavour's own cabinet threatened to resign, and the unexpected force of public opinion made him uncertain until the last minute whether his government could survive.

The sudden revolt in Sicily thus came as a further unwelcome intrusion at a time when matters were already difficult enough. Some prominent Sicilians had consulted him on several occasions between January and March to hear his views on the south, but he had temporized; and though he privately attempted to find whether there were any means of helping them, he had ended up without offering any useful advice.[2] Then, during April and May, he was confronted without warning by a very complicated problem, so complicated that he could not bring himself to follow any consistent policy, but rather abandoned attempts at control and drifted before the current of events. Over his action, or lack of action at this point, there began to grow up a legend which eventually was to portray him as all-wise and all-successful in his conduct throughout the year. La Farina and Admiral Persano later tried to show that Cavour had aided Garibaldi's expedition 'with every possible means'.[3] In fact this was an attempt to justify their own part

[1] 23 May, *Il Diritto*.
[2] L. La Bella, 'V. Fardella, Marchese di Torrearsa', *Archivio Storico per la Sicilia Orientale*, 1932, p. 473.
[3] La Farina in parliament, 18 June 1863, *Atti Parlamentari*; C. di Persano, *Diario privato-politico-militare...nella campagna navale degli anni 1860 e 1861*, part I, 1869, pp. 14–17.

3 ⋆

in the revolution. Subsequent historians have usually accepted their account, and have rationalized what appear to be contradictory facts by saying that he positively helped the expedition while cleverly seeming not to. But this should rather be put the other way round, for in fact he gave no help, while skilfully letting the patriots think that he might do so at any moment.[1] He was in a position where the appearance of patriotism was more important to him than being a patriot in deed. Since his faith was in the methods of diplomacy, his first and essential object was to remain friendly with the cabinets of Europe, and it was on this very point that Garibaldi's venture threatened to ruin his whole policy of cautious gradualism.

The expedition of the Thousand had taken place against Cavour's express advice, and was apparently inspired by his political opponents. To him it was Mazzinian in origin, inexpedient in manner and timing, and extremely dangerous from the point of view of its possible effects. As to its composition, while there were undoubtedly one or two republicans, it had no strong political stamp; but there was a distinct regional preponderance of Lombards and Venetians in this expeditionary force, and there were hardly any Piedmontese at all. Cavour had no confidence in its leaders, and saw that so long as they held the initiative, his own hand would continually be forced by events outside his control. There was an acute risk that something might go wrong: it might be that, without Piedmontese help, a Bourbon counter-revolution would prevail just as in 1849; alternatively Mazzini might capture the rebellion and direct it for his own sinister purposes; perhaps the Sicilian autonomists would use the interregnum to carry their views and make Sicily a separate state. Garibaldi was clearly in the hands of hot-headed, inexperienced men, people with a grievance like Crispi. If they reached Rome they might try to impose conditions on the north; that is to say they might challenge the Piedmontese hegemony in Italy. They might even summon a constituent assembly and call in question fundamental principles of the constitution, or might ask the king to

---

[1] The evidence for this is discussed in D. Mack Smith, 'Cavour's attitude to Garibaldi's expedition to Sicily', *The Cambridge Historical Journal*, vol. IX, 1949, pp. 359–70. The contrary view is stated by W. R. Thayer, *The life and times of Cavour*, vol. II, 1911, pp. 268–9; P. Matter, *Cavour et l'unité Italienne*, vol. III, 1927, pp. 343–6; A. J. Whyte, *The evolution of modern Italy*, 1944, p. 134.

dismiss Cavour himself. Cavour of late had not been on good terms with the king, and indeed Victor Emanuel was rash and self-willed enough to have dismissed him and supported a victorious Garibaldi. It was suspected on good evidence that both Ricasoli and Rattazzi were being actively considered as alternative candidates for the premiership. This weakened Cavour considerably, and made it unwise for him at this moment to take any strong action for or against Garibaldi. If he had been ready to allow discussion of fundamentals, he might have won over the radicals by himself proposing a constituent assembly; but after the loss of Savoy it was more important for him to make concessions to the Right than to the Left. He also could not help but go on looking at the problem as a diplomatist, with the international complications uppermost in his mind. Since all his hopes centred on French support, and as Rome had a French garrison, he was understandably terrified that the democrats' policy of advancing on Rome would bring about a clash with his patron in Paris. His own preference—and it was a reasonable one—was to negotiate with Louis Napoleon for the withdrawal of that garrison in Rome. Another revolution in Italy was of all things most likely to make such negotiations fail.

Cavour therefore did all he could, short of using force, to prevent Garibaldi setting out for Sicily. When at the last minute it appeared that the radical leader would not listen to advice, he even ordered his navy to arrest the expedition '*at all costs*' (the words of his original order were underlined). But he had not dared to be so bold until the volunteers had openly and unexpectedly put themselves in the wrong by leaving port, and fortunate circumstances then took them on a circuitous route safely to their destination. Public opinion in the north had apparently abandoned Cavour for Garibaldi, and public opinion, if not the king himself, might well have unseated the prime minister if he had gone directly against the current. At this moment the parliamentary elections were taking place, and the administrative officers of the crown were fully occupied in trying to return a government majority. There was in any case a serious ministerial crisis, made all the more difficult by the prospect of a difficult debate over Nice. Cavour therefore held his hand. He could not afford to use force until Garibaldi had openly defied him, and even then there were all these other reasons why he should lie low and hope for the best. Once the expedition had escaped interception by his navy, there was little he could do but wait to see whether it would have to be disowned or exploited. He naturally did not wish to compromise himself unnecessarily until one side had emerged victorious. He did not know the extent of his own success in the elections until 10–12 May, by which time Garibaldi had safely landed. After that, as the Turin newspapers show, the imminent debate over Savoy and Nice made any serious consideration of Sicilian affairs impossible. Only on 29 May did Cavour know he had a firm majority in parliament; only on the 31st did he hear of the capture of Palermo. These two pieces of information at last made it possible for the government to assert itself, and also indicated how the expedition might be useful after all. What Cavour then had to do was to bring this private army under a moderating influence. As soon as Palermo had fallen, active but still unofficial aid was therefore given by the king's government in forming a second expedition of reinforcements. After these weeks of delay, however, it was not quite so easy to make up for lost time and exploit Garibaldi's unexpected success. The Thousand, with their rusty converted flintlocks, might well have perished on their own, and Garibaldi in the meantime had only been confirmed in his belief that Cavour could not have the interests of Italy at heart.

It would be wrong to tax Cavour with deficiency of confidence and idealism over this, for it was hardly possible to guess in early May that the revolution would be so successful, or indeed to be sure that France and Austria would omit to veto what was happening. In the general uncertainty, his safest plan was to suspect the worst of Garibaldi, and to place his entire trust in Louis Napoleon. He was seriously worried that France might withdraw her benevolent support from Piedmont, especially as Dr Bertani, Garibaldi's chief organizer in Genoa, had orders to carry out Mazzini's plan for another insurrection in the Papal States.[1] If any of the bigger volunteer expeditions had gone to the Papal States instead of Sicily, it might have brought about the end of diplomatic non-intervention. In order to show that he would by no

---

[1] 13 May, Garibaldi to Bertani, giving orders that Medici should concentrate with his second expedition of volunteers on the Papal States; and 25 May, Bertani to Garibaldi, explaining that Medici had let himself be diverted from this plan (ACM). On 16 June, Bertani asked Garibaldi to instruct Cosenz to attack the Papal States with the third expedition (Crispi, *Memoirs*, vol. I, pp. 277–8).

means countenance such an occurrence, Cavour had to arrest one of Garibaldi's senior officers, Colonel Zambianchi, whom he then illegally kept in prison without trial for almost a year. When Cavour subsequently gave secret help to the two relief expeditions of Medici in June and Cosenz in July, he was in part moved by this same necessity of canalizing the volunteers towards Sicily and diverting them from Rome. His motive, that is to say, was shrewd common sense as well as patriotic enthusiasm; perhaps it was less eagerness to unify the whole of Italy, than fear that France might upset that degree of unification already achieved. Cavour made another serious effort to appease Napoleon III by ordering Mazzini's arrest, though his police failed to locate the culprit. Many people in Paris and Turin continued to believe—although on the very slenderest evidence—that the Sicilian expedition might end in a victory for the republicans. Garibaldi was not in fact a republican, but he was a sworn enemy to the present government. If there were some in northern Italy who could even rejoice when the brave and selfless radical leader, Rosolino Pilo, was killed with the volunteers in Sicily, one can understand how many more feared the influence which a victorious Garibaldi might wield in parliament on his return.[1]

Cavour was not a man who normally lacked courage or vision. Nevertheless it must be admitted that other Italians were bolder, and some among his fellow diplomats more far-sighted. For instance, the United States minister at Turin wrote home with a remarkably clear appreciation of the possibilities of the moment:

before this year is ended, it is quite possible that the entire Italian peninsula with the exception of Venice and perhaps the city of Rome *intra muros* will be united under the sceptre of Victor Emanuel. Only one thing can prevent it—a great effort and an actively conducted war by the Austrian Empire. It is said that the King of Naples has already demanded the armed intervention of that power in his affairs. It is quite improbable that he will receive it. The battles of last summer have prostrated Austria. All the pride and spirit was then taken from her. She rests an inert mass on the bank, while the river of Italian revolution runs a straight, and now an unresisted, course.[2]

[1] This is described in a letter of 4 June, from Cordova to Torrearsa (FT).
[2] 4 June, Daniel to secretary of state Cass (copy in MRR).

To take another example, Bettino Ricasoli, the governor of Tuscany, did not cease to blame the government for abandoning the direction of the Italian movement to Garibaldi. It was pointed out that the world was bound to put responsibility upon Turin for events in Sicily, especially as the revolutionary government at Palermo headed all its enactments with the name of Victor Emanuel. Cavour had been forced into a position where his own cause was bound up with that of the revolution, and where he could hardly stop short of active participation without being ruined; whether the Bourbons won, or whether Garibaldi won without Piedmontese help, the cause of Italy would alike be imperilled. Ricasoli put it to him that the revolutionaries were out-pacing the liberal-conservatives. Therefore, to save the prestige of the king, he should not hesitate to invade the Papal States himself; for, as this pious Catholic concluded, 'we must destroy the temporal power soon, completely and for always'.[1] Much the same advice came from Valerio, the prefect of Como, who wrote to urge that Cavour must either outdo Mazzini or yield: to retain his position he had to make up what he had lost in prestige over the surrender of Nice; otherwise Murat, or Napoleon, or the 'reds' would have an open field for their own private schemes.[2]

So far the opposition had had free rein for its criticism of Cavour's actions and omissions during May. He was charged with 'having done all he could to prevent the expedition, only stopping short before the danger of *civil war*';[3] and the accusation was made that he had then waited to see if Garibaldi won or lost before making any further decision, 'although in a thousand ways the government could have given help without anyone knowing'.[4] Once the volunteers had begun to win, it was a different story. Cavour had spent too much time during May in telling the world how little he approved of Garibaldi's foolhardy venture, so that it was a difficult task to adjust himself in June to the revolutionary victories. Nevertheless, it was essential to change round to try and win Garibaldi's confidence. One thing he could do without prejudice was to hold the ring for a fair fight, and on 1 June he published a statement invoking and restating the doctrine of non-

[1] 11, 16 and 28 June, Ricasoli to Cavour (*Lettere e Documenti del Barone Bettino Ricasoli*, ed. A. Gotti and M. Tabarrini, vol. v, 1890, pp. 119, 126, 145).

[2] 16 June, Valerio to Castelli (*Carteggio politico di Michelangelo Castelli*, ed. Luigi Chiala, vol. I, 1890, pp. 307–8).   [3] 15 May, *Il Diritto* (Turin).   [4] 14 June, *ibid.*

intervention—a protest in advance against armed intervention by any third party in the south. Even this step he did not take until the news of the fall of Palermo had suggested how the government might be able to profit from what was happening. There subsequently arrived from Paris another highly welcome message, to say that France could not help but accept any free vote by Sicilians in favour of union with Piedmont. He therefore allowed that the government might intervene actively but secretly in sending arms to the volunteer army. While still preserving the public fiction of disapproval and non-intervention, he sent out unofficially his friend La Farina to examine the possibility of setting up a regular Sicilian government.

This was a distinct change of attitude.[1] Cavour had been frankly delighted, but no less delighted than astonished, to find that 'the expedition of Garibaldi has turned out to be the most poetic fact of the century, and is praised by almost the whole of Europe'.[2] It had come as a real surprise that Garibaldi, far from having fallen for a completely Mazzinian programme, had mitigated his animosity of a month earlier and confirmed his acceptance of Manin's formula 'Italy and Victor Emanuel'.[3] The Thousand had landed in Sicily, and not in the Papal States as had been feared. The king was for the moment more friendly.[4] There was also the consideration that the recent elections had given Cavour a more comfortable parliamentary majority than many people had expected, and he now felt that this afforded him the support he required for the difficult task of moderating the revolution.[5] While he waited for La Farina's letters to give him some idea of the state of affairs in Sicily, he helped to equip Medici's expedition which sailed on 10 June, and sent back to Palermo certain other Sicilian exiles whose

[1] The National Edition confuses this fact, inadvertently printing the same letter twice with two different dates (*CC Cavour-Nigra*, vol. III, 1928, p. 289; vol. IV, 1929, p. 19). Cavour's change of mind is thus wrongly ascribed to early May.

[2] 6 June, Cavour to G. Durando (*Una silloge di lettere del Risorgimento, 1839–73*, ed. C. Bollea, 1919, p. 260).

[3] 2 June, note by G. Pallavicino Trivulzio (*Memorie pubblicate dalla figlia*, 1883, vol. III, p. 582); 9 June, Farini to Ricasoli (*Lettere di Ricasoli*, ed. Tabarrini, vol. V, p. 113).

[4] 17 May, Cavour to Cugia (*CC Lib. del Mezz.* vol. I, 1949, p. 108).

[5] 11 June, Brofferio to Bertani, where he admits that Cavour had been cleverer than the opposition in the elections (ABM); 15 June, Cavour to E. d'Azeglio (*CC Ing.* vol. II, part II, 1933, p. 81).

intelligence and social standing he calculated would have the right effect on the leading citizens of the island. La Farina's correspondence shows that this help was given on the assumption that Sicily would soon be withdrawn from Garibaldi's purview and annexed to Piedmont. The change in Cavour's attitude, from unhelpfulness to encouragement, was thus described by his friend Hudson, the British minister:

at the outset nobody believed in the possibility of Garibaldi's success, and Cavour, and *tutti quanti*, thought the country well rid of him and of the unquiet spirits who went with him. The argument was—if he fails we are rid of a troublesome fellow, and if he succeeds Italy will derive some profit from his success. It succeeded so quickly that Cavour was forced to look the Sicilian question fairly in the face: and he found the general opinion in upper Italy to be for uniting all Italy under Victor Emanuel.[1]

Such a change of mind came none too soon. Five weeks had passed after Garibaldi's departure before Medici left to follow him with these reinforcements.

As always, Cavour showed himself second to none in his readiness to follow public opinion; and, as on at least one major occasion before, it is likely that he was also swayed against his own first intentions by the impetuosity of the king, who was now an enthusiastic Garibaldian.[2] In the middle of June Cavour even tried to negotiate with Bertani and adopt something of the radical policy of action, 'either in order to regain part of the popularity lost over the cession of Nice, or because of recognition of the irresistible force of events', as one of his opponents put it.[3] The problem was already presenting itself of how he could take away from Garibaldi the active control of affairs, above all how to do so without falling out of step with public opinion.[4] It was his hope that La Farina would eventually find some way to recapture the initiative in Sicily. For the moment, however, Cavour instructed the Sicilian liberals to play second fiddle, and to try and win the dictator's good opinion. They still needed Garibaldi for military victory. In any case

---

[1] 28 June, Hudson to Russell (RP G.D. 22/66).

[2] 1 July, La Varenne to Crispi, 'the king is with you body and soul; he has full confidence in Garibaldi' (quoted in A. Comandini, *L'Italia nei cento anni del secolo XIX*, vol. III, 1918, p. 1496).

[3] 16 June, Bargoni to Bertani (*Memorie di Bargoni*, pp. 106–7).

[4] 18 June, Cavour to Prince Eugenio (*CC Lib. del Mezz.* vol. I, p. 217).

it was likely that the radicals would soon wear out their own reputation by the mere process of trying to govern such a country at such a time. Far better, too, that Garibaldi should be persuaded to carry out the annexation of Sicily to Piedmont of his own accord.

Cavour's general aim thenceforward remained constant, to annex Sicily as soon as might be; and the chosen method was to be that of a popular vote, either a direct vote through a plebiscite, or an indirect vote through a popularly elected Sicilian parliament. In principle he was opposed to universal suffrage, which he once said was incompatible with constitutional monarchy; but the experience of this year taught him that there might be extraordinary circumstances when its use was highly convenient. For a time he thought of trying to recall the Sicilian parliament of 1848. But he was warned that such an assembly would give free rein to the Sicilian autonomists. He was too perceptive a politician not to recognize how successful had been the plebiscitarian system in France, and he also hoped that the patronage of Napoleon III might be won by judicious emulation of his example. Earlier in this year he had agreed to use the method of a plebiscite in Nice and Savoy, both to justify in the eyes of parliament his prearranged cession of these provinces, and also to compromise Napoleon into supporting any extension of this same system to other parts of Italy. France would in all appearance have a great deal to lose from the achievement of Italian unity; nevertheless, Napoleon would have fewer grounds for objection if Sicily voted for union by the same method which French constitutional law had already declared sacrosanct. There was also the point that Piedmontese annexation of Sicily would be in French eyes a concealed and welcome blow against the supposed ambitions of England. Early in June, therefore, Cavour was able to extract from the Emperor of the French a verbal agreement to respect a vote by Sicilians, and he soon began to intrigue actively through La Farina for a plebiscite, as something that would at once satisfy Napoleon and effectively tame the revolution. Paris was a very sensitive spot for his policy, so he lavished money in subsidies to the French press.[1] It was a safe assumption that, if the making of Italy could be no longer postponed, France would want the new nation to be her friend rather than her enemy.

[1] 31 May, Farini (minister of the interior) to Nigra, complains that the subsidies to French papers have already exhausted his Estimates (CF Ravenna).

Fortunately, France and Britain were more afraid of each other than they were of Italian unification. Without the encouragement or at least the toleration of the Great Powers—a toleration broken only by shocked asides and an occasional obedience to the conventions by with-drawal of diplomatic representation—Italy might have been as un-fortunate as Poland in her national aspirations. British policy during 1860 was a good deal less ambivalent than French, and surely no less important for Italy, though it is still sometimes misunderstood. In practice that policy was built up on one simple proposition, that 'Her Majesty's government have always been of opinion that the Italians should be left to settle their own affairs'.[1] This implied a virtual guarantee against intervention by any other Power, and so gave powerful support to the cause of unification. The only conditions attached were that Cavour should not bargain away any more provinces to France, and that he should not try to seize Venice from the Austrian Emperor with whom Britain was in friendly relations. Cavour depended upon this tacit understanding. He wrote in May that, 'comme j'ai peu d'espoir que la France nous aide à Naples et en Sicile, je voudrais engager l'Angleterre à faire au midi de l'Italie ce que la France a fait au Nord. L'Angleterre le pourrait à peu de frais et sans se départir de son égoïsme habituel.'[2]

This trust in England is one of the keys to Cavour's policy in 1860. The private convictions of Palmerston and the new Whig government were for him. Gladstone, for instance, had written in 1859: 'I have not viewed the aggrandizement of Piedmont as an object in itself desirable. When it has reached a certain point, a new set of dangers may spring from it. But as matters now stand it seems to be the most likely course for averting far worse and more pressing evils.'[3] Lord John Russell, the British foreign minister, also had some shrewd comments to make on the situation. He thought that

a Kingdom of Northern Italy, strong and compact, including Florence and Modena, would I believe be an excellent thing for that mechanical con-trivance the balance of power. At all events it is enough that the Tuscan people wish it....I dare say the dreamers wish to unite Naples and Sicily and

[1] 9 July, Russell to Elliot (F.O. 70/312).
[2] 18 May, Cavour to Nigra (*CC Cavour-Nigra*, vol. III, 1928, pp. 303–4).
[3] 22 August 1859, Gladstone to Russell (RP G.D. 22/19).

make a Kingdom of the whole of Italy. But that is wild and foolish. It would make a despotism instead of a free government, an unwieldy power instead of a compact one, and it would increase tenfold the European difficulties.[1]

Russell had already told the Sardinian ambassador that he feared the return of republicanism, as in 1848, and he therefore hoped that Victor Emanuel would take over all those provinces of Italy which might declare for unification. He was deeply distressed at Neapolitan misgovernment, and even regarded this as a breach of treaty obligations with Great Britain.[2] While he wished Sicily still attached to Naples, and while he would certainly give no assistance to rebellion, he also refused to guarantee the Bourbon government even if there should be a reconcession of the 1812 constitution; and the criticisms of Bourbon tyranny made in public by him and his colleagues 'undoubtedly encouraged the revolutionary spirit'.[3] Working in the same direction there was Protestant anti-papalism. Russell stated that he was on the Ghibelline side in the war against the neo-Guelphs; and his nephew, the British minister in Rome, wrote home: 'I cannot conceal my deep conviction that the sooner the Pope's temporal Power is abolished, the better for Italy and Humanity in general.'[4]

Cavour was thus able to rely on the support of Protestant and humanitarian sentiment in Britain, and this regained for Piedmont some of the sympathy which had been lost there by his bare-faced deceit over the cession of Savoy. Opinion in London was also conditioned in favour of Italy through the great enthusiasm aroused by Garibaldi. This heroic and picturesque figure had already captivated English public opinion before his descent on Sicily. As one small indication of this, there exists a letter from Thackeray to Garibaldi early in 1860; Thackeray was hoping to obtain an autobiographical article for the *Cornhill*.[5] The

[1] 25 August 1859, Russell to Corbett (RP G.D. 22/109).

[2] 11 August 1859, Russell to Elliot (RP G.D. 22/111).

[3] 15 April 1860, U.S. minister Chandler at Naples to secretary of state Cass (copy in MRR); 10 May, Daniel at Turin to Cass, 'the Nation which has hardly finished in India the bloodiest series of executions and massacres that the world has heard of since the 14th Century [Great Britain] is horrorstruck to know that the King of Naples imprisons his subjects for political offences' (MRR).

[4] 29 June, Odo Russell to Lord John (RP G.D. 22/75).

[5] 2 February, Thackeray to Garibaldi (Archivio Garibaldi MRR).

Sardinian ambassador in London, when writing to confirm that Britain would oppose Austrian intervention in southern Italy, added that 'les Ministres...s'ils ne sont pas très Cavouriens, ils sont Garibaldiens plus qu'on ne saurait l'imaginer'; and Cavour replied to him with an exhortation to make the most of this.[1] Still more in Italy's favour was the traditional British fear and suspicion of France. The Whig government was afraid that Cavour, by his sacrifice of Savoy, had placed his country in the hands of France. Russell therefore had to satisfy himself first that a movement in Italy would not leave France the gainer by any further alienation of Genoa or Sardinia as the price of services rendered.[2] Once this was certain, he had no further doubts. His ambassador at Turin, Sir James Hudson, was an enthusiastic Italophile, who yet claimed to study the Italian question in the light of 'British interests'. Hudson did not cease to send back unsolicited advice to the cabinet. 'For my part I am all for making a strong Italy and for doubling our naval strength in the Mediterranean: we shall want Italy when we speak with L. Nap. on the Eastern question.' 'Either Italy must be Italian, or she will again be either Austrian or French.'[3] Cavour had cause to be very grateful to Hudson and the Whigs—it was his earnest prayer not to have a Tory ministry in Great Britain until the national revolution was complete—yet even the conservative Malmesbury later confessed that his 'private sympathies were with Italian regeneration'.[4] Queen Victoria continued throughout the year to protest strongly against this 'partnership with the Italian Revolution', pointing out that Victor Emanuel had no 'rights' at all in the rest of the peninsula, whereas the Austrian Emperor had at least a reversionary claim upon Tuscany; but Russell enjoyed himself reminding her of the precedents furnished against the divine right of kings by William III and by Leopold of Belgium.[5]

When Garibaldi landed in Sicily, therefore, the British government,

---

[1] 6 June, E. d'Azeglio to Cavour (*CC Ing.* vol. II, part II, p. 77); and Cavour's replies of 18 and 21 June (*ibid.* pp. 81, 85).

[2] E.g. 10 July, Elliot to Russell, 'except Hudson there are few people in their senses who believe that France would consent to an united Italy without exacting at least an equivalent' (RP G.D. 22/85).

[3] 25 March, 28 June, Hudson to Russell (RP G.D. 22/66).

[4] 14 December 1873, Malmesbury to Massari (Archivio Massari MRR).

[5] 11 January, Queen Victoria to Russell; 12 January, Russell to the Queen (RP G.D. 22/14).

much to the queen's annoyance, proclaimed itself 'entirely neutral'. In private, like most of his countrymen, Russell rejoiced at Garibaldi's success, and from the start considered annexation to Piedmont as virtually an accomplished fact.[1] He told Palmerston on 18 May that he could not stomach defending Bourbons: there were good reasons of national interest why 'we ought as much as possible to have the feeling of Italian independence in our favour. One must expect that Umbria and the Marches as well as Naples will fall and proclaim Victor Emanuel.' But he added the warning that, 'unless Venice remains with Austria, all Germany will stir. And Venice, though Italian, may become as much German as Alsace is French.'[2] To the queen he explained himself in more simple terms: 'the counterpoise for Great Britain and for Europe is the independence of Italy, and this counterpoise is far more valuable than Savoy or Nice. Another Prussia has arisen in the South of Europe which will in all probability be a new guarantee for the Balance of Power. The present subjection of Count Cavour to France is not likely to last long, and if it did, would the Italians long submit to be dependent?'[3]

On second thoughts, and to a less critical audience, Russell expressed some doubts about Cavour's good intentions with regard to France. He did not properly understand what was occurring, and was honestly puzzled that Piedmont, like Germany in 1848, was less interested in her own internal liberties than in the conquest of other provinces. When Cavour denied all intention of yielding Genoa and Sardinia to France, this seemed an exact parallel to the mock denials which had been made over Savoy and Nice a few months before: 'I fear Cavour is little more than a Prefect of the Department of the Po. It is a great pity, as he is so able and has rendered such service to his country....If he would but run straight all might be well.'[4] On 25 July, at the Prince Consort's behest, he took Hudson mildly to task: 'you should be very careful to keep the interests of Great Britain always in sight and not to be led too

[1] 22 May, Russell to Corbett, 'Garibaldi seems to be successful, and no one will be sorry for it. I should be glad if he would put up the King of Sardinia's second son, instead of the King himself' (RP G.D. 22/109).

[2] 18 May, Russell to Palmerston (RP G.D. 22/30).

[3] 26 May, Russell to the queen (RP G.D. 22/14).

[4] 26 and 28 May, and 25 June, Russell to Hudson (RP G.D. 22/109).

far by your Italian sympathies'; adding as a postscript, 'but *Evviva
l'Italia* nevertheless'. Garibaldi's next series of victories then happily
obviated the trouble of any further discussion about the relative merits
of Unity or Dualism.[1] The salvation of Italy was coming not from
Great Britain, nor from France, nor even from Cavour; it was in the
hands of Garibaldi and the revolutionaries.

[1] 25 July, 6 August, Russell to Hudson (RP G.D. 22/109).

CHAPTER III

LA FARINA AND CRISPI: JUNE

In the first week of June, Cavour's first envoy to Sicily, Giuseppe La Farina, landed at Palermo, and began actively to work for annexation. La Farina had long since abandoned his early sympathy for the radical unitarians. He had been converted to the 'artichoke' policy, that is to say to Cavour's programme of peeling off the unredeemed provinces slowly and singly, instead of courting disaster by staking the whole process of unification on a single throw. From La Farina's point of view,

what distinguishes Mazzinianism is the mad policy of all or nothing, the policy which imagines you can achieve your end without thinking out convenient means, which ignores the necessity of alliances, which does not proportion forces to their object, and thinks enthusiasm enough for victory, which is perpetually deluded as to the efficacy of its own initiative, and would like to substitute its own adepts for the elected representatives of the nation.[1]

It was on the whole a fair criticism; but in practice this ex-Mazzinian, like so many converts, had become surprisingly bitter against his late comrades. These differences of view were now a fundamental question in dispute between patriotic Italians. What was needed was someone to reconcile, not to aggravate, their disagreements.

Between 1857 and 1859 La Farina had effectively co-operated with Cavour in planning the consolidation of northern Italy, but his influence in Sicily during 1860 was less happy. This was the year of the 'party of action', from which La Farina was estranged. Garibaldi regarded as a positive hindrance people who believed that independence and unity were a utopian condition which Italy could move towards but hardly hope to attain in the foreseeable future.[2] The two had already had more than one quarrel, and Garibaldi held La Farina partly responsible for the invaders of Sicily being supplied with few and defective fire-arms. This

[1] July. G. La Farina, *Scritti Politici*, vol. II, 1870, p. 315.
[2] As La Farina had said in *Sicilia e Piemonte: Lettera ad un amico in Sicilia*, published 12 December 1857.

past history, as well as the unstable judgement and passionate nature of La Farina, should have marked him as quite the wrong person to send out to supervise the revolution.

He was selected for this task because, apart from being a friend of Cavour, he was director of the *Società Nazionale* which had done so much by way of propaganda and material preparation for the work of national regeneration. Moreover, he was the only Sicilian by birth who was in the inner councils of the government, and he had what was thought to be the added advantage of having become by adoption a Piedmontese. It was a pity that Cavour preferred his candidature to that of Depretis, who one month later had to be sent out urgently to remedy the damage which had then been done. The remarkable thing is that one can find nobody else who agreed with his selection of the tactless and ambitious La Farina. Among Cavour's advisers, Ricasoli specifically disapproved.[1] Valerio had just sent to warn Cavour against this very step. 'Let us hope that the government is not thinking of sending La Farina to Sicily', wrote Valerio. 'He is loathed by Garibaldi and his friends, and a breach between them might be very dangerous. Besides, his past history in '48 and '49 is not in his favour.'[2] The king did not like him. Hudson, too, came out strongly against this 'busybody', and made the significant criticism that 'Cavour has not the gift of putting round men into round holes....La Farina is a round man in a square hole in Sicily.'[3] The Marquis di Torrearsa, one of the most generally respected Sicilians, prophesied to Hudson that the choice would lead to a complete fiasco.

If Cavour had been in touch with any wide range of Sicilian exiles he might perhaps have considered that Torrearsa was preferable for such a delicate mission. Torrearsa and Depretis were two men who later on were left to salvage what remained of Cavour's policy after the damage done by La Farina. The bad choice of subordinates, and the ignorance of every other province but his own, were among Cavour's

[1] 13 June, Ricasoli to Cavour (*Lettere di Ricasoli*, ed. Tabarrini, vol. v, p. 121).

[2] 3 June, Valerio to Castelli (*Carteggio di Castelli*, ed. Chiala, vol. i, p. 305).

[3] 28 June, Hudson to Russell (RP G.D. 22/66); and see King Victor Emanuel's criticism of Cavour's 'confiance illimitée qu'il accorde parfois à des gens qui ne la méritent pas', in his letter of 14 April 1859 to Prince Napoleon, published by Luzio in the *Corriere della Sera* of 17 March 1931.

chief weaknesses for his task as a national leader. The history of this year shows as much. On the present occasion his problem had been to find someone who could first persuade Garibaldi to surrender his civil powers, and who could then set up a government in Sicily just as Farini and Ricasoli had done in the central provinces during the emergency of 1859–60. But of all people he had to choose the personal and political enemy of both Garibaldi and Crispi, of the two people, that is to say, whom it was most necessary to conciliate. The inevitable result was that the strife between liberals and radicals, which had flared up over the cession of Nice and Cavour's initial coolness towards the Thousand, was now extended and intensified. The radicals reacted just as might have been expected. Mordini wrote that 'La Farina's presence in Sicily is preordained to raise up a party against Garibaldi. Cavour has committed a grave error.'[1] *Il Diritto* was amazed that Cavour's choice should have fallen on a man who was generally known to have aroused the 'inextinguishable hatred' of part of the liberal party, and commented that, with such a man, the Turin government could never acquire in Sicily the influence which it ought to possess as the representative of the nation.[2] In part this appointment was due to carelessness, in part to Cavour's underestimation of the possibilities of success for Italian independence. In particular it arose from his disbelief in the ability of the volunteers to succeed in their foolhardy venture without coming to beg help of him on his own terms. This can be the only explanation for his sending anyone, let alone this particular person, to ask Garibaldi to hand Mazzini over to justice.[3] The request for Mazzini's arrest was accompanied by an ultimatum that failure to comply would make Piedmont break off relations and withdraw all aid from the revolution. Fortunately Mazzini was not in Sicily at all, so the brusqueness of this unnecessary challenge could be overlooked. It is to Cavour's credit that he soon realized his mistake in this, as he also realized his yet greater mistake of choosing such an agent as La Farina; but the initial

[1] 5 June, Mordini to Cironi (ASF Dono Ricasoli, busta T, fascicolo IV).

[2] 14 and 21 June, *Il Diritto*.

[3] 12 June, Cavour to Persano *via* Mathieu (*Lettere di Camillo Cavour*, ed. Luigi Chiala, vol. III, 1884, p. 263). For some reason this telegram has been overlooked in the recent national edition of Cavour's letters; Persano says that he received it on the 13th.

blunder was his own responsibility. It prevented the establishment of good relations with Garibaldi at a time when there was goodwill on both sides, barely a fortnight after the capture of Palermo; and from this derived the other misfortunes of the year.

La Farina arrived at Palermo on 6 June. His landing from a Sardinian man-of-war hardly confirmed the announcement that 'he has gone on his own initiative without any mission whether official or semi-official'.[1] Cavour had privately instructed Admiral Persano to convoy him, but to divulge neither the purpose of his journey nor even his name, adding that '*Sig*. La Farina enjoys my entire confidence, knows my plans, and so you can heed his words'.[2] The mission mentioned in this letter was that of concocting some scheme to undermine the allegiance of the Bourbon fleet, and Persano was instructed to help in this, even though Piedmont was officially on friendly relations with Francesco II at Naples. But La Farina's more important task, so Cavour wrote to Ricasoli on 3 June, was 'to see to the ordering of a regular government',[3] despite the fact that Garibaldi had so far invited no such intrusion into the affairs of the revolution. Letters warning Garibaldi against the man would have arrived on the same ship as La Farina himself, and perhaps this very same ship brought the news of the final decision of parliament to sacrifice Nice to France. Yet Garibaldi received him courteously; so much so that Cavour's semi-official newspaper incorrectly announced that he had been given the most important post in the revolutionary government. It was not Garibaldi's treatment of him, but La Farina's own subsequent activities, which made his position impossible and endangered the prospects of union between southern and northern Italy.

There was much in his favour at the outset. He arrived well supplied with money, with a titled *aide* to help win over the Sicilian aristocracy, with annexationist leaflets for his propaganda, and with the specially chartered support of the Sardinian naval and consular authorities. He had all the prestige of being known for Cavour's agent and money-bearer, and probably the dispenser of future patronage and promotion. He was supported by his own reputation as a Sicilian patriot returning

[1] 14 June, *L'Opinione* (Turin).
[2] 1 June, Cavour to Persano (*CC Lib. del Mezz.* vol. I, p. 160).
[3] 3 June, Cavour to Ricasoli (*ibid.* p. 163).

from exile, and by the fact that some of his friends were already well placed in the revolutionary government at Palermo. Garibaldi so far had done nothing to provoke political discord, but had instinctively gone out of his way to conciliate all parties in a united front. Although the radical Crispi had been responsible for organizing the government, the other ministers were mostly moderate liberals: Baron Pisani, for instance, the foreign minister, was a man who had been expressly sent back to Sicily by Cavour, and so was Piola the minister of marine.[1] This is convincing testimony to Garibaldi's good sense and moderation. They were all good appointments, said the British consul about this first ministry of 2–27 June;[2] and Goodwin was certainly no radical.

Without more ado, La Farina set to work. A newspaper was founded with the title of *L'Annessione*, and the town was soon plastered with printed notices saying 'we want annexation to the kingdom of Victor Emanuel'.[3] His activity during the next fortnight was thus described by a partisan critic, Crispi:

at first he tried to persuade me through his friends, of the necessity of taking him into the government. Then he began organising hostile demonstrations, which did not succeed, spreading damaging insinuations that failed to affect us, and his last move was an attempt to bring about a ministerial crisis, which resulted in the resignation of three of my colleagues—Torrearsa, Pisani and Guarneri. His lightest accusation is that I am a republican and am endangering the success of the Sicilian revolution....

In this country of ours, with its hot-headed inhabitants, we may look forward to serious danger, if his intriguing is not checked. It is indeed painful to think that, after so many sacrifices, after the spilling of so much blood, they should seek to deprive us of the joy of gathering the fruit of so many years of study and suffering!![4]

One must suppose that La Farina was here exceeding his instructions, or else that Cavour had left not only the execution but the actual formulation of policy to a subordinate. Their obvious interest should

---

[1] 21 May, Mathieu to Cavour (*ibid.* p. 121); 23 June, Cavour to Persano (*ibid.* p. 234).

[2] 5 June (Goodwin's Political Journal no. 5, F.O. 165/134).

[3] 14 June, Admiral Mundy, *H.M.S. Hannibal at Palermo and Naples 1859–61*, 1863, p. 175; 11 June, *Il Garibaldi* (Palermo); 22 June, *Gazzetta di Catania*.

[4] Crispi, *Memoirs*, vol. I, pp. 255–6.

have been to maintain friendly relations with Garibaldi. That friendliness was still possible is proved by Garibaldi's amicable conversations with the Piedmontese Admiral Persano. But La Farina's conduct put Cavour into direct conflict with the dictator. The returned exile, back among the political and family vendettas of his native island, must have lost his sense of proportion. Certainly he must have been insufficiently briefed for his mission; and it seems that, intentionally or unintentionally, Cavour had given him no instructions to be tactful or compromising.

His opposite number in this miniature struggle for power was Crispi, the leading Sicilian among the Italian radicals, and second only to Garibaldi in his influence over the fortunes of Sicily in this year. Garibaldi later called him the man who was 'first in intelligence among our expeditionary force, and the real organiser and ruler in the heroic government of Sicily in 1860'.[1] Crispi was to have a striking future in Italian politics, as one of the architects of the Triple Alliance and the new Italian empire, and as the 'reactionary' prime minister who crushed a Sicilian socialist movement in the nineties. As a young man he had become a lawyer and a journalist of Mazzini's school. Exiled in turn from Sicily, Piedmont, Malta, and France, he always retained some of the venom and irreconcilable temper of the hardened exile. In this respect he was a good match for his one-time colleague and now enemy, La Farina. Both these two shared a strong wish for the creation of a powerful Italy—as prime minister Crispi was later to have the reputation of sternly repressing any move for Sicilian autonomy. They likewise shared a consummate ambition, an authoritarian temperament, and an extreme arrogance and dogmatism in their private and public behaviour. But Crispi, who retained longer than the other a distinct tinge of the Jacobin, was his rival on personal grounds, as well as being strongly opposed to the conservative policy of piecemeal annexation. It was wrong but perhaps excusable in Cavour to think that this young radical was first too contemptible, and then too dangerous a man to be wooed by his ambition into a coalition with orthodoxy. Crispi made unmistakable overtures for an understanding with the liberal-conservatives during 1860, but this necessary task of conversion was left to be carried through by later politicians.

[1] 24 November 1869, Garibaldi to Crispi (printed in the *Giornale d' Italia*, 18 July 1909).

The revolution of 1860 gave Crispi his first experience of power since 1849. To him almost as much as to Garibaldi, and more than to any other, was due the setting out from Genoa of the *Mille*. In 1859, while Cavour and La Farina had been counselling Sicilians to keep quiet so as not to complicate Piedmontese activity in the north, Crispi had left his English exile, and with forged British and American passports had twice visited Sicily in disguise. There he had secretly organized groups of political revolutionaries, showing them how to make home-made bombs, and in general preparing them for the day of deliverance. At Turin he had then tried to bespeak the active interest in his scheme of Rattazzi, who had temporarily succeeded Cavour as the leading figure in the government. When this failed, it was Crispi, together with Bixio and Bertani, who persuaded Garibaldi to lead his piratical expedition.[1] Once arrived in Sicily, Crispi stepped automatically into the position of legislator and statesman of the revolution, organizing the administration in Palermo, and generally acting as Garibaldi's right-hand man.

What were Crispi's politics? When Petruccelli asked him whether he was a Garibaldian or Mazzinian, he replied—neither: 'io sono Crispi'.[2] And indeed he was always too self-confident to take orders or opinions readily from other people. His views were certainly radical, but we shall see that they were not to be completely identified with those of Garibaldi. As to his relations with Mazzini, like so many other Italians of all political shades he had learnt from Mazzini to be a patriot, and to the end of his life he retained a warmer regard for his master's memory than did many others among the former republicans. In 1859 he had stood by Mazzini in opposition to Cavour's war against Austria —a war, incidentally, which Garibaldi supported—and throughout 1860 he remained at least in correspondence with him. But whereas Mazzini had accepted monarchical government contingently and temporarily, Crispi had now done so finally, and there is no evidence that he wavered in his loyalty to the throne. In so far as there was in this year still any rift between Garibaldi and Mazzini, Crispi ranged himself alongside Garibaldi. Although the fact was never quite appreciated or believed at Turin, the real diehard republicans had abandoned the *Mille* in the first fortnight of May, and Crispi had not

[1] *Risposta del Generale Türr all' opuscolo Bertani*, 1869, p. 6.
[2] F. Petruccelli della Gattina, *I Moribondi del Palazzo Carignano*, 1862, p. 170.

been among them. As he wrote to Bertani in June: 'our friends among the republicans accuse us of forsaking the banner; Cavour's followers say we want a republic! What we really want is Italy, and we will have her!'[1]

The making of Italy was Crispi's objective, and the redemption of Sicily but one step towards that end. In this and other respects he was a good deal nearer to the policy of Turin than La Farina allowed Cavour to know. To judge from Crispi's Palermo paper, the *Precursore*, he began by being almost surprisingly moderate in his political views. He stood up for Mazzini personally, while repudiating the more extravagant aspects of his policy, and asserted that frank acceptance of the monarchy was an essential preliminary if it was wished to unite the nation. Cavour and his friends were misinformed or credulous if they thought that Crispi was working to proclaim a republic from Rome.[2] Equally false was the accusation that he was acting on behalf of Sicilian separatism against any form of union with Naples. For in fact, as a convinced unitarian, he was one of the few Sicilians whose hatred of the Bourbons remained unadulterated by dislike of Neapolitans in general.[3]

If these dangerous suspicions gained currency in the north, this was due to La Farina's reports, which were unfortunately the basis on which Cavour built his policy. These put all the disorganization in Palermo down to Crispi's mismanagement, and ignored the fact that five days of street battle, followed by the complete breakdown of Bourbon administration and the improvization of a new government, were bound to leave disorganization behind. Deceptive accounts were also sent back of how Garibaldi's regime was becoming highly unpopular and could hardly last much longer.[4] From these reports, government circles in Turin acquired a hostility not only to the administration of Garibaldi, but even to Sicilians in general.[5] Later historians, too, were mostly to take La Farina's word for what was happening at this time in

[1] Crispi, *Memoirs*, vol. I, p. 266.

[2] 31 August, Crispi to Correnti, asking him 'to present my humble compliments to His Majesty our champion' (ACP, b. 152). It was Crispi who had proclaimed Garibaldi to be dictator 'in the name of Victor Emanuel'.

[3] 26 January, Crispi to Fabrizi (*Crispi: lettere dall' esilio*, ed. T. Palamenghi-Crispi, 1918, p. 201).

[4] 20 June, *L' Opinione* (Turin), reports from Palermo dated 12 and 14 June.

[5] L. Natoli, *Rivendicazioni attraverso le rivoluzioni siciliane del 1848–60*, 1927, p. 194.

the south, not making allowances for his character and the fact that he had an axe to grind. It is probable that he was not above exaggerating difficulties so as to appear the cleverer in correcting them, and his criticism of Crispi was coupled to equally exaggerated and tendentious statements about his own popularity.

There is evidence to suggest that, as early as 16 June, Cavour realized he had made a mistake in sending out this particular man.[1] Quite apart from the unfortunate influence La Farina was having in Sicily, there was the important point that his absence from Turin left the National Society leaderless and disintegrating. Nevertheless, instead of recalling him, Cavour just gave belated instructions not to force a breach with Garibaldi,[2] and hurriedly dispatched Cordova and others of his Sicilian acquaintance after him in the hope that they might prevent an open cleavage and perhaps discover a better policy. Cavour's semi-official newspaper at Turin referred on the 22nd to the deviation of view between the government and its agent, and also mentioned the unanimous feeling among Sicilians that La Farina's failure in the Sicilian revolution of 1848–9 made him unacceptable as a leader in 1860. In view of La Farina's later expulsion, and the criticism of Garibaldi which then ensued, this confession is worthy of note. The king at least, if not Cavour as well, was becoming aware of the necessity of recalling him, and did not hesitate to express indignation.[3] But still nothing was done.

The peak of La Farina's campaign was reached when the civic council of Palermo was persuaded to register an official motion to the dictator in favour of annexation. To this motion, Garibaldi on the 22nd replied in a pronouncement of what henceforward had to be accepted as orthodoxy. 'It was I who gave you the cry of "Italy and Victor Emanuel"....It is now equally in my power by dictatorial act to proclaim annexation....But let us have this quite clear, I came here to fight for the cause of Italy, not just for that of Sicily: and if we do not liberate and unite the whole of Italy, we shall never succeed properly in any of her individual provinces.'[4] This was one of the simplest and

---

[1] 16 June, Bargoni to Bertani, saying that Cavour was now desirous of replacing La Farina (ABCM and *CC Lib. del Mezz.* vol. I, pp. 208, 229).

[2] 23 June, Cavour to Persano (*CC Lib. del Mezz.* vol. I, p. 234).

[3] Crispi, *Memoirs*, vol. I, p. 322; Comandini, *L' Italia nei cento anni*, vol. III, p. 1490; 22 June, *L' Opinione.*   [4] 26 June, *L' Annessione* (Palermo).

clearest statements of Garibaldi's point of view, and the argument behind it had some plausibility and was sincerely believed. It seems to have satisfied the civic council,[1] and so to have ended the attempt to undermine Garibaldi's position through the mayor and corporation.[2] But in one point La Farina had succeeded: by precipitating and publicizing the issue of annexation to Piedmont, he had rallied for this policy enough support to shake Crispi's position in the government. The effects of his campaign were beginning to be felt in Palermo as well as Turin.

[1] 27 June, *Gazzetta di Catania*, report from Palermo dated 22 June.
[2] La Farina's *Gazzetta del Consiglio Civico di Palermo* came to an end after producing its first and only number on 23 June.

CHAPTER IV

ARGUMENTS FOR AND AGAINST ANNEXATION

The political conflict in Sicily between June and October took shape round one central problem, how soon and by what method the island would join up with the existing kingdom in northern Italy. It will help to explain this conflict if a general preview is given of the various arguments brought up by one side or the other. Historians generally used to conclude that 'immediate annexation to Piedmont was the wise policy for Sicily'. Crispi and his friends, in opposing 'the almost universal eagerness of the Sicilians to be annexed', were said by Bolton King to have had 'no excuse'; and they were not even allowed any motive except 'to leave a thorn in the side of the government', and perhaps to upset the monarchy.[1] Such an interpretation, however, is more than just oversimplified, it is inaccurate.

Some of the reasons urged for quick annexation were spurious in the extreme: for instance, that it would stop England from acquiring her coveted foothold in Sicily,[2] or that it would prevent Garibaldi's camarilla from taking all the perquisites and pickings of office;[3] or else that, by making impossible any further expeditions to Rome, it would end the hated novelty of conscription which Garibaldi was trying hard to introduce.[4] Much more weighty than these was the argument that annexation would restore law and order to the country, and compel northern Italy to underwrite the revolution against a Bourbon restora-

[1] Bolton King, *A History of Italian Unity*, vol. II, 1899, pp. 148–9.

[2] 14 June, *L' Unione* (Milan).

[3] 12 July, G. Fiorenza from Palermo to Ricasoli, to be published in the new *Carteggi di Bettino Ricasoli* in course of preparation by M. Nobili and S. Camerani.

[4] 19 August, Major Cadolini from Messina to Bargoni: 'the Sicilians have no wish to become soldiers, and still less to come with us on to Naples. They shout "viva l' Italia", but really have no thoughts except for themselves. They could not put up a worse showing if they tried. The Sicilian government makes no effort to carry out conscription. And the army which is now called "southern" is composed for nine-tenths of northerners' (MRR).

tion. In many parts of Sicily the pent-up communist rebelliousness of the peasants had been released by the war, and Garibaldi's government found itself with no effective police force to keep the peace. The ruling class was predominantly one of landowners, who were particularly anxious for a return to peace and an end of social war. Merchants wanted a conclusion to the war emergency, and most of them felt certain that a close Piedmontese connexion would favour their trade. The important class of lawyers was to be unemployed continuously for five months, and during this time grew increasingly impatient with military rule. For them and the professional classes generally, annexation held out the attraction of more jobs, higher salaries, and a wider audience or *clientèle*.

The convergence of these various motives would suggest that, if Cavour had played his hand well, annexation might have followed almost automatically. After all, Garibaldi on landing had at once proclaimed Victor Emanuel as king, and all his dictatorial edicts were headed with the sovereign's name. Moreover 'spontaneous' adhesion to this procedure and programme had been received from each successive city in the island as it was conquered. On 14 June Garibaldi's foreign minister officially declared to the governments of Europe that Sicily had in this way already 'voted' through its municipal councils; and that, although a plebiscite would probably follow at some time, it would be merely a formality to confirm this manifest intention to join the rest of Italy. On 2 July he even published a statement to say that 'the island regards itself as already part of the kingdom of Italy'. Such was the design of the revolutionary government. But over the application of this design Palermo and Turin were out of step from the start. Being too far away to judge the situation correctly, Cavour was unable to specify or control properly the detailed political tactics of his agents on the spot. La Farina at first thought that he had official approval for refusing to concede any point to the Garibaldian party. Cavour's correspondence shows how many other things had to compete with Sicily for precedence in his mind. In any case, administration was always less interesting to him than diplomacy, and gave less scope for his own peculiar expertise. Hence his failure to take advantage of this general agreement over essentials in Sicily. Garibaldi's moderate appointments, and the foreign minister's proclamation, went unheeded.

Instead, goodwill and agreement were dissipated by bad tactics, by trying to set up an organized opposition to the dictator, and by trying to force a precipitate vote in a way which aroused all his native suspicion. Some of those who later in the year changed their minds, were at this stage convinced that Cavour's campaign for annexation was premature. Others who now supported it, later confessed that they had been wrong to do so, and even *L'Annessione* was grudgingly to admit the wisdom of Garibaldi's repudiation of its own earlier policy on this point.[1] The Milanese *Perseveranza*, which was another conservative journal, did likewise. For it had to be granted that no free vote could be held while Bourbon troops still controlled an important part of Sicily; and equally it was true that Garibaldi's dictatorial powers were still needed for the direction of emergency government and completion of the enemy's defeat. More important still, annexation at this moment would positively have embarrassed Turin, since France and Austria could then have pinned a definite responsibility on Cavour for Sicilian affairs, whereas at present Garibaldi was happily responsible to no one.[2] Europe could have penalized Cavour, where it could not easily penalize Garibaldi. Moreover, Napoleon's subsequent attempt to stop the volunteer army from crossing the Straits might have been irresistible had the island already been formally annexed.[3]

The first argument against prompt annexation was that, if a vote by universal suffrage was necessary to pacify Napoleon, no even remotely plausible vote on this scale could yet be taken. Until the end of July, Garibaldi could not call himself master of the north-eastern sector of the island, and isolated Bourbon garrisons continued to exist in Sicily for a long time after that. Secondly, Garibaldi did not wish to be bothered with elections in the middle of a precarious military campaign. His dislike of La Farina therefore came vividly to life when a group of civilians began this attempt to distract people's energies from the war and to frivol at *piazza* politics. It seemed to him that preparations for a plebiscite would only divert much enthusiasm and organization away from the front line, and this would be merely for something which he and Sicily had already accepted in principle. By stooping to these

[1] 11 September, *L' Annessione*.
[2] 17 September, *La Perseveranza* (Milan).
[3] 1 July, De Sanctis to De Meis (*Lettere dall' esilio*, 1938, ed. Croce, p. 343).

intrigues, La Farina was only damaging his own cause; for the radicals naturally made capital out of this fact when they wanted to convince Garibaldi that there were strong political objections to such suspicious haste.

Of these political objections to an immediate vote, one was that annexation would mean taking away Piedmontese troops from the vulnerable northern frontier; and this in turn might have emboldened the Austrians to abandon their highly precarious attitude of non-intervention. A yet stronger objection was that it threatened to spoil any hope of quick annexation for the rest of the peninsula.[1] Piedmont was technically on friendly terms with Naples, and Cavour therefore, once he was established as ruler of Sicily, would have been much embarrassed if Garibaldi sailed thence on another piratical expedition to the mainland. By annexation of Sicily, the revolutionary initiative might thus be brought to a stop while Rome and Venice still lay subjugated to the foreigner. The radicals were able to point out that something similar had happened in 1859, when Farini and Fanti had held up Garibaldi's march on Rome: once Emilia had been annexed, little interest had been shown by that province in the rest of Italy, and so a chance of advancing further into Umbria and the Marches had been lost. On this analogy, the annexation of Sicily would only clip Garibaldi's wings, and the island would then become, like Emilia, an outlying dependency of Turin instead of a constituent province of a new kingdom of Italy.[2] On 3 August Crispi's paper carried an article with this interpretation:

it is told of a certain prince of Savoy how he once spoke of Italy to one of his courtiers in these terms, 'we shall eat it leaf by leaf like this artichoke'. Such an attitude typifies the narrow national spirit of the Piedmontese: they have never wanted Piedmont for Italy, but always Italy for Piedmont...; except on one occasion when at long last a great prince managed to change their attitude—this prince was Victor Emanuel, and the time was the campaign of '59....

---

[1] 19 July, *Il Precursore*: 'you who cry out for annexation do not want Italy to become one nation, but just desire liberty for Sicily at the expense of more slavery for Naples, Rome and Venice....If we should isolate Sicily from mother Italy in order to annex ourselves separately to Piedmont, this would retard the coming of full unification.'

[2] 11 August, *La Forbice* (Palermo).

As far as Cavour is concerned, however, there has been no radical change. If he were to obtain his wish and Garibaldi were forced to put up his sword, then Sicily would become a province of Piedmont; perhaps the diplomats of Europe would allot us a new master, and instead of Austria we should have the French. Does not Bonaparte's policy make you suspect this? Would not annexation lead us probably to federation instead of unification?[1]

Many educated Sicilians seem to have wanted some degree of home rule, but La Farina's programme rather opened up a prospect of centralization under the government of Turin.[2] Unconditional annexation could therefore be depicted as implying the same mixture of exploitation, neglect and bureaucratic misrule which was causing the island of Sardinia to wither under Torinese administration.[3] The example of Tuscany was yet further evidence that Piedmontese rule did not automatically bring the ordered government that its champions had expected. Observers more perceptive than La Farina might have realized that disorder in Sicily did not come only from Garibaldi's waywardness or inefficiency, but rather from deep social causes which even the skilled bureaucrats of Piedmont were not going to remove. On the other hand, government from the north was bound to bring with it all manner of novel customs and institutions which would offend local tradition and cause difficulties of assimilation.[4] Some of the more far-sighted

---

[1] 3 August, *Il Precursore.*

[2] La Farina, *Credo*, originally published in February 1858; but at least two editions appeared in Sicily during 1860.

[3] 17 August, La Varenne to Crispi: 'ne pas vous livrer *sans conditions* à Turin, tant que M. de Cav. sera là, car vous en verrez de belles et le pays aussi si on tombait dans son arbitraire. Regardez la Sardaigne à deux pas de vous' (ACP, f. 149).

[4] Those in Cavour's party who put down all the troubles of Sicily to Garibaldi's inefficiency might have learnt something from a letter written to Ricasoli by his secretary in September, which showed that there were plentiful disorders in Tuscany still, long after 'annexation': 'the moral unrest in the country is in part due to the ineffective protection given to property and to the liberty of citizens. Outside the cities people may thieve with impunity right and left, and certain people in the guise of liberals tyrannize over the small villages, not allowing even the freedom to think.' Tabarrini added (what in Sicily was to be discovered too late), that a contributory cause of unrest was the great speed of assimilation by Piedmont which was so damaging to morale; and he concluded, 'until Italian affairs have settled down, we must try hard to hold on to our old Tuscan institutions as long as we can' (*Carteggi di Ricasoli*, ed. Nobili and Camerani).

4-2

Sicilians might also have envisaged the likelihood that annexation would bring with it far higher taxes, and they would have to carry their share of the heavy debts already contracted by Piedmont in the wars against Austria. Almost certainly it would lead to the introduction of an efficient and permanent system of conscription, and would soon put an end to fiscal protection for local products in the national market.

There was an alternative line of reasoning which led to a different but even less welcome conclusion. For, as Cavour's negotiations proceeded through July and into August with the Neapolitan envoys who were seeking his alliance against Garibaldi, Sicilians had some inducement to believe that Cavour might prefer to win Neapolitan support against Austria by a sacrifice of Sicily. Surrender to Cavour in that case might mean a return to the hated Bourbon allegiance and to dependence on remote Naples.[1] Alternatively it might mean a further sacrifice of Italian territory to France. Garibaldi was always firmly convinced that there existed in France a well-considered plan for national aggrandizement at Italy's expense, just as he was also sure that Cavour was a lackey of Napoleon: if this was right, the acquisition of still more territory in the south might demand the alienation of yet another Italian province in compensation, just as Cavour had paid for French approval several months earlier by the sacrifice to France of Nice.[2] This was no wildly improbable hypothesis, and it was quite generally held in British government circles. The Italian radicals were convinced of it. As Cattaneo wrote in June: 'if you let Cavour have Sicily, France will take Spezia just as surely as if Garibaldi were handing it over with his own hands.... To avoid all such claims by France it is imperative that Sicily at all costs should remain free as long as possible.... We must make it the barracks and the arsenal for all that still remains to be done.'[3] However unjust this innuendo, precedent made it plausible when viewed alongside the other causes of growing suspicion.

Carlo Cattaneo was here speaking for one section of the radical 'party of action'. Unlike Cavour's disciplined supporters, who were usually united over ends and means as soon as their leader made up his mind on a point, the radicals were almost always divided, and never

[1] 12 October, *L' Assemblea* (Palermo).
[2] 19 July, *Il Precursore*.
[3] 9 June, Cattaneo to the Marios (Archivio J. W. Mario MRR).

formed a cohesive party in more than name. This was one of the strongest points in Cavour's favour. An important division inside the group of radicals was that Cattaneo called himself a federalist, putting the emphasis on individual liberty within the state, while Mazzini was before everything else a unitarian, with the emphasis on nationhood as something sacred and indivisible. Cattaneo would have found general support from the others for allowing Sicily some regional self-government, but only if this were in a general plan of moderate devolution for all the regions of Italy, and only if it would not cause any diminution in national strength and national consciousness.[1] Most of the radicals were strongly nationalistic, and ranged themselves with those who agreed that 'federation would restrict us to the place of a second-rate power'.[2] And on this point Cattaneo and Giuseppe Ferrari were bitterly opposed to the majority.

Compared to Cavour with his 'artichoke' policy, Mazzini was at once more of a political unitarian and less of an administrative centralist. The Mazzinians wanted annexation pure and simple,[3] but they also wanted to postpone the act of union till it might mean something more than mere surrender to Cavour and the conservatives. This policy of postponement arose directly out of their political radicalism, but was also inspired by their desire for national unity. At last they had some power and political status again, and Mazzini sincerely hoped that this might prove to be the salvation of Italy against the defeatist attitude and merely partial ambitions of both Cavour and the local autonomists. He told Crispi to 'support the independence of the revolution as long as ever you can...but if the autonomists agitate then you must precipitate annexation'. We can see from this that he hoped to establish a strong and independent base for future action, and to win the right if necessary to dictate political conditions to Cavour; yet he was quite as anxious as Cavour not to give the Sicilian autonomists any chance to air their views and perhaps capture the revolutionary movement.[4] At this particular moment he was hiding from Cavour's police in Genoa, knowing that he lay under double sentence of death from his own countrymen. As matters turned out, those of his friends who were in

[1] 4 September, *L'Unità Italiana* (Palermo).
[2] 27 August, *ibid.*   [3] 23 August, *ibid.*
[4] 22 June, Mazzini to Crispi (*Epistolario*, vol. XL, p. 96).

Sicily, for example Crispi and Mordini, often ignored his advice, and did not take such a rigid line against the autonomists. This fact was to have considerable importance for the course of the revolution.

One may say in general that the adherents of Cavour and Mazzini, though they differed on points of principle, had much in common when both are set against this third group of Sicilian autonomists. It was not over the general aim of unity or the method of revolution that the main split developed between the 'party of order' and the 'party of action', because each side contained both convinced unitarians and practising revolutionaries. Nor did the split occur over the propriety of annexing Sicily to the kingdom of Piedmont-Sardinia. It developed rather over whether annexation should come sooner or later. Unlike those who wanted special privileges for Sicily, Crispi did not oppose annexation, he just hoped to postpone it. He had no intention of imposing any conditions on Piedmont, except that he wanted to delay until annexation could no longer endanger the achievement of a unity which included also Naples, Rome and Venice. In this straightforward policy of delay he was no doubt moved in part by other reasons as well. For instance, there was the determination to prolong his enjoyment of power; and this was by no means an altogether unworthy motive, for only by such a prolongation could the plans he had taken so long to mature be carried out, and it was a reasonable assumption on his part that only the radicals had much chance or even much intention of capturing Rome. No doubt, too, it would have been his instinct to resist immediate annexation just because this was the means by which La Farina was hoping to replace him and become Royal Commissioner for Sicily. Nevertheless, it remains that Crispi's primary motive in delay was military and strategic. He assured Mazzini that 'annexation...will be established by vote as soon as this can be done without interfering with our operations on the Continent'.[1] The idea of postponement was all based on his magnificent optimism that Rome would be captured, and that this alone mattered. Nor can one ridicule this optimism, since Crispi had been proved correct against the wiseacres in thinking possible the original conquest of Sicily by a few irregulars. It was a fair supposition that Cavour's cold touch might devitalize this second expedition on to Rome, as it had only just failed to do with their first expedition to

[1] 31 July (Crispi, *Memoirs*, vol. 1, p. 363).

Sicily: for Cavour had not been converted to a delight in revolutionary enterprises, and he still feared that France might fight to save Rome for the Papacy.

From these opinions we may derive something like a general picture of radical policy in Sicily. One of its practitioners put it like this.

Sicily has become the centre of operations....Once master of the Nea-politan arsenals and the immense resources of that country, our march of liberation will be all the quicker....And when we have Rome we shall have Italy....We must make a really big military effort....Till now Palermo has not been pulling its weight....For it is in Sicily that we must discipline the armed forces of Italy, since Italian youth has no other secure and independent stronghold for such action.[1]

The function of Sicily in this radical programme was therefore to act as the springboard and the armoury for a war of final liberation.[2] Petruc-celli wrote in June from London to Garibaldi:

whatever you do, avoid becoming the King Lear of Democracy. Hold on to the Two Sicilies for our party...as something to bargain with against the European diplomats. Remember that one day you may have to say to Europe, 'either allow us to unify Italy under Victor Emanuel, or else we turn southern Italy into a republic'....And if you find this responsibility too heavy, associate yourself with a Convention, not one like the French Con-vention of '92, but a real 'Long Parliament' like that of Cromwell.[3]

Subsequent events were to suggest that much of this radical programme was utopian: but that is not to say it was mistakenly held at the time. The great practical function of the 'party of action' during the *risorgi-mento* was to be a prod for use against the liberals, who were thus forced to take over the radical achievements and give them the stamp of orthodoxy and finality. These radicals reasoned that Cavour looked on them as the chief enemy, and on France as the chief friend, of his own hoped-for Italy. La Farina's embassy had done nothing to disillusion them on this point, and for some reason Cavour on this occasion had made no attempt to deceive them into thinking him their friend. The subsequent messengers whom Cavour sent to Garibaldi were thinking

[1] 21 August, *Il Precursore*.
[2] 19 September, Asproni from Naples to Fabrizi (Archivio Fabrizi ASR).
[3] 14 June, *L' Unione* (Milan).

even as early as July of bringing 'large Piedmontese forces' to fight and destroy the radical nest in Sicily.[1] So there was some excuse for those radicals to cling to their foothold in southern Italy as the only basis in the future for their own political existence. To them it must have seemed that, Cavour once master, they would then be again sent into exile, outlawed from active political expression in Italy, and their principles defeated perhaps for ever. Their self-interest, their desire for responsibility and activity and power, were all at stake.

It may perhaps be thought in retrospect that Cavour was not so well served that he could afford lightly to reject the help of so many future ministers of Italy. But so far as he could see, they were but a few reckless hotheads; and since the government majority in parliament was completely safe, there was no need to stretch his gifts for compromise as he had done so cleverly with Rattazzi and the parliamentary Left eight years before. The issue of immediate annexation was one upon which he was ready to do battle.

[1] D. Guerrini, 'La Missione del Conte Litta Modignani in Sicilia 1860', *Il Risorgimento Italiano*, February 1909, pp. 23–4.

CHAPTER V

ARGUMENTS OVER WAYS AND MEANS

These differences of opinion were reflected from the start in practical politics. We have already watched the commencement of La Farina's campaign. But the political scene in Palermo still remained agitated after Garibaldi's rebuff on 22 June to the champions of immediate annexation. On the 23rd, Crispi's government was weakened by the resignation of two leading members of the Sicilian aristocracy, the Marquis di Torrearsa and Baron Pisani. Later in the same day, perhaps as a partial concession, a decree was issued to say that local authorities should draw up electoral registers and have all ready for voting by 20 July.[1] This marks a small but definite retreat by Crispi from the policy of 'nothing at all till Rome' which Garibaldi had proclaimed the day before in his speech to the civic council.[2] It was a new development, which shows that the situation was now becoming more complicated.

In trying to explain this modification of view, it first of all is clear that Crispi's political ascendancy had been shaken by the insinuations of La Farina, and he was therefore in a compromising mood. We know that he was trying to make contact with Cavour at this time, perhaps hoping to displace his rival in Sicily, and to reconcile all parties there by some striking and meritorious act of statesmanship. He had found that he could not ride the radical programme rough-shod over Palermo opinion. Sicilian susceptibilities had been touched by his innovation of conscription, and war conditions were adversely affecting many vested interests in the island. La Farina had an easy task in suggesting that remedial measures could be expected from Cavour as soon as annexation had been accomplished; and public opinion adjusted itself accordingly. There were also other tactical reasons which induced

[1] 23 June, *Raccolta degli atti del governo dittatoriale.*

[2] It was Crispi who proposed this decree and who circularized provincial governors to execute it with especial care; 25 and 28 June, *Giornale Officiale di Sicilia*; 3 July, *L' Annessione.*

Crispi to yield a point. He had if possible to forestall, or compete with, any grant of a constitution by the Bourbons. In fact King Francesco at Naples had already half-decided to concede Sicily her constitution of 1812,[1] so that there was good reason to fear lest he might recapture some popular support before being driven from his last foothold on the island. It was therefore advisable to put up quickly some plausible alternative and one which offered good long-term prospects of stable and enlightened government. The argument was also being advanced by some of the radicals that, while a vote of annexation would always bind Piedmont to help them, any actual execution of what had been voted could perhaps be delayed until the revolution had reached the national capital.[2]

Such were the thoughts which helped to inspire Crispi's decree of 23 June. One detail we can pause to note is that newspapers nearest to Mazzini deplored his decision.[3] Here we have more proof of another significant division among the radicals, and it was a division which Cavour might well have recognized and widened if he had not determined to look on Crispi as an incorrigible enemy. Notwithstanding all the tirades of La Farina, there were no republicans among Garibaldi's ministers, and most of those ministers were still nearer to Cavour than to Mazzini. But this fact was to be ignored at Turin. Instead, errors of policy by Cavour and his subordinates were to compel the radicals into a common front, and so his programme of annexation became the more difficult to carry out. He did not appreciate that, as soon as public opinion revealed itself, Garibaldi's government was ready to make concessions in the interests of common agreement.

Crispi's election decree was intended as a concession, but in fact it had little immediate effect. La Farina's campaign for a vote had not taken into account the difficulties of employing universal suffrage in a region so socially backward, especially when that region was torn by civil war and communistic *jacqueries*. A vote of any sort would have been

---

[1] 20 June, Elliot telegram to Russell (F.O. 70/317).

[2] 1 July, La Varenne from Turin to Crispi: 'même après le vote, vous avez cent moyens de retarder la chose, tout en vous conservant de l'appui (alors forcé) du Piémont. Le temps est tout, et soyez convaincu que M. de C. ne saurait durer beaucoup' (in the Italian edition of Crispi's memoirs, *I Mille*, vol. I, p. 241).

[3] 1 July, *L'Unità Italiana* (Genoa).

impossible at the moment. Most of the new politicians and civil servants were inexperienced; there was almost nothing left of a police force or local government, and most of the capable clerks and administrators had fled or been liquidated. Although the text of Crispi's decree mentioned 20 July as the date by which preparations were to be ready for the vote, this was soon seen to allow far too short an interval to make up for these administrative deficiencies. On 14 and 22 July, and again on 2 and 25 August, the date for completion of the registers had to be pushed further and further away. It is true that many of the common people in the towns inscribed themselves at once on the electoral lists, perhaps attracted by the novelty and the apparent sense of responsibility thus conferred. But the middle and upper classes were too lazy and too disinterested in this incomprehensible device to go to the appointed churches for registration; or else they went, and then could not be bothered to wait a quarter of an hour in the queue with their inferiors.[1] As for the peasants, the following report of how the prospect of universal suffrage was received in the country-side may not be untypical—a local official is writing to Crispi:

despite all my efforts, out of nine thousand people I cannot make more than six hundred inscribe themselves. The reason for this unfortunate fact is the rumour that those who inscribe as electors will be those chosen for conscription. Because of this current impression I summoned the clergy, and arranged that they should give a sermon on the importance of voting.... What was my surprise when Mass began and still the priest made no attempt to mount the pulpit as he had promised. Seeing this, and still hoping for some result, one of the electoral commission stood up and began to speak. But his first words were taken wrongly, and people took fright. Everyone in the church fled into the fields, and most of them heard no Mass that day.[2]

It is obvious that Sicily was not ready for self-government, nor even perhaps for a plebiscite by universal suffrage to decide its own future.

The final decision did not, of course, lie with the common people. Even under 'universal suffrage' it would be the so-called ruling classes who determined the issue; and among these it was not any conventional

---

[1] 29 June, *La Forbice* (Palermo); 4 August, *L' Unità Italiana* (Florence); 29 July, *La Nazione* (Florence); 26 July, 22 September, *L' Annessione.*

[2] 14 August, Sansa from Floridia to Crispi (ACP, b. 155).

radicalism or liberalism which prevailed. The issues which divided
Cavour from Garibaldi, and La Farina from Crispi, were not always
those which were felt most keenly in Sicily. Again one comes back to
that variegated section of municipalists or autonomists, whose views
pervaded public opinion, and whose vote in the end would decide the
whole controversy. Any generalization about these people can be true
only in part, for they differed widely amongst themselves and never
formed a compact political party with common beliefs. We only know
that numbered among them were many of the leading names of
Sicily: many of the lawyers, trained to use Sicilian law, and fearing the
introduction of new codes and an appeal court in Turin; aristocrats who
were immersed in local history and traditions of Sicilian parliamen-
tarism; the clergy, fearing for the great possessions of the Church at the
hands of secularized Piedmont, and jealous for the ancient insular
privilege of apostolic legateship; agriculturalists with special interests
needing protection in a national market; and those numerous people
who feared that a northern government would nationalize the basic salt
and sulphur industries to bring these into line with northern practice,
or would spread out over the whole peninsula the high taxes and
colossal national debt of Piedmont. So far as one can see, the most vocal
and powerful elements in Sicilian society wanted at least some measure
of local autonomy. That is to say, public opinion in the island should be
differentiated on the one hand from Mazzinian unitarians, and on the
other hand from those who wanted a speedy and complete fusion with
Piedmont. We shall see that many of the more moderate among these
autonomists could still want an immediate, and sometimes an unconditional, vote of union with the northern kingdom; but political
union in their minds by no means implied administrative or financial
fusion. The simple alternative between nationalism and 'annexation'
was not one which was either immediately apparent or inherently
attractive to them.

Some few might even now have been content with self-government
under the Bourbons, so long as Sicilian administration was made quite
separate from that of Naples. A very few at the other extreme might
have fancied a completely separate existence, and no connexion with
either Piedmont or Naples. But the more realistic eventually had to
recognize in Piedmontese protection their only guarantee against a

resumption of Neapolitan rule. Furthermore, they had to acknowledge that this was bound to mean something more than a mere union of crowns with Piedmont, however much such a loose connexion might be 'what every Sicilian would dearly love, only none dare ask for'.[1] A favourite system canvassed was the Scots solution of a common parliament but a separate legal system; for the lawyers were obviously attracted by this sort of autonomy. Discussion in pamphlets and newspapers also took into consideration the Swiss and Norwegian constitutions, as well as the American system of a unitary but federal state. One distinct attitude was based on the assumption that Sicily had its own insular nationality, so that, while it might possibly join an Italian federation, it never should form part of a united kingdom.[2] Almost directly opposed to this was the view put forward by Mariano Stabile in a letter to Lady Russell: that if Italy were to emerge as a unitary state well and good; but if, as seemed the more likely possibility early in 1860, Italy were to become a federation, then Sicily would prefer independence to the risk of ending up a mere appendage of Naples.[3]

What is important to grasp is not so much the points of contact and deviation between the different varieties of autonomist, but the fact that they together formed an important background of opinion to the open conflict between the two active and extraneous parties led by Crispi and La Farina. The bulk of them do not seem to have been attached to either of these parties, but sometimes acted as though the only hope of making their own views prevail consisted in a deliberate attempt to widen the breach between the two. This fact lies under the surface of active politics all through these months, and while it is impossible to assay its precise influence at any one moment, yet the knowledge of its existence will often help to unravel the political complications in Palermo.

We may see for instance during June some indication of a change of view by this third and rather amorphous political group. So far, it had been possible to think from Garibaldi's pronouncements that he had been trying to impose annexation on Sicily, and that he had failed in this just because the autonomists wanted only a loose bond with

---

[1] *Cenni sul giusto modo d' intendere l' annessione della Sicilia*, 1860, p. 3 (Biblioteca di Storia Moderna, Rome).

[2] *Appendice all' opuscolo sull' annessione ed autonomia*, 14 August 1860, pp. 20, 29.

[3] 12 January, Stabile to Lady Russell (RP G.D. 22/73).

Piedmont.[1] With new circumstances this situation was almost reversed, and it now appeared that Garibaldi wished for delay, while many of the autonomists paradoxically wanted annexation. The explanation is partly that, although La Farina's party tactlessly went on tilting against the 'imbecile' autonomists,[2] Cavour repaired this by cleverly hinting to these same people that unconditional annexation might be rewarded later by an ample dose of self-government. Cavour had thus been gradually winning over some of their leaders ever since his informal talks with Torrearsa and Cordova earlier in the year. Hence, by June and July, many of them were ready to prefer immediate annexation, trusting that the national parliament would afterwards make a voluntary concession of regional autonomy.

What Cavour gained in this process, Garibaldi lost. Admiration was unbounded for the person of the dictator, but not for his policy of continuing the war. Once Sicily was liberated, the sustaining impulse behind the revolution thus declined. People there were beginning to suspect that Garibaldi was exploiting them in an attempt to link up Sicily and Naples in a common liberation. The hateful province on the continent was to many of them not worth their sacrifice, and they found abhorrent the very thought that Garibaldi might then set up a joint dictatorship over both Sicily and Naples. Before very long, it was the radical party which was referring to these autonomists as 'imbeciles',[3] and Crispi disliked Cavour the more for playing up to their unworthy selfishness. This third party did not consider annexation to be just one step towards a united Italy, as did Garibaldi or Crispi; annexation was rather the only apparent hope of deliverance from Naples the hereditary enemy. They would have felt humiliated to follow behind Naples in yielding to Piedmont, just as they did not want even to find themselves associated with Naples in an act of joint submission. 'The municipalist party in Sicily', wrote Calvino, 'now wants annexation immediately so as to be able to carry this out before Naples has time to do likewise.'[4] In this sense, the movement for immediate annexation to Piedmont was fed by sentiments which were not exactly Italophile, and which even

[1] 20 June, Conte Siracusa to G. Fiorelli (Museo di San Martino, Naples).
[2] 6 July, La Farina to Cavour (CF).
[3] 29 July, *Il Precursore*.
[4] 9 July, Calvino to Bargoni (*Memorie di Bargoni*, p. 133).

could be positively anti-Italian. This helps to explain why the radical unitarians sometimes looked upon that movement with such suspicion.

These, very roughly, were the current political opinions in June, when several of the more moderate and intelligent Sicilians resigned from the government in protest against Crispi's evident wish to postpone annexation indefinitely. But people of the same political tendencies were to side again with the radicals as soon as it became a question, not of the *time*, but of the *method* of annexation.[1] The conservative Cavour was obliged to favour the revolutionary method of a plebiscite, whereas the radicals wanted to supplement this with that highly traditional Sicilian institution, an assembly of elected representatives. On this point the autonomists tended to side with the radicals and tradition. An assembly would be able to debate all the various possible schemes of union, and to bring the free discussion of enlightened minds to bear on the problem. On the other hand, to force upon the illiterate mob a falsely simplified yes or no vote would leave Sicilians but little say in their own future, and the true significance of their eventual choice would remain unclarified. A simple plebiscite was wanted only by those who advocated quick and unconditional annexation; but many of the autonomists would have liked to attach certain conditions to the act of union, and for this a plebiscite was no use.[2] An elected assembly was

---

[1] E.g. 20 October, *L' Annessione*, A. Guarneri's letter to the editor.

[2] 15 August, Elliot to Russell encloses this statement from a Sicilian, dated 10 August: 'we are all quiet here but do not like the proceedings of the Sardinian Government.... The Sicilians do not like the annexation without a concerted plan for the terms of a separate local government: they would *not* send Members of Parliament to either Turin or Rome' (F.O. 165/133). The British had an interest in regional autonomy which was sentimental and something more. Goodwin noted on 1 August, 'a simple or absolute annexation implies the surrender of the national rights, an act of boundless confidence too great to be prudently risked. A conditional annexation is therefore the wiser course. The conditions to be required are five in number, namely Civil Liberty, Municipal Freedom, National Defence, Free Press and Better Education.... The mode of voting the annexation, whether by direct or indirect suffrage, and the establishment of a constitution, whether the Sicilian or Sardinian, are subjects for future consideration' (Political Journal no. 16, F.O. 165/134). Another British point of view was the criticism made about Garibaldi in the *Westminster Review*, April 1861, vol. XIX, pp. 344–5: 'we are rather inclined to regard as an illegal stretch of power the decree of October by which he finally ordered the vote of annexation to be taken by universal suffrage.... As soon as the island was free, it was his duty to summon the

the only method by which they could lay down conditions of annexation and give publicity to the existence of purely Sicilian interests. There was also the point that Tuscany and the central duchies had lately been summoned to vote on this same question by means of elected assemblies, and it would seem doubly offensive if Sicily were singled out for a different procedure, despite her far older and still living traditions of representative government.[1]

If these were the arguments advanced by the autonomists, there were other reasons why, in the next few weeks, many of the radicals should come to share with them this preference for a representative assembly. It is true that Crispi and his friends always tended to look askance on *conditional* annexation as derogating from their ideal concept of United Italy; but they were also set against the policy of administrative centralism with which the parliament at Turin had become associated, and were ready to agree that the best means to their end might be to reconcile unity with the existence of special economic needs and historic rights in each region. Moreover, the word 'assembly' almost carried the same significance as their cherished 'constituent'. Such a body might be induced to make annexation depend on Cavour's acquisition of Rome. It might also prevent him imposing Piedmontese laws and institutions on the south, and might insist on the creation of something quite new, as befitted a newly-constituted kingdom of Italy.[2] It would provide a public platform for the airing of radical opinions. Incidentally it would prolong the process of annexation until Garibaldi had had time to carry the revolution over to the mainland and perhaps on to Rome. By its very existence it would provide a useful bargaining counter, if ever a pact could be struck with the conservatives. The radicals knew, furthermore, that any support for their views was to be found rather among those educated classes who would predominate among

Sicilian Parliament, conformably to the constitution.... That assembly, one of the most venerable in Europe, not only theoretically possessed the right of disposing of the crown, but had actually exercised it, not only in the Middle Ages, by conferring Sicily successively on the Houses of Suabia and Aragon, but as recently as 1848, by electing the Duke of Genoa as King; and the tyranny of the Neapolitans during eleven years assuredly did not suffice legally to abrogate the ancient laws.'

[1] *Assemblea o plebiscito: memoria*, 1860, pp. 7, 14.

[2] 11 August, La Forbice (Palermo).

the deputies to an assembly: whereas on the other hand they feared the ignorance of the common people; and there was always the possibility that a snap plebiscite vote might be manipulated to crush the last hope of carrying through their anti-Cavourian idea of the *risorgimento*.[1] A mass vote by all the people would surely tend to become a vote for safety first and a quiet life, or for giving absolute priority to the interests of Sicily; while the real need was for courage and action, and for an absolute priority to be given to the interests of Italy as a whole.

In this conflict of ideas the scales were heavily weighted in favour of Cavour, for the radicals were too individualistic to agree on the same point at any one moment. If they came near to common agreement over wanting an assembly, this was not altogether of their own free will, but was forced on them by events which they disliked. The impetus towards national unification was always their first consideration, and some of them feared that an assembly might lead towards Sicilian separation or a federal Italy.[2] It was a risk, that is to say; but still it was a risk which had to be run. Eventually the political and military obstacles which held up their march on Rome were to make a postponement more desirable from their point of view, and an assembly that much more welcome. This gradual approximation of view between radicals and autonomists is reflected in the following statement by a Sicilian—it is taken from a pamphlet written in August:

I would prefer a plebiscite if only it were laid down by law that conditions could be arranged later in a constituent assembly held at Rome, and also if we could agree that interim authority should meanwhile rest with dictator or King only in so far as such authority is necessary for the war or for the maintenance of public order.

If agreement on these lines is impossible, I think we ought to vote by means of an assembly, in which we could discuss the pact of union and how to carry it out. So doing, we should avoid binding ourselves hand and foot by the simple monosyllable 'yes'.

The unification of Italy on the doctrinaire French system would be tantamount to preparing civil war....Annexation must be either preceded or followed by the imposition of conditions.[3]

[1] 24 and 25 October, *Il Precursore*, article by F. Lo Presti.
[2] 14 July, Fragala from Catania to Crispi (ACP, f. 138).
[3] L. Vigo, *Sicilia nell' agosto 1860*, 1860, pp. 8–9.

The radicals inevitably took some time to clarify their attitude to this alternative of assembly or plebiscite, and even as late as October some of them were to be uncertain about it at a decisive moment for the fortunes of their party. Only unobtrusively did it emerge as the focal point of political differences. Even Cavour was for a few days unaware that there existed such an alternative, although he was one of the first to see that this particular issue underlay everything else. Once it became clear, he, no less than the radicals, changed his views, in the opposite direction from them. But to start with, he had thought that it might be advisable to call a special Sicilian parliament. Michele Amari thus tells that, when the fall of Palermo convinced Cavour of the viability of Garibaldi's expedition and of the need to canalize such an explosive revolutionary force, a meeting of Sicilian exiles was called in Turin, and Cavour put before it a plan to recall the Sicilian parliament as in 1812 and 1848. This solution no doubt had a *prima facie* appeal for the Turin government, in that it seemed to emphasize the traditional and historic at the expense of the revolutionary. A parliamentary assembly would flatter Sicilian regional sentiment. At the same time it would also invite British support, because it would mean a revival of that 1812 constitution which had been inspired by Lord Bentinck and built on a British model. La Farina had had this in mind when he originally brought Cavour's mandate for Sicily to follow the Tuscan example and call an assembly 'to vote annexation and regulate the decision of the people'. As late as 28 June La Farina's journal, *L'Annessione*, spoke of an assembly as indispensable, and of a plebiscite as just a possible sequence to it. A month later still, Count Litta, an ambassador from the king to Garibaldi, was still talking in terms of an assembly not of a plebiscite.[1] And for some time after this there was still no very clear appreciation in the north of what was involved.[2]

In Sicily, however, the different political implications of these two methods of voting had become an open dispute by the beginning of July.[3] When Crispi issued his decree of 23 June he was yielding a point over the *timing* of the vote, faced as he was by the alliance of La Farinians

[1] 30 July, diary of Count Litta, *Il Risorgimento Italiano*, February 1909, p. 24.

[2] 20 August, Ricasoli to Cavour (*Lettere di Ricasoli*, ed. Tabarrini, vol. v, pp. 201–2).

[3] 10 July, *Gazzetta di Catania*.

and others in favour of a quick decision. But in the process of yielding he transferred his delaying tactics from the question of time to that of *method*. As an attempt to weaken the opposition alliance he inserted in his decree a proviso, namely that the issue might still be decided by either direct or indirect suffrage, and that meanwhile everything should be prepared as if for the second method, that is to say for election of deputies to a parliamentary assembly. From this moment, all those who believed in autonomy or conditional annexation tended to back Crispi in choosing this latter course; and, now that the radicals had shown their hand, Cavour's party changed their minds and opted less equivocally for the alternative method of direct suffrage by plebiscite.

As soon as the terms of the dispute had begun to crystallize, Cavour adjusted his plans. At the beginning of June he had 'thought it more honest and convenient to convene the Sicilian parliament', as being the most legal and traditional way of sampling Sicilian opinion.[1] Amari had then warned him that such a body would voice only the desires of Sicilian regionalists, and any talk of *italianità* would be swamped.[2] The assumption upon which Amari based his advice—and he had good reasons for knowing—was that the weight of Sicilian opinion wanted local self-government before it wanted national unity. But Cavour needed a quick popular vote in favour of unconditional annexation to Piedmont. The right of self-determination therefore had to be invoked, but only within these narrow limits. Cavour needed to confront Europe and Napoleon with 'proof' that annexation represented the will of the people; but he did not wish the will of the people to go further and tie his hands by forcing conditions on him. Nor in his embarrassed diplomatic position could he relish the prospect of interminable debates in a representative assembly, especially as it had been shown at Nice how quickly a plebiscite might act and how surely it could be manipulated to give the desired result. An unqualified vote for 'annexation'—he always used this word—would leave him quite free to take any action which later circumstances might make appear to be desirable.

In order to obtain this result, Cavour moulded his policy so as to win the support of the middle-of-the-road, local-autonomy school of

[1] Ed. d'Ancona, *Carteggio di Amari*, vol. III, p. 231.
[2] *Ibid.* vol. II, 1896, p. 389.

thought. He consequently let it be known, without detailed promises which might later compromise him, that if annexation were quickly voted by plebiscite, some local government would in all likelihood be conceded afterwards *ex gratia* by parliament. At Palermo the news-papers of his party proclaimed the necessity of decentralization.[1] In Turin his minister for internal affairs, Farini, was deputed to work out an official statement to advocate the devolution of power on to the historic regions of the peninsula. This statement was to be given much publicity by Cavour's friends in Sicily. It carried with it the confident expectation that Sicily would be rewarded with regional autonomy and be spared the system of centralization as practised in northern Italy. Cavour may or may not have been very serious in these hints of devolution. In the end they came to nothing, and he did not show much regret over the fact. On the evidence before him in the summer of 1860, however, their publication broadcast was calculated to give him the best hope of an easy and painless annexation of the south.

An interesting memorandum was sent to Cavour early in July by the foremost living Italian economist, Francesco Ferrara, a former colleague of his journalistic days. Ferrara was a man of autonomist sentiments, who would have liked Italy to copy the United States' system of federal government. His memorandum on this theme is too long to quote in full, but the following excerpts will give the substance of his advice and his analysis of the situation.

The fact is that the Sicilian revolution springs solely from the irresistible desire to break free from Naples. The cries raised, the principles invoked, are simple phrases to which recourse is had purely from reasons of political necessity, and which could be altered from one hour to another with any change in circumstances: the words 'nationality' and 'unity' therefore repre-sent means and not ends....

It is important that we should prevent Sicily becoming the running sore of the kingdom of Italy as she has also been of the Bourbon state....The principle of fusion with the north now being preached is the very negation of liberty, concealed under the invocation of liberty itself: it is even a form of political socialism. It would be a fatal error if Italians showed that they could not emerge from the excesses of municipalism without throwing themselves into the other extreme where unity is confused with absorption.

[1] 28 June, *L' Annessione.*

Complete fusion would in any case be quite impossible to carry out in Sicily, simply because of the profound revolution it would involve for the customs of the island.... The public debt would be increased fourfold at one stroke in a country which would not have the resources for it. The system of taxation would have to be completely changed.... Apart from the difficulty of introducing military conscription, many unfortunate changes would be made in the system of administration, in money, weights, even in language; and the supreme court of appeal would also have to be abolished. Further difficulties would arise through the sheer distance away of the new capital, and through the presence in Sicily of non-Sicilian officials.... All these innovations would be found impossible to apply in practice, however simple they may seem in the abstract....

Sicily has never in its history known such a fusion as this except with Naples between 1838 and 1848; and on that occasion it was such a fusion as forced the island into revolution.... Fusion would turn Sicily into the Ireland of Italy, and hence, instead of making our nationality more compact and secure, would be a real and perennial source of weakness from which an enemy could profit.... Whoever knows the country well must be convinced that annexation, on conditions which Sicilians might later regret, would soon generate sentiments not wholly Italian, which interested parties would not omit to nourish....

Ideas of rigid centralization are not native to Italy...and no other part of Italy is so distinctive as Sicily. The government could profitably carry out an experiment there, which could do no harm, and might be a source of precious information for the future.... The American system would conciliate all Sicilians.[1]

Cavour made no direct acknowledgement at all to his former friend for this long and carefully-planned memorandum. Instead of being grateful for well-intentioned advice, he sent a churlish rejoinder through a third party: 'if the Italian idea has no influence in Sicily, if the idea of building a strong and grand nation is not appreciated there, Sicilians would do well to accept the concessions offered by the king of Naples, and not unite themselves to people who could have no sympathy or esteem for them'.[2] This was unkind and unwarranted; and, probably owing to an over-hasty perusal, it quite missed the point. It only added to the internal divergence among the patriots, and deprived Cavour of

[1] 8 (?) July, F. Ferrara to Cavour (*CC Lib. del Mezz.* vol. I, pp. 296–305).
[2] 7 July (*ibid.* p. 305).

the counsel of one of the few men who could have offset the dangerous nonsense talked by La Farina. Henceforward, Ferrara gave his advice only to the other side.

Yet Cavour had reason for being confident at this moment, and could hardly appreciate how many difficulties lay ahead. All he saw was that Garibaldi had not given way to the republicans, and had still received no military check; the Great Powers of Europe had made no serious effort to intervene; and now Crispi's government in Sicily appeared to be giving ground under pressure from La Farina. Cavour could surely imagine that he was more than likely to inherit Garibaldi's conquests, if only he proceeded with firmness and patience. In the meantime he had no wish to hear advice from people like Ferrara and Bertani, who made the situation look more complicated than he thought it was. After certain initial waverings, he now knew his own mind. What he wanted was to absorb Sicily at once, without conditions; and a plebiscite by universal suffrage was the obvious means for this. His representatives in the south were therefore instructed accordingly.

CHAPTER VI

CRISPI LOSES THE FIRST ROUND: JUNE

La Farina had certain distinct advantages in his conflict with Crispi. Being in opposition it was easy to criticize. Cavour could be held up to Sicilians as bearing the promise of peace and gradualism, while Crispi could be associated with revolution, with the continuance of war, and hence apparently with the need for more taxes, more levies of men and material, and continuing disorder. People were told that the policy of holding an assembly was linked with that of continuing the war into the Papal States,. and so with a prolonged emergency, with continued sacrifices, and even the risk of open war with the French garrison at Rome. To a conservative eye, this was to endanger the whole future of united Italy, by attempting too much too soon. Another point was that, as a result of Cavour's alliance with plebiscitary Bonapartism, direct suffrage could now be called 'the only method held to be legal by the public law of Europe'.[1] A plebiscite might therefore be the only means of securing French permission for the annexation of yet another province by Victor Emanuel. Whereas while an assembly debated, all manner of disasters might happen. Perhaps a European war would break out, or else a diplomatic veto might be imposed on Italian unity. In either event—and this was the decisive point—Sicily would be left at the mercy of Naples. As the Marquis di Rudinì was to put it,

some people seem to wish that five hundred deputies for the island of Sicily should sit and chatter, and all for the sole purpose of asking from the Executive, that is to say from a power unable to grant any such request, conditions which would reduce annexation to a contract in which all the gains would be with Sicily and all the disadvantages with the other contracting party.... At any moment now Europe may be thrown into a general war, and then unforeseen events may easily forbid the unification of Italy. In that case, what would become of us in Sicily, isolated and without strong government?[2]

[1] 14 August, *L' Annessione.*   [2] 16 October, *Il Plebiscito.*

A quick vote for annexation would at least make more certain on this score.

Another convincing reason was contributed by the big battalions. People soon knew that Piedmontese moral and material forces were behind the plebiscite, consequently making that a more feasible method by which to end the revolution; and this argument by itself more than made up for the fact that the plebiscite on its own merits might have commanded only minority support.[1] Time also was on its side. The longer that civil war and rule by amateurs was allowed to continue, the more were people ready to sacrifice full liberty of choice in return for the promise of strong and stable government. A quick decision—it was mistakenly thought—would end the internal uncertainty and disorder attendant on an interregnum. Against the convocation of a Sicilian parliament it was feared that, just as twelve years before, such an assembly would mean all talk and no action, and so would leave the country open to a Bourbon counter-attack. This unhappiness about the memories of 1848–9 was widespread, and proved a powerful influence among the waverers. It was also argued that any attempt to impose conditions on Piedmont would set an example which other provinces might follow, and this would imperil the whole structure of a unitary state. What in any case would happen if Piedmont chose not to accept annexation on conditions?

It would be quite wrong [wrote *L' Annessione*] to demand a pact or guarantees from Piedmont, for that province now represents but a tiny fraction of our great family.... Only the full nation represented in parliament can settle the organization of Italy for the future; and there must be one uniform law, not many local privileges.... Otherwise we should justify the calumny which holds that we Italians cannot free ourselves from the inveterate traditions of localism which for so long have kept us divided and in bondage.[2]

The cumulative effect on the autonomists of such reasoning may be seen in the personal history of two great Sicilians who have already been noticed as leaders in the revolution, Professor Michele Amari the historian, and the Marquis di Torrearsa. As with other former

[1] Natoli, *Rivendicazioni*, p. 197.   [2] 6 September, *L' Annessione*.

separatists, long exile in the north had convinced these two that only by taking orders from Turin had they much chance of promoting Sicilian welfare.

Amari was one of those bred in the full tradition of Sicilian independence and autonomy, and he had for long championed that tradition against both Crispi and La Farina.[1] His widely-read history of medieval Sicily, first published in 1842, had been full of insular animosity against Naples. Subsequently the afflictions of exile had changed him, and by way of republicanism and federalism he had finally come round to acceptance of some sort of unitary kingdom under Victor Emanuel. As Garibaldi's foreign secretary in 1860, he appeared to favour Cavour's policy rather than Garibaldi's. It was his view that it should be left to a future Italian parliament to decide what measure of autonomy be allowed in Sicily, and in the meantime annexation should be approved unconditionally. This did not prevent him from desiring autonomy, nor from still wanting an assembly as well as a plebiscite. As he wrote in August: 'we must not lay down *conditions*, but we can still determine the general lines of annexation. After our forty-five years' struggle with Naples, it cannot be that Piedmont should wish to take from us that administrative autonomy which we used to enjoy under the Bourbon yoke....Everyone now sees that Italy wants unity, but not with the French system of centralization'.[2] On the question of timing, Amari opposed La Farina's plan for immediate annexation, and wanted the vote to be held only when Garibaldi should have crossed the straits to Naples. Once this crossing had taken place, however, there would be no more excuse for delay. In the reasons which he then put forward we can trace an echo of his former separatism: annexation was needed 'in order to combat the pretensions of the Neapolitans, who are now taking advantage of Garibaldi's being in the shoes of Francesco II to revive their old metropolitan rights over Sicily'.[3] Amari was clearly some way removed from either of the two extremes, and he claimed to have taken office just in order to help avoid the clash between

[1] B. Marcolongo, 'Le idee politiche di M. Amari', *Archivio Storico Siciliano*, 1911, pp. 191–216.

[2] 28 August, Professor Amari to Count Amari (*Carteggio di Amari*, ed. d'Ancona, vol. II, p. 129).

[3] 11 September (*ibid.* p. 132).

'annexationists' and 'postponed annexationists'.[1] Yet his faith in Cavour's word, and his consequent reluctance to attach any conditions to annexation, made him increasingly firm in favour of submission to Victor Emanuel.

The Marquis di Torrearsa was the leading figure among the aristocracy, the one Sicilian whom Cavour was later to admit had not lost his reputation in these political broils of 1860. In exile he, too, had stood for autonomy against nationalists of both La Farinian and Mazzinian schools.[2] Indeed, he never quite threw off the reputation that he was a separatist at heart, whose chief aim was to break free of Naples.[3] By May 1860, however, he had so far developed his views as to offer the support of his group to Cavour, fearing that Sicily might otherwise fall before the greater evils of republicanism or socialism; and in return, according to his biographer, he was assured by Cavour that the aristocratic element would be allowed to control the revolution.[4] By June he was one of those who wanted quick annexation, but the method should be that of an assembly, and the union was to be hedged with conditions.[5] On 17 June Garibaldi appointed him President of the Council, to act as deputy whenever the dictator was absent; but from this post he resigned after a week, presumably because Garibaldi would not summon a constituent assembly to decide forthwith the island's future.[6] This policy of quick annexation by means of an assembly was not that of either Cavour or Garibaldi; but it represented the view of a real body of interests which was by no means negligible. Andrea Guarneri, who also resigned at the same time from his post as minister

---

[1] 13 July, Amari to W. C. Cartwright (*ibid.* p. 106). On p. 116 he refers to Pisani and Torrearsa as among those who wanted immediate annexation, and says that 'in pure logic they are right; but not so when judged by the logic of politics and revolution'.

[2] U. di Maria, 'Episodi del risorgimento nella corrispondenza del Marchese di Torrearsa', *Archivio Storico Siciliano*, 1915, p. 166.

[3] 9 July, Calvino to Bargoni (*Memorie*, ed. Bargoni, p. 133); 31 July, Cordova to Cavour (*CC Lib. del Mezz.* vol. I, p. 425).

[4] F. de Stefano, 'I Fardella di Torrearsa', *Rassegna Storica del Risorgimento*, 1934, pp. 1310–12.

[5] 7 July, *L' Unità Italiana* (Genoa), report from its Palermo correspondent dated 30 June.

[6] R. di Castel-Maurigi, *Vincenzo Fardella, Marchese di Torrearsa*, 1862, pp. 43–4.

of justice, explained that he had been impelled to this step by his desire for quick annexation; yet, on the actual method to be adopted, he too thought that Sicily should choose for herself, and not have a plebiscite imposed on her by Piedmont.[1]

In theory this was a distinct point of view, but in practice it was more favourable to Cavour than to his radical opponents. For the historic importance of these men lay less in their desire for an assembly, than in their conviction that annexation should not be unduly delayed. The aristocrats at Palermo were not as much favoured by Garibaldi as they would have liked, or as they might have been by Cavour. Their habits and outlook may have differed from those of the northern conservatives, but they far and away preferred Count Cavour to *avvocato* Crispi. It was true of them in general what a conservative newspaper wrote, that 'the people who call out for annexation are the quietists, and the returned *émigrés*, who now find themselves neglected by the new regime'.[2] Another reporter amplified this same idea when he stated that the annexationist party included 'those whose interest was peace and quiet, those who wanted to end the state of war as soon as possible, and so be able to secure tranquillity and to cease their efforts and their sacrifices'.[3] For these reasons in particular, some among the landowning class desired to bring Garibaldi's provisional regime to an immediate end, even before the conquest of Naples—the salvation of Naples held little interest for the majority of Sicilians. La Farina and his friends therefore had a simple task when they tried to poison upper-class society in Palermo with suspicions of Garibaldi's government. Hence the success of their alarmist rumour about 'Mazzinianism' and 'civil war'. Hence the exaggerated reports to Cavour, in which they magnified the inevitable bandits and pick-pockets into an active organization of either counter-revolutionaries or republicans (they were never sure which). Unfortunately, La Farina was allowed to get away with these exaggerations, and soon the issue was so clouded with emotion that rational discussion proved impossible. If only wiser and more moderate men like ·Torrearsa had not subsequently taken political

[1] 20 October, *L' Annessione.*

[2] 27 July, *Il Movimento* (Genoa), report from its Palermo correspondent dated 24 July.

[3] 20 July, *La Nazione* (Florence).

quietism to the point of virtual abstention from politics, if they had only allowed their criticisms of both Garibaldi and Cavour to take political form, perhaps with their great influence in the island they could have made calmer and more sensible counsels prevail. If this difference of opinion could have been debated in a mood of greater compromise, then the later history of Sicily might have proved happier.

By 23 June, when Torrearsa and Guarneri resigned, the chance of finding any compromise agreement between these three groups of opinion was rapidly dwindling. By this time, some people were just beginning to see how much depended on whether there was a plebiscite or an assembly, and on whether annexation was to come sooner or later. Behind these questions there were matters of principle at stake. Some of the background to this first ministerial crisis of the dictatorship is made clearer for us by the views of other members of the cabinet. Baron Pisani, for example, though he was one of those former exiles whom Cavour had sent back to Sicily, had been appointed by Garibaldi to cabinet rank. He was another who resigned on this occasion, and his letter notifying the dictator of the fact refers deferentially but openly to a disagreement on policy.

You with your great heart and lofty mind, brushing aside all difficulties in your path, wish to run directly to our sublime goal; while I in my littleness, and fearful at the sight of difficulties, think that we should go step by step, completing each single success in turn, and only then proceeding to new enterprises—in fact that we should enlarge our nation little by little.

Once I have made this declaration, nothing remains for me but to recommend warmly to you my beloved and battered Sicily. I beseech you to let its future status rest in doubt no longer, and not to leave it a prey to any factions that may arise....I beg you to consider that, if you go on recklessly into Naples, you may perhaps be aiding that person [Mazzini] whom you least expect to help; and he will know how to profit from your work without even being grateful to you for it....Let Sicily be your fatherland; for it is a country not unworthy of so illustrious a son.[1]

Here is an example of how the desire for quick annexation was sometimes intimately connected with an unwillingness to bother about Naples; and also of how it was involved with the fear that government and property might be jeopardized when the military power of

[1] 28 June, *L' Annessione*, letter dated 24 June.

Garibaldi was no longer available in Sicily. It was this strange combination of interests which told so heavily in Cavour's favour.

Another member of the cabinet, Dr Raffaele, gave his reasons for not resigning with the others. He disagreed both with those who wanted an assembly at once, and with those who wanted to postpone annexation until the whole of Italy was free. He censured the civic council of Palermo for its petition on behalf of annexation, using the argument that an administrative body should not try to take on political functions. Against La Farina he pointed out how impossible it was in present circumstances for Sicilian government to be in any sense normal. He agreed with Crispi that the simple publication of a preparatory decree was as far perhaps as one could yet go towards the future elections. Under a dictatorship, moreover, the will of one man must prevail, and criticism should not go beyond a certain point. 'The Sicilian revolution is personified in General Garibaldi. He is the one man necessary for its consolidation. Even when he has ideas conflicting with our own, is it not a duty for all good citizens to stand firmly with him, even to come closer to him, so as to convince him of the reasonableness of their views?'[1]

It is evident that Crispi's government must have been losing public support if it had to be defended, not on grounds of justice, but on those of dictatorial will. Quite likely there was more than merely the annexation controversy behind this loss of esteem, because the opposition seems to have grown after Crispi's decree of 23 June making provision for a popular vote. Probably it was due to a combination of various discontents: over the necessary requisitioning and conscription arising out of the war, over inflation, and in general over the failure to restore order and prosperity after the revolution had triumphed with such large promises and anticipations of Utopia. All this discontent in Palermo was exploited by La Farina, whose personal and political quarrel with Crispi was for the next ten days the dominant factor in Sicilian politics. A reliable observer like Amari easily penetrated behind the façade of political opposition, and noticed that the fundamental disagreements were personal.[2] Foiled successively in his attempts to control both

[1] 3 July, *L'Annessione*, letter dated 1 July.
[2] 3 July, Professor Amari to Count Amari (*Carteggio di Amari*, ed. d'Ancona, vol. II, p. 97).

government and municipality, La Farina then found a new and more efficacious weapon in the *piazza* mob, and on the 27th he instigated some of the common people to demonstrate against the ministry. The dictator's first reaction to this was a sharp threat that he would move his government out of Palermo and away from this danger of popular dictation.[1] But on second thoughts he resolved to accept Crispi's proffered resignation, and to replace him with someone of more nondescript political colour. He meant to see if the critics of Crispi were justified in their complaints, and whether they could do any better themselves. If only Cavour had allowed himself to be better advised, he could have had no better evidence than this of Garibaldi's moderation and good common sense.

Barely a month after the capture of Palermo, it thus seemed that the patriotic party which had emerged victorious from the revolution was beginning to split up into warring factions. The almost inevitable clash of interests over reconstruction was coming to focus on certain constitutional points, and political parties were already growing up around rival policies and rival personal antagonisms. La Farina had found it easy to sow discord in a broadly-based ministry which contained men of such different political tendencies; and after securing the resignation of several leading ministers on the 23rd, he had now obtained the exclusion of Crispi and the rest. The only pity from his point of view was that he had been forced to use mob demonstrations, an expedient which was as easily copied by his adversaries, and which was to be an element as unfortunate as it was incalculable in Sicilian politics. He had also been obliged to draw closer to 'the aristocratic party, which not only does not want an Italian union, but desires annexation on special terms of autonomy for Sicily'.[2] In order to halt the revolution, La Farina had been compelled to try and dissuade Sicilians from assisting in the redemption of other Italian provinces, and in particular he had played on the animosity between them and the Neapolitans.[3] Annexation was presented to people as the easiest and surest method of dissociating from Naples; or as *Il Diritto* contemptuously said, 'so that

[1] 27 June (Goodwin's Political Journal, F.O. 165/134).

[2] 6 July, *Il Movimento* (Genoa), report from Palermo dated 1 July. This paper called itself 'independent liberal'.

[3] 27 June, *ibid.*, report from Palermo dated 23 June.

Sicilians could sleep in peace without having to bother about other Italian provinces which are still enslaved'.[1] His alliance with the autonomists was something of a *volte face*; but it was effective enough, and as such was to be copied by some of the radicals before many more weeks went by.

One side of this story appears from what Crispi had to tell at this moment. Crispi described how La Farina, after being refused a post in the ministry, had

resorted to intrigue and disloyal machinations, which, thanks to General Garibaldi's forbearance, I was obliged to tolerate....At last, on the 27th, with the help of the police, whose chiefs I have been forced to remove owing to their utter faithlessness, La Farina sent a deputation to wait on Garibaldi and demand our withdrawal....The cabinet of June 2 fell, and another took its place, composed of separatists and La Farinian elements.

What will come of all this?...On that day the individual policy gave way to the policy of the streets, and it was the conservatives who brought this about. Those demonstrations will probably be followed by others, and not only will the government fail to obtain a firm footing, but will be ever at the mercy of the first comer. I know that matters have been purposely brought to this pass in order to reduce the country to such a state of weakness and exasperation that she will beg Cavour, as a favour, to annex her to Piedmont.

Farewell, my dear friend. It is painful to reflect that it has been our lot to make all the sacrifices, to risk our lives even, only to see our enemies usurp the power, and ruin the country.[2]

Two other letters from Crispi at this moment show how he had been hoping to win the confidence of the Turin government. They suggest that, had Cavour been ready to withdraw La Farina, he might possibly have neutralized if not actually won over the radical opposition, in the same way that another of his brilliant strokes of opportunism had formerly won over Rattazzi and the 'constitutional Left'. Both letters were addressed to Cesare Correnti, editor of the conservative *Perse-*

[1] 16 July, *Il Diritto* (Turin); 1 July, *ibid.*, letter from Palermo dated 24 June: 'here parties are becoming agitated. The government is being fought by the Lafarinians and the municipalists who are trying to win power, and I cannot see how we shall find a compromise....The municipalists would like immediate annexation, not caring about anything else.'

[2] 3 July, Crispi to Asproni (*Memoirs*, vol. I, pp. 302–3).

veranza to which Crispi sometimes used to contribute, and himself Crispi's chief contact with the Cavourians. On 25 June, at the peak of La Farina's campaign, Crispi had written:

La Varenne [the bearer of this letter] will tell you of the base intrigues of Cavour's agents to get the power out of our hands....Matters being in such a pass, would you let me ask you to be my intermediary with the king, to show him that we are not lacking in loyalty to the cause of Italy which is personified today in the glorious House of Savoy....Our party since its origins in 1831 has been unitarian before everything. On many diverse occasions we have said that we are for the king if he will be for Italy. Now no one in the world can be so blind that he cannot see how today there can be no safety for our country unless under the protection of the cross of Savoy. Do they do us such an injustice as to think that we lack the intelligence to see the signs of the times? Is not Garibaldi's presence at the head of our government a guarantee? Are not the laws we have so far made a sufficient proof?[1]

There is a hint here of what shortly became a major point of difference between conservatives and radicals; for it soon emerged that the radicals, far from being the dangerous republicans which Cavour sometimes depicted them for political reasons, might be believers in almost precisely the opposite, an excess of monarchism. On at least one point Garibaldi agreed with Ricasoli, in advocating that the final making of Italy needed a king vested with fully dictatorial powers, if for no other reason than just because the *Re Galantuomo* would be less prone to hesitate and count the cost than was the quasi-dictatorial prime minister Cavour. One liberal-radical paper was clever enough to notice as much even in June when it wrote: 'this is the real difference between us and La Farina. It is not a question of a republic, but of *galantomismo*.'[2] It was apparent that, in an attempt to counteract this tendency, 'like a clever minister, Cavour tries to make the king think that Garibaldi is using the royal name for a purpose which has nothing whatever to do with monarchy'.[3] But the king was scarcely likely to be deceived for long. Cavour's real cause for opposition to the radicals was not that they rejected the king, for they did no such thing; it was because they were against the ministry in power, and were

[1] 25 June, Crispi to Correnti (ACP, b. 152).   [2] 16 June, *Il Movimento*.
[3] 17 June, *L' Unità Italiana* (Florence).

hoping to use the king to help upset that ministry. Victor Emanuel for his part was quite content to have a foot in either camp and await what happened. As for the radicals, the more they failed to make contact with Cavour, the more they pinned their faith on the monarch.

The second of Crispi's letters to Correnti bears the date of 5 July, a week after his resignation.

Why is Cavour still against me?...Shall we ever make Italy if his attitude continues like this? Listen to me. Here in Sicily there are no unitarians on principle except myself and the nucleus of young men who follow me. The mass of the country is indifferent. People hate the Bourbons only because they have been tormented by them....Among those who in 1848 ruined the Sicilian revolution there is not one who is for national unity. They pretend to wish for union with the other emancipated provinces of Italy, but in their hearts they are searching out every possible manner in which to change their coats and bring back a Sicilian king.

This party suddenly found itself confronted with the prodigious success of Garibaldi and the rapid way in which I organized the country. Then came La Farina, and with him discord entered this poor land. He found no support here, for all distrusted him; and yet he and his friends are now trying to fight us by force and with the vile accusation of republicanism. In this distrustful and suspicious country, every accusation makes an impression; and if till now people loved and respected me for the sacrifices I had made and my love for the country, now they are beginning to doubt my intentions....

I love Italy above everything, and since Italy must be made with the house of Savoy, I accept the king without *arrière pensée*. It was I who first gave Victor Emanuel the title of king of Italy....It is I who can save Italy in Sicily....I assure you that among politicians you will find none like me. Among the petty celebrities of the island I alone can win Sicily for Italy. Do not oppose me in this. But do help me by withdrawing La Farina whom I have twice saved from death and have not arrested or expelled. Talk to Farini [Cavour's minister of the interior] and let me know at once.[1]

Two particular points emerge from this letter: one, that there was not much to choose between Crispi and La Farina in the matter of

---

[1] 5 July, Crispi to Correnti (ACP, f. 138). On 24 June, Calvino wrote to Bargoni that 'the Lafarinians pretend not to know that the "republicans" fought well enough for Victor Emanuel and Italian unity in the past campaign of 1859, and that they came to Sicily to do so again. But you know how people of that type will make use of any means to their end.' *Memorie di Bargoni*, p. 121.

arrogance and self-importance; and the other, that La Farina's new policy of pandering to the autonomists did not as yet present itself to his rival as a matter for emulation. On both these counts Crispi had obviously been becoming unpopular; though it is hard to apportion the responsibility for this between his political programme in itself, and the arrogant, aggressive manner with which he pushed it. As a strong personality, he aroused the most varied feelings in people. To quote Bixio, a sensible Garibaldian officer who cannot be accused of holding any strong political beliefs: 'I am sorry Crispi has fallen from power and so unjustly....Garibaldi did not want him to go, but in view of the developing crisis Crispi chose to resign, although I am told he will not be out of office for long.'[1] Bixio went on: 'One of the leaders of this intrigue is certainly La Farina, who would like to become a minister and govern Garibaldi; but I do not think he will succeed.' Persano, the Piedmontese admiral who had several ships in Palermo harbour, made an interesting entry in his diary for 30 June. He recorded his impression that Crispi, 'besides ability, possesses really elevated qualities'—an appreciation which, incidentally, the admiral did not pass on with his other information to Cavour. But he added that Crispi would have to be opposed for sharing the rash views of Mazzini, 'and these would be the ruin of Italy if ever they were seized on by the masses'.[2] This was a significant, if not very convincing, line of thought among the conservatives. Another witness of these events similarly recalled, in later days, the horror in Palermo society over Crispi's 'semi-republicanism'; and it is important to remember that republicanism usually meant 'red republicanism', and was connected in people's imagination with social revolution on the model of 1848. This same observer added that it was not Crispi's principles, but rather his rough methods of government, which ultimately drove people into protest. He also explained that the opposition had found in popular demonstrations the sole outlet for their feelings which was at once tolerated, effective, and intelligible to the masses. As an example of Crispi's tactlessness he mentioned that, instead of playing up to local feeling, Crispi had offensively suggested that Sicily had been 'conquered' by an invasion of the Thousand from

[1] 2 July, Bixio to Parodi (*Epistolario di Nino Bixio*, ed. Morelli, 1939, vol. I, pp. 359–60).
[2] Persano, *Diario 1860–1*, 1869, part I, p. 52.

Genoa.[1] There had also been against Crispi the understandable animus towards a returned exile; both because an exile must have had more courage than the rest of his class in choosing this fate rather than compromise with his beliefs, and also because he was now coming back with a wider culture and the condescending air of one who was lecturing them on their political backwardness. All this must be kept in mind when trying to explain the temporary resignation of Garibaldi's first government on 27 June. Other things being equal, the Palermo aristocracy would as naturally turn towards Cavour and the monarchy as it would dislike a mere provincial lawyer from Girgenti.

The temporary disappearance of Crispi from active participation in the government of Sicily only reinforced Cavour in the justifiable optimism which took hold of him at the end of June. The radicals were still a force to be reckoned with at Palermo, but they had failed to establish themselves against the liberals. The dictator was clearly going to do nothing against the king he so much admired. Far from abusing his dictatorial power, he had voluntarily dismissed his chief adviser and appointed a new cabinet of moderates which even included the editor of the liberal-conservative *L'Annessione*. The arrival in Sicily of moderate liberals like Cordova and Amari at the end of June was a distinct help in making a restraining influence felt at his headquarters. As it was, the chief radical leaders like Mazzini and Bertani had not left for Sicily, and were proving unable at Genoa to collect enough men to invade the Papal States as they had planned. So confident was Cavour, that he at last felt strong enough to threaten Garibaldi, putting fair words aside. A message was sent to say that no more help would be given from Turin unless Bertani was deprived of all influence in their despatch.[2] But the dictator sensibly chose to ignore this challenge. He was not going to be deterred from his task of winning the war, and it was to need further provocation than this by the 'moderates' before he himself turned back to take sides in the political turmoil which La Farina was stirring up at Palermo.

---

[1] R. Salvo di Pietraganzili, *Il Piemonte e la Sicilia 1850–60*, 1903, vol. II, p. 348.

[2] 28 June, Cavour to Persano (*CC Lib. del Mezz.* vol. I, p. 257). Amari and Cordova arrived in Sicily with this message on the 30th, and Persano describes Garibaldi's reaction on p. 278.

The more Cavour studied the situation, the more he felt encouraged. With those of his correspondents to whom he liked to give the impression of enterprise and audacity, he even began to prospect not only the annexation of Sicily, but the fall of Naples, and even that of Rome and Venice in the fullness of time.[1] Hitherto Cavour's letters had contained far more references to Garibaldi as an embarrassing nuisance than as a national hero, but now he could afford to let himself be carried away by public opinion and confess privately that he was coming round to the doctrine of united Italy. On 4 July he wrote to Nigra in Paris: 'le succès fabuleux de Garibaldi d'un côté, la cruauté, la lâcheté, l'ineptie du Roi de Naples de l'autre, ont donné au sentiment unitaire un pouvoir irrésistible. Les hommes les plus calmes, les plus modérés, les plus conservateurs sont devenus unitaires. Le Prince de Carignan, mon collègue Cassinis, le Baron Ricasoli n'admettent plus d'autre solution.' He candidly admitted in private that it was these successes in Sicily which compelled him to adopt a forward policy. If he held back now, public opinion throughout the north of Italy threatened to overturn him in favour of the revolution. At the same time Cavour believed he had one trump card himself. For Garibaldi could not change his moderate programme of 'Italy and Victor Emanuel' without alienating many of the volunteers, and in that case a few battalions of *bersaglieri* would easily be able to overcome those who remained.[2] The very fact, however, that this thought entered his head, shows how little he understood of his political opponents. Seldom did he come near to appreciating that Garibaldi would sooner cut off his hand than betray the monarchy.

Cavour was, indeed, in a strong position. But he had left out of account the headstrong and unyielding La Farina, who was even more unrestrained after the eclipse of Crispi. Instead of trying to bridge the gap between Cavour and Garibaldi, La Farina was purposely doing his best to widen it and render it unbridgeable. In Turin he was spreading stories that Sicily was lapsing into anarchy, and that Garibaldi might at any moment apostatize to republicanism. In Sicily he was so far hindering the conduct of the war and the maintenance of Garibaldi's government, that the dictator was finally compelled to abandon his policy of moderation.

[1] 27 June, Cavour to Ricasoli (*ibid.* p. 252); 8 July, Cavour to Ricasoli (*ibid.* p. 309).
[2] 4 July, Cavour to Nigra (*CC Cavour-Nigra*, vol. IV, pp. 54–5).

CHAPTER VII

CAVOUR LOSES THE SECOND ROUND: JULY

Crispi was out of office for three weeks after his resignation on 27 June; but although this made it appear as though La Farina had won, the appearance was illusory. La Farina wrote a letter to Cavour early in July which was not published in his *Epistolario*: it is particularly interesting, in that pencil markings round the more fantastic portions suggest that Cavour by now had probably weighed up the character of the man whom he had sent to restore order in Sicily.[1] La Farina reproved Cavour in this letter for still thinking that there might be some good in Garibaldi.

Perhaps, owing to some scruples of delicacy, I have not insisted enough on Garibaldi's attitude to you.... My greatest fault in his eyes is just that of calling myself your friend. Indeed, some people have advised me to feign other sentiments in order to obtain the General's good opinion.... If, therefore, you and your friends think you can win what I have not been able to win, you are quite wrong [pencil mark]. Putting aside my modesty in the interests of the public weal, I tell you that outsiders would lack all my personal relations and knowledge of people and customs here, and also, I may say, that popularity which makes me (excuse the arrogance) a power with whom Garibaldi himself has to count [pencil mark]. And do not think I say this out of personal ambition. You must know me well enough now not to harbour any suspicion of that.

La Farina must have heard that Cavour was planning to replace him, and the letter concluded with a plea against any other official representatives being sent to take over in Sicily, because that would be read as a personal reflexion upon himself. This last point was also underscored in pencil when Cavour passed the letter over to Farini, either to signify appreciation of its truth or its absurdity. What cannot be denied is that La Farina seems to have been more interested in his own reputation than

[1] 5 July, G. La Farina to Cavour (CF).

in the possibility (which still existed, as Depretis and Persano were to show) of Cavour and Garibaldi working together without an open split.

It was already becoming common knowledge throughout Palermo that La Farina was in 'violent opposition' to the government. In public and private he was saying that 'the cause of the revolution was betrayed by Garibaldi'.[1] Giuseppe Abba, the most notable chronicler of the revolution, described a scene which must have taken place about 26–7 June, and

the grave danger in which La Farina put the fortunes of the dictatorship. I recall clearly the demonstration he organized, with a torrent of people shouting outside the palace for annexation..., and 'death to Crispi' was their cry....I said to a friend that a new Sicilian Vespers must have begun.... Crispi came down to the *piazza*, having been refused a hearing from the balcony. In complete silence he spoke just these few words: 'If you want to make a united nation, then leave it to the dictator; but if all you want is your own liberation, we can go away and leave Sicily for good.' It was a miracle of courage! The tempest suddenly changed, and you could hear cries of 'viva Crispi'.[2]

Another witness, Salvatore Calvino, wrote on 9 July:

Crispi ought to have given La Farina his passport a month earlier. If he did not do so it was from generosity, and so as not to be accused of private vengeance. But it was a fatal mistake; for when your country's welfare is at stake, generosity is wrong....La Farina recently held meetings at which even senior military officers attended. He tried to set up a network of supporters among government officials, even aided by some of the ministers, and he once wrote in the *Giornale* that our first expedition was fitted out at the expense of his National Society. The whole country is indignant against him.[3]

La Farina's more open enemies, Raffaele for instance, ascribed his conduct to mere annoyance at the fact that Torrearsa had been made President of the Council rather than himself. Purely out of spite at this he was associating with the dregs of Palermo, and purposely trying to coerce the government by organized *piazza* demonstrations.

In conditions so grave as those of a country in revolution, the government neither could nor should have remained indifferent. And yet La Farina was

[1] 9 July (Goodwin's Political Journal no. 13, F.O. 165/134).
[2] Letter printed in the Como review, *Garibaldi e i Garibaldini*, 15 November 1910.
[3] 9 July, Calvino to Bargoni (*Memorie di Bargoni*, pp. 133–4).

warned to desist or go away—a warning that was repeated at least twice. We even wrote to one of the ministers at Turin begging him to recall La Farina, since his presence at Palermo, far from helping, was actually hindering Cavour's plan....This had no effect....Meanwhile La Farina found that he was in no better position after the fall of Crispi's ministry, since Garibaldi was still an insurmountable barrier to prompt annexation, and thus also a barrier in La Farina's only path towards becoming *commissario regio*.[1]

Garibaldi not unnaturally read into La Farina's conduct a deliberate intention by Cavour to upset the revolutionary government. While certain of the dictator's friends had advised trying to join forces with Cavour, others, even including some among the more moderate, had recently confirmed his own impression, namely that Cavour had lost his liberty of action by submission to France. It could always be plausibly contended that France wanted a divided Italy or at the most a weak federation which she could dominate;[2] and the actions of La Farina could easily be interpreted to fit in with this. It was hard to deny that Cavour's party was deliberately spreading alarm and despondency, and so hindering the war effort. Through one of Garibaldi's own cabinet, moreover, a plot was afoot to place treacherous officers in his ships, with the intention of capturing his tiny fleet as soon as, or if ever, it became necessary.[3] Garibaldi did not know this; but twice in the course of June Cavour had sent direct ultimatums to the government of Palermo, threatening to break off relations with Garibaldi unless Mazzini was arrested and Bertani repudiated. Evidently at Turin they were as much concerned with party politics as with national politics, and more with counter-revolution than revolution.

Until the beginning of July Garibaldi continued to show himself amenable. The king's government was being unduly provocative in response to his moderation, but still its financial help was desirable or even essential if he was to receive adequate military supplies. Then occurred an unfortunate incident. By some slip in Cavour's information services, the Piedmontese admiral tried to ingratiate himself with Garibaldi by reporting two men, Griscelli and Totti, whom he supposed

[1] 11 July, *Il Precursore*.
[2] 19 June, Pallavicino from Turin to Garibaldi (ACM, no. 1169).
[3] 13 July, Cavour to Persano (*CC Lib. del Mezz.* vol. I, p. 322).

7 ★

to be assassins in Bourbon hire. They were thereupon arrested. It was easily established that they were Bourbon spies, and it also transpired that they had been in the employ of Louis Napoleon and the Pope; but remarkably enough these same two men were simultaneously on a mission from Cavour, for which a substantial payment had already been made, and they had also attracted the notice of Garibaldi's police by offering their services to the revolutionary government as well.[1] The police, in their subsequent report, concluded that these two highly doubtful characters were being used by Cavour and perhaps by others for some sinister purpose. When Admiral Persano realized his mistake he was covered with confusion, and had to ask Garibaldi for their release, explaining that they were secret agents of Cavour who in reality were trying to compromise the Bourbon government;[2] but it was an implausible story, and the damage done was by then irremediable.

Coming on top of La Farina's irritating manoeuvres, this incident proved the last straw. Crispi and his friends seized upon it to show the dictator that he was gaining nothing in return for his political neutrality, nothing at least except suspicion and treachery. On 7 July, therefore, Garibaldi sent an order for the *questura* to arrest La Farina and send him back to the north.[3] What made this summary treatment particularly wounding was the statement which appeared in the *Giornale Officiale*. 'By special order of the dictator', it ran, 'there have been expelled from Sicily *signori* La Farina, Griscelli and Totti. *Signori* Griscelli and Totti are of that type who find some way of enrolling among the secret police of every country. The government, which has to see that the public tranquillity is rigidly maintained, could not tolerate any longer among us the presence of these individuals with their wicked intentions.' The announcement went on to belabour the *Società Nazionale*, of which La Farina had been the president, and even to say that the society,

---

[1] Griscelli's signed but undated confession (in Fondo Nelson Gay MRR) is confirmed by other evidence: 14 July, Cavour to La Farina (*Lettere di Cavour*, ed. Chiala, vol. III, p. 290); *Memoires de Griscelli*, 1867 (Bruxelles); police report to Crispi (ACP, f. 138, nos. 4661 and 4662); the Carte Farini at Ravenna and the Carte Bianchi-Ricasoli at ASF Florence also show that he was in touch with the minister of the interior at Turin and the governor of Tuscany; 31 May, Teccio to Cavour referring to payments made by Cavour to Griscelli (*CC Lib. del Mezz.* vol. I, p. 149).

[2] 7 July, Persano to Garibaldi (ACM, no. 1214).

[3] Library of the Società di Storia Patria, Palermo, b. 27.

'reduced in means after Garibaldi had resigned its presidency, was rather a hindrance than a help to the cause for which we fought at Calatafimi and Palermo'.[1] This statement was as uncharitable as the manner of the expulsion was abrupt, but tempers by this time were boiling, and some violent break in the tension was bound to come sooner or later. La Farina, having staked everything on shaking Garibaldi's position, now had to pay the price of failure. He returned home as he had come, on a Piedmontese warship.

We know that, even before hearing of the expulsion, Cavour was assured that La Farina had failed in his allotted task. Without being quite resolute enough to recall him, Cavour was already casting about to find a successor, and by now had written to tell him that this would probably be Depretis.[2] The king had even tried to insist on his recall as a known trouble-maker, being of opinion that 'if only he comes home the annexation of Sicily will follow automatically'.[3] It is just conceivable that Cavour, not liking to confess and atone for his original mistake, had wanted Garibaldi to bear the onus of responsibility for any open breach, so as to terrify the Sicilian nobility into accepting Piedmontese rule as the only practicable alternative to irresponsible dictatorship and red republic.[4] But probably the delay is one more example of Cavour's indecision and procrastination. Persano told him that expulsion was the best thing that could have happened to his envoy. The immediate and deliberate cause of the divergence between liberals and radicals had been La Farina himself. Crispi on one side and Victor Emanuel on the other had good reason to think that, without the presence of this man at Palermo, things would have gone more smoothly. As it was, all the work of people on both sides to secure annexation by agreement was ruined. He had succeeded in creating the impression that he had been sent by Cavour to oppose Garibaldi's policy, and that Cavour was just out for Piedmontese aggrandizement

[1] 9 July, *Giornale Officiale di Sicilia.*

[2] 8 July, Cavour to La Farina (*Il Risorgimento Italiano*, vol. for 1916, p. 274). Neither was this letter published in La Farina's *Epistolario.*

[3] N.d., Victor Emanuel to Farini (*CC Lib. del Mezz.* vol. v).

[4] Gortchakoff 'feared that the Sicilian nobility would throw themselves into the arms of Piedmont in order to escape both republicanism and dictatorship', quoted by Alfredo Zazo, *La politica estera del regno delle Due Sicilie nel 1859–60*, 1940, p. 369.

and no more.[1] This being so, Garibaldi had no choice but to accept the challenge and send him packing. The dictator so far had shown signs of nothing but friendliness towards the liberals, but this gave him the impression that they could not be trusted. While Bourbon soldiers were still on Sicilian soil he could not allow this sort of factious opposition. Even the conservative *Perseveranza* realized that La Farina had been playing with fire when, in such a delicate situation, he had stirred up the fickle *piazza* mob of Palermo against the government.[2]

The same newspaper made another point when commenting upon Cavour's more than friendly attitude at this time towards Naples. For the prime minister gave the impression of being about to discuss preliminaries of an alliance with the very people against whom Garibaldi was engaged in mortal combat.[3] If Cavour was bluffing in this, at least he did not help the dictator to see through his bluff. All the appearances suggested that France was compelling Piedmont to turn against the revolution. Such behaviour seemed to illustrate exactly Mazzini's belief that Cavour would be forced into an unhelpful and un-Italian policy by pressure from Louis Napoleon. And the Garibaldians took note of the probability that, if Sicily were once annexed to Piedmont, diplomatic necessities might *a fortiori* constrain Cavour to stop the further progress of the Italian revolution before the conquest of Naples. The policy of annexation thus came under strong suspicion. It was certainly not reassuring to find the semi-official *L' Opinione* at Turin carrying bitter articles against Garibaldi's government, at a time when the Neapolitan army still controlled part of Sicily.

Even on a more favourable view of Cavour's policy, there was still good reason for the radicals not to give in to his request for immediate annexation. Even had Garibaldi thought more highly of Cavour than he did—if he had believed, for instance, that the northern government was ready to use revolutionary methods and not merely diplomatic bargaining for the achievement of unity—he could still imagine that, in that case, Cavour's campaign for immediate annexation might be but a stratagem to confuse the diplomats until the volunteers had won all southern Italy. It is important to bear in mind that Cavour, crafty politician that he was, had become accustomed to telling untruths. He

---

[1] G. La Cecilia, *Storia dell' insurrezione Siciliana*, 1861, vol. I, p. 169.
[2] 17 July, *La Perseveranza* (Milan).   [3] 14 July, *ibid.*

had informed the world that he was opposed to Garibaldi's expedition; but later, after that expedition had succeeded, he told Italians that this had been but a ruse. Subsequently he was to ask the revolutionaries that they should not cross over to the continent; but this too, after Garibaldi had disobeyed, was later said to have been a ruse. It was not so easy, then, seriously to complain when Garibaldi treated the whole annexation campaign with disrespect. Either that campaign was genuinely meant, in which case it had to be opposed as cowardly and un-Italian; or else it was bogus, designed simply to delude the diplomats of Europe, and in that case it was to be resisted as a practical joke. This was the price paid for Cavour's deeply subtle methods. People could never know whether to take his words at their face value. Not only the disreputable Garibaldi, but also the highly respectable Lord Palmerston and Lord John Russell said that they never would believe him again after his lies over Nice and Savoy. Even when he spoke the truth, people suspected double motives and a double meaning; and Garibaldi had this excuse for treating his public demands with such scant attention.

Over his original attitude to the expedition of the Thousand, Cavour had in fact been deceitful to no purpose; for people had not believed his disclaimer of responsibility, and he had just compromised himself without benefiting either himself or Garibaldi. The facts suggest that neither then, nor throughout June, had he properly made up his mind what to do. It was Cavour's habit to keep many different policies ready for instant adoption. In southern Italy one can watch his technique of employing many agents at once on the same job, sometimes unknown to each other. No one of them was allowed into all his secrets, but each was encouraged to fend for himself, to push at open doors until one or other hit upon what looked like the best policy in the circumstances; Cavour would then adopt that policy with vigour. Such 'tact des choses possibles' was one important explanation of his great success; but it did have the disadvantage that any single subordinate might compromise his master by overreaching himself. La Farina had been sent to Sicily before it was possible to frame any policy in detail, and had meanwhile been allowed to think that he could act on his own authority. The result was that Cavour was committed to a certain line of conduct before he himself quite knew what was happening. His temporizing with the Neapolitan envoys was likewise a method of playing for time, of waiting for the complete context of circumstances to materialize before he framed the plan of action most suitable to it. But in the meantime his co-revolutionary Garibaldi, left in doubt about his real intentions, was compromising him quite as much as had La Farina, and at the same time was putting the worst possible construction on both his words and deeds. Not only were the two great national forces of Italy out of step, but mention was being made of civil war between them.

Cavour's negotiations with Naples in July illustrate the ambivalence and disingenuousness of his policy. So energetically had he protested about Garibaldi being an irresponsible pirate, that the Bourbon government asked and received his permission to send a special embassy to discuss terms of alliance against the revolution. This put the Piedmontese in a false situation: 'trying to keep in both with the unitarians and with diplomacy, Cavour is falling out with both of them', said one newspaper.[1] These negotiations did him more harm than good. They never quite convinced Naples or France of his good intentions, and they damaged both his reputation for sincerity and the esteem in which he was held by Garibaldi and the patriots. The ambiguity of his position over this is one more illustration of the fact that the diplomatic method was attended with serious drawbacks. His readiness to negotiate was yet another result of his dependence on France, like the cession of Nice and the attempt to stop Garibaldi crossing the Straits. But it was also more than this, for, as the opposition papers pointed out, he could easily have temporized and put off negotiation, making the plea that he must wait until the new Neapolitan constitution had proved itself by working.[2] When he deliberately entered upon these discussions he must have known that this would retard the development of any crisis at Naples, in other words that he would be giving positive aid to the Bourbons as well as alienating the revolutionaries. Whether or not he was also deceiving Francesco (as he was certainly deceiving Garibaldi), the fact remains that his action convinced the *italianissimi* that he was still thinking in terms of a Neapolitan alliance and not of Italian unity. The result was to confuse Italian patriots, and to make the radicals yet more distrustful and uncompromising. Moreover, he must have been fully

[1] 30 July, A. Bianchi-Giovini in *L' Unione* (Milan).
[2] 13 August, *Il Diritto*.

aware that his policy would give this impression; and he could have guessed that the Neapolitans would publicize his complaisant attitude in order to divide Garibaldi from the moderates.

The fact that his friendliness to the Bourbons was bound to antagonize Garibaldi constitutes the chief difficulty in explaining his conduct. Cavour's apologists maintain that he had already made up his mind to reject the proffered alliance before the Neapolitan plenipotentiaries, Manna and Winspeare, arrived in Turin on 16 July. But it is unlikely that he would have gratuitously provoked Garibaldi by negotiating if he had made up his mind in advance that there was nothing to gain from an alliance. One would surely expect to find Cavour's duplicity of a subtler order than this. We know that he had to contend with a rapidly changing situation, at a time when the true state of public opinion in the south was unknown to him. Until he could learn what was likely to happen in Naples and Sicily, it might have seemed that his best plan was to play for time. Garibaldi's success had already forced Francesco to grant a liberal constitution at Naples on 25 June. A serious possibility existed thereafter that liberal as well as conservative Neapolitans, in their resentment over the Sicilian rebellion, might rally to the Bourbon throne and agree to work the new constitution; and in that case, if public opinion at Naples preferred the constitution to Garibaldi, Cavour felt that he would have to opt for the liberal Neapolitans against the revolutionary Sicilians. On certain terms, that is to say, he does seem to have been ready to follow French advice and make an alliance with Naples. The Neapolitan government would first have to show that it had some popular backing; it would also have to join a common front with Piedmont to keep Austrian influence out of the peninsula; and it would have to let Sicilians become independent or at least decide their own fate by a vote.[1] An alliance on these terms would fit Cavour's scheme to maintain relations with France; it would also act as an insurance against Garibaldi's possible defeat;[2] it would, furthermore, insure against Francesco trying to make terms with the

[1] 27 June, Cavour to Villamarina (*CC Cavour-Nigra*, vol. IV, p. 43).
[2] Ed. G. Romano, *Memorie politiche di Liborio Romano*, 1873, p. 34. Romano also confirmed how Cavour told the Neapolitan envoys 'not to wait for Garibaldi to attack you always, but go out and beat him, capture and execute him'. *Ibid.* p. 33.

italianissimi and set up in Italy as a rival to Victor Emanuel;[1] it would make possible the concentration of national resources upon the conquest of Venetia, so as to build up a strong northern Italy as Cavour preferred; it would also halt the revolution and prevent complications arising out of Garibaldi's further advance in the south; above all, it would gain time for Cavour to observe the portents and make up his mind how far he could safely allow the Italian movement to progress. One would suspect that these arguments must have been cumulatively persuasive.

At all events, we know that in the middle weeks of July politicians in the north were considering that alliance with Naples, at least on some conditions, might be more in their own interests than was alliance with Garibaldi.[2] Now that La Farina had been banished, the success of the Sicilian revolution looked much less attractive than before. Cavour had to be prepared for anything, for victory either by the revolution or by the counter-revolution. So far as he could see at the moment, it was likely that the Bourbon army would stand firm in eastern Sicily; but still he had to be ready in case it collapsed. If Great Britain supported France in demanding that he should conclude an alliance with Naples, then he would almost certainly have to play for safety and to concur in measures to check Garibaldi's advance. Yet it would be foolish to commit himself against the revolution until either Britain declared herself, or else he himself was quite certain that it could not succeed. As early as 6 July he was preparing to send secret agents to Naples in case the revolution could not be checked on the Straits of Messina.[3] At the same time, it would not be wise to close the door on the possibility of a Neapolitan alliance. No doubt he expected or hoped that an alliance would prove to be not necessary, or else would be rendered impossible by his conditions. He argued that, if Francesco agreed to

[1] 29 June, Cavour to Villamarina (*Lettere di Cavour*, ed. Chiala, vol. III, p. 277).

[2] Another example is Minghetti, who, in an undated draft, mentions that they were debating the alternative policy of either 'annexation or alliance' for Naples (Carteggio Minghetti, Biblioteca communale, Bologna). Cavour agreed to accept the envoys on 7 July, N. Bianchi, *Storia documentata della diplomazia europea in Italia dall' anno 1814 all' anno 1861*, vol. VIII, 1872, p. 666.

[3] 6 July, A. Ronchei from Genoa to Calvino (F. De Stefano, *Salvatore Calvino*, 1942, p. 189).

his stipulation for Sicily to be first given the right of self-determination, the Bourbons would then lose face at Naples, since 'les Napolitains libéraux s'ils doivent renoncer à leur domination sur la Sicile, deviendront tous unitaires: c'est certain'.[1] This was a clever calculation, based on the regional self-esteem of the Neapolitan liberals; and British support for his prior condition about Sicilian self-determination enabled him to adhere firmly to his point.[2] Nevertheless, so long as the liberals showed any signs of supporting a new constitutional regime at Naples, Cavour was obliged to hold the door open, in case he was forced to make a bargain at Garibaldi's expense. This was his view on 12 July;[3] and long after that, Garibaldi's friends were able to go on assuming that the Piedmontese were ready to betray them at the first opportunity.

However mistaken this assumption may have been—probably not very much—it was the impression and not the reality which mattered. Cavour had conversations with Manna and Winspeare on at least twelve occasions between 16 and 31 July. When the minister for internal affairs, Farini, had a talk with these Neapolitan envoys at Turin on the 20th, he told them frankly that a Bourbon victory over Garibaldi would be 'the salvation of Italy'; and with doubtful taste he taunted them to their faces, saying, 'if only I had twenty thousand of our troops, I should have courage enough to throw Garibaldi and his army into the sea'.[4] All this was at once reported back to Naples, and thence was published abroad. Towards the end of the month, after the news of

---

[1] 4 July, Cavour to Nigra (*CC Cavour-Nigra*, vol. IV, p. 55).

[2] 7 July, Cavour telegram to Villamarina (*Lettere di Cavour*, ed. Chiala, vol. III, p. 281).

[3] 12 July, Cavour to Nigra (*CC Cavour-Nigra*, vol. IV, p. 72). On 14 July Cavour's semi-official *Opinione* publicly explained that he had to wait until the Neapolitan parliament met and accepted the new Bourbon constitution before he knew whether he would have to conclude an alliance. On 20 August the same paper remarked that, 'if the government of King Francesco had been solidly supported by the sincere wishes of the people..., Piedmont would have been able to form an alliance with Naples which would have proved useful to Italy'.

[4] 23 July, Winspeare to De Martino (*CC Lib. del Mezz.* vol. v); also 20 July, diary of Manna and Winspeare on their mission (*ibid.*). Of these two, Manna at least was a completely reliable witness. In any case they probably would have lacked the courage and the motive (as well as the deceitfulness) to make such a story up.

Garibaldi's victory at Milazzo had reduced or abolished all chance of completing the alliance, Manna noticed that Cavour's attitude became less friendly and expansive. But again legend was bound to outlive reality. On 25 July a correspondent at Turin wrote: 'Cavour is perhaps not averse to contracting the alliance (of course with the intention of breaking it at a more propitious season) in order to put up a temporary barrier against the march of democracy....The *signor* Count remains a Count despite his liberal mask.'[1] This was a not altogether unfair supposition in the circumstances, and it played a considerable part in the loss of mutual confidence which became so much more noticeable in July. Once having begun negotiations, Cavour had to keep up pretences even when all serious intention of an alliance had left him. As late as 5 September Victor Emanuel apparently advised the Bourbons to attack Garibaldi boldly, adding that he hoped they would win and capture and hang the rebellious general.[2] This sort of ruse can have gained absolutely nothing, and it certainly lost something in honesty. It can only have encouraged the king's enemies, just as the rumours which it engendered must have divided his friends.

La Farina's banishment, in its own turn, made Cavour yet more unwilling to meet Garibaldi half-way, and so caused the growth of even more mistrust. When the unfortunate exile arrived back at Genoa on 11 July, there was no one to contradict his statements, and he easily persuaded Cavour to approve what he had done in Sicily.[3] He purposely exaggerated the political implications of differences which were largely personal, knowing that otherwise his own behaviour would be called in question. He thus frightened people with the spectre of red republicanism in Sicily; although a fortnight earlier, when he had rather been boasting of his own power and popularity in the island, he had repeated more than once that no vestige of republicanism could be found in the south. Again, he blamed upon Crispi all the lack of ordered governance in Palermo; though the day before his expulsion—when his motives had been different—he had written to give Cavour other reasons which

[1] 26 July, *L' Unità Italiana* (Genoa), report from a correspondent at Turin dated 25 July.

[2] 5 September, Winspeare telegram to the foreign minister at Naples on his interview of that date with the king (*CC Lib. del Mezz.* vol. v).

[3] 13 July, Cavour to Persano (*ibid.* vol. i, p. 323).

were perfectly adequate to explain this.[1] In immoderate language born of wounded vanity he informed northerners that

the camarilla round Garibaldi which has the reality of power is a hotch-potch of incorrigible Mazzinians and vituperative Bourbonists—a horde of savage drunkards.[2]

As for me, it is hardly necessary to add that I do not blench, no not even at the prospect of civil war if it is thought necessary to save the country... convinced as I am that a brigade of Piedmontese will suffice in the last resort to snatch Sicily from the hands of all the Mazzinians of Italy together, even if Garibaldi is at their head.[3]

His ambition was just to stir up trouble between Garibaldi and Cavour. He had a plentiful armoury for abusiveness in the gossip he brought from Palermo, and besides circulating rumours of a reign of terror, he spread it abroad that Garibaldi was also meditating an expedition to recapture Nice from France.[4] The implication from this was that the government in Sicily was not only a nuisance, but even hostile and dangerous.

Cavour's reaction to the news of La Farina's expulsion was prompt. This particular agent would in any case have been recalled; but here was an affront to the dignity of the government, and a public criticism of its policy such as could not go unnoticed. On 10 July Cavour therefore sent a peremptory order to Genoa that no more volunteer expeditions were to be allowed to sail. The motive given for this was that Garibaldi had refused to recognize Cavour's good will and was surrounding himself with Mazzinians.[5] Admiral Persano at Palermo

---

[1] 6 July, La Farina to Cavour: 'Sicily is not like central Italy. Here, so long as there are not a thousand *carabinieri* and four regiments of Piedmontese troops, no one will be able to govern except with their own faction of partisans: every other type of government will be impotent and despised' (*CC Lib. del Mezz.* vol. I, p. 292). When the time came for La Farina to form his own government in Sicily at the end of the year, he asked for as many as sixteen thousand armed men (*ibid.* vol. III, p. 245).

[2] 17 July, La Farina to A. Franchi (*Epistolario di Giuseppe La Farina*, ed. Ausonio Franchi, vol. II, 1869, p. 360).

[3] 19 July, La Farina to G. Clementi (*ibid.* p. 370).

[4] 13 July, Ronchei to Calvino (ACM, no. 3061).

[5] 10 July, Cavour telegram to Magenta, Vice-Governor of Genoa (*Lettere di Cavour*, ed. Chiala, vol. VI, p. 569); 18 July, Cavour to Magenta (*CC Lib. del Mezz.* vol. I, p. 349).

meanwhile prepared to arrest Crispi, Mario and Ferrara as soon as Garibaldi was out of the way.[1] To his ambassador at London, Cavour wrote: 'Garibaldi se laisse entraîner par l'enivrement du succès. Au lieu de faire, ou de laisser faire l'annexion, il songe à conquérir Naples et à délivrer l'Italie. . . . L'annexion nous tirerait d'embarras, car elle ferait rentrer Garibaldi dans une position normale.'[2] The radical 'dream' of conquering Naples was thus an 'embarrassment' to Turin. While Cavour would no doubt have liked to bring about the collapse of the Bourbon regime, he was inclined to think that the time was not ripe, and he was certainly not prepared to work for it if the result would be a radical victory, nor unless he had a convincing display of support from opinion in both the south and the north. Only after Garibaldi's victory at Milazzo was Cavour properly convinced that his radical opponents were not the dreamers he had supposed; and of course this same battle was to make them even more of an embarrassment and a menace to him. Above all he did not wish the radicals to have any share in the deliverance of Naples; for once master of that city, Garibaldi might prove irresistible as well as incorrigible.[3]

Cavour's mistaken analysis and maladroit conduct did not pass without criticism, even among the moderates. That conservative southern landowner, Lacaita, wrote from London that 'here people in general approve La Farina's expulsion, and it is thought that annexation at the moment would arrest Garibaldi in Sicily, and so preserve Bourbon rule at Naples. There is strong disapproval of La Farina's *plotting* against Garibaldi.'[4] The moderate and respectable General Türr, from what he had seen himself in Sicily, published a different story from the tittle-tattle which had reached the ears of Cavour.

I can guarantee that every dictatorial order was invariably favourable to the Piedmontese government. If some people privately expressed opinions against one or other minister in the Piedmontese government, that was something which happens at Turin as well as Palermo. And as for dis-

---

[1] 17 July, Persano to Cavour (*ibid.* p. 342).

[2] 12 July, Cavour to E. d'Azeglio (*CC Ing.* vol. II, part II, pp. 93–4).

[3] 12 July, Cavour to Nigra (*CC Cavour-Nigra*, vol. IV, p. 71).

[4] 23 July, Sir James Lacaita to Massari (Archivio Massari MRR); 10 August, Michele Amari to W. C. Cartwright (*Carteggio di Amari*, ed. d'Ancona, vol. II, pp. 119–20).

crediting the Piedmontese ministers, I believe that La Farina has contributed more than anyone to this....I am fully persuaded that, both for La Farina's reputation and for the national cause, it would have been better had he never come to Sicily. For in Sicily, until his arrival, there had reigned a perfect accord among all parties, and this accord did not return until his departure.[1]

The republicans were not a danger. If Cavour had only known, Mazzini was bitterly lamenting his impotence and the fact that Garibaldi would accept advice from the moderates alone.[2] Garibaldi's recruiting officers Cosenz and Sacchi, when they sailed with their volunteers to Sicily, obediently followed Cavour's instructions to keep clear of the Papal States. Cavour himself soon had to recognize these evident facts, and probably for this reason he did not enforce his hasty veto on further expeditions. Conceivably he had known all along how little a danger Mazzini was, and was simply using this particular red rag as a means to frighten Napóleon into backing a Piedmontese Italy as a lesser evil. If he was waiting for an excuse to sever relations, he probably realized on second thoughts that Garibaldi had not yet put himself in the wrong, and had not been deserted by public opinion. Alternatively, perhaps Cavour had just been caught off balance by one of his habitual *fureurs momentanées* brought on by the humiliating expulsion of his representative and the public exposure of a casual but important mistake. Whatever the explanation, his optimism received a temporary check now that he saw that Garibaldi had a mind of his own and was the real master in Sicily. It was easy to conclude that the envious and excitable La Farina should never have been sent with full powers to intrigue against men he so much disliked. But it was not so easy to see how the damage could now be repaired.

---

[1] 24 July, *Il Diritto*, letter of 20 July by Türr written from Aix to the editor.

[2] 25 June, Mazzini to Caroline Stansfeld (*Epistolario*, vol. XL, p. 101); 6 July, Mazzini to Emilie Venturi: 'Dear, Garib. has spoken delay. Bert. yields. It is both individually and collectively, ruin. I never felt more the bitterness, the *scoramento* of finding myself in another man's hand' (*ibid.* p. 142); 9 July, Mazzini to Caroline Stansfeld, that Garibaldi had 'a feeling of jealousy of me which is really unintelligible' (*ibid.* p. 160).

CHAPTER VIII

CAVOUR ADJUSTS HIS POLICY: JULY

Up to the beginning of July Cavour had rather drifted before events; but La Farina's banishment from Sicily was a warning that those events might run away with him if he did not assert himself. The bolder spirits in his party were advising him to launch an expedition against Naples, so as simultaneously to reap the harvest sown by the radicals and to prevent them extending their influence on to the continent.[1] But Cavour was too much dependent on Napoleon III to be able to push matters so fast, and feared the diplomatic difficulties if Naples was brought in as an additional complication. He had made the Emperor of the French his accomplice so far as Sicily was concerned, but there was a strong Napoleonic interest in Naples, just as there continued to be a strong French interest in seeing that Italian unification did not go beyond a certain point. Sicily was ripe for the harvest, Naples not: 'les *macaronis* ne sont pas encore cuits, mais quant aux oranges qui sont déjà sur notre table, nous sommes bien décidés à les manger'.[2] This was the position during June and most of July, while Cavour cast about for a way to annex Sicily. He would never stoop to become an active revolutionary he said, and would on no account foster insurrection at Naples, though in legitimate warfare he was ready to fight the whole world.[3] Only later, when Garibaldi was revealed to be yet more of a menace, did Cavour lower his standards and demean himself to the point of becoming a vulgar revolutionary. For the present he still spoke as an orthodox liberal, who would have liked a united Italy, but only when Italy was ready to unite itself: 'vous savez que l'opinion publique est ma boussole; mon programme est de ne pas imposer l'annexion, mais de braver tous les dangers pour la faire, si les populations la réclament. L'Italie n'aura peut-être jamais une occasion plus belle de

[1] N.d., Prince Eugenio Carignano to Cavour (*CC Lib. del Mezz.* vol. i, p. 262).
[2] 25 June, Cavour to Nigra (*CC Cavour-Nigra*, vol. iv, p. 39).
[3] 18 July, Cavour to Ricasoli (*CC Lib. del Mezz.* vol. i, p. 350).

constituer son unité et son indépendance réelle; mais il faut que les Napolitains le veuillent sérieusement, et nous aident un peu de leur côté.'[1]

In a number of letters Cavour admitted that the time would probably come when he must break openly with Garibaldi; but for the moment he had to be content with less strident measures, surreptitiously trying to cut off the general's reinforcements and to compel his surrender of Sicily.[2] At the same time Garibaldi's better nature was appealed to in a personal letter from the king, which asked in the first place for annexation as soon as possible, and in the second for avoidance of any attack on the coast of Naples. An attempt was also made to persuade the dictator that the king at least, if not the Piedmontese government itself, was but play-acting in its negotiations with Naples.[3] The objective however, remained the same. The hypothesis of a Neapolitan alliance was not yet abandoned, just as the hypothesis of a united Italy was not yet finally accepted. Both were retained until the forces of nationalism could be more accurately measured. In the meantime Cavour was sure of only one thing, that Garibaldi and not Francesco represented the most immediate danger to his system. 'L'annexion de la Sicile', he said, 'est un moyen d'annuller Garibaldi, ou tout au moins d'amoindrir son influence de façon à ce qu'elle ne fût plus dangereuse.'[4] Some weeks earlier Cavour had been ready to allow Garibaldi to cross over to the continent; but by the middle of July he was hoping that this could be prevented. The man was now too dangerous to be given a free hand. He had been too much antagonized by La Farina to be made a friend merely by more fair words, and at the moment fair words were the only commodity which Cavour had to offer him.

Cavour's main strength and weakness lay in the diplomatic situation of Europe. One of his constant preoccupations was to know how far

[1] 7 July, Cavour to Villamarina (N. Bianchi, *Storia documentata della diplomazia europea in Italia*, vol. VIII, 1872, pp. 691–2).

[2] 13 July, Cavour to Persano (*CC Lib. del Mezz.* vol. I, p. 322); 18 July, Cavour to Magenta (*ibid.* p. 349).

[3] 8 July, Victor Emanuel to Garibaldi *via* M. Amari (Comandini, *L' Italia nei cento anni*, vol. III, p. 1502).

[4] 12 July, Cavour to Nigra (*CC Cavour-Nigra*, vol. IV, p. 71); 14 July, Nigra to Cavour: 'ne craignez pas l'influence de cet homme [Garibaldi]. Il s'usera dans l'accomplissement de sa tâche, et ce n'est certes pas lui qui est destiné à recueillir le fruit de ses œuvres. Garibaldi n'est bon qu'à détruire...' (*ibid.* p. 80).

he could go without alienating France, and as he believed that a general European war was not far off, it was all the more necessary to keep his demands within what Napoleon would allow him.[1] Yet he knew that British support would be forthcoming only in so far as he appeared to weaken in his allegiance to Paris. It was fortunate that Napoleon had lost the confidence of Britain as of most other countries, and was therefore having to rely to a considerable degree 'on the popular and revolutionary element' in Europe.[2] With a little cleverness, France as well as Britain might thus be induced to accept the yet further expansion of Piedmont, provided at least that the impulse did not come from any other European power, but appeared to derive from the Italian people themselves. At the end of July Napoleon wrote: 'je désire que l'Italie se pacifie, n'importe comment, mais sans intervention étrangère'.[3] Evidently the Emperor was ready to accept Piedmontese domination of the peninsula if the alternative was Austrian domination in the north, or if either British or Garibaldian influence threatened to prevail in the south. It was the direct opposite with Great Britain. Lord John Russell still feared that Cavour might be forced to make a bargain with France for the purchase of Sicily and Naples at the price of yielding Sardinia and Liguria,[4] even though on this point his ambassador assured him that Cavour had promised to 'run straight'.[5] But this also had compensating advantages as far as Piedmont was concerned. In order to prevent Italy emerging as a client of France, Russell was ready to vie with Napoleon for Cavour's favour and gratitude. The mutual distrust between Britain and France was an invaluable fact, easily exploited in emergencies, and one more indication that fate was on Italy's side.

Cavour was gradually feeling his way towards a more active policy, as he adjusted himself to what had happened since May. In the process

[1] 8 July, Cavour to Ricasoli (*CC Lib. del Mezz.* vol. I, p. 308).

[2] 12 August, Nigra to Cavour (*CC Cavour-Nigra*, vol. IV, pp. 152–3).

[3] 25 July, Napoleon III to Persigny (Paul Matter, *Cavour et l'unité Italienne*, vol. III, 1927, p. 366).

[4] 31 July, Russell to Farini: 'we know that Count Cavour thought himself compelled to yield contrary to his declarations on the subject of Savoy and Nice, so that many say what has happened once may happen again. Too great a desire to possess Naples may lead to an equal desire to possess Venice and Dalmatia' (RP G.D. 22/73).

[5] 16 July, Hudson to Russell (RP G.D. 22/66).

he let himself be converted by Garibaldi's extraordinary success to conceive that Mazzini's unitarian utopia might not be so distant after all. Italian unity had always remotely been a hypothesis for him,[1] but was hardly a working hypothesis even in the first half of 1860, and until lately he had dismissed the idea as 'nonsense'.[2] Now he found, to his surprise and ultimately to his great pleasure, that the general feeling both in Italy and Europe was ahead of him in this. 'Since the affair of Savoy and Nice', said the United States minister, 'public opinion is no longer with Cavour, but it is with Garibaldi. Cavour cannot oppose him.'[3] Hence the government had reluctantly been compelled to allow the Thousand to set out in May; and hence in July, as Garibaldi threatened to become an ever more actual and no longer just a potential danger, Cavour had to catch up quickly with public opinion if he wanted to give a moderate, monarchical, Piedmontese direction to what was happening. It was a case of yielding to the inevitable. Somehow he had to find a way of discreetly accepting and enveloping the revolutionary movement which so far he had openly repudiated. This would for preference have to be done with Garibaldi's good will, because public opinion, which he proudly acknowledged to be his *boussole* or compass, would not at this moment have permitted an open breach with the glamorous and successful *Duce* in Sicily. The only alternative was that he should go one better than the revolutionaries and outbid them in public estimation at their own game. These various considerations now gave Cavour his leading principles of action. While secretly preparing to stop Garibaldi's further progress, he simultaneously had to devise how, if necessary, he might outdistance the dictator in revolutionary zeal. Yet he also had to keep up an appearance of giving cordial assistance to the very man whom he was preparing to defeat; for that man had not only won the admiration of Europe, but had convinced

[1] 2 October 1832, Cavour to Marchesa di Barolo (*Lettere di Cavour*, ed. Chiala, vol. I, 1884, p. 280).

[2] 12 April 1856, Cavour to Rattazzi, saying that Manin 'vuole l' unità d' Italia ed altre corbellerie' (*CC Ing.* vol. I, 1933, p. 463); Chiala typically omits this part of the letter, without even saying that he has made any omission (*Lettere di Cavour*, vol. II, 1883, p. 220).

[3] 24 July, Daniel to Secretary Cass (copy in MRR); and Commander Forbes on 15 July at Genoa wrote 'it is not in the power of the Government to check the movement' (*The Campaign of Garibaldi in the Two Sicilies*, 1861, p. 5).

8 ✱

Cavour himself and many of his countrymen that a kingdom of Italy might almost be a practical possibility.

An ordinary politician might have been baffled by the incongruousness and irreconcilability of this multiple policy. Not so Cavour. But it was these internal inconsistencies which make it so hard for a historian to follow his tracks. From his private letters, however, one does derive the general impression that, if he had one principal aim throughout July, it was not so much to proceed with the unification of Italy, as to stop Garibaldi's progress altogether, leaving any question of acquiring further provinces plenty of time to mature. His difficulty in pursuing this particular aim was simply that he had always to keep up appearances of quite a different sort. This was necessary even inside the liberal-conservative party, for d'Azeglio had to be reassured that Cavour had no territorial ambitions in the south, while Ricasoli had to think the very reverse; politicians at Naples had to be persuaded that he wanted an alliance with the Bourbons, at the same time as Garibaldi and public opinion in liberated Italy had to believe that he was in league with the revolution; the Piedmontese had to be lured by the vision that they were conquering Italy, at the same time as the rest of Italy had to be assured that it was liberating itself, and merely associating voluntarily with Piedmont to create a wholly new kingdom of Italy; the French had to be convinced that Cavour was Napoleon's humble servant, the British that he was no such thing; Louis Napoleon, too, had to be persuaded that he must support Cavour as his only hope of saving Italy from the anti-clericals and the anti-French, while Russell had to be induced to help Cavour in his reputed desire to free himself from French influence and to destroy the temporal power of the Pope; the Austrians also had to think that Cavour had no immediate ambitions in northern Italy, although Kossuth and the Hungarian nationalists were told that he was eager for battle. It was, indeed, a sign of Cavour's skill and courage that he contrived more or less to keep up these contradictory appearances by artful deceit, at the same time as he gradually edged himself into a position where he could once more command and be obeyed. Even if people had now learnt to disbelieve him and distrust his motives, they were still likely to be confused and confounded by a smoke screen on this scale, and behind such a screen he could deploy his forces until he was strong enough to attack.

One essential task in July was to establish contact again with Garibaldi, in order to preserve one more illusion a little longer, and in case it was still possible to repair the damage done by La Farina. The question was, whom to send. Admiral Persano was still in Garibaldi's good books, but he was a serving officer who might be required elsewhere, and his past history did not suggest that he was above average as a politician any more than he was above average as a naval officer. The need was for someone less official, who was an experienced diplomat and administrator, and who in some degree possessed the confidence of both sides. The answer was found in Agostino Depretis, like Crispi to become later one of the most famous prime ministers of Italy after Cavour's death. This year 1860 was to give both these men their first real experience of government. On close study one can already discern in Depretis the qualities which much later became so notorious in the prime minister, the same hesitation and yieldingness, the same tact, moderation and lack of strong conviction, the same administrative ability, diplomatic *savoir faire*, and skill in smoothing over rival people and ideas. Petruccelli summed him up as 'a capable administrator, but completely lacking in political courage'.[1] On both these counts, because of his capability and his meekness, he had good claims to Cavour's consideration. By temperament and ability he was incomparably more suited than La Farina to a job which required someone genial and serene by nature, a natural sceptic who could tack and temporize.

His political history also marked him out as peculiarly suited to the new post. Depretis was in some sort of contact with Cavour and Garibaldi, the king and Mazzini, La Farina and Dr Bertani.[2] From different points of view, both the *Movimento* and the *Corriere Mercantile* at Genoa welcomed his appointment. At Palermo, *L' Annessione* greeted him favourably as a man who was by birth a Piedmontese, and who in politics was a good democrat without being of the radical levelling variety. He belonged to the same political group as Rattazzi, and had some claims to be considered a leader of the parliamentary

---

[1] F. Petruccelli della Gattina, *I moribondi del Palazzo Carignano*, 1862, p. 107. Hudson rather unfairly called Depretis a 'clever unscrupulous man, and I should say not to be trusted', 16 July, Hudson to Russell (RP G.D. 22/66).

[2] E. Librino, 'Agostino Depretis prodittatore in Sicilia', *Nuova Antologia*, December 1930, pp. 462 *et seq.*

Left at Turin. That he was not too radical had been shown by his opposition to Garibaldi over the question of the *Nazione Armata* in January, and also by his serving under Cavour's administration as governor of the province of Brescia. This latter experience of rule over a large area under emergency conditions left him much better equipped than La Farina for his work in Sicily. The extreme radicals, while they saw in him a true patriot and democrat, called him ambitious, cunning and underhand, and continued to be on their guard.[1] Both sides continued to be slightly suspicious of him, yet he skilfully induced both sides to hope that he shared their way of thought. While still governor of Brescia, he actively abetted the revolution by collecting money and arms for the Sicilian expedition;[2] and having resigned from Brescia, he was one of those who had criticized Cavour's cession of Nice, thus ingratiating himself further with Garibaldi.

Bertani, the extreme radical, could never really understand why Garibaldi was so moderate and unrevolutionary as to want a Sardinian commissioner to whom he could hand over the civil government in Sicily. Nor did Cavour understand or appreciate Garibaldi's initial desire to establish this contact with Turin, or else presumably he would have consulted the dictator's wishes before sending out such a man as La Farina. It was not the least of Cavour's tactical errors that he identified Garibaldi with the extreme revolutionaries, and this attitude only drove the dictator more solidly into their ranks. Neither side is free from criticism in the development of this split, but in fairness to the radicals it must be stated that they had asked for Depretis a month before Cavour agreed to let him go. Half-way through June, when the name of Depretis was first mentioned, the chances of co-operation had been at their greatest, because both sides then realized that La Farina was causing discord and making agreement between Palermo and Turin less easy. The initiative in reconciliation at that moment had come from Bargoni, one of the less extreme members of the radical *partito d'azione*. What Bargoni asked was that a man should be sent to Sicily who was not an extreme partisan, but who could interpret one side to

[1] 9 July, Asproni to Crispi (Crispi's *Memoirs*, vol. 1, p. 318).
[2] 27 April, Depretis to Garibaldi (G. E. Curàtulo, *Garibaldi, Vittorio Emanuele, Cavour nei fasti della patria*, 1911, p. 194); and 24 March, Depretis to Garibaldi (ABM).

the other. By that time Cavour had reached the stage of giving secret help to the volunteer committees which were organizing reinforcements for Sicily; for he had convinced himself that the annexation of this province was feasible, and he wanted to keep the Sicilian revolution alive until the island was free, or until the diplomatic and military situation allowed him to fight his own battles himself. Accordingly he replied to Bargoni that he was now willing to help Garibaldi; but that, since he believed Mazzini to be in Sicily (in this he was mistaken), some guarantee of reliability and good faith was needed. What he proposed was that a man should be sent by the government with full powers, to be on the spot in case of need, and he suggested that Garibaldi should choose this man from a list drawn up in Turin. When notified of this proposal, Bertani's reaction was that he could agree to no name but that of Depretis. Garibaldi welcomed this mention of Depretis, and Cavour also agreed when on 19 June Ribotti was sent to ask his consent.[1] Bargoni's scheme, as it then stood, was that Garibaldi should shortly hand over his powers of civil government to Depretis, and so put an end to the growing schism.

At this point there seemed good reason to hope for a settlement. But, though the choice of Depretis had been virtually agreed by 19 June, he was not allowed to set out from Genoa until four weeks later on 16 July, by which time La Farina's uniquely foolish methods of conspiracy and mob agitation against Garibaldi's plans had made an agreed compromise almost impossible. Cavour was strangely reluctant to recall La Farina. He was inevitably out of touch with Sicily, and perhaps had little choice but to believe the reports of this his semi-official representative. These reports had thus spoken at length of La Farina's personal success, and had stressed the inadvisability of sending out a new royal commissioner instead of promoting to that office La Farina himself. Even when doubt had been thrown on the value of this information, some more days went by in second thoughts over who was the right man to be his successor. Cavour gave orders on 7 July that if Garibaldi insisted on Depretis he should have him, but efforts were still to be made to secure acceptance of the more politically reliable Valerio. For some reason or other, Cavour was fond enough to think that Depretis of the 'constitu-

[1] 20 June, Bargoni from Turin to Bertani; 21 June, Bargoni to Calvino (*Memorie di Bargoni*, pp. 106–19, 128).

tional Left' would be tolerated neither by the country nor by Europe.[1] This was a narrow liberalism thus to arrogate to itself a monopoly of respectability and worth. It was also said that Depretis had once been a Mazzinian and still refused to renounce Mazzini explicitly in public. With rather more perception, Cavour added, 'what is more, Depretis, under an austere exterior, and despite manners which would seem to reveal a resolute character, conceals an irresolute and undecided nature that will with difficulty resist unpopularity. He has ability, but lacks that study of politics which makes it possible to judge the opportuneness of acts affecting international policy.'[2] There was some truth in this, but not a great deal; and such truth as there was did not tell altogether against Depretis as a candidate for this particular post.

This was the moment when La Farina's expulsion upset Cavour's nice balance of policy. The prime minister's first reaction, as we have seen, was to stop further supplies going to help the revolution. But on second thoughts he saw that this could gain him nothing. Accordingly, on 14 July, he at last asked Depretis to come to Turin and be coached for his new office. The radicals for a moment took this as their victory. Probably it was Bertani who had been responsible for the repudiation of Valerio, by describing the latter to Garibaldi as 'molto manipolabile' and 'seen to be day and night with Cavour'.[3] The choice of Depretis had certainly lain primarily with the radicals, and on this very 14 July they also sent a separate letter to Depretis with Garibaldi's instructions to leave at once for Sicily.[4] Cavour, however, had correctly read Depretis's character, and knew that he would do nothing very readily that was unpopular or against his own interests and career. To Persano Cavour therefore wrote that, since Depretis was 'a weak character who will allow himself to be easily coaxed', he might be made the instrument for Piedmontese policy—adding that, nevertheless, he should not be trusted too far.[5] The king was then brought in to make Depretis a royal commissioner, although this title was to be kept secret until it was clear that no difficulties would thereby be created with

---

[1] 12 July, Cavour to Nigra (*CC Cavour-Nigra*, vol. IV, p. 71).
[2] 7 July, Cavour to Persano (*CC Lib. del Mezz.* vol. I, p. 295).
[3] 2 July, Bertani to Crispi (ABCM).
[4] 14 July, Macchi to Depretis (Archivio Depretis ASR).
[5] 14 July, Cavour to Persano (*CC Lib. del Mezz.* vol. I, p. 328).

Garibaldi or with Europe. Thus equipped, on the 16th Depretis at last set out.

Some of the radicals soon began to suspect that after all he might be out to betray the revolution.[1] There is little doubt that he gave Cavour to understand that he would work in the interests of Turin, and he was given a special cipher of the Ministry of the Interior in which to make reports.[2] Almost certainly he agreed to engineer annexation as soon as possible. La Farina wrote on 22 July that 'here everyone is anxiously awaiting the outcome of Depretis's mission.... If he cannot achieve anything, this would then be in all probability the signal for breaking off relations between the king's government and Garibaldi.'[3] One of Cavour's most intimate friends, Castelli, reflected the current view when he wrote that 'I hope Depretis will act like a *good Piedmontese*, which for me is the highest praise there could possibly be'.[4] Castelli's correspondent here was Lanza, the President of the Chamber of Deputies at Turin, Depretis being one of its vice-presidents. We shall see that Depretis, as a Piedmontese by birth himself, and having good reason to ingratiate himself with Cavour, was in fact to represent Cavour in Sicily almost as accurately as La Farina himself. Yet he also had enough sense to see that, though the best hope for Sicily lay in annexation to Piedmont, this should be carried out only in Garibaldi's good time.[5] With his lifelong reluctance to hold strong views of any sort, and his considerable ability in reconciliation and compromise, he should have succeeded in this task if any man could; and if he finally failed in his attempt to serve two masters, this was not due only to the ambiguity of his position and that of Cavour, but also to the fact that La Farina's conduct had left people too much embittered for a reconciliation.

[1] 20 July, *L' Unità Italiana* (Genoa).
[2] 6 October, letter from the Ministry to Depretis, asking him to return at once the *chiffrant* given him for his mission in Sicily (Archivio Depretis ASR).
[3] 22 July (wrongly printed as June), La Farina to G. Giunti (*Epistolario di La Farina*, ed. Franchi, p. 378). Montecchi, who was in the Ministry of the Interior, wrote on 19 July to Fiorenzi of these secret undertakings, saying that 'in a few days we shall see the result of the mission he has gone to perform' (E. Montecchi, *M. Montecchi nel risorgimento Italiano*, 1932, p. 153).
[4] 23 July, Castelli to Lanza (A. Arzano, 'Il dissidio fra Garibaldi e Depretis', *Memorie Storiche Militari*, 1913, p. 10).
[5] 11 October, speech by Depretis, *Atti Parlamentari*.

In allowing Depretis to leave on this mission, Cavour was going part of the way to become himself an unconcealed revolutionary. He did not like it, but he saw no option. As he wrote to Nigra on 25 July: 'je ferai tous mes efforts pour empêcher que le mouvement italien cesse d'être national pour devenir révolutionnaire. Je suis prêt à tout pour obtenir ce résultat. Mais pour conserver quelque chance de succès, je ne puis me mettre en lutte avec la véritable opinion publique.'[1] Perhaps it was some consolation that, choosing Depretis, he weakened the leadership of Rattazzi's group. In the same way, by absorbing a small part of the radical programme, he could vindicate himself with public opinion, and also hope to weaken the parliamentary opposition still further. A private letter of 23 July suggests that to divide the opposition may have been specially useful to him at this moment. 'Here there is a ministerial crisis', wrote De Meis the philosopher from Turin. 'People are talking of Rattazzi; and, for my part, after the mistakes made over Nice, I should see Cavour go to the devil without displeasure; the necessary men in Italy now are Victor Emanuel and Garibaldi, perhaps Farini too, but no one else.'[2] Rattazzi had continued to keep up correspondence with Crispi and the Garibaldians, as they were a possible political ally for the future;[3] but he was perceptive enough to see that Cavour's instinct would sooner or later bring the government into line with the great majority,[4] and this took away from the opposition any opportunity to do other than await further developments.

Rattazzi was in any case powerless, so long as parliament remained closed and Cavour treated the king with circumspection. Although representations were made that at this time of all times the Chamber should be open, so that the collective wisdom and force of the nation might be concentrated behind the government, Cavour did not want his hands tied. Hence 'the ministers were able to carry on as though they were servants of an absolute monarch'.[5] During these six months

---

[1] 25 July, Cavour to Nigra (*CC Cavour-Nigra*, vol. IV, p. 107).

[2] 23 July, De Meis to Bertrando Spaventa (*Silvio Spaventa, Dal 1848 al 1861*, ed. Croce, 1923, p. 347).

[3] 4 July, Rattazzi to Crispi (catalogued but missing from b. 142 of Archivio Crispi ASP).

[4] 17 July, Rattazzi to Castelli (*Carteggio di Castelli*, ed. Chiala, vol. I, pp. 309–10).

[5] 14 August, *Il Diritto*.

Rattazzi returned to his legal practice, and the rest of his group had little outlet for their criticisms but the columns of *Il Diritto*. This Turin newspaper repeatedly tried to throw blame on Cavour for having done all he could or dared to oppose Garibaldi's initial expedition to Sicily, and so for flouting the will of the people. Even after the capture of Palermo he had played an ambiguous and ineffective part in events.

In our view it should have been a question of saving appearances, but at the same time of giving real help; whereas the government did precisely the opposite. Cavour boasted about the assistance given, and indeed was so ostentatious about this that he was compromised a thousand times in the eyes of diplomacy; but he never gave as much practical help as a truly national government ought.[1]

La Farina was sent to Sicily, although authoritative people advised against this, with the aim of opposing rather than helping Garibaldi, of sowing doubt and discord....But despite the continuous representations of the independent press, the government never recalled him....

Cavour and Garibaldi may be agreed over their general aims, but there is a wide gulf between them on the means to be used....and it is Garibaldi rather than the prime minister who at this moment represents the nation....

We do not wish to provoke a ministerial crisis. But we do want the government to proceed with more spirit and more frankness; it should associate itself loyally and courageously with Garibaldi (which it could do without any serious danger); it should show itself more independent of French influence, and should have faith in the nation.[2]

On 24 July the *Diritto* came out with a leading article which surely must have been written by Rattazzi himself, and which gives a good summary of the standpoint of the 'constitutional opposition'. Cavour, it was there stated, distrusted the nation, and had repeatedly violated the 'Italian principle', for instance by entering the Crimean War and by his cession of Nice. He was 'entirely and blindly bound to the French alliance', that *connubio fatale*, and so had become 'but an instrument of the Emperor's policy in Italy'. Garibaldi on the other hand represented the national idea and believed in popular initiative. The article gave a partisan but interesting portrait of Cavour.

His political education took place outside Italy. His mind is subtle, lucid, but too clever to be strong, and is lacking in that warmth which comes from the heart....

[1] 27 August, *ibid.*   [2] 27 July, *ibid.*

It is true that he possesses in a high degree the art of managing assemblies, of catching men in the snare of political passions and individual interests; it is true that he knows how to use alternately insolence, invective, or skilful riposte according to his particular adversary of the moment; it is also true that he has a particular tact in handling parties, purchasing the interest of the press, and winning elections. But all this builds up to the fact that he has deprived parliament of its authority. By inconsiderately abusing his majority, and by further abuse of government influence in elections, he has completely undermined the constitution and upset the equilibrium of power.

The day that war began [in 1859] he closed parliament, having been given absolute powers instead of just the special authority strictly needed for the purposes of war. After that he bartered away two provinces as if they were merchandise, openly violating the constitution in doing so; and parliament just cried him *hosanna*.

The result is that, if you ask people what parliament is, they will reply, 'an assembly of talkers which is a useful ladder for titles and jobs'; and Piedmont, which possesses in her parliament the most precious pledge for the future of Italy, now sees it without authority, without influence among people, without influence on the ministers....

Cavour is highly skilled at capturing individuals, but has not the art of befriending the multitude, because he is despotic in his way of government, and careless of public opinion whenever it is against him.

Cavour did not have much to fear from these parliamentary deputies, for the gifts attributed to him in this article had been used to good effect in weakening their strength and composition. True enough, he was to set a fashion in 'parliamentary dictatorship' which later became a norm of government in Italy; but though he himself was often dictatorial in method, in substance he always remained more liberal than his opponents, and they were quite wrong to think that he lightly disregarded public opinion. On the contrary, a more apt accusation might be that, whenever Rattazzi discovered an alternative line of policy or a point of criticism which found some public favour, Cavour used to incorporate it at once in his own system; so that there was seldom a strong independent opposition with a distinct programme of its own, and therefore seldom sufficient chance of obtaining adequate publicity and debate for major differences of principle. Even the *Diritto* had to agree with Cavour over the value of the French alliance,[1] and could find little good

[1] 27 May, 6 June, 18 August, *ibid.*

to say of Mazzini's politics.[1] A dexterous treatment since 1852 had effectively cut off Rattazzi and Brofferio from the radicals round Garibaldi who still acknowledged the old democratic programme.[2]

Mazzini might possibly have been more of a danger to the government than was Rattazzi; but Mazzini had deliberately drawn his own republican fangs, and now hoped for little more startling than that Cavour might be obliged to yield his place to that revolutionary conservative the Baron Ricasoli.[3] It was still Mazzini's intention to organize a volunteer attack on the Papal States, and so to expose Cavour's false position between conservatives and revolutionaries, or at least to force him off the fence. But this never became much more than an intention, and in practice the movement which Mazzini had begun and kept alive in the dark days was slipping ever further out of his control. The 'party of action' was entrenched in Palermo, but it was divided in itself, and had no one leader with the ability and experience to stand up to Cavour. Once they had forced Piedmont to come half-way to meet the revolution, the chief political task of the extreme radicals was almost done.

By emulating the revolutionaries, Cavour was stooping to conquer: there was no alternative. The Neapolitan alliance, if it had ever been much more than an insurance policy, was fading away in front of Garibaldi's victories and the general reaction to them. 'What can we do?', he demanded of Nigra in a letter of 22 July, knowing that this excuse would then reach Napoleon.

An alliance with Naples would now lower our king in the estimation of Italians. From Florence and Milan people are writing to tell me that, if it is signed, serious troubles will break out in those towns....If the king of Naples had only placed himself at the head of his troops and fought boldly, we could have made some *rapprochement* with him, even if he had after all been defeated. But what can you do with a prince who inspires neither confidence nor esteem?[4]

There was nothing else that Cavour could do but accept the revolution in part, so as to defeat the whole. His letters suggest that his main

---

[1] 28 August, *ibid.*   [2] 7 July, *L' Unità Italiana* (Genoa).
[3] July, Mazzini, *Epistolario*, vol. XL, pp. 216–17, 225.
[4] 22 July, Cavour to Nigra (*CC Cavour-Nigra*, vol. IV, p. 93).

object continued to be the defeat of the whole; and although in retrospect he was glad enough incidentally to have accepted the part, at the time he was fearful of what might befall from this, and acted with reluctance. It is true that, when writing to people in contact with Garibaldi, he dropped convenient hints of his own readiness to resign if this would help co-operation between government and revolution,[1] but it is not easy to believe that any such thought seriously crossed his mind, or that he was making more than a tactful gesture. Cavour and his party never looked kindly on the idea of compromise with the revolution, and if he yielded at all it was only so that he might conquer in the end.

Ricasoli went further, and did not cease urging on Cavour to have done alike with Garibaldi in Sicily, with the Pope at Rome, and with the Bourbons in Naples. Ricasoli was convinced that, although Victor Emanuel had had to accept Lombardy as the gift of Napoleon in 1859, it would be too humiliating for the monarch to accept Sicily as the gift of a mere subject.[2] Here was the material for another investiture contest, over whether the king could allow himself to accept investiture for his new kingdom at the hands of Garibaldi. Victor Emanuel himself did not worry much about this, for he was proud to own Garibaldi's affection and loyalty. But many other people in the north disliked what they read as a challenge to the king's prestige, and disliked it more than they liked what the volunteers were doing for Italy—in other words, many, perhaps most, of the liberals put monarchy before national unity in their scale of political values. Some of them, indeed, in the end accepted unification only because it was a method of recovering royal prestige and defending the principles of social conservation.

Cavour had not been able to frame a detailed plan of action until he could feel the pulse of popular opinion, until he could obtain some general idea of the relative strength and potential danger of the forces at play in the revolution. By the middle of July he had some of the information he required, and it was becoming more clear that he could not afford to wait much longer for the rest. Ricasoli's threats on the one

[1] 23 July, Cavour to Persano (*CC Lib. del Mezz.* vol. I, p. 363).
[2] 15 July, Ricasoli to Cavour (*Lettere di Ricasoli*, ed. Tabarrini, vol. v, pp. 161–2); 15 July, Ricasoli to Fabrizi (*ibid.* pp. 159–60).

hand were matched by threats from the radicals on the other. One of
Garibaldi's friends had seen Cavour on 19 July and put to him the direct
alternative, either to become himself a revolutionary, or else to let the
radical democrats carry out the revolution on their own lines.[1] This
was clumsily stated, but there was just enough substance in the threat to
frighten all good liberals. Though the danger was an illusion, it was an
effective illusion. The few real republican leaders, Quadrio, Saffi and
Campanella, were grouped near Mazzini at Genoa. Bertani was now
working more closely with Mazzini, and was preparing an attack
against the Papal States based on Tuscany.[2] Others of the near-
republicans and federalists were congregating in Sicily, where Garibaldi
was dangerously uncontrollable. The longer they were left alone without
any competition from a liberal policy of action, the more likely they
would be to retain the favour of public opinion.

Cavour's slender hold on Garibaldi so far had mainly depended on
the latter's known loyalty to the king; but unfortunately this bond
between sovereign and subject could only be kept in repair at a certain
price, by unintentionally confirming the revolutionaries in their belief
that Victor Emanuel might be at heart on their side. This belief had
emboldened them to think that, despite the policy of his government,
the king personally wished them to advance on Rome. Judging by what
evidence we have, the king did want them to continue their advance,
and apparently his aide-de-camp Marquis Trecchi took them private
messages of encouragement. If this was not his plan, he would surely
have given Garibaldi a specific order not to raise the Roman question,
or at least not to raise it until France was appeased; and there can be
little doubt that such an order would have been obeyed, however
reluctantly. That Cavour apparently did not ask the king to do so,
probably indicates once again that he was not certain of his master, and
also that Victor Emanuel would not commit himself to his ministers'
policy about Rome until he was quite sure Garibaldi could not succeed.
Cavour cannot be blamed for this ambiguity in his government's
policy; but historians must also be chary of blaming Garibaldi if,

---

[1] 21 July, La Masa from Turin to Garibaldi (G. La Masa, *Alcuni fatti e documenti
della rivoluzione dell' Italia meridionale*, 1861, p. 196).

[2] 23 July, Farini to Ricasoli (*Carteggio di Ricasoli*, ed. Nobili and Camerani; volume
to be published).

8-2

because of that ambiguity, he continued to increase the pressure still further.

By the time of the battle of Milazzo on 20 July Garibaldi was bursting with confidence, and this victory then opened up to him the vision of a completely united Italy, with himself offering the king his new crown in the city of Rome itself. The result was that he now appeared to Cavour as being far from just a quaint adventurer whose deeds might be exploited profitably at a suitable moment; he was a positive and immediate danger to the whole idea of solving the Italian question by diplomatic means and the French alliance. The threat of republicanism may have been deliberately exaggerated, but the liberal leader certainly saw embodied in Garibaldi what Omodeo has called 'the dissolution of his own conception of the State'.[1] Hence Cavour's eagerness to halt the volunteers in Sicily and sweep Garibaldianism from the south. Hence his and Farini's apparent annoyance when the Bourbon army proved unable to defeat Garibaldi or keep him out of Messina. During at least one stage in his conversion to revolutionism, Cavour almost seemed to be on the wrong side of the civil war.

[1] A. Omodeo, 'Cavour e l' impresa Garibaldina', *Leonardo*, May 1929, p. 126.

CHAPTER IX

DEPRETIS BEGINS HIS PRODICTATORSHIP: JULY

The expulsion of La Farina had come as a sharp shock to Cavour in Turin. It had also of course upset the party in Sicily which had been organized to campaign for immediate annexation. Many of the moderates, including people who knew La Farina to be unpopular and thought he should have returned home earlier on his own or on Cavour's initiative, still regretted the arrest and ignominious banishment of a Sicilian patriot.[1] Nevertheless, even among those who disliked what had happened, the matter was passed over in silence, and there was apparently no disturbance to public quiet or to Garibaldi's prestige.[2] Most people in Sicily were probably content to believe that the dictator had good reasons for what he had done, and were glad that the national party in Sicily would no longer be so publicly riven in two factions.[3] Some days afterwards Garibaldi changed the composition of his ministry, but the inclusion of moderate 'Cavourians' like Professor Amari testified to the continuity and essential moderation of the dictator's policy.

Evidently La Farina had exaggerated in report as well as exacerbated in person the political divisions which he had found in Palermo. On his return to the north he published a statement to the effect that three hundred townships in Sicily had sent in petitions for prompt annexation; yet only a handful of these petitions have so far been traced.[4] Annoyed though Garibaldi must have been by the evidence of La Farina's intrigues, he did not let this annoyance deflect him from the moderate

---

[1] 12 July, G. Fiorenza from Palermo to Ricasoli (*Carteggio di Ricasoli*, ed. Nobili and Camerani).

[2] 29 July, *La Nazione* (Florence), report from Palermo dated 24 July.

[3] 12 July, *La Forbice* (Palermo).

[4] F. Guardione found only three in the Archivio di Stato at Palermo, *La Sicilia nella rigenerazione politica d' Italia 1798–1860*, 1912, p. 600, commenting on La Farina's statement in *Il Piccolo Corriere d' Italia* for 22 July.

programme which Crispi had outlined in May and June. On 14 July
provincial governors were informed that 'the programme of the
dictator's government is this: slow, gradual annexation, according as
the opportunities become more or less easy; and in the meantime a *de
facto* assimilation of Sicilian administration to the governmental system
of Piedmont'.[1] Notwithstanding anything La Farina told Cavour, this
was no new policy, but something quite explicit in Garibaldi's administrative actions from the very first, and the arrival of neither La Farina
nor Depretis was to make any difference in this respect. From first to
last Garibaldi stood for assimilation of the south by the north, and the
only difference made upon him by La Farina's plotting was that he was
now forewarned and forearmed against Cavour's duplicity. Garibaldi's
policy is often accused of being immoderate and irresponsibly whimsical,
and it is therefore the more important to note that it remained moderate
and constant despite all this subversive conspiracy. It was Cavour's
policy, not Garibaldi's, which was suddenly changed into something
intemperate and uncompromising by La Farina's conduct.

Depretis arrived in Sicily on 21 July. The common opinion, said the
British consul, was that he came as 'a Piedmontese who will represent
the Sardinian Government';[2] but his arrival by mail boat, and not by
warship like La Farina, was typical of his lesser degree of ostentation,
and his determination that unlike his predecessor he would represent
and reconcile both sides of the political conflict. The chief 'annexationist' paper greeted him on the day he landed with a frank approval
of the dictator's policy of delay. Garibaldi, so this journal now asserted,
should for the time being keep Sicily clear from association with the
Turin government, for in this way he would remain free from any
diplomatic pressure which could be brought to bear on Sicily through
Piedmont. The annexation of the island would also make the invasion
of Naples more difficult; for it was important that Naples should seem
to fall before a popular revolution by the irresponsible volunteers, and
not before a 'conquest' by Piedmont which could be resented by the
rest of Europe as an imposition from without.[3] The general feeling in

---

[1] 14 July, La Porta the minister of public security to the governor of Messina at
Barcelona, on note-paper headed 'Gabinetto Segreto', in the file registered as 'Atti
vari sulla rivoluzione del 1860' (Archivio di Stato Messina).

[2] 18 July (Goodwin's Political Journal, F.O. 165/134).   [3] 21 July, *L' Annessione.*

Palermo was against any further agitation of the people for political ends. It was confidently expected that the various parties would come together again in common agreement, and that Depretis would quietly carry through the annexation by plebiscite as soon as Garibaldi crossed over to the continent. Meanwhile, the weapon of mob demonstrations was held in reserve, if need be 'for use at a more opportune moment'.[1]

Depretis's presence was a sedative and a reassurance to people. He arrived as the official bearer of 'instructions' from the king to Garibaldi.[2] Going up at once to the front line, he scored an early success by being given the official title of 'prodictator' and the concession of 'absolute powers'. This confirmed his joint allegiance and responsibility to both Garibaldi and Cavour, and seemed to bring with it the promise of more harmonious relations. Admiral Persano rejoiced at this formal appointment, for he feared that there had been a move among the radicals to clip Depretis's wings, and Garibaldi was thus giving one more indication that concord and impartiality took precedence in his mind over a radical policy.[3] The Piedmontese consul also reported back approvingly on the new prodictator's reception and his conduct.[4] On 27 July Persano wrote to Cavour:

Depretis has shown himself at once firm and gentle; he is certainly most able; he works calmly and yet with perfect determination; he will shortly be promulgating many of our Piedmontese laws; he is both honest and loyal, and hence it was not hard for me to make him devoted to you; he tells me he has admired you for a long time. I had hardly met Depretis before, but I am coming to admire him more every day.[5]

Not only among the moderates, but among the radicals too there was scarcely yet a dissenting voice on the merits of the prodictator. 'Let them do their worst, these La Farinians and separatists and Bourbonists,'

[1] 17 July, Fiorenza to Ricasoli (BR ASF, busta N, fascicolo E).
[2] 16 July, Cavour telegram to Persano (*Lettere di Cavour*, ed. Chiala, vol. III, p. 292).
[3] 22 July, Persano, *Diario 1860–1*, part I, p. 82.
[4] 24 July, consular report to Turin, quoted in Michele Rosi, *Il risorgimento italiano e l' azione d' un patriota*, 1906, p. 199.
[5] 27 July, Persano to Cavour (*Lettere di Cavour*, ed. Chiala, vol. III, p. 304); but in the national edition of Cavour's letters this passage is not included, and perhaps it is one of Persano's (not altogether disinterested) later fabrications.

wrote Calvino, 'for Depretis is the man to put them in their place once and for all.'[1] More to the centre of Sicilian politics, Amari, now a minister, wrote to his cousin on 26 July:

Depretis will succeed to perfection in tranquillizing people about the political direction to be followed, and will do a great deal to reconstitute the public administration after its complete disorganization. I like him very much. On the few occasions we have met so far in council meetings he has shown not less skill than firmness, as well as knowledge of administrative practice and political penetration.... He is the best of guarantees that things will now go well.[2]

Depretis's treatment of the radicals was especially tactful. One of his first actions was to ask Mordini to write and ask Bargoni to come as his personal secretary.[3] Bargoni was one of those working with that committee for aid to Sicily which Bertani had set up to supply the deficiencies of La Farina's *Società Nazionale*; but he was a moderate man, and it had first been his idea to negotiate with Cavour for sending out the new prodictator to Sicily as a man respected and trusted by both sides. Even more than by this appointment, the radicals were con- vinced of the good intentions of Depretis by his confirmation of Crispi as a minister once more. For Depretis saw in Crispi an expert on Sicilian affairs, who was the friend of Garibaldi and the man who had built up the revolutionary government. Crispi for his part had at this stage little suspicion that Depretis might in the end turn out to be more of a partisan than a moderator. Both were at one for the moment, wanting annexation, but only when this would not be a tie on Garibaldi. Amari, it is true, believed that Crispi must have been put on the pro- dictator as a sort of watchman or supervisor, and was bewildered to find no hint that Depretis might be only feigning confidence in him. It seems, nevertheless, that there existed complete confidence between the two. After the first week Crispi even took this confidence to the point of addressing to Garibaldi a request that he might be allowed to rejoin the army, explaining that Depretis was by that time quite

[1] 31 July, Calvino to Bargoni (Rosi, *L' azione d' un patriota*, p. 199).
[2] 26 July, Professor Amari to Count Amari (*Carteggio di Amari*, ed. d'Ancona, vol. II, pp. 107-8).
[3] 25 July, Mordini to Bargoni (MRR 221/6/2).

familiar with his duties and did not need him further.[1] The request was not granted, for Crispi was still required at Palermo.

It is likely that Crispi had returned somewhat to public favour, and that, however much La Farina's friends continued to dislike him, the three weeks of his absence from the government had impressed people with the value of his energy and single-mindedness. On his return to the Home Office, an immediate improvement was noticed in the preservation of law and order, at least by radical sympathizers.[2] The sensible and moderate Amari was suspicious of Crispi as a colleague, but remained personally on good terms with him, and made the shrewd comment that 'he shows intelligence and integrity in business whenever it has nothing to do with either his friends or his enemies'.[3] Calvino, who until lately had always cut Crispi even if they met in the house of a common friend, was now reconciled to him owing to his 'great services, and the abnegation with which he has served the cause of Italian unity'.[4] Another person to speak well of Crispi, despite a strong personal dislike, was Count Litta, when he came to Sicily on a mission from the king. Litta entered in his diary for 31 July that Depretis, 'when asked about Crispi, answered me plainly that he was quite satisfactory, adding that he would even follow out our ideas about immediate annexation...; and also that we ought to use him because of his large following in Sicily, and because he had distinguished himself on every occasion and shown himself a valiant soldier in the battles of Calatafimi and Palermo'.[5] It was hardly likely that a man like Francesco Crispi, with such a temperament, and such a desire to command, after having waited twelve years for this moment, would long remain idle and out of office.

When Depretis arrived in Sicily, Garibaldi had just won his decisive battle at Milazzo on 20 July. This brought the volunteers right up to the

[1] 26 July, Crispi to Garibaldi (*Memoirs*, vol. I, p. 346).

[2] 15 August, *Il Diritto*, report dated Palermo 10 August.

[3] 3 August, Professor Amari to Count Amari (*Carteggio di Amari*, ed. d'Ancona, vol. II, p. 114).

[4] 9 July, Calvino to Bargoni (*Memorie di Bargoni*, pp. 130–1); also 25 June, V. Cordova to Crispi: 'for my part I am convinced that the revolution must be completed by none other than yourself who initiated it' (ACP, f. 138).

[5] 31 July, Guerrini, 'La missione del conte Litta', *Il Risorgimento Italiano*, February 1909, p. 26.

Straits of Messina, and so raised the question of how soon they would be able to cross to the mainland. The dictator was at his most hopeful. So many apparently insuperable difficulties had already been overcome that he refused to flinch before all the political and diplomatic complications which threatened. His mind was as usual preoccupied by military matters, and with some justification he reduced these complications to a mere question of power. If his forces proved sufficient, then advance would be easy; if not, not. It was as simple as that. Not even La Farina's exposure had completely destroyed his faith that co-operation with Turin would prove possible, for he believed he would succeed and that success would have to be condoned and exploited by the king's government. He had written on the 13th to Victor Emanuel, promising to tell him in advance when he felt able to cross the Straits. He frankly acknowledged in this letter that he appreciated the difficulty about Rome, protected as it was by the French; and he explained to the king that, while still preparing a movement in the Papal States, he was recommending no precipitate action there. He further requested Victor Emanuel to look into rumours that the Piedmontese government was starting a separate movement in Naples, because he was not ready for it. Such a movement might well be used to spoil the radical plan of action, and he feared that he would be forced to launch a hurried invasion at the first sign of any insurrection on the mainland.[1] This indicates that he was by no means unaware even at this early date of Cavour's tentative counter scheme to forestall him at Naples. Several days later he wrote to Persano with a *démarche* towards Cavour, for whose eyes it was intended: 'we are all working together to make Italy under our *Re Galantuomo*. As we have the same aim, I hope we shall easily understand one another.'[2] Coming only a week after La Farina's expulsion, this was magnanimous, and also optimistic. Garibaldi seems to have been genuinely convinced at this point that Cavour as well as the king might come in with him, and one may guess that Persano's play-acting was chiefly responsible for this. The admiral's most notable qualities in a long and inglorious career seem to have been a skill in flattery, and a *penchant* for taking imaginative liberties with the truth; and at Palermo he used both assiduously to allay Garibaldi's suspicions. This

---

[1] 13 July, Garibaldi to Victor Emanuel (Bollea, *Una silloge di lettere*, p. 282).
[2] 16 July, Garibaldi to Persano (*CC Lib. del Mezz.* vol. I, p. 344).

helped to keep the dictator in a good temper, but there is little doubt that it also helped, against all Cavour's wishes, to confirm the radicals in their intention to march on Rome.

It was now becoming an important question whether Garibaldi's advance could be stopped in Sicily. A month earlier, before Cavour had properly thought out his policy, he had been hoping that the revolutionary army would cross the Straits. At least he said as much, and perhaps he genuinely supposed that the volunteers would wear out their strength and reputation in Naples and let Sicily be quietly annexed behind them.[1] Before the middle of July he was of a different mind, for the revolution was proving more dangerous and uncontrollable than he had thought. Persano now received a change in orders: 'our policy must be to prevent Garibaldi at all costs from passing over to the continent, and at the same time we must work up a movement in Naples ourselves'.[2] Cavour was here aiming to do precisely the two things which Garibaldi most feared. Despite outward protestations, a first attempt was now made from Turin to stop further reinforcements being recruited to join the volunteers in Sicily. Persano was privately commanded to encourage Piedmontese naval officers to desert semi-officially to Garibaldi's fleet, so that they would be at hand to mutiny if and when Cavour decided he was strong enough to bring his rival policy out into the open. The admiral was also instructed not to give even indirect assistance to Garibaldi, but to keep his ships well away from any fighting.[3] Once the volunteers had cleared the last Bourbon garrisons out of Sicily, their usefulness would cease as far as Cavour could see. Much better that they should not go on towards Naples at all, because their further success might be more disastrous even than their defeat. 'La position est bien compliquée', Cavour told his minister at Naples, Villamarina. 'Nous ne pouvons guère désirer que Garibaldi passe à Naples, car il est si mal entouré, tellement enivré de ses succès, qu'il porterait avec lui le désordre et l'anarchie. Une fois à Naples il voudrait aller à Rome malgré les Français, ce qui serait la ruine de notre

---

[1] 19 June, Cavour to La Farina (*Lettere di Cavour*, ed. Chiala, vol. III, p. 266); Farini, the minister of the interior, thought likewise, see L. Rava, in *Nuova Antologia*, f. 939, 1 February 1911, p. 554.

[2] 14 July, Cavour to Persano (*CC Lib. del Mezz.* vol. I, p. 329).

[3] 23 July, Cavour to Persano (*ibid.* p. 363).

cause.' It was explained that the new liberal constitution published by the Bourbons at Naples had changed everything: for, with even a vaguely liberal government at Naples, either a Garibaldian or a Cavourian *putsch* there would seem morally wrong, and unless well disguised would have a very bad effect on liberal opinion in Europe.[1] Cavour was already beginning preparations in case he might have to attempt a *putsch* of his own against the Bourbon government; but this was under duress, as a last defence against Garibaldi setting off a train of explosions on the mainland. His motives were not strictly those of an unalterably convinced 'unitarian', but rather those of a liberal conservative who still would prefer the Bourbons at Naples if Garibaldi was the alternative.

The dictator and his friends were not to know that Cavour was writing in this sense, but the less charitable among them might have guessed it, and the entertainment of the Neapolitan plenipotentiaries at Turin cannot have inspired them with much confidence. Private letters were arriving in Sicily from Turin which conveyed the impression that an actual alliance with Naples was about to be signed at any moment, and the danger that such a pact might be made must surely have weighed with the dictator as he planned his future policy.[2] Again there were other rumours that Cavour was himself thinking about plans for a counter-revolution at Naples, directed as much against Garibaldi as against Francesco. Probably Cavour was for some time undecided which of these alternative policies would better fit the situation, but both of them were directed against Garibaldi.

On 22 July news reached Turin about the battle of Milazzo. Cavour was warned that the last Bourbon garrison in Sicily might have to

---

[1] 20 July, Cavour to Villamarina (*ibid.* p. 354); 24 July, Cavour to Villamarina: 'permettez moi de croire que de Turin on juge plus sainement la position que de Naples. Il est hautement à désirer que la délivrance de Naples ne soit pas due à Garibaldi, car si cela arrive le système révolutionnaire prendra la place du parti nationale monarchique' (*ibid.* pp. 383-4); 23 July, Lord John Russell to Elliot, with orders to tell Garibaldi that 'he ought to be content with the whole of Sicily and not stir any further the fire of Italian insurrection' (RP G.D. 22/111).

[2] 18 July, G. La Cecilia from Turin to Garibaldi (ACM, no. 1048); 27 July, Frapolli from Turin to Depretis, saying that though the government now seemed to be in favour of national unification, it was slow and inefficient in action, always unprepared, and was more than ever the slave of Napoleon (Archivio Depretis ASR).

surrender, and that insurrections were already breaking out on the mainland. He now had to confess that a Neapolitan alliance was quite unrealistic. When the French proposed to him that they should make a joint guarantee for a six months' truce in Sicily, he had to reply that, however good the idea in theory, there seemed little possibility of now being able to control the volunteers.[1] Public opinion would not have stood for Cavour joining a foreign power to use force against them. He would have to try other methods, even though with small hope of success. So, later on the 22nd, the cabinet officially requested the king to write a direct letter to try and dissuade Garibaldi from crossing the Straits, provided at any rate that Francesco recognized the right of Sicily to determine its own future.[2] At the very best this might have the double result of winning Sicily for Piedmont, as well as halting Garibaldi short of Naples. Cavour suspected that such a letter would arrive too late to have much effect on the dictator, but at the very least it would act as a formal satisfaction to diplomatic convention, and as a reassurance to those who suspected Piedmont of fishing in troubled waters.[3] The king's letter, written on advice from the cabinet, was duly carried to Sicily by his orderly, Count Litta, who sailed on the 23rd and eventually encountered Garibaldi on the 27th.

There is some obscurity about this mission of Litta and the exact messages he took with him. Several versions exist of the king's official letter, and five different versions of Garibaldi's reply, though Curàtulo could find no signed original of either. The generally accepted text of Victor Emanuel's letter mentioned his disapproval of Garibaldi's original expedition, and advised that this civil war between Naples and Sicily should now stop.[4] But a second and more informal letter in the king's own handwriting came to light many years later in 1909, long after Garibaldi and other witnesses who could have confirmed it were dead. This second letter purported to contradict the first, and to give Garibaldi the king's permission to disobey his official communication.

---

[1] 23 July, Cavour to Nigra (*CC Cavour-Nigra*, vol. IV, p. 100); 24 July, Cavour to Talleyrand (*ibid.* p. 103).

[2] 22 July, 'Verbali del Consiglio dei Ministri', E. Artom, *L' opera politica del Senatore I. Artom nel risorgimento italiano*, 1906, p. 277.

[3] 22 July, Cavour to E. d'Azeglio (*CC Ing.* vol. II, part II, p. 102).

[4] 22 July, Victor Emanuel to Garibaldi (*CC Cavour-Nigra*, vol. IV, p. 98).

If genuine it was entirely contrary to the cabinet's positive decision and advice—and surely there would have been no reason for falsification in a secret cabinet minute. It is not printed with the king's first message in the national edition of Cavour's letters. Neither Garibaldi nor Cavour ever made mention of having seen or heard of a second message, and Garibaldi on the contrary often repeated that the Turin government had tried to stop him crossing to Naples.[1] Omodeo thinks Cavour cannot have known of it. The king did not say a word to Ricasoli when they met at the end of July, though Ricasoli was loud in his protests at the king's public behaviour, and it would have been easy and effective for the king to have dropped him a hint. None of the friends who surrounded either dictator or king ever referred to its existence. No one has yet explained these extraordinary facts. Nor has it been explained why this mysterious letter should not have been published after 1860 as a reply to Garibaldi's accusations of governmental obstruction; nor why its advice, if genuinely intended, could not have been more judiciously given by word of mouth; nor, indeed, why it should have been found among Litta's papers rather than Garibaldi's or the king's, and with its seal unbroken.[2] It has been suggested that it may represent the private policy of the king which he tried to undertake without the knowledge of the cabinet.[3] The king certainly wrote this second letter and gave it to Litta at some stage, but the evidence suggests it was not delivered. One explanation which fits many of the facts is probably too far-fetched to be credible, that it was written for the purpose of later justification, but then buried as too compromising. Its content was sensible enough. Possibly the king had instructed his private orderly to sound Garibaldi first, giving him the official letter as the cabinet had asked, but if he found the dictator bent on further conquest he was to hint that success would be condoned. It would have been absurd to protest at something which could not be helped, and dangerous to

[1] E.g. 28 August 1869, *Il Movimento* (Genoa), letter of Garibaldi to Barrili dated 24 August 1869.

[2] D. Guerrini, 'La missione del conte Litta', *Il Risorgimento Italiano*, February 1909, p. 24; Curàtulo's reply, *ibid.* August 1909, pp. 652–9; Curàtulo, *Garibaldi, Vittorio Emanuele, Cavour*, pp. 150–4.

[3] G. Manacorda, in *Nuova Antologia*, 1 June 1910, p. 408; A. Omodeo, 'Cavour e l' impresa Garibaldina', *Leonardo*, May 1929, p. 126.

announce publicly a breach with Garibaldi until either public opinion would sanction such a move, or at the very least until there was something to be gained by it and his further progress could thereby be stopped.

As for Cavour, despite all the legends conveniently built up round this second letter, we know that he did not want Garibaldi to cross the Straits, but hoped that the moderate liberals could if necessary take charge of anything that was to happen in Naples. The difficulty of his position was that Garibaldi could hardly be induced to desist unless the king gave him a formal and definite order to halt, or unless there were evidence that the liberals would actively take over and carry forward the revolution. For the present moment, therefore, nothing much could be done without danger, and so governmental policy still had to be one of watchful waiting. In the meantime the king's official and published letter could at least be used to show Europe that the responsibility for any invasion of Naples lay solely with Garibaldi: it would thus act as an insurance, either in case Garibaldi were defeated, or in case Piedmont had finally to intervene against him in the interests of European peace and Napoleon's commitments to the Pope. As for Cavour's attitude to the problematic second letter, we must be ready to accept a number of interpretations. Perhaps the letter was not sent at all; perhaps it represents the private policy of the king unknown to his ministers; perhaps, as on other occasions, Cavour knew about what the king was doing but pretended not to know. On the most favourable interpretation it was Cavour's project all along; but if so, it was designed only to 'legalize', and to claim some credit for, an action which he regretted but was powerless to stop. Those historians can hardly be correct who say that Cavour was secretly urging Garibaldi to advance,[1] for there is too much other evidence to the contrary.

Cavour was reluctant to take direct responsibility when matters were in so much doubt, and when several lines of retreat could more profitably be left open in each direction. Faced by a difficult choice, he was once more obliged to let Garibaldi take the initiative, confining himself to an attitude of discouragement, but being as far as possible ready and

[1] G. M. Trevelyan, *Garibaldi and the Making of Italy*, 1911, p. 101; I. Nazari-Micheli, *Cavour e Garibaldi nel 1860*, 1911.

free to act in whatever way circumstances might dictate. It was a perfectly justifiable policy in the circumstances, to let Garibaldi take the kicks, but to try and make him hand over any halfpence that might accrue. Meanwhile, Depretis could be relied upon in Sicily to try and keep up for a little longer the appearance that all the patriots, of whatever political colour, were working together in amity.

CHAPTER X

CAVOUR PLANS A REVOLT AT NAPLES: JULY

Cavour was never again to be so passive as he had been when the Thousand first set out. Thereafter, however much he may have been on occasion playing second fiddle to Garibaldi, he always had, if not a positive policy, at least some hypotheses for a policy. The chief difficulty is to disentangle these various hypotheses; for Cavour instinctively tried to keep his freedom of manœuvre so as to be prepared for any eventuality. He had to be ready to accept Garibaldi's success, but also to disown his failure; to accept annexation of the south, but also to score any point against what were called—still with a pejorative connotation —the *italianissimi*.

Throughout June and July his main object was to see that the Sicilian revolution avoided the two extremes of failure or overmuch success; and on occasion he was able to contribute materially towards preserving this nice balance. But it was a delicate and dangerous task. Garibaldi's failure would not have been an unmitigated disaster, for it would have arrested the revolution, and given Cavour the several years he sought to consolidate the existing kingdom of northern Italy. Yet public opinion in Italy would not lightly have forgiven Cavour for allowing its hero to perish, and he would have hopelessly alienated the radical element in Italian politics which he relied on being alternately his stalking-horse, his scapegoat, and the combustible tinder and ignition spark needed for the next insurrection. On the other hand, Garibaldi's success beyond a certain point would have meant handing over the Italian movement to the hotheads, and perhaps thereby causing its collapse; the European Powers would possibly have intervened against it, and Cavour might have been swept out of power before he had been able to shore up some defence against internal and external onslaught.

It was not the danger of Garibaldi's defeat, but the danger that he might win too fast and too completely, which forced Cavour to intervene more directly at the end of July. All over the country people were looking to the king's government for some bold decision, especially as the winding up of the Sicilian campaign brought on as an urgent matter the question of Naples. Some of the liberal-conservatives at Naples had been astonished at the cowardly or underhand appearance so far given by Piedmontese policy. 'I wish Victor Emanuel would throw off the mask like a man and go to war honestly,' wrote the British minister, 'instead of putting on an innocent look and sitting like a receiver of stolen goods opening his pockets to any plunder his children may bring to him.'[1] Correspondents in Naples and Rome had begun to warn Cavour that he was being dwarfed by the revolution, and were begging him to do something about it.[2] Ricasoli at Florence expressed himself deeply humiliated over the king's official letter advising Garibaldi to stay in Sicily, for the king thereby put himself in the wrong with national sentiment at the same time as he knew his advice would be flouted, and this could only have the effect of bringing the monarchy into ridicule and public contempt. Ricasoli threatened to resign if the king did not resume command of the national movement, and he conjured Cavour to 'expose us if you like to war with one or even three powers, but save us from Garibaldian anarchy'.[3] Another government official, Lorenzo Valerio, wrote from Lombardy in a similar vein: 'Cavour and Farini have allowed themselves to be overwhelmed, and it is no longer they who govern. This has inflicted a severe wound on our constitutional regime. God help us.'[4] In Piedmont, the 'Speaker' of the Chamber of Deputies could not understand this lack of courage, and thought that the government could at least have made up its mind either to oppose or to help Garibaldi, instead of wavering in the middle. 'The direction of the Italian movement is no longer in the hands of the

---

[1] 25 June, Elliot to Russell (RP G.D. 22/66); 10 July: 'an underhand intrigue far surpassing anything that could be alleged against the Austrians' (G.D. 22/85).

[2] E.g. 24 July, Pantaleoni from Rome to Cavour (*CC La Questione Romana negli anni 1860–1861*, 1929, p. 31); cf. Marc Monnier at Naples on 24 July: 'la diplomatie, M. de Cavour, Vittorio Emanuele, n'ont pas l'air de s'entendre et agissent séparément. Il n'y a dans tout ceci qu'un homme logique, immuable, inflexible, qui marche droit devant lui—c'est Garibaldi qui prendra Naples'. *Garibaldi, histoire de la conquête des deux Siciles*, 1861, p. 195.

[3] 2 and 3 August, Ricasoli to Cavour (*Lettere di Ricasoli*, ed. Tabarrini, vol. v, pp. 176, 180).

[4] 29 July, Valerio to Castelli (*Carteggio di Castelli*, ed. Chiala, vol. i, p. 310).

government', he bewailed, 'but has passed into the hands of the republicans; and if the government cannot reassert itself they will drag us along behind them.'[1] Another of Cavour's friends, Sir James Hudson at Turin, feared that, if Cavour did not yield to the radical pressure and fight against Naples, then 'half the king of Sardinia's army will desert in order to join Garibaldi'.[2] Instead of having been secretly maturing some fine *coup de théâtre*, Cavour in appearance was just letting matters slide. 'My belief is that he has no plan. He is a waiter upon Providence and the chapter of accidents.' Hudson also envisaged, however, that as Garibaldi threatened to take the revolution into Naples, Cavour would in the end be forced despite himself to outdo Mazzini and 'seek the annexation of the rotten body of Naples to the vigorous North Italy'.[3] The disease would thus bring about its own remedy.

Cavour was never very far behind such a widespread display of opinion, and from a letter written to his London ambassador on 25 July we can tell that by that time he had reached certain interim conclusions about the new situation in the south. In the first place, it was no longer likely that he could ever sign any alliance with the Naples government, for he was now assured that public opinion would in that event turn him out of office. In the second place, the cowardly surrender of Messina finally proved that the Bourbons had lost all dignity and power of resistance, so much so that it was hardly possible for the governments of either Naples or Piedmont to stop Garibaldi's advance into Calabria. Cavour had been informed by his minister at Naples that the Bourbon regime was disintegrating. As a result, he now concluded that the best hope of controlling and profiting from the revolution was himself to adopt and exploit the concept of Italian unity which people apparently found so fascinating.[4]

This left Cavour the problem of how he could remain friendly with the Bourbons at the same time as he planned their destruction, and also the problem of how he could retain the semblance of friendship for Garibaldi while he proceeded to steal the revolutionary thunder.

---

[1] 1 August, Lanza to Cadorna (*Le carte di Giovanni Lanza*, ed. De Vecchi di Val Cismon, vol. II, 1936, p. 169).

[2] 31 July, Hudson to Russell (RP G.D. 22/66).

[3] 27 July, Hudson to Russell (*ibid.*).

[4] 25 July, Cavour to E. d'Azeglio (*CC Ing.* vol. II, part II, pp. 108–9).

Inevitably he had to continue to try and maintain for as long as possible his many-faced attitude to events in the south. Thus to Persano, who was a link with Garibaldi and had retained some of the dictator's confidence, he wrote that the volunteers must be congratulated on their 'splendid victory', and that the national movement could no longer be halted half-way, but that the Piedmontese forces must themselves carry it on into Venice. On the very same day, 28 July, he wrote in a different vein to his minister at Naples. Villamarina was told that the prospect of Garibaldi's further success was 'fâcheux, très fâcheux; mais il faut savoir se résigner à ce qui est inévitable. Garibaldi à Naples est maître de la situation. Il ne trahira pas le Roi, mais il lui imposera sa politique, et sa politique n'admet pas de transaction. Il faut par conséquent se préparer à la guerre avec l'Autriche dans un avenir peu éloigné. Pour ma part, j'y suis tout résigné.' The volunteers were a nuisance, but after Milazzo there was no stopping them, and there was one great compensation: 'le courage déployé par les volontaires est d'un effet moral excellent, il prouve à l'Europe que les Italiens se battent et se battent bien'.[1] To a third correspondent, his minister at Paris who usually received the largest share of his confidence, Cavour wrote stressing those aspects of the situation which were calculated to carry most weight with Louis Napoleon:

Si Garibaldi passe sur le continent et s'empare du Royaume de Naples... il devient maître absolu de la situation. Le Roi Victor Emanuel perd à peu près tout son prestige; il n'est plus aux yeux de la grande majorité des Italiens que l'ami de Garibaldi. Il conservera probablement sa couronne, mais cette couronne ne brillera plus que par le reflet de la lumière qu'un aventurier héroïque jugera bon de jeter sur elle....

Garibaldi..., disposant des ressources d'un royaume de 9,000,000 d'habitants, entouré d'un prestige populaire irrésistible, nous ne pourrons pas lutter avec lui. Il sera plus fort que nous....Le Roi ne peut tenir la couronne d'Italie des mains de Garibaldi: elle chancellerait trop sur sa tête. Pour raffermir son trône il devrait monter à cheval et chercher à faire oublier au centre du fameux quadrilatère les aventures de la Sicile. La prise de Vérone et de Venise feront oublier Palerme et Milazzo....

Elle est inévitable si l'on veut sauver le principe monarchique. Pour un Prince de la Maison de Savoie mieux vaut périr par la guerre, que par la

[1] 28 July, Cavour to Villamarina (*CC Lib. del Mezz.* vol. i, pp. 400–1); 28 July, Cavour to Persano (*ibid.* p. 401).

révolution. Une dynastie peut se relever si elle tombe sur un champ de bataille, son sort est scellé à jamais si on la traîne dans un ruisseau.[1]

If Cavour's opponents had known what he was writing here, they would have called this just one more proof that, though he was a nationalist after a sort, he yet put the interests of the dynasty before those of the nation.

Cavour was no better informed about affairs in Naples than he had been about Sicily, and until the second half of July he had to rely on the reports of his not very competent minister there, bolstered up by the current gossip among the Neapolitan exiles at Turin. It is instructive to note that *L'Opinione*, the newspaper which carried his officially inspired pronouncements, had no regular correspondence at all from southern Italy, but concentrated its news services on Paris and the Austrian frontier where Cavour's chief interest lay. This helps to explain why he had to formulate his Neapolitan policy on evidence which was insufficient in quality and quantity. From the information at his disposal, he had at first hoped that terror of Garibaldi would bring the Bourbons into an alliance with Piedmont against Austria and the Pope; for though Louis Napoleon had not put up much opposition against Piedmont's having Sicily, there were political, dynastic and religious reasons why France should want to preserve an independent Naples. Cavour's negotiations for an alliance with Naples in the middle of July have already been described. But Garibaldi's victories and Italian public opinion very soon ruled out the possibility of any such alliance, and by that time Cavour was ready with an alternative and far bolder policy. The Marquis de Villamarina had sent more than one report to say that Neapolitans had no other wish than for annexation to Piedmont. So limited was Villamarina in his sources of information and knowledge of human nature, that he had even expected a rebellion with this object to break out in Naples by the end of July.[2] In consequence, Cavour came to imagine that his best policy now might be to anticipate Garibaldi by a liberal rising on the mainland.

Since Villamarina continued to be so confident about the general feeling for annexation at Naples, Cavour, who had no personal knowledge at all of Naples and little enough of Neapolitans, had to believe

---

[1] 1 August, Cavour to Nigra (*CC Cavour-Nigra*, vol. IV, pp. 122–3).
[2] 9 July, Villamarina to Cavour (*CC Lib. del Mezz.* vol. I, p. 311).

him. Massimo d'Azeglio knew better from personal experience. It was nonsense, said d'Azeglio, to think that more than one in twenty Neapolitans really wanted annexation, and this being so it would be a labour of Hercules for Piedmont to try and clean out that particular stable.[1] There were others who agreed with this former prime minister that the rest of Italy was not ripe for such a union. 'Naples', wrote Casalis, 'is considered a country which, because of the number of its inhabitants, their corruption, ignorance and lack of national spirit, especially among the masses, will present great and almost insuperable difficulties for the country which tries to absorb it.'[2] This was the misfortune of Naples, to be regarded either with thoughtless contempt or thoughtless over-confidence; and, as a result of this mistake, the policy of northerners towards the south was put on a wrong footing from the start.

If Villamarina had looked further into people's motives, he might have perceived that with many Neapolitans the desire for annexation was more apparent than real. All too often it was a projection of the fear that Garibaldi would arrive first and instigate a civil and social war from which they were bound to suffer. A simple annexation to Piedmont, they imagined, would avoid or mitigate this disaster and guarantee the continuance of conservative government. For the common people were becoming increasingly restive as the Bourbon administration began to crumble. The British consul had a report from Taranto on 6 July to say that the lower classes were on the brink of revolution, not out of liberal sentiments, since they were quite indifferent to mere forms of government, but as an excuse to pillage the property of their betters; and it was stated that 'moderate citizens' therefore feared lest Garibaldi should come to 'spread intestine disorder in these districts, which will become a prey to blood and the devastation of civil war'.[3] At Salerno the common people had already taken the occasion of the

[1] 2 July, M. d'Azeglio to Castelli (Raccolta Azegliana MRR).

[2] 29 July, Casalis from Parma to Depretis (ASR).

[3] 6 July, Vice-consul Randone from Taranto to Consul Bonham at Naples: 'the labouring class, numerous and often wanting daily bread,...if now in some measure leagued with the party in favour of unity, is nevertheless always ready to take advantage of the smallest disturbance to pillage and lay hands on other people's property: it breathes only anarchy and disorder, and is indifferent to the form of Government' (F.O. 165/134).

Bourbon grant of a constitution to rise and demand a division of the land.[1] The police records at Naples are full of similar accounts from other provinces. At Avellino, according to reports of 3 and 28 July, there had been local risings against the constitution, against the *galantuomini* and the national guard, and significantly their cry was *Viva il Re*, by which was meant Francesco and not Victor Emanuel. On 19 July the sub-intendant of Vasto told of hundreds of peasants, armed with scythes and bill-hooks, advancing to claim their old rights to enclosed land. The mayor of Venafro on the 24th sent in an account of how the country folk had been attacking 'honest citizens' and the national guard; and at Chieti on the 29th they had managed to burn the prison registers.[2] Just as in Sicily, that is to say, the common people were taking advantage of the evident collapse of civil government. Fear of this submerged revolt is an important reason why so many of the honest citizens in Naples were busy whispering their desire for annexation to Piedmont. On precisely the same grounds, however, the very same people were anxious not to stir a finger to hasten the revolution, until they knew that a Piedmontese army was approaching the frontier to come and restore order if necessary. The same reasons why in theory they supported Cavour, in practice made them unwillingly but decisively aid Garibaldi.

Villamarina did not understand the social *malaise* of the Napoletano, and so could not explain it to his government. Cavour was thus persuaded into a new policy by facts which, had they been correctly interpreted, might have suggested a very different reaction. He was also put at cross purposes with the Neapolitan liberals; for while they wanted the Piedmontese to arrive and give them the excuse for rebellion, he was not going to intervene unless they first rose and gave him the excuse to put his armies in motion. Officially, in the eyes of Europe, he was still not a recognized participant in the revolution that was afoot; indeed he was excluded from it by the doctrine of non-intervention; and if ever he was to violate this doctrine he would need some popular call to make his intervention something other than shameless aggression. So, while he still did not break off his *pourparlers*

[1] 26 June, G. Mottola's diary (*Archivio Storico della Provincia di Salerno*, June 1924); also 14 June, the Intendant of Salerno (in Archivio di Stato, Salerno, Affari Politici, b. 9).

[2] Documents in Archivio di Stato, Naples, Dicastero Polizia.

for an alliance with the Bourbons, he also laid plans in case the exact opposite policy became more possible or advisable. From Villamarina's reports he received the impression that, with a little mild encouragement, the south might rise in revolt; and by the middle of July he had also been informed that Nunziante and other generals in the Neapolitan army might be ready to play the traitor if allowed to change sides without losing their rank.[1] All this opened up another possible line of action.

Certain southerners exiled in Turin, notably Bonghi, Nisco, Mezzacapo and Pisanelli, were therefore summoned, along with other young and enterprising men like Ribotti, Zanardelli and Visconti-Venosta, and all sent off to Naples. Their mission was exploratory in the first place; but they also had to prepare the ground for an insurrection, in case the Piedmontese should want an excuse to step in and forestall Garibaldi. If the liberals could only stage a revolt in advance of the radicals, they would succeed in preventing Garibaldi's march via Naples to Rome; and in the process they would also prevent the indignity of a rebellious subject seeming to hand over Naples to a supplicant King Victor Emanuel. In other words, they would save the moderates from losing control of the national movement.[2] The first batch of these potential *agents provocateurs* had arrived at Naples on 16 July, and the fact that on this same day Cavour had his first meeting with the Neapolitan envoys shows how he simultaneously maintained two contradictory policies. After an unconscionably few hours in which to observe the situation, Visconti-Venosta wrote back with a cheerful confirmation of Villamarina's reports, saying that he could find no trace of an autonomist party, and that the exiles had nothing to teach the local citizens in *italianità*.[3] This was good news for Turin, and the task ahead was thus made to seem far easier than it proved to be in reality. People in the north also imagined that *amour propre*, if nothing else, would force Neapolitans to start a rebellion themselves; for otherwise Naples might have both to submit to the radicals, and also to receive a humiliating salvation at the hand of their former dependents in Sicily.[4]

---

[1] 14 July, Prince Eugenio to Cavour (*CC Lib. del Mezz.* vol. I, p. 327).

[2] 3 August 1912, note by Visconti-Venosta (*ibid.* p. 340).

[3] 17 July, Visconti-Venosta to Farini (*ibid.* pp. 340–2).

[4] 10 August, Poerio to De Lequile (G. Bandini, 'Lettere di C. Poerio nel 1860', *Rassegna Storica del Risorgimento*, xxx, 1943, p. 493); cf. 16 April, Elliot to Russell:

Unfortunately Visconti-Venosta had spoken too soon, and his government therefore was not able to gauge the situation accurately. As a result, Cavour for a time still refused to implicate himself more than he need in the encouragement of violent revolution. The assumption was that the ripe pear would fall and not have to be plucked. On 23 July he was quite hopeful that, with no extraordinary action, he could expect to record the success of Villamarina's Neapolitan rebellion 'in a few days' time'.[1]

Until 26 July, indeed, it was not known that the British government would refuse to join France and Piedmont in their joint plan to halt Garibaldi and reconcile the Bourbons to the loss of Sicily.[2] Until that date, Louis Napoleon had been hoping that Cavour would conclude an alliance with Naples, and that the Great Powers would intervene and stop Garibaldi crossing to Naples. Cavour had not liked this French proposal for foreign intervention in the south, since any such intervention was bound to be to some extent at Piedmontese expense, and would emphasize Italy's servile status. But he had not allowed his minister in London to oppose it openly, for he did not dare contradict his powerful ally; and there was also the point that, once Garibaldi had completed the liberation of Sicily, the interests of Piedmont might equally be endangered by his further progress on to the mainland. People have usually interpreted Cavour's inaction as evidence of his patriotic desire 'to clear the way for Garibaldi's passage of the Straits';[3] but more likely it was the exact opposite. Lacaita's dramatic mission to Russell, moreover, turns out to be less important than was once thought.[4] Cavour's secret orders to Admiral Persano were that he should not help Garibaldi's crossing, and should rather try to 'delay it by indirect

'the Neapolitans...almost all of them, whether liberals or not, feel irritated that the Sicilians refuse to accept the portion of a Neapolitan Province which they think their proper place' (RP G.D. 22/85).

[1] 23 July, Cavour to Villamarina (*CC Lib. del Mezz.* vol. 1, p. 362); 16 July, Cavour to Prince Eugenio, shows that Cavour still believed it would be too dangerous to give money or arms to those who were conspiring at Naples (*ibid.* p. 333).

[2] 26 July, Russell telegram to Elliot (F.O. 70/312).

[3] Trevelyan, *Garibaldi and the Making of Italy*, p. 100.

[4] M. Avetta, 'Studi cavouriani. Una "vexata quaestio" alla luce dei carteggi cavouriani', *Rassegna Storica del Risorgimento*, vol. XXI, 1934, pp. 52–71.

methods as long as possible';[1] and these orders must be read in the light
of Persano's conviction that Garibaldi could not easily cross the Straits
of Messina without the protection of more ships than the revolutionaries
themselves possessed.[2] Cavour was if anything on the side of France
against Garibaldi; but Britain for her part did not need much persuading
to stand up for Garibaldi against the French—not only because she liked
Garibaldi more, but chiefly because she liked France less. At Turin they
feared that Britain would prefer Garibaldi rather than Cavour at Naples,
'even though it meant anarchy and revolution'.[3] This was true in part;
but Russell's real suspicions were of Napoleon, and he suspected Cavour
only in so far as Cavour was a client of the emperor. British policy
remained constant for non-intervention, just because this offered the
best hope of a stable solution being reached in Italy; and especially was
this so when intervention only threatened to increase French influence
at Naples. It was not so much, therefore, that Cavour patriotically
contrived to make Russell change his policy, as that Russell's rejection
of the French proposal made Cavour change his; for the last obstacle in
the path of the revolution had thereby been removed. The collapse of
Napoleon's attempt to mediate brought Garibaldi within dangerous
reach of Naples and Rome, and Piedmontese policy had to be adjusted
accordingly.

At the end of July, Cavour had to admit that the situation was out
of his control and called for quite exceptional methods. Alarming
information came in from Naples as well as from London and Paris.
Letters were written to him on the 23rd from the south which told of
the evacuation of Messina by the Bourbons, and of the likelihood that
Garibaldi could no longer be checked short of Naples. Turin was also
informed that the liberal middle classes in the south were after all
proving too craven to initiate any spontaneous insurrection before the
radicals arrived, while the poor *lazzaroni* were keenly looking forward
to Garibaldi's arrival and already associating the liberator's name with
a Golden Age and dreams of hitherto unknown prosperity.[4] This was

[1] 1 August, Cavour to Persano (*CC Lib. del Mezz.* vol. II, 1949, p. 2).
[2] 2 August, Persano to Cavour (*ibid.* p. 8).
[3] 1 August, Cavour to E. d'Azeglio (*CC Ing.* vol. II, part II, p. 118).
[4] 23 July, Villamarina to Cavour (*CC Lib. del Mezz.* vol. I, pp. 367–70); 23 July,
Visconti-Venosta to Farini (*ibid.* pp. 377–83).

doubly dangerous. What Cavour must have found even more threatening, an army of six thousand well-armed and well-organized irregulars had been quietly collected by Bertani in Genoa and Tuscany, and this army was now preparing to attack the Papal States in a pincer movement to join with Garibaldi at Rome.[1] If he put off much longer making a choice between his various hypotheses of action, it might well be too late for his decision to have any influence on events.

Agostino Bertani was by profession a doctor of medicine with a substantial clientèle in Genoa, but he was also a member of the Turin parliament and among the most active of radical politicians. Though he had broken from Mazzini in 1859, and though he now adhered steadfastly to Garibaldi's programme of 'Italy and Victor Emanuel', he was still not far enough removed from the republicans to make Cavour feel safe.[2] It was his great weakness to regard himself as little less in stature as a politician than Mazzini or Garibaldi, and he did not willingly take orders from anyone. Ever since May, Bertani had been the chief organizer of the volunteer brigades at Genoa, and officially in charge of Garibaldi's principal base in the north. In that capacity he had obstinately maintained that any agreement with Cavour would check the overflow of revolutionary ferment in Italy, and emasculate the 'party of action'. He had much better reasons for this contention than historians have often allowed him; but it cannot be said that he conducted himself with much tact, moderation or skill, and he proved to be almost as much a barrier to good relations between radicals and moderates as was La Farina himself.

Bertani had all along determined to prepare an invasion of the Papal States so as to link up with Garibaldi farther south; and in this he had had the active co-operation of Mazzini, who feared that Garibaldi might come to terms with Cavour if the conflagration were not quickly stoked up in this new quarter. The proposed expedition was in part a political venture, and was intended as a deliberate challenge to Cavour's policy of avoiding the 'Roman question' in deference to France. The extreme radicals were most anxious to raise the question of Rome, so as to break free of French influence, and to confound Cavour, and to

[1] A. Bertani, *Ire politiche d' oltre tomba*, 1869, p. 65; G. Maraldi, *La spedizione dei mille e l' opera di A. Bertani*, 1940, pp. 88–98.

[2] G. Maraldi, 'La rivoluzione siciliana del 1860', *Rassegna Storica del Risorgimento*, vol. XIX, 1932, p. 534.

oppose a 'unitarian' against a purely 'Piedmontese' solution for the problem of Italy. Garibaldi approved of this idea for an attack on Papal territory, but regarded it first of all as a military matter, as a diversionary movement. Medici in June and Cosenz in early July had together forced a postponement of the planned attack, by obeying Cavour and leading all the available volunteers from Genoa to Sicily. But at the end of July Bertani had a larger and better equipped expedition than ever, and was determined 'to have done with Cavour, once and for all'.[1]

It is important to stress these different motives inside the radical camp. Unlike the extremists, Garibaldi had viewed this diversion as something directed not against, but in conjunction with, the government of Turin. He had encouraged Bertani to prepare it, but at a later stage had insisted that he wait until a landing was first effected on the Neapolitan coast, shrewdly judging that France should not be provoked until the revolution was solidly entrenched on the southern mainland.[2] Towards the middle of July, Garibaldi had written to tell the king of his intentions, and had offered to put this new army of volunteers at the king's disposal if he would but lead the diversion. Victor Emanuel was by no means averse in principle to the project. Up to the last moment, indeed, there continued to be a fair chance that radicals and moderates might meet amicably in such an expedition. Farini as well as Ricasoli was in the plot,[3] and it is less likely that this was bluff on their part than that Cavour was keeping it in reserve as yet one more insurance policy; in other words that he was just waiting to see whether this, or a Neapolitan alliance, or a Neapolitan rebellion would best serve his interests. The testing point came at the end of July. On the 30th Garibaldi wrote to tell both Bertani and Ricasoli that he would be ready to cross the Straits in a fortnight's time, and now needed a strong invasion simultaneously from the north.[4] The fact that he told Ricasoli shows that in

[1] 30 July, Bertani to Crispi (this is missing from ACP, b. 135, but there is a copy in ABCM).

[2] 2 July, Sacchi from Palermo to Bertani, on a conversation he had had with Garibaldi on 1 July (MRR); Bollea, *Una silloge di lettere*, p. 282.

[3] 28 July, Farini to Depretis (copy, CF).

[4] 30 July, Garibaldi to Ricasoli (*Lettere di Ricasoli*, ed. Tabarrini, vol. v, p. 171); 30 July, Garibaldi to Bertani (ABM).

his mind it was no underhand Mazzinian plot, but rather something quite open, for which he might get official help. The precipitate course of events was now forcing the moderates to abandon their policy of watchful waiting, and their intention was not to help but to hinder. In view of the rival projects which Cavour had lately been maturing, both the timing and the probable leadership of this proposed invasion might prove most inexpedient for him. In any case, information was now arriving that in France there existed 'a reaction in favour of Naples'.[1] Bertani had his own plans to start a blaze everywhere. He was already sending arms to Naples and the Abruzzi,[2] and a responsible official described how 'things have reached such a point that in Genoa Bertani is stronger than the government'.[3] Neither this state of affairs, nor the imminent invasion of the Papal States in defiance of France, could be tolerated by the liberals if they wished to retain their position of influence, because Bertani with an army behind him was far more politically dangerous than Garibaldi. Above all, the French alliance must be preserved intact, even if it meant combating the *italianissimi* by force of arms. Cavour therefore could no longer put off becoming a revolutionary himself. He had at once to compete with the radicals on their own ground.

On 29 July Ricasoli arrived by summons at Turin for a hurried consultation with Cavour and the king, and a policy was devised 'to make the national principle triumph at Naples without the intervention of Garibaldi'.[4] The intention was to make another and bolder effort to provoke a 'spontaneous' rising before the dictator arrived. Such a rising would in effect defeat the radicals, and would also establish that the annexation of Naples was based not on right of conquest, but on the manifest wishes of public opinion. For this purpose arms were to be sent from Genoa, and Piedmontese troops were to be held in readiness for prompt invasion of Naples in gracious response to such an undeniable demonstration of popular feeling. A provisional government was also to be prepared in advance, ready to take office under Liborio

[1] 27 July, Nigra to Cavour (*CC Cavour-Nigra*, vol. IV, p. 109).

[2] 30 July, Bertani to Crispi (Crispi's *Memoirs*, vol. I, p. 328).

[3] 2 August, Lanza to Castelli (*Carteggio di Castelli*, ed. Chiala, vol. I, p. 311). Lanza was the future prime minister.

[4] 30 July, Cavour to Persano (*CC Lib. del Mezz.* vol. I, p. 412).

Romano, one of the present Bourbon ministers whose allegiance had been secretly suborned.[1] Ricasoli, who did not mince his words, called this a '*coup d'état* after the Napoleonic manner'. He also hinted that, in their consultation at Turin, they had discussed and even accepted the possibility that it might provoke a war with Austria.[2]

Evidently Cavour had by now been induced to master his earlier resolution that he would never follow the contemptible radicals in using the methods of underhand conspiracy. Since the Neapolitan liberals were clearly not going to stir of their own accord until Garibaldi's arrival, this new plan of sending secret help and positive orders offered the northern liberals their only chance of success. The idea was that Liborio Romano should use the arms sent him and set up a provisional government, which in turn would invoke the protection of Piedmont. Victor Emanuel would then accept the protectorate thus pressed upon him, and his troops would land to maintain order and hold up Garibaldi. In later years, some of the agents of this policy tried to persuade themselves that Cavour had been intending all the time to work in collusion with Garibaldi, not against him; and some historians swallowed this attempt at self-justification.[3] But in reality the whole point of the plan was for the king to take over government 'au nom de l'ordre, de l'humanité en arrachant des mains de Garibaldi la direction suprême du mouvement italien'. Cavour knew what he was doing. 'Le plan que j'ai adopté a des dangers. Mais l'entrée de Garibaldi à Naples en a de plus grands encore. Si cela arrive, c'est lui et non Victor Emanuel qui sera le véritable Roi d'Italie.'[4]

It was to be hoped that the king in the last resort would begin to see matters in this light, and could be converted into feeling some resentment at the rising power and arrogance of the revolutionary party. Cavour's ability at the eleventh hour to win over the king against Garibaldi was eventually to take its place among the decisive facts of the *risorgimento*. At the beginning of August, however, Victor Emanuel

---

[1] 30 July, Cavour to Villamarina (*CC Lib. del Mezz.* vol. I, p. 411).

[2] 31 July, Ricasoli to Cavour (*Lettere di Ricasoli*, ed. Tabarrini); 31 July, Ricasoli telegram to Cavour (BR ASF, f. Z).

[3] E.g. Alessandro Luzio, *Garibaldi, Cavour, Verdi*, 1924, p. 190.

[4] 1 August, Cavour to Nigra (*CC Cavour-Nigra*, vol. IV, p. 123); 1 August, Cavour to Villamarina (*CC Lib. del Mezz.* vol. II, p. 2).

continued to have an independent and more 'Garibaldian' policy of his own, somewhat distinct from that of his ministers; and probably he was still ready—or even still hoping—for Garibaldi to reach Rome and make possible a change in government. We shall see in a later chapter how Cavour addressed himself to this delicate problem. He still had to persuade the king to be a Cavourian and not a Garibaldian, and to back his constitutional minister instead of assuming for the monarchy a revolutionary dictatorship.

CHAPTER XI

CAVOUR FAILS AT NAPLES: AUGUST

Cavour's decision no longer to be a virtually passive spectator of the revolution was to destroy Garibaldi's occasional hopes that the northern government might connive in his plan to create an immediate diversion on Papal territory. Cavour wanted no movement in the Papal States, at all events not unless Napoleon gave him permission, nor until he could feel more confident about the success of his *agents provocateurs* at Naples.[1] He acted only just in time to stop what was happening, for Bertani had begun to mobilize his men, and Garibaldi had written on, 30 July with orders to launch the expedition at once. Luckily for Cavour, the dictator's letter took a fortnight to reach its destination, and by the time it arrived the government had been able to defeat the Genoese radicals and break up their army.

What happened was this. On 31 July Farini, the minister of the interior, had hurried to Genoa to see if, in a private talk with Bertani, he could dissuade the radicals without using force. This called for a little mild deceit. Bertani was told that the government had at last decided to intervene openly in aid of Garibaldi, and that the revolutionary committee had better ship their volunteers to Sicily so that France should not be provoked into vetoing what was afoot. After various threats and promises had been made, Bertani was given one day to think the matter over, and on 2 August he agreed to go quietly.[2] Mazzini at first understood by this that Bertani merely intended to placate the government with apparent connivance, and that instead of sailing for Sicily he meant to land in the Papal States; but by the 6th even Mazzini was in despair, convinced that Bertani like so many others

[1] 30 July, La Masa from Genoa to Garibaldi (La Masa, *Alcuni fatti e documenti della rivoluzione dell' Italia meridionale*, 1861, p. 199); 1 August, Cavour to Nigra (*CC Cavour-Nigra*, vol. IV, p. 125).

[2] 1 August, Farini telegram to Ricasoli (BR ASF, f. Z); 5 August, Farini's circular to all governors (*ibid.* b. N, f. B).

of his former friends had fallen away to the government side.[1] Bertani had in fact been allowed by Farini to think that, once his volunteers had satisfied the conventions by breaking up their encampment at Genoa, no obstacle would be made to their concentrating off Sardinia, so that they might then invade the Pope's dominions without compromising the Turin government. This was a justifiable ruse. Cavour's new object was no longer merely to avoid being compromised. At last he had an active policy of his own.[2] What happened in practice was that Bertani went off to tell Garibaldi about this new turn in events, and persuaded him to come and collect these five thousand men waiting off Sardinia, the intention being to lead them thence in a direct landing on the coast of either Naples or the Roman provinces. The two men then sailed to Sardinia for this very purpose, only to find that the bulk of the expedition had in the interval been forced by Piedmontese warships to leave for Sicily.[3] Cavour by this means reasserted the authority of the government. He had split up the volunteer force, and averted the immediate danger of a diversion. Garibaldi, not best pleased with either Cavour or Bertani, had to return to his original project of moving up from Messina through Calabria, and Bertani soon led the rest of his men southwards to join him.

One last effort was made by some of the radicals in the north. As soon as Cavour had regained his firm control of Genoa, Mazzini moved to more likely ground nearer the Papal frontier. Mazzini's newspaper at Genoa had been censored and confiscated more and more frequently as the moderates recaptured their position,[4] and towards the middle of August he left his hiding-place and moved south to Tuscany. Here there existed a sizeable undercurrent of discontent with Piedmontese rule.[5]

[1] 4 August, Mazzini to Caroline Stansfeld (*Epistolario*, vol. XL, pp. 268–73); 6 August, Mazzini to Emilie Venturi (*ibid.* p. 276). Vol. XL of this national edition of Mazzini's correspondence gives thirty-six letters from Mazzini to Bertani during July 1860, and one letter only during August; but vol. XLI, covering the months from August to February 1861, contains no letters to Bertani at all.

[2] Maraldi, *La spedizione dei mille e l' opera di Bertani*, pp. 95–9.

[3] *Edizione nazionale degli scritti di Giuseppe Garibaldi*, vol. I, *Memorie*, 1932, pp. 315–16. [4] *L' Unità Italiana* was confiscated on 3 and 6 August.

[5] 4 August, a police report to Ricasoli on public opinion in Tuscany: 'a Piedmontese party proper does not exist at all among us. The idea of absorption arouses an ever more pronounced disgust.... The systematic predilection for everything Piedmontese

Ricasoli had so far managed to retain a considerable degree of provincial autonomy at Florence; and one sign of this was that he had allowed, and even encouraged, Baron Nicotera to organize a band of volunteers not very much smaller than that which had just left Genoa. Ricasoli and Nicotera had originally intended to work in with Bertani for a joint march on Rome. Cavour's changed attitude towards the volunteers was thus not altogether approved or understood by his colleague in Florence. Despite frenzied notes from Cavour and Farini, Ricasoli either would not or perhaps could not find and arrest Mazzini. Nor were Nicotera's volunteers dissolved. For one thing, the governor of Tuscany was by no means convinced that Cavour was being as bold as the situation required. He himself was a firm monarchist, for only the monarchy would guarantee the 'conservation of social principles'; but he had nevertheless come to a private arrangement with the semi-republican Nicotera, whom he wanted available with his men for a time of more forceful action; and he even dropped a hint that, if Piedmont finally refused to allow a movement in the Papal States, then he would side openly with the revolution.[1] Again he asked Cavour directly to intervene against Rome.[2] He also once more threatened to resign if his own independence of the central government was not confirmed.[3] One way and another his rashness and uncontrollability in this state of exaltation gave Cavour many anxious moments.

Giovanni Nicotera was one of the more rabid of the radicals. Though he had momentarily accepted the Garibaldian programme, he was less ready to compromise on the republican issue than was Mazzini. He regarded himself as having an entirely independent command over his

...and the imposition upon Tuscany of a collection of new and barbarous phrases... make a very bad impression indeed.' So far only military matters had come under Turin directly, but all who had come into contact with the government on this complained of the haughty and knavish behaviour they had met; and if Piedmont ever made an alliance with Naples, or did not accept the idea of unification, this would become open opposition. (BR ASF, b. P, f. A.)

[1] 9 August, Ricasoli to Corsi (*Carteggio di Ricasoli*, ed. Nobili and Camerani); and Nicotera's statement about Ricasoli's complicity in *Il Garibaldi* (Naples) of 19 September.

[2] 9 August, Ricasoli telegram to Cavour (BR ASF, f. Z).

[3] 8 August, Ricasoli to Carignano, he had only accepted this post on the understanding he had 'freedom to operate according to my conscience' (*Carteggio di Ricasoli*, ed. Nobili and Camerani).

volunteers in Tuscany, and to be answerable to no one, not even to Garibaldi. In future years he was to become a leading minister of the Italian crown, but even then he was to be notorious for his authoritarian temperament and ungovernable temper. In 1860, this unexpectedly truculent opposition from Cavour was too much for him. In one letter of 4 August, which Ricasoli after his usual manner intercepted, he spoke of continuing his plan to invade Papal territory even if it meant fighting the Piedmontese.[1] Such a suggestion did him no credit. But despite these outbursts, he went on receiving protection from the governor of Tuscany. These two barons, one of them a conservative monarchist, the other a democrat and republican, occasionally thought and acted on much the same lines.

Cavour found Ricasoli's conduct so insupportable that he could not bring himself to write to him for more than a fortnight. Matters were difficult enough without this degree of obtuseness and irresponsibility. Such little news as arrived from Naples suggested that no insurrection might now be possible without the help of Garibaldi, since Neapolitans seemed to want annexation not because it was positively desirable, but negatively as a lesser evil to the revolution.[2] Cavour felt sure that he could regain his influence in Italy once he could reach a point where it was possible to come out into the open with a regular declaration of war; but if at Naples he could not bring about an incident 'which appears to be spontaneous', he would not be able to rely on the approval of France and England, and without their connivance it was not so easy to be confident.[3] The ambiguity and embarrassment of his position was simply this, that he needed an 'incident', and yet could not risk trying

[1] 4 August, Nicotera to Bertani (copy in BR ASF, b. T, f. P); in busta G and busta T there are letters and diplomatic documents to Cardinal Antonelli, to the French and Spanish ambassadors in Rome, diplomatic correspondence of Prussian consuls with their home government, some original letters of Nicotera and Guerrazzi which Ricasoli must have confiscated outright, and copies of Elliot's telegrams to Russell, all intercepted in Tuscany.

[2] 6 August, Cavour to Prince Eugenio (*CC Lib. del Mezz.* vol. II, p. 17); 7 August, Ribotti from Naples to Eugenio and Cavour (*ibid.* p. 36). In messages of 9, 16 and 22 August to Nigra, Cavour and his secretary could not give much news of Naples except what was in the papers (*CC Cavour-Nigra*, vol. IV, pp. 146, 164, 176).

[3] 5 August, Cavour to Nigra (*CC Cavour-Nigra*, vol. IV, p. 138); 9 August, Cavour to Persano (*Lib. del Mezz.* vol. II, p. 48).

1 1

to create one too openly. He desired the benefits which Garibaldi had taught him might accrue from revolution, but without the drawbacks and without the reputation of being a revolutionary.

Il est évident que le Roi de Sardaigne ne peut pas envahir le Royaume de Naples en pleine paix; ni se mettre à conspirer ouvertement contre son Souverain. Je ne sais pas ce qui arrivera si Garibaldi s'empare de Naples; mais ce que je sais c'est que si nous suivions une politique d'aventurier... nous serions mis au ban de l'Europe, et quelques vaisseaux de ligne nous mettraient à la raison.[1]

Cavour thus had to steer a careful course between European disapproval of an active policy on the one hand, and the growing sentiment in Italy for adventurousness on the other. He could never on any occasion afford to flout Louis Napoleon, but he also had to pick his ground carefully before provoking a public quarrel with Garibaldi. In one of his most perceptive and magnanimous letters, he wrote on 9 August to tell Nigra that he dare not openly challenge Garibaldi unless the radicals involved him with France or threatened to upset his whole political system. Nor yet did he dare to resort to his favourite political weapon and recall parliament.

Pour faire l'Italie à l'heure qu'il est, il ne faut pas mettre en opposition Victor Emmanuel et Garibaldi.... Si demain j'entrais en lutte avec Garibaldi, il est possible que j'eusse pour moi la majorité des vieux diplomates, mais l'opinion publique européenne serait contre moi, et l'opinion publique aurait raison, car Garibaldi a rendu à l'Italie les plus grands services qu'un homme pût lui rendre : il a donné aux Italiens confiance en eux-mêmes : il a prouvé à l'Europe que les Italiens savaient se battre et mourir sur les champs de bataille pour reconquérir une patrie.[2]

This was generously and sincerely said. Kind words apart, however, he was all the more convinced that Garibaldi was a dangerous character who must somehow be arrested. For the moment there was little he could do about it. He could only reconcile himself to Garibaldi crossing the Straits of Messina, and then wait a little longer to see what happened.[3]

---

[1] 6 August, Cavour to Prince Eugenio (*CC Lib. del Mezz.* vol. II, p. 18).
[2] 9 August, Cavour to Nigra (*CC Cavour-Nigra*, vol. IV, pp. 144–5).
[3] 10 August, Hudson to Russell: 'the fact is neither here nor at Naples does either Government seem to know what to do. Both Governments see Garibaldi looming in the distance and the prospect is not agreeable to either of them' (RP G.D. 22/66).

What could be done in preparation for this he did. Money and arms were sent so that Liborio Romano would be encouraged to raise an insurrection ahead of Garibaldi in Naples. As a yet more decisive step, on 15 August a battalion of Piedmontese *bersaglieri* arrived secretly in Naples harbour, to be held ready under hatches for Admiral Persano to use in any profitable emergency.[1] Many reports meanwhile began to circulate in the north about preparations for a possible war, and rumours spread fast about orders given to munitions factories and of national guard officers called up for service.[2] Cavour had to recognize that there was a serious danger of Austria choosing this moment to attack and regain what had been lost in 1859; but he boldly asserted that he would not fight shy of such a war 'if it is the only means of saving us from the revolution'.[3] He even recognized and accepted the possibility that Austria might win and so prejudice the whole cause of national independence.[4] In other words, the king's government had been forced into the terrible position where they would rather be beaten by Austria than allow Garibaldi to win on his own, and where they would prefer to plunge the country into a fruitless and disastrous foreign war rather than themselves try and find common ground with the Italian radicals. It was still possible and even likely, one must remember, that if liberal and radical patriots did not stand together, the Bourbons might defeat Garibaldi during his perilous crossing; and Cavour well knew that in that event the national cause would receive a calamitous setback, and he himself might have to make way for another prime minister whom the rest of Europe would find more trustworthy.[5] Garibaldi's failure or success might therefore prove equally dangerous. This was the fact which inhibited the Piedmontese from taking any constructive action in these critical weeks. Cavour's hope was that he might still be able to arrive at Naples before Garibaldi, but he could be none too confident of success. On 16 August he wrote: 'we have given Naples everything

[1] 12 August, instructions to Captain Wright (*Lettere di Cavour*, ed. Chiala, vol. III, pp. 324–5).

[2] 13 August, *La Perseveranza*; 14 August (copy of note by U.S. minister Daniel to Cass, MRR).

[3] 14 August, Cavour to Nigra (*CC Cavour-Nigra*, vol. IV, p. 157).

[4] 16 August, Cavour to Ricasoli (*CC Lib. del Mezz.* vol. II, p. 92).

[5] 16 August, Cavour to Cassinis (*ibid.* pp. 90–1).

necessary for a revolution, arms, money, soldiers, men of counsel and men of action. If after all this the kingdom turns out to be so rotten as to be incapable of action, I do not know what to do; and we must resign ourselves to the triumph either of Garibaldi or of the reactionaries.'[1] Here he was underestimating his own courage and resourcefulness.

While he waited for news of Romano's insurrection and Garibaldi's crossing, Cavour did what he could and what he dared to make events move in his favour. His success in breaking up Bertani's private army now emboldened him to make one more attempt to stop the whole recruiting drive upon which Garibaldi relied for building up his revolutionary forces. On 7 August, a preliminary circular from Farini at the Home Office warned all the provinces that the increase of desertions to Garibaldi was gravely compromising the discipline of the royal army;[2] and then, on the 13th, another and more peremptory circular forbad all further recruitment of volunteers. 'The government is firm in its intention not to let itself be overcome by those who have no mandate or responsibility given them by the king and the nation.... The government must fulfil its duty to act as supreme moderator of the national movement.'[3] This was a new voice for any public pronouncement, or at least it was a voice which Italians had not heard for three months. Evidently the government really had a plan and was confident about it. What people still could not quite understand was that to resume charge of the national movement meant for some reason opposing Garibaldi rather than joining him. This abrupt prohibition of recruitment was to arouse great resentment in the south, even among Cavour's friends who could not see what he was about.[4] Garibaldi naturally read it as damning evidence that Cavour's only wish was to curry favour with France. It made Nicotera almost ungovernable. But Cavour kept his own counsel. At this stage he could no longer afford to be so delicate and nice about annoying the volunteers, and such a prohibition was a sure method of cutting off their sources of

---

[1] 16 August, Cavour to Ricasoli (*CC Lib. del Mezz.* vol. II, p. 92); this part of the letter was omitted by Chiala (vol. III, p. 331), so as not to give offence.

[2] 7 August. One copy of Farini's circular is in BR ASF, b. N, f. B.

[3] 13 August, *Gazzetta Ufficiale di Torino*; 14 August, Valerio's protest from Como (*Carteggio di Castelli*, ed. Chiala, vol. I, p. 313).

[4] 16 August, *Il Nazionale* (Bonghi's paper at Naples).

supply, as well as of husbanding Piedmontese resources against the day when Victor Emanuel could openly lead his men into battle. Before long it might even become a positive advantage for Garibaldi to be annoyed with the northern government, because he might lose his temper in some public pronouncement, and so give Cavour a long-awaited chance to pose as an offended party.

When on 18–19 August Garibaldi crossed the Straits—a fact which Cavour knew on the 20th—the time seemed ripe for yet more resolute action. This was the moment when Cavour prepared a plan to invade the Papal States himself. Some historians have assumed that Cavour had determined upon such an invasion as early as 1 August;[1] and they then built upon this fact an argument which made out Cavour's earlier policy to have been more logical and self-conscious than it probably was. The evidence cited for these interpretations does not bear this inference. Through the first three weeks of August the hypothesis of this invasion was no doubt maturing in Cavour's mind, but he still waited until he had more information about the fate of his own plot at Naples and of Garibaldi's landing in Calabria. As soon as he had enough information, he made up his mind to a move which was calculated with extraordinary skill and courage. In one sense it was as courageous as Garibaldi's first expedition to Sicily in May, for though Cavour had many more chances of success than had the Thousand, he knowingly risked the terrible chance of civil war against the *italianissimi*. He was also planning to lead a Catholic country in fighting the Pope by force of arms, and somehow he had to do this while still retaining the support of his Catholic ally in Paris. The stakes were high, but the prospective winnings were enormous, nothing less than Sicily, Naples, and the papal provinces of Umbria and the Marches; in other words a half of the whole peninsula. Equally important was the fact that once more the liberal-conservatives would be able to call the tune, and the king could again overtop that overmighty subject Garibaldi.

The latter purpose of course could not yet be publicly acknowledged. Cavour still went on using a simple ambidexterity to confuse people's

---

[1] E.g. Trevelyan, *Garibaldi and the Making of Italy*, pp. 116–17, 169, 211. This was based on E. d'Azeglio's recollections twenty-five years later (*La politique du comte Camille de Cavour 1852–61*, ed. N. Bianchi, 1885, p. 379). But these recollections were inaccurate here as elsewhere, and Cavour's letters tell a different story.

minds. The revolutionaries were encouraged in the illusion that, by invading Papal territory, the king was coming to their aid; while Louis Napoleon was simultaneously wheedled with the suggestion that, in a Piedmontese invasion of the south, he had the only method of forcing back the Italian movement into a conservative channel. There have not been lacking interpretations which made out that Cavour had all the time intended his invasion to be in aid of Garibaldi, as a support without which the revolution could not have survived much longer.[1] But this was yet another rationalization invented later for political purposes in order to justify the official policy: for at this particular moment Garibaldi's course through Calabria was at its most headlong and successful; he was least in need of aid, and most to be feared. Cavour's skill is seen at its best in the way he both confused appearances and also found many and even contradictory reasons for doing the selfsame thing. On this occasion he was making a great virtue out of a hard necessity forced upon him. He was obliged to move fast if he wanted to crush the revolution; and yet, as he himself confessed, if he had allowed his true motives to become known, public opinion would have been against him and the plan would have failed. The only hope of success was to give the illusion that his motives were the very opposite of what in fact they were.

The invasion of Umbria and the Marches had been originally a radical project, and this project Cavour just took over and improved upon. Something of this sort had been constantly in the minds of Mazzini and Bertani since May, and Garibaldi had always intended that his revolution in the south should be assisted by a parallel movement in the centre. Bertani's mobilization for this particular invasion at the end of July had been one compelling argument behind Cavour's decision to forestall him, so that the popularity of this move could be stolen for the liberals and the king—just as Bertani's threat to invade had also conveniently given Cavour the wherewithal to justify his own counter-invasion in the eyes of European statesmen. For some months Cavour had been urged by his colleagues to invade the Marches, on the grounds that this would be the best or the only way to provoke and canalize a revolution in Naples. Such a scheme had been put to him five months

[1] E.g. D. Zanichelli, *Cavour*, 1926, pp. 389–90; A. J. Whyte, *The political life and letters of Cavour*, 1930, p. 423.

earlier by Pantaleoni from Rome.[1] In April the king himself had privately assured the Garibaldians that he meant to synchronize their movement in the south with one of his own in the centre.[2] General Fanti, Cavour's minister of war, had more recently been laying independent plans for such an invasion, hoping it would restore the morale of the regular forces and win them some of the glory which they so much envied Garibaldi.[3] Ricasoli too, as we have noticed, had continuously advocated imposing a violent solution of the Roman question, and by early August was already well advanced in a private plot of his own to bribe the Pope's Swiss Guard.[4] The prime minister had thus been subjected to a good deal of advice and prodding in this direction. Almost certainly the question of the Papal States had been discussed in general terms at that meeting towards the end of July between Cavour, Ricasoli and the king; and the British minister had already been casually informed that the Pope, if he left, might be offered alternative accommodation in Sardinia.[5] The time came for Cavour to make up his mind to an actual invasion when he began to fear the failure of his first plan to seize Naples before Garibaldi arrived. How he carried out his bold project of aggression must be left for consideration later. It is sufficient for the moment to say that it was the threat of Garibaldi's advance upon Naples which at once gave colour to Cavour's invasion of the centre and made it necessary. Once again it was opposition to the revolution rather than motives of high patriotism which was the immediate stimulus to action.

Many reasons have been produced to explain why Cavour failed in his first scheme for a *pronunciamento* at Naples. Garibaldi was far stronger than the moderates in the south, and had a much clearer idea of what he wanted, and could act openly instead of by underhand means. Cavour also tried to work through too many unco-ordinated individuals, most of them former exiles sent back to act more or less independently in the city of Naples. There was not sufficient co-operation between his

[1] 20 March, Pantaleoni to Cavour (*CC La Questione Romana 1860–1*, vol. I, p. 14).
[2] 25 April, Türr to Bertani (Archivio J. W. Mario MRR).
[3] 5 June, Fanti to his brother Gaetano (*Il Risorgimento Italiano*, vol. for 1914, p. 255).
[4] 3 August, Ricasoli to Cavour, *Carteggio di Ricasoli*, ed. Nobili and Camerani; this fact is not given in Tabarrini's edition.
[5] 31 July, Hudson to Russell (RP G.D. 22/66).

agents, and perhaps they were not given either sufficient powers of independent initiative or sufficient clear instructions on possible lines of action to be adopted in varying circumstances. Cavour habitually relied too much on untried men and mediocrities for this sort of employment. He always disliked using strong people of independent character like Depretis or Crispi, Ricasoli or Garibaldi. Principally for this reason he was not usually successful in picking his subordinates, and it is striking how, man for man, Garibaldi's chosen lieutenants in southern Italy were far superior to his. Villamarina and Persano were both mediocrities, Villamarina dangerously so; and it made matters worse that ambassador and admiral shared a mutual jealousy and dislike. Both suspected, with some reason, that their master was putting on a different face to each of them. Each wrote home to complain of the other, and both of them feared for their dignity whenever they had to try and co-operate harmoniously on the same programme. Apart from these, there were two or three people in Naples who seem to have had secret and separate supplies of money from Cavour. Of this money a disproportionate amount was spent with small effect on bribes to seedy members of the aristocracy.[1] Cavour's subsidies do not seem either to have been sufficient for his purpose,[2] or to have been sufficiently concentrated in one place and in one direction. The truth probably is that he was too fully preoccupied with difficult problems of diplomacy to have much time for such matters. He was personally disinclined to, and relatively unskilled in, the detailed workings of administration. Moreover, like all the moderate liberals as a class, he sometimes proved to be not quite versatile or reckless enough to make a good revolutionary.

One of the most busy of the returned exiles was Baron Nicolò Nisco, who arrived at Naples on 3 August with a cargo of three thousand guns.[3] Nisco's particular scheme was to try and work towards proclaiming the regency of the Count of Syracuse on the collapse of the present Neapolitan government.[4] This Syracuse was a penniless Bourbon

[1] Note by Borromeo (*CC Lib. del Mezz.* vol. II, p. 17).

[2] 28 August, Ronchei to Bargoni (MRR); 24 August, Persano to Cavour (*CC Lib. del Mezz.* vol. II, p. 145).

[3] N. Nisco, *Storia del reame di Napoli 1824–60*, 1908 (5th ed.), pp. xxix–xxx.

[4] 4 August, Nisco to Ricasoli, he hoped 'this would stop Garibaldi's march' (*Carteggio di Ricasoli*, ed. Nobili and Camerani).

princeling, of irregular private life, quite without influence in the country, and said by Nisco's colleagues to be a positive obstacle to action. To this man Cavour paid considerable advances in cash. It was an anomalous situation to find the moderates thus driven to want rule by such a hireling traitor of a discredited dynasty rather than by Garibaldi. Another well-placed traitor was General Nunziante, upon whom Cavour set special store. Nunziante had been in his time a notorious reactionary, and was 'considered by the public one of the worst of the Camarilla'.[1] His conversion to liberalism, well timed in August, was shortly to earn better promotion in the Italian army than fell to the lot of many senior Garibaldian officers who had fought with greater loyalty and self-sacrifice for their king and country. It was his appointed job to spread disloyalty among the Bourbon army; but he, too, turned out not to be worth what he cost, and he quite spoilt Nisco's plan by threatening to leave Naples unless the candidature of Syracuse was dropped.[2] Syracuse, Nunziante, and Liborio Romano who was simultaneously one of King Francesco's sworn ministers and one of Cavour's trusted agents, were certainly an odd trio on whom to bank the fortunes of a revolution.

Most of Cavour's spies soon enough convinced themselves that Villamarina's reports, on the strength of which they had acted in the first place, were quite wrong, and that southerners were either too fearful or too little interested to revolt. Except in some parts of the provinces, people preferred to wait until Garibaldi arrived and carried out the dangerous part of the revolution on their behalf. Cavour was soon speaking of Neapolitans with contemptuous disparagement as 'ces poules mouillées'.[3] That future premier of Italy, the tolerant Zanardelli, found it impossible to work with them, and he added that the returned exiles were little better than they as instruments of bold and decisive action.[4] The British minister Elliot, when he heard of Cavour's plan to engineer a revolution, gave it as his view on 11 August that he doubted if Neapolitans had enough pluck.[5]

[1] 5 July, Elliot to Russell (F.O. 70/318/342).
[2] 25 August, Villamarina to Cavour (*CC Lib. del Mezz.* vol. II, p. 151).
[3] 13 August, Cavour to Persano (*ibid.* p. 71).
[4] 29 August, Zanardelli from Brescia to Depretis (ASP Min. Luogo. Interno, b. 4165).
[5] 11 August, Elliot to Russell (RP G.D. 22/85).

Another obstacle was that some former exiles, especially among the old Neapolitan aristocracy, preferred to play a quite different and less dangerous game. Since Francesco was trying to work his new constitution by holding elections, they chose to accept nomination for the Neapolitan parliament.[1] Their idea was probably to have a representative body all ready in existence to vote against Garibaldi when Cavour's troops should arrive. But such a policy was quite contrary to the plan for revolutionary action.[2] Garibaldi had an easy target when he saw Cavour's men thus favouring the Bourbon constitution rather than the radical revolution. Their conduct only gave substance to the Mazzinian indictment that Cavour was flirting with the Neapolitan autonomists. In terms of practical politics, it split the liberal committee in Naples into two warring factions, the party of order and the party of action; and in general it set a bad example and diminished popular ardour. Villamarina had to report back to Turin that these men would have done well to stay in exile, since their return had only divided the patriots and contributed to paralyse any hope of a revolt.[3] Here is another indication that the simultaneous pursuit of many complementary or contradictory policies by the northern government did not always work out for the best.

Cavour was in this way publicly competing with both Garibaldi and King Francesco for public favour in Naples. This was neither dignified nor politic, and in these circumstances the natural reaction of most Neapolitans was simply to wait and see which of the three contestants proved most powerful. People knew throughout August that Cavour was still entertaining Winspeare the Bourbon plenipotentiary, and believed no doubt that Piedmont was always ready to make an alliance with Francesco if ever the Bourbon army could hold fast against the revolutionaries. Cavour's insurance policy of negotiating or pretending to negotiate an alliance was thus being shown up as a tactical error: for

[1] 8 August, *Il Diritto* in this connexion gives the names of Bellelli, D'Afflitto, Pisanelli, Silvio Spaventa, Lequile, D'Ayala.

[2] 6 August, G. Matina from Naples to Garibaldi (ACM 1101); 23 August, Poerio to Mascilli (*Nuova Antologia*, 16 January 1912, p. 324); 17 July, Visconti-Venosta to Farini (*CC Lib. del Mezz.* vol. I, pp. 340–2); August, Nisco to Cavour (*ibid.* vol. II, pp. 203–4).

[3] 21 July, Villamarina to Cavour (*ibid.* vol. I, p. 357); 15 August, Villamarina to Cavour (*ibid.* vol. II, pp. 85–6).

not only had it antagonized Garibaldi, but it was helping to defeat the simultaneous scheme to precipitate a liberal *pronunciamento* at Naples, and was generally creating distrust about Cavour's motives. The attitude of most Neapolitans was probably expressed by Elliot, when he said of Cavour's policy that 'open war would be infinitely more creditable, and it would avoid all the dangers both of Mazzinianism and reaction through which we shall otherwise have to pass'.[1] This was a timid, but not an altogether unjustifiable, point of view for southerners to hold. The warning signs of a peasants' revolt were a powerful argument against making any precipitate move before it was absolutely clear that Cavour would commit himself irretrievably and guarantee them against failure. He wanted to keep his hands free; they wanted to commit him; and neither he nor they wanted to risk a first and un-retraceable step into the unknown.

Cavour's recognition of this state of mind was one of the factors which helped to make him finally decide that he must set his own armies in motion and take part in the civil war himself. He expressed indignation that the Neapolitans preferred to let others relieve them of the Bourbons; but in reality his anger was due to the fact that they would not relieve him of Garibaldi. Francesco, Napoleon, and also the Neapolitan people, had each in succession failed to arrest the revolutionaries for him, so he had now no option but to attack this task himself. Perhaps he hoped that, when they knew that the Piedmontese were actually on the march, the liberal Neapolitans would still rise and appeal for annexation in time for him to move in before the volunteers could arrive. Preparations for armed intervention were therefore set more urgently on foot, both to go directly by sea to Naples, and also to march south through the States of the Church.

Garibaldi's crossing of the Straits on 19 August had been a considerable military feat. The transports which conveyed his army had no proper navy to protect them, and his commissariat had to meet great difficulties in improvising food supplies for so many men in rapid movement. But one of the chief obstacles in his path went unobserved, for he had no idea that the northern government was so far opposed to him and so far advanced as this with a counter-plan of its own. The rumour had already arrived in his camp before this time that Cavour might be

---

[1] 20 August, Elliot to Russell (RP G.D. 22/85).

intending to invade the Papal States, but there was little thought yet that this might not be a friendly act.[1] Garibaldi continued to believe that royal favour would follow him so long as he was successful, no matter what the king might have to say in public. Certainly Victor Emanuel was much less of a politician than Cavour, and, unlike the latter, hardly seems to have changed his policy very much during the course of the southern revolution. On 5 August or soon afterwards he sent a message by word of mouth to encourage Garibaldi to go ahead and even attack the Papal States.[2] Just possibly this was merely a recognition of what could not be helped, in an attempt to keep the dictator's confidence. More likely it represents the real wishes of the king as distinct from those of Cavour, the king being as headstrong and enthusiastic as the prime minister was cautious and fearful. At all events, its effect was to make Garibaldi over-confident. Now was the time when he became really excited over the prospect of reaching Rome, and the historians who censure him for this excitement must take into account the king's perhaps ill-considered words.

But an ominous note was beginning to intrude into this apparent concord, as the volunteers realized that the king's words were not always supported by the actions of his government. During a critical moment in the passage of the Straits, a Piedmontese warship appeared in Messina harbour, but without stirring even unobtrusively to help Garibaldi in his hazardous enterprise. When one of his transports ran aground in passage and had to be burnt, still the Piedmontese ship answered all pleas for aid with a dead silence.[3] In view of Persano's many private protestations of amity, this could not but be taken amiss. It seemed to correspond all too well with Farini's deception of Bertani at Genoa, and his recent proclamation against any further recruitment of volunteers. Cavour's smoke screen could not much longer conceal

[1] 18 August, Commander Forbes at Messina, *The Campaign of Garibaldi in the Two Sicilies*, adding that 'Cavour has, at least for the moment, ceased to push for immediate annexation, and a thoroughly cordial understanding exists between the King and the Dictator', pp. 123, 137.

[2] G. Manacorda, 'Vittorio Emanuele II e Garibaldi nel 1860 secondo le carte Trecchi', *Nuova Antologia*, f. 923, 1 June 1910, pp. 413, 426.

[3] 20 August, G. Medici to Cavour (*CC Lib. del Mezz.* vol. II, p. 112); 13 August, Persano to Cavour (*ibid.* p. 74); 17 August, Professor Amari to Count Amari (*Carteggio di Amari*, ed. d'Ancona, vol. II, p. 123).

that this new Machiavelli had also the faces of Janus. On 23 August *Il Diritto* finally wrote that, 'after all these equivocations and contradictions, the government has at last come out in open opposition to the movement led by General Garibaldi'. Sooner or later the dictator would see this for himself.

Once ashore on the opposite side, however, Garibaldi needed no help but that of Bertani's reinforcements, and for some time he paid little attention to politics. The conquest of Naples which Cavour had dreaded so much was now on the way to becoming an accomplished fact. Enthusiasm for Garibaldi's name tore like a forest fire through Calabria, and the moderate liberals who had been hoping to take over government in the provinces before his arrival were quite outstripped.[1] Everywhere the liberals seemed by comparison weighed down with inertia, and it was the radicals who acted.[2] Just as in Sicily, the lower classes pictured Garibaldi as a god bringing with him comfort and prosperity; and he played up to their ideal by at once reducing the price of salt, abolishing food taxes, and opening up the recently enclosed pasture land on the Sila to the peasants. On the other hand, among the wealthier citizens, 'many who a short time ago were anxiously looking forward for the arrival of Garibaldi now anticipate with fear the moment of his coming, as likely to be the commencement of a period of anarchy and confusion'.[3] On 28 August the Marquis D'Afflitto expressed the fear felt by the liberal leaders at Naples: 'pray God', he wrote earnestly, 'that the movement is not discredited by any lack of respect towards property'.[4] But the rights of property were in fact being trodden underfoot indiscriminately, as peasants armed with

[1] 25 August, G. Devincenzi to Cavour (*CC Lib. del Mezz.* vol. II, p. 156).

[2] 27 August, Persano telegram to Cavour (*ibid.* p. 167); 29 August, Mazzini to L. Ferrari (*Epistolario*, vol. XLI, 1935, p. 13); 8 September, M. Guerri (Ricasoli's agent at Penne) to Ricasoli: 'this is what the nation may expect from the doctrinaires' (BR ASF, b. N).

[3] 15 August, Elliot to Russell (F.O. 165/133/443); 4 September: 'in various parts of the country Communist tendencies are already making themselves apparent. Some large estates have been regularly parcled (*sic*) out for division, while in other cases the timber is being openly cut and carried away by the new self-constituted proprietors' (F.O. 165/133/492).

[4] 28 August, D'Afflitto from Naples to Albanese (F. Zervella, 'La reazione di Ariano nel 1860', *Samnium*, January 1943, p. 40).

scythes occupied the land, turned their cattle loose on the 'commons', burnt charters and title-deeds, and diverted streams away from their lord's mill.[1] Perhaps in sum this did not amount to very much. Nevertheless, the very fear that such things were happening paralysed the middle classes with terror at Garibaldi's approach, and at the same time was enough to leave the common people most unwilling to take any counter-action on behalf of Cavour's rival programme. Furthermore, it soon made even the liberals and the landowners most anxious to establish Garibaldi's provisional government, for this would be their only hope of preserving law and order during the most vulnerable days of emergency. These sentiments of fear put the finishing touches to the collapse of the Bourbon regime in the provinces, just as they also inhibited the action of those liberals who worked for Cavour. Once again the peasants were proving to be an important factor in Garibaldi's success, as they frightened their betters into at least a temporary, allegiance to him.

During the last ten days of August Cavour's attention was concentrated on preparations for central Italy, and he had little time to make any detailed plans for the swiftly changing situation at Naples. He remained clear about his main intention, which was to 'fight the revolution with all the means in my power'.[2] For awhile it was confidently expected that General Cialdini would have time to beat Garibaldi to Naples and so be able to 'dominate the revolution'.[3] If it came to the worst, Persano or Villamarina might lead a last-minute revolution and set themselves up in charge of a puppet government. By 27–8 August, however, his mood had swung back into pessimism at the 'conduite ignominieuse' of the Neapolitans, and they were being spoken of scornfully as 'abrutis' who 'n'ont pas du sang dans les veines'. As Cavour put it, 'la conduite des Napolitains est dégoûtante: s'ils ne veulent rien faire avant l'arrivée de Garibaldi, ils méritent d'être gouvernés comme les Siciliens par des Crispis'.[4] These snap judgements

---

[1] E.g. the graphic description in *Il Nazionale* of 16 August and 20 September; and police reports in Archivio di Stato, Naples.

[2] 21 August, Cavour to Ricasoli (*CC Lib. del Mezz.* vol. II, p. 118).

[3] 26 August, Farini to Ricasoli (CF).

[4] 27 August, Cavour to Villamarina (*CC Lib. del Mezz.* vol. II, p. 169); 28 August, Villamarina to Cavour (*ibid.* p. 176).

were made in a moment of great tension, and this will explain the lack of sympathy or psychological penetration. Cavour's agents of course were already busy excusing their own and his deficiencies by blaming the Neapolitans collectively, and he for his part did not see that, in a situation where even his own orders had to be so vague and indecisive, a whole people could be forgiven if they did not manage to think quickly and act effectively. Confronted with contradictory advice from Persano and Visconti-Venosta, Cavour in fact changed his mind from day to day on whether he should or should not antagonize Garibaldi yet further by trying to set up a puppet government of liberals. This created even more confusion.[1] But in practice there was nothing helpful Cavour could do, simply because the Bourbon army had not put up the resistance which he had expected of them.[2]

No mere formulations of policy could now prevent the radicals reaching Naples first, and this in turn was bound to force upon Cavour another change of policy. In a sense it was true that he was beginning to regain control of the situation; but in another and paradoxical sense the initiative even in this new phase remained with Garibaldi, because the only excuse for invading Papal territory was the presence of the dictator at Naples. The radicals thus forced Cavour to invade the centre; for, quite apart from the need to save the Pope from red revolution, if the radical advance could not be checked farther south, Italy might be 'liberated' not only up to Rome but up to and including Turin as well. Not only the radicals around Garibaldi, but also some of the opposition deputies at Turin were hoping as much; and in government circles this produced an anti-Jacobin panic, which strangely developed into being a major impulse behind the making of a united nation.

[1] 31 August, Visconti-Venosta protests to Cavour (*ibid.* pp. 194-5).

[2] Elliot called this Cavour's fault for not coming into the open and fighting the Bourbons fairly and 'like a gentleman'. His conduct was 'as discreditable as anything ever done by a Bourbon' (Sir Henry Elliot, *Some Revolutions and other Diplomatic Experiences*, 1922, p. 55).

CHAPTER XII

POLITICAL DIFFERENCES IN SICILY: AUGUST

Since early July, when La Farina left Sicily, the political climate of Palermo had remained more or less equable. Depretis had arrived on 21 July, determined to try and restore confidence between Garibaldi and Cavour, and hoping to find an agreed policy in annexing Sicily to Piedmont with Garibaldi's good will. In his talks with Victor Emanuel and Farini preparatory to leaving on this difficult mission, Depretis had been given to expect material help in his task of restoring order in the island, but assistance was made conditional on evidence of his good faith in preparing the ground for a plebiscite and annexation. Cavour intended that, as soon as possible, Depretis should publish the Pied-montese constitution as the first step towards union, and the induce-ment was held out that this would make it easier to find money for the Sicilian government. Here was the first step in a programme upon which moderates and radicals were not far from agreement.

The arrangement of forces in Palermo at the beginning of August does not show a straight fight between moderates and radicals. On the contrary, Crispi for the moment was surprisingly enough on the same side as Depretis and Cavour, while in so far as there was an opposition it was to be found in the bulk of those who wanted only a conditional union with the north. Many of the autonomists had been hoping to have a proper Sicilian parliament, and to restore the island constitution of 1812 and 1848. But they were prevented, for on 3 August Depretis and Crispi followed Cavour's behest in both signing the preamble to a proclamation bestowing on Sicily the Piedmontese *statuto*, and calling this 'an inviolable pact binding Italy to Victor Emanuel'.[1] It was also decreed that public officials should swear loyalty to Victor Emanuel and the northern constitution, or else be dismissed.[2] On the 9th this was followed by the introduction of Sardinian laws on the mercantile

[1] *Raccolta degli atti del governo dittatoriale e prodittatoriale in Sicilia*, 1861.
[2] 15 August, *L' Unità Italiana* (Genoa), in a report from Palermo dated 10 August.

marine, on the 18th by that of Sardinian copyright laws, on the 26th by introduction of the communal and provincial law of the 'Regno d'Italia', on the 28th by the military penal code, and on the 30th by the northern laws on public security. A decree of 17 August also declared the northern *lira* with the head of Victor Emanuel to be the only currency, doing away with the *oncie* and *tari* peculiar to Sicily. Such administrative edicts by Garibaldi's government were of course pre-judging the very issue of annexation which Cavour had thought to be the principal matter in dispute, yet here they were proposed and supported by both radicals and moderates. Even if there was inevitably much more of intention than achievement about them—for example, the old coinage and even many outward signs of a 'natural' economy were to be found in Sicily up to the end of the century—they appeared to bear out Cavour's policy to the letter.[1] The diary of Count Litta tells us that Crispi as well as Depretis had begun to talk in favour of immediate annexation at the end of July, and now the formal introduction of Piedmontese laws by Crispi himself seemed a virtual recognition on his part that annexation was almost an accomplished fact. Confirmation by popular vote still had to follow, but the presumption was that a plebiscite would be held as soon as formal union with Piedmont could be carried through without giving the European Powers an opening to thwart Garibaldi's further progress. In all appearance Depretis had thus succeeded in harmonizing the radical and liberal policies, and this was taken as a defeat for the autonomists, a guarantee that formal annexation would follow as soon as possible.[2]

But Cavour in his ignorance of Sicily—an ignorance unhappily fostered and exploited by La Farina—did not understand that this proclamation of the *statuto* was an agreed policy between Depretis, Cordova and Crispi, and that Crispi's *Precursore*, of all the Palermitan newspapers, gave it unqualified welcome.[3] The fact that Cavour did not know of, and so could not use, this growing approximation of opinion in Palermo, must be put down to poor liaison and bad advice, unless we assume that he was in principle averse from any alliance at all with the radicals, that he was more against revolutionism than he was in favour

---

[1] 16 August, Cavour to Cassinis (*CC Lib. del Mezz.* vol. II, p. 90).
[2] 15 August, Elliot to Russell (F.O. 165/133/440).
[3] 5 August, *Il Precursore*.

of nationalism. For some reason he had now made up his mind that he could not trust even Depretis, and so there was no one authoritative in Sicily with whom he could speak frankly about the development of affairs. Depretis was thus left without a lead, and without the assistance he had been led to expect, while the patriots were able to read into Cavour's inaction a lack of confidence in the possibilities of Italian unity. Cavour still believed Crispi to be a red republican, and people in Turin thought that the introduction of the *statuto* was simply the work of Filippo Cordova, the Sicilian who had succeeded La Farina as leader of the Cavourian party.[1] Neither supposition was true. Crispi was the minister responsible for promulgating the *statuto*, and he had sworn the oath of allegiance to Victor Emanuel on 9 August along with the rest of the cabinet. On the other hand, the so-called Cavourian or 'annexationist' papers in Palermo had at once found fault with the proclamation, for the very reason that Crispi was one of its authors; they argued that it was something which should have followed and not preceded a popular vote.[2] The autonomists were to put their criticism even more strongly. 'Are we going to become Italians or Piedmontese?', asked one Palermo newspaper.[3] Another called this decree 'a violation of the principle of national sovereignty', implying that the northern constitution was being imposed on a sovereign people by force.[4] La Farina's old paper, *L' Annessione*, was now veering towards the autonomists in order to find an ally against Crispi;[5] whereas Crispi himself was so much a nationalist that he wanted unqualified annexation as soon as this would not hamper Garibaldi's progress. 'Sicily shall be annexed unconditionally, and Italy shall *be*!', he wrote with emphasis to Mazzini.[6]

In this way a bitter conflict, partly over personalities, partly out of sheer ignorance and doctrinaire reasoning, grew up to spoil the relative harmony between the chief factions in Sicily. The month of August had

---

[1] August, Cavour to Cordova: 'I hope that Depretis will break free of Crispi's influence and on your advice publish our *statuto*' (*Lettere di Cavour*, ed. Chiala, vol. VI, p. 576).

[2] 8 August, *L' Annessione*; 9 August, Cordova to Cavour (*CC Lib. del Mezz.* vol. II, p. 52).

[3] 11 August, *La Forbice.*   [4] 21 September, *Tom Pouce* (Palermo).

[5] 8 August, *L' Annessione*; 13 August, letter by Perez intercepted by Ricasoli (BR ASF, b. N, f. N).

[6] 31 July, Crispi to Mazzini (Crispi's *Memoirs*, vol. I, p. 364).

begun quietly enough. A correspondent of the moderate and Cavourian *L' Opinione* had written on 3 August that, 'as for different parties, you will not find a trace of such among us here'.[1] Then the *statuto* decree, instead of confirming this agreement as one might have expected, was made a cause of further discord; and a pamphlet on the 8th could speak of how 'everywhere there was nothing but talk of fusionists, unitarians, autonomists and separatists'.[2] One or other of these labels was adopted by each of the leading journals, and what until now had seemed but subtle gradations of opinion soon developed into apparently irreconcilable opposites. At Messina one paper came out with the at first sight surprising statement that, 'between the hypothesis of gradual unification and that of complete Italian unity there exists an abyss'.[3] Depretis made some effort to bring all parties together on better personal terms, and began to send out general invitations to an occasional soirée.[4] A slight relaxation of tension was noticed for a while, and it was hoped that in a few days most people might again be in agreement.[5] But suspicions had returned to antagonize people beyond the possibility of reconciliation, and the two main parties, radical and liberal, were to grow further and further apart during the course of the month.

Depretis himself, nevertheless, continued to try and run with both hare and hounds. In important respects he still adhered to Garibaldi's programme as distinct from Cavour's, and was thus thinking of a fairly swift passage on to Rome and even to Venice.[6] When explaining his views later in parliament, he said that in such military matters Garibaldi was to be trusted. As far as internal politics were concerned, his first principle was to try and reconcile both sides with a 'formula', and his natural disposition was to commit himself to neither side until circumstances forced a choice. The widening gap in Sicilian politics now put him in an ever more false position. The radicals later claimed that he must have been working all the time in secret collusion with Cavour,

[1] 7 August, *L' Opinione* (Turin), report from Palermo dated 3 August.

[2] P. Bozzo, *Sull' annessione al regno Italiano della Sicilia*, dated 8 August, p. 1.

[3] 18 August, *L' Indipendente* (Messina).

[4] 11 September, Nievo to Melzi (Dino Mantovani, *Il poeta soldato Ippolito Nievo*, 1900, p. 371).

[5] 10 August, *L' Annessione*.

[6] 20 August, Bargoni to De Bianchi (*Memorie di Bargoni*, pp. 141–2); 6 August, Depretis to Garibaldi (ACM).

and just waiting for Garibaldi to be safely out of the island. The accusation was even made by the autonomists that he had purposely kept Sicily without law and order so as to create a panic, which he could then use for pushing through annexation.[1] This was nonsense; but even so he certainly gave Cavour to understand that he was not fully behind Garibaldi, and he kept in touch with the prime minister at Turin both directly and through intermediaries like Farini, Cordova and Amari.[2] It was also true, as Palamenghi-Crispi said, that 'he was already in possession of a royal decree, with the date left blank, that appointed him royal commissioner...as soon as the annexation should be proclaimed'.[3] This simultaneous allegiance to both king and dictator was bound to present insoluble difficulties as soon as Cavour decided that the monarch must declare war on the revolution.

As Garibaldi moved farther away from Palermo, Depretis found himself more and more left to his own devices, his own responsibility growing, and a decision less and less easy to postpone. Before long he was so far out of touch with the dictator as to have to learn the news of the war from reports in the daily press.[4] On 14 August Amari noted that the prodictator was thinking in terms of a quick conclusion by formal annexation,[5] and Cordova confirms this.[6] The ambitious politician in Depretis also let it be known again at Turin that he would like a coalition between Cavour and his own parliamentary party, so as to put up a common front during the national emergency.[7] Yet he could not go on playing for the gratitude and esteem of Cavour without this losing him the esteem of Garibaldi. To break with either might ruin his career, and might even be a signal for the outbreak of civil war, as La Farina was almost pleased to note.[8] Depretis was still carefully

---

[1] 25 September, *Tom Pouce* (Palermo).

[2] E.g. 17 August, Farini to Depretis (*CC Lib. del Mezz.* vol. II, p. 99).

[3] Crispi, *Memoirs*, vol. I, p. 342 (edited after his death by T. Palamenghi-Crispi).

[4] 9 August, Depretis to Amari (*Carteggio di Amari*, ed. d'Ancona, vol. II, p. 115).

[5] 14 August, Professor Amari to Count Amari (*ibid.* p. 123).

[6] August, Martini to Castelli (*Carteggio di Castelli*, ed. Chiala, vol. I, p. 312).

[7] *Ibid.*

[8] Franchi deliberately omitted the most hostile and offensive remarks in La Farina's letters, but there are still plentiful references to possible 'civil war' between moderates and radicals; e.g. *Epistolario di La Farina*, ed. Franchi, p. 361 (17 July), p. 370 (19 July), p. 411 (22 August),

feeling every step of his way, trying to preserve the alliance, but never liking—Cavour had noticed this—to affront public opinion, and never being absolutely clear in his own mind what precisely he wanted or how to attain it. People generally agreed that his first motive was ambition;[1] but, if he had any strong views one way or the other, they were so shrouded in caution and indecision that not even his secretary quite knew what they were.[2]

The moment for a choice seemed to have come when on 19 August Garibaldi departed from Sicily on his lightning passage to Naples. Many Sicilians who had hitherto been willing to leave all to the dictator's wisdom now saw that, with him gone about other business, and Piedmontese laws being brought in one after the other by his deputy, they were likely to lose all say in settling the future status of their country if they did not vote soon.[3] Those who wanted only a loose union with Piedmont would have agreed with those who wanted outright annexation, in considering this matter of self-determination a point of 'face' and prestige. For these reasons Depretis hoped that he could proceed to hold a plebiscite in Sicily. He had understood from Garibaldi ever since July that annexation would not be delayed beyond the moment when the revolution no longer needed Sicily as a base for operations, and there was good reason to think that this time had come.

Perhaps Depretis did not realize that some arguments still told in the other direction. Even after the capture of Naples on 7 September, Sicily could still be regarded as a source of soldiers and war material; and Garibaldi knew that, once the moderates were in control of Sicily, they would hardly help their political opponents to carry out the very expedition on Rome which they dreaded above everything. Garibaldi's lack of confidence in Cavour's good faith had lately received further confirmation from a number of different directions. It had been feared since July that Cavour was actively preparing for either an alliance with the Bourbons or a *pronunciamento* at Naples, and both alternatives carried a threat to the radical policy of revolution. In August there had already

---

[1] 5 August, Pallavicino to Garibaldi (G. Pallavicino Trivulzio, *Le Memorie*, vol. III, 1882–95, p. 600).

[2] 20 September, Bargoni to Depretis (Archivio Depretis ASR).

[3] 6 September, *Il Regno d' Italia* (Palermo).

been the dissolution of Bertani's army and the prohibition of further recruitment of volunteers in the north. Garibaldi was therefore able to claim with good reason that he still needed his dictatorial powers in Sicily; and this claim proved to be justified in the end, since the island was required as a base and an insurance against defeat right up until the threat of Bourbon counter-attacks disappeared in October.

Nevertheless, Cavour had by now rendered all such discussion more or less academic, for he had taken his decision to march through the Papal States and stop Garibaldi's further advance. The plan for invasion was synchronized to take place along with an intensification of his propaganda campaign in Sicily, the intention of which was to weaken Garibaldi and if possible to delay him further. Meanwhile, Persano, it was hoped, might be able to take over the town of Naples with the troops he already had available on board ship in the bay. In so far as it affected Sicily, this plan included a well-subsidized attempt to turn public opinion towards demanding an immediate plebiscite. Depretis certainly connived at this, even if he took no very active part in it. His policy till now had been to put through a vote of annexation as soon as ever Garibaldi could be persuaded that the military situation allowed it; but now he was ready to go further, and to encourage the familiar 'spontaneous' movements as a means of bringing political pressure on the dictator.

Garibaldi had nominally given complete powers to Depretis, and was still trusting him implicitly: 'do whatever you think best and I shall approve it', so the dictator had written to him as lately as 10 August.[1] But it had been tacitly recognized that the annexation question was a reserved point which involved strategic considerations, and upon which therefore Garibaldi alone could pronounce. Depretis now led Cordova to believe that he was on the point of carrying out a palace revolution and announcing the plebiscite on his own responsibility.[2] Probably Cordova was wrong about this, whether intentionally or unintentionally. The prodictator knew that there were political as well as military considerations beyond his competence and his knowledge, and he must also have been aware that these political considerations would enter

---

[1] E. Librino, 'Agostino Depretis Prodittatore in Sicilia', *Nuova Antologia*, December 1930, p. 479.

[2] 24 August, Cordova to Cavour (*CC Lib. del Mezz.* vol. II, p. 138).

more and more into the situation as Cavour regained the initiative. Depretis retained at least a partial loyalty to Garibaldi, and knew that he could hardly survive at Palermo without it; but this did not make his position any more simple or his various responsibilities any easier to reconcile. Another element in the rising temperature of politics in the south was the arrival of that fiery radical Bertani to take up the post of first political adviser in Garibaldi's entourage. Bertani brought with him more confirmation that Cavour had all along been guilty of duplicity in regard to the southern revolution. The growing indignation, especially over the news of Farini's veto on further reinforcements, made it less likely that Garibaldi would allow a plebiscite, and also more difficult for Depretis to carry out anything like a palace revolution on his own. Only if he could persuade the dictator to agree could Depretis hope to emerge successfully from such an ambiguous position between two masters; and this would be the more difficult in that Bertani was hourly at Garibaldi's side, while he himself was falling ever farther behind.

Such, very roughly, was the position in the second half of August. A minute of the Turin cabinet on the 20th shows that, as soon as it became clear that Garibaldi was on the move again, Cavour decided to take special measures for obtaining the Sicilian plebiscite.[1] He explained to Depretis that annexation would solve everything, since, 'in the enthusiasm such an act would arouse, all these party bickerings and personal animosities would be forgotten'.[2] At once, says Amari, the prodictator became 'resolute for annexation, and even Crispi does not now disagree; though Depretis is afraid that Garibaldi in his exasperation may refuse if we first ask his permission, and may create a scandal if we do not ask him at all'. Evidently it was still possible for Crispi as well as Depretis to want quick and unconditional annexation. Even when Cavour began to move his troops towards the south, some of the radicals could still hope for a time that this meant, not antagonism, but grudging acceptance of Garibaldi's programme to conquer Rome.

Depretis had been forced to discard candour and honesty to the point of keeping not only his secretary, but even Crispi his chief minister, unaware that he might be working with Cordova to halt Garibaldi and

---

[1] E. Artom, *L' opera politica del Artom*, p. 278.
[2] 27 August, Cavour to Depretis (*CC Lib. del Mezz.* vol. II, p. 170).

bring the revolution to an end.[1] He later tried to maintain that he had allowed no one to oppose the dictator's wishes; but there is evidence that the opposition leaders had first secured his approval for their campaign,[2] and Crispi stated that some of the propaganda literature sent round the island betrayed by its seal and paper an origin in the prodictator's own office.[3] Depretis tried to keep at least the semblance of impartiality by retaining Crispi in office, even though the radical leader stood under Cavour's severe censure; but Crispi was not deceived by this, and Cavour took it as yet more evidence of untrustworthiness. The prodictator was evidently appreciated by neither side. Persano 'thought' that Depretis led the right wing of the revolutionary party, and believed that he sincerely wanted annexation, but 'not even this right-wing party offers our Piedmontese government any opening for interference in Sicily. The party of Depretis is nevertheless the only group which even goes so far as wishing us to interfere, and I think that we shall have to try and get on with it as best we can.'[4] On the 29th Asproni gave Crispi a quite different view of the situation, as seen by a radical: 'Depretis wishes to open a way to power for himself, in Turin. He has no liking for Cavour, but he will second him with this end in view. Cajoled by Cordova into the belief that he is winning Cavour's favour by listening to his advice and virtually surrendering his own will to him, he regards your achievements and your presence in the ministry with secret disapproval.'[5] The peacemaker was becoming suspected by both sides, and not without reason.

In the absence of a candid statement of policy by Depretis, political interest concentrates on the duel between Crispi and Cordova. Filippo Cordova was a very able Sicilian lawyer, in Cavour's opinion the most capable of all Sicilians, and later to be a minister at Turin. He was another of those Sicilian autonomists whom long residence in Turin had turned into what he himself styled 'the most Turinese of all

[1] 30 August, draft letter of Crispi to Garibaldi (ACP, f. 135); 20 September, draft of Crispi to Scelsi (ACP, b. 152).

[2] Ed. V. Cordova, *Filippo Cordova...Discorsi...Scritti...Ricordi*, 1889, vol. 1, p. 108.

[3] Crispi, *Memoirs*, vol. 1, p. 402.

[4] 4 September, Persano to M. d'Azeglio (Raccolta Azegliana MRR).

[5] 29 August, Asproni to Crispi (Crispi, *Memoirs*, vol. 1, pp. 402–3).

Turinese in the world'.[1] He had been an old colleague of Cavour's journalistic days, who had then become a civil servant in Piedmont. In June 1860 he had been sent to Palermo so that he might repair some of the harm done by La Farina in baiting Garibaldi. The dictator had received him well. Some of the other radicals, however, remembered against him how he had at first ridiculed as lunacy their plan for a Sicilian expedition,[2] and he was looked upon as one coming to take lucrative office under Garibaldi only when the fighting and the danger were over, perhaps even as an instrument to undermine the dictator's position.[3] At first they thought he was still something of an autonomist. But soon, when Depretis showed himself too scrupulous to indulge in blatantly disobeying Garibaldi, it was Cordova with whom Cavour most frequently corresponded, and who had obviously inherited the leadership of the plebiscite party. Cordova first tried to reach some understanding with the prodictator, and after frequent interviews the latter seems to have arranged to allow the circulation of annexationist propaganda in the provinces.[4] This plan of campaign was decided at a meeting on 1 August to which were called all those prominent citizens who wanted immediate annexation. At this meeting Cordova made special provision for those who still hoped to secure some local autonomy, and even for those who wanted annexation only upon special conditions laid down in advance. Attractive schemes of administrative decentralization were propounded for their benefit, and a speech by Farini on this subject was specially reprinted for wide distribution among those who liked to think of Palermo as a regional capital with a governor-general of its own.[5] This helped to win the alliance of a most important, probably the most important, body of opinion in the island.

Depretis, still trying to bridge the gap, at one point offered to make Cordova minister of finance; but the latter refused because Crispi still

[1] 1 September, Cordova to Castelli (*Carteggio di Castelli*, ed. Chiala, vol. I, p. 319).
[2] 9 July, Asproni to Crispi (Crispi, *Memoirs*, vol. I, p. 318).
[3] 16 October, *L' Unità Italiana* (Genoa), report from Palermo dated 5 October; 18 November (*ibid.*, report dated 9 November).
[4] 2 August, Natoli to La Farina (*Epistolario di La Farina*, ed. Franchi, vol. II, p. 388); V. Cordova, *Filippo Cordova*, vol. I, p. 108.
[5] 30 August, Cordova to Cavour (*CC Lib. del Mezz.* vol. II, p. 189).

held his post as minister for internal affairs. Cavour knew that 'Cordova is the only man capable of administering the finances of Sicily',[1] yet he specially instructed him on this occasion to refuse this appointment in the government,[2] and then went on accusing the revolutionary government of doing irreparable damage to the financial situation of the island. On receiving these instructions Cordova turned down all office involving political responsibility. But it was noticed that he had no scruples in taking salaried government employment in the shape of the biggest official legal post at Palermo; and this, moreover, did not prevent him still carrying on agitations all over the island against Garibaldi's published policy.[3] A fortnight before Cordova accepted this post, the same office had been—perhaps over-ostentatiously—refused by Crispi on the grounds that he had not come to Sicily in search of jobs and salaries. Cordova was a highly respectable person, who was carrying on what he thought to be the best policy by the best available means. But in admitting this, one must also point out that, in any comparison of worth, morality and self-sacrifice, the radicals do not emerge nearly so badly as some of the liberal historians were wont to assume.

Cordova's chief opponent in the government may have been a man of less common sense and less moderation, but he also had more vision, more energy and more loyalty than members of the liberal 'party of order'. Since the middle of July Crispi had again been in control of the pivotal department of the interior, an office which in Italy has usually carried enough powers of police and patronage and local gerrymandering to make it the real centrepiece of government. Crispi's views differed from those of many other radicals; and since until the middle of September he was to be the leading spokesman of this faction in Sicily, the singularities of his creed must be carefully distinguished. It is difficult to know which he held to be the greater enemy of united Italy, whether it was the narrow-minded Sicilian municipalists, or else that party at Turin which put the emphasis on a greater Piedmont. What is certain is that, unlike Mordini who succeeded as leader of the radicals when Crispi left to join Garibaldi at Naples, he did not try to compete

---

[1] 29 November, Cavour to Victor Emanuel (*CC Cavour-Nigra*, vol. IV, p. 280).
[2] 9 August, Cavour to Cordova (*CC Lib. del Mezz.* vol. II, p. 49).
[3] 1 September, Governor of Catania to Crispi (ACP, f. 143).

with Cordova for the alliance of those Sicilians who wanted special conditions of entry into the framework of united Italy. It was Crispi who had proposed and secured the proclamation of the Piedmontese *statuto*, when many others would have preferred to restore the Sicilian constitutional law of 1848. His *Precursore* strongly criticized the selfishness and foolishness of autonomy,[1] and was itself reviled by other papers for sacrificing Sicilian interests to the idea of a unitary state.[2]

Another common accusation against Crispi was that he was a republican, all the more dangerous for being so in secret. It is true that he was still friendly to Mazzini, but Crispi had finally renounced his own republicanism, and his hope now was that the king would overturn Cavour and unite all Italians round Garibaldi's revolutionary programme.[3] We have already noticed how Crispi's monarchism had reached the point of sending his friend La Varenne in secret to see the king, and of dispatching humble tributes of loyalty through Correnti. The radicals continually returned in this way to the hope that they could fall back on the monarchy against Cavour; and perhaps Cavour, by exploiting in emergencies the king's friendly relations with Garibaldi, gave Crispi too much confidence on this point and let him set too fast a pace. As for the federalists and autonomists, Crispi regarded them as mostly traitors,[4] and their policy as just playing the old French game to keep Italy weak and divided. There is no doubt that he backed the cause of annexation in the cabinet throughout August. Despite all La Farina said, Crispi's policy had been (so he wrote to Mazzini) that 'as to annexation, it will be established by vote as soon as this can be done without interfering with our operations on the Continent.... The separationists...now demand the convocation of the assembly and conditional annexation. But we shall overpower them in the end.'[5] Like Cavour, he did not want conditions and did not really want an assembly. He chiefly differed from the moderate liberals in wishing to wait for annexation until Garibaldi was well established on the continent, and in considering any differences about the method and timing of a vote as altogether subsidiary to military operations.

---

[1] E.g. 29 July, *Il Precursore*.   [2] 6 September, *Tom Pouce*.

[3] 23 July: 'let Cavour go on eating his artichoke; but as for our *Re galantuomo*, he has never been an egoist like that, and he wants what we are wanting', *Il Precursore*.

[4] 23 September, *ibid.*   [5] 31 July, Crispi to Mazzini (*Memoirs*, vol. I, pp. 363–4).

Crispi was to change these views only in the last days of August when he discovered that Depretis was in reality a 'lieutenant of Cavour' with ulterior motives, and that the annexation which he had himself also been striving for was secretly intended by Cordova simply as a means to cut short the revolution. He then realized that the moderates had in mind the continued alienation of Rome and Venice, and the triumph of a 'greater Piedmont' policy over that which aimed to build a new kingdom of Italy. The cause of immediate annexation thus threatened Crispi personally with political defeat and possibly with a return to exile in England. Suddenly it dawned on him how Cavour had discovered a way to recapture the initiative after four months of waiting upon Garibaldi's good will. Sicilian politics therefore took on a new virulence at the end of August, especially with the arrival of yet more imperious envoys from Cavour like Casalis and Bottero, and of other prominent radicals like Asproni and Friscia.

Even more decisive in causing Crispi's change of front was the suspicion that Rome might after all be out of Garibaldi's reach. So far the plausible assumption had been that they would march on Rome and thence offer Victor Emanuel the crown of Italy. This may have been foolishly optimistic, but surely no more so than Crispi's sustaining faith which had originally overcome Garibaldi's reluctance to set sail for Sicily. Crispi had built his political programme on the knowledge that 'Garibaldi had sworn he would not sheathe his sword till he had accomplished the double mission of achieving the independence and the unification of Italy....He therefore does not wish to compromise the cause of unity by premature annexation of Sicily'.[1] The radicals firmly believed that 'the achievement of unity does not depend on an immediate annexation, or on the method of annexation, but just on Garibaldi and his valiant army'[2]—that is to say, on the conquest of Rome. Now Garibaldi had hitherto reckoned on the Pope leaving Rome just as in 1848–9, and on the practical certainty that the French garrison then would also leave, since it would have nothing left to protect. Many of Cavour's party, too, had believed or hoped as much. Cavour himself and Napoleon III had regarded this as a possible outcome of events, and even in the Papal Curia there were some who favoured a flight from

[1] 23 July, Crispi to La Varenne (ACP, b. 140).
[2] Bozzo, *Sull' annessione al regno Italiano*, p. 17.

Rome. But at the end of August circumstances were changing; the likelihood was that after all the Pope would stay, and that additional French reinforcements might even be sent to defend him. If this likelihood was verified it would probably make Garibaldi's main project impossible.

It was such developments which eventually made Crispi change over to join those of the radicals and the autonomists who wanted delayed annexation by an elected assembly. Nothing was certain yet, but as Rome receded a little from the foreground of the picture, he came to recognize that delay was requisite and that the timing and the manner of a popular vote were more important than he had imagined. Immediate annexation would mean surrendering the one place where the revolution was firmly entrenched, long before that revolution had reached its goal. In other words it would signify the defeat of the revolutionaries by the conservatives. The failure to organize a new Italy round Rome would make what was happening seem as if it were no more than the conquest of other Italian provinces by Piedmont. Crispi was not far wrong in thinking that to make Sicily something like a province of Piedmont was the surest way of forcing by reaction a revulsion of feeling towards separatism. An immediate and unqualified annexation would in this manner threaten his dream of a united Italy.[1] Some of the other radicals had been even quicker to see this point, and had already begun to seek an opportunist alliance with their enemies of yesterday, the autonomists who wanted a deliberative assembly. There was no deep logic about this, but in the sudden collapse of all their great hopes, it was a question of a last-minute defence to salvage something. Instead of being accepted on their own estimation as conquerors, king-makers negotiating on equal terms with Cavour, the radicals were finding themselves faced with the prospect of being cast off again by their countrymen as pariahs. It would have been strange if, after such a sudden change of fortune, they had not been thrown off their balance.

[1] 10 October, *Il Precursore*.

CHAPTER XIII

CAVOUR FORCES DEPRETIS TO A CHOICE: 1–8 SEPTEMBER

Once Cavour had reached the decision—with whatever justice—that he would gain nothing from an alliance with the revolutionary forces, once he no longer needed Garibaldi as a stalking-horse, it was natural that he should do his utmost to crush the revolution everywhere. In the north his army was gradually moving into position, ready to repel the 'unprovoked aggression' from Papal mercenaries which he had timed to take place on 8 September. In the south he continued with added vigour his attempt to coax or coerce the Sicilian government into holding an immediate plebiscite. It was his hope that the concert of, Europe would consider such a popular vote to be a valid excuse for adding yet another province to his master's kingdom.

For three months now Cavour had been trying to engineer this plebiscite. He had first employed La Farina as his instrument, with lamentable results. Then he had hoped to achieve something by the more refined methods of the tactful Depretis, only to find him too scrupulous in respecting Garibaldi's wishes to make any overt move. So he next turned to another less scrupulous official of Garibaldi's, and tried out Cordova's scheme of promoting a big propaganda campaign all through the provinces, to work up the appearance or the reality of a popular agitation which might be used to force Depretis to take sides. Towards the end of August he decided to send in reinforcement a Turin newspaper editor, Giovanni Bottero, to present Depretis with an actual ultimatum.[1] The intention was (as one of the more influential government newspapers unambiguously and rather naïvely put it) to 'win over that rich and noble province of Sicily so that its resources may be employed for the needs of Italy'.[2] Bottero was one of Garibaldi's fellow-townsmen, a faithful henchman of Cavour, but with one foot in the camp of that dubious parliamentary Left-centre which Cavour

[1] 23 August, Cabinet minute, E. Artom, *L' opera politica del Senatore I. Artom*, p. 279.

[2] 4 September, *L' Annessione*, quoting *Il Corriere Mercantile*.

husbanded so skilfully. This man was sent to demand from Depretis a plebiscite by 15 September, and for this purpose he was armed with the threat that otherwise the Sicilian government would be treated by Turin as 'an adversary'.[1] Moreover, Depretis, though nettled by Cavour's abruptness and lack of *finesse*, had to face the compelling argument that Bottero was the long-awaited bearer of a loan, part of which was payable only if the prodictator cut clean away from the dictator's policy of procrastination.

Under this pressure Depretis agreed to fix a term for annexation,[2] and had to hope that a threat of resignation might secure Garibaldi's consent to this. He himself was convinced that a plebiscite was now possible and desirable. The passage of time had only tended to reinforce the case for immediate annexation among the undecided middle of Sicilian opinion. Even among those who almost automatically followed Garibaldi's wishes, there were many who in his absence just assumed his consent to a course of action which carried the greatest promise of tranquillity and stable government. These were the very people whose non-partisan adherence to common sense ultimately decided most of the successive political crises of Sicily in this year. The dictator had at first asked them for delay, but he was now far away and busy about other things. Surely he was now less in need of a respite, and perhaps he had even forgotten all about them. Bottero's ultimatum, on the other hand, was backed by the certainty that failure to comply with what he asked would make Sicily be considered by Piedmont as an enemy. Crispi and his long-term plans thus began to appear ever more obviously the chief obstacle between them and a return to peace and order.[3]

Cavour's project was simple; but he was not free from criticism over the manner of its execution. Depretis had done his best to reconcile

---

[1] 26 August, La Farina to Cordova (Carte Cordova MRR); 26 August, La Farina to Gramignani (*Lettere di Cavour*, ed. Chiala, vol. VI, p. 582).

[2] 1 September, Professor Amari to Count Amari (*La Sicilia nel Risorgimento Italiano*, 1931, p. 119); 4 September, *Il Diritto*; and Scelsi's remarks in *L' Annessione* of 6 November.

[3] Undated letter to Crispi: 'for my part I think that the Cavourians have taken this step in order to alarm the quietists and impel them against the policy of Garibaldi, in other words against you, Crispi, whom they consider an obstacle between them and the annexation which they equate with tranquillity' (ACP, b. 156, no. 78).

radicals and liberals and to work by compromise; but Cavour had deliberately acted to make compromise impossible, and had seemed to care little for the damage thereby inflicted on the growth of good will and mutual confidence among Italians. Depretis and not Cavour was here the exponent of a *juste milieu*. If Cavour's method had been quicker and more certain in achieving its aim, there would have been less cause for complaint; but writing to Cavour on 1 September Depretis squarely blamed the prime minister for any delay in settling the Sicilian question.

If only you had helped me as you had promised, things in Sicily would be better than they actually are, and annexation would by now be an accomplished fact, and the Neapolitan business much nearer to a happy ending....

I may incidentally assure Your Excellency that all my ministers without exception have been agreed on hurrying up annexation....If there now seem to be obstacles in the way of this annexation, not least among the reasons for this is the abandonment in which you have left me for the last forty days.[1]

Depretis never had occasion to address Garibaldi in such a tone of protest as he here employed towards Cavour. Perhaps this letter may in part be explained as an attempt by the prodictator to find a scapegoat for his own inability to fulfil the tentative programme he had settled with Cavour on 14 July; perhaps, too, there is something in it of a mere angry *tu quoque* in rejoinder to Bottero's accusation of weakness. Nevertheless, there was plenty of justification for taxing Cavour with errors which had arisen directly from his reliance upon partisan and inaccurate information. If the politicians of Turin had not underestimated the difficulties of government in Sicily, the liberals by now might have won, and won without splitting the patriots into warring factions. Once again there is the implication that Cavour was more concerned to beat the radicals than to create a united Italy.

It must be admitted that Cavour had left Depretis with no information about his own larger policy, and without any helpful advice on how to overcome Garibaldi's objections to an immediate plebiscite. In particular Cavour had had no troops to spare for Sicily, and sent

[1] 1 September, Depretis to Cavour (G. Maraldi, 'La rivoluzione siciliana del 1860', *Rassegna Storica del Risorgimento*, 1932, p. 515; *CC Lib. del Mezz.* vol. II, pp. 208–9).

none of the arranged quotas of police or money until it was too late for this to have the political effect he intended. He did not appreciate that the tax system there had quite broken down, and that the problems of keeping order and rebuilding the administration were quite as urgent as the political question of annexation which filled the picture seen from Turin. Depretis had asked for two hundred policemen as an earnest of what Cavour had promised him in July, but Cavour said he could not afford a quarter of this number, and he purposely delayed sending these until he had more certain news of the plebiscite.[1] There was also a consignment of cannon and rifles which did not arrive as promised. The explanation cannot have been simply that Piedmont could not spare the help that was required, because later in the year four hundred policemen were produced for the south within a few hours of Farini asking for them. The basic reason was political. Cavour did not trust Depretis. To this extent he had himself to thank when the latter's efforts on behalf of annexation went askew. Depretis was surprised and annoyed that the Piedmontese were so lax in helping Sicily and conciliating Garibaldi. It was pointed out that even what little they did do to help could have been done with more promptness and less irritation.[2] The prodictator had been striving to improvise food, clothing and arms for twenty thousand men, though Sicily was a poor country which had just passed through civil war and revolution; but when Cavour was appealed to for a loan, this could only be provided after a month's delay, and then was hedged about with conditions which made it not an aid to Garibaldi but a weapon for his overthrow. The result was that, far from finding such belated help a contribution towards the desired aim of immediate annexation, the patriots in Sicily were divided even more than before. The radicals were presented with evidence which could only mean that Cavour did not want the revolution to succeed too easily or too well. The fiction of a common front was abruptly disproved, and the old agitation and faction was revived just at the

[1] 17 August, Farini to Depretis (*CC Lib. del Mezz.* vol. II, p. 99); 31 August, Governor Mathieu of Cagliari to Depretis, that at last he could send the twenty-five policemen and two officers (Archivio Depretis ASR).

[2] 3 and 28 August, Professor Amari to Count Amari (*Carteggio di Amari*, ed. d'Ancona, vol. II, pp. 111–12, 127–9); 21 August, draft of letter from Depretis to Count Amari (Archivio Depretis ASR).

1 3

moment when—so claimed Crispi's friends—the country had been returning to something like peace and normality.[1] Crispi could not deny the lack of law and order; but he accused Cavour's party of deliberately provoking and exaggerating disorder, and then exaggerating reports of it, so that people would blame Garibaldi's government and look to Piedmont for deliverance.

Depretis himself was the first to complain when Bottero arrived in Palermo with instructions compiled by people who had little idea of the true situation in Sicily. In his letter of protest to Cavour, the prodictator reproved the prime minister for 'fallacious judgements on Sicilian affairs, since these affairs cannot be weighed up properly from afar, especially by *ex parte* observers'. An ultimatum for a plebiscite could hardly do much good, because the prodictator was already persuaded in his own mind that Sicily should be annexed as soon as possible; and Cavour's new envoy found immediately that he was preaching to the converted. In fact, Bottero's arrival was likely to become a positive hindrance, since both Garibaldi and Sicilian public opinion would resent the implication that annexation was not freely willed but rather imposed on them by Turin.[2] Depretis even asserted that the effect of his arrival would probably be to ruin any chance of effecting this annexation in the near future.[3] When Bottero told Depretis to rid himself of Crispi, the advice was indignantly rejected: 'do write and tell them at Turin to stop harping on these questions of personalities. So long as annexation is carried out, what does it matter whether this is done by Crispi or by another?' The only result of such advice was to make Crispi suspicious of Depretis, and more ready to take counter-action. Bottero thus brought with him not peace, only further cause of division; and it was upon division, not reconciliation, that Cavour and Cordova were now bent. In a letter of 4 September Cordova said that he was not working in collusion with Depretis over his propaganda campaign in the provinces; but he added that he was going to persevere with his plan to force the prodictator's hand, and 'if Garibaldi does not agree, we are ready to do anything to obtain what he is unwilling to grant'.[4] There was not much room for compromise here.

---

[1] 11 September, *Il Precursore*.
[2] 1 September, Bottero to Cavour (*CC Lib. del Mezz.* vol. II, pp. 209–10).
[3] 4 September, Cordova to Cavour (*ibid.* p. 240).   [4] *Ibid.* pp. 241–2.

At the end of August and throughout the first week in September Depretis was desperately trying to avoid an irreparable breach inside his cabinet. His chief problem was with Crispi, who was now in a most equivocal position. As late as 24 August the ministry was apparently still agreed on prompt annexation, and Amari said that Crispi did not demur to this.[1] But Depretis and the ministers were afraid that Garibaldi might disapprove when he heard of what they proposed. On the 28th Amari told how Crispi was the only minister not 'impatient' for annexation, yet that he did not openly oppose it, but just raised obstacles to create delay. The arrival of Bottero then was a final cause of division. On the 30th, Crispi's bewilderment at the prodictator's apparent *volte face* was clearly expressed in a letter to Garibaldi. 'Sicily is in the hands of one of Cavour's substitutes', he wrote. 'Immediate annexation is being openly discussed, and it is said that you not only desire it, but have ordered it yourself. Can this be possible? Let me know.'[2] Pending the dictator's reply, Crispi did not dare to give way to public recriminations. He was beginning to realize that he might have been caught in the wrong camp, but he could not change sides until he was more certain of what Garibaldi and Depretis each intended. Amari wrote on 1 September:

in the cabinet we are all agreed, even Crispi. And since public opinion must accuse Crispi always, they have now chosen to accuse him of wanting to hurry up annexation for reasons of ambition. I wish we could get it over quickly and so put an end to this pandemonium into which Sicily is rapidly falling. They are expecting an armed demonstration tomorrow, though I cannot tell you yet which party is responsible for this.[3]

Depretis, too, confirmed that Crispi stood 'fully in agreement' with the other ministers for immediate annexation.[4]

There are a number of points to remember when trying to identify and explain Crispi's attitude at this moment. He had always strongly

---

[1] 24 August, Professor Amari to Count Amari (*Carteggio di Amari*, ed. d'Ancona, vol. II, pp. 126–7).

[2] 30 August, Crispi to Garibaldi (*Memoirs*, vol. I, p. 403).

[3] *La Sicilia nel Risorgimento Italiano*, 1931, p. 121.

[4] 1 September, Depretis to Garibaldi (A. Colombo, *Contributo alla storia della prodittatura di Depretis*, 1911, p. 17); as late as 4 September we have corroborative evidence from Amari (*Carteggio di Amari*, ed. d'Ancona, vol. II, p. 131).

advocated the union of north and south Italy, and had never wanted delay for the sake of delay. Nor had he at any time been opposed to a plebiscite, whether or not this was to be held in conjunction with the deliberations of an elected assembly; and he was in fact shortly to sign a decree authorizing a vote by plebiscite alone. His leading principle had been to subordinate everything to the development of Garibaldi's strategy. Ever since the revolutionary army had left Sicily on 19 August he had been out of touch with what was happening at the front, and would therefore have been surprised but not wholly incredulous when assured that the dictator now wanted an immediate vote in the island. Perhaps for a moment Garibaldi's astonishingly swift movement up the toe of Italy may have convinced him that an immediate plebiscite could no longer hinder the strategy of the war. Such at least was Amari's interpretation of Crispi's position.[1] He could not yet foresee all the obstacles in the way of an immediate march on Rome; and there also seemed a reasonable chance that Cavour might be bluffing the diplomats again, and might be ready in the case of Rome as of Sicily to 'pleurer et prener'. One more reason for Crispi's relative quiescence was the fact that Sicilian public opinion, which had never liked the idea of unnecessary prolongation of provisional and makeshift government, was becoming less and less friendly towards the radical programme.[2] Most of his radical friends had gone off to Naples with the fighting forces, and he therefore felt the more isolated. His intention now was just to play for time while Garibaldi was consulted, and meanwhile to hold his place in the cabinet for as long as this was possible without prejudice to his political conscience or his allegiance to the dictator.[3]

All depended on what Garibaldi should decide. On 1 September Captain Piola left with an explanatory message from Depretis to the general, while Palermo was left tensely expectant as to what the reply would be. The prodictator hoped that Piola would secure permission to hold a vote forthwith. 'Without the security for the future which

---

[1] 7 October, Amari to Cartwright (*ibid.* vol. II, p. 135).

[2] 1 September, Bagnasco to Crispi: 'I have many letters from Palermo, and they tell of the general indignation against you and how your very life is in danger' (ACP, b. 152); 7 September, Bargoni to Calvino (Curàtulo, *Garibaldi, Vittorio Emanuele, Cavour*, p. 382).

[3] 20 September, Crispi to Scelsi (ACP, b. 152).

annexation would bring,' he explained, 'the capitalists and property-owning classes will lend us no money here. I could of course compel them, but the means at our disposal are slender, and it might compromise us abroad.'[1] Piola was away for four days, but there was little remission of the struggle in his absence. On 3 September, Depretis held one of the receptions in which he used to sound the opinion of Palermo society; and it was noted that Bottero and the Piedmontese consul were present. The latter was being used by Cavour as an intermediary for sending instructions about the plebiscite campaign to his agents in various parts of Sicily.[2] As for Bottero, he had recently been having further consultations with members of the government,[3] and was living with Depretis in the Royal Palace.[4] It was known all over Sicily that, from this august address, he was carrying on propaganda for annexation.[5]

In the first days of September the radical cause was reinforced by the arrival at Palermo of Nicotera and his expedition. Baron Nicotera was a man more Mazzinian than Mazzini himself, a man who until the revolution broke out in Sicily this year had been confined in a Bourbon prison. He had then formed a contingent of volunteers in Tuscany, but this had been captured by Cavour and shipped off to Sicily as to a sort of isolation hospital. Depretis in Palermo then refused this contingent permission to follow on after Garibaldi until their more republican officers had resigned. Nicotera was so incensed with this treatment that, against Mazzini's wishes, he refused to accept Garibaldi's monarchical programme.[6] His presence in Sicily for those few days was hardly calculated to aid Depretis in his task of reconciliation, and Cavour's party took it as evidence that the republicans might at any moment throw off the mask and repudiate their contingent loyalty to the throne. But Nicotera was too bitter, too much of an extremist, and too un-

[1] 1 September, Depretis to Garibaldi (Colombo, *Contributo alla storia*, p. 17).

[2] 4 September, Consul's report to Cavour, quoted in Maraldi, *Rassegna Storica*, 1932, p. 566.

[3] 2 September, Depretis to Crispi (ACP, f. 138).

[4] 18 September, *L' Opinione*, report from Palermo dated 7 September.

[5] 16 September, *La Perseveranza*, report from Messina dated 9 September.

[6] 12 September, Mazzini to Caroline Stansfeld (*Epistolario*, vol. XLII, p. 67); 24 September, *La Gazzetta del Popolo* (Turin) gives Nicotera's letter of 13 September to *Il Lampo* (Milan), saying that he never had shouted and never would shout 'Viva il Re'.

trustworthy to be given much confidence by the other revolutionary leaders, and he had little influence in the south during the remainder of this year.

The activity of these days of waiting was described by Professor Amari, who was now in the cabinet. 'We are taking every step we can to push through the vote, and also to see that we secure a majority for annexation, though without letting it appear that the government is exerting any pressure. In any case', he continued ingenuously, 'how could we exert pressure? All the soldiers have gone off to the front and the national guard only expresses the state of public opinion.'[1] On the 4th Amari himself drew up a form of proclamation for the plebiscite, so as to have all in readiness for Piola's return: his draft was approved by Depretis 'and by my colleagues', which presumably included Crispi. It is interesting and important to note that, at the same time, the cabinet approved another complementary document outlining the special franchises and privileges which Sicily should be given under the new regime from Turin; this document, too, was drawn up by Amari, and the intention of its author was to specify in more detail the concessions which he understood Cavour was ready to make in answer to demands for local self-government.[2] Some of the autonomists were flattered in this way with expectation of favours to come if only they would vote for annexation unconditionally. Amari's second document was afterwards to be conveniently forgotten, but he himself at the time wrote it in complete good faith.

Outside the cabinet room the state of agitation in Palermo looked dangerous. This agitation ran at a deeper level than mere politics, as one can see from the fact that it continued much the same whether under the Bourbons, under Garibaldi, or under Cavour after November. Some people were always ready to exploit disturbances for private interest, and to others a riot was as good as a play. Sometimes the successive *piazza* demonstrations seemed to be on the point of merging into a class war like that which had been disturbing the big estates of the interior. The Marchese Torrearsa feared that private passions were in this way creating a conflict from which even civil war might

---

[1] 4 September, Professor Amari to Count Amari (*Carteggio di Amari*, ed. d'Ancona, vol. II, p. 131).

[2] 7 October, Amari to Cartwright (*ibid.* p. 137).

result.[1] La Farina's example had thus been followed by various agitators who exploited political disagreements to incite the mob to violent action.[2] Each political group in turn was claiming to have genuine popular feeling on its own side and to be opposed by merely artificial demonstrations from the other. That is to say, each put its own interpretation on the facts. One report thus ascribed this febrile agitation to the frustrated wish of everyone for early union with Piedmont.[3] Another gave a different explanation:

on 5 September Palermo was a real battlefield. . . .Petitions of all varieties rained in from every quarter. Some wanted annexation today, others only on Garibaldi's arrival in Naples, and others after the conquest of Venice; but the greater number wanted annexation only when Garibaldi should find it most convenient. . . .Round these petitions there joined up demonstrations, and the public peace was in real danger.[4]

There was further disagreement on the method to be used. Some people wanted a plebiscite. Eight hundred others signed a petition for annexation to be carried out as soon as convenient by means of an assembly.[5] The middle and upper levels of society were naturally frightened at the prospect of lower-class unrest, and hoped for a quick resolution of the political impasse such as would guarantee security and peace. Some preferred conditional annexation, others unconditional, some a plebiscite and some an assembly; but, even for those who normally had no strong political views, annexation at almost any price was likely to offer very solid advantages. Only an explicit pronouncement by Garibaldi could at this stage have persuaded the majority to favour further postponement.

Depretis was waiting anxiously to hear from Piola that Garibaldi approved his change of mind, since on this the success or failure of his whole mission depended. When Piola at last caught the advancing army at Fortino on 4 September, Garibaldi was fully taken up with

---

[1] Ed. De Stefano, 'Documenti del Risorgimento negli archivi privati di Trapani', *Rassegna Storica*, 1942, p. 799.

[2] 4 and 6 September, *Tom Pouce* (Palermo).

[3] 12 September, *La Perseveranza*, quoting the Palermo correspondent of *L' Opinione* in a report dated 7 September.

[4] 11 September, *Il Precursore*.

[5] 4 September (Archivio Depretis ASR).

directing the headlong march on Naples, and he hurriedly dictated a reply to confirm that Depretis might act in whatever manner he thought fit. Evidently Garibaldi was still convinced that Cavour either would not or could not stand out against the revolution. But Bertani happened to overhear what had been said, and at once remonstrated that it was tantamount to abdication: the annexation of Sicily would cut Garibaldi off from his base, and after Farini's circular against the volunteers there was no guarantee that Cavour would not use this to hinder rather than to help. The dictator therefore altered his reply to the Sicilian government, and on second thoughts wrote instead: 'I am always disposed to do what you recommend, but on this one point of annexation I think that Bonaparte must wait a little longer. I prefer that all should be done simultaneously when we reach Rome.'[1] In principle Garibaldi was never anything but in favour of annexation, and moreover he wanted it with no conditions attached so long as this did not mean that the revolution had been defeated and brought to a close. But he instinctively felt that Cavour was playing a deep and reprehensible game. To his simple mind, the policy of annexation seemed to have been designed by Napoleon and then imposed on a not unwilling Cavour just in order to pull the fangs of the red revolutionaries. Bertani had amplified and exploited this suspicion, and Garibaldi therefore, on thinking again, drew up this unequivocal negative, adding like a true dictator that Depretis should expel half a dozen of those troublesome conspirators who were disturbing Sicily in his absence.

When Piola arrived back at Palermo with this answer on 5 September, he found the town more disturbed than ever. Crispi and Cordova had just been having a public scene with a brisk exchange of insults. Cordova had been circularizing the urban and provincial authorities in the island to persuade them that they should send in reports of the widespread desire for a plebiscite, and some local officials had replied that Crispi threatened them with expulsion if they did any such thing. On the 4th Crispi had been openly charged with this in front of Depretis, and denied all knowledge of it. As a counter-charge he accused Cordova of conspiracy against the government.[2] Both parties to this controversy

[1] A. Bertani, *Ire politiche d' oltre tomba*, pp. 74–7.
[2] 7 September, Sardinian consul to Cavour, quoted by Maraldi, *Rassegna Storica*, 1932, p. 567.

were so self-righteous about their own inaccuracy, and so deaf to any information or advice which did not come from their immediate friends, that neither can be considered a reliable witness as to the state of public opinion. Crispi, conceited as ever, thus described the atmosphere of mutual recrimination and the reception of Piola's message from Garibaldi: 'the ministers and the prodictator were confused and frightened. Only the minister for internal affairs remained impassive, saying that the agitation in the town was factitious, and that immediate annexation would be dangerous. But he stood alone, and it was even proposed that the annexation should be ordered in despite of Garibaldi's opposition.'[1] No decision was taken yet on this proposal, although there was general agreement that Garibaldi's answer was unacceptable. It was decided that they dared not publish his reply, on the grounds that publication would merely prolong the uncertain situation in which the government had a dual responsibility to two incompatible persons and programmes. We may guess, on the contrary, that its publication would have converted many of the waverers to Garibaldi's policy of postponement; but this would still have left Depretis with all the difficulties of provisional government, and irreparably at odds with Cavour.

This rebellion in the cabinet against the dictator's ruling compelled Crispi finally to make up his mind. Early the following day, at 7 a.m. on 6 September, he presented his resignation. 'Depretis pleaded with me again and again to stay at my post, but I was adamant. The conduct of Bottero and Cordova has been such that I made their expulsion from the island a condition of my return to power....And so Depretis is trying to find my successor, although nobody wants the job owing to the difficulty of keeping public order with three thousand escaped prisoners still at large.' The day continued in general scenes of agitation. 'An immense crowd of people walked up and down the Toledo bewailing my resignation and demanding the dismissal of the other ministers.'[2] These demonstrators carried the slogan of 'we want annexation, but only when Garibaldi says so'.[3] Later in the day Crispi sent off a personal messenger to tell Garibaldi what was happening. The man chosen was Paolo Orlando, one of the famous family of radical-minded industrialists from Sampierdarena. He was to explain to the

[1] 7 September, Crispi to 'Luigi' (Orlando?; ACP, b. 152).   [2] *Ibid.*
[3] 11 September, *L' Opinione*, report from Palermo.

dictator that Crispi had resigned because 'Depretis had promised Cavour to secure the plebiscite. And between you and Cavour, between Italy and the foreigner, I had no doubts about my choice.'[1] Crispi's statement continued:

it is not true that the country really desires immediate annexation. The communal councils have either completely disregarded the pressure brought to bear by our enemies, or have voted in an entirely different direction.... I regret not to have been able to join you, but Depretis forbade my going, fearing I should enlighten you on the true state of affairs.... From this distance I can only warn you not to believe the prophecies of imaginary danger in case you are really opposed to annexation. Sicily will obey your slightest sign. If Depretis, Cordova, Bottero and their helpers had not stirred up the country, no one in Sicily would have given a thought to immediate annexation. Drive out the agitators, issue a programme that shall clearly set forth your views, and the country will at once be quieted.

Crispi was a ferocious partisan, and we cannot know whether this interpretation of public opinion was accurate. But it would be hard to say either that the author of these words disbelieved what he said, or indeed that they do not contain at least a good deal of the truth.

While Orlando went to state Crispi's case, Piola was sent back again by Depretis to Garibaldi with a warning that five of the ministers would have to resign if a popular vote were not taken at once.[2] Further delay, said the prodictator, would make the country ungovernable. He too, but only vaguely, hinted at resignation. He insisted that he was under no pressure from Cavour, but had reached this decision by an independent study of affairs in Sicily. Answering one of Crispi's objections, he stressed that there would be plenty of time between the vote itself and the actual surrender of power 'during which no one could trouble us'. He concluded by saying that he would have come in person to put this case, but feared what would happen while he was away. Bargoni, his secretary, had even thought for a moment that Cordova and Torrearsa were purposely trying to entice Depretis to go and see Garibaldi, so that they might then use the mob in his absence to carry

[1] 6 September, Crispi's draft (ACP, f. 135); the English edition of Crispi's *Memoirs* gives the date wrongly as 10 September, vol. I, pp. 407–8; 6 September, Sacchi from Palermo to Bertani: 'this prodictator is more for Cavour than for Garibaldi' (MRR).

[2] 6 September, Depretis to Garibaldi (Archivio Depretis ASR and ABM).

themselves into power. This fact will serve as a reminder that Depretis was by no means entirely identified with the party of Cordova, just as he never succeeded at any point in winning Cavour's confidence. Bargoni states in a letter of the 7th that Depretis never would have decreed the plebiscite without Garibaldi's prior consent, and this belief was probably correct.[1] But at the same time the prodictator also believed that the welfare of Sicily and his own future career depended on his ability to secure that consent.

The day of 7 September brought a slight relaxation of tension. Crispi wrote to Garibaldi once more, this time to recall the radical programme of 22 June when the dictator had preached to the Palermo municipality on the text of 'no annexation before Rome'. Crispi earnestly besought him not to weaken when so near to the consummation of the whole *risorgimento*.[2] A second letter was written by the radical minister to Luigi Orlando, the brother of Paolo, which indicates that the prodictator had momentarily yielded a point to keep Crispi from open opposition while Garibaldi was consulted. 'Today the agitation has changed a little, though it is not exhausted. Cordova and Bottero have disappeared. Depretis is now of the opinion that annexation cannot be immediate, and that we must wait.'[3] On Crispi's suggestion Bottero had been requested to leave Sicily,[4] even if another of Cavour's agents, Casalis, had just arrived to take his place.[5] Crispi was now able to admit that his own resignation had been little more than a point of personal dignity, in that 'Depretis had preferred Cordova to me'.[6]

The prodictator had known his man, as he was again to do twenty-five years later when Crispi was once more his minister for internal

[1] 7 September, Bargoni to Calvino (ACM, no. 2988).

[2] 7 September, Crispi to Garibaldi (ACP, f. 135); at the same time he wrote to Depretis insisting that he be allowed to resign, and Depretis in reply begged him not to abandon his post but to come and discuss new proposals (*ibid.* f. 138).

[3] 7 September, Crispi to Orlando (ACP, b. 152).

[4] 11 September, Sardinian consul to Cavour, quoted by Maraldi, *Rassegna Storica*, 1932, p. 569.

[5] 7 September, Bargoni to Calvino: 'Casalis arrived yesterday from Turin and is preaching annexation like a man possessed....He and Sant' Onofrio are most active' (ACM).

[6] 7 September, Crispi to Correnti (ACP, f. 135).

affairs and he premier of all Italy. Depretis feared not only Garibaldi's resentment but also the mischief Crispi might make at Naples if allowed to resign, and probably he also still valued the other's tremendous drive and energy too much. This was why he made sufficient concessions to tide over the next day or two. 'I am tired, absolutely worn out', wrote Depretis, 'and but little satisfied with people and the march of events in Sicily.' It was greatly to his credit that, two months after La Farina's expulsion, he still held at least the partial allegiance of both radicals and moderates; but the cracks were now widening, and the effort to be tactful in so many directions simultaneously was proving too strenuous. With desperate cleverness he held out the bribe to Bertani's 'Committee in Aid of Garibaldi' that, until the plebiscite was held, it would be hard to find the expected contribution to their funds: 'for unfortunately our affairs in Sicily are still much upset by agitation, and if the country does not emerge quickly from the crisis, it will be difficult, very difficult indeed, to restore the finances'.[1] In two further letters dated this same 7 September, Depretis repeated to his *carissimo amico* Garibaldi an admonition that further postponement would but play into the hands of 'the few but busy separatists'; whereas on the other hand, a plebiscite would remove uncertainty about the future, and so would restore enough credit and financial stability to permit a better flow of military equipment for the volunteers.[2] It may be imagined how puzzled Garibaldi must have been when presented with such contradictory pieces of advice.

A cross-section of Palermo opinion in the newspapers of 8 September shows that there was still a wide divergence of views. The *Annessione* and the *Precursore* took their usual opposite stands, the one against Crispi, the other for him. It was clear that the radicals were unpopular both with those who wanted quick annexation by plebiscite, and also with the municipalists who resented their authoritarian and premature introduction of Piedmontese laws. The quasi-Mazzinian *Unità Italiana*

[1] 7 September, Depretis to Macchi (Archivio Depretis ASR).

[2] 7 September, Depretis to Garibaldi: 'all I want is to come and talk to you...for I am sure I can be of as much help to you at the front as here. You may rest assured, however, that while I remain in Sicily, I shall do my utmost so that your intentions and your orders are exactly executed'; he also mentioned 'a certain bettering of conditions in the country, especially in its financial situation' (ABM).

of Palermo noted a general rejoicing after Crispi's resignation, and commented that the high hopes once entertained of him had now been destroyed. But its sister paper, Quadrio's *Unità Italiana* of Genoa, carried a quite different picture in a report from its Palermo correspondent of this very same day: 'public opinion is on Crispi's side.... The better sort of people [*i buoni*] reproach Depretis with not publishing Garibaldi's reply, which would have decided the whole question and tranquillized people's minds.'[1] The *Cicala Italiana* expressed astonishment that the same old agitation for annexation had so soon begun all over again, and exclaimed that Cavour was going on the wrong tack if he really wanted national unity: 'everyone who opposes the will of our liberator is putting party spirit before the good of the country, and stands for opinions which are false and which will have unfortunate results for us'.[2] *Tom Pouce* tilted against both parties, against Cordova's plot for an immediate plebiscite, and against Crispi's intention to vote upon annexation only when Garibaldi wished it.

They both represent factions in disguise.... We do not deny that there must exist a right of petition under a dictatorship, but we cannot tolerate the jesuitical way in which people are going around houses and shops to extort signatures for a petition which must be unintelligible to most of those who read it.... It is for us to await the moment of our complete redemption. ...Either the annexation must be put off, or else, if it is to come soon, then it should be attended by conditions.[3]

In these remarks we again meet the conviction of the autonomists that Crispi stood for an attitude not identical with that of Garibaldi, but that he rather represented a faction whose proclamation of the Piedmontese *statuto* revealed an intention to by-pass Sicilians and impose on them an alien law. If people were impatient with the extreme radicals that is to say, it was often because by a mistaken analysis they were thought to be more Cavourian than Cavour. Sicily now had a free press for the first time in twelve years, and after this lapse of time most of the writers perforce belonged to one of these two

[1] Cf. 8 September, *L' Unità Italiana* (Palermo), with 13 September, *L' Unità Italiana* (Genoa).

[2] 8 September, *La Cicala Italiana* (Palermo).

[3] 8 September, *Tom Pouce*.

external 'factions', and had received their training in politics and journalism either at Turin or among the Mazzinians of the diaspora. It is not among these exotics, but rather among the independent journals which could criticize both sides, that one must look for hints about the real sentiments of Sicilian 'public opinion'. One will then see that there was far from being a straight fight between Cavour and Garibaldi, between liberal patriots and radical patriots. And one will also see that Sicilians were far from being unanimous about the merits of quick and unconditional annexation.

CHAPTER XIV

DEPRETIS FAILS TO PERSUADE GARIBALDI: 8–14 SEPTEMBER

On 8 September, the temporary lull in Palermo was disturbed by the arrival of two pieces of information. Too late for inclusion in the evening papers came the eagerly awaited telegram from Bertani to say that Garibaldi had entered Naples in triumph on the 7th; and at once Depretis sent off to notify Crispi of the fact, hoping no doubt that he would now think the capture of Rome sufficiently near for the plebiscite to be held.[1] But Crispi had already heard of a second piece of news which complicated the issue, namely that Piedmontese troop movements were being reported in the north. This tallied with other information received during the past three weeks which suggested that the Turin government might be meditating some more active intervention in the Italian civil war. It might signify that Cavour had decided to throw in his lot with Garibaldi. Alternatively, it might mean that he was invading the centre and south only to defend the cause of order and the French alliance against the advance of red revolution. Crispi's present mood was to expect the worst. Although Cavour might let it be inferred that his aim was to help, some of the radicals already feared, and correctly feared, that it would rather be to hinder.[2] For this reason the good news of the conquest of Naples did not resolve the ministerial tension.

In the streets of Palermo, however, Garibaldi's triumph at Naples was greeted with tremendous enthusiasm, and a dangerous turbulence was converted into general festivity. The gainers from this were the third force in Sicily, people who were happy neither with Cavour's policy of immediate annexation, nor with the revolutionary extremism of Crispi. Bargoni wrote that

the triumph of Garibaldi at Naples...was providential from our point of view, because the drive for annexation had become very strong. Apparently

[1] 8 September, Depretis to Crispi (ACP, f. 138).
[2] 11 September, *Il Precursore*, notice dated 8 September; 6 September, *Il Diritto*.

the plan had been to overthrow Garibaldi's dictatorship in Sicily, while simultaneously on the mainland the Cavourians would try to precipitate the annexation of Naples before the revolutionaries could forestall them. Garibaldi would then have had to continue the national *risorgimento* in his island home of Caprera. But now things are changing, and the agitators have disappeared.[1]

At the same time Bargoni's statement shows that people were losing patience with the tactless and intransigent Crispi: 'rightly or wrongly, his continuance in office was thought to be impossible'. This seems to have been a general impression.

By 9 September Crispi's proffered resignation had still not been formally accepted. Depretis was hoping that, if Piola brought back a helpful reply from Naples, it might yet prove possible to hold the cabinet together, round an agreed policy of annexation with Garibaldi's consent. On the 9th Crispi's friends organized another demonstration for his return to power, apparently without his knowledge.[2] The demonstration was broken up by the police, and arrests were made of two 'avvocati' and others 'who said they were representatives of the people'.[3] The police were no longer taking orders from Crispi, and quite rightly so, since he had followed his offer of resignation by a refusal to attend to his ministerial duties; but hereafter he had the additional grievance against Depretis that favourable discrimination was being accorded to demonstrations from the opposite side. The party of Cordova thought it was entitled to some revenge for the arrests Crispi had made when he was unassailable, and now it was reinforced by Bottero who had returned and was directing political operations from a Sardinian frigate in the bay.[4]

If Crispi had fallen from the active exercise of power, his eclipse did not automatically involve that of all the other radicals who made up the 'party of action'. Probably the policy which most accurately represented the radicals was that which can be associated with the more moderate Bargoni. Much of the unrest in Palermo had grown up out

---

[1] 9 September, Bargoni to Mordini (AMB).

[2] 20 September, Crispi to Mordini (AMB).

[3] 21 September, *Il Nazionale* (Naples), report dated 9 September.

[4] 11 September, Sardinian consul to Cavour (quoted by Maraldi, *Rassegna Storica*, 1932, p. 569).

of personal hostility to the vain, unscrupulous, if brave and single-minded Crispi. Now that this personal obstacle was removed, some of the autonomists near the centre of enlightened public opinion were to discover a new sympathy with the main group of his fellow-workers. Many others who were not sympathizers still disapproved of the methods and suspected the motives of Cordova and company. They could see that the race between Cavour and Garibaldi to reach Naples first had been easily won by the latter, and realists had to adjust themselves to this victory for radicalism. Crispi must have told everyone that Garibaldi had specifically confirmed his own opposition to an immediate plebiscite, and that Depretis had nevertheless refused to publish or to accept the dictator's orders on this point. People like Torrearsa, who wanted good government and hence quick annexation, also recognized how futile it was to plunge Palermo into dangerous faction fights when all would really have to be settled at Naples. If only Cavour had managed to win the race, well and good: he would have imposed annexation, and they would have had to fight rather for the preservation of their local institutions. Instead, Garibaldi had won. The hope of all realistic annexationists who were not fanatically devoted to Piedmont or Cavour ought therefore to be that, first accepting Garibaldi's wishes for temporary postponement, they might then prevail on Cavour to meet Garibaldi half-way and concede a representative assembly as well as a plebiscite.[1]

Public opinion is indefinable and essentially unascertainable. It is not easy to agree with Bolton King when he assumes that public opinion at this, or indeed at any time, definitely favoured Cavour's solution of unconditional annexation which finally prevailed. There can be little doubt that most educated Sicilians were eager for some form of union with the north, even if they would not have used Cavour's word 'annexation' with its slightly unfortunate implications. But here the differences began. On this same 9 September, a correspondent of the liberal-conservative *Perseveranza* wrote from Messina that even the most earnest annexationists in that 'Cavourian' town wanted a maximum of administrative and judicial autonomy. This particular correspondent himself had sympathized when Crispi, countering Bottero's

[1] Ed. De Stefano, 'Documenti del Risorgimento negli archivi privati di Trapani', *Rassegna Storica*, 1942, p. 799.

unwarranted attempt to 'arrange annexation', had made answer that Sicilians as a free and proud people would rather ask Piedmont to join herself by vote to them.[1] The same writer added that those who favoured deferring the vote were gaining converts in Messina. They were using to good effect the argument of 'no ingratitude to Garibaldi', 'no talking to the man at the wheel'. Once more we have an example here of the influence wielded in Sicilian politics by an apotheosized Garibaldi the Liberator, all-wise and generous. Admiration for the dictator, if it was not always unbounded, was a stronger sentiment than the respect reserved for that cold, remote intellect which most Sicilians hardly knew by the name of Cavour; and this admiration was always there to attract some people to the dictator's policy of waiting to proclaim national union in Rome. Likewise the tremendous pride of Sicilians in themselves and their island told in favour of the policy of conditional annexation by means of an assembly. Surprisingly enough it was Crispi, smarting under the sense of being deceived and defeated, who now voiced these sentiments. Underneath his outward showing he occasionally revealed some of the deepest prejudices of his fellow-islanders. 'Cavour thought he had to deal with Emilia and Tuscany. But he was wrong. Sicily is something quite different, and must receive different treatment than other provinces.'[2] Now that matters were not going so well for them, the radicals were evidently changing course.

Meanwhile, Piola had been gone for several days on his second mission to find Garibaldi and present him with Depretis's new protest. When late at night on the 7th he caught up with the general, the latter was in bed after his entry into Naples, and too exhausted to hear Piola's business. Crispi's rival embassy of Orlando and four other friends may have already forearmed Garibaldi with the other side of the story. At all events on the 8th Piola had again to report failure. 'The dictator', he wrote, 'does not understand the sad state of Sicily, and does not believe your government to be so lacking in force that it cannot wait any longer.'[3] Garibaldi's orders were that Depretis should take no action for another fortnight until the prospects of advance on Rome became clearer. The political difficulties in Palermo bulked less large when

[1] 16 September, *La Perseveranza* (Milan), report from Messina dated 9 September.
[2] 7 September, Crispi to Correnti (ACP, f. 135).
[3] 8 September, Piola from Naples to Depretis (Archivio Depretis ASR).

viewed from Naples. Instead of Piola being allowed to return with an explanation of these new orders, he was even instructed to stand by in Naples to help with a naval landing at Ostia. This shows the true bent of Garibaldi's mind. The general had no patience with civilian wranglers who purposely or accidentally acted to hamstring him and restrict his freedom of movement in the middle of such a campaign. He was convinced that, were he himself at Palermo, his policy would be accepted whatever it was. He did not understand how his deputy could be any less respected than himself, and he cannot have known that Depretis had kept Sicily ignorant of his recent instructions to postpone a vote. On this 8th of September his mind was probably filled with thoughts of Rome, at last after many years almost within his grasp.

A second letter from Piola later on the 8th gave Depretis the information that Garibaldi planned to move on Rome within three days, but made no mention of Piola's original mission to secure approval for a plebiscite. The atmosphere of Naples had apparently prevailed on him too, and he seemed more interested in whether Cavour would promote him for his services during the Sicilian revolution.[1] The dictator himself wrote to Depretis on the 9th, and as the draft for this letter reposes in the *Archivio Bertani*, with corrections by Bertani upon it, we may recognize the source of Garibaldi's political inspiration at this time. Bertani had a special grudge to wipe off against Cavour, since the latter, after much public abuse, had recently prevented his own projected invasion of the Papal States. Bertani's advice to Garibaldi continued to be that he should oppose Cavour's conspiracy for engineering annexation: once the revolution was victorious at Rome, Victor Emanuel could be offered the crown of a united Italy; this would constitute a final triumph of the revolution, and perhaps could be accompanied by a demand for Cavour's dismissal. Garibaldi's letter to Depretis therefore argued that, 'if I must once again deny myself the pleasure of annexation', this would only be because the proclamation of United Italy must come from the Capitol and not be the result of piecemeal declarations from provincial capitals. 'You know that your project of annexation means tearing away one province from its revolutionary

[1] 8 September, Piola from Sapri to Depretis (Archivio Depretis ASR); 12 September, Persano to Depretis, 'Piola has failed in his duty by not returning with an answer to your demand' (*ibid.*).

solidarity with the others. By the revolution and not by annexation shall we be redeemed.'[1] Surely Sicily could wait another two weeks.

During 9 and 10 September nothing of all this was known at Palermo. Depretis was still playing for time until he heard from the dictator. He spoke fairly and civilly to a deputation of worthy Palermitans who called on him to ask for a representative assembly to be summoned.[2] Crispi wrote to him each day in case there was a ship leaving for Naples, but every time was met with some such reply as: 'nothing today, but do come and talk things over'.[3] Meanwhile, to the extreme annoyance of the prodictator, Bottero had defied the ban put upon him and landed in Sicily once more.[4] Depretis mournfully saw himself alone, 'abandoned', without force to keep order and carry out his decrees, without good trustworthy subordinates, without the moral courage to decide frankly for either Cavour or Garibaldi, yet distrusted by both sides. Openly to gainsay Garibaldi would be dangerously like political suicide. On the other hand, as La Farina wrote to Cordova, 'either Depretis will carry through the annexation, or else our armies will do so—it is for him to decide if he will return to Turin hissed or applauded'.[5] This was a hard choice. In despair he wrote off to Admiral Persano, hoping it might be possible to spare some warships. Perhaps, with armed forces at his command, he would be strengthened against the ebb and flow of public feeling in Palermo.[6]

There were a number of far-fetched rumours abroad in the city. It was being said, for instance, that Cordova and Bottero were plotting to make one of Victor Emanuel's children into king of Sicily. Another rumour was current about Crispi attempting to reunite Sicily and Naples into a joint southern state. 'Nothing can equal the febrile agitation of public opinion in the last three days', wrote *L' Annessione*. In streets and cafés there were animated discussions, some groups holding that any decision should be left to Garibaldi, and that the

[1] 9 September, draft of Garibaldi's letter to Depretis (ABM).
[2] 11 September, Professor Amari to Count Amari (*Carteggio di Amari*, ed. d'Ancona, vol. II, p. 133).
[3] 10 September, Depretis to Crispi (ACP, f. 138).
[4] 11 September, Melino to Cavour (*CC Lib. del Mezz.* vol. II, pp. 280–1).
[5] 11 September, La Farina to Cordova (Carte Cordova MRR).
[6] 10 September, Depretis to Persano (Archivio Depretis ASR).

annexationist party was ruining the country, others that Garibaldi really wanted annexation and was only being dissuaded by Bertani; but everyone of course 'claimed to speak in the name of the *people*'.[1] The *Precursore* boasted that the capture of Naples had brought over more people to the radical way of thinking, because 'while annexation was necessary so long as the Bourbons ruled at Naples, to annex now that Garibaldi is there would be tantamount to snatching Sicily from its liberator and throwing it to the person who had sold Nice. . . . Now that the moment has come to create the new monarchy of Italy, this is no time for annexations! We must go full out for Rome.'[2]

All these rumours and disputations were then suddenly emptied of importance by the arrival, on the 11th, of Piola's report, and by the knowledge that Garibaldi had for the second time rejected Depretis's proposal for an immediate plebiscite. Crispi was jubilant; the annexation party was quite confounded. Amari, with typical moderation and common sense, reacted at once: 'Garibaldi says he only asks for a fortnight's delay before annexation. How could we possibly deny this request to him after he had handed over to Persano all the Neapolitan fleet!'[3] The surrender of the fleet to the Piedmontese authorities was surely convincing testimony of the general's good faith. It might also be assumed that he could see matters in better perspective from Naples than they could in Palermo.

But what line was Depretis to take? He could hardly agree with Amari, who cannot have known the extent of his undertakings to Cavour. Nor did he like the idea that Crispi might go alone to Naples and poison Garibaldi's mind by a partisan account. There was, however, a fair chance that, since the dictator had once been swayed by Bertani, with a little more persuasion he might change his mind back again. Depretis therefore decided to go in person to Naples, stating decisively that he would not return unless with authorization for what he wanted.[4] Possibly Garibaldi's letter of the 9th let Depretis think himself indispensable and so made him over-confident. But in any case

---

[1] 11 September, *L' Annessione*, notice dated 9 September.

[2] 11 September, *Il Precursore*.

[3] 11 September, Professor Amari to Count Amari (*Carteggio di Amari*, ed. d'Ancona, p. 132).

[4] 14 September, Cordova to La Farina (quoted in Crispi, *Memoirs*, vol. I, p. 411).

14 ★

some drastic resolution of the deadlock was necessary. Either Cavour and Garibaldi had to be reconciled in a common policy, or someone else should take over the government who could rule in the name of one or other without ambiguity. Failing this, the administration at Palermo would continue paralysed, and in the absence of policy and of police, of confidence and common enthusiasm, mob agitation would have free rein. Persano had sent none of the ships which the Sicilian government had requested. Too late did Cavour realize Depretis's predicament and promise the immediate despatch of a much-needed, much-requested battalion of soldiers, and the remainder of his agreed loan.[1] This was not a spontaneous assistance for Sicily, but only a last-minute effort to strengthen Depretis. A concurrent plan was now hastily improvised to bring back part of the Piedmontese fleet and capture Sicily with the prodictator's connivance. But by the time that the news of this wild scheme reached the island, Depretis had set off on his journey to Naples.

He started off before noon on 11 September, arrived at dawn on the 12th, and saw Garibaldi at 9 a.m. On the same boat with him travelled Crispi and the Baron Nicotera. Depretis had been hoping to return immediately with everything settled, but once at Naples he found that nothing could be decided during two days of 'stormy discussions'.[2] In his absence from Palermo an insurrection by Cordova had been feared,[3] but the deputy prodictator sent reassuring telegrams.[4] A calm had settled over the Sicilian capital, for now that positive and apparent steps were being taken to resolve their political disagreement, the factious conspiracy of both extremes was temporarily stayed. People welcomed this attempt to compel Garibaldi back into Sicilian politics to choose what was best for them: it had been his absence and his preoccupation with Naples which had lain at the root of their uneasiness, and they had been jealous of Naples for usurping his attention. 'There is now no

---

[1] 10 September, Vice-Governor Magenta of Genoa to Depretis, with orders from Farini (Archivio Depretis ASR).

[2] 25 September, Professor Amari to Cartwright (*Carteggio di Amari*, ed. d'Ancona, vol. III, p. 212).

[3] 18 September, *L' Unità Italiana* (Genoa), report from Palermo of 13 September.

[4] Three or four of these exist in the Archivio Depretis and the Archivio Mordini at Barga.

further question of precipitate annexation,' said one paper: 'the people are quite satisfied with the knowledge that Garibaldi is to decide their fate.'[1]

We have three separate drafts of an edict which Depretis took for Garibaldi to sign, his intention being to establish the fact that he still possessed the dictator's confidence, and hence that he should return to Sicily with a programme of reform, concord and immediate annexation.[2] This suggestion provoked considerable debate, as we can see from three other drafts which represent counter-proposals by Garibaldi and Bertani, each of them progressively modifying the prodictator's demands. The first of these counter-suggestions was that the following reply be made to Depretis:

I do not accept the resignation you have offered me. This is no moment for good citizens to stand down from their office when they are helping me in the holy war of national unity. Go back to Palermo. Continue your reform of the laws in the direction of making more uniform the institutions of our common country. Try and conciliate people by filling their minds with the sentiment of nationality, the love of Italy, and devotion to Victor Emanuel. I am sure that the Sicilian people will help me in our task.

After this text had presumably been rejected as offering no new contribution, a second draft, also dated the 14th, was a little more explicit. 'Go back to Sicily with full powers as before, but with one limitation, that of not speaking further of annexation.' It went on to say that annexation would follow as soon as Rome fell, when Garibaldi would offer a kingdom to Victor Emanuel on two conditions: first, that the officers of the revolutionary army should be compensated for their loss of livelihood and be allowed to transfer their commissions to the regular army; and secondly, 'that His Majesty will promise me on his word as our *Re galantuomo* to prosecute the Italian movement until we possess our natural frontiers entire, and that meanwhile he will allow me to march with my army of volunteers to the present boundaries of the state in order to prepare for this final war of liberation'. The thought here is Garibaldi's to the letter. But its cut-and-dried manner of expression, and the doctrinaire defiance of all considerations not only of

[1] 12 September, *Tom Pouce* (Palermo).
[2] All are in the Archivio Depretis ASR.

diplomacy but of personal pride in the king and in Cavour, also reveal the hand of Bertani. Its rejection along with the first brings us to the third and final form of reply to Depretis, which we possess in Bertani's own handwriting and which speaks for itself: 'the present state of affairs in Sicily makes it advisable for me to accept your resignation and that of your ministers. With my whole heart I thank you for all the good you have done.'[1]

During the two days from the 12th to the 14th Garibaldi had been unwilling to admit the existence of such a split as this implied. But the firm refusal of Depretis to accept these proposed half-measures left only one way out, and the prodictator's resignation is dated 14 September.[2] Perhaps it was Depretis's misfortune to have arrived at Naples in the short period when Bertani was established as the ruling force of the civil government, with Crispi now by his side to provide chapter and verse in criticism of the prodictator's conduct of affairs. Depretis was unwilling to return to Sicily unless he could promote his career by obtaining annexation and becoming royal commissioner in the island. That truly would have been a great achievement. But, failing that, he had to confess defeat; and he did so with a good grace. At Palermo they had expected Depretis back on the 14th, and the national guard was out all day ready to welcome him home.[3] Amari had been confident that he would return with some agreed programme, and was now writing that Crispi's policy could not possibly win, since 'the only force left in Sicily which is worth anything at all is the national guard, and that force will have none of Crispi at any price'.[4] But Amari, like Depretis, was counting without his host.

At all events, the radicals and moderates in Sicily could no longer continue after 15 September in the illusion that each party was covertly working for the other, and that Cavour and Garibaldi were acting in harmony. Realization of this fact eventually forced the undecided middle in Sicilian politics to distribute itself, and this in the end was to go far in helping to resolve the whole political controversy. Before

[1] All three are in Archivio Bertani MRM.
[2] 14 September, Garibaldi's acceptance in Archivio Depretis ASR.
[3] 15 September, *L' Annessione*.
[4] 14 September, Professor Amari to Count Amari (*Carteggio di Amari*, ed. d'Ancona, vol. II, p. 133).

such a result could happen, however, the same realization infused a greater virulence into both sides. With the Cavourians it was the cue for a more relentless and intensified campaign on behalf of annexation. To many others in Sicily it made clear that, since an ultimate Piedmontese victory seemed certain in the very near future, a guarantee of insular autonomy might have to be won now or never, if need be by more forceful measures. In this way there was generated a last-ditch bitterness among all those who wanted an alternative system to the Piedmontese: and this included regionalists, separatists, republicans, federalists, and all the various sects inside the radical 'party of action'.

CHAPTER XV

GARIBALDI SUCCEEDS AT NAPLES:
1–15 SEPTEMBER

Outside the narrow world of Palermo, in the first fortnight of September the whole condition of southern Italy was rapidly changing. It was a new complication in the story that the national movement henceforward had three or more separate centres of policy-making. In addition to Palermo there was Turin, and now there was also Garibaldi's swiftly-moving headquarters on the mainland. Activity at the two capital cities of Sicily and Piedmont henceforward had to take into account the problems which arose and the decisions which were made at this third centre of operations; and the inevitable delays in communication put yet another obstacle in the way of synchronizing and harmonizing policy.

Until the last moment Cavour never quite gave up hope that he might forestall Garibaldi and arrive first in Naples. As he told Nigra privately—sending different 'official reasons' separately for reference to Napoleon—'vous savez tout ce que j'ai fait pour devancer Garibaldi à Naples. J'ai poussé l'audace jusqu'au point où elle pouvait aller sans courir le risque de voir éclater la guerre civile; et je n'aurais pas même reculé devant cette extrémité, si j'avais pu espérer d'avoir pour moi l'opinion publique.'[1] It may be that in making this extraordinary statement Cavour was not being strictly truthful, but was just concerned to induce in Nigra a useful state of mind. Against this, however, one must remember that Nigra was his most trusted confidant and already knew the extent of Cavour's multiple policy.[2] One must also keep in mind those different 'official reasons' which were sent in a regular despatch. The English habit of publishing official correspondence had forced Cavour to reserve his secret thoughts for a parallel series of private letters, 'destinée à n'être jamais publiée, ni même communiquée

---

[1] 12 September, Cavour to Nigra (*CC Cavour-Nigra*, vol. IV, p. 202).

[2] E.g. 28 November 1858, Cavour to Nigra (*ibid.* vol. I, 1926, p. 221); 1 March 1860, Cavour to De Roussy (*ibid.* vol. III, p. 131); 9 January 1861, Cavour to Lady Holland (*Lettere di Cavour*, ed. Chiala, vol. VI, p. 667).

à de nouveaux ministres..., avec la certitude qu'ils seront maintenus secrets, maintenant et dans l'avenir'.[1] In this case a private letter to his favourite minister suggests that his hostility to Garibaldi was unbounded, or at least was limited only by the instinct of self-preservation. The clash which now developed is almost always blamed squarely on Garibaldi, who is said to have showed incapacity and pettiness against Cavour's moderation and statesmanship. But this thesis needs revision.

In the first week of September Cavour's many agents in the south were busily at work, some of them trying to anticipate Garibaldi by springing a palace revolution of their own, others hoping to neutralize the effect of Garibaldi's probable victory by first winning control of the navy and the forts commanding Naples. Their general orders had been to secure 'l'appui des classes sociales les plus élevées et les plus intelli-gentes' against the radicals,[2] and in this they had registered some minor success. Without much hesitation the Bourbon Count of Syracuse had accepted a sizeable monetary inducement,[3] and Persano optimistically hoped that with a few thousand ducats he had already won over the royal Neapolitan navy.[4] It should perhaps be stated that the existence of this subterranean plot was generally known, at least by the end of August,[5] and cannot have come as a surprise either to Francesco or Garibaldi. In the long run it did no good and much harm.

One particular respect in which Cavour's activity glaringly con-tradicted Garibaldi's was in the attempt he made to preserve the Bourbon army from disintegration. While Garibaldi was striving with all his power to defeat this army, some of its senior officers were secretly working in Cavour's employ to keep it in being for later use if need be on other purposes. Not only this, but many people suspected that these other purposes, as well as including another national war, might also include the more immediate function of checking Garibaldi's advance. By 4 September this whole plan was shown to be as impolitic as it had

[1] 23 January 1860, Cavour to Desambrois (*CC Cavour-Nigra*, vol. III, p. 19).

[2] 2 September, Cavour to Villamarina (*CC Lib. del Mezz.* vol. II, p. 213).

[3] 19 October, Farini to Cavour (*ibid.* vol. III, 1952, p. 141).

[4] 6 September, Persano to Cavour (*ibid.* vol. II, pp. 246–7).

[5] 30 August, *Il Diritto* quotes *Il Movimento*, to say that Cavour planned 'to use the alarm and confusion at Naples to proclaim a provisional government containing those Cavourian exiles who have returned with the task of causing a revolution there without Garibaldi and before Garibaldi'.

been ineffective. Persano realized that the employment of the dubious General Nunziante had been a mistake, for it had alienated many of the Neapolitan liberals from Cavour's programme. By delaying the break-up of the Bourbon army, of course, it had also been an unambiguous challenge to Garibaldi. The newly-formed Committee of Order at Naples thereby came under grave suspicion of being as much opposed to Garibaldi as to Francesco; and when the liberals at last put out a petition for annexing Naples to Piedmont, no one would sign it. Cavour's original plan had thus served only to discredit the moderate cause. It had quite failed in its more immediate purpose, for by this time hardly any units of the Bourbon army remained intact.[1] Persano concluded, somewhat late in the day, that it would be wise to change about and seek some agreement with the less extreme among the revolutionaries. A few weeks earlier such a *volte face* might perhaps have reconciled people, and have averted some of the subsequent troubles.

The parallel, and not always wholly co-operative, activity of Villamarina had proved equally stultifying. Cavour's official representative at the Bourbon court had rather built his hopes of an insurrection on one of Francesco's chief ministers, Don Liborio Romano, who had secretly promised to change sides as soon as his master's position proved hopeless. The plan was that Romano should then form a provisional government, and should formally request Cavour to land his troops from Piedmontese ships waiting for this very purpose in the harbour. Here was another scheme to try and save Naples from Garibaldi. But Liborio Romano turned out to be a frail and undependable ally, and as soon as Garibaldi was undeniably leading in the race for Naples he transferred his treachery into the radical-revolutionary camp. Villamarina thus had to fall back on his second line of defence, and worked upon the liberal Committee of Order to try and incite them to over-throw the Bourbon government.[2] The ambassador's simultaneous negotiations with both the ministry and the committee were inconsistent, and only aroused suspicions all round. As a third line of defence he had also tried to purchase the support of the mob leaders in the city.[3] This last action cannot have helped his standing with the middle and upper

---

[1] 4 September, Persano to M. d'Azeglio (Raccolta Azegliana MRR, 564/10/9).

[2] 7 September, E. Villamarina to Cavour (*CC Lib. del Mezz.* vol. II, pp. 250–1).

[3] 8 September, S. Villamarina to Cavour (*ibid.* pp. 262–3).

classes upon whom success in the last resort depended. All 'honest citizens' were at this moment in terror of a *jacquerie*, since disorders were already breaking out on their country estates at the approaching collapse of civil government.[1] Almost all the nobility had by now fled abroad from Naples.[2] Most other people in the town were waiting tensely and without committing themselves until they knew the upshot of this three-sided political quarrel. Villamarina wrote in disgust to Cavour on the 7th about their supine and cowardly inaction: 'dans la rue quelques individus du peuple crient, mais la masse demeure d'une apathie indigne et ne se prête à aucune démonstration qui puisse forcer la main au Général. Pas de caractère, de dignité ni de courage; c'est dégoûtant.' And he added: 'jusqu'à présent il nous a été impossible d'obtenir que la flotte arbore le pavillon Sarde et se mette sous les ordres de Persano; ils ont peur de Garibaldi'.[3]

Zanardelli and others among Cavour's *agents provocateurs* had already recognized defeat and left Naples before Garibaldi arrived there on the 7th. Shortly afterwards Ribotti and Mezzacapo, the two senior officers of the northern army who had been sent to Naples, were ordered home to rejoin their corps; and the rest followed later. Garibaldi had won the race, and this clumsy effort to beat him had considerably strengthened Bertani and the extremists. The dictator had no particular affection for Bertani, but he was easily convinced by what he saw of this plot that the revolution would have to remain strictly autonomous and un-compromising. A fortnight earlier, when passing through Calabria, he had strongly favoured political collaboration, and the newly appointed civil and military authorities there had been obliged to take an oath to Victor Emanuel and the Piedmontese constitution.[4] But on arrival at Naples he was going to find evidence that Cavour had been trying to halt the revolution and simply annex Naples to a greater Piedmont.[5] Alongside this there was another impressive fact. For Garibaldi had

[1] 11 September, Brenier from Naples to Thouvenel (C. Maraldi, *Documenti francesi sulla caduta del regno meridionale*, ed. Omodeo, 1935, p. 169).

[2] 31 August, Villamarina to Cavour (*CC Lib. del Mezz.* vol. ii, p. 197).

[3] 7 September, Villamarina to Cavour (*ibid.* p. 251).

[4] 30 August, Governor Plutino from Reggio to Cavour (E. Artom, *L' opera politica del Senatore Artom*, p. 145).

[5] 1 September, *L' Amico del Popolo* (Naples); 4 September, *Il Garibaldi* (Naples).

found in the provinces that it was the radicals and not the moderates who showed themselves most public-spirited, most careless of counting the cost, most willing to sacrifice themselves in aid of his advance. As usual it was the 'party of action' and not the 'party of order' which had risen to this particular kind of occasion, and 'honest citizens' therefore had only themselves and Cavour's party to thank if nearly always the radicals had come to power in the towns and villages of the countryside.[1]

At the eleventh hour the Committee of Order in Naples did make an effort to forestall the revolution and set up a provisional government, hoping thereby to demonstrate that they had revolted spontaneously without waiting to be 'conquered', and so could claim to have some say in the new government; but this move of theirs came far too late to be of any help to Garibaldi, and he merely looked on it as another attempt by the Cavourians to usurp his power. Commander Forbes, described how a deputation from Naples came to meet the dictator on the 5th: 'Dr Tommasi, of the Cavourian party, had the audacity to read him an address, tantamount to saying that he was a very fine fellow, but that he was not wanted in Naples, where they were going to form a provisional government and to annex immediately; at the same time he presented a printed list of its members.' Forbes commented on this that 'their conduct was not only ungracious but ungenerous to the last degree, and that it paved the way for that wretched system of intrigue between the two factions which was so speedily to follow Garibaldi's entry into Naples, where his presence had now become a necessity, not only to prevent a civil war in the streets, but a disruption which might cause an infinity of harm to the national cause'.[2] The moderate Bonghi, as well as Persano, agreed that the Committee of Order fell lamentably in popular estimation when it appeared that it was as much directed against Garibaldi as the Bourbons.[3] The miscalculations of Cavour and his subordinates had thus rather lessened than improved the chances of the moderates coming into power at Naples. At the same time they were also to give Garibaldi yet more evidence

---

[1] 8 September, *La Perseveranza* (Milan), correspondence from Naples dated 4 September.

[2] 7 September, C. S. Forbes, *The Campaign of Garibaldi in the Two Sicilies*, pp. 228–9.

[3] *c.* 4 September, Bonghi to Cavour (*CC Lib. del Mezz.* vol. II, p. 238).

that Cavour was his bitter enemy. Not many more days were to go by before all pretence had to be dropped and the latent quarrel came into the open.

By 7 September, however, Cavour had momentarily been forced to change the emphasis of his policy, and to try once more to convince Garibaldi that he was a friend who could be trusted. His *coup* had failed and it remained to put the best face possible on the fact. He therefore wrote with orders that Persano should go and see the general and try to persuade him that they should jointly prepare the conquest of Venice.[1] Cavour at this moment was just on the point of launching his army on Naples by way of the Papal States, but it was obviously in his interest to play for time and to confuse public opinion about his intentions. In truth it was not Venice which filled his mind, but rather this other subtle plan to ward off the revolutionaries from their objective in Rome. To this object he now bent his whole attention.

Admiral Persano at this point sent back to Turin an alarmist telegram which was to have some importance. It stated that Garibaldi was bitterly critical of Cavour's behaviour, and that he was under the influence of the republicans and was determined upon challenging Louis Napoleon at Rome.[2] This telegram was written before Persano had spoken to the general himself. It was based merely on hearsay evidence supplied by that same Tommasi who had just aroused Garibaldi's worst anger by his tactless address. It was also written 'in the certainty that there was nothing to get alarmed about'.[3] But it will be seen in the next chapter that Cavour either became, or pretended to become, very alarmed indeed. While still keeping up the outward illusion of friendship, at heart Cavour became the more convinced that an open cleavage could not be put off much longer. This particular telegram had mentioned that Garibaldi was making outrageous statements against Cavour, and its recipient now began to fear more particularly than before that the revolutionaries were planning to displace him in the king's favour. The premier was therefore able to use this casual but opportune report from Persano to prejudice the king against Garibaldi, and no doubt he particularly stressed its hint about the danger

---

[1] 7 September, Cavour to Persano (*ibid.* pp. 252–3).
[2] 7 September, Persano to Cavour (*ibid.* p. 250).
[3] C. Di Persano, *Diario 1860–1*, part II, 1870, p. 112.

of republicanism. It does not matter that in tenor it was an isolated exception among the admiral's communications, nor that it was not taken very seriously by those who knew its author.[1] The next day, as soon as Persano had been able to see Garibaldi for himself, he corrected this previous statement. He now reported to Turin that the dictator had conceded everything, that the new ministers chosen for Naples were good men and Cavourians, and that the republicans had been quite routed.[2] This was a fair apology and partial redress, but it was contained in a letter sent through the post and did not reach Cavour for some days. The Piedmontese invasion of the Marches at this moment had just severed telegraphic communication between north and south, and no telegrams at all could be received in Turin from Naples between 9 and 28 September. In the interim, communications were slow, and Persano's original telegram thus helped to set the tone for Cavour's policy at a crucial period. It was in these few days after the 9th that government and revolutionaries became publicly irreconcilable.

Hearsay and misconstruction apart, the actual deeds of Garibaldi upon his arrival in Naples were noteworthy for their moderation and statesmanship.[3] He showed far more sense of good will and compromise towards his political opponents either than they credited him with, or than they were prepared to show him in return. Instead of Persano having to try and capture the port and the strategic forts which dominated the city of Naples, Garibaldi actually requested that the Piedmontese soldiers in the bay should be disembarked from their troop-carriers in order to garrison the town. Enactments of the revolutionary government were all given out in the name of 'Italy and Victor Emanuel'. The first number of the new *Giornale Officiale* carried the cross of Savoy—although the printer in error used the pre-constitutional form which had been disused in Piedmont since the absolutist days of 1848. Garibaldi's very first decree of all, moreover, gave the whole Bourbon

---

[1] 8 September, Nigra to Cavour: 'je crois cependant que Persano exagère un peu, selon son habitude' (*CC Cavour-Nigra*, vol. IV, p. 197).

[2] 8 September, Persano to Cavour (*CC Lib. del Mezz.* vol. II, pp. 261–2); also 11 September, Persano to Cavour: 'if I am not mistaken I think that Garibaldi is now convinced of the necessity of following your policy, and abandoning his own more rash and risky one' (*ibid.* p. 272).

[3] A. J. Whyte, on the other hand, called them 'deplorable' (*The political life and letters of Cavour*, p. 428).

fleet to Admiral Persano. This act alone might well have shamed Cavour's hostile suspicions. Piedmont was being presented with a more substantial navy than she already possessed, in which there were five ships able to outgun any of her own.[1] What was more important, they were the only ships that the revolutionaries could have used in the combined operations now being set on foot against Rome. Cavour was in fact receiving the most valuable gift he could have been given, and some of the extreme radicals at once recognized it as a signal loss to their cause.[2]

The only explanation for this moderation is that Garibaldi must surely have expected Persano to aid him in his next move upon Rome. Otherwise to surrender those ships was virtual abdication. Evidently he still felt that the government at Turin would be swept on by the momentum of public opinion; or else that Cavour once more must be opposing him only verbally and for form's sake; and in either case that, in the last resort, the king would accept anything from the revolutionaries so long as they were successful. Twice already this year, over the expedition to Sicily and the crossing from Sicily to Naples, Cavour had purposely allowed the revolutionaries to think that his public statements might have been 'for diplomatic consumption only', not necessarily to be taken at their face value. With one hand he had tried hard to dissuade, but the other was held ready to help if and when success was recorded. This had been a policy of opportunism, not of design. It was not long-premeditated, but rather stumbled upon, and then rationalized *ex post facto* and lifted to the dignity of being called a programme. For otherwise Cavour would surely have devised some arrangement whereby Garibaldi would have known when the government was in earnest and when only pretending. The limitations of such opportunism now became apparent, for Garibaldi imagined that, as in Sicily and Naples, he would also be given a fair chance to succeed against Rome. The result was that Cavour found himself in a position where he had to face the possibility of fighting a civil war against his fellow-patriots.

At Turin, Garibaldi's surrender of the fleet was probably taken as yet more evidence that he was nothing more than 'a well-meaning goose'

---

[1] The superiority of the Neapolitan fleet is underestimated by C. Randaccio, *Storia della marina militare Italiana 1860–70*, vol. I, 1886, pp. 196–9; see Elliot's dispatch of 26 September, F.O. 165/135.

[2] 22 September, *L' Unità Italiana* (Genoa), report from Naples dated 12 September.

—-the description is Sir James Hudson's. True enough, the dictator was a simple-minded man with little keenness of intelligence, and so was an easy butt for the clever politicians in the north. But if Cavour and the others had been still cleverer than they were, perhaps they would not have made the cardinal error of underestimating Garibaldi out of what was sometimes mere snobbery and priggishness. They took his foolishness and incapacity so much for granted that they never gave him the credit that was his due. They all too often assumed or pretended that he was a puppet of the republicans. It seldom occurred to them that he could be more popular than they were, or even in his own way more efficient in governing southern Italy at such a time. Garibaldi's instinctive feeling for public opinion sometimes made him the equal of Cavour in knowing what was expedient. The dictator's obeisance to St Gennaro at Naples in September, for instance, or to St Rosalia at Palermo in July, exemplified his political tact at its most successful, though this was a quality which the liberals refused to allow him. Indeed, it showed a politic deference to public superstition against his own private convictions such as was not in keeping with Cavour's nature to have ever displayed. This anxiety not to shock local susceptibilities was the very point upon which subsequent Piedmontese rulers in Naples were to be by comparison most open to criticism.

The common people of Naples were conquered at once by his benevolence and his success. Marc Monnier noted that 'Garibaldi est un saint pour les lazzarones. C'est Dieu qui l'envoie pour sauver le pays; plusieurs l'appellent Jésus-Christ; ses officiers sont les apôtres.'[1] Depretis wrote to Cavour from Naples on the 13th: 'the government must not forget that the popularity of the general is immense. He is accompanied by a torrent, which can have its course regulated, but not be dammed up.'[2] For many Neapolitans, no doubt, the delight over Garibaldi's *joyeuse entrée* was mixed up with a moderate dose of straightforward carnival spirit. Probably it did not betray intelligent appreciation of altered political conditions, so much as relief at escape from a half-known danger, and perhaps a willingness to welcome whatever king might reign. Different levels of society must have viewed him with very different feelings. The possessing classes were always terrified

---

[1] Marc Monnier, *Histoire de la conquête des deux Siciles*, 1861, p. 302.
[2] 13 September, Depretis to Cavour (*CC Lib. del Mezz.* vol. II, p. 290).

that the revolution might cut society into two halves,[1] and many were soon hoping that Piedmontese forces would shortly arrive to save them from social anarchy or a Bourbon counter-attack. The dictator's greater interest in conquering Rome than in defending their big estates from damage was to them as inexplicable as it was deplorable. As early as 9 September, the British minister remarked how the fear that Garibaldi 'was determined to pursue his theory of Italian unity to its most extreme length filled the reflecting portion of the community with apprehension and gloomy foreboding'.[2] A week later, and the national guard was sometimes firing on the Garibaldians. Many of the Neapolitans 'would give their ears to get rid of him and are quite astonished to find that he did not come here in order to be their very humble servant'.[3] The appearance of such sentiments among the politically conscious classes was to be historically important, but it never much affected the enthusiasm for the dictator among the common people. In later years these few months were often looked back to with regret. Despite all the disadvantages of civil war and insecurity, there was still some attraction in being ruled *con amore* instead of *con forza*.

Garibaldi's policy after 7 September continued to be as empirical as ever, pursuing his advance until he met a force too strong for him. His interest was almost entirely in the military situation and not in politics. He was in a hurry, because his campaign would have to be over before the winter rains came in November, and already on 8 September he was planning to move on towards Rome in three days' time.[4] His sole concern was the Holy City. On the 10th he sent a note for publication in Sicily, to confirm once more that union with the kingdom of Sardinia would be effected only when the acquisition of Rome made possible a full union of all Italy.[5] When he heard about Cavour's invasion of the Papal States, his instinctive reaction was to fit this into his own scheme, and to hope that the king's ministers must have been carried away by success, by public opinion, by the king himself, and perhaps also by

[1] 10 September, *Il Nazionale* (Naples).
[2] 9 September, Elliot to Russell (F.O. 165/133/499).
[3] 18 September, Elliot to Russell (RP G.D. 22/85).
[4] 8 September, Piola from Sapri to Depretis (Archivio Depretis ASR).
[5] 10 September, *Edizione nazionale degli scritti di Giuseppe Garibaldi*, vol. IV, 1934, pp. 298–9.

their own better nature, to connive at a march on Rome. 'Garibaldi a été on ne peut plus charmé de la décision que vous avez prise d'occuper l'Umbrie et les Marches', wrote Villamarina to Cavour on the 10th. But the dictator had then gone on to express some doubts which he hoped would be forwarded to Turin: 'si cette décision avait été prise avec la pensée de former un cordon autour du Pape pour sauver une partie de ses États, elle produirait le plus mauvais effet'. He already told Villamarina that he was shocked to find signs at Naples of another propaganda campaign for annexation such as he had already met in Sicily. He repeated that he had no confidence in diplomacy as a method, yet he allowed it to be known that he would first wait to see if the French could be induced to leave Rome of their own accord.[1] This was an attitude of guarded optimism, but by no means one of irreconcilability or defiance.

In another interview of this same day with Elliot and Admiral Mundy, Garibaldi gave the impression that he was 'an enthusiast, who had determined to risk all on the prosecution of his idea of Italian unity'.[2] On the subject of Venice, 'he was confident in the present humour of the Italian people, that the King could not decline the undertaking without the sacrifice of his whole position and popularity.... Garibaldi answered that he had no alternative but to go to Rome, and he declared that he did not even look upon it as an enterprise of any considerable difficulty.'[3] Obviously he would have shared the general belief that the Bourbon columns retreating upon Capua and Gaeta would crumble just as the rest of Francesco's army had disintegrated all the way from Palermo.[4] At Naples, and even at Turin, it was quite possible to believe that the French would prefer to abandon Rome rather than risk a war with the last ally they had left in Europe. So long as the nation was really united, it would not be worth Napoleon's while to pit himself against it by force of arms. On this hypothesis, Cavour could only be waiting for Garibaldi to occupy the city with his 'irresponsible' and 'uncontrollable' forces, so giving Victor Emanuel the excuse to arrive and 'restore order' in the accepted manner. Garibaldi, now as always,

[1] 10 September, Villamarina to Cavour (*CC Lib. del Mezz.* vol. II, p. 273).
[2] Mundy, *H.M.S. Hannibal at Palermo and Naples*, p. 244.
[3] 10 September, Elliot to Russell (F.O. 165/133/502).
[4] *The Westminster Review*, January 1861, vol. XIX, p. 133.

was quite ready to be disowned in the event of failure; but as success would make Italy a nation state at last, the gamble seemed well worth the risk. No one who was grateful to him for his defiance of all caution and prudence in May could blame him for now wanting to chance his hand again. However mad his plans may have seemed to a moderate man like Elliot, 'one must admit that his landing at Marsala did not appear a much less desperate undertaking'.[1] Thayer, Bolton King, Trevelyan and Whyte were all agreed in deploring Garibaldi's 'mad design on Rome' as something supremely nonsensical and unrealistic; but there was something to be said in its favour; and there is some significance in the fact that the king and Cavour made such half-hearted efforts to argue him out of it.

No doubt sheer lack of brains also played its part in making Garibaldi misunderstand or fail to sympathize with Cavour's position. But if misunderstandings had accumulated all through the summer, the chief responsibility for them must be sought elsewhere. Garibaldi had never concealed his intentions and never deviated one jot from his published programme; but Cavour on the other hand had never once published what anyone could feel sure was his real purpose, and even today it is hard to judge from his many contradictory statements what were his true opinions at any one moment. What historians cannot know for certain today, Garibaldi can be forgiven for not knowing amid all the uncertainties of the actual moment. The lack of co-ordination between north and south became much more pronounced after 9 September, for communications had become so slow that any threat or friendly message from either party took up to a week to reach its destination, and often arrived in a quite different context from that for which it had been devised.[2] In the absence of definite information, the wildest rumours were current in the south. It was said for instance that Cavour might be forced to change his cabinet, to eliminate Garibaldi's particular *bêtes noires* Farini and Fanti, and so to make possible more co-operation with the radical programme.[3] There was another rumour that

---

[1] 11 September, Elliot to Russell (RP G.D. 22/85).

[2] E.g. the letter written on 14 September by Kossuth to Garibaldi at Cavour's request did not reach its destination until the 21st (*Politica segreta di Napoleone III e di Cavour in Italia e in Ungheria 1858–61*, 1895, ed. L. Chiala, pp. 134–40).

[3] 14 September, *Il Nazionale* (Naples).

the king was being kept in a state of ignorance by Cavour and was secretly searching once more for occasion to break out and accept the full unitarian policy.[1] Garibaldi was in the middle of a confused medley of hints and threats and advice, but the northern government never dared to give him an honest statement of their real policy. All things considered, he can hardly be blamed for thinking the accomplishment of the great ambition of his life to be at last within his grasp.

It must be remembered that the Piedmontese prime minister was looked on by many of the radicals as a *défaitiste*, and even as an actual traitor tied to Napoleon's apron strings, as someone who was more anxious on behalf of Piedmont and the institution of monarchy than on behalf of Italy and Italians. That this should be so was in part a failure of publicity and human relations. When Cavour dealt with rough men of the common people like Garibaldi he proved to be much more unapproachable and embarrassed than was Victor Emanuel. Surprisingly little effort was made to extend any confidence towards Garibaldi, or even to treat him as worthy of much consideration; and the result was to confirm the dictator in the impression that he was being deceived and exploited. But besides this failure to treat Garibaldi fairly and with respect, there were incidents which could not easily be explained away. Cavour had tried hard to stop the Thousand setting out in the first place. Garibaldi's store of rifles had been impounded at Milan in May, and other munitions had been sequestered later. Although subsequent reinforcements under Medici and Cosenz had received official aid from Turin, it was significant that these expeditions had sailed while La Farina still hoped to win the government of Sicily on behalf of Cavour. It could not be denied that La Farina had set on foot a most tactless assault on Garibaldi's authority, and had done so in the name of the Piedmontese government itself. After that, when these means had failed to capture the revolution, the enrolment of volunteers in the north had been abruptly forbidden, without satisfactory explanation, and Bertani's expedition had been forcibly diverted, first on one pretence to Sardinia, then on another to Sicily. For eight weeks negotiations had been going on at Turin for an alliance between the House of Savoy and the very Bourbons against whom the volunteers were fighting. In the meantime Garibaldi's agents in the north had on

[1] 16 September, A. Scialoia to Cavour (*CC Lib. del Mezz.* vol. II, pp. 310–11).

frequent occasions been hindered, and one envoy who had been sent expressly to negotiate with the government had simply been dismissed offhand as an impostor. An attempt had then been made to stop Garibaldi from continuing his advance beyond Sicily. Undertakings to send money and policemen to help restore law and order in Sicily had not been honoured. Admiral Persano had given many private words of sympathy to the volunteers, but his practical insincerity was exposed when the Piedmontese ships had stood aloof and unhelpful during Garibaldi's perilous crossing of the Straits. Finally, instead of assisting the volunteers to conquer Naples, a heavily subsidized counter-plot had been directed against Garibaldi as well as against Francesco. These were accumulated grievances which Garibaldi had at the back of his mind.[1] If on any point they were based on misunderstanding, Cavour had not done much to explain his conduct. But in fact they were not based on misunderstanding. Garibaldi was quite correct to think of Cavour as his enemy, even necessarily his enemy. Cavour needed this enmity in order to retain the French alliance and win the support of conservative Naples.

In the second week of September at Naples this conflict came to a head. Garibaldi by now had learnt to expect more hindrance than help from Cavour, but still trusted that victory in the south might force the government of Turin into a more open and co-operative policy. Even this last hope could not be held much longer. Already the more perceptive among the radicals were realizing that Cavour's unexpected initiative in Naples and Umbria might conceal beneath its specious exterior an intent to excommunicate the 'party of action'.[2] The opposition newspapers at Turin had been hinting, at least from 6 September onwards, that Cavour might be intending by this move to oppose rather than to co-operate with the revolution.[3]

According to Villamarina, Garibaldi's attitude was still far from unfriendly as late as the 10th. But the realities of the political and military situation were beginning to dawn upon him, and while he continued to put his trust in Victor Emanuel, he became ever more impatient with

[1] *Edizione nazionale degli scritti di Garibaldi*, vol. IV, pp. 382–90.
[2] 31 August, G. Deideri from Genoa to Garibaldi (ACM, no. 916); 1 September, Mazzini to Caroline Stansfeld (*Epistolario*, vol. XLI, p. 27).
[3] 6 September, *Il Diritto* (Turin).

Cavour, and ever more assured in his 'holy horror of diplomatists'.[1] On the 11th Garibaldi wrote directly to the king, asking him to send a man who could take over the civil government of Naples, but asking also whether Cavour and Farini could be replaced in the government.[2] This was a decisive moment in the development of the breach between dictator and prime minister, and it shows that Garibaldi still thought the king was on his side. The arrival of Depretis at Naples with his resignation then revealed that Cavour's propaganda for annexation had successfully upset the chances of compromise government in Sicily, and in addition to all these other grievances Garibaldi therefore found himself obliged to leave the front at a critical moment to go and pacify the factions at Palermo. During the three days he was away, the bad generalship of one of the more 'Cavourian' among his subordinates was to earn the volunteers what turned out to be their first real military defeat of the year. It was a small check, but important in its effects, and it was to mark the furthest limit of his advance. Garibaldi never forgave Cavour for thus forcing him to leave the battle area, but Cavour had good reason to look upon this Bourbon success at Caiazzo as a real triumph for the liberal cause.

Meanwhile the identical faction fight over annexation was developing at Naples as in Sicily, with the same object and the same result. The following account by Commander Forbes must surely have been a little excessive, but it shows what a bad impression was being created on one neutral observer by the conduct of Cavour's party at Naples. Forbes told of the

immediate annexationists, who, finding they cannot attain their wishes by fair means, do not scruple to foster anarchy in every possible way, not even disdaining to make use of reactionary plots. In short, the game at Turin is becoming more and more apparent; the Piedmontese would create anarchy in the South in order to have a plausible pretext for action.... Though committing an act of revolution, Piedmont must step in as a conservative power to stay anarchy and stifle republicanism; and if they do not exist, the world must be made to believe so.[3]

[1] 11 September, Elliot to Russell (RP G.D. 22/85).

[2] 11 September, Garibaldi to Victor Emanuel (*CC Cavour-Nigra*, vol. IV, pp. 212–13).

[3] 11 September, Forbes, *Campaign of Garibaldi in the Two Sicilies*, pp. 241–2.

Though perhaps exaggerated, there was more than a little truth in this, more anyhow than in the counter-accusation that the radicals were purposely abetting anarchy to prepare the ground for social revolution and republicanism.

On 13 September the Sardinian ambassador at Naples addressed Garibaldi some slightly tactless remarks about hurrying up the process of annexation. This made a bad impression, but not quite so bad as Villamarina's refusal to let the Sardinian troops now on shore in Naples go out and help the volunteers at the front.[1] Garibaldi had invited these troops to garrison the city, and they had accepted his invitation even though Piedmont was at peace with the Bourbons. When therefore they refused his second request to help in fighting the Bourbon army, this can hardly have been due to a wish to avoid being compromised. The fact that they preferred to stay behind the lines and control the city of Naples was bound to give the appearance that their primary intention was to check the revolution rather than fight the Neapolitan king. Possibly the situation might have been handled with greater tact if only someone other than the vain and petty Villamarina had been on the spot to represent Cavour's views; but Villamarina had none of the arts of a diplomat,[2] he did not even possess the confidence of Cavour and the king,[3] and in any case he had been left several weeks without news from the north.[4] Garibaldi was allowed to see that Cavour was plotting behind his back, buying up newspapers in Naples, making bad blood between him and the king, and allowing the two battalions of *bersaglieri* to land on the pretext of helping him but really to see that he did not escape.[5] 'At Palermo they wanted annexation so that I should not cross the Straits; at Naples they want annexation so that I cannot cross the Volturno'—so he now told the Sicilians.[6] The belief in Cavour's double-dealing thus came to overlay every other thought in his mind, and the worst possible construction was now put on the

[1] 13 September, Villamarina to Cavour (*CC Lib. del Mezz.* vol. II, p. 289).
[2] 18 September, P. S. Leopardi to Cavour (*ibid.* p. 319).
[3] 12 October, Farini to Cavour (*ibid.* vol. III, p. 92).
[4] 15 September, Villamarina to Cavour (*ibid.* vol. II, p. 303).
[5] Garibaldi, *Memorie Autobiografiche*, 1888, pp. 382–4.
[6] 17 September, Garibaldi's proclamation, *Edizione nazionale degli scritti di Garibaldi*, vol. IV, p. 301.

invasion of the Marches which a few days ago had seemed such a hopeful augury.

This sharp worsening of relations became publicly known on the 15th. On that date the *Giornale Officiale* at Naples made public a private letter from Garibaldi to Brusco in which the general forswore reconciliation to the man who had sold Nice to the French. Possibly this letter was in fact written by Bertani; or else Bertani just seized on a momentary aberration of an annoyed Garibaldi and saw to the publication of this tactless and ill-tempered letter so as to drive another wedge between minister and dictator. It came very opportunely for Cavour, who was already seeking the best ground for a public separation, and at the worst was even ready for a civil war. Here he was provided with a gratuitous and plausible pretext. Garibaldi's request to the king for the prime minister's dismissal had been a gage of defiance, and Cavour was now able to accept the challenge with some confidence. The whole, incident is one more example of the difference in mettle and tact and cleverness between these two great national leaders. It was Garibaldi's letter to Brusco which provoked the open clash between them, and for this reason he is usually taxed with responsibility for the cleavage. But what on his side was an unpremeditated outburst in a fit of bad temper when things were going badly, on the other side was something more calculated and deliberate. It must also be remembered that, while to Garibaldi the prospect of civil war against Cavour was inconceivable, to Cavour himself it was something which had already been accepted as a possible outcome of a consciously-adopted line of action. Until the end of October, and indeed even throughout November and December, Cavour went on fearing that he might possibly have to repress the volunteers by force.

It will be realized that this was the outcome of a difference in political theory as well as in political practice. To the great majority of radicals the nation was something sacred and indivisible, something which was ideologically sacrosanct and which in itself constituted a wholly sufficient justification for what they were doing. Cavour on the other hand should perhaps be called a patriot rather than a nationalist. In his own way he was like them an idealist, but he was far more pragmatic and empirical in his approach to the national problem. Whereas the radicals argued from the theory to the facts, he began with the facts and was ready to fight for national unification only when the facts seemed to justify it, only when the forces making for unification seemed to be sufficient and to have enough momentum of their own. Whereas his political opponents had all the virtues and faults of one-track single-mindedness, he saw the complexity of *res publica*. He believed for instance that good government might be more important than self-determination. In his opinion the aim of statecraft was not simply to achieve nationhood, but was also concerned with such things as constitutional government, free trade, 'the principles of social conservation', respectability, the *juste milieu*, and a *tact des choses possibles*. In the name of these other principles of action he could do what to the radicals would seem something sacrilegious. Not only Garibaldi, but also Mazzini and even Victor Emanuel said at various times, and surely meant, that the making of Italy was more important than any other political principle whatsoever, whether monarchy or republic, conservatism or radicalism, or the primacy of any one province over the rest. But on this point—and not entirely to his discredit—Cavour disagreed. In the middle of September 1860 he was far more acutely aware of what was happening than the others, and now knew his own mind better than they did theirs. If he had artfully manoeuvred into a position where he could and did claim to be an aggrieved party, this must not be allowed to conceal from us that he had most to gain from this cleavage with Garibaldi, that he had planned it, and that he alone was ready for it when it came. The story therefore must now be looked at in more detail from his point of view.

CHAPTER XVI

CAVOUR BREAKS WITH GARIBALDI: SEPTEMBER

Cavour at Turin naturally looked upon this widening gap very differently from Garibaldi at Naples. By the beginning of September he realized that he had reached what he himself felt to be the supreme and critical phase of the *risorgimento*.[1] Appreciative as he was of some of the great things Garibaldi had done for Italy, he was now convinced even more that the man was fundamentally a menace and a nuisance. He had told Nigra that he would not shrink from civil war against the radicals if only he could win public opinion; but his own conduct over Nice and Garibaldi's conduct in Sicily had left him for some months without enough public support, and it was a difficult question how far and how directly and when he could dare to oppose the radicals and yet have public opinion on his side. A decision could not be put off much longer. The more territory Garibaldi won, the greater would be the momentum of the revolutionaries, the larger their army, the more they would be master of the situation, the more difficult to resist them, the more they would be able to speak on terms of equality with Cavour, and the more humiliating it would be for Piedmont and the king. Garibaldi nominally ruled over as large a territory and as many Italians in the south as did Victor Emanuel in the north. There was serious danger that, by comparison with the victorious dictator, the warlike reputation built up with such difficulty by northerners for their king would be lost, and Victor Emanuel would appear to be merely a friend of Garibaldi the kingmaker. By 1 September Ricasoli was desperately and insolently addressing the government on this theme, saying that 'les Italiens cherchent en vain leur Roi'; and so touched both Cavour and His Majesty on the raw.[2] Garibaldi was almost within striking distance of Rome, and his arrival there—so at least Cavour imagined—

[1] 8 September, Cavour to Plutino (*CC Lib. del Mezz.* vol. II, p. 260).

[2] 1 September, Ricasoli to Cavour (*ibid.* p. 207); 2 September, Cavour to Ricasoli (*ibid.* p. 212).

would undermine both the royal prestige and the French alliance on which the liberal-conservatives based their policy, and perhaps also would invite the foreign intervention in Italy which Cavour had done so much to avert. It might even threaten the Piedmontese constitution: for though Cavour was probably not altogether deceived by his own propaganda about the dangers of republicanism, still after 11 September a dictator who held power by right of conquest was asking the king to dismiss the elected and responsible representative of 'the people' in parliament. Quite apart from this there was also the fact, as the British minister at Naples put it, that 'no country has a greater interest than Piedmont in the prevention of the spread of extreme revolutionary doctrines'.[1] Almost any risk was worth running rather than let Garibaldi proceed on his way unopposed; but better if possible to let the radicals make a false step, and so bring upon themselves responsibility for a breach which Cavour could pretend to deplore.

Cavour had been preparing for this contingency at least since the middle of August. The circular of 13 August forbidding the enrolment of volunteers had been the first unambiguous action taken. But he also recognized frankly that the only way to win public opinion was to capture some of Garibaldi's prestige. He would therefore have to join in the revolution, in order to inherit and legitimize what the radicals had gained for Italy. The real test would be whether he could dethrone them and become their heir without positively fighting them, whether he could win without seeming mean and ungrateful, and in practical terms whether he could reach Naples in time. Hence his decision to attack the Pope, so as to steal the revolutionary thunder at the same time as he secured a passage to the south for his troops. This was what G. M. Trevelyan called 'the crowning act of Cavour's life, and the greatest example of his political genius'.[2] Military units were first called up in readiness for 'autumn manoeuvres' on the frontier.[3] Nicotera's volunteers in Tuscany, which had been allowed and even encouraged to gather there before this change in policy,[4] were broken up despite

[1] 31 August, Elliot's memorandum (F.O. 70/319).
[2] Trevelyan, *Garibaldi and the making of Italy*, p. 209.
[3] 18 August, *L' Opinione* (Turin).
[4] 23 August, Ricasoli to Cavour (*Lettere di Ricasoli*, ed. Tabarrini, vol. v, p. 213); 26 August, Ricasoli to Farini (BR ASF, b. T, f. P).

Ricasoli's violent protest. If the compulsory disbandment of the Genoese volunteers earlier in the month had been due rather to French susceptibilities over any invasion of Papal territory, the disbandment of those in Tuscany was now due to Cavour's plan for invading that territory himself. The volunteers would have been useful to him as auxiliaries in this campaign, but there were political reasons why the royal army and the king's government should monopolize what prestige was attached to this bold venture. A mixture of tact, firmness and deceit[1] was needed to inveigle Nicotera away to remote Sicily at the beginning of September, but this delicate move was just effected in time.[2] On 29 August the cabinet formally decided to invade the Papal States, but Cavour and Farini had irrevocably decided as much on their own initiative at least since the 26th.[3] For some reason Depretis was told of this plan but not Garibaldi, Persano but not yet Villamarina. Probably the whole episode was much more impetuous and empirical,, much less considered and organized, than one might suppose.

No doubt it had suddenly struck Cavour that, since Garibaldi might in any case cross the Papal frontier soon and spread the conflagration into central Italy, he himself could gain nothing and might lose much from standing idle. He believed that France would probably oppose a Garibaldian invasion, whereas she might possibly be induced to favour an alternative Piedmontese invasion if this was put to her as a less expensive way of preventing the spread of revolution and saving at least Rome to the Pope. If France could only be persuaded to accept this policy, such an invasion was likely to pick up for Sardinia *en passant* the Papal provinces of Umbria and the Marches, and presumably the southern provinces of Naples and Sicily as well. It would provide Italians with an alternative focus of enthusiasm to Garibaldi, perhaps outshining the latter in military prowess, as well as preventing his

[1] 31 August, Nicotera's protest to the Governor of Leghorn (BR ASF, b. A, f. P).
[2] The Governor of Leghorn reported that all the volunteer units left between 1–7 September. News had come in just before this that 145 English volunteers had captured the island of Montecristo as a first step to landing on the Papal coast; 27 August, Ricasoli to Cavour (BR ASF, f. Z).
[3] 26 August, Farini to Depretis (quoted by Librino, in *Nuova Antologia*, December 1930, p. 485); 28 August, Cavour to Prince di Carignano: 'nous avons décidé d'intervenir dans les Marches et dans l'Umbrie en suscitant un mouvement dans ces provinces qui justifie l'entrée de nos troupes' (*CC Cavour-Nigra*, vol. IV, p. 185).

further march up the peninsula. Cavour thus had everything to gain. If he also stood to lose a little, at least it was tolerably certain that on any other calculation his losses would be yet greater; for if he remained inactive or followed any other line of action, then Europe might end the policy of non-intervention; and yet if he stood out any longer against the current of national feeling, it would assuredly sweep him away.[1] All through the *risorgimento* Piedmont was able to take risks in the happy conviction that, while she had the whole peninsula to gain, her own existing frontier was virtually guaranteed against defeat by the strong interest of France against Austrian encroachment.

Judging by Cavour's private as well as public pronouncements—and to people of different political allegiances—his main object was to 'combat the influence of Garibaldi', and 'to prevent the revolution extending into our kingdom'.[2] It was more important at this moment to fight against the revolution than against Austria, and risks would have to be taken against the revolution which would not for instance be worth taking simply to win Venice from Austria.[3] He was going to invade the Papal States because 'it is at Ancona that we shall gain the moral force we need to be able to dominate the revolution'.[4] This was an example of that attitude of mind which made the radicals say that Cavour was only half a patriot. They did not allow that there might be good reason for him to lack confidence in the force of nationalism. In their eyes he was guilty of the moral blemish of preferring to expand Piedmont rather than make Italy, to fight Garibaldi rather than co-operate with him. The radicals wanted to make Italy, and on this point they were more realistic than their opponents admitted; but although their own more apocalyptic and catastrophic programme was in a sense to be justified by its own success, it was unfair of them to deny that Cavour too might have his own realism in advocating a more Fabian, but still surprisingly radical, strategy.

[1] 28 August, U.S. Minister Daniel to Cass: 'the Sardinian Government will not have the power to arrest the current. It would be destroyed if it attempted to do so' (copy in MRR).

[2] 31 August, Cavour to Persano (*CC Lib. del Mezz.* vol. II, p. 192); 4 September, Cavour to Carignano (*ibid.* p. 223); E. Della Rocca, *Autobiografia di un veterano*, vol. II, 1898, p. 35.

[3] 27 August, Cavour to Valerio (*Lettere di Cavour*, ed. Chiala, vol. III, p. 351).

[4] 3 September, Cavour to Persano (*CC Lib. del Mezz.* vol. II, p. 218).

If Garibaldi's lodestar stood above Rome, Cavour's was fixed in the firmament above Paris, and at the end of August Farini went off post haste to Chambéry in the hope that Louis Napoleon would agree to what the Piedmontese government now proposed.[1] Napoleon was probably as imprecise as ever, but our knowledge of this interview is even more shadowy and partisan than of that at Plombières in 1858. He certainly gave Farini to understand that, things being as they were, he would allow the Piedmontese to go and restore order in central and southern Italy, or in other words that the doctrine of non-intervention did not apply to this one sub-alpine state. His only conditions seem to have been that Cavour should be both quick and successful, and also that the invasion should appear to onlookers not as a conquest, but as the response to a spontaneous insurrection which indicated beyond dispute the manifest wish of the people. Apparently it had not been difficult to bring Napoleon to this pitch. Cavour's representative at Paris had helped matters by insisting with the Emperor that Garibaldi stood for Britain, and was being backed by Lord John Russell to reduce French influence in southern Italy.[2] French public opinion, as seen in the *Revue des Deux Mondes*, the *Temps*, the *Constitutionnel*, and the *Patrie*, had been becoming increasingly alarmed by Garibaldi and the Mazzinians.[3] The Catholics in France had to admit that, if they did not want their country herself to have the expense of fighting Garibaldi's forty thousand volunteers, then Cavour's scheme offered the best hope of saving their pockets and at least guaranteeing the Pope his asylum in Rome. The Emperor personally was aware that a moderately strong Italy, while it might have other disadvantages, would at least help to hold Austria on the Mincio frontier, and so give him scope to develop his own private schemes on the Rhine. For these various reasons, Cavour could feel cautiously sure that in the last resort Napoleon would have to stand by 'the only ally which France possesses'.[4]

[1] For some reason, Massari, writing in 1872, tried to deny that Cavour was here trying to obtain Napoleon's consent (G. Massari, *Il Conte di Cavour*, 1935 ed. Milan, p. 328).

[2] 23 August, Cavour to Nigra (*CC Cavour-Nigra*, vol. IV, p. 177).

[3] 24 August, G. Lanza to Castelli (*Carteggio di Castelli*, ed. Chiala, vol. I, p. 316).

[4] 31 August, Cavour to Bruno the Sardinian consul at Geneva (P. Matter, *Cavour et l'unité Italienne*, vol. III, p. 382).

The rest of Europe needed less careful handling. Cavour continued to keep in mind that Austria might choose to attack while his armies were engaged in the centre: but he calculated that this was unlikely, since in Austria's present state the least military reverse might cause the collapse of her whole empire;[1] and Britain at least, if not France as well, gave 'the most categoric guarantee' to Piedmont against an Austrian attack at this difficult moment.[2] He made a special effort to neutralize feeling in northern Germany, and for this purpose boldly advocated the unification of Germany as well as of Italy. As Cavour saw it, these two states would become 'les deux pierres angulaires du nouvel édifice européen', for they did not exclude, but rather implied, each other;[3] at least it was politic to say as much, even if he did not intend a great deal by the words.

In Great Britain, Lord John Russell had already been won over by Garibaldi to see that the Neapolitan Bourbons could no longer survive, and that Italy must be a single and not a dual state.[4] Russell was not yet ready to permit the upset in political balance which would follow the acquisition of Venice; and Cavour—no doubt advised by Hudson—made clever use of this point, announcing that his invasion in the Marches was precisely 'to avoid the Venetian difficulty'.[5] Such an attack upon the Pope's dominion was especially gratifying to Protestant England. Lord Shaftesbury wrote to Cavour with the *nihil obstat* of Exeter Hall, to say that 'your revolution is the most wonderful, the most honourable, and the most unexpected manifestation of courage, virtue and self-control the world has ever seen!'[6] It was Garibaldi whom Cavour should have thanked for this. Englishmen had made of

[1] 13 September, Cavour to General Lamarmora (N. Bianchi, *Storia documentata della diplomazia europea in Italia*, vol. VIII, pp. 692–3); 20 October (*ibid.* pp. 693–4).

[2] 24 September, Emilio Visconti-Venosta from Turin to his brother Gino (AME).

[3] 9 September, Cavour to the editor of the *Deutsche Zeitung* (CC *Lib. del Mezz.* vol. II, 268).

[4] 6 August, Russell to Hudson (RP G.D. 22/109); 6 August, Russell to Elliot: 'the Bourbons of Sicily seem determined to be faithless to the end....The trick about evacuating Sicily shall be the last that they shall play me....Do not follow the King to Gaeta or any other place where he may lay his false head on his uneasy pillow' (RP G.D. 22/111).   [5] 7 September, Hudson to Russell (RP G.D. 22/66).

[6] 12 September, Lord Shaftesbury from Paris to Cavour (CC *Ing.* vol. II, part II, p. 123).

15-2

the general their hero, and had erected him into the great rationalist, not to say Protestant, who would clear up the hocus-pocus of Rome. *The Times*, for instance, hoped that he would submit the liquefying *ampoule* of St Gennaro's blood at Naples to chemical analysis. The son of one British cabinet minister, the Duke of Somerset, had joined Garibaldi's volunteers in the south. The Duke of Wellington had secretly sent him £50. In London his picture had sold 'by the million' to help pay for the revolution. Workmen in Glasgow gave up their half-holidays to make munitions for him, and a collection at the Athenaeum on his behalf had realized £300 in one night.[1] G. M. Trevelyan has shown in his three books on Garibaldi how British public opinion learnt to idealize him as a model of gallantry and chivalry, and how, largely through him, they came to contemplate the *risorgimento* as a liberal protest against tyranny and reaction.

Once satisfied about the attitude of the Powers, Cavour gave the order to launch the spontaneous insurrection which Napoleon required. A revolt was engineered by Ricasoli, timed to break out the other side of the border on 8 September.[2] Where possible, Papal troops were first corrupted with cash.[3] On 5 September the National Society sent round to its adepts in the Marches a circular with details of how much pay the 'volunteers' should receive, and with instructions about how deputations could be sent to invoke the aid of Victor Emanuel against the oppression they were suffering. Ever since the end of August, General Fanti had been making preparations for his offensive, spreading the convenient rumour that this was in some way intended to help

[1] One contemporary diary at Naples describes the persecution of Garibaldi by his English fans: 'some ladies who sought an interview with him later at the Hotel d'Angleterre, asked him for a kiss a-piece, and that each might cut off a lock of his hair. General Türr...looked somewhat out of patience, standing guard over Garibaldi with a comb, and raking down his head after each operation.' 'Extracts from the journal of an Englishman at Naples', *Macmillan's Magazine*, December 1860, vol. III, p. 154.

[2] 30 August, Ricasoli telegram to Farini to say that all was arranged (BR ASF, f. Z); even Hudson knew about it more or less accurately: 'the insurrection, I expect, will break out on the 9th inst., and the Sardinian intervention will be almost simultaneous' (report dated 7 September, RP G.D. 22/66).

[3] 31 August, Ricasoli to Farini, mentions having already spent about £15,000 (*Carteggio di Ricasoli*, ed. Nobili and Camerani; omitted from Tabarrini's collection).

Garibaldi at Naples. On the 5th it was announced that, as minister of war, he was leaving to inspect the troops on their autumn manoeuvres.[1] No one could have been very surprised when an ultimatum was then sent to Cardinal Antonelli on the 7th, protesting against certain not very clearly specified massacres perpetrated by General Lamoricière's mercenary army, and threatening invasion if this army were not dismissed. A deputation from over the border duly arrived more or less on time at Turin to ask for Victor Emanuel's intervention. The prepared insurrection also broke out according to plan on the 8th, but unfortunately it misfired.[2] Cavour bewailed in private that 'l'insurrection de l'Ombrie est très peu de chose. C'est déplorable. Nos amis veulent-ils conquérir l'indépendance sans sacrifices?'[3] But since news of the ultimatum was by this time public property, it was all the more necessary to expedite the invasion; for otherwise the French might have time to protest, and Antonelli could present a reasoned reply, and the hesitant insurrectionaries would be altogether subdued.

Cavour of course kept up the pretence and the confusion by giving out different explanations of what he was up to, one explanation for the Garibaldians, another for home opinion in the north, others to Britain and France. The most important person to placate was the Emperor of the French, who was certainly not an enthusiastic observer of what was afoot. Napoleon's conditional approval at Chambéry must now have weakened considerably after this partial failure to meet his stipulations: the spontaneous insurrection had not materialized, and Garibaldi had not yet begun the march on Rome which was to have been the excuse to make Cavour's aggressive action seem plausible. For this reason Cavour was driven into exaggerating his legend about *sansculottes* at Naples and Palermo, and Persano's misguided but in one sense timely alarmist telegram of the 7th was immediately sent off to Paris for use as

[1] 5 September, *La Perseveranza* (Milan).

[2] 8 September, Vincenzo Ricasoli to his brother Bettino: 'we are really surprised that the inhabitants of the Papal States are so afraid and will not make up their minds to do anything at all....I have done everything to send them men and help....The Italians are a lot of big sheep, and the heroism of Garibaldi is easily acquired when dealing with this sort of person.' To be published in the edition by Nobili and Camerani, *Carteggio di Ricasoli*. Vincenzo was a spy, but in Tabarrini's edition of these letters the ugly word is excised from Fanti's letter of 9 September.

[3] 10 September, Cavour to Ricasoli (*CC Lib. del Mezz.* vol. II, pp. 270–1).

necessary.[1] These minor hitches in Cavour's engineered revolt were thus a contributory cause of his clash with Garibaldi, for a public breach now became all the more a necessary element in self-justification. Italy (as well as Garibaldi) had to suffer for this fact. Another result was that the French alliance received a setback. Napoleon's subsequent with-drawal of his legation from Turin can only in part be explained as a fiction to keep up appearances. It also expressed a feeling that he had been deceived, because Farini had given him to understand that Pied-mont would wait for a proper pretext such as would give the impression she had right on her side.[2] As things had turned out, the whole of Europe, and his own subjects in particular, could appreciate the patent fraud. To Frenchmen the Pope had been put in the right against Cavour, and to the British so had Garibaldi. Grammont indignantly commented on the invasion and its mock motives that 'c'est créer le désordre pour avoir le droit de rétablir l'ordre'.[3] Antonelli was also enabled to make a dignified rebuttal of the ultimatum, pointing out that Cavour's principles of conduct were clearly uncivilized, or at least that they compared badly with those observed by governments which he had the effrontery to call harsh and oppressive. Cavour himself was launching a cruel and unprovoked war on false pretences: 'you, *signor conte*, know perfectly well how those outbreaks arose, whence came the money and arms for them, and whence the instructions to commence'. Reason, law and morality were against the Piedmontese, and what they were doing they did only in the name of brute force.[4]

Cavour had, however, gained his main point, and France did not intervene. The Emperor had been made an accomplice, first by his acceptance of Nice, and then by his irresolution at Chambéry; and also by the fact that Piedmont was now an indispensable buffer state, for the creation of which thousands of Frenchmen had died at Magenta and Solferino. Furthermore, Victor Emanuel was at last forced definitely to choose his minister's side against Garibaldi. Another sign of success was that the regular army was soon winning what Cavour hoped would be 'a prestige quite overshadowing such glory as a run

[1] 8 September, Cavour to Nigra (*CC Cavour-Nigra*, vol. IV, p. 197).
[2] 26 September, Nigra to Cavour (*ibid.* pp. 233–4).
[3] 9 September, Grammont to Thouvenel (Matter, *Cavour*, vol. III, p. 385).
[4] 12 September, *Il Giornale di Roma*, reply dated 11 September.

of good luck had conferred on Garibaldi and his volunteers'.[1] This was perhaps an unfortunate comparison to challenge, since all the concentrated efforts of official Piedmontese historiography were never quite able to make Cialdini's march to Ancona as glorious as Garibaldi's progress from Quarto to the Volturno. But at all events it was true that the skilfully-provoked engagement at Castelfidardo on 18 September brought about a rout of the untrained Papal army barely a week after hostilities had begun. Although Cavour himself was far from thinking so, some moderate and responsible Italians were led by this success to agree with Garibaldi that they were within sight of Rome itself and the culmination of Italian unity.[2] Garibaldi's views on this point are customarily taken as proof of his folly and unrealism, so it is as well to stress that, if so, he stood in good company. Not everyone had been so sure that France would intervene against Garibaldi's march on Rome. Cavour's own intervention, therefore, could still for a time seem different from what it really was; that is to say it could appear not as a move to by-pass Rome in the interests of the French alliance, but rather as an attempt to settle the Roman question quickly before the French could stop him, and before the Garibaldian anti-clericals could reach Rome from the opposite direction.

Cavour no doubt was delighted that people could so misinterpret his motives, because this all helped to confuse his opponents in the south. Not the centre but the south was his chief preoccupation, and once his invasion had been successfully launched, he could turn again to see what was happening to Garibaldi at Naples. On 7 September Persano had

---

[1] 21 September, Cavour to Cialdini (*CC Lib. del Mezz.* vol. II, p. 336).

[2] 10 September, Bettino Ricasoli to his brother (*Lettere di Ricasoli*, ed. Tabarrini, vol. v, p. 234); 29 September (*ibid.* p. 244); 21 August, Dr Pantaleoni to Cavour (*CC La Questione Romana 1860-1*, vol. I, pp. 33-4); 27 September, Poerio from Turin to Lequile and de Simone (G. Bandini, 'Lettere di C. Poerio nel 1860', *Rassegna Storica del Risorgimento*, 1943, pp. 501-2); 27 September, G. Lanza, the Speaker of the House of Deputies, to Castelli (*Carteggio di Castelli*, ed. Chiala, p. 326); 29 September, Emilio Visconti-Venosta to his brother Gino (AME). All these were roughly in agreement with Garibaldi. Against them were those like d'Azeglio who were frightened that the Pope might leave Rome, and those like Cavour who thought that the French alliance was too important to be worth the risk. On 20 September, Cavour's semi-official paper *L' Opinione* announced that the presence of the French garrison at Rome was not to be considered as incompatible with Italian independence.

sent his alarmist telegram, a telegram which, true or untrue in what it said, was a providential weapon in turning the king against Garibaldi and justifying the invasion in the eyes of Napoleon. Garibaldi at Naples had to be opposed. If Cavour had any serious thought of compromise, he would surely have made a greater effort to show how he had lately been converted to many of the dictator's views. It is true that the previous week he had written some outwardly friendly words in one of the few letters he ever sent to Garibaldi;[1] but this temporary descent from his dignified aloofness was in reality another direct result of the cabinet decision to invade the south, and can only have been intended to keep Garibaldi quiet while he completed his own preparations to crush the revolution. The decision was now taken and was irrevocable. We do not know if Cavour's messenger ever reached Garibaldi on this occasion; but only deeds and not words would have counted for much at this point, and now that the liberals had the initiative again, they argued that there was less need for them to concede anything substantial.

However surprised and pleased Cavour was to be when he heard of Garibaldi's first moderate actions at Naples,[2] this could not move him from his obvious duty. He had already decided upon a split. The first step was to find out how far the king would stand by him now that Garibaldi was challenging his right to represent the nation in this new revolutionary phase. Armed with Persano's telegram, he and Farini had gone to see the king on the 8th, and after dwelling on the disagreements in policy between government and revolutionaries, had offered to resign if Victor Emanuel could find other ministers more capable of collaboration with the radicals. According to Cavour's own account of this meeting, he explained that new ministers could at this point be appointed without offence, whereas a change in government could never be made once Garibaldi's defiance became public, for then people would take it to be the result of unconstitutional pressure by a self-appointed dictator. On these representations the king loyally and 'constitutionally' confirmed his support of the ministry, and added (says Cavour) that if necessary he would oppose Garibaldi by force.[3]

[1] 31 August, Cavour to Garibaldi (*CC Lib. del Mezz.* vol. II, p. 191).

[2] 10 September, Cavour to Villamarina (*ibid.* p. 271); 11 September, Cavour to Fanti (*ibid.* p. 275); 11 September, *L'Opinione* (Turin).

[3] 8 September, Cavour's memorandum (*CC Lib. del Mezz.* vol. II, pp. 258–9).

Obviously this was something which had been demanded by the prime minister as a matter of confidence.

Judging by the king's quite unusual impatience against Garibaldi in the next few days, Cavour must have put his case very well in this interview. Such an assurance by the king gave Cavour the confidence to proceed to his next step. Till now he had never been at all sure of his master, who had more than once seemed to be rather in Garibaldi's camp than his own. The radicals for their part were still confident that the monarch was an orthodox Garibaldian in secret.[1] The dictator was acting at this moment on the tacit assumption that, in the last resort, he could appeal to the Throne against the government.[2] He had also an explicit conviction that the Court would approve of his invading the Papal States.[3] When on 11 September Garibaldi wrote to the king asking him to dismiss Cavour and Farini, we have Bixio's evidence that the dictator here had believed with good reason that he was playing not so much his own game as the king's.[4] Bixio explained that Garibaldi would always obey a royal order, even to the point of renouncing his advance on Rome; but the king not only made no such precise order, but had apparently given Garibaldi the impression that he was anxious to get rid of his prime minister and adopt a bolder policy. The implication drawn, and probably intended, was that Victor Emanuel did not want Garibaldi to desist until quite sure that Rome was out of his grasp. Thus the king as well as Cavour had a double policy. Probably no harm was meant by it, and there was nothing in Sardinian constitutional law which made it illegal. But in fact it had had most unfortunate results. The king was severally encouraging both Cavour and Garibaldi in policies which were inconsistent with each other and which now threatened to collide, knowing or hoping that he could accept whichever succeeded and disown whichever lost. This plan brought its own

[1] 9 September, Sineo to Garibaldi (ACM, no. 1291); 5 October, Sineo's letter printed in *Il Risorgimento Italiano*, January 1908, p. 10.

[2] There had been a long history of personal messages between them via Amari, La Masa, Litta, Trecchi, and others; *Carteggio di Amari*, ed. d'Ancona, vol. II, p. 108; E. Librino, in *Nuova Antologia*, December 1930, p. 471; M. Rosi, *Il risorgimento italiano e l' azione d' un patriota*, p. 199.

[3] G. Manacorda, 'Vittorio Emanuele II e Garibaldi nel 1860 secondo le carte Trecchi', *Nuova Antologia*, fasc. 923, 1 June 1910, p. 413.

[4] 18 September, Astengo to Cavour (*CC Lib. del Mezz.* vol. II, pp. 316–17).

defeat. Cavour chose his moment cleverly to drag out this ambiguous dealing into the open, and forced an embarrassed sovereign to choose between being a constitutional or an unconstitutional monarch. The king prudently decided to be constitutional and to drop his unofficial allies on the Left.

Persano's somewhat irresponsible communication had served the prime minister well. It may be appreciated that Cavour did not want the radicals to seem too friendly at this moment, for on the legend of their relentless and uncompromising opposition depended his only good excuse for Piedmont invading the Papal States. It was indeed far more important to win Napoleon's collaboration at this moment than Garibaldi's, and Cavour therefore exaggerated the import of a few isolated and unrepresentative remarks in order to commit both Napoleon and Victor Emanuel to his policy. This may have had the incidental result of dividing Italians from each other, but in other respects it was a useful expedient well adapted to his prime object. Garibaldi's political actions when he arrived in Naples had been moderate, so much so that both autonomists and Mazzinians were even accusing him of favouritism towards Piedmont;[1] but when seen from Turin, this was quite outweighed by the dictator's unalterable opposition to Cavour personally and to the French. Pretences were kept up for a few days more. On 12 September the king wrote a letter to Garibaldi with congratulations upon taking Naples; but he now added an admonition that the regular army and the volunteers would have to co-ordinate their advance, so that Garibaldi should keep the king fully informed of his plans, and take his next forward step only with royal consent.[2] Garibaldi obediently submitted to this. It is notable, however, that even though the king had now decided in favour of Cavour and moderation, his letter still put no specific veto on the Roman expedition, and indeed did not mention the city. Presumably it was intended as a means to slow down Garibaldi's march, by letting him continue in the belief that government and volunteers might both be converging on the Holy City and so needed to act in concert. The king had allowed himself to

[1] 14 September, Brenier from Naples to Thouvenel (Maraldi, *Documenti francesi sulla caduta del regno meridionale*, pp. 170–1).

[2] 12 September, Victor Emanuel to Garibaldi (Curàtulo, *Garibaldi, Vittorio Emanuele, Cavour*, p. 351).

be convinced by Cavour that Garibaldi was now a rebel against the sovereign, not just a political opponent of the minister. He therefore did not dare even now say to Garibaldi in so many words that he must desist entirely from thoughts of Rome; and consequently the ambiguity remained, and the revolutionaries were still left to imagine that the king was secretly on their side. This lack of frankness succeeded in its aim of keeping Garibaldi loyal to the throne; it also had the effect, perhaps not altogether unwelcome to Cavour, of making the dictator more confident in publicising his strictures against the ministry.

The true policy of the northern government only gradually became manifest. On 11 September it was still possible for the Turin public to think that there was no conflict, and that Garibaldi's first actions in Naples proved that he 'is not a man of party but a man of the whole nation'.[1] But in private La Farina had already been writing cheerfully on the 10th that 'the breach between General Garibaldi and the king's government is imminent, I would say is almost a *fait accompli*'. La Farina added in more detail that the king was going to stop the march on Rome, by force of arms if necessary, and also had a plan for sending troops to take over Sicily from the dictator.[2] This of course must have represented the upshot of Cavour's interview with Victor Emanuel on the 8th. To see the significance of this change in policy one must remember that it all took place while Garibaldi was more or less amicable. Not until the 11th did Garibaldi write his letter to the king requesting the replacement of the existing ministry. By the 14th, Cavour would have known about this letter, and would have noted Garibaldi's resolve to advance as soon as possible on Rome.[3] The telegraph lines from south to north had been cut on 8–9 September, and the greater difficulty of communication must have added to the growing suspicion on both sides. The last telegrams received by northern papers from Naples were dated the 8th, and after that the published correspondence from

[1] 11 September, *Il Diritto*.
[2] 10 September, La Farina to G. Ingrassia (*Epistolario di La Farina*, ed. Franchi, vol. II, p. 417).
[3] 14 September, Cavour to Nigra shows that Cavour had received it (*CC Cavour-Nigra*, vol. IV, p. 211); Trevelyan has this episode wrongly, *Garibaldi and the making of Italy*, p. 191.

southern Italy was almost always five days in arrears.[1] On 14 September Napoleon announced that he was withdrawing his minister from Turin in protest against Cavour's conduct, and this would have made the feeling of tension far worse.

The populace of Turin knew all this on the 15th. They were also informed that Count Trecchi had arrived in Turin with important letters to the king from Garibaldi, and the purport of these letters might have been guessed from the tone of Garibaldi's proclamation of five days before which received publication in the newspapers of this date.[2] The general public in Piedmont learnt with dismay of the dictator's protest against 'those miserable people who...while others were fighting on the barricades of Palermo for the freedom of Italy...were talking of the annexation of Sicily....If I had listened to them, should I have been able to continue the fight for Italy?...Annexation will come soon, but only when we can proclaim it from the top of the, Quirinal hill.' This news of Garibaldi's intentions came to most people as a complete surprise. *Il Diritto*, for instance, which claimed to be the best-informed paper for radical policy, had repeatedly given positive assurances that he did not mean to march on Rome and risk war with the French. This journal now tried to explain Garibaldi's proclamation away, by saying that he would surely change his plans when he heard of Cavour's invasion of the Marches.[3] Such a lame excuse was insufficient to conceal the growing political division from the multitude; but this no longer mattered so much to Cavour, because he was at long last finding that the whole length of Italy for the first time responded to his direction.

All this was much less clear at Naples than it was at Turin. Another week went by before Garibaldi himself properly knew how fast the initiative was passing to the opposite camp. Appearances still suggested that the king stood with him against Cavour, and he hoped that the Piedmontese would find themselves obliged to co-operate in the capture of Rome. On the 17th his official *Giornale* at Naples announced

[1] E.g. 21 September, Cavour to Valerio, says that he has had no news from Naples for five days (*CC Lib. del Mezz.* vol. II, p. 338); 21 September, *La Perseveranza* reported that the last news from Naples which had reached Milan was dated 11 September.

[2] 15 September, *Il Diritto*; 17 September, *La Nazione* (Florence), report from Turin dated 15 September.   [3] 16 September, *Il Diritto*.

proudly that Perugia had been taken by the soldiers 'of our king'. Then on the 18th arrived Vimercati with the king's reply to the letter in which Garibaldi on the 11th had asked for Cavour's dismissal. One might expect that Vimercati in private must have tried to make the dictator see reason and postpone his advance on Rome; but, to judge by his official communication, once more something of the same vagueness and ambiguity was deliberately retained. The king's reply simply said that a change of ministry was inopportune 'for the moment', and it was signed 'your most affectionate Victor Emanuel'.[1] Vimercati's private thoughts were anything but friendly, and even before seeing Garibaldi he managed to convince himself that Naples was full of irreconcilable revolutionaries, and that king and dictator could no longer run together.[2] Putting all these facts together, one will see that the official Piedmontese policy was now quite clear, but yet that it had also been decided to continue in the dangerous attempt to keep Garibaldi confused about what was being planned. It was still important not to offend him by any outward sign of antagonism; but if, short of this, he could be gently dissuaded from any rash initiative, then this might gain time for the Piedmontese troops to reach the frontier of Naples before the volunteers could cross into Papal territory.

In the meantime, Cavour on 16 September appointed parliament to meet after a long recess, fixing the date of convocation at 2 October. His idea was that Garibaldi's programme might then receive a public and authoritative repudiation, and also that the policy of invading the Marches might be formally and retrospectively approved by the legal representatives of the people. The publication of Garibaldi's intention in the newspapers made it impossible to keep up much longer the pretence of amity and collusion; but luckily Cavour was now arguing from strength, and the weapon of parliament, long held in reserve, could be brought out with confidence. On the 17th the premier wrote to Villamarina that 'le projet d'attaquer les Français annoncé à l'Europe nous oblige de séparer notre cause de celle de Garibaldi'.[3] The ministerial

---

[1] N.d., Victor Emanuel to Garibaldi (Curàtulo, *Garibaldi, Vittorio Emanuele, Cavour*, p. 353).

[2] 18 September, Vimercati to Castelli (*Carteggio di Castelli*, ed. Chiala, vol. I, pp. 323–5).

[3] 17 September, Cavour to Villamarina (*CC Lib. del Mezz.* vol. II, p. 308).

press now became suddenly and sharply critical of the government at Palermo and Naples. But no anathema was pronounced until it was known how the dictator would react to Vimercati's mission. On the 21st Garibaldi replied that 'he would like to go to Rome, but submits himself to the orders of the king':[1] nevertheless, this reply would not have been received in the north for some days yet, and in Cavour's present mood it would hardly have been trusted; and in any case it still suffered from the ambiguity that the king's orders carried an implication of delay only. Before it arrived there was another catastrophe, for Garibaldi's defiant letter to Brusco against Cavour was printed in the papers of Turin on 22 September. Cavour could now afford to be righteously indignant. As he said, 'Garibaldi, enivré par le succès, s'est cru le maître des destinées de l'Italie'.[2] People at Turin were astonished and scandalized. The *Gazzetta del Popolo* called it 'a national disaster' that such a manifest dualism had begun in Italy. Even *Il Diritto* now gave up hope of a reconciliation and said that one or other party would have to give way. The breach, that is to say, was at last public property. But Cavour had at least secured that he himself appeared the innocent and offended party. Public opinion showed a mixture of alarm and fear. At Turin people were increasingly apprehensive that, if the revolutionary army once reached the Papal States, then the doctrines of the revolution might even penetrate through into Piedmont. This pervasive sentiment of fear was all that Cavour needed to make him feel completely confident. Tell the Emperor, he wrote to Nigra, that

si Garibaldi persévère dans la voie funeste où il est engagé, dans quinze jours nous irons rétablir l'ordre à Naples et à Palerme, fallût-il pour cela jeter tous les Garibaldiens à la mer.

L'immense majorité de la nation est avec nous. Les débuts [*recte* débats] du Parlement le prouveront. Gianduia est furieux contre Garibaldi. La Garde Nationale de Turin marcherait contre lui si besoin était. Les soldats de Fanti et de Cialdini ne demandent pas mieux que de débarrasser le pays des chemises rouges....

Nous avons été conciliant, même faible en apparence, pour avoir le droit de frapper et de frapper fort lorsque le moment serait venu. Il fallait attendre

[1] 21 September, catalogue of royal archives, quoted by Bollea, *Il Risorgimento Italiano*, November 1917, p. 456.

[2] 22 September, Cavour to E. d'Azeglio (*CC Ing.* vol. II, part II, p. 127).

que ces Messieurs jettassent le masque monarchique qu'ils portaient. Maintenant le masque est jeté, et nous irons de l'avant. Le Roi est décidé à en finir.[1]

It was Cavour who this time was quite carried away by his own
success. More than once in these days he repeated that Garibaldi was in
league with Mazzini,[2] and perhaps he believed as much. He even took
urgent steps to put the port of Genoa in a state of readiness lest the rebels
were meditating an attack on Piedmont itself. This was all as excessive
as his original analysis was inaccurate. Garibaldi was in fact casting off no
mask, for he had never concealed his views. On the other hand, Cavour
himself, by his own confession here, had spoken fair words so that he
might strike and strike hard when he was strong enough. All this talk
of civil war, moreover, was perhaps a little too enthusiastic in tone to
be quite seemly in the mouth of a responsible minister, especially as it was
directed against the man who had just conquered half Italy for the king.

No doubt the problems in Cavour's path were too manifold and
difficult for him to remain quite as equable as he was wont. At all
events he was to prove nowhere near so magnanimous in victory as he
had been in defeat. He revelled in these difficulties, the more of them
the better.[3] By his own choice he was obliged to be diplomat, politician,
administrator and even general all in one; for he had never collected
about him enough good men to take some of the responsibility off his
shoulders. This made it all the more exciting that such a great success
was now within his grasp. The radicals had been cleverly and decisively
out-manoeuvred, and he could move over to the offensive both against
them and against the other enemies of Italy. His own kingdom of
Sardinia, with its population of eleven millions, looked like inheriting
two millions more in the centre and nine in the south. The remote dream
of Dante and Machiavelli was suddenly becoming real, and the vision
blinded him to some of the more delicate colours which were already
coming into the picture.

---

[1] 22 September, Cavour to Nigra (*CC Cavour-Nigra*, vol. IV, pp. 221-2).

[2] 24 September, Cavour to Magenta (*CC Lib. del Mezz.* vol. II, p. 352); 24 September, Cavour to E. d'Azeglio: 'il a fait lui-même sa paix avec Mazzini' (*CC Ing.*
vol. II, part II, p. 128).

[3] 28 September, Cavour's words reported by H. d'Ideville: '"j'aime les situations
difficiles et je suis servi à souhait, cette fois", fit-il en riant et en se frottant les mains.'
Journal d'un diplomate en Italie, vol. I, 1872 (2nd ed.), p. 163.

CHAPTER XVII

THE RADICALS AT BAY:
SEPTEMBER

In this rapid development of the political conflict the views of the government were clear enough. The manifold views of the opposition leaders, however, were probably not clear even to themselves. Events were moving too fast for them. And not only were their ideas confused, but also, in consequence, even the rough strength of the various forces ranged against the government was—and still is—hard to assay. For there were too many separate groups in opposition, and their respective followings are too shadowy for proper analysis. It is not even easy to, be sure whether or no they were a real danger; nor whether Cavour's expressions of fear and horror over the 'party of action' represent his conviction or were simply a pretext. We know that he was going to defeat the opposition from the Left, as in a previous critical phase of Piedmontese history he had defeated the opposition from the Right. But one must not postulate the result before tracing the process. Nor must one automatically take his own valuation of the politics of the revolutionary party. For he tended to underestimate their sense and their loyalty and readiness to compromise, as sometimes he overestimated alike their wickedness, their folly, and their internal cohesion.

If his opponents lost, it was not just because individually they lacked his great skill. They were also quite hopelessly divided among themselves. It was a fact that the strongest among them were not the dangerous extremists he imagined. For example, the two prodictators whom Garibaldi chose in the south, Depretis and Pallavicino, were both moderate and conciliatory men, as well as good at their job, and both of them retained a fundamental and overmastering loyalty to the government of Turin. Yet Cavour had little use for them, either for their ideas or for their efficiency; and in a number of ways he made their task more difficult by his aristocratic contempt and uncooperativeness. It is instructive to find that Cavour's special representatives in the south, notably La Farina and Farini, proved on comparison to be more incompetent than these two prodictators; and furthermore, it is difficult to believe that Cavour can have selected them without this being for the very reason that they were known enemies of the radicals. It was, indeed, part of Cavour's considered scheme to be uncompromising—in which point he differed both from Mazzini and from the king his master. Garibaldi's lieutenants whom he ranted against as concealed Mazzinians were really working for him far better than he knew, and were even covering up some of his own mistakes. He could afford to write them off as incapable; but at their worst they were no more incapable than Villamarina or his other select counter-revolutionaries at Naples. Their disreputability was certainly no greater than that of the unspeakable Griscelli, nor their lack of political tact more notable than what lay in his own resort to such a vile instrument. Their headstrong defiance of diplomacy in wanting to attack Rome had, if anything, been exceeded by that of Ricasoli. They had acted illegally and dictatorially without a doubt, but no more so than Cavour when he held the Garibaldian Colonel Zambianchi in prison for ten months without trial or charge. Their attitude to the king was often as respectful as, and often more respectful than, his own. Certainly they had been reckless and had arrogantly flouted Cavour's advice; but their doing so after all proved to be one of the most important contributory factors in the making of Italy. We shall also see how, only a few weeks after Cavour took over the south from the radicals, all the accusations which he had lightly made against Garibaldi's government were being made with redoubled force against his own.

Cavour's superlative qualities as a diplomatist are unchallenged, but they do not make him necessarily more reliable a judge in his own cause than were his opponents. Doubtless some of these radicals were often incompetent, and sometimes all of them were outrageous, but it could be maintained that on the whole they had proved to be the better Italians. Garibaldi and Mazzini were both ready to buy national unity at any price, even if it meant giving up republicanism, committing political suicide, and surrendering to their lifelong personal enemies. Victor Emanuel, like them in this, said he was ready to become simple *monsu Savoia* and clap his hands at Mazzini's success if this sacrifice were necessary for the making of Italy.[1] But Cavour, until a few years back,

[1] *c.* 31 August, N. Nisco on his visit to the king (*Storia civile del regno d' Italia*, vol. IV, 1888, p. 339).

had considered talk of Italian unity as 'silly nonsense'; and if he was now changing his mind, he showed remarkably little generosity or acknowledgement to the people who taught him that he had been misreading the times. He was right to be impatient with their incapacity, but Italy would have been more solidly built had he known how to be more friendly to other people who were fighting in the van of the national movement. In this he proved to be a victim as well as a beneficiary of the type of parliamentary system he had developed, for he found that this system enabled him to proceed without being obliged to take account of any criticism to the left of Rattazzi.

Urbano Rattazzi and the parliamentary Left were too little aware of what was going on and of what Cavour had up his sleeve to be much of a danger to him at this moment; nevertheless it is interesting to note their views. During August and September the attitude of this 'constitutional opposition' altered more than once with the development of events. When in mid-August Cavour made his first overt move to stop further units going to reinforce the volunteers, it must then have seemed to Rattazzi that diplomatic considerations were forcing the prime minister into line with the reactionaries. For Cavour could not say publicly that he was preparing to be more revolutionary than the revolutionaries. Politicians at the time, like historians since, therefore had to guess whether his main motive really was the fear of Mazzini and 'the return of the *party of action* on the political scene'.[1] Probably it was. At all events the opposition press drew the conclusion that Cavour had broken with Garibaldi. They pointed out that he was going back on his promise in cutting off vital supplies to the south.[2] Instead of being a symbol of Italian independence, his name now 'stood for Italian dependence on the foreigner'.[3] His action might even result in Garibaldi's march being checked, and in that case 'Italian unity will be postponed for twenty years'.[4] 'But *we* believe', said *Il Diritto*,

---

[1] 26 August, *L' Opinione*, Cavour's semi-official paper, said that it was.

[2] 25 August, *Il Movimento* (Genoa) said that Farini's suspension of recruitment had at first been taken as something designed for diplomatic consumption only, but now the order was apparently being enforced; although Farini had promised Brusco in Cavour's presence that the government would not cut off Garibaldi's supplies.

[3] 24 August, *L' Unione* (Milan).

[4] 10 September, *L' Unità Italiana* (Genoa).

'that Italy will be made by the exertions of Victor Emanuel and Garibaldi, without reference to Cavour, and even if necessary against him.'[1]

When after all this Cavour suddenly launched his invasion, for a brief moment the Piedmontese radicals changed their reproaches into joyful excitement. 'The monarchy has crossed the Rubicon, it has given way to the pressure of national aspirations.'[2] Only the more skilled parliamentarians realized that there was more in this than was at first apparent. Francesco Guerrazzi and others met on 9 September to discuss this new development, and decided to warn Garibaldi that Cavour was working in a contrary direction. Some of the radical deputies were then sent south to put to the dictator how he might co-operate with the parliamentary opposition in overthrowing the ministry.[3] Among these radicals there were some who were close to the throne, whom the king used to patronize in his frequent moments of impatience with Cavour. Ferrari was one of the opposition deputies to sail for Naples, and he took Garibaldi a message from Sineo which said that the king approved of his project to advance on Rome, adding that there seemed good chances of success.[4] From our knowledge of the king, it is more than possible that this was an authorized indiscretion, made before seeing Cavour on the 8th; and from our knowledge of Riccardo Sineo, it is unlikely that this radical deputy would have risked his reputation if the message had not been genuine. In later days Sineo gave further information about this. He asserted that, at one moment in September, the king privately admitted that he was going to replace Cavour and Farini by a Rattazzi government in which Garibaldi had confidence.[5] Quite possibly Garibaldi possessed information about this episode when on 11 September he wrote to ask the king for this very replacement: because the dictator's letter was certainly written on advice from someone, and the mention of Farini's name as well by both Sineo and Garibaldi, when this is read

[1] 1 September, *Il Diritto* (Turin).
[2] 11 September, *L' Unità Italiana* (Genoa).
[3] 13 September, *Il Diritto*; 11 September, F. Campanella from Genoa to Dolfi, confiscated by Ricasoli's police (BR ASF, b. T, f. C).
[4] 9 September, Sineo to Garibaldi (ACM, no. 1291); later in September, Sineo himself travelled to Naples.
[5] 5 October, Sineo's letter, *Il Risorgimento Italiano*, January 1908, p. 10.

in conjunction with Bixio's statement (see above, p. 233), gives all the more point to the fact that Garibaldi thought he was obeying the king. If so, then the breach between Cavour and Garibaldi was in one sense just another aspect of the tension between minister and sovereign. Sineo went on to say that Cavour got wind of this plot and exerted all his powers to convince Rattazzi and the king that it was too dangerous a game for them to attempt. Perhaps the embarrassment at exposure of his 'unconstitutional' behaviour was one reason why the king now became so annoyed and so outspoken against Garibaldi. In other words Victor Emanuel, having thoughtlessly assisted in causing this split, then with equal thoughtlessness widened it further in an endeavour to cover his own initial responsibility. This conclusion is based on circumstantial evidence, but it is a convenient and likely as well as a specious argument. The Royal Archives are still secret; but as more and more becomes known about Victor Emanuel, it is clear that he lies at the bottom of more than one apparent enigma in *risorgimento* history. The monarchy was determined to win, heads or tails; and quite rightly so, except that such Machiavellism can be justified only by success, and in the present instance it was not altogether successful.

Some of the northern radicals had also welcomed and helped to augment these differences growing up between Turin and Naples. Rattazzi and Brofferio had both kept up direct correspondence with their friends round Garibaldi, for they never lost sight of the fact that the revolution had happened in Cavour's despite and might possibly be used to unseat him. Their hopes had rather grown during the summer as Garibaldi's popularity outshone that of Cavour, and until quite lately they believed that the ministry at Turin was not very firmly established.[1] When Cavour managed to reassert himself and to impress the king with the terrible prospect of Garibaldi provoking war with the French, messages were urgently sent by Rattazzi's party to dissuade the dictator from any further thought of Rome. They particularly asked him to reassure people publicly about this; and they also suggested that he should write a moderate letter to the king promising to annex the

---

[1] 2 September, Rattazzi to Depretis (Archivio Depretis ASR); also cf. 14 August, Brofferio to Crispi (ACP, f. 135); 6 December, Brofferio to Garibaldi, complaining that the dictator had not answered his three or four letters earlier this year (ACM, no. 844).

south at once if only Cavour resigned.[1] In other words, the opposition leaders in Turin were exploiting Garibaldi in order to overturn Cavour. Presumably they imagined that the volunteers would even renounce the culminating expedition on Rome merely in order to assist their own parliamentary *coup*. The suggestion was made that Garibaldi might leave the front line and appear in parliament, so as to strengthen their chances of defeating the ministry.[2] Letters were written to stir him up against Cavour, and to make him understand that the moderates had declared war on the radicals, so that he must look to his own defence.[3] When the existence of this 'tremendous duel' between the two men could no longer be denied, the *Diritto* finally called on Cavour to abdicate and so save Italy from civil war.[4] Arguments were put forward to say that both sides were now agreed over their general aims, the disagreement being merely based on personalities, so that if only Cavour put his country before his desire for power, he would resign.[5] At the end of September, Asproni gave expression to these secret hopes of the parliamentary Left: 'I think that we shall be able to strike Cavour down from Naples; that is to say we shall do so if only Garibaldi begins to understand something of political matters... or at least puts some trust in his real and wiser friends.'[6]

This effort to widen the gap between Cavour and Garibaldi did no service to Italy. If the intention was to make both of them more suspicious of each other and more irreconcilable, it certainly succeeded. In other respects it was wasted effort, because Garibaldi was interested only in Rome, not in parlour politics. If he distrusted Cavour, this was only because the latter showed so little enthusiasm for unifying Italy; but he also retained an equal dislike and distrust for Rattazzi. This latest

[1] 17 September, Marazio editor of *Il Diritto* to Macchi, Luzio, *Garibaldi, Cavour, Verdi*, pp. 216–17; 25 September, Macchi from Genoa to Cattaneo (ACP, f. 127); as late as 2 October, *Il Diritto* went on saying that it had never occurred to Garibaldi to march against the French in Rome.

[2] 22 September, Galeotti from Florence to Massari (Archivio Massari MRR).

[3] 26 September, Macchi to Cattaneo (ACP, f. 127); 27 September, F. Gola to Garibaldi (ACM, no. 1012).

[4] 24 September, *Il Diritto*.   [5] 28 September, *ibid.*

[6] 29 September, Asproni to Brofferio (Raccolta Martini MRR, 342/23/9); 21 August, another letter from Asproni to Brofferio had hoped and expected that the results of Garibaldi's advance would shortly be felt at Turin (*ibid.*).

manoeuvre was assuredly not one which inspired confidence in the latter as an alternative candidate for the premiership.

Cavour knew he had not much to fear from Rattazzi and the parliamentary opposition, provided at least that the government did not allow Garibaldi to get away with a monopoly of national sentiment. The person who appeared to worry him most was still Mazzini, now dangerously close to Garibaldi at Naples. Mazzini continued to be considered a cloak-and-dagger assassin. His ideas and his moral integrity were both completely underestimated and misunderstood at Turin.[1] The terror he managed to inspire in people was quite extraordinary. Italy later claimed him as a hero, but only after his death, when he was no longer thought dangerous; for during his lifetime this lonely exile with his tiny band of followers was believed to be turning Italy upside down. On 17 September, after hiding in Genoa and Florence for four months, escaping arrest 'like an eel',[2] Mazzini had eventually reached Naples on the same boat as Vimercati. This added very considerably to the alarm of all 'honest citizens', Cavour among them; and for the purposes of history it is perhaps more important to observe that alarm than to explain how unjustified it was. Republicanism was a purely mythical spectre, but like other myths its power was quite out of relation to its veracity.

Legend apart, Mazzini could in fact claim that 'not a single word about a republic or about anything which could divide Italians into two camps has passed our lips for the last three years'.[3] During his London exile, although the Sardinian ambassador had been careful to see that articles against him regularly appeared in the English press, Mazzini had never once replied with public criticism of the Sardinian government which he so much detested.[4] Poor and despised, he could still show himself morally superior to the government by which he had

---

[1] 25 September, U.S. Minister Daniel writing to Cass about the Mazzinians: 'they care nothing in fact for a republic or for Italy. Their real object is *Power*, and they are endeavouring to establish a gulf between [Garibaldi] and Piedmont for the sole purpose of setting up a government under their own auspices' (MRR).

[2] 16 May, Cavour to Talleyrand, asking him (just as in former years) for the loan of French policemen to come to Italy and help track Mazzini down (*CC Cavour-Nigra*, vol. III, p. 297).

[3] 1 August, *Scritti politici di Mazzini*, ed. naz., vol. XXIII, 1933, p. 146.

[4] E. Morelli, *Atti del XXIV congresso di storia del risorgimento 1936*, 1941, p. 422.

been condemned. The making of Italy was what mattered most to him, under whatever auspices; and while it stuck in his gorge to raise his own voice for Victor Emanuel, he accepted and in a sense welcomed what was happening, and said that he would actively try and prevent anyone campaigning for a republic.[1] The monarchy was winning, but he was proud to note that this was only by public conversion to his methods and his aim of unity. His own technique of revolution had turned out to be completely successful in the south, despite all Cavour's contempt for it as unrealistic. Mazzini had there proved his point that popular initiative could sometimes be worth more than a foreign ally. Garibaldi had used this technique not only in conquering a whole kingdom, but also in restoring to Italians a priceless self-confidence, as some of the moderates themselves confessed. The events of this year had only confirmed Mazzini in disgust at Cavour's alternative method of diplomatic calculus and 'Machiavellism'. The myth of 'Italy', on the other hand, had proved to be another most powerful incentive to action, far outweighing nice calculations of what was possible or expedient. Honest faith in a mission or a principle, said Mazzini, was worth a great deal more even in practical politics than Cavour would allow, more than a French alliance for instance, which might fail you at any moment, more than a calculating guile which could deceive even your own friends. The method of merely calculating what was expedient had already proved on numberless occasions to be a paralysing influence against action. The method of diplomacy was often useless, and sometimes harmful.[2]

Mazzini had changed his mind more than once during the recent rapid succession of events. He had been overcome with despair on hearing of Cavour's decision in August to forbid the further recruitment of volunteers. Then he had received inside information that Cavour genuinely intended to invade the Papal States, and his dismay changed

---

[1] 21 August, Mazzini to F. Stanzani (*Epistolario*, vol. XL, pp. 338–9).

[2] 1 September, *L' Unità Italiana* (Florence): 'diplomacy signifies the treaties of 1815...; or Germans invading Naples and Piedmont, as in 1821...; or the French occupation of Rome and the Austrian occupation of the legations...; Nice and Savoy snatched away from Italy....Diplomacy means a wavering indecision before the idea of unity...and negotiations with the Bourbons at Naples....Diplomacy means leaving Garibaldi to fight his battles alone.'

to a momentary satisfaction.[1] As early as 7 September, however, he had already realized that Cavour's motive was not to win Rome, but rather to save Rome from Garibaldi, and he guessed that only a further reckless initiative by the radicals could fend off such a result.[2] He had had small hope of achieving this when he set out himself for Naples, but nevertheless his arrival there caused great panic.[3] Afterwards it came as a surprise to the moderates when they discovered how little political influence he had managed to win during his stay in the south.[4] In their great fear of republicanism, they had not believed at the time in his tactical conversion to more moderate counsels, nor in his casual and distant treatment by Garibaldi. There are nine letters extant from Mazzini to Garibaldi between September and November, but these do not show that he aspired to a directing hand in affairs; and while they reveal mutual sympathy and admiration, there is little real cordiality in them, and not a little distrust.[5] Whereas newspapers in northern Italy went on saying that Mazzini was 'ruling' in Naples and Sicily,[6] in reality he was out of touch with the dictator, and spent his time in retirement, writing or visiting Pompeii and Paestum. In so far as he had any influence it was not so insidious as some people have imagined.[7] He candidly reproached the more extreme republicans like Nicotera with refusing to collaborate with Victor Emanuel,[8] and personally he was now reconciled to the position of camp follower in the triumph of the monarchy.[9]

---

[1] 2 September, Mazzini to Botta (*Epistolario*, vol. XLI, p. 36).

[2] 7 September, Mazzini to Sacchi (*ibid.* p. 49); 7 September, Mazzini to Crispi (*ibid.* p. 50).   [3] 18 September, *Il Nazionale* (Naples).

[4] 25 September, Fasciotti the Sardinian consul at Naples to Cavour (*CC Lib. del Mezz.* vol. II, p. 365); Maxime du Camp, who disagreed with Mazzini, yet wrote of what he had seen that 'je dois dire qu'à Naples il fut admirable de dévouement et d'abnégation. Avant d'aimer une forme politique, il aime sa patrie' (*Expédition des Deux Siciles*, 1861, pp. 248–9).

[5] Before long Garibaldi had reached the point of calling Mazzini 'a real obstacle to the unification of Italy' (MRR, 395/20/3).

[6] 13 October, *La Nazione* (Florence).

[7] Nazari-Micheli, for example, concluded of this year that 'the real struggle was not between Cavour and Garibaldi, but between Cavour and Mazzini' (*Cavour e Garibaldi nel 1860*, p. 195; Thayer, *Life and times of Cavour*, vol. II, p. 379).

[8] *c.* 22 September, Mazzini to Caroline Stansfeld (*Epistolario*, vol. XLI, pp. 98–100).

[9] 19 September, Mazzini to Matilda Biggs (*ibid.* pp. 92–3).

Mazzini lives by himself [wrote Asproni with some perplexity], aloof from everything, a spectator of what is going on. Not only does he not put forward his republican ideas, but he restrains the haste of the more impatient, and preaches that it is imperative to subordinate every sentiment to unity. He has aged considerably, and his face shows how much he has suffered. I think this man has a gigantic spirit and an intellect above everyone's.[1]

Mazzini was not to be feared at Naples, and he does not figure prominently in any of the political struggles which were to follow there. But one cannot deny that his presence accidentally did the revolutionaries a great disservice. It played Cavour's game by frightening the moderates, and certainly took its share in turning them and the king against Garibaldi.

More dangerous in practice was Bertani, who had brought his large reinforcement of volunteers to join Garibaldi's forces at the end of August. On arrival at Naples, Bertani in his usual dynamic fashion set about organizing everyone, including the dictator. Garibaldi never showed much cordiality towards him, because several times recently the man had shown that he could follow an independent and irresponsible line of policy. Nevertheless Bertani was welcome. He came with yet more confirmation of the glad news that there were fair chances of receiving royal support in deposing Cavour and completing the march on Rome. Bertani was a single-minded man, an idealist, a man of great energy, and a good organizer. Where others failed to prevail by sweet reasonableness on the mind of Garibaldi, his self-confidence and blustering efficiency sometimes succeeded; and for a fortnight, during Garibaldi's more intransigent phase in the middle of September, Bertani was the keeper of the dictator's conscience, and corrected and probably wrote some of his official letters. Cavour's agents on the spot sent back word that he was a secret republican.[2] These agents do not always seem to have been able to distinguish radicalism from republicanism, and in consequence they sent home misleading reports, which then had a big effect on Turin opinion. One result of this was that Cavour misunderstood and exaggerated Bertani's

---

[1] 29 September, Asproni to Brofferio (Raccolta Martini MRR).

[2] 25 September, Fusco from Naples to Ranucci (CF); Nazari-Micheli repeated the story that he was a blind follower of Mazzini (*Cavour e Garibaldi nel 1860*, 1911, p. 158; Thayer, *Life and times of Cavour*, vol. II, p. 374).

influence on the conduct of affairs.[1] Nevertheless, as Garibaldi was too busy fighting to bother much about civilian affairs, such a man in this position could do much harm. He had certainly encouraged Garibaldi to think that the king was on his side in order to convince him that there was no need to be half-hearted about the advance on Rome.[2] He also antagonized the liberals by using this chance to introduce fantastic measures of social reform.[3] In the end it was Bertani's extremism and hot temper which did as much as anything to lose the day for his party, since he was loath to concede very much to expediency or even to good manners. The more respectable elements in Neapolitan society were soon crying for his blood,[4] and towards the end of the month Garibaldi sent him back to Genoa. This action is convincing testimony of Garibaldi's will to compromise. Perhaps it speaks less well for his good sense that he had not acted sooner. But his forced visit to Sicily, and then the battle of Caiazzo, had not left him much time for Neapolitan politics; and it was not Garibaldi's fault that Pallavicino did not arrive earlier to take up the burden of civil government.

Most of the other radical leaders also came to Naples in the first week of Garibaldi's dictatorship. Crispi, Nicotera and Depretis landed from Sicily on the 12th. Alberto Mario and his wife Jessie White Mario were already there. In the same boat which brought Mazzini on the 17th arrived Aurelio Saffi and Professor Saliceti. Carlo Cattaneo and Giuseppe Ferrari, the two chief federalists in Italy and two of the strongest intellects among the deputies in parliament, also came to Naples. Cattaneo ranks in Italian history rather as an educator than as a politician. His federal views never became a principle of political action in Italy. He had been persuaded by Bertani against his own will

---

[1] N. Nisco, who was an agent of Cavour at Naples, later confirmed from his own personal knowledge that they had been in error here (*Storia del reame di Napoli 1824–60*, vol. III, 1908, p. 129).

[2] E.g. 17 September, Bertani's telegram to say that 'the Marches are in full insurrection, and 20,000 Piedmontese soldiers are supporting the volunteers', in Paternò's bulletin (ASP collezione particolare).

[3] J. W. Mario, *Agostino Bertani e i suoi tempi*, vol. II, 1888, pp. 198–202.

[4] 23 September, *Il Nazionale*, referred to one of Bertani's measures as 'a challenge to society, a negation of the moral principles on which society rests...the exaggeration of popular sovereignty, of the absolute right to work, of a contempt for every social distinction'.

to come south and give advice, but he was not a practical man. It was a source of discord that he criticized Mazzini almost as much as he did Cavour. He told Bertani that the main body of radicals was too much like Cavour in wanting to impose a programme by force. He called them half Jacobin and half Bonapartist, and he blamed them for never questioning whether an imposed unification of Italy was as desirable as a free association of autonomous states.[1] 'Sicily and Naples are not regions...but states', he wrote.[2] Federalism, like liberty, was in his view a point of principle, republicanism only a matter of convenience; and federalism to him was the only form of national union compatible with liberty. In holding such views, Cattaneo in fact was being too theoretical, perhaps also too much of a 'liberal', and certainly was showing too little national arrogance, to do more than confuse counsel at Garibaldi's headquarters. The one political axiom which at this time it was impermissible to call in question was that of unification. In this sense, but in this sense alone, he must be called an eccentric.

Garibaldi had never been in a situation where he had to choose between so much miscellaneous and even contradictory advice. His mind was not naturally tempered to submit so many distinct choices to any adequate process of reasoning, but as usual he proceeded by instinct, judging in the main by what seemed militarily possible.[3] Probably he could not understand Cattaneo's federal doctrine at all. He was too distrustful of Mazzini to put much faith in that quarter. He cannot be said to have liked Bertani, and he had a poor opinion of Rattazzi and his parliamentary party.[4] The one person he would instinctively obey, the king, sent him only vague letters which, under a non-committal friendliness, thinly concealed a new note of acerbity and mistrust. Garibaldi himself could not penetrate the secret of this dubiety. The explanation is either that Victor Emanuel was embarrassed over leaving the general in the lurch after earlier hints of good will; or else it was because in Turin they did not wish Garibaldi to know yet that Rome

[1] Undated draft letter from Cattaneo to Bertani (Archivio Cattaneo MRM).

[2] C. Cattaneo, *Stati uniti d' Italia* (1861), ed. N. Bobbio, 1945, pp. 190–1.

[3] G. Guerzoni, *Garibaldi*, vol. II, 1882, p. 215. Guerzoni was with Garibaldi at this moment.

[4] 9 September, Astengo from Naples to Cavour (*CC Lib. del Mezz.* vol. II, p. 269).

would be by-passed; and probably, too, they wanted the volunteers to become properly involved in the Roman question, so that their own invasion of the Marches could be more readily justified. Garibaldi was a man to be feared, a man who also had to be made out as a dangerous enemy, yet whose open hostility could not be provoked for the moment without some risk.

Once again a complicated political conflict was to be resolved in military terms. On 17 September the Garibaldians could still be hopeful that an agreement was being reached by which the French garrison would leave Rome and allow them to advance.[1] As late as the 19th, Garibaldi issued a proclamation for volunteers to come in by land and sea so that they might all join in this final phase of action, his idea being to meet the Piedmontese in Rome and thence march with them against Venice.[2] But on this same day, the 19th, Türr's miscalculation in Garibaldi's absence exposed the volunteer army to the military reverse, which has already been described. The immediate strategical problem had been how to cross the Volturno and outflank Capua, but Türr's over-hasty tactical advance left them with a highly vulnerable salient at Caiazzo, and they shortly had to fall back again upon the river. The recapture of Caiazzo by the Bourbons on the 21st even opened up the possibility of a counter-attack on Naples, and a panic began in the city. Garibaldi had been away at the time, for this was the very moment when Cordova's intrigues had compelled him to go and appoint a new prodictator in Palermo. It made him realize that there was stiffer opposition ahead than had been expected, and that he might have to adjust his plans in consequence. Vimercati said more than once that, for all he could see, the Rome expedition was being abandoned.[3]

As long ago as 11 September Garibaldi had sent to ask the king to let him have the Marquis Giorgio Pallavicino as a prodictator to run the government at Naples. After a week's delay Pallavicino set out, and on 22 September he arrived on the same boat as Cattaneo. The marquis belonged to one of the richest and noblest families of Lombardy. Twenty years before, he had been a national hero, after imprisonment

---

[1] 18 September, Elliot to Russell (RP G.D. 22/85).

[2] 19 September, *Edizione nazionale degli scritti di Garibaldi*, vol. IV, p. 305.

[3] 20–1 September, Brenier from Naples to Thouvenel (Maraldi, *Documenti francesi*, pp. 176–8).

by the Austrians in the fortress of Spielberg. Once he had been a disciple of Mazzini, but he had now decisively broken with republicanism.[1] While by no means a friend of Cavour, he was at least in occasional correspondence with him. Pallavicino was a moderate radical, who had once been president of the National Society, and never forgot that Piedmont possessed resources without which Italy could not be made into a nation. If he did not go and visit Cavour before leaving Turin, this was so as not to arouse the suspicions of Garibaldi, for unlike La Farina and Depretis he wanted to arrive in the south without any entangling commitments. Partly as a result of this, Cavour had no good words for him or his mission.[2] Garibaldi saw Pallavicino on the 22nd, and told him that he had no intention of being duped again by Cavour and Fanti as he had been in similar circumstances during 1859. But the marquis nevertheless received the impression from this interview that Garibaldi's criticism of the government was in part a matter of misunderstanding on both sides, and that it still left room for negotiation; accordingly he returned home at once so as to discuss the possibility of compromise with Cavour and the king. It was noticed at Naples that his own calmer counsels had made some impression on the dictator; Garibaldi was now ready to be more friendly if only Cavour would but guarantee that those volunteers who wished to join the national army would not be turned adrift.[3]

Back at Turin on the 23rd, Pallavicino found that Vimercati had preceded him with a less conciliatory tale, and that Cavour had managed to prevail upon the king. A personal letter from Garibaldi was presented to Victor Emanuel, but the latter put the message rudely in his pocket unread, and began a tirade against the impertinence of one who claimed to be on a level with his king. He became quite furious when Pallavicino interpolated that Garibaldi had after all done some things which merited gratitude.[4] While Garibaldi was apparently still open to persuasion, the king clearly was not. Pallavicino then saw

[1] 19 June, Pallavicino from Turin to Garibaldi, 'distrust Mazzini and the Mazzinians: they spoil everything they touch' (ACM, no. 1169).

[2] 21 September, Cavour to Valerio (*CC Lib. del Mezz.* vol. II, p. 338).

[3] 22 September, Cordova to Cavour (*ibid.* pp. 346–7); 25 September, *Il Nazionale* (Naples).

[4] G. Pallavicino-Trivulzio, *Le Memorie*, vol. III, pp. 605–9.

Cavour on the 24th, and found him at first quite reasonable and even ready or feigning to give way. At a second meeting on the 25th the prime minister was quite changed, and said he was ready to combat Garibaldi and take the consequences. Pallavicino was shocked, and pointed out that this might leave the way open for the Mazzinians to take over at Naples; to which Cavour replied 'so much the better', for this would give an excuse to obliterate them. Pallavicino could only expostulate that the Mazzinians were not Croats, but Italians, and that war against Garibaldi would be fratricidal. This had no effect. On the way back to take up his post at Naples, he wrote to explain once more that Garibaldi had the same aims as the Turin government, but was just afraid that Cavour might be creating only a new cisalpine Gaul dependent on France.[1] If unwarranted, this fear could surely be allayed without difficulty.

The result of these exchanges was not known to Garibaldi for three or four days. In the interval he continued to show signs that his momentary rage was passing. Perhaps he still had hopes that Victor Emanuel would dismiss Cavour after hearing what Pallavicino had to say. He told people that he had not deserved harsh treatment from the king. Gradually he was becoming reconciled to the situation. Piedmontese troops were known to be moving up towards a position where shortly they might stand between him and Rome, so that one way or the other the future would depend upon them. So while Bertani wanted to halt General Cialdini on the frontier, Garibaldi now expressed the hope that the Piedmontese would soon cross into Neapolitan territory.[2] When his secretary ran into angry opposition from the liberal ministers at Naples, he confirmed the latter in office[3] and refused to sign some of Bertani's decrees.[4] On the 25th, Bertani therefore gave up his post. Mazzini sadly read into these events the conclusion that there was no further possibility or intention of moving on Rome. The rumour had already reached him of the dictator's truly Garibaldian answer to the

[1] 26 September, Pallavicino to Cavour (*CC Lib. del Mezz.* vol. II, pp. 371-2).

[2] 26 September, Villamarina to Cavour (*ibid.* pp. 374-5); 26 September, Astengo to Cavour (*ibid.* p. 377).

[3] 22 September, Villamarina to Cavour (*ibid.* p. 345).

[4] 23 September, three of Bertani's decrees were repudiated by Garibaldi (ACP, f. 138); 25 September, Bertani to Garibaldi (ACM, nos. 813, 814).

king, 'Sire je vous obéirai'. 'He is dejected, discouraged, quotes lines of our poets, and talks of Caprera.... The weakness of the man is something fabulous', wrote Mazzini.[1] 'Gar after plenty of waverings and steps taken towards us has yielded to the King and to the moderates here.... Bertani is going to be sacrificed by him to the *moderates*.'[2] On the 27th, in the first decree for some time which he had signed alone without Bertani's countersignature, Garibaldi welcomed 'our brothers of the Italian army commanded by the brave General Cialdini.... In a short while we shall be able to shake them by the hand.'[3] This was sensible and realistic. Garibaldi, one might say, was now being more moderate than the moderates themselves.

Pallavicino returned to Naples on the 27th, and the next day went to report to Garibaldi at Caserta. The dictator was perplexed and disappointed to discover that the king had been so surly and abrupt; yet he had no thought of rebellion. His attitude was a placid one of acceptance and resignation. Elliot now added his own impression that, although no announcement had yet been made, Garibaldi had been persuaded by this news not to continue his advance.[4] The general confessed amazement that Mazzini should be considered in the north as so dangerous, and put forward the shrewd suggestion that Cavour must be just using the name as a scarecrow to frighten people into supporting a conservative policy.[5] Whether intentionally or unintentionally, Cavour was not behaving as though he properly understood the situation at Naples. Villamarina himself wrote at this time to warn Cavour that the information on which he had latterly built his policy had been incorrect, since the dictator would in no circumstances disobey the king or think of proclaiming a republic.[6] Medici also sent a letter to Cavour on the 28th to put him on guard against some of his more partisan advisers, for if anyone said that Garibaldi's entourage was dangerous they must be judging from passion and not from reason.[7] But these warnings

---

[1] 25 September, Mazzini to Caroline Stansfeld (*Epistolario*, vol. XLI, pp. 106–8).

[2] 27 September, Mazzini to Emilie Venturi (*ibid.* pp. 115–16, 118).

[3] 27 September, *Il Giornale Officiale di Napoli*.

[4] 28 September, Elliot to Russell (F.O. 70/320/536).

[5] 28 September, Pallavicino, *Le Memorie*, vol. III, p. 609.

[6] 29 September, Villamarina to Cavour (*CC Lib. del Mezz.* vol. II, p. 390).

[7] 28 September, Medici to Cavour (*ibid.* pp. 387–8). ·

carried no weight at Turin, where in the flush of success people had no room for second thoughts.

The news brought by Pallavicino aroused mixed feelings in Naples itself. The conservatives tended to be overjoyed, the radicals disconcerted. Probably among most people there was distress to learn that Garibaldi and Cavour had not been reconciled, and this was sometimes ascribed to the extremist views and bad tactics of the men round each of them.[1] One thing which cleared the air a little after the 30th was the departure for the north of some of the secondary leaders among the various factions, bound for Turin where parliament was about to open. As Cavour regained the initiative, the centre of gravity of the Italian revolution was shifting northwards, and Bertani, Ferrari, Asproni, Depretis, Cordova and Scialoia took themselves off in pursuit of it. Political disagreements were then a little less bitter for a few days.

As Garibaldi became more subdued, Cavour became more confident, and excited. He no longer had to make shift to adapt himself to Garibaldi's unaccountable whims, but was himself once more in charge of events. His invasion of the Papal States had evoked but little opposition throughout the rest of Italy. D'Azeglio, it is true, had resigned from his post as governor of Milan, prophesying doom to come,[2] and the aristocrats of the old school did make some protest at the immorality of attacking Pius IX and King Francesco on such a trumpery excuse.[3] But the most prominent reaction was one of delight. Cavour found few voices to criticize him when he justified his conduct by *raison d'état*. 'I do not know if the means adopted were perfectly regular', he was to tell parliament afterwards; 'but I do know that the end was holy, and that the end will justify any irregularities there may have been in the means.... Never was war conducted with greater generosity,

[1] 30 September, *Il Nazionale*.

[2] 12 September, M. d'Azeglio to Castelli (*Carteggio di Castelli*, ed. Chiala, vol. I, p. 322); 16 September, d'Azeglio to Arese (copy in Raccolta Azegliana MRR); 7 June 1861, d'Azeglio to Pacetto (MRR); all these contradict and illuminate Cavour's statement in *L' Opinione* of 25 September that d'Azeglio's resignation had no political implication.

[3] E.g. 16 October, Brignole-Sale in the Senate: 'were we not at peace with that king?...Had not our government publicly and frequently disapproved the Sicilian revolution?...Had not the king of the Two Sicilies given to his people a constitution which had been the object of our hopes and advice to him?' (*Atti Parlamentari*).

magnanimity and justice.'[1] This last phrase was a little excessive. Many people who resisted Cialdini's attack had inevitably been dressed in civilian clothes, and many peasants and even some of the clergy were therefore being shot summarily on capture for the crime of defending their religion, their legitimate sovereign and their fatherland, or even for no crime at all. Some people preferred to use the word 'barbarous' when describing this conduct; and the Bourbon government at Gaeta wondered how Victor Emanuel could stoop to this level when he himself made such extensive use of irregular volunteers.[2] Fortunately the army continued its quick and triumphant progress, and ten days after Castelfidardo the town of Ancona had fallen.[3] Royal commissioners were appointed as civil governors, Valerio in the Marches, since his appointment might please the democrats, and in Umbria Napoleon's cousin, Pepoli, to pacify the French. The political absorption of these central provinces was already beginning as advance troops moved down towards the Neapolitan frontier.

Towards the end of September the success of the war made it possible for Cavour to think more seriously again about what General Fanti called 'operation Naples'. Advice was now coming in from people so diverse as Gladstone, Napoleon, Nigra, and even princes of the House of Savoy, that he should at this point make some magnanimous gesture towards Garibaldi; in this way the radicals and the south might be conquered by generosity, and the victory of Piedmont would not be marred by bitterness and division.[4] Louis Napoleon was particularly anxious lest Garibaldi should be made into a popular martyr and

---

[1] 16 October, Cavour in the Senate. *Ibid.*

[2] 23 October, Elliot to Russell; 26 October, Casella to Elliot (F.O. 70/321).

[3] Incidentally the army had no maps of the Napoletano until Villamarina sent some in October, and Admiral Persano had to sail his ships to Ancona with no charts of the Adriatic. In other words, national unification had not even been a remote hypothesis for the planning staffs at Turin.

[4] 16 September, Gladstone to Lacaita: 'Garibaldi has shown such admirable intelligence and good sense along with all his other fine qualities that one must not distrust him in anything' (Charles Lacaita, *An Italian Englishman Sir James Lacaita*, 1933, p. 151); 16 September, Prince di Carignano to Cavour (*CC Lib. del Mezz.* vol. II, p. 305); 24 September, Nigra telegram to Cavour: 'faites une dernière tentative de conciliation et tâchez de gagner ces hommes en leur faisant de larges concessions' (*CC Cavour-Nigra*, vol. IV, p. 222); 22 September, *Il Nazionale*.

Cavour labelled as an ingrate.[1] Lord Palmerston gave his gratuitous opinion that the government 'ought to treat Garibaldi as an ally and not as an enemy'.[2] Palmerston also pointed out that Garibaldi had put himself in the right by his steadfast loyalty to Victor Emanuel, and by such actions as his voluntary cession of the Neapolitan fleet.[3] But Cavour was adamant: 'il n'y a pas de conciliation possible entre Garibaldi et le Gouvernement du Roi.'[4] Fanti had express orders to use force if necessary to disarm the volunteers;[5] though, when a false rumour spread that Garibaldi had given similar orders against the Piedmontese, the liberals held up their hands in pious horror. Cavour thought for a moment of going south himself,[6] but on second thoughts decided to send Farini as civil governor of Naples[7] and Ricasoli for the same post in Sicily.[8] These decisions, it must be remembered, were taken long before there had been any plebiscite in the south, and even without any state of war being declared between Piedmont and the recognized king of Naples; but Cavour was not the man to wait for nice formalities to give him technical justification for what he intended to do.

Cavour felt sure that right as well as might was on his side. He carefully selected certain arguments which he thought would satisfy Palmerston and sent them to London:

Garibaldi n'a aucune idée politique précise. Il rêve une espèce de dictature populaire, sans parlement et avec peu de liberté. Ses adeptes Bertani et autres acceptent sa dictature comme un moyen d'arriver à la Constituante et de la Constituante à la république.

Vous ne pouvez pas vous faire une idée du désordre qui règne à Naples. Les fous de toute l'Europe s'y sont donné rendez-vous. Jersey tout entier s'y est transporté.[9]

[1] 1 October, Panizzi from the British Museum to Cavour, that Napoleon had said as much to him personally (*Lettere di Cavour*, ed. Chiala, vol. VI, p. 606).

[2] 28 September, Palmerston to Russell (RP G.D. 22/21).

[3] 24 September, E. d'Azeglio to Cavour (*CC Ing.* vol. II, part II, pp. 129–30).

[4] 27 September, Cavour to Villamarina (*CC Lib. del Mezz.* vol. II, p. 383).

[5] 21 September, Cavour telegram to Fanti (*ibid.* p. 333).

[6] 22 September, Cavour to Nigra (*CC Cavour-Nigra*, vol. IV, p. 222).

[7] 24 September, Emilio Visconti-Venosta to his brother Gino (AME).

[8] *c.* 26 September, Farini to Ricasoli, adding that the plan was to go 'and establish monarchic authority, morality and common sense in Naples and Sicily' (*Carteggio di Ricasoli*, ed. Nobili and Camerani; to be published).

[9] 27 September, Cavour to E. d'Azeglio (*CC Ing.* vol. II, part II, p. 133).

Cavour still misread Garibaldi's character enough to be worried that the latter might try to oppose the advance of Fanti,[1] and he instructed Villamarina in that case not to hesitate before overturning him and setting up a provisional government in collaboration with General Medici.[2] His chief strength was that he had momentarily prevailed upon the king to distrust Garibaldi and resent the appeal for the dismissal of a constitutional ministry. As Poerio described in a letter of the 27th, 'the king is indignant, and if there were once some differences between him and Cavour, these have now been dispersed...Rattazzi has spontaneously given his support to the ministry, and I do not think that in the Chamber there will be twenty votes supporting Guerrazzi.'[3] It was on this day, the 27th, that the details were finally decided for the plan which this more favourable situation made possible. Cavour sent off to tell Nigra what was proposed, that the king 's'est décidé...à marcher sur Naples pour mettre Garibaldi à la raison et jeter à la mer ce nid de républicains rouges et de démagogues socialistes qui s'est formé autour de lui....C'est *l'ultimatum* insolent apporté par cet imbécile de George Pallavicini qui a décidé le Roi.'[4] No doubt Cavour had made as much of this 'ultimatum' as he could. All had depended on the king's decision. Fortunately Garibaldi had been induced to overreach himself, and in the selfsame action had both antagonized the king and attracted public responsibility for the clash between north and south. The radicals had again been outmanoeuvred.

In being so uncompromising and ruthless, Cavour had been moved in part by Garibaldi's request to the king for his replacement, but in part also by the unexpected sharpness of Napoleon's protest against his attack on the Pope. 'It is by driving the Mazzinians into the sea that we shall receive from Napoleon a plenary absolution', he wrote.[5] If only France could be mollified, the rest was easy. In northern Italy, public opinion was already on his side, as a *juste milieu* which saved them from

[1] 29 September, R. de Cesare, *Una famiglia di patrioti*, 1889, p. ccxiii, on what Cavour had just said to Spaventa.

[2] 25 September, Cavour to Villamarina (*CC Lib. del Mezz.* vol. II, p. 361).

[3] 27 September, Poerio to Lequile (G. Bandini, 'Lettere di C. Poerio nel 1860', *Rassegna Storica del Risorgimento*, 1943, pp. 501–2).

[4] 27 September, Cavour to Prince di Carignano (*CC Cavour-Nigra*, vol. IV, pp. 235–6).

[5] 30 September, Cavour to Pepoli (*CC La Questione Romana*, vol. I, p. 44).

the Pope and Mazzini. Cavour had never been so popular in Piedmont as he was now that he had regained the initiative for Turin and for conservatism,[1] and this popularity gave him the firm impression that the cult of Garibaldi was on the wane and could be attacked with impunity. He could not guess what would be the price to be paid for this in the future. 'The Garibalditis is on the way to a cure', he told Pepoli, and 'I flatter myself that the discussions in the Chamber will finish it off.'[2]

The prospect of parliament reopening came to Cavour as a tonic. It was not only that he knew himself to be a master of parliamentary technique; but also, like a true liberal, he preferred to encounter his enemies in public debate. He knew that those most prone to Garibalditis were not prominent in either Senate or Chamber of Deputies. It is true that Garibaldi was himself a member of parliament; and ironically enough, earlier in the year it had been he who denounced Cavour in the Chamber for violating the constitution by ceding Nice and Savoy. But that episode had only confirmed the radical general in his abiding contempt for a body which could slavishly ratify this violation of national territory. Cavour was thus quite right to say that Garibaldi's favourite form of government was a popular dictatorship,[3] and the knowledge was particularly instrumental in making parliament look on the *invitto duce* of southern Italy with fear and distaste. The prime minister knew that he was sure of a large majority as soon as the Chamber reopened on 2 October, when all these disagreements could be brought safely into the open.

[1] 28 September, H. d'Ideville at Turin, 'il est impossible d'être aussi populaire', *Journal d'un diplomate en Italie*, vol. I, p. 163.

[2] 30 September, Cavour to Pepoli (*CC La Questione Romana*, vol. I, p. 44).

[3] E.g. G. Tivaroni, 'Garibaldi e la dottrina della dittatura', prints Garibaldi's letter to Lallemand of 3 December 1869, *Rivista del Risorgimento*, 1897, pp. 669–71.

CHAPTER XVIII

MORDINI THE NEW PRODICTATOR: 17-25 SEPTEMBER

By the middle of September, Italian affairs in general were driving on at what Lord Palmerston called 'railway speed', but the island of Sicily seemed to have been left in something of a backwater, and Sicilian politics had again taken on the appearance of being more local than national. As a French observer in the south commented on 18 September, 'on ne semble être d'accord en Sicile que sur un seul point, la haine du nom napolitain, et de tout lien politique, même abstrait, avec ce royaume'.[1] Apart from this one point of agreement, Sicilians were becoming ever more restless and anxious as the battle moved farther away. Depretis's attempt to find a highest common factor of consent had ended in his resignation on the 14th. As a result of this, Garibaldi had most reluctantly to leave his military preoccupations in order to come and repair these growing differences. On the 17th the dictator arrived unexpectedly in Palermo for a six-hour visit, intending to find out for himself what was amiss and to select a new civil governor.

Crispi's candidacy for the vacant prodictatorship was out of the question, since he had aroused too much personal antipathy to be the instrument of pacification, and was too much of a partisan and too little of a diplomat to be able to find a compromise and secure people's consent to it. Before returning to Sicily the dictator had, it is true, asked Crispi to come with him as adviser, but the latter was too much frightened of the changed atmosphere of backbiting and popular demonstrations, and was too eager to remain on the centre of the stage at Naples. There is not much doubt that his presence in Sicily at this moment would have been more hindrance than help. But possibly it was an error of judgement on his part thus to minimize the importance of Sicily for the fortunes of his party, and not to be at hand to take an active share in the choice of Depretis's successor.

[1] 18 September, Brenier to Thouvenel (Maraldi, *Documenti francesi sulla caduta del regno meridionale*, p. 175).

Bertani was more far-sighted than this. Probably he had been behind the approach made to Aurelio Saffi, former triumvir of the Roman republic of 1848, to come and accept the post of prodictator,[1] and then he even took it upon himself to write out and sign a decree nominating Calvino to this position.[2] Bertani's views, however, did not prevail with Garibaldi nearly as often as the moderate liberals chose to think; nor did they prevail on this occasion. A description of the actual election was sent to Crispi by one of the prodictatorial secretariat who was a radical but also a friend of Cordova:

No sooner had Garibaldi arrived than he tackled the reform of the government. He first put up Parisi as prodictator, on your recommendation I should imagine. But such a choice would have been the downfall of our party. Parisi betrayed us under Depretis; and then, when he saw us back in power again, pretended as hard as he could to be on our side; or perhaps he is indeed with us for the moment, but then would betray us again as easily if it should ever serve his turn....He ought not even to remain Minister of the Interior as he is now....The only suitable Minister of the Interior is yourself. Everyone now is unanimous in calling eagerly for you, for what Garibaldi said here has completed the restoration of your reputation and your political beliefs....

But to return—when I saw the decree nominating Parisi as prodictator I was dismayed, knowing what our friends would say about it....Like everyone else I was despairing of any alternative, when suddenly my eye caught Mordini, and I knew he was the man. Some people turned up their noses when I proposed him, and said he was too close to the republicans; others said, 'Mordini? Who knows *him*?' But my proposal met with support from Sutera, Cacioppo, Ugdulena and Calvino; he was put up to the General and was accepted instead of Parisi.

It was all very fortunate, for Mordini's appointment has been welcomed by everyone, even by our enemies. He is courteous but strong: his published programme is that of Garibaldi, and his first acts have won him both love and respect....He has reappointed Bargoni as secretary-general to the government. Bargoni has a good reputation, though my own view is that as a Tuscan he is something of a 'municipalist', that is to say he does not love us Sicilians as he ought. But we shall see.[3]

[1] 22 September, *L' Unità Italiana* (Genoa); 7 October, *Il Nazionale* (Naples) contains a letter from Saffi about this.

[2] 14 September (ABM).   [3] 22 September, Navarra to Crispi (ACP, f. 135).

In the circumstances Antonio Mordini was an excellent choice. He had been born into the small agricultural nobility of Tuscany, and had distinguished himself in the 1848 wars of liberation at Florence and Venice. At the present moment he was a lieutenant-colonel and auditor-general of Garibaldi's army. While belonging to the 'party of action', and though further towards the left than Depretis, he was also a loyal deputy in the Piedmontese parliament. He had voted in the Tuscan assembly for the annexation of his home province to the kingdom of Victor Emanuel, and since then had taken an oath of allegiance to the king. In addition to having done good service for Garibaldi and for Sicily in 1860, he was already known in the south as a distinguished patriot,[1] and he combined in himself the loyal monarchist and the radical, the convinced annexationist and the non-Piedmontese. Yet for all that, Mordini's appointment was not liked at Turin. Cavour gave undue regard to the fact that he had once been a republican (like many of the liberal-conservatives!), and soon transformed him imaginatively into a rabid follower of Mazzini.[2] Mordini had in fact split off from Mazzini at the time of the Genoese insurrection of 1857, and subsequently had supported the Piedmontese war of 1859. Earlier in 1860 he had again specifically renounced the republican leader.[3] Cavour's successors after 1860 were to find in him a capable prefect and minister, and he finished life as a respectable senator, if anything rather to the Right of Italian politics.

This was the man whom Garibaldi now presented to the citizens of Palermo as his deputy. In a public speech to them the dictator reaffirmed his own determination to push on to Rome. Not until Rome had fallen did he mean to proclaim the new kingdom of Italy under the gallant monarch of Sardinia in whose name he had already conquered the south. Far from opposing annexation, he wanted only to postpone it

[1] 20 June, *Il Paese* (Palermo).

[2] Nazari-Micheli still refers to him as a 'secret Mazzinian', *Cavour e Garibaldi nel 1860*, p. 166; Whyte also calls him a republican, *The political life and letters of Cavour*, p. 428.

[3] 5 June, Mordini to P. Cironi (who was editor of the radical *Unità Italiana* of Florence and a friend of Mazzini): 'just as Cavour committed a grave error in sending La Farina to Sicily, so others are equally wrong to push forward the name of Mazzini. What we need now is *abnegation* of our own private wishes in the interests of *concord*' (Rosi, *Il risorgimento e l' azione d' un patriota*, p. 197).

in the interests of other yet unredeemed provinces of Italy; and he gave his audience to understand that he was agreed on this principle with the king, but that Cavour alone stood against it. This was not an accurate statement of the situation, but Garibaldi still thought it was true, and had good reason to do so. At all events his confident assertion must have carried conviction with the Palermitans. To understand their reaction to Garibaldi's speech, we must forget that he was not to reach Rome and that the king had by now decided against him; for he himself did not know this yet, and his assurance to the contrary must have done much to calm Sicilians and unite them behind his apparently irresistible advance.[1]

A radical newspaper thus described the sudden effect on people: 'the miracle happened and in a few hours Palermo was bewitched. Dare we hope that these *signori annessionisti* will have done with their trouble-making now that Garibaldi has silenced them?'[2] The party of Cavour was momentarily at a loss, and even the irreconcilables must have seen the uselessness of further agitation. Those who objected found it best to keep silent. Their chief hope was to wait for the arrival of the Piedmontese, whose armies were now winning their first victory in the north at the very moment that Garibaldi's were suffering their first military reverse. With General Fanti approaching the Neapolitan frontier, the long-term prospects for the liberals were good. It must have seemed that there would be not long to wait until Cavour re-imposed his will upon the revolutionary movement, either to crush it or to co-operate with it. Whether for one reason or the other, the febrile agitation of Depretis's last days now diminished a little, at least for a day or two.

Nevertheless, though active propaganda weakened, private sentiment in favour of annexation (if perhaps only in Garibaldi's good time) was bound to grow stronger unless the new administration could effect a second miracle and increase the efficiency of government. The wildest opinions continued to circulate in Sicily, and Cordova's friends naturally exploited whatever discontent and opposition they could find. One of Ricasoli's informants wrote privately on 19 September in stronger terms than anyone ever dared to voice in public. 'We are now

---

[1] G. Oddo, *I mille di Marsala*, 1867, p. 891.
[2] 20 September, *L' Unità Italiana* (Palermo).

drifting into civil war.... The national guard will not support this new ministerial combination.... In Sicily all are unanimous in favour of annexation, and differences exist only about the method of its accomplishment; these differences, too, will disappear the moment it is possible to emerge from this inferno of a most tyrannical dictatorship.'[1] A more dispassionate judgement would perhaps not have found very much tyrannical about a government which tried to rule a naturally anarchical country during a civil war with no censorship, no armed forces to spare for domestic affairs, and only a tiny body of police. This qualification, however, does not altogether invalidate the political criticism. Many people continued to have private doubts about Garibaldi's obstinate adherence to his earlier policy.

The moderate and sensible Amari for this reason refused to join Mordini's cabinet: 'the country wants annexation and quiet,' he said, 'all except a small knot of crack-brains and mischief-makers. Garibaldi's presence here has made us swallow the pill, but it is not so certain that we shall digest it.'[2] Some days later, Amari wrote to a friendly politician in England that the fall of Depretis had been caused by a combination of place hunters, Mazzinians, Garibaldians and autonomists; and he bewailed that 'le bas peuple dans son honnête naïveté adore en Garibaldi le héros du mythe, qui, par conséquent, a toujours raison vis-à-vis des hommes politiques sans sabre ni chemise rouge'. Amari's one hope was that the Piedmontese army would soon arrive in Sicily. If they were not careful, he thought, there might be a rebellion against Garibaldi, a rebellion which would bring about a civil war in which Garibaldi would triumph.[3] Torrearsa on the other hand, who was but little removed politically from Amari, chose to support the new prodictator,[4] and his provisional and conditional support was perhaps more typical of the general opinion. There were doubts and suspicions on more sides than one, but the most sensible attitude was to wait and see. A reassuring

[1] 19 September, G. Fiorenza to Ricasoli (*Carteggio di Ricasoli*, ed. Nobili and Camerani).

[2] 18 September, Professor Amari to G. P. Vieusseux (*Carteggio di Amari*, ed. d'Ancona, vol. III, p. 209).

[3] 7 October, Amari to Cartwright (*ibid.* vol. II, p. 134).

[4] 20 September, Marchese Torrearsa to his brother Giambattista ('Documenti del risorgimento negli archivi privati di Trapani', *Rassegna Storica del Risorgimento*, 1942, p. 800).

comment which has come down to us from 20 September remarked that
'the country is now quieter, though much doubting the good faith of
the annexationists'.[1] Members of Cavour's party also noted this restoration of tranquillity.[2] It should have been some satisfaction to them
when Mordini's ministers took the oath to Victor Emanuel and the
Piedmontese *statuto*.[3] In the provinces Mordini had a good response
when he asked for moderation, calmness and unity.[4] On the whole a
satisfactory reception was accorded to the new prodictatorial regime,
and Garibaldi's personal recommendation gave it a flying start among
'le bas peuple'.

One reassuring influence with members of the annexation party was
the widespread belief that Mordini could not last more than a fortnight.[5]
At the very worst they felt sure that Garibaldi would hardly choose
civil war when Cavour at last revealed his intentions and offered combat
as the only alternative to surrender.[6] But the new prodictator was in
fact to remain in power for seven weeks, skilfully piloting his government through many storms. The change in personnel of his new regime
helped to cut out some of the old personal animosities from politics.[7]
The radicals were in a cheerful and generous mood, because so far as they
could see the capture of Rome was imminent. Even Crispi himself now
laid down as Mordini's first duty the preparation of the island for a vote.
Apart from preparing for this act of union, the prodictator had to
organize men and munitions for Garibaldi's advance, to try and create

[1] 20 September, Chiarenze from Palermo to Crispi (ACP, b. 156).

[2] 21 September, Sardinian consul from Palermo to Cavour (*CC Lib. del Mezz*
vol. v).

[3] 22 September, *L' Annessione.*

[4] 18 September, the governor of Catania wrote to Mordini to say that everyone
in his province agreed with the dictator, and 'any move against his policy has been
rejected' (MRR); 20 September, the governor of Castroreale told Mordini that
'public spirit here moves with the general current and is developing satisfactorily'
(MRR, 221/23/9); 18 September, governor of Catania in a telegram to Mordini
described how 'your prodictatorial pronouncement is published here and has brought
joy and confidence to people once more' (AMB).

[5] 25 September, *La Gazzetta del Popolo* (Turin), report from Palermo dated
21 September.

[6] 25 September, Amari to Cartwright (*Carteggio di Amari*, ed. d'Ancona, vol. III,
p. 212).

[7] 28 September, Mordini to Bertani (ABM).

a body of police to enforce the law in Sicily, and to improve the administration at Palermo. He addressed himself to all these tasks. Mordini was like Depretis in possessing a conciliatory disposition, and this must have helped him keep the peace so that political problems could resolve themselves with time. His policy was to make another attempt at reconciliation and compromise, and he was not to know that a compromise solution now had little chance of success. In practice, while everyone cried concord, one side interpreted this to mean that Garibaldi should surrender, the other that Cavour should resign.[1] Such a difference of opinion could not continue for long unresolved, but the prodictator managed, partly from policy, partly from weakness,[2] to postpone his decision.

After the first week it still seemed that things were 'not going at all badly when you remember the great difficulties of the situation'.[3] There was certainly some opposition to Mordini but it was not alarming, and while it was realized that matters could not continue indefinitely in this state of suspension, there was nevertheless little to fear immediately unless Cavour decided to take over Sicily by force. On 24 September the official *Giornale* criticized those who made up the opposition, on the grounds that they were trying to precipitate annexation. For however desirable this end might be in itself, the common cause might suffer if it were enacted with too much haste.

The government will act severely against those who disturb the mutual confidence between it and the people, and if necessary will take such special steps as would be its right and its duty in these circumstances....
All of us in Sicily are annexationists, and none more so than the present ministers.... The champions of precipitate annexation know this perfectly well, but for their own private purposes they choose to turn a mere question

---

[1] 26 September, *La Cicala Italiana* (Palermo).

[2] 3 November, *La Valle di Giosaffat* (Palermo): 'Mordini has the kindest of hearts, is affable, weak of character, and knows nothing of the country; so that he lets himself be influenced now by the aristocracy, now by the populace. The result is that, continually oscillating between these two extremes, despite his sincere and noble declaration that he will not represent a government by party, he comes to represent a government by the *piazza*.'

[3] 25 September, S. Castiglia from Palermo to Crispi (ACP, f. 135); 26 September, Mordini to Crispi: 'I think I have now been able to acquire sufficient force in the country' (ACP, f. 140).

of timing into a major question of substance. The clear proof of their sinister designs is the insinuation that differences of opinion exist between General Garibaldi and our *Re Galantuomo*; as if it were not notorious that one and other are bound by indestructible ties of affection and esteem, and that both have but one aspiration, the making of Italy.[1]

There can be no doubt that Mordini believed this doctrine of the harmony of interests, and the fact continues to be an important clue to both his motives and Garibaldi's in continuing their defiance of Cavour.

If these were his public statements, Mordini's private views can be found in a letter to Bertani which he wrote on the 25th to describe what was happening:

I at once set about getting to know the public and making myself known by them. The composition of the new ministry created an excellent impression. The country can see from this that we represent no exclusive view;, and while we shall be firm in following the programme of Garibaldi, we have no intention of making our government represent a single party. This is one proof the more that we have no special axe to grind, for there exists only one political path we can follow. Our full attention is concentrated on administration, which for one cause or another is in a chaotic condition here.

In such a state of chaos the arrival of Casalis was fatal. Not that he carries much influence. But his previous conduct, as Crispi will know, should have prevented him coming. His first move was to go and see Cordova.... And he lost no time in spreading about the rumour that Depretis would soon be back here as royal commissioner at the head of four thousand Piedmontese soldiers. In my position, without material forces to aid me, it will be disastrous if people undermine the moral force upon which alone we have to rely, that is to say by spreading it about that my government is a matter of only a few days.

The agitators are taking advantage of the presence of Casalis, and make out that this confers on them *from above* an authorization to intrigue. They are going about to extract signatures for an address beseeching the king to send soldiers to the island. But fortunately they are meeting a general rebuff from the common sense of the people. They also tried to make the Civic Council follow up this address, but I forbad it. Their actions have helped to disturb the general calm here...so much so that, after leaving Casalis free

[1] 24 September, *Il Giornale Officiale di Sicilia*.

to sow his wild oats in order to find out what he was really up to, I took steps to have him put under arrest.... The Sardinian consul then asked if he might have him in custody at his own house, and I agreed.[1]

Cordova and Casalis had evidently not delayed for long in renewing their propaganda campaign for annexation. This campaign was well organized. It had begun in August by the formation of a central committee in Palermo, with the purpose of persuading local authorities everywhere to send in reports to convince Depretis and Garibaldi of the 'unanimous wish' of their locality for immediate annexation. Cavour had been kept in touch with the development of the movement by his consul at Palermo, and during the first ten days of September, until Depretis fell, he had been confident of its success.[2] The consul's correspondence shows that most of the details had been worked out with the active aid of this official representative of Piedmont. He attended meetings of the committee, and Cavour already in September was making a note that he should be given the Cross of St Maurice for his political activity against Garibaldi's government.[3] This same man did his best to impress upon Cavour that Mordini, despite the fact that he had voted for annexation in the recent Tuscan assembly, was at heart a republican.[4] After Mordini's appointment the collection of signatures for annexation still continued in the streets and cafés.[5] The governor of the province of Noto discovered that Bottero had been the medium for passing on instructions from Cavour to the Piedmontese vice-consul at Messina, and this official had been retailing these instructions to all other consular officials in eastern Sicily. Their orders were that they should each try and make the provincial governors raise a subscription and use it to oppose the policy of Garibaldi's government.[6] By mischance it happened that the governor of Noto was loyal, and so reported what he heard to the government; but for the most part Crispi had appointed to governorships those local figures whose territorial

[1] 25 September, Mordini to Bertani (ACP, f. 140).

[2] 4 September, Cavour to Prince di Carignano (*CC Lib. del Mezz.* vol. II, p. 223).

[3] Cavour's note written on the letter sent by Rocca from Palermo on 25 September (*ibid.* vol. v). The decoration was duly given him in April 1861.

[4] 21 September, Rocca to Cavour (*ibid.* vol. v).

[5] 20 September, *Giornale di Catania*; cf. 8 September, *Tom Pouce* (Palermo).

[6] 22 September, the governor of Noto to Mordini (AMB, b. 28).

position gave them the most influence, and these men often pursued independent policies of their own against that of the Palermo government to which they were nominally responsible. Of course it sometimes happened that Cordova slipped up and selected as recipient for his propaganda some man who disapproved of this method of procedure: in that case the 'unanimous wish' of this or that locality was likely to be reported as being against immediate annexation. But whichever way they told, reports of this type are fallible as evidence of the state of public opinion. People's views were surely more diverse, more complicated, more unreasonable, even more unintelligible than such crude statements tried to make out. As one of these provincial radicals had ruefully and ingenuously commented, 'in general the interior districts of Sicily reveal a great ignorance of political principles, so that little or no difference is made between annexation to Piedmont and Italian Unity'.[1] The subtleties of the political conflict were far above the heads of ordinary Sicilians; and as for the dominant personalities in local government, they would always tend to put a simple return to peace and quiet in the centre of their political programme.

Crispi in August, when he was minister for internal affairs, had chosen to take a firm stand against disaffection. There was good reason for a government to resent disloyalty among its own appointed servants, and to be impatient of opposition in a time of war emergency under a dictatorial regime. The government had originally been organized as a dictatorship because, for a country like Sicily, dictatorship was the only organization of power which could satisfy the demands of war and the rebuilding of a totally wrecked administration. Crispi therefore claimed that there should be only one policy, laid down by the government, and that party strife ought to await quieter times. He told Garibaldi that he had documentary proofs of how Cordova, though still nominally a judge in the Palermo court of appeal, was obstructing the policy and administration of the dictator's government. In reply had come a telegram on 12 September ordering Cordova at once to answer these charges at Naples. This was still before the resignation of Depretis.

After Cordova, Crispi and Depretis had all left Sicily, Bartolomeo Casalis became the leader of the annexation movement with whom

[1]   27 August, questura of Piazza to Crispi (ACP, b. 152).

Mordini had to deal. Casalis first made some attempt to induce Mordini's colleagues to desert him and so force the prodictator's submission. He also let fall a hint that people should hesitate before collaborating with a man on the Piedmontese black list who was shortly and inevitably to be dismissed with all his followers. This was accompanied by the other actions described in Mordini's letter quoted above. On 24 September Casalis wrote a letter to Bottero, which illustrates in the first place the degree of misconception about the new prodictator, and in the second place the extent to which Cavour was fomenting rebellion against Garibaldi. In this letter Casalis explained that he intended to leave shortly for Naples, 'because all my work here is now ready':

> Mellino has been able to do his part admirably: he has won over the artillery units in Palermo to place themselves at his disposition, and the regiment of cavalry too; and he has arranged everything else with the more influential citizens of Palermo whom you know about.
>
> So here we have everything ready and are only waiting for the order to move. The deputation to the king is leaving on the same boat which brings you this letter, that is if the government does not stop it. *Mordini's government is like that at Naples in working against annexation and for a republic.* Mazzinian propaganda is being carried out with an admirable activity and a mint of money. I wrote formerly from Naples to tell Cavour what I now tell you, that it is time to end this business. A breach is now unavoidable, and we must therefore bring it about quickly before they can prevail on public opinion to support them. Otherwise the advance of Mazzinianism will precipitate a bloody civil war. We must move at once. Mellino has also paid careful attention to the press, with the result that all papers are on our side except the *Precursore*. . . .
>
> Depretis did well to resign and leave Garibaldi isolated among Bertani and Crispi and the other more or less disguised Mazzinians. Thus, when our government thinks the moment ripe to break with these fools who are compromising our cause, Depretis will be able to return on one of our warships to Palermo as royal commissioner.[1]

Not unsurprisingly, Casalis was arrested on this same day, before he could carry out his plan. The Piedmontese consul had already prepared for the eventuality of his arrest, and was ready with his offer to Mordini

[1] 24 September, Casalis to Bottero (Bollea, *Una silloge di lettere del risorgimento*, p. 346).

that he himself should be allowed to look after the prisoner in his own consulate. Mordini, perhaps weakly, agreed to this proposal, and so incurred the odium of oppression without its advantages. A moderate and fully justifiable action was now publicized to the world as an act of gross tyranny. On the 25th Casalis and Mellino took ship for Naples.

Cavour knew about what was happening in his name. He had been already informed that his friends in Palermo 'had a scheme ready for a *pronunciamento*, which would substitute a new provisional government for that of Garibaldi, and would proceed to annex the island immediately'.[1] His informants give the impression of being more extreme and alarmist in their letters to Cavour than when writing to their other friends, perhaps purposely exaggerating the difficulties in Sicily so that Mordini might seem the more a villain and they themselves the more heroic. But it was on such information that Cavour made up his mind that henceforward he would exclude all idea of, compromise. He even decided to take away the few policemen he had formerly sent to help Depretis in the maintenance of law and order, making the excuse that they now might be used to serve Mazzini instead of the king, and adding in explanation that there was no more room for reconciliation between Garibaldi's government and the king's.[2] Probably this was also because he did not want Mordini to win the reputation of being able to restore order on his own. Annexation must be forced on an unwilling government—if necessary by adding to the anarchy in Sicily, so that the radicals would lose and the liberal-conservatives would gain in popular estimation.

House-arrest and expulsion were mild answers to the activity of Casalis, but they were enough to colour the accusation that this was a dictatorial reign of terror. On 24 September, as part of the same plot, there fled from Sicily to Genoa several former Piedmontese officials. These men had originally been allowed by Cavour to go and fill senior posts in Garibaldi's ministry of marine, in case it ever became necessary to usurp control of the Sicilian navy.[3] On their return to Genoa they

---

[1] 18 September, Cordova to Cavour (*CC Lib. del Mezz.* vol. II, p. 321).

[2] 27 September, Cavour to Villamarina (*ibid.* pp. 383–4).

[3] 20 September, *La Gazzetta del Popolo* (Bottero's paper at Turin), report from Palermo dated 25 September; 30 September, Dafieno from Genoa to Depretis (Archivio Depretis ASR).

made statements to the press, which Mordini wisely published in the official *Giornale* at Palermo so that the public could judge of their truth:

In Palermo the police are carrying out a real terror. The populace is waiting with the greatest anxiety for the armed assistance of Piedmont. No one is any longer sure of being able to sleep in his own house. Public opinion in Palermo is even beginning to come out with recriminations against Piedmont for its delay in helping the island. Everyone now believes that the present prodictator and his ministry are aiming to create a republic, and people are furious at the fact.[1]

This legend was easily enough believed by northerners, for whose consumption it had of course been devised. The familiar bogey of republicanism could always be brought out with good effect on special occasions like this, even though there was not the least chance of republicanism emerging triumphant from southern Italy, or even of being freely propagated there. The whole issue had been prejudged, to Mazzini's dismay, from the first moment that Garibaldi had landed at Marsala in the name of the king. The only active republican leader in Sicily had been Nicotera, and he was deprived of his command because of this very fact. Republicanism was merely a *revenant*, and it was dragged back into active life just because it had some political usefulness as a scare to the politically neutral. No doubt these statements to the press would have been generally believed in the north, where it was important to work up feeling against the radicals before parliament met on 2 October. The sense of mission and manifest destiny among the Piedmontese would simultaneously be flattered, for the article assured them that the northern troops were eagerly awaited in Sicily as deliverers from the hated dictatorship of Garibaldi.

Mordini, however, would hardly look on matters in that light. Garibaldi had again confirmed the radical programme in his speech of 17 September, and this had virtually forced the new prodictator into a more coercive policy than that of Depretis. Such a coercive policy was at least partially successful in checking the organized disloyalty among local authorities and the notorious beguiling of the armed forces from their allegiance.[2] Conspiracy had to be quelled. There was hardly any

[1] 4 October, *Giornale Officiale di Sicilia*, quoting the *Gazzetta di Genova* of 1 October.
[2] 4 October, *L' Annessione* admits this.

real danger of governmental terror when news was freely published, especially as almost all the press had apparently been bought by Cavour's agents. With so little physical force to back him, Mordini had rather to rule by the moral force of the admiration which Garibaldi's personality inspired. The programme of his government, too, was not so very unwise and dangerous as the moderates made out. At all events, it seemed obvious enough to an observer in England that Garibaldi had good arguments for delaying annexation, because the annexation of Sicily would deprive him of his base, and of further supplies of munitions and troops.[1] If there was any lack of wisdom, it was certainly not all on one side. Cavour himself was being accused of short-sightedness in his policy of quick, unconditional annexation. 'If his campaign succeeds, he will pay dearly for his victory', said Asproni: 'in less than six months we shall have a bloody and fatal conflagration. Neither Naples nor Sicily will endure in peace the yoke of Turin and the laws of Piedmont.'[2] This prophecy was not far wrong. If Mordini did not succeed in what he tried to do, neither did the moderates when it was their turn to try and rule in southern Italy. If his methods and policy were foolish, it is possible to argue that theirs were equally so.

Mordini did his best to carry out Garibaldi's political programme. What he could not do in a few weeks was to remedy the economic unrest, the agrarian disorder, the high prices, the administrative disorganization, the lack of police and revenue, all of which made everyone long for the end of the war and the restoration of regular government. These deficiencies were serious; but to put this in perspective it may be noted that much the same accusations were being made by Guerrazzi and others against Cavour's administration in the north at this time; and Cavour was having to make precisely the same reply as Mordini, that in an emergency politics had to come first, and administrative reorganization could only follow afterwards when political questions were less exacting. It was not just a group of politicians, that is to say, who stood in the way of law and order. The very same criticisms were also to be made by Sicilians against Cavour after Mordini had yielded up his power in November. For Sicilian discontent

[1] 28 September, Lord Palmerston to Russell (RP G.D. 22/21).

[2] 29 September, Asproni from Naples to Brofferio (Raccolta Martini MRR, no. 342/23/9).

was as much social as political in origin, and it was to continue under successive liberal governments quite as strongly, if not more so, than now under the radicals. All one can say for the present is that in September 1860 it was a powerful reinforcement to the cause of annexation, the objective towards which many people looked as if it were a magic refuge from all their troubles.

It was on 24 September that Mordini handed over Casalis to the custody of the Piedmontese consul and deprived the absent Cordova of his post as procurator-general of the Palermo government. Then on the 25th a number of Sicilian notables left individually from various parts of Sicily to go and ask Cavour if he would lend armed support to the champions of annexation. As Garibaldi had not been impressed by their desire to end the revolution, Casalis had decided that they ought to appeal directly to the king in whose name the dictator claimed to be ruling. The deputation was headed by Father Lanza and Prince Belmonte, its main support coming from the Palermitan aristocracy.[1] After having led numerous Sicilian revolutions during centuries of foreign domination, the titular aristocracy in Sicily were now alarmed to find themselves entirely excluded from the new revolutionary government, and even sometimes threatened in their lordship over the provinces. Ever since Marchese Torrearsa and Baron Pisani had resigned in June, the nobles had scarcely been represented at all in Garibaldi's successive ministries. Cavour on the other hand had courted them, despite their autonomist instincts; for he knew that they would find Garibaldi's government too radical, and that they would prefer submission to Piedmont as a lesser evil if this meant the return of order and monarchy. Mordini was to them a Tuscan 'foreigner', who ruled through a combination of other foreigners and Sicilian intellectuals and lawyers. The revolutionary government was also supported by a large 'foreign' army, which claimed to have 'conquered' Sicily, and this fact was by no means always well received by natives of the island.

No doubt most of the nobles would have liked to receive some degree of local self-government in Sicily with all the confirmation of their power and position it would imply. But they had some reason at first for thinking that this would come more readily from Cavour than from

[1] 25 September, De Stefano Rosario to Crispi (ACP, f. 135); 11 October, *L'Assemblea* (Palermo).

the radical unitarians, and they were not yet to know that liberal Piedmont was to be less lenient on this point than either Garibaldi or even the tyrannical Bourbons. Their secular strife with Naples made them the first to react against the radicals when Garibaldi tried to reimpose upon Sicily submission to a remote secretariat in Naples. They also could argue that the absence of law and order might sooner be eradicated with the help of Piedmontese men and money. Communal anarchy and the dislocation of trade would hardly be remedied as quickly by a temporary prodictator. It seemed to them that Mordini's real intention was to postpone the advent of settled government in the interests of other Neapolitan and Roman provinces for which most Sicilians had little or no feeling but one of resentment. All this contributed to weaken the prodictator's position, especially with the aristocracy whose landed property made them particularly vulnerable in times of disorder. Mordini took good note of their attitude, and was soon looking about him for some way to capture the interest of this important element in public opinion.

CHAPTER XIX

FURTHER CONTROVERSY
OVER ANNEXATION:
SEPTEMBER–OCTOBER

During the first ten days of Mordini's rule, the old labels of annexationist, delayed-annexationist and conditional-annexationist were shuffled again, as gradual y the true political bent of the new pro-dictatorship revealed itself. Depretis had come to grief over attempting to hasten the union of Sicily and the north, because he had here been pitting himself against the indifference of Garibaldi and the hostility of the radicals and autonomists. Mordini therefore decided to try and make an alliance between the radicals on the one hand, and a group of autonomists on the other, hoping to secure a common agreement for postponing and limiting the vote of union. The formation of this alliance, and its provision of greater strength to the cause of Garibaldi, was later to be Mordini's proud boast.[1] But the more extreme members of the 'party of action' were at first only confused by it, for they were far more interested in creating unified central government than in qualifying this by the acquisition of local autonomy.

Those who thought of the new prodictator as just another of the radicals thus missed an important political distinction. There was, for instance, a certain coolness which now grew up between Mordini and Crispi. The former criticized both Crispi and Cordova for letting a mere rivalry of personalities obtrude to confound politics and weaken administration; and his remarks on this point came to the ears of Crispi, who took offence at them.[2] Mordini then set himself deliberately to associate with the group of people who put Sicily first, and who resented the action of both Crispi and Cordova to superimpose either

[1] 24 January 1861, Mordini to Crispi: 'the present force behind Garibaldi is based on the alliance of our party with the old autonomists, an alliance which I formed during the prodictatorship' (ACP, f. 140).

[2] 2 October, Calvino from Naples to Mordini (AMB, b. 30).

national or Piedmontese interests upon them. This association in people's minds of Crispi and Cordova is one example of how the two active parties were still looked upon as extraneous, and as having more similarities than incompatibilities between them. There was certainly one element in the radical party which thought of itself as having more in common with Cordova than with the 'little Sicilian' party which wanted local autonomy.[1] Another illuminating point was that, although the main body of radicals disliked Cordova, they did so precisely because his past history made him suspected of autonomist predilections, and by no means just because he now seemed to champion a greater Piedmont.[2] These confusions all helped Mordini in his early experiment with what in later Italian history became known as 'transformism'. Instead of accepting the party system as he found it, his object was to split up the existing groups and fabricate as many pieces as possible into a new broadly-based ministerial coalition. He arrived with the reputation of being a radical, but he quickly adapted himself to try and establish that he was independent of both extraneous factions, both the nationalist and the Piedmontese. How far he had succeeded by the end of the month may be seen in the following anecdote related by one of Crispi's friends in the government of Palermo:

Last night at the theatre, the Duke of Verdura [mayor of the city] was heard to make the following remarks: 'Mordini is on the right lines, and even though he arrived in Sicily with ideas contrary to our own, nevertheless new acquaintance with the needs of the island has brought him round to our point of view. He first wanted to introduce a certain special law, but when he found it was against our wishes he abandoned it.'

I do not know if the Duke was just flattering himself; but I do know that our local aristocrats are showing themselves expert at winning Mordini's ear, and that none of our party is near him. Even though he has some regard for me personally, yet I have scarcely seen him at all.[3]

The same shift in the prodictator's policy is evident in an important difference which developed between him and Bertani. Bertani had become Garibaldi's secretary at Naples, and was determined that Mordini and Sicily should not be allowed to abandon orthodox

[1] 22 September, Navarra to Crispi (ACP, f. 135).
[2] 18 September, *L' Unità Italiana* (Genoa), report from Palermo dated 13 September.
[3] 2 October, V. Cacioppo to Crispi (ACP, b. 156).

radicalism. In order to preserve the political solidarity of the south he had therefore introduced into decrees the ominous words 'Dictatorship of the Two Sicilies'. To observers in Palermo this implied a continuance of the loathed Neapolitan connexion, and even carried a hint that, when Garibaldi had moved on to Rome, Sicily might be left under the rule of a Neapolitan prodictator. Just as many liberal Neapolitans had aided the Bourbons rather than lose their domination over Sicily, so there were many Sicilians who might have opposed even Garibaldi rather than submit again to their dependence on Naples. This mutual animosity, that is to say, was sometimes stronger than any liberal or national sentiments; and we have already seen that, paradoxically enough, it had been perhaps the mainspring of action in this the most decisive of all the revolutions for the making of Italy. Regional jealousy was quickly stirred up again when, in two decrees of 16 and 20 September, Bertani took further and more practical steps to centralize government at Naples. The intention here was only to establish a strong, unitary dictatorship such as could stand up to Cavour and prepare the conquest of Rome. But the Sicilian government protested at such an under-mining of its authority and prestige, and pointed out very pertinently that Cavour's party could at least offer something preferable to making the island a subordinate province under Naples.[1] Bertani replied to this protest by repeating the mistake most northerners tended to make, saying that the autonomists were indistinguishable from separatists and therefore were enemies to be resisted.[2] Mordini, far from agreeing with this crude diagnosis, had properly seized on the distinction between autonomists and separatists, and by allying with the former had averted the danger of their union. Basing himself on this alliance, the prodictator was to succeed in keeping Sicily independent for several more weeks; and then, when this no longer served Garibaldi's purpose, he was to use the alliance to pilot Sicily through further political storms to the safe harbour of union with the other provinces of Italy.

First, he set himself to repair the damage done to morale through Bertani's centralization decrees. By moderate action he might hope to

[1] 20 September, *L' Unità Italiana* (Palermo); 25 September, Castiglia to Crispi (ACP, f. 135).

[2] 21 September (copy), Bertani from Naples to Mordini (AMB; the original is in the Carte Bargoni).

convert some of those who put local autonomy above immediate surrender to Piedmont; and he might then form an alliance between this group and those other people who preferred a completely unified Italy to the immediate economic advantages of 'annexation'. As a Tuscan, Mordini would be aware that there was already considerable feeling in other provinces against the over-hasty imposition from Turin of uniformity on the Piedmontese model. Furthermore, having so little in the way of police or financial resources behind him, he was obliged to walk warily and to try and keep in with as many as possible of the various currents in local sentiment. Both these facts led him half-way to meet the party of Ferrara and Emerico Amari. One of Cavour's agents reported that, if the autonomists were in a numerical minority, they were yet as a group 'stronger and more energetic' than those who wanted unqualified annexation.[1] They also included some of the most intelligent and popular people in Sicily among their number.[2] When Mordini formed his coalition between various shades of radical and liberal, this new coalition was said to outnumber those who wanted immediate and unqualified annexation.[3]

Within a fortnight he had made much progress. Four days after his appointment he had begun to insist with Garibaldi on the special position and special needs of Sicily, and between this date and 4 October the alliance between 'Mazzinians and autonomists'—as one paper a little misleadingly put it—became an accomplished fact.[4] The apparent anomaly was striking, and Crispi's more strictly unitarian friends at Palermo wondered what on earth was happening to the radical pro-gramme. The people who were profiting from the replacement of Depretis by Mordini seemed to be, not the radicals, but the autono-mists. The one minister to survive the replacement was Enrico Parisi, who had first won Garibaldi's attention on 17 September, and then managed to nominate most of Mordini's cabinet before Mordini was himself appointed. The result was that four of the ministers had autonomist leanings, including this same Parisi in the important position

[1]   16 September, the Sardinian consul at Messina to Villamarina (AME).

[2]   16 October, P. Morello from Palermo to Ricasoli (*Carteggio di Ricasoli*, ed. Nobili and Camerani).

[3]   29 September, Bargoni from Palermo to Bertani (ACP, f. 140).

[4]   4 October, *L'Annessione*.

of minister for internal affairs.[1] Their influence on the prodictator was bound to be strong. It was with their help and advice that Mordini was to win over the mayor of Palermo; and the importance of this may be gauged from the fact that the civic authorities at Naples were in similar circumstances to lead the opposition against Garibaldi's radical policy. One description of what was happening told how, while Depretis had always remained a continental, Mordini in this way 'made himself a Sicilian'.[2] The mayor for this year was the Duke of Verdura, and he had hitherto been associating with that group of aristocrats which would have welcomed annexation in preference to Bertani's enforced junction of Sicily and Naples. Mordini's intelligent cultivation of their local pride now gave such people another choice. Instead of ignoring local sentiment like Bertani, the prodictator frankly recognized that some Sicilians wanted freedom from Naples at any cost. Union with Piedmont was to some of them, not something inherently desirable, so much as the price they would willingly but not enthusiastically pay for this freedom. The motives behind the annexation campaign were thus by no means always patriotic. Some people would have been positively glad to have Naples stay outside the union, and were quite ready to sacrifice the mainland provinces to the ambition of a Lucien Murat or a Prince Napoleon.[3]

This loose but effective coalition took some of the sting out of the aristocratic deputation which set off for Turin on 25 September. Father Lanza's deputation had been designed essentially as a propaganda gesture, to provide Cavour with an excuse for claiming to possess the support of public opinion if ever it became necessary to eject the Garibaldians forcibly from the south. Mordini ascribed little importance to it, since clearly the deputation had no mandate from any body of

[1] 22 September, Cacioppo to Crispi (ACP, f. 135). This radical says that Raffaele was the leader of the 'separatists', together with Emerico Amari, Ferrara, Fiorenza, Marchese Roccaforte, Guarneri, Costantino, Parisi, Piraino, Peranni and Scrofani, the last four of whom were ministers actually in office. He added that these three had figured among the authors of a petition on 3 September asking for an assembly for Sicily and repudiating Victor Emanuel. Cacioppo hoped that the 'annexation' party would not combine with these separatists, especially as these latter found support right down among the plebs.

[2] Quoted by Rosi, *Il risorgimento e l' azione d' un patriota*, p. 211.

[3] 13 June, *L' Italia Una* (Palermo), in which E. Navarra complains of this fact.

people, but merely expressed individual opinions.[1] Nevertheless, he was wrong to be so little concerned. Lanza arrived in Piedmont on 1 October, just when Cavour was about to inform parliament of the attitude he intended to take towards Garibaldi, and possibly the prime minister would have been influenced to take a yet stronger line by this access of local support for his defiance of radicalism. In return Cavour told this small group of Sicilian notables that, in his opinion, Turin could not be the capital of the new Italy.[2] This audacious statement must have helped to allay the fears about Piedmontese provincialism on which Mordini thrived; and it suggested that Cavour was not going to leave Garibaldi a monopoly of the magic appeal of Rome.

As events moved fast towards the incorporation of the south into the kingdom of northern Italy, the principal arguments ceased to revolve round the question of a plebiscite in Sicily. Taking the plebiscite for granted, the real question became whether it should be accompanied by a representative and deliberative assembly. In the first fortnight of October this problem was to dominate Sicilian politics.

Those who wanted a plebiscite, and nothing else, had on their side the important and ultimately decisive fact that the financial and military support of Piedmont was mobilized against the very idea of an assembly. Northerners had good reason to fear that such a quasi-parliament might try to impose conditions or discuss constitutional fundamentals. It certainly would delay annexation at a critical moment when all Italian provinces ought to be ranged under one supreme authority against the danger of Austrian invasion. From Cavour's point of view, Garibaldi's independent dictatorship had to be terminated quickly, especially as it was now so near to provoking war with France.[3] The solid and substantial *La Perseveranza*, one of the leading newspapers of northern Italy, while it allowed that a representative assembly might have served some purpose once, as a limitation on dictatorial power, now held that it would be superfluous, since Sicilians would soon be

---

[1] 4 October, *L' Unità Italiana* (Palermo); 7 October, *Il Diritto* (Turin); 25 September, Mordini to Bertani: 'not a few of the aristocrats are favourable to my government', A. Arzano, *Il dissidio fra Garibaldi e Depretis*, 1913, p. 57.

[2] 14 October, *Il Plebiscito* (Palermo), Raeli's report from Turin dated 7 October.

[3] 22 September, G. Dina (editor of *L' Opinione*) to I. La Lumia (MSS La Lumia, Biblioteca Communale Palermo).

represented in an Italian parliament. And it added that 'the wish to dictate conditions for entry into the kingdom of Italy would be a contradiction of the principle of unity which has already been proposed and accepted....It would be a challenge to national sovereignty, and a wrong done to other regions which have also contributed their share to the liberation of the south.'[1]

Several months earlier Cavour's party had been all for calling a Sicilian assembly, but now they feared that, instead of being a rubber stamp to seal annexation to the existing kingdom of Piedmont, it might turn out to be a constituent assembly, and proceed to discuss a new constitution and the inauguration of a new state. As an example of the kind of danger which threatened, one Palermo paper pointedly mentioned that Sicilians wanted Victor Emanuel the *First*, king of a new Italy; they did not like Cavour's offer of Victor Emanuel the *Second* of a kingdom already based on Turin.[2] Here was dangerous heresy indeed. Public discussion of such heterodox views by the southern intelligentsia was bound to be dangerous. It was all the more imperative to rush Sicily into a quick act of abdication by plebiscite. The influence of republicanism seemed to be discernible in the fact that annexation was being postponed even after the acquisition of Naples had removed earlier reasons for delay. Perhaps Cavour had sounded the alarm too often not to be himself occasionally deceived by his own diplomatic propaganda into thinking Mazzinianism a real danger which only outlawry and persecution could subdue. The personal enemies of Bertani and Garibaldi constantly assured the prime minister that these men were tools of Mazzini. The prophet himself had been for some months at large in Italy, eluding the diligent searches of Cavour's police, and was now on the scene of action in Naples. La Farina was even developing the wild theory that the Mazzinians in Sicily were in league with both the reactionaries and the separatists, and were bent only on destroying the region from which they would soon be evicted by the advancing armies of Victor Emanuel.[3]

Cavour was thus ready to increase his pressure on Sicily for a plebiscite. He had spread abroad his wishes, both through the agency of official

---

[1] 12 October, *La Perseveranza.*   [2] 27 September, *Tom Pouce.*

[3] 7 October and 21 October, *Il Piccolo Corriere d' Italia* (in G. La Farina, *Scritti Politici,* vol. II, 1876, pp. 344–6).

representatives, consuls and naval officers, and unofficially through La Farina, Cordova, Bottero, Casalis, Mellino and others whom he had sent for the purpose. He was in personal correspondence with some of Garibaldi's generals. His agents controlled a number of papers in the chief cities of Sicily, and Mellino had won over nearly all the Palermo press with subventions. Through these newspapers he had let it be known that unconditional annexation through a plebiscite might be rewarded by a liberal allowance of local autonomy, and in this way he was competing with Mordini for the allegiance of the more moderate autonomists. The influential Michele Amari, for instance, pinned his faith for the future in these hints from Turin, and proclaimed:

pas de conditions dans l'annexion! Il sera seulement entendu que la Sicile gardera toutes les libertés administratives compatibles avec l'unité politique de la nation. Le programme de Farini les a indiquées à peu près pour toutes les *régions* composant l'Italie. D'autres exceptions seraient nécessaires pour une île comme la Sicile....[1]

Two of the leading papers in Palermo, which were especially active in helping to spread this belief, printed documents purporting to show Cavour's special regard for the need of Sicily to have its own peculiar institutions.[2] These same papers also put it about that the national parliament would later make a free concession of 'conditions' to the island, so that a plebiscite would not prevent, but would rather lead directly to, the grant of local autonomy. In *Il Plebiscito*, the young Marquis di Rudinì, who in later days was himself to inherit Cavour's office, wrote as follows:

there are some people who would like five hundred Sicilian deputies to spend time in vain chatter and demand conditions from an executive authority which has no right to grant them. Such conditions would reduce the annexation to a contract in which all the advantages would be for Sicily and all the disadvantages for the other party....Meanwhile the whole of Europe may be plunged into war, or something else may occur to prevent Italy being formed. And then what would happen to us?...

In any case we may be sure that *regional* liberty cannot be denied us. Parliament will have to provide for it, for in the national parliament all Italy

---

[1] 7 October, Amari to Cartwright (*Carteggio di Amari*, ed. d'Ancona, pp. 136–7).
[2] *L' Annessione* (e.g. 27 September), and *Il Plebiscito*.

will be represented, and we shall be in a majority by reason of our community of interests with our brothers on the continent. Moreover, let it not be said that we cannot rely on the word of Victor Emanuel.[1]

This article by di Rudinì very clearly states the fear of many leading Sicilians that an assembly would now be fatal to the cause of annexation. On the one hand, a debate upon this highly controversial subject would prolong matters unduly: in the meantime an invasion by Austria might give an opening for another European congress to intervene in Italy, and then Catholic and legitimist pressure might prevail to stop the whole process of unification. On the other hand, there was also the point that an assembly might haggle for prior terms, and Piedmont might then refuse to accept an offer of conditional annexation. The result would only be to throw Sicily back into the scrummage between Garibaldi and the Bourbons.

Cavour was to exploit both these sentiments. But yet more decisive was the fact that he now could hold over Sicilians the argument of *force majeure*. Many of those who earlier had opposed annexation had to recognize the uselessness of its further postponement once Piedmontese troops had reached Ancona on 28 September.[2] Cavour already had it in mind to send Persano with warships and troops to Sicily if Garibaldi resisted much longer,[3] and the general expectancy of such an invasion sufficed to turn many people away from the project of an assembly.[4]

Besides this direct pressure from Turin, there were certain miscellaneous and even opposite interests in the south which were becoming bound up with the cause of quick annexation. La Farina thus summarized some of them:

the national party wanted annexation as one step towards the speedy constitution of national unity; the timid because it would insure them against

---

[1] 16 October, *Il Plebiscito*.

[2] G. Cadolini, *Memorie del risorgimento*, 1911, p. 457.

[3] 12 October, Farini to Cavour: 'a short time back you were thinking of sending Persano and the fleet to make an armed demonstration [*a rompere i vetri*] at Palermo. It seems to me that if you now sent Cordova, Casalis and Melino with the fleet, and they issued an appeal to the Sicilians, it should not be hard to put an end to the Mordini regime' (*CC Lib. del Mezz.* vol. II, p. 93).

[4] 7 October, Sutera to Crispi (ACP, b. 139); 26 September, Mordini to Crispi (ACP, f. 140); 20 September, *L' Annessione*.

the dangers of more war and more revolution; merchants and industrialists in order that they might take up again in peace the exercise of their commerce and industry; the landowners to recover their lapsed rents; and all honest men so as to end a state of affairs where there was no law and no magistrates.[1]

The class of lawyers, which in Sicily comprised a large proportion of the politically minded, sought in annexation the reopening of the courts and hence re-employment after months of practical idleness.[2] Again, those Sicilians who were already fighting or were liable to conscription could not help but associate Garibaldi's policy with the need for further exertions on their part; whereas annexation would put all the responsibility and the exertion on to the shoulders of Piedmont and her army.

Another interesting point of view was put forward by the governor of Patti, who wrote to tell Mordini that he had full confidence in whatever Garibaldi decided, and was eager for national unification, but yet that, for the immediate needs of the present, annexation was essential. Annexation would bring 'the supreme advantage of associating ourselves with a people which is distinguished for its sense of the practicable, a calm and disciplined people which has been already accustomed to free constitutional life for a dozen years'.[3] He went on to say that the Piedmontese connexion would no doubt mean more public works and educational advances, and 'credit for the development of agriculture and industry, as well as laws to release us from the tyranny of ecclesiastical mortmain'; and also soldiers to keep order in the countryside. It would satisfy the general wish of ordinary citizens to settle down and terminate the period of revolution, and fulfil their hope of being at last able to organize government properly. 'For the idea that everything is provisional has become so firmly established that everything proceeds more slowly and insecurely than it should.'

This fact, that the revolutionary government was thought to be not properly set up, was most important. Not only had Garibaldi laid it down that administrative reorganization must be subordinated to the main task of military provision, but Cordova and Casalis had started

---

[1] 3 March 1861, La Farina, *Scritti politici*, vol. II, p. 359.
[2] 30 August, *L' Annessione* prints a protest by the lawyers.
[3] 19 September, governor of Patti to Mordini (MRR, 221/23/8).

a rumour that the enactments and appointments of the revolutionary government were but temporary and would be soon quashed by the Piedmontese. It was partly for this reason that taxes were not paid, that new laws and decrees were disregarded, and that those men best fitted for government service often refused to compromise themselves by taking up appointments. The state treasury being empty, and confidence low, many government employees found that their salaries were more than two months in arrears.[1] There was thus a good response when even the mildly autonomist *La Forbice* mentioned the hope of better government to come:

If a division of Piedmontese troops arrived tomorrow, conscription could be enforced automatically. . . . And as for our capitalists, why, with a strong government they could trust, they would rush to contribute. . . . On the other hand, a provisional government has no prestige, its employees have no security of office and know it, nor is there enough money to pay for all the things that ought to be done. Every official is irked by this knowledge, and the public service suffers accordingly. . . . And the minister who knows that tomorrow he will no longer be minister is reluctant to make any energetic or vigorous dispositions.[2]

For the same reason, there had been very few subscriptions in answer to an appeal for a government loan launched on 27 August. People evidently did not have faith that a provisional government could guarantee their money.[3] All these facts told the same story. Even Crispi's paper once had had to admit that 'every day which goes by brings an additional argument for ending this transition stage as soon as possible'.[4]

There were still more arguments which counted in the same direction. One carried special conviction with the important class of high-ranking officers in Garibaldi's army. For these valiant and self-sacrificing men had little chance of retaining their rank, or even of continuing in their profession, unless they could make their peace with Cavour. Since General Fanti was already half-way through the Papal States, it was evident to them as to others that the revolution was virtually at an end, and so there was a noticeable tendency among them

---

[1] 27 September, Scavo to Crispi (ACP, b. 155).
[2] 7 October, *La Forbice*.
[3] 16 September, Sardinian consul at Messina to Villamarina (AME).
[4] 21 August, *Il Precursore*.

to bow to the rising sun.[1] For another and much more numerous group of people in Sicily, the general hatred of Naples took shape in a wish not to be forestalled by that province in joining the new kingdom of Italy, and equally in a determination not to wait until a joint annexation might be arranged by Garibaldi for both southern provinces in one. The fear was even being expressed that Naples was trying to reassert again through Garibaldi the metropolitan claims which she had lately exercised over Sicily.[2]

Evidently the glamour and prestige of Garibaldi had diminished since the magnetism of his personality had been transferred to distant Naples. He had departed from Sicily on 19 August and, though his return for six hours on 17 September momentarily revived all the old enthusiasm, he did not revisit the island again this year. Had he possessed any idea of antagonism or disloyalty to Victor Emanuel, he would no doubt have responded to the appeals of the radicals, and would have returned, to reorganize his volunteers. But he did not return. In his absence on other business the Sicilians felt leaderless, forgotten by the one man who had so inspired them. It was but a short step from this to feeling exploited by a prodictator whose ideas they not unjustly thought to differ from his, and misled by doctrinaire unitarians who appeared to work more in Neapolitan than Sicilian interests. Garibaldi had flattered their self-esteem and brought out the best in them. But, once he had gone, this same self-esteem was wounded by the tactless tendency of his ministers to 'exasperate Sicilians by treating them as *conquered* people who must submit to the will of their conquerors'.[3] They had also denuded Sicily of troops, and left good citizens in the fear of civil war and social revolt.[4] In this natural desire for self-esteem, for peace, quiet and prosperity, we have the measure of Sicilian liberal sentiment in this year: it had first been directed against the Bourbons, it was now resulting in opposition to the prodictatorship, and it was finally to turn

---

[1]   25 October, *L' Unità Italiana* (Palermo).

[2]   11 September, Professor Amari to Count Amari (*Carteggio di Amari*, ed. d'Ancona, vol. II, p. 132).

[3]   26 September, *Il Nazionale*. It was Crispi who made this 'theory of conquest official and strong.... And hence the separatists, with their various sections of autonomists, conditionalists, Bourbonists, and the formalists who want a Sicilian assembly, all regained ground and influence.'

[4]   17 September, Sardinian consul at Palermo to Cavour (*CC Lib. del Mezz.* vol. v).

people against Piedmont, from whom in its turn salvation had been expected. Unfortunately these popular wishes were mostly unrealizable, and for reasons which lay deeper than politics. Salvation for this much-conquered island was hardly to come in the next few years from the north, any more than in times past it had come from most other points of the compass in succession.

The fundamental problem of Sicily was economic and social. Though this is not the place to pursue in detail the social question, it must be mentioned as something which had considerable repercussions on politics. The middle and upper classes, though they contained people holding all manner of opinions, were collectively becoming more anxious for a settlement at any price; and, as events were developing, the obvious settlement was an adherence to Cavour's demand for annexation to the kingdom of Piedmont-Sardinia. No other practical alternative, whether of a republic, a federal state, an independent king-dom, or of foreign absorption, had so far emerged as a likely possibility from the confused history of their revolution. Meantime trade was languishing, rents were unpaid, and there was fear of the violence of the common people.[1] August had seen the climax in a long story of peasant unruliness, rick-burning, cattle-slaughter, tax-avoiding, charter-destroying, frequent land-occupation, and in many cases assassination and *jacquerie*.[2] No sooner was it clear that the revolutionary govern-ment had not the resources for an adequate defence of life and property, than the most powerful of human sentiments was thrown into the scales on behalf of Piedmont. It was especially important that the people most affected by disorder were of particular strength in local government; and they considered themselves as the voice of public opinion, as not only the most vociferous but also the only weighty element in politics.

It was these same people who made up the national guard, a force which in Sicily and Naples was to be a political as well as a military organ,[3]

---

[1] 12 September, *L' Indipendente* (Messina).

[2] D. Mack Smith, 'The peasants' revolt of Sicily in 1860', in *Studi in onore di Gino Luzzatto*, vol. III, 1950, pp. 227–34.

[3] E.g. 6 September, F. Ugdulena to Crispi, describing how a move to put up a rival candidate for governor of Messina was defeated by the national guard, because Fabrizi its leader happened to be a radical (ACP, f. 135). Elsewhere, of course, the national guard was almost always to take a conservative line.

and which opposed in turn both Crispi[1] and Mordini.[2] The national guardsmen were to be a fine means of propaganda for annexation,[3] and the officers casually disobeyed military orders whenever these conflicted at all sharply with their political views.[4] Moreover, the dispatch of all available troops to help Garibaldi in his great battle on the Volturno had left them the only organized force in the country. In Palermo, and still more at Naples, they were to exert a well-directed pressure in the final political crisis over the plebiscite.

This middle- and upper-class element in the population was particularly strong at Messina, a town which by reason both of its position and its character was to prove more important than Palermo in the *dénouement* of this political conflict. The privileged port of Messina was the seat of the largest mercantile community in the island, and its dockyards and also its rich countryside had been very much disturbed by war conditions. In July, before Garibaldi arrived there, a report had described how, 'Messina is in a miserable state. Skilled men are unemployed, the owning classes ruined, commerce is at a standstill.'[5] On 1 September the director of customs wrote to tell Crispi about the numerous assassinations lately recorded to the account of the so-called *camorristi*. 'Messina is stricken with horror.... Many officials are abandoning their posts....Anarchy re gns supreme.'[6] This was no isolated piece of evidence. The governor, Ugdulena, wrote on the 20th: 'on my arrival here I found Messina dominated by a handful of cut-throats...who were in league with the smugglers.'[7] Meanwhile, the scanty forces of

[1] 12 September, *L' Italia* (Messina).

[2] 19 September, Fiorenza to Ricasoli (*Carteggio di Ricasoli*, ed. Nobili and Camerani).

[3] E.g. 25 October, *La Perseveranza* says that for three days before the plebiscite they wore the cockades of the annexation party.

[4] 22 October, *L' Annessione*: 'everyone knows that the national guard is not purely a military body, but rather, and chiefly, a political organization, formed as a guarantee for the constitution....For this reason there can be no doubt but that it has a right to question its orders when there is a danger to the state of which its members are citizens and whose liberties they have to defend.'

[5] 12 July, *La Costanza* (Palermo); 15 August, the head of the carabinieri said it was still impossible to collect the customs (ASP Ministero Polizia, b. 1548).

[6] 1 September, director of customs from Messina to Crispi (ASP, f. 138).

[7] 20 September, Ugdulena to Mordini (ASP Ministero Polizia, b. 1548); 12 October, report by the head of the carabinieri (ASP Segreteria di Stato, b. 1561).

public order at Messina had to be depleted in order to save the Lipari Islands from anarchy.[1] There were several pirate ships working off the coast.[2] All the time the town had to continue in a state of siege because of the Bourbon garrison still holding out in the citadel, and armistices were periodically interrupted by shelling and sorties which made life dangerous and insecure. The result of all this was that the arrival of regular Piedmontese troops and Persano's navy was eagerly awaited. It was not so much a question of politics as of security. Since there were only two battalions of volunteers available to contain the citadel, reinforcements were badly needed,[3] but Garibaldi could not spare a man from the main theatre of war. The Messinese had consequently felt abandoned by him, ever since he had left for the continent without reducing this enemy strongpost.

This all helps to explain the mixture of fear and dissatisfaction in this peculiarly vulnerable, but also politically most important, corner of Sicily. The fear of anarchy and private vendettas made 'honest citizens' yearn for the restoration of peace and quiet. There was little temptation for them to confuse this simple issue by the addition of complicated political questions like radicalism and nationality. At all events these honest citizens openly 'professed to remain detached from the national movement'.[4] It was for administrative rather than political reasons that the civic council at Messina memorialized Garibaldi to ask for annexation as quickly as possible.[5] On 5 October the Piedmontese consul had to report that everyone was flying from the city with all their possessions, for about the fifth or sixth time in as many months; and he guessed that in two days' time no one would be left at all. Hence arose the 'hatred' against the government. A plebiscite was considered 'the only way to solve the question of the Bourbon garrison in the citadel.... People are speaking publicly against Garibaldi as against a traitor'.[6] The

---

[1] 10 October, governor of Messina to Bargoni (AMB).

[2] 16 October, governor of Messina telegram to minister of public security (ASP Segreteria di Stato, b. 1561).

[3] 1 October, Mordini telegram to Garibaldi (AMB).

[4] 2 September, Sardinian consul at Messina to Cavour (*CC Lib. del Mezz.* vol. v).

[5] 8 September, *L' Annessione* prints their memorandum of 28 August; 19 August, Sardinian consul at Messina to Villamarina shows that the civic council voted for annexation at its very first meeting after being liberated (AME); 15 October, *Il Pungolo* (Naples).   [6] 5 October, Sardinian consul to Villamarina (AME).

holding of an assembly was feared because it might lead to the introduction of 'a system of abhorred separatism';[1] for there were special reasons why a close connexion with northern Italy would be particularly advantageous to a trading community. It contributed even more to the discontent of the provinces that the old civic antagonism against Palermo was still alive. During earlier Sicilian rebellions in this century, many prominent citizens of Messina had sided with the Neapolitans against Palermo. Differences were intensified in 1860 by the complaint that Palermo was monopolizing the jobbery and appointments and contracts of war.[2] Added to all this, the sudden necessity to provision Garibaldi's army when it was preparing to cross the Straits, and then the equally sudden reduction of that army to a simple garrison, had caused a boom, then a slump, and so unemployment.[3] Economic unrest thus merged with political discontent against the provisional government at Palermo. Not many days in October were to pass before these cumulative grievances were to have their effect on the course of the revolution. Messina was an important town, and we shall see that its wishes could not be left unheard.

[1] 17 October, *Omnivagus* (Messina).

[2] 27 October, *La Valle di Giosaffat*; the seamen of Messina complained that there were no Messinese in the national marine (petition in AMB, b. 30); 6 September, the director of customs reported that his men were not being paid; in the Archivio di Stato, Messina (*Atti vari del 1860*), there are references to civic funds being requisitioned by Garibaldi's army, and factories being taken over; 6 September, Ugdulena to Crispi, passes on the lawyers' complaint that at Messina the courts were so long in abeyance (ACP, f. 135).

[3] 16 August, *La Cicala Italiana* (Palermo).

CHAPTER XX

MORDINI SUMMONS AN ASSEMBLY: 5 OCTOBER

By the beginning of October, some formerly doubtful points had been more or less settled so far as Sicily was concerned. First, the postponement of at least the outward form of union with Piedmont was hardly possible much longer. Secondly, this would have to be decided by a plebiscite, with or without the addition of a representative assembly to decide ways and means. Some men of high standing and repute continued to advocate that there should be this prior summons of a constitutional assembly, just as there had been local parliaments in Tuscany and Emilia when those other provinces had considered the same question of annexation some months earlier. Among Sicilians there was a number who would have welcomed this as a good chance to debate the terms on which annexation should be voted. Not many people outside Sicily would have looked very favourably on this idea at the time, but in later years the impression was to gain ground that some good might have been done, and some evil have been avoided, had Sicily either demanded or else been spontaneously granted partial autonomy from the first. Arguments were frequently put forward in 1860 to show that the island had special needs and interests which a parliament at Turin or Rome would never have the time and knowledge to attend to; and hence, that Sicilians should thrust them forward for consideration while their island still had some independent status. Probably most of those who wanted autonomy were also hoping for a speedy union with Piedmont; but their ambition was for a union tempered by conditions. The radicals round Crispi had different ideas about this: they rather wanted to delay annexation, so as to keep for themselves and the revolution some further freedom of movement; but, provided they could gain this one point, they would then have been reluctant to make any conditions which might prejudice the formation of a unitary state. We have already seen how this inherent difference of approach was partially overcome by Mordini, as some of the radicals and the autonomists were drawn together. The common denominator between them was found in this proposal to call an assembly, the radicals seeing in it a means of delay, and the autonomists an assertion of the right of Sicily to have some particular say in her own affairs.

On 1 October a dozen prominent men, styling themselves members of the 'Sicilian parliament', wrote to Mordini with an official request that he should call an assembly as well as hold a plebiscite. The parliament of which they claimed membership was that of 1848. Since it had never been 'legally' dissolved, it offered some constitutional basis for a representative assembly to meet once more. Their petition incidentally mentioned that they hoped it would be possible to achieve 'the formation of an Italy strong, free and independent, and they were ready to sacrifice everything necessary to this end'. But they were also proud that 'Sicily had now regained its own distinct personality and assured its emancipation from any government based on Naples'. Although they wanted national unity, it should be accompanied by conditions, 'by measures and restrictions which would ensure that the needs of each region, and inveterate local customs, and the forces of tradition were all duly respected'.[1] Even more interesting was their belief that, if only Garibaldi would decree the indispensable separation of Sicily from Naples, this fact alone would pacify the island and free it 'from all that might be harmful in the uncertainty of provisional government'. Hitherto this argument from 'uncertainty' had been used rather to justify the alternative thesis of straight annexation by plebiscite. On 3 and 5 October these same dozen Sicilians, including ministers, peers of the realm, and members of the 1848 parliament, submitted further memoranda to Mordini to ask that a vote might be held without more delay. These autonomists were thus agreed with Cavour's party in trying to force Mordini and the radicals to give up their policy of indefinite delay, and this fact must have counted a good deal with the prodictator, since he now needed their support. In order to keep his new coalition intact, he would have to try and meet their wishes.

But if these petitioners were grouped with the Cavourians in wanting a speedy conclusion to the revolution, they clearly did not agree with

---

[1] 1 October (petition in AMB); the signatories included the director of the bank of Sicily, the president of the Palermo civic council, and the director-general of excise.

the idea of a straightforward annexation by plebiscite. This was what gave Mordini his cue. One might even say that the main interest of the petitioners was not in the matter of timing, so much as in the method to be used for a vote:

A people cannot be said to have full freedom in voting unless there has been previously the free exercise of the right to formulate the alternatives to be voted on. And the exercise of this right cannot be conceived or assured except by means of an assembly freely chosen by the people.... All the more is this true of Sicily, where the principle of constitutional representation has formed for so long such a vital part of our laws and customs.[1]

It was the proud contention of Sicilians that they possessed the oldest parliamentary institutions in Europe, and this insular school of thought thus put the emphasis firmly on ancestral tradition and constitutional precedent. Such a view sharply differentiated them from those who stood behind Cavour in his appeal to the foreign, new-fangled (and even revolutionary) doctrine of a plebiscite by universal suffrage.

The opening days of October in this way witnessed a further narrowing of the terms of conflict. Mordini's chief preoccupation remained that of how to reconcile Garibaldi's programme with the exigencies of public opinion, and these petitions must have suggested that he could not put off some form of popular vote much longer. He had already persuaded Garibaldi to override Bertani's centralizing decrees and confirm the administrative independence of Sicily from Naples. The result of this had been both to strengthen his hand with the autonomists, and at the same time to give him back some of the powers withdrawn from his armoury by Bertani. Both of these facts in their turn were to lead on 5 October to Mordini's publication of a decree summoning an assembly. In this decree he made no mention at all of a plebiscite; and the assembly was to be for Sicily alone, without any mention of Naples. As far as he could see, this was the only method now left by which he could satisfy public opinion while still postponing the surrender of power.

Postponement and delay had become the first principle of his strategy. As a mere prodictator under Garibaldi he was unwilling to take much positive initiative on his own, nor could he be sufficiently in touch with

[1] 3 October and 5 October (AMB, b. 30).

2 0 ✶

policy as it was developing at Naples and Turin to feel confident in doing anything much but await events. He could not know yet that Garibaldi had no hope of reaching Rome. He was fully aware that Cavour was trying to force through immediate annexation, but he also believed that Garibaldi was acting in full accord with the king and was even in negotiation with the cabinet at Turin.[1] He may have suspected that Cavour's apparent opposition was a mere bluff to deceive the rest of Europe, while Garibaldi went on to take Rome. No enlightenment on the broader political situation had been forthcoming from Naples. It is important to know that Sicily was left without instructions during this vital week, since the dictator was fully occupied with the Volturno battle and its aftermath. Mordini, therefore, had no option but to go on trying to play for time, so as to leave Garibaldi's hands as free as possible. But he had to reconcile this with the growing concentration of opinion against any continuance of the state of uncertainty. These two considerations met together in his decision to call an assembly.

By 5 October, even some of the more extreme radicals could see that only by making considerable concessions to other points of view could they succeed in keeping any initiative for themselves. One of Mordini's less moderate associates wrote on that day to Crispi at Naples: 'I feel we are going under, and that the reactionaries [*i tristi*] will triumph yet again, and that our United Italy will be still to seek. All the same', he added, 'I shall do what I can, and shall not neglect any chance of kicking the Cavourian carcass.'[2] The precarious situation at Palermo made it hard to be dispassionate. Plots against the prodictator were being hatched by officers of the guard and certain leaders of the aristocracy.[3] For the last fortnight the Piedmontese consul had been agitating for Cavour to send him 'a few Piedmontese regiments',[4] and we know that Cavour did have plans for sending troops to take over the island by force. On the 2nd Crispi wrote to warn Mordini that 'a reaction had

[1] Mordini's letter of 3 or 4 October to Crispi (ACP, f. 140).

[2] 5 October, Navarra to Crispi (ACP, b. 156).

[3] 19 and 20 October, *L' Annessione*: the opposition meetings were held in the house of the Prince Pignatelli, who was commandant of Garibaldi's Guardia Dittatoriale, and those present included Baron Pisani, I. La Lumia the editor of the *Giornale Officiale*, Marchese di Rudinì, and other prominent aristocrats like Scalia, S. Elia and Florio.

[4] 21 September, Sardinian consul to Cavour (*CC Lib. del Mezz.* vol. v).

been planned to take place at Palermo by means of the militia with the aid of troops summoned from Turin to help enforce prompt annexation'.[1] In such a situation the radicals could not afford to remain fixed in their old ideas. Bertani admitted to Mordini that they were rapidly losing ground, and now sent words of encouragement for this change of mind:

as for this assembly idea, I as a unitarian do not like it, and yet in the face of so imminent a danger of our absorption by Turin without guarantees, and without the acquisition of Rome or Venice, I think it is the only possible expedient. If you are decided, and if Garibaldi agrees, go ahead at once, *absolutely at once*....Perhaps after receiving his vote of confidence in parliament Cavour will strike....It is important for us to provide not only for possible victory, but for a last-ditch defence and the best way of retreat. So let us have the assembly, if Garibaldi agrees.[2]

To Cattaneo, on the same day, Bertani wrote that 'the prompt reunion of parliament in Sicily and Naples is our only hope now'.[3] This was a significant use of words—'parliament' and 'reunion'. Nothing but a free vote of the people could avail to put pressure on Cavour; because Cavour had apparently decided on intervention in Sicily, and Bertani knew that it would be immoral, even if it were possible, to resist him by arms. The physical weakness of the government at Palermo was sharply stressed on this very 5 October by the embarkation of the last remaining soldiers and artillery for Naples. Morally, however, the government might still be made strong if there was yet time to summon a parliament; for this would link up with previous traditions of representative government, and if only such a parliament could once meet, Cavour would hardly dare to dissolve it or disregard its wishes, claiming as he did to act in the name of the people.

Such considerations as these would no doubt have been discussed by the ministers when on the 5th they met with the prodictator and decided unanimously to call an assembly. Perhaps they also still hoped to make the surrender of Sicily conditional on Cavour's capture of Rome, as well as on the grant of local self-government. By this logic Sicily would be preserved for united Italy, and would not become just

[1] 2 October, Crispi to Mordini (ACP, f. 135).
[2] 6 October, Bertani to Mordini (AMB, b. 30).
[3] 6 October, Bertani to Cattaneo (ACP, f. 135).

an appendage of Piedmont. A decision reached in a freely elected Sicilian assembly would obviously carry great importance with European opinion, 'and whatever happens on the continent, Sicily may thus be made into a pivot for any national movement in the future'.[1] It would also be a safeguard against any subsequent attempt to sacrifice Sicily like Nice as the purchase price of a French or Bourbon alliance.

There was no time to ask Garibaldi's opinion on this proposed step. The telegraph line to Naples was interrupted, and when telegrams did arrive they were often undecipherable, even to the point where treason in the post office was suspected.[2] Three ships had arrived in succession from Naples without a single word from the dictator, because, unknown to Mordini, the battle of 1–2 October had left Garibaldi with no time to think of Sicilian politics. The prodictator felt a heavy responsibility on himself, to make some decision which would at once appease Sicilians, and yet which would still preserve intact the programme which Garibaldi had laid down in his Palermo speech of 17 September. He was entitled to believe that he would have been informed if ever that programme was to be altered.

Certain evidence about the development of Garibaldi's views reached Palermo in successive reports from three envoys whom Mordini had sent to discover what exactly was happening on the mainland. The first of these envoys was Count Castellani-Fantoni, one of the opposition deputies who had recently arrived from Turin, and who had set off again for Naples on 21 September. This man had written back on the 27th to say that Garibaldi was veering towards immediate annexation. 'The misgovernment at Naples has generated the need, or at least the desire, for immediate annexation, and personally I think we should be foolish to oppose it. Garibaldi feels this too, and an order of the day by him in the official *Giornale* this evening leaves no doubt on the point, to everyone's satisfaction.'[3] This letter must certainly have arrived and been seen by Mordini before 5 October. But though it showed that Garibaldi was weakening in his resolve, it said nothing about the method to be used for annexation, and on the matter of timing it was

---

[1] 5 October, Bargoni to Calvino (ACM, no. 2989).

[2] 29 September, Bargoni to Bertani (ACP, f. 140); Crispi's telegram from Naples of the 4th was delivered in Palermo only on the 6th (ACP, f. 143).

[3] 27 September, Castellani-Fantoni to Mordini (AMB).

contradicted by what little news had come from Bertani and Crispi. Mordini probably saw the actual order of the day in the Naples *Giornale Officiale*, and if so he would have observed that in fact it marked no fundamental change in the dictator's plans. He would also have noticed in the same issue the fall of the Pisanelli-D'Afflitto cabinet at Naples. This cabinet had been closely associated with the policy of immediate annexation, and its resignation appeared to indicate the triumph of postponement. There was some truth in this appearance. Garibaldi had, it is true, been weakening between 20 and 30 September, but in fact it was only the stalemate on the River Volturno in October which finally thwarted his intention to win Rome before holding a popular vote.

The second envoy was Saverio Friscia, whose report from Naples was probably the latest indication of Garibaldi's policy which Mordini received before deciding to call a Sicilian parliament. Dr Friscia probably returned to Palermo on 4 October, which is the date of his long report published on the 5th in the *Giornale Officiale di Sicilia*. He was a former exile from Sicily who in politics was a Mazzinian radical. He had originally been sent to Naples a fortnight before to protest against Bertani's centralization decrees of 16 and 20 September, but Garibaldi's reply to him was now received by Mordini in a different context to that for which it had been designed. Friscia's report tells how the dictator 'said that he placed the very fullest confidence in Mordini to carry out the programme Garibaldi had put before the people...and charged him to use *largamente* the powers given him and hereby take full latitude to act in that sense...and to receive praise in advance for whatever he might decide to do'. This report would now be interpreted as an obvious encouragement for Mordini to choose an assembly, and the reference to Garibaldi's original programme would have signified the 'march on Rome' quite as much as 'submission to Victor Emanuel'. Friscia had, however, even more encouragement to give than this. 'Garibaldi protested that it was his firm wish that the administrative autonomy of Sicily should be respected, for this autonomy was just and sacred, and...Sicily and Naples were administratively separate and were under one government only in so far as this was necessary to achieve the unity of Italy.' In all likelihood this reply from Garibaldi had been designed simply to reassure Sicily about its independence of

Naples; coming on 4 October, however, it must have had the further
effect of inciting Mordini not to wait on Naples, but to summon a
separate assembly if local conditions made it seem desirable.

What Mordini was not to know was that, since giving his message
to Dr Friscia, Garibaldi's views would have been sensibly modified by
the intervening battle of the Volturno. A third Sicilian envoy at the
front, Salvatore Calvino, thus drew up a despatch on the 4th, which
was not sent till the 5th, and which then arrived in Sicily too late to
affect the issue. Its substance was that 'dictator approves *conciliatory
policy, no longer hopes to go on to Rome*'. The italics here are from
Calvino's draft. The telegram then continued: 'if Piedmontese troops
come, let them land as at Naples. Manufacture and send rifle bullets
especially for Enfields.'[1] This was unequivocal; but it was too late.

Garibaldi was out of touch with Sicilian affairs. Communications
were slow, and in any case he was fully taken up with the biggest battle,
he ever encountered. He can have had little idea how, during his own
absence from Sicily, the unanimity of adoration which always greeted
him personally might be less willingly accorded to his deputies; nor
can he have known how the enthusiasm of an earlier date was being
clouded over by economic and political unrest. It had come as a surprise
when Mordini sent Friscia to ask for the restoration to Sicily of those
government departments which Bertani had transferred from Palermo
to his central secretariat at Naples; because Garibaldi had not appreciated
that Sicilians would continue to dislike Neapolitans even after the
Bourbons had been removed. For the moment he was in no position
to be bothered with political strategy, with the petty *trasformismo*
politics of Palermo, or even with planning how to make radicalism
prevail in the long run against the orthodox liberalism of Cavour. His
chief concern with Sicily was that the island should send him more and
more munitions. Though Calvino had arrived in Naples on 30 September, Garibaldi saw him only on 3 October, and then detained him
altogether for a week longer without letting him return. Mordini had
sent Ca vino to present Garibaldi with certain definite and urgent
requests: namely, that he should allow more arms and men to remain
in Sicily; that he should give the Palermo government more power and
prestige, and not for instance transfer the Sicilian ministries of war and

[1] 5 October, Calvino to Mordini (AMB, b. 28; the draft is in ACM).

marine to the continent; and that he should not communicate with provincial governors and service chiefs in Sicily except through the medium of the prodictator. But Garibaldi seemingly cared for none of these things, and Calvino's replies therefore arrived in Sicily too late to affect the issue. Mordini made his decision of 5 October in ignorance of the fact that events had now overtaken him.

The cabinet meeting of 5 October in Palermo is partially known to us through a minute which runs as follows:

discussion was opened on the condition of the country, in the light of the continued progress of the national cause on the continent, and of the repeated announcements of a possible armed intervention in Sicily. As it was considered that such intervention might give a preponderant voice to one special party, thus disturbing the free manifestation of opinion, the Council unanimously agreed that the electoral colleges should be summoned on the basis of the dictator's decree of 23 June 1860, in order to launch the country along a path that might assure it the free declaration of its wishes. The Council also agreed that an exact account of this intention should be made to the dictator, so that we might have his final determination in the matter.[1]

There was also a published version of this cabinet decision, and it was significantly different in some respects from the private minute. Its stated reason for holding a vote was not the fear of armed intervention, but simply because 'the day is coming ever nearer when the kingdom of Italy will be formed under the constitutional sceptre of Victor Emanuel'. Of course the public statement said nothing of foreign pressure or the danger of a Piedmontese invasion. Nor did it say anything about seeking Garibaldi's approval; on the contrary, an announcement was to be made at once which carried the implication that the calling of a deliberative assembly was the dictator's preordained policy.[2]

Mordini felt a little guilty about what he was doing, for he knew that he was committing Garibaldi on what might be a highly important point. He therefore sent off to Naples a copy of his decree, with the explanation that it was only a tactical move made under pressure, and that pending the dictator's orders there had been no pronouncement on

[1] 5 October (MRR, cartella 221).
[2] 5 October, *Raccolta degli atti del governo dittatoriale*, 1861.

when exactly the assembly should meet.[1] The next day he followed this with another note to elaborate the point that the decree would not tie Garibaldi's hands, for the assembly would not meet yet, and then would take up further time in discussion; and in any case Garibaldi would be under no obligation to give practical application to its advice until his own good time. If necessary he could delay matters still more by having a subsequent plebiscite to confirm its decisions. This is important evidence for any judgement on Mordini, and it tells against the general assumption later made in the north that a rabid prodictator had unscrupulously lured an unwitting Garibaldi from the true patriotic and liberal path. Evidently Mordini's guilty conscience was not for having chosen an assembly rather than a plebiscite; it was for having chosen anything at all. His genuine assumption was still that Garibaldi required him to postpone annexation in order to make time for developing the revolution. He was at pains to make it clear that 'by this method I have left the dictator all the time he may require to push on with his own policy as he best knows how'. That is to say, Mordini was still thinking in terms of the Rome expedition which, unknown to him, had now been rendered impracticable. His justification was that the assembly decree had been 'merely a step to ward off the Cavourian tempest...to conserve the island for Italy and for Garibaldi'.[2] All this, he insisted, merited that Garibaldi should approve his action and send confirmation at once.

Mordini scarcely need have worried on this last point. The face of the revolution was rapidly changing, but Garibaldi had meant what he said when he gave back a free hand in politics to his prodictator. Events had been succeeding each other too fast for there to be any intricate plan of policy which Mordini could upset, and Garibaldi was as usual being ruled rather by instinct and opportunism. The centralizing decrees subordinating Sicily to Naples had come not out of Garibaldi's head, but from the radicals round Bertani who had taken it upon themselves to try and mould the dictator's policy for him. Since the end of September, Bertani had given way to Crispi as Garibaldi's right-hand man; and circumstances now forced both Crispi and Bertani to see that Mordini's alternative scheme offered the radicals their only hope of

---

[1] 5 October, Mordini to Garibaldi (ACP, f. 140).
[2] 6 October, Mordini to Garibaldi (ACP, f. 140).

even partial victory in the struggle for political survival. Crispi sent off a telegram as soon as he heard of it: 'the dictator approves the decree for electing deputies. Summon assembly for the day which suits you best. For this purpose we revoke the law of 16 September, and leave you with a free hand as you request. Bravo Mordini. Get on with the elections, and campaign for some good deputies.'[1] In the light of Mordini's future action it is important to note this justification of his policy by Garibaldi's secretary. He must have received Crispi's message with some relief.

As for the immediate reaction of Sicily to the decree, Mordini reported that it was 'prodigioso eccellente'.[2] Most of the provinces welcomed the news almost with exaggerated applause.[3] Even Messina reported that the great majority received it very warmly.[4] Another doubtful city, Catania, hailed the decree 'with satisfaction, yet [*però*] considering it to be the natural fulfilment of previous dictatorial pronouncements'.[5] It is clear, that is to say, that the opposition to Mordini had as yet no fault to find with what a week later was to be described as the most controversial and sinister of measures. Far from the assembly being unwelcome, the grudging word *però* indicates that this decree was only logical and should perhaps have come long ago. Cavour himself at an earlier stage would have been extremely glad at the announcement of such an assembly, though now he was one move ahead of his partisans at Palermo, and had learnt to see how dangerous this particular institution might be. Cavour's friends in Sicily, however, were jubilant, because to their untutored eye the decree seemed to imply that the provisional regime would soon be ending, and there was little thought that underneath might be concealed a different inspiration. In all

---

[1] Undated draft in MRR, 221/31/1; 15 October, *Il Giornale Officiale di Sicilia* published a decree to this effect signed by Garibaldi and Crispi at Caserta on 7 October.

[2] 7 October, Mordini to Garibaldi (Carte Sirtori, Ambrosiana Library, Milan).

[3] Many reports are in MRR: Trapani reported great public joy and bands playing; Sciacca told of 'an inexpressible joy'; Girgenti said that 'the impression created could not have been better'; Patti reported 'enormous applause...and all apprehensions have now disappeared, everyone saying that the future of the country is assured'; at Castroreale there had been 'an explosion of enthusiasm which is quite indescribable'.

[4] 7 October, governor of Messina to Mordini (MRR).

[5] 8 October, governor of Catania to Mordini (AMB, b. 28).

appearance, the implications of the choice between plebiscite and assembly had still not been generally grasped.

For the best cross-section of contemporary opinion we may turn once more to comments in the local press. *La Forbice's* conclusion was 'better late than never',[1] and 'the assembly decree has been published only after the government had lost highly precious time in blessed somnolence'.[2] The strongly Cavourian *Regno d' Italia*, which had been agitating unequivocally for the plebiscite, now took Mordini's move as a convenient basis for compromise; and 'since they offer us an assembly instead, let us take it'.[3] Still more positive was the comment of La Farina's old paper, *L' Annessione*. A fortnight later this journal tried to create the legend that the decree of 5 October had encountered an indifferent silence.[4] But on the 8th it expressly mentioned the popular joy at its reception, and again on the 9th it referred to the general exultation. True, there was already a suspicion that there might be a catch somewhere, since the complete unexpectedness of Mordini's announcement had left people 'without time to think'. But the comments made by this paper in its issue of the 9th were if anything more favourable and bore fewer reservations than in that of the day before. It considered that Mordini's instructions to provincial governors about the assembly were admirable, and agreed that Sicily had received the decree with exultation, but only warned Mordini not to let it lead to long discussions and delay.[5] This suggests that general approval was maintained between the 5th and the 9th. Mordini had succeeded for the moment in satisfying most people who mattered, Garibaldi on the one hand and the local Cavourians on the other. Had he acted earlier, he might conceivably have won the day.

Remarkably and significantly enough, the only Sicilians who positively objected to his decree from the first were the extreme radicals of Mazzinian colour, whose overriding concern for unity made them fear in an assembly the utterance of latent separatism. By a strange irony, the people whom Cavour always considered the villains were once more the very people who almost alone with him now deplored anything like a Sicilian parliament. In the opinion of orthodox liberals,

[1] 7 October, *La Forbice*.   [2] 16 October, *ibid.*
[3] 6 October, *Il Regno d' Italia*.   [4] 17 October, *L' Annessione*.
[5] 9 October, *ibid.*

Mordini was by definition a Mazzinian *pur sang*, and therefore the existence of an extremely useful political distinction escaped them. They did not know, for instance, that the radical governor of Noto accepted the assembly decree under protest: he would have preferred a straight plebiscite by universal suffrage, and took what was offered merely because it carried with it some possibility of conciliation; but he fore-told that many deputies would turn up to the assembly simply to vote for unconditional annexation.[1] The governors of Corleone and Aci disliked the new decree heartily. The latter, for instance, sent to say that 'a very sinister effect has been produced by this convocation of deputies in Palermo; in view of the dictator's promise, we had been hoping for representatives of the people to meet only on the Capitol in Rome'. He concluded by asking Mordini if Garibaldi's specific warrant could be shown for this change of front, since he himself at Acireale had no intention of executing the decree until a satisfactory explanation could be made.[2] An answer duly came from Bargoni, secretary-general to the Palermo government, explaining that, if Garibaldi had once thought of waiting until he could hold an assembly at Rome, now he had changed or amplified his views and wanted one first in Palermo. The rejoinder to this from the recalcitrant governor was a brusque resignation.[3] Yet another radical, Navarra, a leader-writer for the *Precursore* whom Crispi had left behind with instructions to watch over and report on Mordini, feared that with this assembly 'the Sicilians will end up by proclaiming their autonomy under a king of their own'.[4] This was a possibility which the radical unitarians would have deplored above everything.

For the only other class of people who reacted immediately against the proclamation, we must look to the north of Italy. Only one motive was there allowed to the prodictator, that of wanting an assembly just in order to hinder Cavour's policy of simple annexation.[5] In Sicily itself, however, at least until the new *mot d'ordre* came from Turin, Cavour's supporters gave Mordini at any rate a grudging approval, and his decree had a smooth passage for four or five days. Crispi's telegram of the 6th giving Garibaldi's blessing to the assembly reached Palermo

[1] 13 October, Scelsi to Mordini (MRR, 221/31).
[2] 10 October, governor of Acireale telegram to Mordini (AMB, b. 28).
[3] 12 October, *ibid.* (MRR).
[4] 8 October, Navarra to Crispi (ACP, b. 156).   [5] 9 October, *La Perseveranza*.

on the 7th,[1] and this contributed its part to the general pacification. The preponderance of common-sense opinion in the centre of Sicilian politics was probably quite agreeable to what was proposed. *La Forbice* came out once more against any fusion with Piedmont, that is to say against any annexation which meant the simple acceptance of the Piedmontese constitution and laws. It also opposed the other extreme of making Sicily a separate kingdom, for the convincing reason 'that in the present state of affairs we could find absolutely no one to take on the post of king'. No, Sicily should vote to become part of a kingdom of *Italy* under King Victor Emanuel, and not a state of its own. The same paper then went on to reject as invalid the parallel of Tuscany—for this province had been quoted by Cavour's party as having voted for union not with Italy, but with the existing kingdom of Sardinia. The cases were not parallel, for earlier in the year the goal of unity had seemed distant, whereas now a new kingdom of Italy was almost in being.[2]

The Palermitans in general probably waited only to know Garibaldi's mind before being quite certain of their own. It was often difficult for them to understand either of the active parties, which both seemed to have concealed and possibly disreputable motives, 'and which were fighting without understanding one another, like the Jesuits and Jansenists'.[3] But after Garibaldi's confirmation became known on the 7th, there was little further reason for them to doubt Mordini's good intentions. At Messina, too, there was a relaxation of tension; and after a truce with the Bourbon garrison on the 8th had allayed fears somewhat, the radical governor intervened in the theatre amid cheers to read out that Victor Emanuel had begun his march towards Naples.[4] The full width of the gap dividing radicals and moderates could have been appreciated at this point by Cavour alone, since he now had the picture in perspective and at last saw his goal clearly before him. It was but imperfectly or spasmodically perceived by Garibaldi, and hardly at all by the generality of Sicilians. Their thoughts were fathered by the hope that they might be able to combine the security represented by Victor Emanuel with the enthusiasm and lofty ideals generated by their dictator.

[1] The date of receipt is marked on the form (AMB, b. 28).
[2] 8 October, *La Forbice*.
[3] G. Crescenti, in a pamphlet *Il nuovo regno d' Italia*, dated Palermo 27 September, p. 4.
[4] 8 October, report by the Sardinian consul at Messina (AME).

CHAPTER XXI

PALLAVICINO FIGHTS FOR A PLEBISCITE: 8 OCTOBER

For a few days after Mordini made his decision of 5 October, Sicilian politicians were able to continue within the bounds of their closed world, little regarding and little able to regard the course of events at Turin and Naples. The difficulty of communication was such that, although Cavour in the north knew on the 6th about Mordini's decree of the day before, people in Sicily did not know for a full week about Cavour's speech of the 2nd to parliament. During this week, owing to their ignorance of Cavour's attitude, even the most conservative daily papers at Palermo had no major disagreement with Mordini's new statement of policy, and people were content to know that a Sicilian assembly would soon be meeting. The position was described on the 9th by consul Goodwin to Lord John Russell—Lord John being now a convert to united Italy, but Goodwin still sharing some of the autonomist sentiments he found about him in Palermo.

The decree of the 5th convoking the electoral colleges on the 21st inst. for the election of a national assembly has been favourably received. Preparations are making to give effect to its provisions by all political parties. The day for the meeting of the assembly will be shortly fixed, and an early day is confidently looked for. The sole business of the assembly will be to lay down the conditions for the entrance of Sicily into the Italian union.[1]

By itself this would be too partisan a testimony to carry much assurance. But from other sources we have already seen that the bulk of Sicilian opinion on the 9th was still expecting a local parliament to meet and discuss what conditions they would attach to annexation. This was regarded as the most likely way to reach a highest common factor of agreement about their future status. A description of the current state of mind was given by Goodwin, who expanded his statement yet more explicitly:

among these conditions, which at present are subjects of speculation, the following appear indispensable...first, the provision for the payment of the

[1] 9 October, Goodwin to Russell (F.O. 165/134).

interest of the national debt at present amounting to a million of ducats per annum, exclusive of 600,000 ducats for the interest of the floating debt: secondly, the determination of the quota to be contributed by Sicily towards the common expenses of the states: and thirdly, the retention of the laws and tribunals. For the last forty years Sicily has possessed a code of laws and a system of judicature framed on French models, which however exceptionable on the score of centralization, have on the whole well answered their purpose. The abolition of the Court of Cassation and the removal of the seal of justice, in the last resort, to a foreign capital would entail upon suitors long voyages by sea and great loss of time besides heavy expenses.

While informal discussion was already beginning on these conditions of union, Mordini, reinforced by approval from Naples, set about his preparations for convening the assembly. On the 7th he had written round to all provincial governors explaining the idea of such a convention. 'I am not one of those who think that the government ought to have its own candidates in the elections', he said. 'Governors, therefore, must not even indirectly suggest candidates for their districts.' Their job was just to see that everyone was encouraged to vote, and that no party should by deceit or intimidation bring such pressure to bear that voting was blind or unspontaneous.[1] Mordini assured them that a plebiscite by universal suffrage would follow afterwards as the final consecration of union. He explained that, if it had been thought necessary to precede the plebiscite by an assembly, this was meant as an act of concord to pacify growing differences of opinion; for it would serve as a forum where they could freely discuss those differences without fear of outside pressure.[2] Mordini by now really does seem to have thought of what he had done as an act of concord. Although he had begun by calling it a check to Cavour, the favourable reception on all sides in Palermo had been so impressive that by the 9th he even thought the news would be well received in Turin.[3] He now appointed 4 November as the date for this local parliament to meet.[4]

[1] 7 October, *Il Giornale Officiale di Sicilia*; the next issue announced the appointment of a committee of architects to choose a building to house the assembly.

[2] 9 October, a second letter to governors, signed by Mordini and Bargoni (MRR, cartella 221).

[3] 9 October, Mordini to Mangini (copy in AMB).

[4] 9 October (Raccolta degli atti del governo dittatoriale).

Late on 9 October Mordini sent off a telegram to tell Garibaldi what a good effect had been scored by his proclamation for a Sicilian assembly;[1] but there were nevertheless several details about this message and its despatch which suggested that all was not quite well with his plans. There was, for instance, the great difficulty in communication which it reflected: for though sent on the 9th, this telegram did not reach even the other side of the Straits until after noon on the 11th. A second and more ominous sign was the fact that Mordini should have needed once more to ask Garibaldi to send back occasional informatory letters, or at very least the reports of the Stefani agency; for the prodictator's government was inviting ridicule by never knowing on time either Garibaldi's policy or the military bulletins from the front, and sometimes it had to await the Genoa newspapers to learn even the chief items of news from Naples. The same telegram also contained the complaint that, though a ship had just arrived from Naples, it was without Parisi or Calvino; for these two Sicilians were both urgently wanted back for their important jobs at Palermo, and originally had been sent only to discover what was happening on the mainland. As a final point, the text reveals that Cavour's speech given to parliament a week earlier was at last known in Sicily. On 2 October Cavour had publicly placed his veto on any solution other than unqualified annexation by plebiscite. The arrival of this ultimatum must have given Mordini serious cause to worry about what effect it would have on Sicilian opinion.

The reports from Turin about the proceedings in parliament were in fact going to change the whole aspect of affairs in the south. They had reached Naples two days before, with the result that events there had already changed direction before Mordini could take stock of the new situation. There was by now another complication, in that Garibaldi's headquarters at Caserta had become one more centre of action and policy-making, along with Naples, Turin and Palermo. Indeed, Palermo was now the least important of these four centres. Mordini did not fully realize it, but in fact the Sicilian government henceforward was too far out of touch with what was happening to preserve much initiative or even much freedom of movement on its own. Those party leaders who had not gone northwards for the opening of parliament had naturally tended to congregate round the person of the dictator. For

[1] 9 October, Mordini to Garibaldi (Archivio Garibaldi MRR).

this reason one has to follow events at Caserta and Naples before their repercussions can be identified in Palermo at several days' remove.

The political situation at Naples was roughly this. Since 1 October, Garibaldi's chief adviser and secretary had been no longer Bertani but Crispi, another of the *enragés* but a cleverer and slightly more moderate and tactful man than his predecessor. Garibaldi was by no means proving himself the uncompromising and reckless revolutionary which Cavour supposed. Though many of the radical leaders had arrived in Naples, they were there as soldiers or private citizens, and Crispi alone had been given important political office. Against the urgent advice of his secretary, Garibaldi had appointed a cabinet of ministers as a self-imposed check upon his dictatorial will. He had even dismissed Bertani at the request of the more conservative Neapolitans, and had nominated two successive ministries of moderate liberals who were perpetually at odds with his secretariat and enthusiastic for the ideas of Cavour. He had followed this up by appointing a predictator for Naples in the person of Marquis Pallavicino, a man of compromise and moderation who had already decided that it was his first duty to secure immediate and unconditional annexation to Piedmont. Certainly Mazzini was still in Naples: but, although Cavour chose to think Garibaldi a mere tool of this arch-agitator, in fact Mazzini was quite off the stage upon which all these rivalries of interest and doctrine were to be played out, and by this time had given up Garibaldi for politically lost.[1]

The dictator had personally been hoping to abstain from politics, and had rather been engrossed throughout the first few days of the month in his close-fought battle along the River Volturno. On 1 October the royalists made their first big attack of the whole southern campaign, but the volunteers held firm all along the line, and over two thousand prisoners were taken. For political reasons this engagement was going to be played down by northern generals and military historians.[2] In reality it was one of Garibaldi's finest military ventures, in which he defied the pundits by showing himself a master of defensive strategy, and in which he proved fully able to control a larger force of men than

[1] 2 October, Mazzini to Caroline Stansfeld: 'nothing can be done without him—very little, I fear, with him' (*Epistolario*, vol. XLI, p. 126).

[2] Colonel C. Cesari, *La campagna di Garibaldi nell' Italia meridionale, 1860*, p. 193, published by Ministero della Guerra, Ufficio Storico, 1928.

the Piedmontese regulars had numbered at Castelfidardo or indeed in
the whole of the Crimean War. Some of the Piedmontese troops who
had been already landed at Naples, and who so far had been obliged to
refuse Garibaldi's urgent requests for aid, were at last permitted by
Villamarina to join in the battle, because of the danger of a counter-
attack on the city. Between three and four hundred of them came up
in the later stages of the fight, and suffered half-a-dozen casualties from
shell-fire.[1] This must have had considerable moral effect, just as did the
presence of British sailors 'on leave' helping to man the guns. It was
the first occasion Piedmontese troops had fought side to side with the
volunteers; and it warned the Bourbons that Cavour was going to pay
no regard to the diplomatic niceties of breaking off diplomatic relations
and declaring war. Furthermore, it carried the implication that the
Piedmontese were no longer worried that the volunteers could continue
their march upon Rome. In reality Villamarina had had to act on his
own authority, for Cavour had left him no instructions to cover such
a situation. The ambassador had been confronted with the fact that the
Piedmontese were already compromised against the Bourbons by their
military occupation of the port and fortresses of Naples. If he refused
to give yet more material help to Garibaldi at a moment of such peril,
this refusal would only be interpreted as a wish that Garibaldi might
lose, and it would have the worst possible effect on Cavour's reputation
among liberal Neapolitans.[2] It did not matter that the Piedmontese
troops were abruptly withdrawn once the immediate danger was over.
The important fact was that, without being consulted, and without any
enthusiasm, Cavour had momentarily found his men fighting alongside
the volunteers.

It is usually stated that Garibaldi's new-found docility henceforward
was due to the stiffer resistance he met on the Volturno, and to the fact
that his almost complete lack of artillery and cavalry now became
important for the first time in these different conditions of warfare.
But the political effect of Villamarina's decision was quite as important,
for this went part of the way to restore Garibaldi's faith in the good
intentions of the Piedmontese.[3] Until now, the fair words of the Turin

---

[1] 3 October, Colonel Santa Rosa to Fanti (*CC Lib. del Mezz.* vol. III, 1952,
pp. 25–6).　　　　[2] 2 October, Nisco to Cavour (*ibid.* p. 14).

[3] 5 October, Villamarina to Cavour (*ibid.* p. 45).

government had been contradicted by almost all the appearances, in particular by the presence of three thousand soldiers waiting idly at Naples; but after 2 October there was more tangible evidence of a positive will to collaborate. Garibaldi still seems to have been hoping that Cavour might eventually be dismissed and that the king would then make Rome the object of the campaign;[1] but by 5 October he had given up hope of being able to proceed much farther before the Piedmontese advance column arrived from the north, and he was already beginning to prepare his volunteers for the next campaigning season in the spring of 1861.[2] With the realization that there was small possibility of further advance at the moment, he was also brought up sharply and most reluctantly against the political struggle developing behind the lines. In his ignorance of politics, he had not realized that a prodictator, a cabinet of ministers, and a secretary-general, all with more or less undefined powers, might sometimes collide and bring government to a stop.

Back in the city of Naples, the more respectable citizens were in much the same state of alarm that they had been before Garibaldi's arrival a month before. They were terrified either that the Bourbons would return victorious and let loose the *lazzaroni* in a counter-revolution, or else that Garibaldi would risk his forces in a drive on Rome and leave them without defences or orderly government. Garibaldi's invasion, coming on top of the breakdown of the Bourbon administration, had exaggerated the natural lawlessness of the city and district of Naples, and there were dangerous signs that lower-class unrest was becom ng associated with political reaction and loyalty to Throne and Altar. The liberating army had not proved universally popular, because of its rowdyism, its deserters and its requisitioning of private property, and above all because it had not eliminated the fear of a Bourbon counter-attack.[3] Admiral Mundy reported that, though there were some thousands of Calabrians with the volunteers, only ten Neapolitans had

---

[1] 4 October, Elliot to Russell (F.O. 70/320/549).

[2] 6 October, Garibaldi's proclamation to Molise, *Edizione nazionale degli scritti di Garibaldi*, vol. IV, p. 312.

[3] 8 October, Elliot to Russell: 'the decline of Garibaldi's popularity has been one of the most curious things imaginable...if the Sardinians do not quickly come to save him he will rapidly lose more ground' (RP G.D. 22/85).

joined the patriot forces [1]—Commander Forbes ironically put the figure at a single man,[2] and Türr said it was eighty.[3] At all events the number was remarkably small, and there is little doubt that the war of liberation was felt less keenly at Naples than in some other parts of Italy. Mindful of what had chanced on other occasions, the citizens were judiciously waiting to see who won before committing themselves. They even showed reluctance to attend gala occasions in the San Carlo theatre, in case this might turn out in the end to be public alignment with the losing side. The sense of regional separatism was probably less strong with them than among Sicilians, but one visiting deputy from Turin was impressed to find a 'universal' desire to keep their own laws and autonomy, and was already foretelling a revolutionary secession of the south if the northern system of union was imposed there too unyieldingly.[4]

Early in October the Neapolitans were more interested in an immediate restoration of law and order than in what long-term arrangements would come about thereafter. They knew that Cavour had called parliament to meet on 2 October, and it was to be expected that he would then ask for special powers to annex the south by simple decree and so end the state of uncertainty and provisional government.[5] In the meantime, while they waited for news of this to filter through from Turin, the new prodictator Pallavicino issued a proclamation to raise their spirits, promising them a splendid future. 'Under the rule of Victor Emanuel, I promise you order and liberty, the impartial adminis- tration of justice...expansion of the national guard, schools for the people, railways, and encouragement of all types of agriculture, com- merce and industry.'[6] All this alluring prospect was held out to Neapolitans if only they accepted Pallavicino's offer of a plebiscite and immediate annexation. The alternative offered by Crispi, on the other hand, would involve them in further fighting and a prolongation of the state of emergency. The radicals were known to stand for a continuation of war and revolution, as well as for anti-clericalism, and any number

[1] 16 October, Mundy, *H.M.S. Hannibal at Palermo and Naples*, p. 324.
[2] Forbes, *The campaign of Garibaldi in the Two Sicilies*, pp. 314–15.
[3] 16 October, Elliot to Russell (RP, G.D. 22/85).
[4] 5 October, *Il Diritto*, letter from Cavalleri.
[5] 5 October, *Il Giornale Officiale di Napoli*.　　[6] 6 October, *ibid*.

of utopian political ideas, all the things that is to say which good honest citizens most disliked. The wealthier classes had an abiding dread of Mazzinianism, which was often identified with social as well as political revolution. They were particularly worried that Garibaldi seemed to place more confidence in the *canaglia* than in the *galantuomini*.[1] They also suspected the radicals of wanting to call an assembly as a way of prolonging the emergency and perhaps tying the hands of Cavour. The suspicion was fully justified. If people had only known, one of Bertani's last acts before falling from grace had been to ask Garibaldi what he thought about the 'idea of calling a parliament in this part of Italy as a counter-balance to that of Turin'.[2] Perhaps this proposal for a southern parliament had hardly been a very serious suggestion at the time, but the threat became dangerously real when on 6 October there was published in Naples the news of Mordini's pronouncement about the assembly in Sicily. This news horrified the Neapolitan conservatives, and was just the lead which the radicals had been waiting for. After the collapse of their own private schemes for the conquest of Rome, Crispi and his friends had to recognize that Mordini had surpassed them in perception and skill. Crispi at once proposed in council that Naples should fall into line with Palermo, and at this suggestion all the latent political differences came to the surface.[3]

For one day discussion was adjourned. Garibaldi, who had hitherto maintained that any form of vote should be put off until the end of the war, had lately been wondering whether there was anything further to gain by postponement. He had empowered Mordini to modify his original plan if local conditions made it necessary, and now assumed that his prodictator in Sicily must have acted for the best. Accordingly, his first reaction was to give Mordini's decree his formal approval, and —so said Crispi—to order a corresponding assembly for the mainland provinces of the south.[4] His ministers at Naples had already discussed this very question on 2 October, with much heat and to little purpose. But on hearing of Mordini's action they now met again on the 7th,

---

[1] 13 October, vice-consul Astengo to Cavour (*CC Lib. del Mezz.* vol. III, p. 107).

[2] 23 September, Bertani to Garibaldi (Curàtulo, *Garibaldi, Vittorio Emanuele, Cavour*, p. 386).

[3] 16 October, *L' Indipendente* (Naples).

[4] 18 March 1865, Crispi to Mazzini (Crispi, *Memoirs*, vol. I, p. 442).

clearly shaken by the news and by Garibaldi's reaction to it. After some debate they voted by three against two in favour of following the Sicilian example as the dictator suggested. One of the minority was Raffaele Conforti who nominally presided in the cabinet, but even he was wavering, and earlier in the day had apparently favoured an assembly.[1] Crispi described how Pallavicino was present at the discussion and opposed the decision with all his might. Then, unable to give a casting vote, the prodictator had gone off immediately to put his views at Garibaldi's headquarters in Caserta. Pallavicino at this point began to hint at resignation, and perhaps this threat helped to carry his views, for Garibaldi now overrode the ministerial decision and gave him a mandate for a plebiscite. This appeared to be a rebuff not only to the cabinet, but even more to the dictator's radical secretariat. Crispi nevertheless saw a way to reconcile this new decision with the old. Far from making difficulties, he even smoothed the way to a settlement. His compromise suggestion was that Garibaldi's mandate must be taken, not as alternative, but as something complementary to the ministerial decision, in other words that Naples should have both assembly and plebiscite, the latter merely to indicate the general opinion whether for union or no, and the former to discuss, implement and apply the findings of the general will. Crispi says that he therefore 'arranged matters' accordingly.[2]

Further light is thrown on this change in Garibaldi's and Crispi's views by Francesco De Sanctis, the great literary critic and future national minister of education. De Sanctis was at this time serving under Garibaldi as governor of Avellino in the hinterland of Naples, and was perhaps the most moderate, balanced and acute intellect of all the actors on this particular stage. Until now he had adhered to the radical programme of proceeding to Rome, and had loyally discountenanced the premature campaign for precipitate annexation. But on 6 October he saw Garibaldi and told him that the invasion of the Marches by Cavour, together with the threat of intervention in Italy by the other states of Europe, had changed his mind. In his opinion there was no longer any alternative to falling in with the wishes of Turin if the

[1] 8 October, Parisi to Mordini (Rosi, *Il risorgimento e l' azione d' un patriota*, p. 418); 12 October, Cattaneo to Bertani (Archivio Cattaneo MRM).

[2] Crispi, *Memoirs*, vol. I, p. 443.

revolution was to be concluded without disaster. De Sanctis left Garibaldi on the 6th under the impression that he had carried his point; but when he returned on the 7th, he found the dictator talking with Crispi, and once more of the opinion that annexation should be made *conditional* on the redemption of Rome and Venice—this obviously had been the substance of Crispi's advice in the interval. So De Sanctis went back to seek out Pallavicino at Naples, where he must have arrived just after the Neapolitan cabinet had voted in favour of calling an assembly. Both of them then returned together to put the opposition case at Caserta. 'The discussions were long and lively', said De Sanctis, 'but Crispi showed himself generous, and not only yielded but induced Garibaldi to yield too.' Garibaldi insisted on one point only, that the wording of the plebiscite should mention Italy united and 'indivisible', so as to render the vote invalid if Cavour failed to reach Rome or ceded any more provinces in compensation to France.[1] This mild and un-, prejudiced account of events shows that tempers were still more or less unruffled, and that Crispi was still ready for compromise, while Garibaldi as usual was wavering between confused alternatives, swayed this way and that in each successive interview. It hints also that Crispi may have kept his thoughts about an assembly to himself.

This brings us to the moment, late on the 7th, when some news arrived from Turin to embitter the feelings of those who fought each other in the dictator's presence. This was the account of Cavour's speech to parliament on the 2nd. Contrary to the advice of Cavour's best Neapolitan counsellors,[2] this speech had insisted quite firmly on the unconditional surrender of the south, and had employed the provocative and somewhat humiliating word 'annexation' which a growing body of opinion in Naples and Sicily was now trying to avoid. The receipt of this news coincided with a report that the Piedmontese General Fanti, a strong personal enemy of the dictator, was about to send his advance troops across the northern frontier into Neapolitan territory.[3] This had all the appearance of being a joint political and military offensive against the radicals. Evidently Cavour had no intention of waiting upon the

[1] F. De Sanctis, *Opere complete*, ed. N. Cortese, vol. xiv, 1938, p. 53.

[2] E.g. 14 September and 4 October, *Il Nazionale* (Bonghi's paper at Naples).

[3] Telegram from the governor of Teramo, received in Naples on 6 October (ACP, f. 143).

result of a popular vote before taking over southern Italy; on the contrary, he seemed suspiciously eager that the plebiscite should be conducted in the presence of Sardinian troops. The implication of all this for Garibaldi was, first, that 'compromise' would now mean capitulation; secondly, that there was but little time left if he wanted any other policy than that of unconditional surrender to prevail; and thirdly, perhaps also that his own eventual submission could hardly be much longer delayed. Yet another piece of news also arrived at the same time, namely that on 3 October Victor Emanuel had arrived at Ancona to assume command of the northern army. Hitherto Fanti and Cialdini had been in command, until it was quite certain that there was no further danger of any military check. What remained now was for the king to win the political battle against the Garibaldians. Cavour's expectation was that Garibaldi, who had also held the rank of general in the royal service, would not submit easily to General Fanti whom he so much disliked; whereas he would loyally obey if called to order by the king. Hence Victor Emanuel's arrival at Ancona at this precise moment.

Naples knew of all this by 7 October, and the various parties in the south reacted to the news according to their kind. Garibaldi's mood was one of resignation. He was miserable about it, but passively resigned, and still retained some slight hope that the king might have some hidden purpose. As for Crispi and the more extreme radicals, they must have realized that for them it was now or never. Cavour's public challenge put them on the defensive, and left them altogether at a disadvantage tactically. To Pallavicino and the liberal-conservatives, on the other hand, Cavour's words and the king's presence near the frontier brought an enormous access of support.

On 8 October, as a result of the news from Turin, and of Garibaldi's meeting with Pallavicino and De Sanctis, the same ministers at Naples who by a majority had decided for an assembly the day before, changed their minds and voted unanimously for a plebiscite. Crispi was one of them—since he had arrogated to himself the slightly ridiculous title of 'minister of foreign affairs' with a seat in the cabinet. His vote on this occasion shows that, if not fully convinced, at least he had been forced to transfer his attack from the principle to its application and wording.[1]

[1] Pallavicino, *Le Memorie*, vol. III, p. 626.

Later on he recounted what he had said at the meeting which took this decision:

I declared that the Southern provinces, owing to the special conditions under which their revolution had taken place and in consideration of the importance of their position as regards the rest of Italy, could not accept the formula that had been adopted when the people of Tuscany and Emilia had cast their vote. Our country must not *give* herself to another, must not *annex* herself, which verb savours overmuch of servitude, but must rather express her desire that union be achieved....A plebiscite under the conditions that prevailed in the Central provinces might now be regarded not as a simple halt by the way, but as a complete renunciation of our determination to redeem the entire peninsula.[1]

These doubts were to be partially resolved by the wording of the decree, wherein it was said that the plebiscite would be for an 'indivisible' Italy; and it was to such a carefully phrased conclusion that all the ministers at last agreed.[2] October 21 was fixed for the vote.

This agreement lasted but a few hours, yet it was enough to have an important effect on more than just Naples or southern Italy. Why did Crispi give his consent to this decree? Probably because he still hoped that a plebiscite could be held conjointly with an assembly which would give him all he wanted in delay and publicity. It may be that he was also relying on Mordini to keep Sicily free and independent after the annexation of Naples, as a fortress and a centre of operations for the radicals. It is likely, moreover, that he feared that Garibaldi might have definitely changed his mind in favour of a quick vote: in which case the most that could be obtained was a declaration in favour of 'Italy one and indivisible'. This particular wording, if ever the occasion arose, could always be interpreted to mean postponement of the actual union until after the fall of Rome and Venice.

It was only when Crispi had time to reassure himself about Garibaldi's real opinion in another interview, and to reflect on how unlikely it was for Cavour to be moved by a mere form of words, that he reverted in his tactics to an aggressive championing of the assembly. Garibaldi, too, changed his mind again almost at once in the same direction. But by then it was too late. The plebiscite decree of the 8th, unsigned it is true

[1] Crispi, *Memoirs*, vol. I, p. 443.
[2] 8 October, *Il Giornale Officiale di Napoli*.

by Garibaldi, but approved by all the ministers including Crispi, was telegraphed by Pallavicino to all provinces, and was to leak through *via* Reggio into Sicily. Once known in Messina and Palermo it was to destroy all possibility of Mordini being able to proceed with his plan to call a local parliament, because it gave Sicilians the impression that Garibaldi had rejected the idea of a similar assembly at Naples, and hence that Mordini on 5 October must have been acting disloyally and on his own initiative. For this result Crispi must be held largely responsible. He had misread the situation.

The dramatic irony of the situation did not stop at this. It will be seen in a later chapter how, a few days afterwards, the policy of conditional annexation by assembly again prevailed in Naples, and once more Crispi had a brief moment of triumph, once more Pallavicino was in despair. But the news then came back from Sicily that Pallavicino's decree of the 8th had been seized on delightedly bv the plebiscitarians in Palermo, and that Mordini had had to yield to their pressure. This news in turn had repercussions in Naples. The result was that Sicily, having first been compelled by Naples to change over from an assembly to a plebiscite, then forced Naples to follow Sicily on precisely the same issue. There is a sense in which Crispi's government in the south can be said to have died by its own hand.

CHAPTER XXII

PARLIAMENT SUPPORTS CAVOUR: OCTOBER

Cavour would not have understood very accurately what was going on at Naples and Palermo, especially during the three weeks' break in the telegraph service in September. But this hardly mattered, since at last he knew his own mind and could take positive action in accordance with what he knew. While Fanti carried out the military invasion of pontifical and Neapolitan territory, Cavour concentrated on dealing with all the diplomatic and political repercussions of this invasion as they arose. He first applied himself to the problem of how to meet the angry protests, which had come in from Russia, Prussia and Spain against the illegality and immorality of his war policy. They had complained that he had neither awaited the Pope's reply to his ultimatum, nor declared war; and that he had flagrantly violated the very principle of non-intervention from which he had formerly derived so much benefit. But to these protests Cavour was able to oppose the active encouragement of Great Britain and the passive connivance of France. The balance of power was thus on his side, as it was invariably on Italy's side during the later and successful years of the *risorgimento*.

A second problem was more difficult. For a long time he had been perplexed how to combat the revolution without openly attacking Garibaldi. His difficulty was to catch up with the remarkable conversion of public opinion to Garibaldi's beliefs, yet to do this without having publicly to acknowledge either his former impercipience, or his present debt to the revolutionaries. He had, if possible, to retain all the advantages, with none of the disadvantages, of being at once their enemy and their friend. By the beginning of October, however, certain points told strongly in his favour when he came to tackle this acrobatic feat. There was first the tremendous fact that the invasion of central Italy had now restored his popularity. At the very same time, the volunteers were suffering their first military check on the Volturno. His information now led him to believe that Garibaldi was no longer in any position to make difficulties over the entry of Piedmontese troops into the south of Italy.[1] Another point was that Cavour had outflanked Rattazzi, so that the parliamentary Left had no alternative policy to offer, and did not even know the facts on which to base one. At Turin, 'public opinion is ferociously anti-Garibaldian, and insists that we end a system of government that so much dishonours Italy and the cause of liberty'.[2] People there were in general most enthusiastic over the assertion of Piedmontese influence in the peninsula. Most of them were sufficiently anxious about losing the privileged position of a capital city not to be too eager for Garibaldi to reach Rome,[3] and they were also burning with monarchist zeal against this self-appointed upstart dictator in the south. Asproni wrote from Turin on the 4th to Crispi that 'the king is completely back in Cavour's hand'; and he added maliciously that Rosina, the king's mistress who had had a considerable share in the former breach between monarch and minister, 'has been placated with large gifts, and now is all in favour of Cavour'.[4] According to Bertani, himself now in Turin, people there were so excited and incensed as to call Garibaldi 'a traitor and a rebel'.[5] This was the result of reports sent back by Piedmontese agents in the south; for the terror of social revolution, together with a lack of understanding about their opponents, and a desire to overdarken the picture for purposes of self-justification, had combined to make these agents mislead northern opinion on the subject of Naples and Sicily. But Cavour was delighted at the result, because an irate public opinion made things easier for when he could launch his campaign against the 'Garibaldian hordes'. The long-term results of this were to be most unfortunate. For the moment, however, it gave him just the right atmosphere to win the vote of confidence he required; and in these circumstances a parliamentary debate was the natural expedient to which he turned.

[1] 2 October, Cavour telegram to Fanti (*CC Lib. del Mezz.* vol. III, 1952, p. 6).

[2] 2 October, Cavour to Victor Emanuel (*ibid.* p. 9).

[3] 4 October, Asproni (a deputy) from Turin to Crispi: 'all speak of Garibaldi with anger and contempt....The secret motive for this is neither love and esteem for Cavour nor hatred of Garibaldi—it is the fear of losing the Capital that is driving them all crazy' (Crispi, *Memoirs*, vol. I, p. 434).

[4] *Ibid.* These words were excised from the published version, but can be seen in the original (ACP, f. 138).

[5] 6 October, copy of Bertani to Cattaneo (ABCM).

The Baron Ricasoli at Florence was advocating a different system. Ricasoli and Medici represented another current of opinion among the 'moderates', which would have preferred the king to be proclaimed a dictator until the emergency had passed and the process of unification was complete. 'Royal dictatorship will be the proof of the practical sense of Italians', wrote the governor of Tuscany in a remarkable statement on 1 October. 'Dictatorship will inaugurate stupendously the new monarchy. No one will deny the magic significance of this word.'[1] Ricasoli thought that a dictator was necessary if the Italians were to round off the kingdom by incorporating Rome, and he was beginning to suspect that Cavour was too much of a Piedmontese to want the completion of Italian unity.[2] He had little enough sympathy with the radicals who were ruling at Naples, 'those swindlers and madmen' as he called them;[3] but nevertheless his confidence in the king, and his distrust of Cavour, brought him far closer to Garibaldi than he can have suspected. In his almost mystical desire to reach Rome, his voice sounded like that of Mazzini himself. 'Without Rome Italian life will be sterile, and the achievement of nationality will mean little more than mere economic betterment. It will be a union of territory and not a real fusion of interests. Turin municipalism once again will interfere with the need for a truly national life.'[4] This might have been Mazzini writing. No wonder Cavour brought his correspondence with Ricasoli once again to an angry stop; for the prime minister now had less need of the other's help, and he realized the danger implicit in this fundamental difference of approach. An attempt was made to try and induce the Iron Baron to go and become royal commissioner in Sicily, but the latter interpreted this as just a plot by the Piedmontese so that they might the more easily control Tuscany in his absence. 'I prefer to stay here and keep alight the Italian flame, and to combat the most infamous, vile, stupid, immoral and senseless domination [of Cavour's government from Turin].... Without Rome we shall not have Italy....

[1] 1 October, Ricasoli to Bianchi at Turin (*Lettere di Ricasoli*, ed. Tabarrini, vol. v, pp. 253–5).
[2] 3 October, Ricasoli to Bianchi (*ibid.* p. 257).
[3] 3 October, Ricasoli to Silvistrelli (*Carteggio di Ricasoli*, ed. Nobili and Camerani; not given by Tabarrini).
[4] 7 October, Ricasoli to Bianchi (BR ASF, b. N, f. H).

Though we are now twenty-two millions in number, we are acting as
if we were only two.'[1] Ricasoli was confident—as much so as Garibaldi
—that a show of force against Louis Napoleon would suffice for the
attainment of Rome; and when parliament did nothing to demonstrate
this *antica virtù* which he felt, he reviled it for such humiliating behaviour.
In parliament they were just making empty speeches and empty laws,
when as yet Italy did not exist.[2] Ricasoli's anxious longing for a
dictatorship shows that he was not properly in touch with the liberal
majority in parliament upon which Cavour so much relied. The
deputies at Turin would hardly propose that Victor Emanuel became
a dictator, for this would be at their own expense. They and Cavour
distrusted the king, and feared that he might exploit any increase in
power by breaking loose from their tutelage to back a triumphant
Garibaldi.[3]

During all these months before October, Cavour had not bothered
to call parliament, because he had not needed its approval for any of his
successive policies towards Garibaldi's revolution. Nor had he even
thought fit to consult the deputies about his invasion of the Marches.
If he had now decided that he would drive the Garibaldians 'into the
sea', this too was quite on his own initiative. Parliament, in fact, was
not really so active a force in the constitution as Cavour sometimes
liked people to think. What he himself prized about it was its very
passiveness. It was useful as an inactive partner; as a dead weight which
could sometimes be brought in with good effect against the king and
Garibaldi; as a platform and a means of publicity, through which
Cavour could create and reinforce the impression that he was a liberal
fighting against both revolutionaries and reactionaries. The Turin
parliament was a largely hand-picked and submissive body, and Cavour
knew that it made a minister stronger to have such an instrument ready
for emergencies. If he ever were obliged to suppress Garibaldi by force,
there would be an obvious advantage if he could 'colour his design
better'[4] in a parliamentary statement which would admit just enough

[1] 7 October, Ricasoli to Bianchi (BR ASF, b. N, f. H).
[2] 9 October, Ricasoli to Bianchi (*ibid.*).
[3] 8 October, Bianchi to Ricasoli (*Carteggio di Ricasoli*, ed. Nobili and Camerani;
not given in Tabarrini).
[4] N.d. (late September?) Farini to Ricasoli (*ibid.*).

21-2

of the truth to make him appear even more in the right. Until this moment in the year he would have found it very hard to colour his various designs publicly in a manner which redounded wholly to his credit. But now Garibaldi had put himself in the wrong and published his criticisms of Cavour; whereas the Piedmontese had at last put themselves in the right by a 'national' policy in the Marches. If the duality of power and policy within the state could no longer continue unresolved without prejudice to the national cause, now was the moment to recall parliament after its long recess throughout the summer. A free vote was worth more than any dictatorship, said Cavour. 'I think that for Italy to have constituted herself a nation without sacrificing liberty to independence is not her least title to fame. She has not passed through the dictatorial hands of a Cromwell. She has freed herself from monarchical absolutism, but without falling into revolutionary despotism.....Parliament is the only moral force capable of overcoming the sects and winning us the sympathy of liberal Europe.' So wrote Cavour, in a fine statement of his liberal creed, on the day that parliament was opened.[1]

In his speech to the Chamber of Deputies on 2 October, Cavour defined his new attitude to the situation in southern Italy with comprehension and skill. All his rhetorical gifts were needed to patch over the inconsistencies. His object was twofold: to secure approval for the annexation of the south, and to win what amounted to a vote or censure on the radicals. In other words he had simultaneously to condemn the revolution and to accept its fruits. Indeed, he had to force the radicals to yield up those fruits as to their rightful owner, making himself out to be at once Garibaldi's natural heir and also his conqueror. With an eye to the public record, he carefully paid tribute to Garibaldi, 'a name so justly dear to the multitudes'. Yet, as kindly as he could, he told the deputies that they would have to choose one thing or the other. 'Revolution and constitutional government cannot coexist for long in Italy without their dualism producing an opposition which can benefit only our common enemy.' 'There must be no more revolutions, or else Europe will have reason to think that revolution is not for us a means but an end, and in that case Europe would cease to give us help.' Cavour no longer disowned Garibaldi's invasion of southern Italy as he

[1] 2 October, Cavour to V. Salvagnoli (*CC Lib. del Mezz.* vol. III, p. 12).

had done in his previous statements of policy; indeed he went to the other extreme, and claimed that it was 'a necessary consequence of the policy initiated by Charles Albert and followed for twelve years by the government of Victor Emanuel'. This was a concession to the Savoyard diehards, whose thoughts never stretched much beyond Turin, and who needed to be convinced that legitimism and Catholicism and 'Piedmontism' were not being trodden underfoot by the newly-theorized popular sovereignty of a united kingdom. With this same audience in mind, Cavour carefully left out any mention of Rome; and he even made the positive statement that, once Venice had been acquired, 'the era of wars and revolutions in southern Europe would be closed for ever'. Perhaps Cavour was here just sounding out opinion, to discover how far he could go without offending the majority. But it was a portion of his speech which particularly annoyed Ricasoli; for, without Rome as the new national capital, Florence and the other provincial capitals would continue to be dependent on the 'infamous' domination of Turin.

Turning to southern Italy, Cavour tried to establish that his government had a right to interfere in what was happening there. If Garibaldi continued in power much longer, it would be the Mazzinians who came out on top.

Garibaldi's expedition sailed in the name of Victor Emanuel.... The king and parliament cannot now allow provinces recently emancipated to remain for long in the uncertainty of provisional government....

The generous prince whom all Italy proclaims as the initiator and *duce* of the national *risorgimento* has special obligations towards the people of south Italy, for their liberation took place in his name, and he is responsible for their fate before Europe and before posterity. Not that he means in any sense to *dispose* of the peoples of southern Italy by his sovereign fiat; it is just that he has a duty incumbent on him to give them the chance of emerging from provisional government by the free manifestation of their wishes.... Whatever their choice, it will be religiously respected.

Cavour spoke of free wishes to be 'religiously respected', but then went on to limit the very narrow bounds within which those wishes must lie. Southerners were, indeed, to have only one choice after all, either to approve or disapprove a circumscribed formula of annexation.

We must give it as our opinion that annexation ought not to be accepted [by parliament] if it were offered to us only under special conditions. For that would be to shackle the future ordering of the nation, and would introduce a radical fault which would be the seed of discord and antagonism to come.

He conceded that a federal form of state might sometimes justifiably exist 'in certain peculiar conditions'; yet a pact of surrender which was made dependent on the continuance of local autonomy would be 'contrary to the trends of modern society...and would constitute a real relic of the middle ages'.[1]

On the basis of these arguments, Cavour asked to be empowered by parliament to arrange by decree for the assimilation of all provinces that might vote for 'annexation to the state'. In the analogous case of Tuscany, earlier in the year, parliament had been called on simply to accept or reject a popular vote which had already occurred; but in the case of Sicily and Naples Cavour thought it necessary to put a 'moral compulsion' on the voters well in advance, before they took other ideas into their heads.[2] Here was another anomaly, for while any stipulation of conditions by southerners was specifically ruled out, Cavour carefully stipulated his own. Northerners were thus taking advantage of the fact that their own 'assembly' was already in existence, whereas the south so far had none. Sicily and Naples were now told that they had to vote in a plebiscite by universal suffrage; for anything else would prove unacceptable to Louis Napoleon; and it was also feared that a select assembly of notables would be much harder to manipulate. Then Cavour made quite clear that the plebiscite could choose nothing else but simple 'annexation'; so that, for instance, there could be no question of common submission by both Piedmont and Sicily to an altogether new state of Italy. After all, was he not addressing his speech to the parliament of Turin, where even the radicals and the reactionaries had this local pride in common? What he now demanded from parliament was powers to accept and 'regulate' all those provinces which might decide in a plebiscite to 'make part of our constitutional monarchy'. He was in a mood which was at once defiant and triumphant. An opposition request for papers he rejected out of hand, giving the remarkable reason that in the British parliament—so he thought—papers were only laid after the events with which they dealt had been

[1] 2 October, *Atti Parlamentari.*
[2] 4 October, *Il Diritto* (Turin) deplores this compulsion.

concluded.[1] He was already looking forward to revoking some of Garibaldi's enactments in the south, and with this in mind he made a point of publicly stating that some of the dictator's legislation was *ultra vires*. It was perhaps a strange doctrine to maintain that dictatorial powers were limited so precisely; and equally strange was the implication that Cavour and the Turin parliament, as well as knowing the exact extent of Garibaldi's provisional authority better than the general himself, were virtually sovereign already over affairs in the south. Cavour also asked parliament to authorize him to dispense with the legal need to give the south as many representatives in parliament as existing laws would allow, since this would slow up business in the Chamber; and he explained further that there was a smaller number of wealthy families in the south whose position was such that they could provide a deputy to carry the responsibility of self-government.[2]

This partial disenfranchisement of the south, and the treatment of Naples and Sicily as if already subject to Turin, did not pass without criticism. Cavour's parliamentary legerdemain was notorious, even among people who frankly admired him as the greatest statesman Italy had ever produced.[3] But the tone of parliament at this particular moment of national triumph was not friendly to would-be critics. Giuseppe Ferrari was not well received when he replied to Cavour on the 8th with facts he had found and opinions he had formed during his recent stay in Naples. Ferrari claimed to speak on behalf of those Garibaldians who were not able to come and speak for themselves. These men were about to be excluded from government and deprived of rank by others who had sat comfortably at home while they themselves were on the battlefield. They had conquered half of Italy for the crown, and so deserved at least that their views should receive some respect and consideration. Ferrari maintained that, despite all the difficulties of a large-scale civil war, Garibaldi's government had proved far better than that of Farini in Emilia during the revolution of 1859; and he also asserted that, if there was unruliness and anarchy in the south,

[1] 5 October, *Atti Parlamentari*.   [2] 6 October, *ibid.*
[3] E.g. A. Biar.chi-Giovini in *L' Unione* (Milan) of 24 July—adding: 'in his ministers Cavour likes to find servants not colleagues, and in parliament he sees a meeting of pupils rather than a deliberating assembly....He is intolerant of every shadow of opposition....Under Cavour's despotism the constitution is derisory.'

22 ★

this was in part because the natural disorder of a revolution had been aggravated by artificial agitation stimulated by Cavour's envoys in order to force through a precipitate annexation. He then went on to castigate the 'racial contempt' of the Piedmontese for other provinces:

Wherein consists the Piedmontese system? It consists in imposing one single state upon all the other states of Italy.... Unconditional surrender of the south would mean that Piedmont could abolish all the Neapolitan laws and replace them with her own.... Whereas the legal system now prevailing in the Two Sicilies is very good...and better than any other at present existing in Italy.

Ferrari's speech was frequently interrupted, and he was called to order by the chair for criticizing the Cavourian party in Sicily, though he spoke in terms far more mild and respectful than those being used by other deputies against the Garibaldians. People did not like to hear him publicly assert that there was a cleavage between upper and lower Italy,[1] a cleavage which was geographical, climatic, social, economic, cultural, linguistic, political, and even racial; nor did they like it when he accused Cavour's government of making this division still worse. The task of solidifying a national consciousness was obviously going to prove so difficult that a conspiracy of silence was beginning even now about the 'southern question'. The need to create a sentiment of common nationality was so urgent in people's minds that all talk of provincial differences and rivalries had to be kept to a minimum. By tacit agreement of the liberal party, any ideas which could be thought of as tainted with federalism or republicanism were not to be discussed, not even in parliament.

This intolerant and peremptory attitude of the majority makes it the more interesting to see what other arguments were being put forward by the opposition. Ferrari was an eccentric federalist. Guerrazzi was ill and did not speak. Rattazzi was probably too anxious for his reputation and his sovereign's good opinion to give any lead, and Cavour skilfully kept his leading opponent quiet, with private offers of jobs and public expressions of esteem. But Sineo had less to gain or lose, and

[1] 8 October, Ferrari: 'the literary separation between north and south Italy is so deep that we know the literature of St Petersburg far better than that of Naples, and through no fault of our own' (*Atti Parlamentari*).

spoke up for Garibaldi in the parliamentary session of the 8th. He pointed out that Garibaldi and his generals had had no time in the fighting of the previous month to answer the malicious stories about them in the press. Sineo himself had found no republicanism at Naples when he visited it. If Mazzini was there it was because Naples was still a free country like England—and 'unlike Piedmont' was the barbed implication. Cavour had never in his life been in such peril as Garibaldi had known in Sicily; and yet Cavour had added to that peril, deliberately arousing opposition against the revolutionary government while Bourbon armies were still fighting in both Sicily and Naples. Parliament had not protested in 1859 when during the revolutions of central Italy Farini and Ricasoli had had to suspend freedom of the press; but under Garibaldi the press had been free and altogether there was really less to protest about. The revolutionary government in Sicily had expelled La Farina and Cordova, but cases of arbitrary imprisonment and expulsion had been taken for granted in central and northern Italy. Sineo pointedly stressed that, when Tuscany had joined Piedmont, no emphasis had been put on the word 'annexation', and there had been no parliamentary censure of 'anarchy' and 'misgovernment'. The reason for this discrimination, he said, could only be that in central Italy the government had been conservative, while in southern Italy it was radical. Another interesting point of comparison was that Farini in Emilia had become dictator after a practically bloodless revolution in which society had not disintegrated; but Garibaldi had had to rule a far larger and more insubordinate country after it had been torn by civil war and social revolution. Far more pressing problems had presented themselves in Sicily than in Emilia, said Sineo, and they had not been bungled as people supposed, but had rather been attacked with surprising success.

The discussion was taken up again on the 9th. Desiderato Chiaves, a conservative from Turin, reminded the more radical deputies that Piedmont was the province which had borne the burden and heat of the day, and which had kept alight the flame of Italian nationalism when the rest of the peninsula was in bondage. Something was surely due to Piedmont for having made greater sacrifices than any other region of Italy. After Chiaves, a speech by Bertani was heard in dead silence. In view of what the press had been saying about him, people had not expected this firebrand to be so pacific; but Bertani was not the man to browbeat parliament, and his only significant contribution to the debate was the suggestion that Cavour should go to Naples and shake Garibaldi by the hand. Filippo Mellana, another member of the Left, defended Garibaldi's refusal to annex Sicily earlier. While Messina was still in Bourbon hands, and while a Bourbon ambassador was still accepted in Turin, surely the dictator could not have handed over the revolution to Cavour without bringing it to a standstill. Piedmont was obliged to work by diplomatic methods, the same which had forced the surrender of Nice to France as a payment for her help. Far from the diplomatic method being obviously better than the revolutionary, the very contrary was arguable: even the other countries of Europe would rather Italy was made by revolution than that she should again be beholden to France for her liberation. Mellana foretold that the implied vote of censure in this motion before parliament would only result in Garibaldi retiring to Caprera, and the army of volunteers built up with such difficulty would then dissolve instead of being kept in being for the next step against Venice. Any censure of Garibaldi would be resented in the south; especially as the whole issue had been quite unnecessarily raised in parliament. It was known that Cavour already had adequate powers to act. By coming to request a specific and unnecessary parliamentary vote on this issue, when other and graver issues of peace and war had gone without notice, he was gratuitously and it seemed deliberately antagonizing some of the boldest and most worthy spirits in the country. His action was an intentional rebuff to people who had selflessly sacrificed themselves to win half Italy for the monarchy of Savoy.

These were the main criticisms made by opposition speakers; but when it came to a vote, most of them tried to preserve the illusion of a national front. It was recognized that the government had had difficult decisions to take, and that, once taken, people should rally together if possible, and not vitiate the new nation at birth by exaggerating opposition beyond a certain point. After such a gruesome civil war, the need was above all for concord. When La Farina began describing to the chamber how Sicily still lacked some of the basic sanctions of a civilized society, the Genoese Lorenzo Pareto expressed the general horror that any Italian, let alone a Sicilian, should demonstrate such shameful things to any foreign observer. Italy should be united and strong, said Pareto, and not waste time in talk. Antonio Mosca of Milan agreed with him that Cavour must have his affirmative vote: the motion as presented was, in Mosca's view, infelicitously expressed, impolitic, and unnecessary since Cavour knew that he had the requisite powers already; yet the ground had been so chosen that every liberal must vote in favour of it. Even Bertani had to agree with this. It was evident, explained Marco Minghetti on behalf of the cabinet, that Europe might tolerate, but could hardly approve, what was happening in Italy; and it was therefore necessary to hurry up the process of annexation, so as to present the world with a *fait accompli*. This was an argument which would have had an appeal for all sides, and as the opposition saw that they themselves had now no chance of prevailing, better far that Cavour should succeed than that a divided nation be exploited again by the rest of Europe.

Cavour concluded the debate with his trump card. Whether he had been impressed by the sense of the meeting, or whether he realized he would have to go one more step towards the revolution if he was to hold an adequate majority, on 11 October he explicitly said that Rome would one day have to become the capital of Italy. This evoked tremendous enthusiasm. In a sense it might have seemed a dangerous statement, for it risked losing the support of sincere Catholics in order to win that of the patriots from Ricasoli to Garibaldi. But the patriots were by now almost irresistible; and Cavour had collected enough evidence over the past eight years to show that many or most educated Catholics put the nation first, so much so that they were ready to face interdict and anathema for their national faith. In any case, public opinion in the north was hopeful that the Pope and the French would abandon Rome, and Cavour could hardly afford to stand out against it.[1] Even Mazzini must have been tempted to cheer at this belated conversion of a new pupil. The Chamber, now aroused to great excitement, first gave a unanimous vote of gratitude to Garibaldi, and then by 290 to 6 decided to accept the unconditional 'annexation' of any provinces which asked for it. On 16 October Cavour spoke again, this time in the Senate, stressing to this rather different audience that his

[1] 30 September, *Il Diritto*; 1 October, Panizzi to Cavour, that even Napoleon believed as much (*CC Lib. del Mezz.* vol. III, p. 40).

policy had been essentially conservative and not revolutionary; in fact boasting that he had fought against the revolutionary principle and defeated it. The end would justify the irregular means he had had to use, or so at least he said. This was the occasion when he made his comparison of Piedmont and Prussia, and foretold that by 'putting herself at the head of the German movement, Prussia will continue gradually to develop her liberal institutions'. At this date it would have been heresy to suggest, as Cattaneo was suggesting, that nationalism might not after all prove to be so liberal and liberating a force. Cattaneo was now a deputy for Milan, and went on being repeatedly elected, but he never brought himself to attend in parliament to take his oath of allegiance to the 'perversion of liberalism' which had won the day. The rest of parliament did not agree with him in this diagnosis. There were eighty-four senators in favour and twelve against Cavour's motion. On the 19th, this short session of parliament, having done its job, was closed.,

Cavour had been quite confident that he would find parliament an enthusiastic supporter, for he knew its composition, and he had proved its mettle in the debate over Nice in May. Experience had also shown that his most powerful opponents were a danger only when they could work secretly upon the king while the Chamber was not in session. He therefore had already been preparing the detailed application of his victory over the radicals. In a sense his triumph had been too complete. He had done all he could to diminish the prestige of Garibaldi,[1] and had succeeded so well that he had deluded himself into underestimating the dangers which a different parliamentary situation might have exposed. It did not occur to him that any of the opposition criticisms put forward in the Chamber were anything else than 'foolish' or 'boring'.[2] He was certainly surprised and delighted at the extent of his success.[3] Perhaps this helped to blind him to the advantages of going himself to Naples, and seeing for himself whether the state of society and opinion there

[1] 20 September, *Il Diritto*: 'evidently the government has tipped off all its journals to denigrate Garibaldi...to discredit him before public opinion. A government has a thousand means of directing public opinion; it has money, newspapers, governors, intendants, mayors, armed forces, authority, the arm of justice, and inducements and threats of every conceivable variety.'

[2] 10 October, Cavour to Victor Emanuel (*CC Lib. del Mezz.* vol. III, p. 75).

[3] 13 October, Cavour to Farini (*ibid.* pp. 100–1).

justified making concessions to Garibaldi. He had once thought of travelling to the south along with the king, but had now given up the idea. Just before parliament met he helped to neutralize Rattazzi by dangling before him the offer of becoming a viceroy in Sicily or Naples.[1] A week later he rejected this plan too. On one point alone he was quite sure, that the king would have to go first and meet Garibaldi, for Victor Emanuel was the one man with whom the dictator was properly submissive. Cavour could not himself have endured the ordeal of personal relations with the king on such a mission, and Rattazzi was too keen a monarchist and a courtier to be given so much independent authority.

For the delicate task of advising the king and taking over the government from Garibaldi, Cavour finally chose Farini and Fanti for Naples, and Montezemolo, aided by La Farina and Cordova, for Sicily. It can hardly have been an accident that these five men were among those whom the Garibaldians most detested, the very men above all to whom they would have felt most humiliated and aggrieved to hand over their command and the fruit of all their labours. The coincidence was too extraordinary to have been unintentional. Not only were they Garibaldi's personal enemies, but La Farina and Cordova had recently been expelled from Sicily for disturbing the peace, and their return might be expected at once to revive all the passionate factiousness which had been allayed by the prospect of regular and conservative government. Italy was most of all in need of conciliation at this moment, and the king suggested sending Valerio instead to Sicily as a man more in Garibaldi's confidence. Cavour replied by offering to resign.[2] The threat of resignation was repeated later on a similar point, and such a rare and remarkable fact suggests that he felt as strongly over this as upon any act of his political life. The appointments were clearly deliberate, and anti-Jacobinism was the most important criterion of choice, not co-operativeness, nor administrative ability. They were certainly not calculated to weld people into a common front on this critical birthday of a new nation.

The opposition was bitterly offended at these nominations, and so were many of the moderates. Admiral Persano protested to Cavour on

---

[1] 2 October, Cavour to Farini (*ibid.* p. 10).
[2] 3 October, Cavour telegram to Farini (*ibid.* p. 19).

6 October against sending Farini, since Garibaldi was known to dislike him intensely: but Cavour replied that he was frightened lest others should try to influence the king's mind at Naples, and Farini alone could be relied on to remain unyielding.[1] Pallavicino likewise wrote in protest, seeing that the appointment was likely to arouse the sleeping lion in Garibaldi and make the essential task of carrying through the plebiscite still more difficult.[2] Ricasoli was altogether contemptuous of Farini's suitability for this administrative post,[3] and the event was to prove his worst fears justified. But Cavour resented the accusation of tactlessness more perhaps than anything else. He was still being guided by people who either knew nothing of southern affairs, or had a lamentable *parti pris*. Public opinion in the north laboured under the same handicap. Most of those who became correspondents in Naples and Sicily for northern newspapers were of the same political party, nearly all of them being former exiles who were chosen for this task because they were safe Cavourians. The public in Piedmont was therefore influenced by people who were out of touch with the south, and out of sympathy with Garibaldi; and the result was that most northerners, Cavour himself included, were ill-informed about southern opinion. Even when a liberal Neapolitan like Mancini wrote against this appointment of Farini, Cavour took no heed.[4] He soon enough acknowledged that it was going too far to send General Fanti to Naples, but he was not prepared to discuss his other nominations even with the king, and all five people, Fanti included, were shortly on their way to the south.

On 3 October the king landed at Ancona with Farini, who was now his viceroy designate of Naples. There he joined his troops, and together they began their march towards the Neapolitan frontier. A request was first sent back to enquire of Cavour whether the chief aim was to save the town of Naples, or to defeat the Bourbon army, or to suppress Garibaldi.[5] It is interesting to note that it had not been thought

[1] 6 October, Persano, *Diario 1860–1*, part III, pp. 98–9.

[2] 10 October, Pallavicino, *Le Memorie*, vol. III, p. 624; there is also an undated protest by General Medici (Archivio Medici MRR).

[3] 3 October, Ricasoli to Bianchi (*Carteggio di Ricasoli*, ed. Nobili and Camerani).

[4] 27 October, Cavour to Mancini (*CC Lib. del Mezz.* vol. III, p. 207).

[5] 1 October, Fanti telegram to Cavour (*ibid.* pp. 3–4).

desirable or possible to settle this important question before they left Turin. Cavour's answer shows that even he could not yet be very clear about it: they were told to march towards the frontier, hoping that the armies of Garibaldi and Francesco would dissolve at the news of their coming, but also ready to intervene in case a Bourbon counter-attack threatened to recapture Naples.[1] Farini made a half-hearted protest against Cavour's dispatches, and the fact that he was apparently 'too much preoccupied with Garibaldi, and too little with the king of Naples'.[2] But Napoleon's orders were that the Bourbon armies must remain for the moment unchallenged. Cavour's only excuse for invading the Marches had been that he must bring Garibaldi to heel, and France would only have allowed Victor Emanuel to move if his proclaimed enemy was 'the revolution'. So Cavour told Farini on the 5th that he should 'first restore order at Naples' and bundle Garibaldi off to Caprera. He should then form a new cabinet in Naples, and 'work up unanimous manifestations in favour of annexation'.[3] Technically the Piedmontese troops had no right to cross into the southern kingdom, but this was an unimportant detail.[4] Cavour now told the Bourbon minister at Turin that Francesco had abandoned his capital, and so had in fact abdicated; and that the consequent anarchy in the south forced King Victor Emanuel to go and re-establish order.[5] Fortunately Lord John Russell, after hearing a fortnight before of Bertani's casual suggestion to make Saffi prodictator of Sicily, was counselling an immediate invasion to restore conservative government in the south.[6] When Garibaldi himself asked Cialdini to cross the frontier, there was no further reason for delay.

It is evident that Victor Emanuel and Farini (who was still minister for internal affairs) had set out before Cavour had been able to decide

[1] 1 October, two telegrams from Cavour to Fanti (*ibid.* pp. 1, 4).

[2] 5 October, Farini to Cavour (*ibid.* p. 43).

[3] 5 October, Cavour to Farini (*ibid.* pp. 38–9).

[4] 8 October, *La Perseveranza* remarked on the presence of a Bourbon ambassador still in Turin, but explained that 'if there is anything anomalous or bizarre in the situation, it certainly is not on the part of our government, but rather on that of the Bourbons, for they obstinately try and maintain regular diplomatic relations with us'.

[5] 6 October, Cavour to Winspeare (*CC Lib. del Mezz.* vol. v).

[6] 1 October, Lacaita to Massari, quoting Russell (*ibid.* vol. III, p. 5).

what precise attitude should be adopted towards Garibaldi, and as a result they were soon issuing orders at cross-purposes from Ancona and Turin. When the prime minister had decided not to accompany the king he had presumably weighed this up, because he was quite aware of the possibility that 'camp politics' might even lead the country to 'another Villafranca'.[1] The analogies with 1859 were, indeed, far from pleasant. Sometimes it was only by the long-distance threat of resignation that he managed to prevent the king making some small concessions to Garibaldianism.[2] As new information arrived at Turin he inevitably had to change his mind on the detailed application of policy, and his efforts to control matters from afar therefore could not help but sometimes be confusing. On 3 October he was hoping that the king would proclaim himself a dictator; but on the 4th he was already reproving Farini for signs of a separate 'politique au camp'. Before many weeks had gone by he had given up hope of being able to restrain the king any further, and was only anxious for the latter to come home quickly so that he could do no more mischief.

The one principle of conduct which Cavour thought they had agreed upon in advance was a refusal to compromise with the radicals. He repeatedly insisted upon an 'inexorable' attitude to all Garibaldi's civilian followers. In this he was seconded by Farini, who had already made up his mind even before crossing the frontier that 'in Sicily and Naples people are finding the rule of these vulgar proconsuls as odious as that of the Bourbons'.[3] It was an unhappy augury for the future government of southern Italy that this doctrinaire conviction was already so unquestioned, for there was much good as well as bad in Garibaldi's rule, and the subsequent application of this warped standard of political values to the south was going to have bad results. Farini, moreover, went on mistakenly assuming that Garibaldi would have liked to resist the northern army if only he had the means.[4] This, too, helped to put their relations on a wrong footing from the very start.

---

[1] 4 October, Cavour telegram to Farini (*CC Lib. del Mezz.* vol. III, p. 31).

[2] A. J. Whyte repeats the legend that it was the other way about, Cavour being moderate and generous and the king intransigent (*The political life and letters of Cavour 1848–61*, p. 436).

[3] 6 October, Farini to Borromeo (*CC Lib. del Mezz.* vol. III, p. 53).

[4] 6 October, Farini to Cavour (*ibid.* p. 49).

Worse still, the refusal to compromise was based on an inner contradiction which was not properly understood. Cavour thus wrote to the
king on the 2nd that 'we must employ the greatest regard towards
Garibaldi, but without accepting the least compromise with the system
he represents'. Again on the 4th he told Farini that, 'without ceding
an iota to Garibaldi, we must not irritate him, or else public opinion
would abandon us'. Farini was instructed to be 'inexorable' and yet
not show himself ungrateful; for if the national hero were treated badly,
then the present 'ferociously anti-Garibaldian' sentiments of the public
would swing back violently to become a 'tremendous reaction' against
the government. The distinction implicit in all this advice was not a
good one, whether judged by morals or politics. It may be assumed
that even Cavour himself, had he gone to the south, would have been
unable to resolve such an inner incompatibility; and he may even have
realized as much when he made up his mind to stay at home. There
were some arguments against being generous, but also others against
being ruthless; and the eventual attempt by default to be both generous
and ruthless at once would have needed, to say the least, great *finesse* in
execution. As things turned out, the subordinates he chose for this task
were not fitted either by temperament or ability to work out on their
own what he omitted to tell them.

During the first fortnight of October, while parliament was still
debating what to do, the Piedmontese troops moved down to the
frontier and entered the Abruzzi. Villamarina sent them from Naples
a rough map of the countryside, enclosing with it for Farini's benefit
a paean of praise about Garibaldi's good faith and rectitude and his
prowess comparable with that of Homer's heroes.[1] Now that the lion
was tamed, his good qualities apparently were becoming more
appreciable, and were sometimes more appreciated. Garibaldi himself
belied Farini's suspicious hostility by writing to congratulate the king
on the success of the royal army against the Papalists. The dictator
promised to come half-way to meet them, in order to present his
homage and receive his orders for the rest of the campaign.[2] He still
did not quite understand that Farini's first objective was Naples and not

[1] 8 October, Villamarina to Farini (CF).
[2] 4 October, Garibaldi to Victor Emanuel (*Epistolario di Giuseppe Garibaldi*, ed.
E. E. Ximenes, vol. I, 1885, p. 135).

the Bourbon stronghold of Gaeta. The king then replied with congratulations to Garibaldi on the battle of the Volturno.[1]

Farini was not up to the level of this mutual admiration. He had the task of writing a proclamation which the king issued on 9 October from Ancona, addressed to his future subjects in southern Italy. One must remember that this was a fortnight before the plebiscite, and a full month before Garibaldi finally handed over power in the south. This proclamation was not in all respects very happily phrased. When Cavour read it he was not pleased to see the French soldiers of the Pope dismissed as 'a set of cosmopolitan ruffians'. Nor was it politic to claim for the king a right to speak in the name of the people of Italy against 'a faction that was ready to sacrifice the national triumph to dreams of fanatical ambition'. This, presumably, was a reference to Garibaldi and his radical friends. The king undertook in his proclamation that he 'would never allow Italy to become the roost of cosmopolitan sects'. 'People of southern Italy! my troops are advancing among you to restore order. I am not coming to impose my will on you, but to see that your will is respected. I know that in Italy I am closing the era of revolutions.'[2] The implication of this was that Garibaldi governed against the wishes of the people, and that his government was needlessly inefficient and disorderly. It also announced publicly that the king was coming, not to accept the revolution with gratitude, but rather to terminate it as something disreputable. To judge from this proclamation, all seemed to be over except the voting. Cavour even began to refer in official decrees to 'those provinces not yet annexed'. Already the prime minister was looking forward to when Farini would be properly installed as 'dictator' of Naples.[3] If necessary he and Fanti were ready to use force; and if Garibaldi did not publish the plebiscite on his own, then they were going to use their troops to organize a vote in his despite.[4] Cavour said, and perhaps was not talking only for the record, that he would rather resign than appear to be ungrateful to

---

[1] 9 October, Victor Emanuel to Garibaldi (Curàtulo, *Garibaldi, Vittorio Emanuele, Cavour*, p. 354).

[2] 16 October, *Il Giornale Officiale di Napoli*.

[3] 10 October, Cavour to Farini (*CC Lib. del Mezz.* vol. III, p. 76); 16 October, Cavour to Farini (*ibid.* p. 122).

[4] 12 October, Farini to Cavour (*ibid.* pp. 92–4).

Garibaldi;[1] but this policy was bound to carry with it the appearance as well as the reality of ingratitude. In any case, his appointed deputy now was out of immediate range and beyond restraint. Farini was determined 'to clear away all traces of Garibaldianism'. As he wrote to Cavour on the 13th, 'it is said that they intend to proclaim a constituent assembly. Just let them try it! I shall then carry out another "second of December" on 26 October.'[2]

Garibaldi at Caserta did not know that his chosen successor was nurturing such unfriendly sentiments. But he soon read the menacing phrase about 'closing the era of revolutions', and the other about driving out the 'sects' which were said to be sacrificing the nation to their own ambitions. This could only mean that Venice and Rome were being repudiated, and that the sectarian Garibaldi was to be treated as a nuisance and an enemy rather than as a friend and deliverer. The Piedmontese had certainly chosen their tactics clumsily. They were allowing it to be believed that they opposed nationalism as well as radicalism. There was a glaring contrast between Russell's justification of Piedmontese action—namely that Italians should decide their own fate by themselves—and Farini's argument that the king was advancing merely because of the urgent need to restore order. The latter excuse had been used to justify the Austrian invasion of 1859, and might as easily be used to support a Bourbon counter-revolution in 1861 if Victor Emanuel failed in his set task. For this reason the royal proclamation was sharply attacked in the opposition press, both for its angry and provocative language against Garibaldi, and for its gratuitous resuscitation of the republican spectre, and in general for the way it 'awakened ungrateful memories, offended legitimate pride, and embittered people by sowing hatred and rancour'. Garibaldi had sent a letter of submission, and this was the public reply to him.[3] Reports of this proclamation reached the dictator not long after the news that Cavour had unjustifiably proposed to parliament the 'annexation' of the south. Confronted by such evidence of personal mistrust and political enmity, Garibaldi's conciliatory mood left him as suddenly as it had come; and the political situation at Caserta and Naples once more became tense and dangerous.

[1] 8 October, Cavour to Farini (*ibid.* pp. 63–4).
[2] 13 October, Farini to Cavour (*ibid.* p. 103).
[3] 14 October, *Il Diritto* (Turin).

CHAPTER XXIII

MORDINI CHANGES HIS MIND:
9–13 OCTOBER

Cavour's first speech to parliament, moderate in phraseology but uncompromising in tone, was known in Sicily on 9 October, a week late,
and was published in the newspapers of Palermo on the 10th. This was
the first time Cavour had pronounced so outspokenly on the affairs of
southern Italy, and the fact that he was speaking *ex officio* made his
challenge to the revolution even more startling. It remained to see
what effect this would have on Mordini, and whether the prodictatorial
government would surrender quietly and without making further
trouble.

Several communications sent to Sicily from the north give us some
idea of early reactions against what Cavour had said. The Genoese
correspondent of the Palermo *L'Assemblea* thus wrote a letter from the
point of view of an autonomist, full of astonishment at Cavour's *volte
face*, and giving his explanation of the reasons for it. The prime minister
had formerly assured him many times, and in the presence of Count
Amari, that Sicily had a just title to self-government. They had pointed
out to Cavour how, even in the worst days of Neapolitan domination,
Sicily had never been deprived of her supreme court, or of her distinct
financial system with its separate treasury and national debt. But if she
were now to be merged in with the rest of Italy, these old privileges
would be threatened. Under a centralized system she would be less free
than before; and there would be the added disadvantage that, instead
of the capital city being twelve to fourteen hours distant at Naples, it
would lie half-way across Europe in remote Turin. These arguments
had been put to Cavour, and apparently he had once been convinced
by them. If he had now changed his mind, this particular correspondent
put it down to his wish for northern Italy to share in the profits from
the immense patrimony of mortmain property in the island; because
Sicily was mistakenly thought in the north to be a wealthy country,
which could and should contribute a large quota to the expenses of

union. Another point in Cavour's change of mind might have been that the deputation of Sicilian nobility had just arrived in Turin, for this would have shown that he was on stronger ground than he had at first imagined; indeed that he could make almost whatever demands he liked, in the confidence that Sicilians would pay any price to emerge from revolutionary government and war conditions. This same communication from Genoa then pointed out to readers at Palermo that Cavour had discreetly left open a line of retreat, in case the Sicilian vote did insist on imposing conditions. Cavour in parliament had only said 'it is our *opinion* that no conditions should be allowed', not that this had actually been decided. What was more, the correspondent added, 'Victor Emanuel had always declared that for his part he would accept a conditional vote by Sicily'. Much anxiety was felt in Genoa lest Cavour had wounded the *amour propre* of Sicilians, and so reduced the chances of forming a national union. Sicily was advised to retrieve the position by voting for conditional annexation as if nothing had happened, confidently assuming that Cavour would accept the accomplished fact if his bluff were called.[1]

For a second reaction to Cavour's speech, we have a letter written to Mordini by the editor of *Il Diritto*, Annibale Marazio, expressing the views of the parliamentary opposition at Turin before they heard of Mordini's proposal to hold an assembly. The first fact to face, he wrote, was that Cavour had won this particular round. Parliament at Turin would be solidly behind the government against the extra-parliamentary left-wing agitation of a military dictator, and if necessary would send Victor Emanuel into the field against the volunteer army in the south. The opposition deputies had therefore agreed that they should give up their earlier plan to postpone annexation until the fall of Rome and Venice. The only hope of retrieving their position was to surrender gracefully, *pour mieux sauter* later on. Mordini was told that:

you must first persuade public opinion through the press that Cavour's proposal to parliament is an outrage, insulting alike to Garibaldi, and to the historic traditions of Sicily, and her right to express her opinions freely in a vote. You must prepare a legal agitation against the proposal and its author.

The bearer of this letter, *Sig.* Guarneri, thinks it might be best to call an assembly on a restricted suffrage. I support this plan provided you can carry

[1] 11 October, *L' Assemblea*, report from Genoa of 5 October.

it out in a few days, and provided you can determine clearly in advance the terms of reference for the assembly in such a way as absolutely to exclude the possibility of separatism. In this way Sicily would keep its local autonomy, and be guaranteed against any supersession of its laws or any mania for fusion. ...But I do not think it would ever do for Sicily to be given a viceroy, a separate ministry or a distinct parliament.

If this assembly can meet before the arrival of the royal troops, its very existence will be a protest against the policy of Cavour....For if Cavour were to dissolve it, he would incur strong opposition.

But, came the conclusion, assembly or no, the essential task remains the same, first to inform public opinion of the implications of Cavour's latest step, and then for the revolutionary government to abdicate at a sign from Garibaldi, without any open opposition or recrimination. This would give the parliamentary Left the most favourable ground on which to prepare a subsequent attack against the government at Turin.[1]

These counsels would probably have been known in Sicily by 10 October, the day on which Mordini printed the text of Cavour's speech in the *Giornale Officiale*. Notwithstanding everything Cavour said in that speech, the prodictator was determined to try and hold on to his assembly, and in the same issue of the 10th he printed another denial of the persistent rumours that Garibaldi was not agreeable to his doing so. For several days more, indeed, it seemed likely that the Palermo government might be able to continue undisturbed in its project. On the 11th Mordini told Garibaldi that perfect tranquillity continued;[2] and even at Messina, a town which was always in the van of any opposition to Mordini, the first news of Cavour's speech seemed to provoke talk only, not active opposition.[3] In all appearance, that is to say, the first public evidence of a clear-cut defiance of Garibaldi by Cavour was not in itself enough to deflect Sicilians from their allegiance to the dictator's government. True enough, people were much worried by this evident cleavage inside the nationalist party, and began to question Mordini's policy more often. But governors continued to

[1] 4 October, Marazio to Mordini (AMB, b. 30).
[2] 11 October, Mordini telegram to Garibaldi (Carte Sirtori, Ambrosiana Library, Milan).
[3] 11 October, governor of Messina to Mordini (AMB, b. 28).

report that their provinces would scrupulously follow whatever Garibaldi's wishes were known to be.[1]

At Palermo there was immense activity in preparation for the election of deputies. Rival programmes were being canvassed and discussed.[2] As late as the 14th the autonomist *L'Assemblea* spoke of a frenzy of electioneering, with a hundred rival lists of candidates, ranging from Bourbonist, absolutist and liberal-separatist, down to the other extreme of those who wanted the most complete assimilation into Piedmont. The partisans of immediate annexation were themselves divided deeply by considerations of method and timing. There were those of the French centralist faith, who declared that prosperity depended on strong, centralized government. Or there were those who hoped and believed that Cavour was working on a plan for regional devolution and local self-government, from which Sicily in particular stood to benefit. Others were for delay in annexation: some because Garibaldi appeared to desire it; some because they hoped thereby to obtain an altogether new constitution for Italy; others because they resented the prospect of Piedmontese absorption, and because a delay would leave them more time and opportunity to secure satisfactory safeguards. Among people who wanted to impose conditions there was also appearing yet another division, between those who required 'administrative' devolution only, and those who demanded a full 'governmental' devolution.[3] Some Sicilians were against any idea of annexation at all. This category included the separatists; but it also included their extreme opposite, those who were uncompromising unitarians before everything, whether monarchist or republican, and who feared that an incomplete union might weaken the desire and pursuit of the whole.

If the reception of Cavour's speech did not at once put an end to this canvassing between rival factions, it did nevertheless suffice to give the

[1] 10 October, governor of Modica telegram to Mordini, showing that he had only just heard on the 9th of Mordini's decree of the 5th (AMB); 13 October, governor of Syracuse to Mordini, using the term 'constituent assembly' (MRR, cartella 221).

[2] 12 October and 13 October, *La Forbice* (Palermo); 15 October (Goodwin's Political Journal, F.O. 165/134).

[3] 14 October, *L'Assemblea* (Palermo); in its issue of the 12th it said that the 'inexorable annexationists' were all standing together in one single electoral committee, while the other groups were split and weak.

opposition to Mordini what for five days it had lacked, a policy. Published by Mordini on the 10th, the press of that date took sides over it. *Il Regno d' Italia*, which a few days earlier had accepted the assembly, if with reluctance, now recognized it as a new waste of time, as an attempt to set up a constituent on the 1848 model with a Mazzinian stamp, and hence as a danger to Italy and to France and to all Europe.[1] *L'Annessione* thought it could discover in Cavour's speech a clue to explain Mordini's concession of a vote on the 5th: never had the Mazzinians been so clever in their deceit. Very pertinently it pointed out that, although Mordini's government had sworn an oath to the king and issued all its acts 'in the name of Victor Emanuel', now it had been placed in opposition to the policy of that king's legally constituted government.[2] This would make Mordini not only a political opponent, but a rebel who could be forcibly corrected. A third annexationist paper, *Il Plebiscito*, led off in its first number with an eloquent and persuasive appeal to Sicilians:

For us in Sicily, annexation means order and justice. . . .It will destroy any possibility of the Bourbons returning. . . .We shall annex ourselves independently of Naples, and we shall lose none of our rights in doing so, because we shall be joining not Piedmont but Italy. . . .Perhaps we shall even be able to change the institutions of Piedmont, because these institutions will not be so suitable in a new state which includes the whole of Italy. . . .

To insist on conditions would now imply that we did not want Italian unity: it would signify a wish to separate off from the kingdom of Victor Emanuel, either to fall again under Francesco, or to turn republican, or else to remain in our present transitory state of uncertainty. . . .

We of the annexed provinces will together make up eighteen millions, while the province of Piedmont numbers but four; and so with five times the number of deputies we shall lay down the law, not have it imposed on us. . . .

Now that our gracious king is threatened by the Pope, by Austria, and by the Bourbons in Gaeta and Messina, will you add to his difficulties? No, in God's name.[3]

Of the other Palermo newspapers, *La Forbice* as usual took a middle view, this time if anything rather inclined to that of Cavour. It agreed

[1] 10 October, *Il Regno d' Italia*.
[2] 10 October and 12 October, *L' Annessione*.
[3] 12 October, *Il Plebiscito*.

that no conditions should now be attached to union, for Sicily could not claim to be ruled differently from other provinces, and neither could Piedmont accept conditions on behalf of a future parliament of all Italy. Moreover, if Cavour should take it into his head to refuse acceptance, a vote for conditional annexation would create a highly indecorous and inconvenient situation. The paper also agreed on giving pride of place to a plebiscite over an assembly, since the former method was that favoured by the French Emperor whose good will had to be cultivated. Nevertheless, it added, now that the decree of 5 October had stipulated for an assembly, to change this plan just because of Cavour's speech would cover Sicily with ridicule. Even though they might not want to alarm Europe by calling a constituent assembly, it would yet be necessary to alter the Piedmontese constitution, and this representative meeting of Sicilian notables would thus have a useful advisory task to perform. One more point made by *La Forbice* was to deplore Cavour's failure to state that he meant to declare the existence of a new kingdom of Italy.[1]

Crispi's former journal, *Il Precursore*, took much the same line, representative in this case of those stricter radicals who looked askance on Mordini's attempt to compromise with autonomism. This paper claimed to speak for the great majority of Sicilians in wanting annexation without any conditions.

Hence there is no need to fear that we shall attach conditions to annexation. The only thing Cavour has to fear is that the assembly will vote annexation, not to Piedmont, but to a kingdom of Italy under the constitutional sceptre of Victor Emanuel.... Cavour is devoured by the ambition to *piedmontise* Italy, and for this reason imposes on us annexation to Piedmont, thus preventing the formation of the great nation promised us by the king.... Above all we put our faith in the king.[2]

Let us be under no illusion: if they force southern Italy simply to join itself to Piedmont, it will not be long before we see the south making every effort to regain its autonomy, with immense loss to the national cause.[3]

In this prophetic utterance is to be found the logic which led many strict unitarians to oppose Cavour's demand for annexation.

[1] 10 October, *La Forbice*.   [2] 12 October, *Il Precursore*.
[3] 10 October, *ibid.*

Another paper, *La Valle di Giosaffat*, commenting afterwards on the disappointment with which Cavour's public statement had been received, wondered very pertinently how he could both reject the stipulation of any conditions by Sicily, at the same time as he himself laid down very narrow conditions indeed on which alone he would agree to union. It added that this very Cavour, who now wanted precipitate annexation, was the same who earlier this year refused to stir a finger when Sicilians had pleaded with him for help, the same who had given as his grounds for inaction that 'a Sicilian revolution would be a premature movement, so Piedmont could not help you'.[1] This was an accurate statement of Cavour's views a few months earlier, but it was perhaps a more spiteful than helpful reminder in the present circumstances. Several days later the same paper wrote another article of protest with a more substantial criticism:

Naples and Sicily both wanted annexation, yet we never gave the Turin parliament any right to impose on us the form and the substance of our terms of annexation. It is a strange case, and perhaps unparalleled in history, when the representatives of eleven million Italians usurp the right to vote an anticipatory law imposing conditions on more than eleven million other Italians who as yet have no legal representation in their parliament.[2]

L' Assemblea, the journal associated with Francesco Ferrara the autonomist, pointed out a further contradiction in Cavour's scheme: for how could he both repudiate any conditions and also promise to respect the vote religiously whatever it should be? Despite all Cavour's hints about local autonomy, wrote Ferrara, here he had at last thrown off his mask to reveal a plot of protracted deception. The result could only be to give votes to the party in favour of a separate island state, and would merely confuse those annexationists who had been promising Sicily local self-government in the name of Cavour himself. Compared with the enlightened deliberations of an assembly, a vote by direct suffrage under the present conditions prevailing in Sicily would in any case be utterly capricious and unrevealing.[3] And how could Cavour honestly think that Sicily was imposing her will on other provinces if she merely decided not to depend on Naples for judicial appeals, or if she desired some financial independence for purely local affairs?[4]

[1] 27 October, *La Valle di Giosaffat*.　　[2] 1 November, *ibid.*
[3] 10 October, *L' Assemblea*.　　[4] 12 October, *ibid.*

It was a significant commentary on public opinion in Sicily that, when it was finally decided in favour of the plebiscite, this was due not to Cavour's statement but to a message seeming to come from Garibaldi. While the issue was still in doubt, the town of Reggio received Pallavicino's decree dated the 8th which purported to give the approval of Garibaldi for a plebiscite at Naples. The arrival of this news was shortly going to clinch matters in favour of the plebiscite both in Sicily and on the continent. Reggio Calabria was a town lying on the straits, almost opposite to Messina, and all telegrams between Naples and Palermo stopped there. This breach in the telegraph line had helped to cause the irregularities and inaccuracies in transmission, and so had contributed to keep the two capitals out of step. It also had meant that news from Naples sometimes reached Sicily as a secondhand report by the governor of Reggio, a fact which gave that functionary some importance. This governor was one Antonio Plutino, a patriot and owner of large estates in Calabria, who had contributed largely to the expenses of Garibaldi's expedition and had valiantly led his *contadini* during the revolution. Politically he was a liberal-conservative, and he was one of the few people in the south to be directly in correspondence with Cavour. As both governor and *latifondista*, the lack of governance in his province made him doubly eager for a plebiscite and the speedy arrival of northern troops.

On the evening of 11 October, many printed copies of the Neapolitan plebiscite decree arrived in Messina 'by private hand' from Reggio. This was the information which induced people to suspect that Garibaldi was after all in agreement with Cavour for a plebiscite.[1] Plutino was later accused of flooding Messina with copies of the decree on purpose to embarrass the government.[2] If he really did so, it would have been quite understandable on his part. But however it came about, the obvious conclusion drawn in Messina was that Mordini must have been deceiving people as to Garibaldi's real wishes, and covertly working for quite a separate radical-autonomist policy of his own. This suspicion connected up with the other notion that the prodictator was too much a representative of the rival city of Palermo, that he was the mouthpiece of those bureaucrats in the capital who wanted in their own

[1] 13 October, governor of Messina to Mordini (MRR, no. 221/31/8).
[2] 13 October, Mordini in code to Crispi (ACP, f. 138).

interest to postpone the surrender of power. No less disliked would have been the possibility that, with Pallavicino's simple plebiscite, Naples might steal a march on Sicily and annex herself at once, while Sicilians lost their just priority and had to endure the *longueurs* and dissensions of an assembly.

The news from Reggio was known to the people of Messina about 9 p.m. on the 11th. Early the next morning a large crowd came to the central piazza and sent a deputation to the provincial governor. He replied that he knew nothing about the decree, but to pacify them said he would make enquiries.[1] Francesco Ugdulena, the governor of Messina, was a friend of Crispi, but not one of the extremists. In his private opinion he claimed to be dismayed at the idea of a plebiscite,[2] but in his public practice he proved to be one of those trimmers whose common sense made them yield to superior force rather than stand unshakable on a preconceived doctrine. Both sides were to revile him, for his part in this business: some of the radicals blamed him for the collapse of their hopes for an assembly,[3] and a few weeks later Cavour rewarded his help by dismissing him from office.[4] In reality he was one of those radicals who allowed the exercise of power to modify their idealism, and who put unconditional unification of the various regions of Italy above any mere tactical alliance with local autonomism.

Ugdulena found the decree from Reggio quite unexpected; and he became really alarmed when, 'the news once public, almost the whole population of Messina made a peaceful but imposing demonstration, including the military garrison and the national guard'.[5] A slightly different version came from a person who said that the great majority, even of those who wanted a plebiscite, still disapproved of the demonstration. 'It was organized and led by a handful of quite ridiculous people, of the kind who are always ready to shout in the market place, but who are the first to hide when things threaten to become

[1] 12 October, Sardinian consul at Messina to Villamarina (AME).

[2] 25 October, Ugdulena to Crispi (ACP, f. 138).

[3] 25 October, Asproni from Palermo to Crispi: 'that wretch Ugdulena had no little influence in wrecking our plan for an assembly (ACP, f. 138); 13 October, Ugdulena telegram to Garibaldi, advocating a plebiscite as 'more conformable to the public law of Europe' (Carte Sirtori, Ambrosiana, Milan).

[4] 8 December, *Il Precursore*.   [5] 13 October, Ugdulena to Mordini (MRR).

violent.'[1] Nevertheless, there were armed men in the demonstration, soldiers on edge because of the powerful Bourbon garrison still in the citadel and because of their arrears of pay, national guardsmen because of their political alignment and middle-class representation; and this was what persuaded Ugdulena to warn Mordini that in his view an assembly was now out of the question. Moreover, 'on 12 October the civic council of Messina held an extraordinary session to consider the news that the plebiscite had been proclaimed on the continent, and *Signor* Cacopardo, the chairman of the council, sent circulars round the island to protest against the prodictator's forcible imposition upon us of an assembly'.[2] As before at Palermo, the civic authorities were claiming to pronounce on national politics, on the grounds that no other representative body existed to champion sectional interests against the radical democrats in power.

While Messina was being thus thrown into confusion, Mordini at Palermo had been proceeding on the assumption that his assembly was generally acceptable. On 12 October a wild exchange of telegrams marked the development of this new crisis. At 6 a.m. Ugdulena telegraphed to Mordini the bare news of the decree brought over from Reggio the previous evening, and warned him that a strong party would exploit it as corroboration for their own desire to have a plebiscite.[3] This notice was probably sent before the demonstration occurred. Mordini replied as soon as he received a second telegram with news of this popular outburst. He told Ugdulena that

you should reject anything from Reggio which concerns the mainland provinces and not ours, and whose introduction into Sicily may foment party strife here. I am sorry that you did not tell me at once this morning of the demonstration. I should have given you more explicit instructions if you did not think yourself competent to act energetically on your own. You must not allow people to discuss governmental action, for in calling an assembly we acted with the dictator's approval and had his subsequent confirmation and praise. Yesterday I received a telegram from Crispi, and today another from the minister of war at Naples, but neither contained a word about this plebiscite decree, precisely because it does not concern Sicily.

[1] 13 October, V. Cianciolo from Messina to Mordini (AMB, b. 31).
[2] *Gli ultimi conati del Borbonismo e Mazzinismo*, Italia, 1860, pp. 64–5.
[3] 12 October, Ugdulena to Mordini (MRR).

He added, what was later confirmed to be true, that in all probability the decree was signed not by Garibaldi, but simply by the Neapolitan prodictator Pallavicino; and he charged Ugdulena to calm people and keep Palermo informed while the dictator was consulted once more about this latest turn of events.[1]

During the course of the 12th at least three other telegrams were sent to Ugdulena by Mordini, though it is impossible to know the time or even with certainty the sequence of their despatch.[2] One just asked for the full text of the Reggio decree. A second insisted that 'the convocation of the electoral colleges had Garibaldi's full approbation. The date fixed for the assembly was his own suggestion. The different conditions of Sicily and Naples made it advisable to have different methods of voting in each. It is essential that people respect the decisions we have taken. No party must be allowed to impose its will on the dictator and his representatives. You must see that no disorderly manifestation takes place.' It can be seen from this response that Mordini's composure and self-confidence had been seriously shaken, so that he had to fashion a not very convincing excuse for Garibaldi's apparent sanction of one thing in Naples and another in Sicily. In a third telegram he showed himself obviously aware that, despite his own excuses, all was not well, and he was beginning to have serious doubts whether Garibaldi might not have changed his mind. 'Remember that the telegraph line must be completely closed except for government service. Tell me at once if ever you hear of this Naples decree from any other source. And let me know if you are sure of its authenticity, and whether it has any particular reference to Sicily.'

In reply to these various communications from Palermo, Ugdulena sent a succession of despatches later in the day. One at noon told of the demonstration of the Messinese, and of how he had calmed it by saying that he would send off to Reggio for more information about the news from Naples: 'had it not been for this wretched decree, the people, if somewhat reluctantly, would have obeyed the wishes of the government'. Towards nightfall he sent three more telegrams to Palermo. The first of these was obviously in reply to Mordini's question: 'the decree has no mention of Sicily, but its authenticity has

---

[1] 12 October, Mordini to Ugdulena (AMB).
[2] 12 October, Ugdulena telegrams to Mordini (MRR, cartella 221).

been guaranteed to me by the governor of Reggio.' The second ran
as follows:

8 p.m. At this very moment has arrived a ship from the governor of
Reggio with a bundle of copies for me of the Naples plebiscite decree. Since
this morning, no further manifestation has occurred in the streets....People
think that a plebiscite would be more conformable to international law. They
fear that any other method will put Sicily below Naples, and make Sicilians
seem less reasonable and their vote less acceptable. During the period in
which the assembly dragged out its debates, Sicily would remain isolated
and separate, what time Naples became part of Italy. You will have to explain
all this to the country, and we shall have trouble unless you change your
manner of voting.

The note went on to say that the people of Messina had observed that
the plebiscite decree emanated from Naples, where Garibaldi was
thought to be, while the assembly decree came only from Palermo.
Hence arose the suspicion that Mordini was working against Garibaldi,
a suspicion reinforced by the popular belief that the dictator was in close
touch with Victor Emanuel whose government in Turin had now come
out publicly for annexation by plebiscite. Hence also the cry of the
demonstration in Messina that morning, 'down with the deputies who
are betraying us'. Five minutes afterwards Ugdulena sent his third
dispatch: 'a telegram has arrived from the governor at Reggio with
further assurance that the decree is genuine. Messina is deluged with an
infinite number of copies, and this will make the summoning of an
assembly most difficult, for it will now be thwarted in all manner of
ways.'

In actual fact, despite all appearances, on this 12 October Garibaldi
had still not decided conclusively in favour of Pallavicino's plebiscite;
but this was of little importance against the other fact, that Pallavicino
and Plutino had secured the arrival of 'an infinite number' of leaflets in
Messina which gave the contrary impression. Too late did Mordini
commandeer the telegraph system for government service only, because
soon after midday the Piedmontese vice-consul at Catania had already
sent the news to his colleague the consul at Palermo,[1] and this was a sure
means of dispersing it throughout the island. Mordini simultaneously
felt himself threatened from the other side, for he had just heard of the

[1] 12 October (AMB).

resignation of another radical governor who maintained that the summoning of a Sicilian assembly ran right against Garibaldi's plan to hold a constituent assembly at Rome. The prodictator's decree of the 5th was caught between fire from two directions at once, from radicals on one side and Cavourians on the other. He could not help but be impressed by the growing sense of alarm. Cavour's friend, General Carini, was even writing to warn him of nothing less than civil war, and to point out that certain of the clergy were already preaching that all annexationists were traitors to Sicily.[1]

Mordini continued to hold some hope that he could calm things down, and either reconcile or contradict the strange news from Reggio. At some moment in the day he sent off a message to all provinces explaining that, as there had so far been no confirmation of the Reggio decree, they should therefore 'go on with the work of preparing calmly for the elections'.[2] To Naples he sent further telegrams asking why no one ever bothered to keep Palermo instructed officially about developments on the mainland, and in particular why his messengers Calvino and Parisi were still unaccountably detained. Crispi was asked, 'tell me whether this decree is genuine, and why no one informed me—it is beyond belief'. To Garibaldi he sent a note in code with a desperate suggestion of how to retrieve the situation: 'it is absolutely necessary for you to come in person and open the assembly on 4 November. I expect a categorical answer at once to say you will come.'[3] This latter request was despatched at 10.30 a.m., and this shows that, even before hearing in detail from Ugdulena at Messina, Mordini recognized that only an explicit and public declaration by Garibaldi could now save the day. It is also important that the message was received in Naples the same evening, so that (as will be seen in the next chapter) this sign of weakening in Palermo would have been known to Garibaldi in time to influence him in favour of yielding finally to the plebiscitarians.

On 13 October the news received from Reggio was in all the papers of Palermo. The *Giornale Officiale* just remarked that the decree bore the signature only of Pallavicino not of Garibaldi, and mentioned that the Palermo government had once more asked the dictator for his

---

[1] 13 October, Carini to Mordini (AMB, b. 30).
[2] 12 October, Mordini to governors (MRR).
[3] 12 October (ACP, f. 135).

instructions. The party of Cavour was greatly excited, and took steps to publicize the decree in meetings.[1] Deputations were sent to Mordini, but he refused to see them. What irked him most was not so much the fact of what had happened, but the manner of its happening: once again the lack of consideration for Sicilian affairs by the radicals at Naples was resulting in the prestige and authority of his government being challenged. Early in the day he worked off some of his dissatisfaction upon Ugdulena:

instead of sending me the text of this decree, you just asked me what you should do about it. I replied with a request for you to send me at least that part of it which would tell us if it was in the form usually adopted by Pallavicino. I still have had no reply. Be careful not to hold out promises or hopes to the people.... Again last night I received despatches from Naples without a word of this decree. Meanwhile the government is ready to follow either course, but cannot exceed its powers and change on its own initiative a line of conduct so much approved by the dictator.[2]

It is just conceivable that Mordini was here being disingenuous, but it is not likely. Garibaldi's silence was inexplicable unless there was some special reason why he wished Sicily to have an assembly. Perhaps, like Bertani and the extreme radicals, the dictator wanted to hold on to Sicily as a basis for action in the future, and so to delay annexation there, while yielding on the mainland. There was still no absolute certainty that the Neapolitan plebiscite decree of the 8th was genuine. But whatever the explanation of the apparent discrepancy, Mordini must surely have expected that his assembly plan was consonant with Garibaldi's wishes, since a week had gone by without his receiving any instructions but those approving his action. What was more, having had to act once already without specific instructions on the 5th, he would be more anxious than ever not to force the dictator's hand again by unilateral action and without particular authorization. For the moment, therefore, everything was suspended until Garibaldi chose to clear up the contradiction by a personal message.

Messina meanwhile continued to force the pace. Ugdulena replied: 'this evening the civic council met, and instead of preparing for the

---

[1] 16 October, P. Morello from Palermo to Ricasoli (*Carteggio di Ricasoli*, ed. Nobili and Camerani).

[2] 13 October, Mordini to Ugdulena (AMB).

election of deputies, voted an address to yourself and to the dictator in favour of a plebiscite. Since the movement is general, you will perceive how impossible it is to make any frontal attack upon it. The demonstration contained both soldiers and national guardsmen.'[1] This address by the civic council made an express appeal to the moderates, by insisting that a plebiscite would end the state of alarm more expeditiously; but it also appealed to that section of the radicals which regarded the assembly as 'a kind of abhorrent separatism'. Once again we meet this tactical alliance of Left and Right against Mordini's experiment in transformism; and its force was far from being one of mere inertia. The municipality's resolution did not stop at giving advice, but even stated in so many words that Messina would suspend the elections.[2]

Such an open strike of local authorities must have been a strong influence on the government. There was also the ominous suspicion that, while telegrams from Naples to Sicily were now coming through well enough, the absence from those telegrams of any reply to reiterated demands for enlightenment suggested that some messages to Naples were being held up, probably at Reggio and possibly by design. In consequence it was now decided to send a ship to Naples, as the only certain way to obtain an answer, and with the intention of forestalling a deputation to Garibaldi which was said to be leaving from Messina. A ship was duly provided for this purpose by Admiral Persano. But before it could sail, the situation had developed to the point where Mordini was forced to yield and concede a plebiscite.

The prodictator had prided himself on not being deaf to the voice of public opinion, and the impact of the recent news from Naples now made that voice unmistakable. The changing strength of opinion at Palermo can be gauged through successive communications in cipher with Naples during the course of the 13th. Mordini first told Garibaldi that 'the situation continues most difficult. Messina asks for a plebiscite ...I cannot understand what has prevented Calvino or Parisi returning or writing.' Then, in case the dictator was perhaps too busy to reply, Mordini sent a note to Pallavicino, asking him to press the matter and find out why Palermo had been given no news for four days.[3] At

---

[1] 13 October, Ugdulena to Mordini (MRR).
[2] 15 October, vice-consul Richards sends a copy to Elliot (F.O. 165/134).
[3] 13 October, Mordini to Pallavicino (AMB).

10.45 a.m. he also sent a telegram to Crispi, though it arrived at Naples only the next morning: 'the decree of the 9th for a plebiscite has produced the worst possible effect, all the more so in that I was told nothing about it in time.' Still without information, he was at last forced to give up the struggle. In the afternoon he sent three despairing telegrams to Garibaldi in succession:

In order to obtain concord [he wrote], I now think it necessary to have a plebiscite. I would have already published a decree about this, but I feared it might be against your wishes. It is inexplicable that Crispi, Calvino and Parisi should have left me without a word for four entire days, and that no one in Naples should have foreseen the entry of your decree of the 7th into Sicily and have given me the necessary instructions about it. I beg you to let me have a reply and tell me what you want me to do. Perhaps I shall have to make some decision on my own authority if I see that the public good demands it.

More imperative still was the next:

If you want an assembly, come here at once in person, and send a telegram with your actual signature which I can publish. The provinces have decided for a plebiscite. In any assembly now I visualize a great deal of trouble, and I repeat that it will not be possible without your coming in person.

As there was still no reply, he followed this with an ultimatum:

If the dictator does not agree I shall be compelled to resign.
The situation today is such that you must authorize me imperatively and at once to alter the election into a general plebiscite.[1]

[1] Undated draft (MRR, no. 221/23/20).

CHAPTER XXIV

GARIBALDI MAKES HIS DECISION:
9–13 OCTOBER

Mordini had been forced into his desperate position by the swift change in Sicilian opinion, and by the failure of either Garibaldi or Crispi to send him instructions. He was unwilling for the second time to act altogether on his own at Palermo, especially as political developments in Sicily had become so much dependent upon events at Naples. But then the news of Pallavicino's decree had finally allowed him to think that Garibaldi at Naples could not really object if Sicily came into line by giving up her elected assembly: and on the strength of this he gave in.

His impression, however, was incorrect. Garibaldi's characteristic vacillation was never more in evidence than now. On the 6th Crispi had found the dictator favouring an assembly. But on the next day the news of Cavour's speech had arrived at Naples, and produced 'très bon effet sur l'esprit de Garibaldi'.[1] Pallavicino came away from him on the 7th with the conviction that he was now for a plebiscite, and on this basis the Neapolitan government had issued the decree which threw Mordini into such despair. The more conservative papers at Naples announced with much satisfaction that Pallavicino had triumphed over Crispi, the conservative ministry over the radical secretariat.[2] 'In the short space of twenty-four hours the position has been completely changed. We have stopped short on the brink of anarchy....The sectarians had just begun to spread among the people a discontent with the new order of things...and were providing food for the general sentiment of anxiety which prevails among the multitude'; but then the prodictator's intervention had saved the day.[3] On the 8th, however, the pendulum began to swing back once again, and when in the evening a crestfallen Crispi accompanied Mordini's emissary Parisi out to Caserta, he surprisingly won from the dictator an opinion which implied

---

[1] 8 October, Villamarina telegram to Cavour (*CC Cavour-Nigra*, vol. IV, p. 244).
[2] E.g. 8 October, *Il Nazionale*.   [3] 9 October, *ibid.*

that Pallavicino had misinterpreted his words the day before. Garibaldi, it now seemed, really wanted just the same system for Naples that Mordini had already selected for Sicily on the 5th, and it therefore appeared that the plebiscite decree had been forced through by Pallavicino under false pretences.

After this there was inevitably a return to discord and confusion. Alexandre Dumas's paper, *L'Indipendente*, wrote that 'from the 8th to the 11th *signori* Parisi and Pallavicino spent their time in going to and fro between Naples and Caserta, one after the other; and curiously enough they each brought back different answers'.[1] Crispi maintained that, for these three days, Garibaldi remained 'staunchly in favour of the Assembly',[2] The Neapolitan prodictator would perhaps have interpreted the situation in a quite different sense. But whichever came nearer the truth, of one thing there can be little doubt, that Pallavicino's plebiscite decree of the 8th had in a sense been premature, and did not coincide with any firm opinion in the dictator's mind.

On the 9th Garibaldi summoned Pallavicino to come and see him about revoking this decree. Crispi's diary recorded: 'Mistake in the hour. We do not arrive until after Pallavicino has left. Garibaldi declares he has arranged with Pallavicino for an assembly. We submit the draft to him which Cattaneo has prepared, and he endorses it.'[3] Cattaneo also went out to Caserta on the 9th, and after waiting several hours found Garibaldi free to discuss the situation. His version of the interview stated that Crispi received orders to present his project for an assembly to Pallavicino and talk the matter over.[4] Cattaneo gave a

---

[1] 16 October, *L' Indipendente*. This and other early numbers of Dumas's paper are missing from the bound copy in the Biblioteca Nazionale, Naples; but this loose copy is to be found in ACP, f. 127.

[2] 13 October, Crispi to Bertani (Crispi, *Memoirs*, vol. I, p. 451).

[3] 9 October, *ibid.* p. 483. Writing some years later to Mazzini about this same day, Crispi said: 'I do not know what passed between the General and his Pro-Dictator... Garibaldi, however, assured me that the idea of an Assembly had been accepted. It is a fact that he lent his approval to the draft of the decree that was presented to him, and with his own hand wrote the following words beneath it, which were addressed to Pallavicino:—"This appears to me to represent precisely what we agreed upon together, and is perfectly satisfactory to me. If you consent to all this, send me a copy of the above decree, duly endorsed, and I will sign it also"' (*Ibid.* p. 445).

[4] 10 October, Cattaneo to Lemmi (Archivio Lemmi MRR).

picture of the situation as he saw it in a letter written in English to his
English wife:

the Sicilians are decided to have an Assembly, to look about every thing
that concerns the annexation to *all Italy* (not directly to Piedmont). The
General wishes that the Neapolitans should do the same. Pallavicino does
not like the idea of an Assembly, but he will be forced to yield to a stronger
will. What is really ridiculous is that M. [Mazzini] is now for an Assembly
and is beginning to be federal.[1]

Carlo Cattaneo himself was a warm champion of the assembly, and
not only for tactical reasons like Crispi, but also as a point of dogma
which related to his whole scheme of political thought. Indeed, as the
leading Italian federalist, his ideas were almost as divergent from those
of Crispi as they were from those of Cavour. It was true, nevertheless,
that the radicals of both persuasions were at one over the tactics of the
moment, and in this critical position their various shades of disagreement
were less pronounced than at most other times during the *risorgimento*.
Mazzini was present only in the background, as a fount of advice which
was not often taken. It surprised many to find him at this moment
scarcely differing at all from his life-long opponents, the federalists.
The coalition between them, however, was fighting in a hopeless cause,
for by 9 October Garibaldi had now lost both military and political
initiative. The armies of Victor Emanuel were on the point of entering
the *Regno*, and between two and three thousand additional Piedmontese
troops landed at Naples from Genoa on this very day. These political
questions were usually solved in the last resort by considerations of
power, not by considerations of cleverness, or good intentions, or even
justice; and while Piedmontese power was growing, the check to
Garibaldi's momentum was already resulting in a sudden increase of
desertions from his volunteer army, so that the ratio of strength between
the two armies was rapidly altering.

Despite Garibaldi's vacillation, Pallavicino for his part was therefore
still able to hope on the 10th that the plebiscite would follow as
arranged. The prodictator sent off to ask Cavour not to let the king
come to Naples until the vote had been taken, or otherwise Europe
might say that voting had been under pressure. He apologized that the

[1] 11 October, Cattaneo to his wife (ACP, f. 127).

wording had to be for 'Italia una e indivisibile', but explained that 'it would have been impossible for me to make these seven million Italians swallow the bitter pill of simple annexation to the ancient monarchy of Savoy'; and he added, 'I have reason to think that the result of the plebiscite will conform to our wishes'.[1] It may be noted in parenthesis that Pallavicino himself, before many months went by, was to rally again to the radical opposition against Cavour's policy of annexation and absorption. For the moment, however, he was primarily concerned to oppose the radical policy of delay and discussion, and preferred to force matters through by a snap vote, relying on the wisdom of his fellow northerners to concede freely in more tranquil times the devolution which they would not yield in a crisis and to force.

As the temper of politics grew hotter in Naples, Bonghi's *Nazionale* went so far as to group all the radicals together under the name of 'republicans', and began to imagine republican plots everywhere; though the same paper had hitherto been loud in its denial that such views existed at all in the south. A few days earlier this same conservative journal had been criticizing Cavour's project for 'annexing' the south;[2] but now it substantially changed its ground, terrified that 'Mazzini is bent on social revolution'.[3] There was enough reason already for opposition to the radicals without having to resort to this old republican *canard*. By their obstinate refusal to surrender to uncompromising and superior force, Crispi and his friends were open to the accusation of imperilling the future of Italy. Bertani himself, who as a deputy had publicly voted at Turin in favour of Cavour's 'law of annexation', was covertly writing to Cattaneo that 'the immediate reunion of the Neapolitan and Sicilian parliaments is now our only hope'.[4] This was far more deceitful than was the plan of those who aimed to win annexation through the verbal fiction of united Italy. The radicals were exasperated and angry at what was happening. They still clung to power, even when there was not much left for them to do with it.

The political conflict was intensified on the 11th. Crispi saw the dictator at dawn.[5] Garibaldi was also visited by representatives of the

[1] Pallavicino, *Le Memorie*, vol. III, pp. 623–4.
[2] 4 October, *Il Nazionale*.   [3] 10 October, *ibid*.
[4] 6 October, Bertani to Cattaneo (ABCM).
[5] 11 October, Crispi's diary, *Memoirs*, vol. I, p. 483.

national guard wanting a plebiscite,[1] and then by representatives of the 'National Association' asking for an assembly.[2] Back at Naples there was a cabinet meeting at midday.[3] All the ministers except Crispi were now behind Pallavicino, despite their majority vote on the 7th for an assembly.[4] In order to thrash the matter out, the dictator therefore called an *ad hoc* council, which was attended by Pallavicino, Crispi, Cattaneo, Calvino, Parisi, Mario and Caranti among others.

L'Indipendente gave a long account of this meeting, writing from the radical-federalist standpoint favoured by Alexandre Dumas its editor. 'Pallavicino was against the other members of the council, and pointed out how that in this country, where the spirit of autonomy was so strong, an assembly and its attendant discussions would even imperil the success of any vote in favour of annexation.' The prodictator then spoke of the danger of civil war; but the very mention of such a possibility so angered Garibaldi that 'he burst out in an eloquent attack on the prodictator's government'. At this Pallavicino resigned, and turning in Crispi's direction said: 'there is the man who has caused all the discord between us. Without him Italy would by now have been united, and with him we shall get no further towards our goal.' Crispi remained dumb with astonishment for a moment, and then was said to have replied quietly and respectfully. Garibaldi for his part retorted to Pallavicino: '*signor* Crispi is the best of my friends. He is courageous and disinterested. He has shared all the dangers I have had to endure, and has been more useful to me than anyone else.'[5]

So much for Dumas's version of this meeting on the 11th. Crispi's account of the controversy told much the same story.[6] Pallavicino in his diary also confirmed how Garibaldi accused him of 'Cavourianism'; and admitted that he had been 'cut to the very quick by Garibaldi's praise of Crispi as the necessary man who was more useful to him at the

---

[1] 15 October, *La Bandiera Italiana* (Naples). Copy in Biblioteca Universitaria, Naples.

[2] 18 October, *Il Popolo d' Italia* (Naples).

[3] Summons to Crispi (ACP, f. 135).

[4] B. Caranti, *Alcune notizie sul plebiscito delle provincie Napoletane*, 1864, p. 35; but one authority says that Anguissola sided with Crispi, *Gli ultimi conati del Borbonismo e Mazzinismo*, 1860, p. 62.

[5] 16 October, *L' Indipendente*.

[6] 13 October, Crispi to Bertani (*Memoirs*, vol. 1, p. 451).

moment than anyone else'.[1] Pallavicino was so 'convulsed by grief and rage' that Caranti had almost to carry him to the station on their return to Naples.[2]

This prodictator who had momentarily resigned was a nobleman whose politics normally ran closer to Garibaldi than to Cavour, even if much nearer to Cavour than to Mazzini. His position at this moment was therefore most significant, as that of a near-radical who yet saw that united Italy could hardly be won except by making accommodations to Cavour's policy. The one thing he wanted to avoid at all costs, and which now seemed to threaten him, was a deadlock and even possible civil war between Cavour's party and Garibaldi's. And as the Turin parliament had decided against accepting a conditional annexation, it appeared to him that any talk of an assembly could gain nothing and would only be an element of discord. Two forces were contending for political primacy in Italy; and if conflict between them was avoided, it was due in part to Pallavicino. In part it was also due to Mordini. And in part it should be ascribed to the complicated accidents of chronology which in this critical week kept Naples and Sicily out of step.

The next day, 12 October, was a time of great confusion. Pallavicino's adherents in Naples had been busy overnight to repair the damage done at Caserta, and at the café d'Europa 'had concerted a great annexationist demonstration to take place during the day of the 12th'.[3] Everywhere there was a noticeable feeling of disquiet. Rumours had been circulated among the national guardsmen that Mazzini was on the point of proclaiming a republic. The senior officers of this civic militia even took it upon themselves to mobilize their men against this feared rising by the 'party of action';[4] and before long their show of force had an important effect on politics. The leading conservative paper in the town wanted a special effort to be made against the threat of republicanism, and for this purpose invoked the aid of the twelve thousand national guardsmen as well as the seven thousand Piedmontese soldiers who were garrisoning the Neapolitan forts.[5] This same paper made out that Crispi

[1] 12 October, Pallavicino's diary, *Le Memorie*, vol. III, p. 627.
[2] Caranti, *Alcune notizie sul plebiscito*, p. 36.
[3] D. Salazaro, *Cenni sulla rivoluzione Italiana del 1860*, 1866, p. 67.
[4] 17 October, *L' Unità Italiana* (Genoa), report from Naples dated 13 October.
[5] 12 October, *Il Nazionale*.

had attempted a *coup d'état* in order to push through his idea of an assembly, and explained that what the radicals intended by this assembly was a constituent body packed with their own nominees for the purpose of imposing a republic.[1] This was well calculated to frighten people at Naples, for a republic was dreaded as something 'red' and anarchic, associated with *émeutes* and the guillotine, and the civil population was in no position to know that the editor's statement was a wild exaggeration.

The news of Pallavicino's resignation was common property in Naples quite early on the 12th, and caused great excitement there. The day soon became noisy with popular demonstrations and clamours, when, as Crispi said, 'we were one and all cursed and applauded by turn'.[2] The shouts of *Down with Crispi* 'were the most frequent of all', so the victim himself confessed, though he claimed that the police were instigating the crowd to demonstrate.[3] The generality of citizens of course cannot have known of the political struggle going on round Garibaldi, and can have but partly guessed at the issues in dispute and the size of the controversy. One rumour contributing to the popular alarm was that Garibaldi had been killed, and that the news of his death was being hushed up until Victor Emanuel arrived.[4] The crowd was fickle as always, and with sufficient inducement could probably have thrown its weight on either side.

Both main factions among the politicians in Naples appealed to the dictator to come from Caserta and quieten the populace.[5] Garibaldi at

[1] 17 October, *ibid.*

[2] 18 March 1865, Crispi to Mazzini (Crispi, *Memoirs*, vol. 1, p. 446).

[3] 18 October, Crispi to Bertani (*ibid.* pp. 453–4). Another picturesque episode, related by *L' Unità Italiana* (Genoa) of 1 December, told about La Sangiovannara, a Neapolitan woman of the common people, whose popularity gave her an unofficial leadership among the *lazzaroni*. 'She was a real woman of the people, that is to say an excellent woman at heart, but ignorant, and prone to follow the first suggestions, whether good or bad, which came to her from the people she trusted. Now the moderate party had been able to get hold of her, and to use her as one of the most active propagandists for immediate annexation....The good woman confessed ingenuously that she had believed those who depicted Mazzini to her as a friend of the Bourbons and of the Pope, and she told how she contributed to the agitations crying "death to Mazzini".'

[4] 12 October, Cattaneo to Bertani (Archivio Cattaneo MRM).

[5] Cattaneo and Türr—see Türr's note scribbled on the back of Gusmaroli's telegram of 13 October (MRR, no. 168/49).

last reluctantly consented to leave the front line once more and play the politician himself. Later on he was to accuse Cavour's government of again having intrigued behind his back expressly to weaken him and divert his attention from defeating the Bourbon army. Instead of being able to concentrate on attacking Capua, he had had to return first to Palermo in September, and now to Naples in October, this being the only method of pacifying angry political demonstrations which—it was claimed—had been engineered for the purpose by paid agitators.[1] The northern government had intervened to stop him on three occasions, so he wrote at about this date: first in May to prevent him going to Sicily, secondly in July to prevent him crossing the Straits of Messina, and thirdly in October to prevent him crossing the river Volturno.[2] There is no doubt that Cavour had hindered as well as helped the military campaign in the south. He had wanted Garibaldi to succeed in part, but not too much, and not too easily; and for most of the time he had been more anxious to hinder than to help. To that extent the dictator had just cause for recrimination.

One person who had visited Garibaldi on the 11th had then found him again expecting that a march on Rome might still be possible, perhaps with aid from the king.[3] Probably his own political opinions were much the same, or rather his lack of confirmed opinion was still maintained. He certainly went on hoping for the capture of Rome, whether this year, next year, or sometime. He had strong criticisms against Cavour and the Neapolitan conservatives, but in the main he just wanted both political factions to keep quiet while he was able to continue with the war. And yet the vagueness of his political ideas, when taken together with his conciliatory disposition, had given each faction to believe that he might be on their side, and this had only encouraged both to intransigence. The same fact explains why conservatives and radicals should have combined on the 12th in asking him to come to Naples, since each faction hoped for his support. General Türr thought that the dictator would simply proclaim a plebiscite and restore Pallavicino to office; while the radical *Iride* gave out that he

[1] Note by Garibaldi, probably written in 1861, *Il Risorgimento Italiano*, January 1908, p. 8.

[2] *Edizione nazionale degli scritti di Garibaldi*, vol. IV, p. 313.

[3] 11 October, Persano, *Diario 1860–1*, part IV, pp. 15–18.

would convoke an assembly, 'to prevent us being just handed over bound hand and foot to Piedmont'.[1]

Amid an 'indescribable din' in Naples, Cattaneo wrote on the 12th depicting the situation to Bertani, and referring to Pallavicino as 'a simple unfortunate, with ideas that cannot be his own'. In another note, written in English and possibly intended for the London press, he said that Pallavicino still allowed the principle of a representative assembly for Sicily, while opposing it for Naples[2]—and in this statement he was probably correct. Cattaneo also wrote to Pallavicino personally:

the general says he will be in Naples at midday for a meeting of the cabinet in the Palazzo d'Angri; and he has asked me to let you know in friendly terms that he hopes you too will come to the meeting, since it concerns the future of our country....

Let me for my own part...remind you that in your house, on the 7th, Conforti [the chief minister in Pallavicino's government] was in favour of an assembly, but on the 8th he changed his mind. It is people like this who are now under suspicion of holding up munitions supplies to our armies, and who are refusing to give Garibaldi eighty thousand francs to pay for firearms which have been already ordered and received.

You are wrong to think that there could be any dualism between an assembly in Naples which met to cede the country, and the national parliament which accepted that cession. There could be no dualism between the men that electors would return to our local assembly, and those, practically the same, they would send to the national parliament. Nothing of the sort has appeared in the local assemblies of Switzerland or the United States, though these particular bodies are actually invested with sovereign powers. Your objection is a mere dream, and one suggested to you from outside.

For my part I even believe in the need for permanent local assemblies, not only to bring internal concord, but as instruments of progress in their own right. Surely we are out to bring the people of Italy together as brothers, not to suppress or silence them. The real dualism today is rather that disastrous cleavage between our virtuous and warlike leader and those who have said that they are ready to consider even the prospect of civil war. And which of these two sides are you on? A Garibaldian ministry is now our only hope.[3]

Cattaneo was a great Italian. But like Mazzini he was far greater as a prophet or thinker than as a practical politician. It had been only

[1] 12 October, *L' Iride* (Naples).   [2] 12 October (ACP, f. 127).
[3] 12 October, Cattaneo to Pallavicino (Archivio Cattaneo MRM).

by using great pressure that Bertani had persuaded him at all to come south to Naples, and now he was ill and anxious to return home. For him an assembly was desirable chiefly in so far as it signified a constituent assembly, the means whereby annexation could be made conditional on local autonomy, if not on the creation of a federal state. To the radicals round Crispi, on the other hand, it was rather a means to postpone annexation until the moment when a united kingdom of all Italy could be formed; they thought of it as an instigation to make Piedmont co-operate in attaining unity, an attempt to avoid the imposition of a provincial hegemony from the north. Cattaneo's letter is interesting in its suggestion of how near this leading federalist stood at this moment to Garibaldi and the unitarians. Its reasoning was by no means negligible, however much its manner of presentation was deficient in tact. It was at least a fair statement of the wider views of one school of thought, and it also mentions the immediate criticisms which were being made against the conservative ministry of Conforti. Pallavicino gave a short reply to it, also dated the 12th: 'your letter is a tissue of sophistries, and unworthy of your great ability. I have not the time to confute it. I have given in my resignation, and will not retract it. Either Mazzini and Crispi go at once, or else I shall leave myself on the first ship.'[1]

Meantime, Garibaldi arrived back in Naples from Caserta, and the second council meeting took place as arranged.[2] The *Giornale Officiale* carried Conforti's detailed description of what happened. According to this account, Garibaldi first reproached the conservative ministers for their lack of solicitude in providing him with adequate money and munitions, and also for their dismissal of several radical governors who had been appointed in the provinces. To this Conforti made formal answer in his capacity as minister for internal affairs; but the reply left Garibaldi still dubious, and Conforti then suggested that, if he lacked confidence in them, they should resign. Garibaldi thought this over awhile, and then agreed. The ministers therefore all signed a form of resignation, and Garibaldi just asked them to remain in office until he

---

[1] 12 October, Pallavicino to Cattaneo (*ibid.*).

[2] Pallavicino says that Garibaldi never came to Naples on the 12th at all (*Le Memorie*, vol. III, p. 629); but these memoirs were written at a much later date.

had appointed their successors.[1] Slight variations on this official version occur in the account given in Dumas's *Indipendente*, where Garibaldi was said to have accused the ministers of replacing his own nominees in the provinces with new governors who were actually reactionary, that is to say involved with the *ancien régime*.[2] This vexed question of whether radicals or conservatives should govern in the provinces had been the subject of bitter dispute for the past month between the ministry and the dictator's secretariat, and Conforti had taken advantage of Bertani's disgrace and Garibaldi's absence at Caserta to make important changes in the governorships. It is interesting that Conforti's account of this meeting made no mention of the political issue of plebiscite *versus* assembly, but confirmed Cattaneo's statement that the ministers' loss of face arose first of all out of their misconduct of administration. Dumas agreed about this, and even added (what can hardly be true) that the ministers seemed to care little one way or the other about the purely political controversy.[3]

Once the ministry had resigned, Garibaldi had to look around for a successor. He did not agree with Crispi that a dictator should rule dictatorially through mere technical, non-political administrators, but obstinately believed that there should be ministers who in some way represented public opinion. His notions of dictatorship were not nearly so austere as Cavour imagined. Indeed, all the half dozen or so ministries which he appointed in the south were either entirely composed of moderates, or at least had only a minority of radicals; but this fact was never understood in Turin. On 12 October he found himself without a responsible cabinet, and though his secretary was delighted about this, he himself was really uncomfortable. It even looked as though, with no responsible government in office, and with only nine days to go, either plebiscite or assembly would turn out to be impossible by the specified date of voting, 21 October.[4]

For a few hours Crispi, as secretary-general to the dictator, was left in sole charge of affairs, and he made what use he could of the brief interval. His diary for the 12th runs: 'Garibaldi entrusts the government to the heads of departments and myself until the assembly be convoked. The decree is signed.' The decree here mentioned was one

[1] 17 October, *Il Giornale Officiale di Napoli*.   [2] 16 October, *L' Indipendente*.
[3] 19 October, *ibid*.   [4] 12 October, Elliot to Russell (F.O. 165/133).

for an assembly, conformable with that already published in Sicily seven days before, and complementary to that decree of four days earlier which had prescribed a plebiscite for Naples. Crispi wanted both plebiscite and assembly. For a time he had even persuaded Pallavicino to agree on this; and Garibaldi gave his signature to his proposal,[1] whereas so far as we know the dictator had not signed Pallavicino's earlier decree of the 8th for a plebiscite alone. Another ordinance then brought both southern provinces into line, by giving Sicily a plebiscite to accompany the assembly already proclaimed in Palermo. The radicals at last thought that they might have found an acceptable compromise which gave them the substance of victory, and news of all these proceedings was at once despatched to Mordini. Unfortunately for Crispi this news was to arrive in Sicily too late to save the situation. Pallavicino, even though technically out of office, had in fact already won a decisive victory by his earlier plebiscite decree of the 8th, for this had by now reached Sicily and forced Mordini to yield. The only hope for Crispi was at Naples. He did make some effort there to publicize his new decree of the 12th for the convocation of an assembly;[2] but he was handicapped by the fact that the police force and the official *Giornale* were still controlled by the resigning ministers. Conforti and the others were evidently looking on their resignation as a tactical gesture rather than as anything permanent.

While Crispi had been busy in this direction, Garibaldi was being unsuccessful in his attempt to form a new ministry. Colonna, the mayor of Naples, nearly succeeded in completing an administration,[3] but early on the 13th he was dissuaded from this by Pallavicino.[4] Crispi wrote to tell Bertani on the 13th that 'up to the present we have no ministry, and the General is disinclined to form one'.[5] Crispi was still hoping that

---

[1] Crispi, *Memoirs*, vol. I, pp. 456–7.

[2] 12 October, a fragment in English exists among Crispi's papers, evidently intended for the English press: '...General Garibaldi does not approve of an irregular votation such as took place at Nice...M. Pallavicino admitted the principle [i.e. of an assembly] for Sicily, but opposed it for Naples...' (ACP, f. 127).

[3] 13 October, Colonna to Garibaldi, saying that his task was rendered harder by the general belief that Crispi (who as a Sicilian was unpopular at Naples) would remain in office (ACM, no. 889).

[4] Salazaro, *Cenni sulla rivoluzione del 1860*, p. 68.

[5] Crispi, *Memoirs*, vol. I, p. 453.

Garibaldi would fail to find a new ministry and a new prodictator, and would have to bring the various governmental departments directly under himself and his secretariat. But this was counting without Pallavicino, who wrote to the dictator later on the 13th virtually returning himself to power; like the ministers, he had decided to stay in office, on the plea that 'to leave the country without a government would be a crime'.[1]

It is easy enough to reconstruct the motives of the prodictator. Pallavicino had just told Cattaneo that he would not retract his resignation, and indeed this resignation had been already accepted; but he had been dismayed to find that his bluff was being called, that his enemy Crispi was not expelled, as he demanded, but even called by Garibaldi 'the necessary man who is more useful to me than anyone else'. The conservatives had not gained by the prodictator's disappearance. On the contrary, a decree for an assembly had received Garibaldi's signature, in the interval. Pallavicino would not have known yet the news from Sicily, where his plebiscite decree of the 8th had by now arrived and succeeded so well. What he might have feared was that the absence of Garibaldi's signature on that original decree of the 8th would by now have told against the plebiscite, especially when Sicilians came to hear about Crispi's new assembly decree of the 12th which Garibaldi had personally signed. All this helps to explain why Pallavicino was now attempting a return to power, sincerely convinced that such a plan alone would save the cause he had been fighting for. It was presumably a calculated step, for his former prime minister, Conforti, simultaneously made a public speech in which he was quoted as saying that, despite their voluntary resignation of the 12th, the ministers would not leave their posts except 'under coercion'.[2]

On his return to Naples the next day, 13 October, Garibaldi began by clearly supporting the policy of Crispi. His first step was to arrest the chief of police, who was accused of working on Conforti's orders to manipulate the mob for political purposes.[3] He then personally

[1] 13 October, Pallavicino to Garibaldi (ACM, no. 1168).
[2] 18 October, Crispi to Bertani (ABCM).
[3] 13 October, Crispi's diary (*Memoirs*, vol. I, p. 484); on the 14th Garibaldi said he could be released again, but Türr thought it inadvisable, see notes by Garibaldi and Türr dated 14 October (MRR).

addressed the people from the balcony of one of the public buildings, and told them to stop their agitation and their shouting of 'Death to Mazzini'. As usual the effect of his words was magical.[1] Crispi called this speech 'Garibaldi's last triumph; because he was soon afterwards overcome by the evil genius which presented itself to him under the name of "concord", and so asked for another conference'.[2] The dictator never liked to flout any manifestation of what he took to be genuine public opinion, and he had to recognize that no liberal and responsible Neapolitan politician would join an administration unless Crispi's radical programme was dropped. Garibaldi's refusal to stand on his dignity is another testimony to his realistic approach, his essential moderation, and his good sense. It was on this day that he must have received the king's letter from Ancona, the same which congratulated him on the Volturno battle and looked forward to an early meeting between them both. This, too, would have helped to open his mind to concession.

The third and last conference between the various disputants took place at 2.00 p.m. on the 13th. A representative selection of the leading politicians in Naples was summoned to it, leaving out Mazzini of course who continued to remain inactive. Pallavicino, Conforti, and Francesco De Luca led for the moderates, Crispi, Cattaneo, Aurelio Saliceti for the various shades of radical. The *Giornale Officiale* described how Garibaldi first put to them the question 'whether we should follow the plebiscite by an assembly as in Sicily'.[3] An affirmative answer came from Cattaneo, who proclaimed his federal views, and was for making the Italian union conditional on terms. Conforti argued against this that, once the people had voted by universal suffrage, there could be no question of any assembly to judge or alter the expressed will of the majority. Conforti continued:

the Turin parliament has voted not to accept conditional annexation. Shall we then force a division in Italy? Shall we lengthen the life of our interim government? Shall we prove those foreigners right who ridicule our internal

[1] 19 October, *L' Unità Italiana* (Genoa), report from Naples dated 13 October, 'as if by magic, the General had hardly finished speaking when all the white favours for annexation disappeared from people's hats'; also 14 October, *Il Nazionale*.

[2] 18 October, Crispi to Bertani (ABCM).

[3] 17 October, *Il Giornale Officiale di Napoli*.

discords? No! we Neapolitans must not haggle over conditions, as if we had not yet emerged from the middle ages. We are not giving ourselves to any foreign power on whom we must impose conditions; we are giving ourselves to ourselves.... We Neapolitans, who have been so much calumniated by the world, certainly have no intention of increasing these calumnies by insisting on our municipal claims; all we want is that Italy should be made, and quickly.

L'Indipendente gave some variations on this official account. 'None of those who opposed Pallavicino and Conforti mentioned the imposition of conditions on the union of south to north Italy.... Only Saliceti, speaking of the defects of the Sardinian *statuto* and of the other laws of Piedmont, indicated that the assembly would have to decide what reforms might be desirable.'[1] Another description of events came from Professor De Luca. His version of this dispute recounted how, when Pallavicino referred to the veto placed on an assembly by the vote of the Turin parliament, Cattaneo leaped up and pointed out that this parliament represented only part of Italy, not the whole, so that Cavour's refusal to accept conditions was itself a condition imposed by one province upon others. De Luca added that Saliceti called the plebiscite superfluous, seeing that the one point it could decide, namely the sovereignty of Victor Emanuel, had been formally proclaimed since May in all the decrees of the revolutionary government, as well as by all the municipalities severally and also by popular acclamation; there was in fact nothing for a mere plebiscite to do, since the government of southern Italy had been already carried on for some time in the name of the king of Sardinia. Saliceti thereupon proposed the calling of a Neapolitan assembly, so that there would be some body to discuss the difficult questions of the transition and the transference of power. This proposal was not agreed to by the meeting, and De Luca himself put forward the opinion that, in view of the publication of Pallavicino's decree of the 8th, to call an assembly without a plebiscite would now make people suspicious of a plot. He added, nevertheless, that in his opinion a plebiscite should be followed by an assembly, 'not with the idea of approving or rejecting what will have been decided by popular vote, but in order to complete it politically, and to advise on the method of unification, this being a question which the plebiscite by itself could

[1] 19 October, *L' Indipendente*.

not deal with'. De Luca added 'that the mode of voting so far chosen would discredit us abroad, because being open and public it would arouse suspicions of pressure'. Apparently Conforti agreed with this diagnosis, and promised to try a different procedure.[1]

Aurelio Saliceti, the former triumvir of the Roman republic, was another person to give his story of what happened in this conference. He began by saying that Conforti's account was a complete fabrication 'in every syllable'. He then distinguished himself clearly from Pallavicino and the plebiscitarians on the one hand, and from Cattaneo and the federalists on the other. What he wanted was first a declaration of union with the north, then the summons of a southern parliament to debate the terms of this union, and then a plebiscitary referendum to confirm both the union and the terms. His own contribution to the debate had included the following words:

the revolution preceded and did not succeed the arrival of General Garibaldi; it made possible his entry into Naples.... Thus the choice of a king and of union with the rest of Italy had been decided as a *fait accompli*, and it would be absurd to ask the people who accomplished this whether they now desired it.

If there was one thing the revolution could not do in itself, this was to establish on what terms the union should be carried out. To a question of this nature you could not reply with a simple 'yes' or 'no'. The extremely complex nature of the problem, the dignity of the country, and the greatness of its interests, all demanded tranquil and mature discussion; and this could take place only in a parliament elected by universal suffrage, whose proposals could then be submitted for popular approval, just as had already happened in the central Duchies and Tuscany, and was about to happen in Sicily.... The approval which the people would then give to the deliberations of this parliament would constitute the plebiscite which the decree of 8 October called for.[2]

The dramatic conclusion to this conference was described some months afterwards by Cattaneo. The sense of the meeting had favoured the radicals, and a decision was reached which might easily have had far-reaching results.

I left Garibaldi half an hour after the dissolution of the meeting in which five votes against two had recognized the necessity of an assembly like that

[1] 20 October, *ibid.*
[2] 23 October, *ibid.*, letter from Saliceti dated 18 October.

which had been chosen in Sicily. But after this decision had been reached, Pallavicino once more resigned his office and inveighed against Crispi. At last Garibaldi lost patience, and got to his feet saying, 'if you will not have the assembly, to hell with the assembly; I am off to Caprera'. No one present made the slightest observation. Only when Pallavicino offered to shake hands, I refused, and told him what I thought of him.[1]

Cattaneo was hardly master of his feelings at this moment, for all his hopes and plans had suddenly collapsed as soon as Garibaldi gave up the effort to understand and reconcile these two points of view. Up to the very last moment the radicals had felt themselves on the brink of a local and yet important success. But the Piedmontese army was by now only a few hundred miles away, and as Farini had every intention of using force to prevent an assembly meeting, it was perhaps as well for Italy that the dictator's common sense prevailed once again. 'In the end Garibaldi, exhausted by the obstinacy of the two parties, decided that each prodictator should act as he thought best, and that in consequence there should be a plebiscite in Naples and an assembly in Sicily.'[2]

The losing party not unnaturally discovered in this turn of events a carefully planned *coup de théâtre*, and there was some truth in what they said. *L'Indipendente*, for instance, told how at the critical moment of the meeting petitions were handed in by the military, covered with a volume of signatures 'which they had been gathering for the previous twenty-four hours at great expense of the secret funds which we had thought abolished'. So far as can be seen, the really decisive stroke with Garibaldi was this intervention of the soldiers and the national guard. In particular there was the action of General Türr, that gallant Hungarian of Garibaldi's irregulars. This man was of all Garibaldi's senior officers the one nearest to Cavour, and not only because of his politics, or because his future career was at stake, but also because Cavour was secretly exploring the possibility of an alliance with the people of Hungary against the Austrian Empire. Türr's own military future, now that Garibaldi's star was waning, lay on the chance of transferring to the regular army of the king. At this moment he had been sent back from the front to take over as commanding officer in the city of Naples.

---

[1] 26 April 1861, Cattaneo to his wife (Archivio Cattaneo MRM); 19 October, *L' Unità Italiana* (Genoa).

[2] 16 October, *L' Indipendente*.

He was living there at the same house and table as Pallavicino,[1] and it is easy to guess where he absorbed the opinions which made him one of the chief instruments in Garibaldi's change of mind.

General Türr, by the afternoon of 13 October, had in his possession numerous letters and petitions drawn up by the commanders of the national guard. Certain senior officers of this essentially middle-class and conservative organization had met together after Pallavicino's resignation on 11 October, and told the ex-prodictator that 'they promised to *initiate* a petition at once among their men on behalf of the plebiscite'.[2] Pallavicino was thus aware quite early of this move on the part of the chief organized force in the city, and the knowledge may well have helped to influence him in deciding to take office again. The two generals in charge of the national guard for the city and province of Naples had then written a joint letter to Garibaldi on the 12th, claiming to speak on behalf of the whole force; and they told how 'the national guard is gravely concerned to see the country moved by further agitation which is threatening public order and tranquillity.... We turn to beg our idolized Giuseppe Garibaldi that his handiwork shall remain intact, and that the disasters threatening us and all Italy may be avoided. Indeed for our part we are determined to avoid them at all costs.'[3] It was said that this address 'had a great effect on the dictator, who set great store by such demonstrations', especially since the national guard was his chief defence against the social disorder to which this letter referred. Just as in previous moments of the *risorgimento*, the guard was proving to be a political as well as a military organization, and acted as though possessing a right of initiative in political matters. Without waiting for any government permission, it had been mobilized by its officers on 12 October against the 'danger of republicanism'. On the following day 'the national guard had gathered together under arms and stood with the rest of the population behind the ideas of Pallavicino'.[4] Its officers had their petition ready for the dictator at this final council meeting; and just when Pallavicino had resigned a second time, Türr entered the council chamber with a handful of addresses for

[1] G. Locatelli Milesi, 'L'epopea Garibaldina del 1860', *Tridentum*, May 1910, p. 210.

[2] Salazaro, *Cenni sulla rivoluzione del 1860*, p. 67.   [3] *Ibid.* pp. 70–1.

[4] Caranti, *Alcune notizie sul plebiscito*, pp. 39–42. Caranti was Pallavicino's secretary.

presentation. Garibaldi had his head swimming with the subtleties of half a dozen clever and opinionated lawyers, contending with each other over a problem which was far from simple. Türr's intervention then proved to be the last straw. The dictator's curt phrase brought the meeting to an end: 'if this really is the desire of the Neapolitan people, let it be so.'[1]

These several versions tell much the same tale, from widely varying points of view. Garibaldi's changefulness had continued up to the very last minute; but the moderates had finally won, and a simple plebiscite by itself had been assured, at least for the mainland province of Naples. Conforti now issued a simple statement to say that Garibaldi had confirmed the former ministry in office.[2] As one witness commented, 'in this way was resolved the question which was so important that for one moment it had threatened the whole outcome of Italian unity'.[3] Slightly different was the verdict of *Il Pungolo*, which upbraided both parties in the dispute. The people of the capital, said this newspaper, had been kept entirely uninformed about the issues of the controversy, and it was precisely their fear of what they did not understand which had caused all the alarm and agitation at Naples. The *Pungolo* first indicted *Il Nazionale*, which had tried to tell the people that the dispute was no more than a question of personalities, with Crispi as the chief villain. But it also blamed the *Indipendente* on the other side for romanticizing the conflict, and likewise those other papers which had just portrayed what had happened as a mere palace revolution. 'The project of assembly had nothing wrong about it except inopportuneness. One month ago it would have been possible, but now no longer.' Luckily for Italy, this paper concluded, when Garibaldi's friends tried to make of him a Cromwell, he stayed a Garibaldi.[4]

This was a realistic and intelligent acceptance of the situation. 'What would once have been a generous thought, would now be a deplorable error. For now the question is one of very existence, not of the particular manner of existence. The congress of diplomats meeting in Warsaw threatens us with the end of non-intervention. Hence we must

---

[1] Salazaro, *Cenni sulla rivoluzione del 1860*, p. 81.
[2] 13 October, *Il Giornale Officiale di Napoli*.
[3] Salazaro, *Cenni sulla rivoluzione del 1860*, p. 80.
[4] 15 October, *Il Pungolo* (Naples).

answer this threat at once with a *fait accompli*.'[1] In accepting this logic, the dictator's luminous intuition had once more decided what his intellect and his heart had not been able to settle. Evidently he was a dictator with a difference. Despite Bertani's representations on the one hand, and La Farina's misrepresentations on the other, he believed in public opinion as much as did Cavour. Indeed, this faith was almost an obsession with him. He was thus quite ready to resign his powers when he felt this to be the will of the people.

[1] Explanatory proclamation to the citizens of Salento, among miscellaneous 'proclami' in Biblioteca Nazionale MSS, Naples.

CHAPTER XXV

THE PLEBISCITE IN SICILY: OCTOBER

Although they had failed to carry Garibaldi with them at Naples, the radicals clung for a few more hours to the hope that they might keep their foothold in Sicily. But by 13 October, though Crispi did not yet realize it, his foolish omission to keep Palermo informed had forced Mordini into surrender. Crispi should no doubt have visualized earlier that there was the possibility of serious trouble arising from the slowness in communications with Sicily. Briefly recapitulated, the situation at Palermo was that Mordini's project for an assembly had seemed widely acceptable, at least until the 11th. Then on the 12th there had spread rumours of Pallavicino's decision for a plebiscite; and especially as this decision was mistakenly believed to be Garibaldi's, it had successfully captured public opinion. Mordini's despairing account of this fact was contained in perhaps the only telegram during this period to reach Naples in less than twelve hours, and what it said may well have had an influence on Garibaldi's mind. Its effect on Crispi had been to make him suddenly aware that his preoccupation with Naples might be losing him Sicily too; and so he had bent all his efforts to what then seemed the best compromise still attainable, that Sicily as well as Naples should each have both plebiscite and assembly.[1] This device now offered the only chance of keeping radical supremacy in the south, at least for a little longer, and so of forcing Cavour to sacrifice some of his more extreme claims before the revolution was concluded.

It was in the afternoon of the 13th that Garibaldi ruined this desperate hope and decided that each prodictator should decide as the situation in his particular area suggested, which meant that Naples at least would have a plebiscite only. This left Crispi no hope at all except in Sicily, where a local parliament had been summoned to meet in three weeks' time. At once he sent Mordini a belated explanation of what had been happening, and tried to excuse his earlier silence on the grounds that he

[1] 12 October, draft decree (MRR).

had hoped to arrange a joint policy for both provinces together. Now that this wish had been disappointed, he was sending two decrees to Sicily with Garibaldi's signature, confirming the previous grant of full powers of initiative upon the prodictator, and ratifying actions which the Sicilian government had already taken. 'Keep steadily on at your post. You have a great mission to fulfil, and I am sure that you will not fail. They are now attacking the honour of the men on our side.'[1] This message, with the attached decrees, Crispi consigned to Calvino and Parisi who were at last allowed to return. But bad weather held up their departure for a further day, and the two decrees could not be published in Sicily until the 15th, by which time Mordini had given up all hope and capitulated.

The events of these two intervening days had shown what might be expected from Naples and Palermo being so far out of touch with each other. On the evening of the 13th, although Mordini had already reached the conclusion that Sicily could not hold out much longer, a telegram sent by Parisi from Naples at 6 p.m. indicated that on the mainland the matter was still under discussion, and that the Sicilian envoys at Garibaldi's side even thought that their mission was going well.[2] An hour later Crispi was still optimistic. 'The dictator received all your telegrams', he told Mordini, 'and will come in person if possible to open the assembly. You will receive an answer to your questions by Parisi and Calvino who will return as soon as the weather clears up.'[3] Crispi continued on the 14th to imagine that something could yet be salvaged from the wreck. Three more telegrams which he sent on this day to Mordini confirmed that the latest decision for a plebiscite concerned Naples alone and not Sicily, and that Mordini's decree of the 5th for a Sicilian assembly still stood intact. Perhaps Garibaldi—and certainly Crispi—would come to Palermo for the inauguration of this regional parliament.[4]

---

[1] 13 October, Crispi to Mordini (ACP, f. 135).
[2] 13 October, Parisi to Mordini (AMB).
[3] 13 October, Crispi to Mordini (MRR, cartella 221).
[4] 14 October, Crispi to Ugdulena: 'the plebiscite is for Naples, not for Sicily. It was decreed by the Neapolitan prodictator and not by Garibaldi. In Sicily you can have a plebiscite later if the assembly thinks fit' (ACP, f. 135). Also 14 October, Crispi to Mordini: 'the dictator decided yesterday that there should be no change in

These communications all arrived too late. For by now Mordini was in despair. On the evening of the 13th he had been threatening to resign. But then came Crispi's sudden burst of reassuring messages, which only left him more perplexed than before. We have seven telegrams that he sent or at least drafted to Garibaldi on the 14th, and know that they were taking twenty-four hours to reach their destination.

The position is untenable. Believe one of your most faithful followers, and authorize me to proclaim a plebiscite here. Every hour and even moment is precious.[1]

Again:

from Crispi's dispatch I understand that you are still decided for a Sicilian assembly. But I assure you that, if the assembly was necessary at one stage, it has now become impossible owing to the decree at Naples authorized by yourself which gave out that a plebiscite would be for the benefit of the country....I have made unbelievable efforts to procrastinate today. There is no knowing about tomorrow. But if you persist you will have to come here yourself and at once.[2]

It must have helped to influence Mordini's judgement that the city council of Palermo met on the 14th and followed that of Messina in electing to send a deputation to Victor Emanuel.[3] Even his former friends among the autonomists were now swinging over against him. Naples would take pride of place if she annexed herself to Piedmont through her plebiscite on 21 October, because Sicily would have to wait until 4 November before her assembly could hold even its first meeting. The prospect of having to follow on behind Naples was humiliating. The councils of Caltanisetta and Syracuse also, being like other municipal councils representative of propertied interests in the island, passed formal votes in favour of a plebiscite as the quickest way

what you enacted for Sicily and Pallavicino for Naples. Because of this falling out of step of the two provinces I have resigned and shall return to Sicily in order to sit in the assembly. Garibaldi will come and open it if he can' (*ibid.*).

[1] 14 October, Mordini to Garibaldi (AMB).

[2] 14 October, Mordini to Garibaldi (Archivio Garibaldi MRR and Carte Sirtori, Ambrosiana, Milan).

[3] 16 October, *L'Annessione* (Palermo).

of ending the revolution.[1] This was a concerted policy to employ the only representative organs in existence for expressing the general sentiments of liberal–conservative opinion. The mayor of Caltanisetta was Baron Trabonella, a man of consequence in local affairs, and the owner of most of the sulphur mines, but his political horizon was a narrow one. So far as we know, he had favoured the Bourbons in April; he certainly supported Garibaldi in June, and Piedmont in October. In each case, that is to say, his vote went to the government which offered the best hope of law and order at the moment. This attitude was fully justifiable, and probably it was not untypical either. One may even suspect that it was the most common of all sentiments during this year of national revolution, and that it was as powerful as the more specialized impulse of patriotism in helping to form a national state.

Faced by non–cooperation or passive resistance on the part of the classes which were most politically conscious and socially powerful, Mordini first tried to restore his position by announcing that Ugdulena had been sent to request Garibaldi to allow a plebiscite; and in the meantime he pressed Crispi to hurry on Garibaldi to give his permission. Still no news came through, and Mordini saw that, in case he was forced to act on his own initiative again, he had better prepare some sort of justification. So he sent round to all provincial governors to ask what they would advise him to do now it was official that Naples at least was to vote by plebiscite. Some remote parts of Sicily were cut off from events, and Syracuse in the south-east, for example, had only just heard of Mordini's notice of 9 October in favour of the assembly. The governor of Syracuse had even written on the 13th welcoming this Sicilian parliament and contradicting the vote of his municipality.[2] Apparently the governor of Caltagirone only heard on the 13th about Cavour's speech of the 2nd, and he on the other hand reported that it had converted his district to the plebiscite.[3] This was without any doubt the more representative view, and most of the provinces now replied to Mordini's latest request by asking him to follow Pallavicino's example.

[1] 16 October, Bargoni telegram to governor of Caltanisetta (AMB); and 15 October, minutes of the Syracuse civic council (MRR).

[2] 13 October, governor of Syracuse to Mordini (MRR).

[3] 13 October, governor of Caltagirone to Mordini (MRR).

It seems reasonably clear that, if Mordini had hitherto been reluctant to order any change in his public policy, this must have been due to his belief that Garibaldi was against the immediate annexation of Sicily by plebiscite. Whether the dictator still intended to march on Rome, or whether he had some other plan in mind, his former instructions made it certain that he had wanted some delay in annexation. In Mordini's frantic appeals to Garibaldi on the 13th and 14th one can find little support for La Farina's accusation that the prodictator was defying public opinion and trying to stay in power. On the contrary, in so far as we can ever identify public opinion, it seems to have been Mordini's nature and policy to follow it whenever he could. Public opinion had welcomed his project for an assembly after 5 October; but after 12 October it had changed to want a plebiscite; and he had done his best to persuade Garibaldi to sanction first the one and then the other.

On 15 October the political unrest in Palermo found its final resolu-, tion. Parisi must have arrived back from Naples early in the morning with Garibaldi's decrees and Crispi's advice to hold out. Then at 2 p.m. came a message from the dictator: 'in answer to your note of the 13th, do just as you wish and I shall approve your action'. If the prodictator had really been trying merely to hold on to power, he could have con- tinued with his assembly and justified himself with this latest authoriza- tion; but he chose not to. Whatever Crispi may have hoped that he might do after receiving this message, there was no doubt about it in his own mind, and he replied: 'Parisi and Calvino have arrived and told me of your patriotic intentions. So I have ordered the publication of the decree prescribing a plebiscite for 21 October, and with the same wording as that at Naples.'[1] It is significant of the change of temper in Sicily that it was Parisi himself, with his autonomist reputation, who as minister for internal affairs officially made the proposal on which this new decision was taken. A decree announcing the plebiscite was ready for insertion in the *Giornale Officiale* of the 15th, and that evening special messengers left Palermo to carry its text to all parts of Sicily. Only six days remained in which to alter the whole machinery of annexation. Mordini gave the governors of each province a public explanation of recent events, assuring them that Garibaldi's wishes had really been for

[1] 15 October, Mordini to Garibaldi (AMB, b. 28, and Carte Sirtori, Ambrosiana, Milan).

an assembly, but that at Naples, where matters were less tranquil than in Sicily, a quick and final settlement of affairs had become so urgent that a plebiscite was necessary. Once the dictator had acknowledged this priority of the expedient over the desirable, Sicily could not help but do the same, he explained, since regional pride would not admit of her trailing behind Naples in union with the kingdom of Italy. On this point the ministers in council were as unanimous as they had formerly been over the assembly.[1]

The immediate reaction throughout Sicily was one of great relief. To all appearances the danger of Garibaldi pitting himself against Cavour was over, and there was a good chance of quickly being able to bring the revolution to an end. People at large would have been ignorant of all the back-stage wrangling and disagreement, and would see only that Garibaldi had found a compromise formula which they might assume to be the best solution in the circumstances. Even the unitarian radicals tried to look on the better side of it. 'They were assured that the wording of the plebiscite made no mention of either annexation or conditions, and did not in the least compromise the cause which is so vital to Sicily and Italy.'[2] Under the new decree, people were to be asked to vote on the following proposition: that 'the Sicilian people desire to form an integral part of Italy one and indivisible under Victor Emanuel as their constitutional king'. To this they could say only 'yes' or 'no'. The particular phrasing had been chosen so as not to offend by any suggestion of 'annexation' to the kingdom of Piedmont-Sardinia. It had further given the radicals to believe that their constituent assembly would in any case have to follow some time, for the implication was that they were voting to join a new state of Italy, and not an already existing state possessed of a ready-formulated constitution.[3] Some people, indeed, regarded the use of these words as imposing yet another very important condition on Cavour; for it would allow them to hold that the vote was nullified if ever Cavour took it into his head to cede any further part of Italian territory to France, or even if he failed to carry on the revolutionary momentum until the final consummation of the national movement. Thus the *Precursore*, until it

[1] 15 October and 16 October, announcements by Mordini in *Il Giornale Officiale di Sicilia.*

[2] 25 October, *L' Unità Italiana* (Palermo).   [3] 20 October, *ibid.*

understood that the new policy meant the defeat and resignation of Crispi, at first tried to make out that a plebiscite on such terms was a victory for Garibaldi over Cavour.[1] Likewise the radical *Indipendente* of Messina now agreed that a plebiscite with this particular formula was welcome; and it praised Pallavicino for having thus healed the division between radicals and moderates which had persisted ever since Garibaldi's breach with Cavour had become public a month before.[2]

In more conservative and in Piedmontese circles there was naturally some cavilling over the heretical phrase 'Italia una e indivisibile'— Villamarina thought it 'bad taste'[3]—but on the whole the party of Cavour in Sicily was well pleased. *Il Regno d' Italia* gave thanks to Mordini for so well interpreting the people's wishes: a plebiscite was quick and safe, and would solve the main issue, while leaving the question of conditions to be argued out if necessary in a future parliament.[4] The satisfaction was even more general over Mordini's plebiscite decree of the 15th than it had formerly been over his assembly decree ten days before. Messina reported that 'the government is everywhere acclaimed'.[5] Even the two leading 'autonomists', Dr Raffaele and Professor Ferrara, were so far carried away by the excitement as to wear the token '*si*' which was in everyone's hat to signify their acceptance of union with the north.[6] Mordini himself had a great reception at the theatre with the mayor of Palermo and the commandant of the national guard, and a large crowd came to the Royal Palace and cheered a speech he made from the balcony.[7] He sent to tell Garibaldi of the general enthusiasm and how Palermo was illuminated each night in celebration.

If there was any doubt about the way that people would vote, it was removed by Garibaldi's statement on the 15th that the two Sicilies 'already formed an integral part of Italy one and indivisible', and that he proposed to hand over to King Victor Emanuel the dictatorial

[1] 15 October, *Il Precursore.*
[2] 18 October, *L' Indipendente* (Messina), Mario's paper.
[3] 11 October, Villamarina to Cavour (*CC Lib. del Mezz.* vol. III, p. 85).
[4] 15 October, *Il Regno d' Italia* (Palermo).
[5] 15 October, Ugdulena's secretary to Mordini (AMB, b. 28).
[6] 30 October, *La Perseveranza* (Milan), report from Palermo dated 24 October.
[7] 17 October, *Il Giornale Officiale di Sicilia.*

powers conferred on him by the nation.[1] In sending this information
to Mordini, the dictator instructed him to welcome any landing of
Piedmontese troops, but not to relinquish the government itself until
he received express orders.[2] Mordini then followed Garibaldi in
publishing a declaration that he intended to yield power to the king,
and he virtually directed Sicilians to confirm this by a favourable vote
on the 21st.[3] Not everyone in southern Italy was pleased by these
premature and peremptory demands. Elliot described how Garibaldi's
decree of the 15th 'has, I am told, given considerable offence to the
Neapolitans, who would rather have had the appearance of themselves
deciding on their future condition instead of having by their votes on
the 21st simply to ratify the transfer of the Kingdom to Victor Emanuel
which has thus been decreed by the Dictator'.[4] But at the same
time that Garibaldi's decree was published, the *Giornale Officiale*
printed the king's advance proclamation to the people of southern Italy
as if they were already his subjects.[5] Both king and dictator were
looking on the plebiscite as a mere formality. Just as Cavour was
issuing decrees 'for those provinces not yet annexed', so official notices
were already being given out in Naples 'by approval of the king'.
General Cialdini with his northern army was already over the frontier,
and he was communicating directly with local officials in the Neapolitan
provinces.[6]

Preparations in Sicily were hurried through so that the plebiscite
might without fail take place on the 21st and so coincide with that of
Naples. In the city of Palermo itself, out of a total population of a
quarter of a million, there were only just over forty thousand registered
voters, of whom thirty-six thousand were to vote. 'Universal suffrage'
was thus something of a misnomer. Many citizens had not enrolled on
the register at all, 'misunderstanding its importance; and many others
in five months had lost their identification cards, often not knowing
what they had been intended for'.[7] On the day before the election the

---

[1] 15 October (*Raçcolta degli atti del governo dittatoriale*).
[2] 18 October, Garibaldi to Mordini (AMB).
[3] 17 October, *Il Giornale Officiale di Sicilia*.
[4] 18 October, Elliot to Russell (F.O. 70/321/585).
[5] 16 October, *Il Giornale Officiale di Napoli*.   [6] 20 October, *ibid*.
[7] 17 October, *Il Regno d' Italia*.

register had to be opened again.[1] The original decree of 23 June about the conduct of the vote had allowed each locality to make its own regulations about this. Messina now asked, vainly, for ten more days of preparation. Syracuse had formed no electoral roll, and a proclamation invited people merely to sign on in an open register. At Palermo, 'great crowds' had to vote without any previous formality at all.[2]

The excitement in the capital city was immense over this novel form of *festa*, and everyone in the street embraced everyone else. People became quite frenetic when, on the 20th, Mordini made the gesture of handing over all public order to the sole care and trust of citizens. All-night festivities preceded the great day in most places, with nocturnal illuminations, and the streets 'beautifully decorated with tapestry and Sardinian flags'.[3] The 21st was a Sunday, and voting was generally conducted in the churches after mass. The prodictator with the ministers and civil servants and the archbishop all voted in the cathedral. When, evening came many people had still forgotten to vote, so the city council decided that it would be in order to keep the poll open all through the next day as well.[4] Consul Goodwin reported that 'in Palermo the election was conducted with good humour and good order'.[5] Crispi's *Precursore* became eloquent and hyperbolical:

to a person coming from England, that is to say from the first country of the world, where the most liberal institutions have been rooted for centuries and have reached their most extended manifestation, to a person coming from great Albion nothing could arouse greater admiration than to see our people voting with order and dignity on a matter of such weight.... The history of constitutional states tells us that the people are usually indifferent at the first exercise of their new rights, so that the first elections normally show a very small number of votes. Yet in Sicily there was no elector who did not crowd to the booths to record his vote. Oh! what a miracle has Garibaldi's genius inspired.[6]

[1] 20 October, *ibid.*
[2] 8 November, *L' Indipendente* (Naples), report from Syracuse dated 27 October; 22 October, *L' Annessione* (Palermo).
[3] 22 October, vice-consul Richards from Messina to Elliot (F.O. 165/134).
[4] 25 October, *L' Unità Italiana* (Palermo).
[5] 25 October (Goodwin's Political Journal, no. 23; F.O. 165/134).
[6] 23 October, *Il Precursore.*

It would be easy to show how in many particulars the system adopted was not a good method of testing the will of the people. Voting was public, on a rostrum, with two open urns for all to see which was selected; and one imaginative pro-Bourbon described the *mise en scène* as being 'before a semicircle of disguised Lafarinian agents, with crabbed faces and an air of mystery, seated in the centre of the nave'.[1] Outside the big towns, in areas where the villages were still feudal and where landowners had made up their minds that Piedmont offered the best hope of restoring order, the publicity which surrounded the voting meant an almost compulsory '*sì*'. In some places, for instance Trapani and the island of Ischia, the ignorant peasantry fled to the mountains, under the impression that the voting was only a plot to inveigle them into an ambush and then press them for military service.[2] A correspondent of one paper described how, in his own village, the head of the *municipio* first rose to explain the significance of 'yes' or 'no', only to be met by voices crying 'we want neither Victor Emanuel nor Francesco, but Don Peppino'—that is to say, Giuseppe Garibaldi—at which the speaker, somewhat nonplussed, told them that in that case they should vote 'yes', which accordingly they did.[3] One governor had written to draw attention to this sort of problem, and to state that the complete illiteracy of nearly all the peasants made a secret ballot impossible. He received the following unhelpful reply from the government: 'if an illiterate voter is at the mercy of the presiding official, the defect lies in the fact not in the law.'[4]

Small wonder that some few looked on with amazement at handing over such responsibility to the ignorant mob, and prophesied doom to follow.[5] But as a device carefully suited to a certain limited objective there was much to be said for it. The moderates had known what they were about when adopting such a bold innovation. From their point of view it was essential that the people should give the semblance of

[1] P. Oliveri, *Episodi della rivoluzione Siciliana*, 1865, p. 64.

[2] 30 October, governor of Trapani telegram to Mordini (AMB, b. 28); 25 October, *L' Indipendente* (Naples).

[3] 1 November, *L' Unità Italiana* (Palermo).

[4] 8 October and 11 October, correspondence between the government and the governor of Mazzara (MRR).

[5] Oliveri, *Episodi della rivoluzione Siciliana*, p. 61.

popular approval to annexation; and they could feel quite sure that, with the national guard on duty, with a public ballot, with Garibaldi's personal directive, and presiding magistrates all of whom had taken an oath of loyalty to King Victor Emanuel two months before, there could be no doubt of the results. All that was needed was to combine discipline with excitement. The national guard was therefore marched down to the poll as a body and in uniform to give the example of a solid vote, bearing flags and favours for '*sì*'.[1]

The existence of minor irregularities is comparatively unimportant, but deserves some passing notice in view of later doubts about the validity of the plebiscite. Not only had the compilation of the register been mishandled, but electoral tickets sometimes fetched a price on the black market.[2] Although Mordini did more than Pallavicino to keep the forms of a free election, provincial governors were less educated than he in 'constitutional rule'. The governor of Caltanisetta made odd use of Mordini's prohibition against employing patent government pressure; and both purposely and unwarrantably he read into it an implication that the electoral manifestations of the opposition, of autonomist 'agitators' with their 'clandestine press', were likewise to be forbidden.[3] The prodictator had prided himself on allowing freedom of expression in the press for the annexation party—more at least than Cavour usually allowed to the Mazzinians—but here one of that party was taking pride in having driven all opposition groups underground in his province. Perhaps more typical was the governor of Girgenti, who reconciled the double pull of his conscience by instructing his subordinates 'not to influence the freedom of the vote, but nevertheless to elevate public spirit up to that height which the interests of Italy and the common aspirations of all Sicily demand'.[4] In Noto and Modica, and perhaps elsewhere, the provincial governors practised a venial form of deceit when they chose not to risk the continuation of conscription for the moment, and suspended the levy until after the voting was

---

[1] 25 October, *La Perseveranza*; 22 October, report by the commander of the national guard at Milazzo to his inspector-general at Palermo (MRR).

[2] 11 October, P. Grofani gave the price as two *scudi* each, writing to Mordini (AMB); 12 October, *L' Assemblea* made it five francs each.

[3] 13 October, governor of Caltanisetta to Mordini (MRR).

[4] 29 October, governor of Girgenti to Mordini (MRR).

over.[1] One of the big differences between Victor Emanuel's rule and Francesco's was going to be this novelty of conscription, and it was on this head more than any other that the subsequent rebellion was to develop against Piedmontese domination.

It would, of course, have been quite impossible to avoid all use of what one may call false pretences. Imperative reasons of state demanded that a tremendous majority should emerge from the poll, and the authorities would have been more than human if they had not made the most of an unlearned and gullible electorate. It had not been accidental that Cavour had chosen the method of 'universal suffrage', a method which in theory he disapproved, and which to some people seemed highly dangerous. His most loyal supporter among southern newspaper editors fearfully pointed out how even England had not yet arrived at such an advanced degree of democracy. Ruggero Bonghi thought that universal suffrage was 'quite unsuited yet to the social, moral and educational conditions of the people of Italy and especially of Neapolitans'.[2] To give one small example, Maxime du Camp described what he saw in Naples at the time of the plebiscite, when 'bien des gens des quartiers populaires, après avoir crié "vive l'Italie une!", nous disaient: "L'Italie, qu'est-ce que c'est? une, qu'est-ce que cela signifie?".'[3] The general ignorance would have been even worse in Sicily. Yet it was this same fact which made a popular vote safe for Cavour. Lord John Russell missed the point here. The English minister wrote to Elliot that 'universal suffrage is no favourite of mine, and I should be afraid that a few sweating madonnas and canting friars might pervert that mode of voting into a machinery for restoring Francesco II of pious memory.... The project has indeed a Gallic taste in it which I do not fancy.' He added, however, that doubtless Cavour knew his own business best.[4] In reply to this, Cavour through Hudson 'said he disliked it as much as you do, but it is his only weapon against France, which is doing all she can to trip up Italy's heels'.[5] This was a good

[1] 10 October, governor of Modica to Mordini (MRR); and *Gli ultimi conati del Borbonismo e Mazzinismo*, Italia, 1860, p. 66.

[2] 18 December, *Il Nazionale* (Naples).

[3] Maxime du Camp, *Revue des Deux Mondes*, 1 September 1862, p. 8.

[4] 11 October, Russell to Elliot (RP G.D. 22/109).

[5] 19 October, Hudson to Russell (RP G.D. 22/66).

argument *ad hominem*, but there were yet more realistic reasons still. Elliot wrote as follows about this system of voting: 'I do not apprehend that the proportion of negative votes would under any circumstances have been very large, but with the present arrangement there is still less chance of it.' So far as he could judge 'there are still, especially in the capital, many persons forming a large proportion of the educated classes who would prefer that Naples should remain a separate kingdom, provided they were secure from the return of the Bourbon dynasty'. In these circumstances, voting by universal suffrage presented no test of public opinion, for it offered only one simple question, and the answer to that question could be no more than yes or no. This really meant that there was no choice at all, since everyone would have to vote 'yes' if they wanted to emerge from uncertainty and disorder. 'Many who are separatists will therefore give the affirmative vote. In fact both the terms of the vote and the manner in which it is to be taken are well calculated to secure the largest possible majority for the annexation, but not so well fitted to ascertain the real wishes of the country.'[1]

To vote 'no' indeed had no meaning at all, for the only alternative to Victor Emanuel was Francesco, and the clock could not have been put back short of a bloody counter-revolution, and perhaps could not have been put back at all. In any case, the long history of numberless revolutions in southern Italy had instilled into people an automatic sense of the little gain derivative from revolution, as well as a temperamental inclination to approve whatever king might reign. Garibaldi had won the ordeal by battle, and this made a vote for the Bourbons unrealistic. There was little or no idea among the people that he might represent a different principle from Victor Emanuel, and so the course before them was clear. The really live issues between radicalism and conservatism, or between autonomism and centralism, were not at this time up for consideration, let alone the more rarefied notions of republic or federation. But all parties would have been positively or negatively agreed together in voting for Victor Emanuel, whether what they wanted was to prevent reaction or to stop revolution. Marc Monnier noted on the 22nd that 'd'opinions franchement, positivement annexionistes, il n'y en a guère; mais l'annexion est la seule solution

[1] 16 October. Elliot to Russell (F.O. 165/133/579); Mundy, *H.M.S. Hannibal at Palermo and Naples*, p. 256; Elliot, *Some Revolutions...*, pp. 97, 101.

possible'. He went on to describe how the common people exercised their vote:

depuis quarante siècles qu'il existe, c'est la première fois qu'on le consulte sur ses destinées.... Il fallait donc les voir hier, ces va-nu-pieds devenus citoyens et tenant dans leurs doigts cette carte d'électeur qu'ils ne savaient pas lire. Ils se réunissaient par groupes, musique en tête et bannières déployées, en chantant l'hymne de Garibaldi; ils criaient à tue-tête en chœur, 'Sì, Sì'... et entouraient des hourras dignes des fêtes britanniques.[1]

On 21 October the people of Sicily voted by 432,053 votes against 667 'to form an integral part of Italy one and indivisible under Victor Emanuel as their constitutional king'. The complementary figures for Naples were 1,302,064 in favour, and 10,312 against, which still amounted to a more than ninety-nine per cent majority.[2] With three separate armies fighting in the former *regno*, this result hardly represented a free and accurate test of opinion. The Bourbon forces were still in Messina, Gaeta, Capua and other smaller fortress towns. The city of Naples already contained seven thousand Piedmontese troops who had come by sea, and another still larger column had lately crossed the Abruzzi frontier. Just when a free ballot was meant to be taking place, General Cialdini in one province was summarily shooting all peasants found with firearms.[3] But Sicily was a good deal more settled than this, and the majority there was larger. Rather less than one-fifth of the population voted.[4] The details from each village were given in driblets by the *Giornale Officiale* as they came in. Out of a total of 292 Sicilian districts, it seems that there were 238 with no negative votes at all. Perhaps no less surprising is that there should have been only eighteen districts where the authorities made return of any votes which were null and void. In one case mentioned by the *Giornale*, 'the excess for this commune of ninety-four voters over and above its registered number is due to the presence of voters from other communes'.[5] Equally

[1] Marc Monnier, *Garibaldi: histoire de la conquête des deux Siciles: notes prises sur place de jour en jour*, 1861, pp. 367–8.

[2] 3 November, *Il Giornale Officiale di Napoli* gives the final figures.

[3] 21 October, L. Zambeccari to Pallavicino (*CC Lib. del Mezz.* vol. III, pp. 164–5).

[4] 29 October, *L' Indipendente* (Naples) said that the number of abstentions was high, owing to the propaganda of the clergy; 21 October, Elliot telegram to Russell, says that there were not so many abstentions as he had expected (F.O. 165/133).

[5] 25 October, *Giornale Officiale di Napoli*.

remarkable, but more typical, the returns from Patti show that, out of 1646 eligible voters, everyone voted and every single person for '*sì*'. At Palermo, out of forty thousand registered, there were more than four thousand abstentions and only twenty negatives. Messina, out of twenty-four thousand actually voting, had only eight negatives. *La Forbice* apologized for the fourteen negative votes out of three thousand at Alcamo, saying that their existence did at least serve to show how free was the vote.[1] Alcara had even more, twenty-seven negatives out of 384; Caltabellotta, forty-seven out of five hundred. But these were exceptional.

The largest number of hostile votes in any one district was at Girgenti, with seventy out of a possible two thousand five hundred. *Il Regno d' Italia* could not conceive how there could be so many 'inept' voters bold enough to declare against the majority; the figure was said to be 'shameful and irritating', and it was some relief to know that 'the citizens of Girgenti have protested in the most clamorous demonstrations against the horde of imbeciles' who had caused it.[2] Such was the scandal in this instance that the governor had to write full of contrition. It was due, he lamely apologized, not to his failure in preparing the elections, but to the abnormal influence of the clergy in his area.[3] This particular calumny on the clergy, one may note, was not perhaps altogether disinterested. The same governor had already been writing to Mordini about the 'material interests' which argued for the secularization of Church lands in Sicily.[4] Evidently the landowning class which was emerging with even greater strength from the revolution was already bent on making the most of its victory. The dissolution of the monasteries, and the sale at cheap prices of the nationalized ecclesiastical lands, was to be one of the most important factors in the growth of a newly-rich class after 1860.

La Farina at Turin was overjoyed at the results of the plebiscite. He interpreted them to mean that all Cavour's enemies in Sicily numbered less than one per cent of the people, including in this number Bourbonists, Papalists, separatists, autonomists, federalists and Mazzinians. 'It was a victory no less important and striking than that of Magenta

---

[1] 23 October, *La Forbice* (Palermo).   [2] 3 November, *Il Regno d' Italia*.
[3] 29 October, governor of Girgenti to Mordini (MRR).
[4] 20 October, governor of Girgenti to Mordini (AMB).

and Solferino.'[1] Mordini, however, somewhat naturally read the results in a different light, and was equally delighted that he had been able to follow public opinion and yet see Garibaldi's policy reconciled with that of Cavour, without bloodshed, and by means of a compromise formula that seemed so far to satisfy almost everyone. Some newspapers of the other party generously paid tribute to the prodictator for having followed public opinion as soon as ever it had decided for a plebiscite.[2] The civic council of Palermo had unanimously made him a citizen so that he should be able to head the vote himself. With justifiable pride he addressed to the people a public pronouncement after the results were known:

> Italy exists, and it has been created by the plebiscite.... One step more and we shall have a nation which will be strong and feared, protected by its girdle of Alpine frontiers. And then we shall see what can be done by the genius of a country which has already been mother to three civilizations.[3]

'Everyone has won and no one has lost', he said when thanking his ministers for their collaboration. 'If there is anything lacking it is only that time did not permit us to fulfil all the glorious mission left us by Garibaldi.'[4]

[1] 21 October and 28 October, *Il Piccolo Corriere d' Italia*, quoted in G. La Farina, *Scritti politici*, vol. II, pp. 345–6.

[2] 3 November, *La Perseveranza*, report from Palermo dated 27 October; 21 October, *Il Pungolo* (Naples), report from Palermo dated 18 October.

[3] 24 October, Mordini's printed proclamation (MRR).

[4] 22 October, Mordini to his ministers (MRR 221/23/9).

CHAPTER XXVI

THE DOUBTFUL SIGNIFICANCE
OF THE VOTE:
OCTOBER–NOVEMBER

The terms in which the plebiscite had been cast made it difficult to establish the precise significance of this overwhelming majority vote. Most of the leading political figures claimed for one reason or another to be more than satisfied with what had occurred, Garibaldi as well as Cavour, Mordini as well as La Farina. If what had been achieved was less than the radicals had hoped a month earlier, it was far more than might have been expected in May when they first conceived their outrageously daring expedition to the south. But this multiplicity of approval only serves to show how variously these results could be interpreted. Cavour was the man who had tried hardest to bring the plebiscite about, and his only concern had been to settle matters quickly by an impressive vote of whatever sort. He had not been able to consider whether, and if so how, he could also sound southerners about their more detailed wishes; because this would have added yet a further complication, and his other plans might well have collapsed under it. Hence his interpretation of this simple 'yes' and its significance had to be intuitive. Important consequences were soon to follow from the fact that his particular interpretation was not to be in all respects accurate or justifiable. It was easy enough to see that the vote signified a universal desire to return to peace and quiet and good governance. But beyond this point there were many varying reasons, both ideal and material, why different people should have wanted to put themselves under the constitutional monarchy of Piedmont-Sardinia.

It was a fair preliminary assumption that many people had voted consciously out of national sentiment. If the ordinary citizens of the south sometimes did not know what the word 'Italy' meant, the concept of national unity had at all events penetrated the *esprits forts*, the thinking and acting leaven of middle-class liberals who were such an initiating

force in the national movement. Crispi and La Farina were each at the
centre of a small and rival group of patriotic Sicilian intellectuals.
Something can be learnt from the fact that La Farina's *Credo Politico*,
written originally as a programme for the National Society several
years before, was specially republished in its eighth edition at Palermo
just before the vote took place. The intention was probably to instruct
Sicilians about what had been going on in the north during their years
of cultural and political isolation, and no doubt this publication was
meant to influence the plebiscite. La Farina in this essay gave as a
principal argument for national unification the economic and military
power which it would bring. A unified Italy would make possible more
government enterprise in economic affairs, a greater planned concentration of capital, a larger internal market, and the deliberate creation of
outlets for commerce abroad. This pamphlet thus twisted Mazzini's
mystical idea of unity almost out of recognition, infusing into it new
theories from the school of Friedrich List in Germany. But the particular twist was well calculated to attract a class of people hitherto
resistant to pure Mazzinianism. A new level of smaller and less hide-
bound landowners had appeared in the south since the 'abolition' of
feudalism and entails earlier in the century, and now formed an upper
middle class in the countryside which could appreciate the doctrines of
economic nationalism quite as well as could the merchants of Messina.
These landowners had good reason to hope that the anti-clerical government of Turin might secularize for their profit the enormous ecclesiastical estates, which for centuries had been growing ever larger in
mortmain on the close alliance of Church and State. In these and other
ways, the more politically important elements in Sicilian society would
see great material advantages in annexation. They stood to profit very
considerably from the paradoxical fact that annexation would give
them at once more political radicalism and more social conservatism
than they had known under the *ancien régime*. The poorer classes no
doubt would have much preferred the reverse combination of political
conservatism and social radicalism; but luckily the poor did not matter
so much, and had no adequate representation in Cavour's parliament.
It was important that the Italian radicals were politicians rather than
social reformers. Garibaldi in Sicily had, it is true, linked up his
movement with a peasants' revolt; but Garibaldi was primarily a

nationalist, and by August he had deliberately turned against his earlier allies as soon as he realized their divergence of aim. By that time the socially-conservative classes had also realized that to accept the national revolution might be the best means of retaining their status and improving their prosperity.

The affirmative vote was generally taken to be a vote for both nationalism and social conservation; but though this was technically correct, one significant qualification to this truth went unobserved, and certain dubious inferences were improperly drawn from it. The conservative newspapers had for tactical reasons laid undue stress on the half-truth that Mazzini was a social revolutionary. This had at least been effective in practice, for one Swiss observer noticed that 'la peur de Mazzini les a tous rendus emmanuélistes'.[1] But Cavour went yet further, and was remote enough from Sicily to ascribe the favourable vote in part to what he termed the fear of 'Garibaldianism'. This was a good deal less than a half-truth, and in practice it amounted to a major error of judgement. It contributed largely to the general misunderstanding at the time, and later to the selection of unsuitable treatment for the south. Other conservatives like Bonghi, who had been watching matters from closer at hand, recognized on the contrary that, if the *popolo minuto* was now beginning to conceive of Italy and national independence, this was simply due to Garibaldi and his enormous prestige.[2] Pasquale Mancini, the future foreign minister of the 1880's, was hardly a radical Garibaldian, but his diary in Naples at this time records one entry that, 'if the people now accept union with Piedmont, it is because Garibaldi wished it.... He could have proclaimed himself king like Masaniello.'[3] Depretis in parliament was bold to give Cavour the lie direct on this point, saying that 'in fact Garibaldi will turn out to have been the greatest annexationist of us all, since the annexation of half Italy we can consider his handiwork'; but the deputies listened to this contradiction of their cherished assumptions in a profound and sceptical silence.[4] A corroborative opinion came from the British minister at Naples. Elliot had for some time been saying that, without

[1] 16 October, Marc Monnier, *Garibaldi: histoire de la conquête des deux Siciles*, p. 361. [2] 9 October, *Il Nazionale*.

[3] 12 November, G. P. Mancini, *Impressioni e ricordi 1856–1864*, 1908, p. 177.

[4] 11 October, Depretis, *Atti Parlamentari*.

the enthusiasm generated by Garibaldi, Sicilians would have reverted to their 1812 constitution in preference to the Piedmontese *statuto*.[1] It was this same opinion of Elliot's about Garibaldi's influence which had converted Lord John Russell to believe in Italian nationalism, and thus had had a quite decisive effect just when France had been on the point of bringing the revolution to a stop. The radical Quadrio, indeed, took this argument so far as to make it a positive accusation against Garibaldi, on the grounds that he had prejudged and predisposed the future of Sicily by imposing annexation on the people through his dictatorial will.[2]

Cavour, on the other hand, continued to believe that Garibaldi had combated annexation, and hence that the plebiscite was a vote against the dictator and all his works. This in turn led him to imagine that public opinion would permit a completely intransigent attitude towards the radicals, and even that sternness would be welcomed. In what was taken to be an intentional snub he wrote to thank Pallavicino for these splendid results, implying that they were due to the prodictator and in spite of Garibaldi. For a brief moment after 22 October, when a sudden threat from Austria made him appreciate the need for national unity, he showed a kindlier attitude towards the volunteers and hinted that he might need their help in the north. But a few days later, as soon as Britain and France had guaranteed him from this particular danger, he was urging Farini to take a whip and 'throw them into the sea', to 'play the dictator in fact if not in name...and pitilessly sweep away the ordure left by Bertani in that stable'.[3] This was more than a lack of charity; it was a lack of common sense. Events were to show that Cavour did not possess adequate resources to subdue the south, and he might have been well advised to retain the volunteers as an auxiliary to help in keeping order and in assaulting Gaeta. Instead they were dissolved for what were essentially political reasons; and, being treated as a nuisance, they accordingly behaved as such.

Cavour made the excuse that the radicals were irreconcilable; but now that he had publicly announced his conversion to the doctrine of Italian unity, this was not true, and Cavour must have known it was

---

[1] 1 June, Elliot to Russell (F.O. 70/317/243).

[2] M. Quadrio, *Il libro dei mille del Generale Giuseppe Garibaldi*, 1879, p. 185.

[3] 2 November, Cavour to Farini (*CC Lib. del Mezz.* vol. III, p. 261); 3 November, Cavour to Farini (*ibid.* p. 275); *c.* 4 November, Cavour to Farini (*ibid.* p. 287).

not true. No effort was made to concede any substantial point to the dictator, and sometimes not even to show him the most elementary courtesies. Certainly Garibaldi replied churlishly, but it must be re-membered that he had just been called upon to surrender a life-long ambition. The radical leader was in any case known to be no politician, and to be rather a man who acted in temper and on impulse. This was the big difference between them. Garibaldi's bark was worse than his bite, and though he said ill-tempered things, still he told Mancini that Cavour should come south in preference to Farini.[1] This was not irreconcilability. But no concessions were made, and, as a result, in the next six months Garibaldi's petulant but justifiable irritation was to become a grave cause of weakness to the state. He would certainly have been a difficult person to deal with as a national figurehead, but he could have been invaluable in helping to rally the south during the testing period which lay ahead. The evidence suggests, however, that, Cavour did not think this worth the trouble. Indeed, he was ready to go to extraordinary lengths to avoid it. By deliberate calculation he did not want the radicals to have more status and influence in the new Italy than he could help. His information was that Gaeta would fall without much difficulty, and that the south was praying for the king to come and deliver them from a revolutionary dictatorship. He there-fore did not need Garibaldi's help, and yet would positively gain from his enmity. Cavour's political supporters in the south were now referring to Garibaldi as a 'beast' and a 'madman', and were going to all lengths so that Cavour should give no credit to their local enemies who had done so much more for the national cause than they. This sort of information and advice only influenced the northern government to mould its policy on the basis of a false premise.

Another false and dangerous assumption was that the almost unani-mous vote of the south signified a ready willingness to be absorbed into the northern kingdom. Here was plenty of scope for disagreement and misunderstanding. Cavour had purposely gone on using the word 'annexation', notably in his motion to parliament. Garibaldi had purposely preferred a more non-committal terminology. But however much care was taken over the exact wording of the plebiscite, the very fact that it was a plebiscite and not an assembly ruled out any subtleties

[1] 21 October, Mancini to Cavour (*ibid.* p. 161).

of differentiation and inference. Cavour therefore did not know how little expectation or desire there was in Sicily and Naples for a rigidly centralized administration under Turin. He had been told that much discussion was going on in the south about the future organization of the state, about where the national capital should be located and so forth;[1] but his own preoccupation was rather to see that such discussion was kept as subdued as possible. Perhaps he then became the victim of his own propaganda; for southerners were so convinced of his liberal sentiments that they trusted him, and as discussion never turned into agitation he was not fully aware of their strength of feeling.

One might say that the misunderstanding here was almost deliberately cultivated. The newspapers of Cavour's party in Sicily had always carefully avoided any hint of absorption of the south by the north, and had rather paid lip-service to the need for administrative devolution in the Italy that was to come.[2] When Farini, as minister for internal affairs at Turin, had been deputed by Cavour to work out an official statement of policy about local government, he had publicly recommended the devolution of power on to the historic regions of the peninsula, and the abandonment of the system of highly centralized departments hitherto practised in north Italy. Farini's statement of policy, seemingly so full of promise for the future, was expressly published at Palermo on 30 August, and Cordova had specially sent copies all through the interior of the island for the deliberate purpose of winning over the autonomists to the cause of annexation. A correspondent noted that 'the effect it made has been enormous....People here think that it must have been designed on purpose for Sicily, where more than anywhere else special insular conditions make us feel the need of an administrative autonomy for running internal affairs.'[3]

Another medium for the communication of these same sentiments had been the Sicilian Count Amari. This man technically held the post of Garibaldi's representative attached to the government of Cavour, though his politics and conduct in fact made him more representative of Cavour than of Garibaldi. At the end of August he was briefed by

[1] 21 October, Mancini to Cavour (*ibid.* p. 158).

[2] E.g. 28 June, *L' Annessione* (Palermo).

[3] 5 September, *La Perseveranza* prints a report from the Palermo correspondent of *L' Opinione* dated 31 August.

Cavour to pass on further hints to Sicily, and to say that as much regional autonomy would be allowed as was compatible with national unity. He wrote in this sense to his cousin, Professor Amari, who was then a minister in the government at Palermo: 'conclude the annexation at once and you will then receive everything you desire.'[1] The professor took him at his word, and based his campaign for the plebiscite on the assumption that Farini's scheme to set up distinct and autonomous regions in Italy was a foregone conclusion. He even was given to understand that there would be a special concession to Sicily of some political as well as administrative devolution, with the appointment of 'pseudo-ministères'; and it was said that 'Cavour, si je ne me trompe, est bien disposé à cela'.[2] In October Cavour was to write personally to the Sicilian General Carini with a gloss on this theme for him to publish: 'Sicily can count on my ministry to promote a system of wide administrative decentralization. The government will put before parliament its project to introduce this system of regions, and then it will be for parliament to push it through.'[3]

All this was good strategy—it would be wrong to call it simply a stratagem—if Cavour wanted to bring over to the cause of unqualified annexation men of autonomist inclinations. Even if he was sincere, however, this idea of local self-government was never much more for him than something speculative and theoretical, and once the immediate political advantage had been gained, it turned out that the cabinet was not sufficiently agreed to bring it anywhere near to practical application. Accordingly this scheme for dividing Italy into partially autonomous regions died before birth. Cavour had been well aware of its publicity value,[4] and some people had said from the start that the proposal was no more than 'a mere hoax to attract the public opinion of Naples and Sicily'.[5] At any rate there was a widespread misunderstanding about what he intended, and the extent of this misunderstanding is shown by the fact that even newspapers of Cavour's own party continued to

---

[1] 31 August, Count Amari to Professor Amari (*Carteggio di Amari*, ed. d'Ancona, vol. II, p. 130).

[2] 7 October, Professor Amari to Cartwright (*ibid.* p. 137).

[3] 24 October, *Il Regno d' Italia*, letter from Cavour dated 19 October.

[4] 29 August, Cavour to Nigra (*CC Cavour-Nigra*, vol. IV, p. 186).

[5] Cattaneo's magazine *Il Politecnico* (Milan), vol. IX, September 1860, p. 285.

insist on the necessity for some kind of local autonomy, being sincerely convinced that it was desirable.[1] The later policy of centralization, though it had some compensations, was taken by many people in the south to be both foolish and a breach of implied contract; and this assisted in giving the union a bad start. It all went back to the fact that annexation had to be carried through by plebiscite and not by assembly. Not only just the south, but the whole of Italy was to suffer for the vote having had to be taken under these pretences.

Palermo newspapers before the end of October already bore signs that there was misunderstanding about what had happened and what was going to happen. *La Valle di Giosaffat*, for instance, speaking for some of the moderate autonomists, still thought and hoped that an assembly was going to follow on after the plebiscite. This paper had opposed Mordini's government, and wanted a quick union with Piedmont, but it also warned Cavour not to take away from Sicily those institutions and privileges which even the Bourbons of Naples had not dared to touch. Although the thinking classes might believe liberty to be worth paying for, the common people 'understand nothing of liberty, just as they understand nothing about annexation'; and if they were now to find that they had to pay more taxes or had to depend on Turin for legal redress, they would revolt in a matter of months.[2] This was a frightening thought. Union with northern Italy had been put to the common people as an automatic solution to their troubles. Few of them had stopped to think, for instance, that 'Italy one and indivisible' might need an enormous government bureaucracy, and an astronomical

---

[1] E.g. 12 September, *Il Nazionale*. The doyen of Neapolitan exiles, Poerio, had told Hudson 'that the majority of their Countrymen will accept the Constitution with the Bourbons rather than lose what they call the *Autonomia Neapolitana*', 16 July, Hudson to Russell (RP G.D. 22/66). Elliot also had an interesting comment to Russell on 6 August: 'the most thinking people here, without being themselves favourable to [union], are almost all of opinion that it is not now possible to arrive at any solution without in the first place passing through the annexation which they believe will be found impracticable, and that the permanent arrangements will rise out of its ruins.... But the very softness of the Neapolitans, and their inability to make any effort by themselves to escape from a system they dislike, may perhaps be the means of the annexation going on longer than is expected even though the country is not satisfied' (RP G.D. 22/85).

[2] 27 October, *La Valle di Giosaffat*, report from Messina dated 22 October; 1 November, *ibid.*

expenditure on armaments and railways and the other appurtenances of a Great Power. No doubt there were many who stood to gain materially and at once from unification; but for the vast majority of southerners its first impact was to be a heavy increase in taxation and the cost of living, with little immediate and apparent gain therefrom. When one Sicilian in January 1861 was asked who Cavour was, the reply came that he was a cigar merchant who had increased the price of tobacco [1]—such was the first impression produced on one level of society by united Italy. For Cavour was not even going to wait for the relevant facts to be ascertained; he just assumed that, if the Genoese could pay taxes on a Piedmontese scale without rebellion, so could other Italians. [2] This was bad logic. Northerners could rarely get it out of their heads that 'Naples and Sicily were among the richest provinces of Italy', [3] and so a sad disillusionment was in store for both sides.

Another and more dreadful warning came from *Il Precursore*. 'If, Piedmont is deceiving us and forcing through a premature vote in order to make us subject to another province of Italy and not to a unified state, if she is going to treat us as a conquered people, applying to us her own inferior system of laws, then you may be sure that tomorrow the revolution will break out more violently than ever.' [4] This radical paper specifically claimed that the acceptance of the plebiscite by Turin constituted a bilateral contract: the wording of the plebiscite was significantly and designedly different from that used in Tuscany, and the vote had been cast in such terms that it would be invalidated by any failure on Cavour's side to place the acquisition of Rome in the forefront of his programme. [5] Crispi, whose mouthpiece this journal was, later embroidered the same theme in a letter to Mazzini:

The plebiscite of the Southerners did not signify the *annexation* of the former kingdom of Sicily to the Sardinian provinces, and even where this was implied, it did not mean that annexation was to be *immediate.*...The honest men of either party should have been satisfied, for all possibility either

[1]   3 January 1861, La Farina to Cavour (*CC Lib. del Mezz.* vol. IV).

[2]   30 October, Cavour to Valerio (*ibid.* vol. III, p. 232).

[3]   28 September, *La Gazzetta del Popolo* (Turin); 9 December, Cassinis to Cavour: 'this island is the paradise of Italy...an eternal spring...immense wealth...' (*CC Lib. del Mezz.* vol. IV).

[4]   25 October, *Il Precursore* (F. Lo Presti).   [5]   21 November, *ibid.*

of federation or of a republic was thus excluded. Meanwhile, as the means by which union was to be achieved could not be established by direct suffrage, this must be done by the Assemblies. Those who were opposed to the Assemblies either did not understand the decree of October 8, or wilfully misinterpreted its meaning. Consequently the ministers at Turin were entrusted with a mission that should have been fulfilled by the local parliaments.[1]

Another paper, *L'Unità Italiana*, though it had recommended people to vote 'yes', maintained all the same that one could vote thus and still expect a later constituent assembly to model a fundamental constitution for the Italian kingdom.[2] This journal had supported annexation pure and simple, but had also assumed that the acquisition of Rome would sooner or later demand the convention of an assembly where the old Piedmontese *statuto* could be debated and if necessary modified.[3] Just before the plebiscite was held, it printed a statement from the former minister Guarneri, saying: 'I shall vote for annexation, but only on the understanding that the plebiscite will determine the *time* and not the *method* of our merger into the Italian state.'[4] Of course no such private interpretation was in any way binding on the new rulers of Italy, and probably they would have looked upon this statement as belonging to a lunatic fringe beyond the bounds of respectable political intercourse. In any case they knew of many counter-arguments in favour of making the process of unification as quick and simple as possible, and it might have seemed a fair gamble that, so doing, things would probably turn out for the best. There was, however, a price to be paid for speed and convenience. The idea was beginning to gain currency that the Piedmontese had all along in this year acted with a disingenuous and Machiavellian lack of frankness, and that one of their chief aims from the start had been to exploit national feeling simply for purposes of provincial self-aggrandizement.[5] This thought did not help to reconcile the different sections of the nation to each other.

[1] 18 March 1865, Crispi to Mazzini (Crispi, *Memoirs*, vol. I, p. 447).
[2] 20 and 25 October, *L' Unità Italiana* (Palermo).
[3] 23 August, *ibid.*   [4] 20 October, *ibid.*
[5] E.g. 26 October, Mérimée from Paris to Panizzi: 'les Piémontais...ont manqué à toutes les conventions politiques, à tous les principes internationaux, et ce qui à mes yeux est le pire, c'est qu'ils n'ont jamais agi avec franchise' (*Il Risorgimento Italiano*, April 1920, p. 181); E. Cenni, *Napoli e l' Italia: considerazioni*, 1861, p. 77; C. Baldi, *Breve studio sulla letteratura storica-politica del risorgimento italiano 1860–1*, 1907, p. 63.

This was the start of plentiful misunderstanding on both sides, and suspicion and mistrust were not long in germinating. On 16 October Professor Amari had written to ask the prodictator for an *ad hoc* council to consider the peculiar interests of Sicily. As Amari had fought hard for the plebiscite and on behalf of unconditional annexation, no one could call him partisan, he said; and yet here he was, acting on the conviction that the new government in the north would make special arrangements for the island, and hence that an advisory body should be appointed.[1] This preliminary council at Palermo would perform one function of the representative assembly about which so much had been spoken; but as it would be advisory only, and in no sense a constituent body, Amari thought that the government of Turin would look upon it as an acceptable compromise which did not derogate from parliamentary sovereignty. On 19 October this council was duly appointed, two days before the plebiscite took place, and no doubt this appointment must have had an important effect in reassuring the voters that Cavour's undertaking about decentralized government was receiving serious consideration. When the vote was over, however, it gradually became clear that Cavour was adamant against anything which savoured in the very least of a representative assembly, because he feared that this would favour those autonomists or radicals who wanted to call his system in question. He was quite ready for Sicilian members to attend the parliament at Turin, where tempers were cooler, the environment more inhibiting, where old traditions of thought and behaviour were stronger, and where straightforward annexation would be defended by a comfortable ministerial majority. But a purely Sicilian body meeting in Palermo was obviously dangerous, and if Sicilians had not taken this point already, so much the worse for them. Perhaps Cavour did not properly appreciate that, intentionally or unintentionally, most of those who voted had not been allowed to know what the vote was really about. The Marquis di Rudinì had just been persuading his fellow Sicilians to approve unconditional annexation on grounds which now almost seem like deliberate deceit—namely that regional self-government could not be denied by Piedmont, and that the word of Victor Emanuel was pledged on this point.[2] The process of deception then came full circle;

[1] 16 October, Professor Amari to Mordini (AMB, b. 30).
[2] 16 October, *Il Plebiscito*, article by di Rudinì.

for Cavour did not appreciate that the docility of the south was something artificial, and he therefore based his policy on the assumption that no special concessions were needed. People's memories in politics are short, and these intimations and half-promises were forgotten as the centralistic implications of 'unconditional annexation' gradually became evident. Amari's council of state duly published a report in November,[1] but its recommendations were discarded with contumely by Cavour. Sicilian autonomy was hardly thought of again as a practical proposition until eighty-five years had gone by.

One cannot say that everyone was completely taken by surprise. On 25 October the British consul at Palermo, Goodwin, prosily remarked that 'the step taken by the Sicilians in annexing their island to the Italian States without limit or condition is a leap in the dark fraught peradventure with serious consequences'.[2] The leading radicals and autonomists were already aware, before the vote was taken, that they had been beaten. 'Cavour has won', lamented *L' Unità Italiana* of Genoa: 'the first act of the drama ended at Villafranca, the second is now ending at Naples. God help Italy!'[3] The southern radicals saw that they were being tricked into a sham plebiscite in which their real views could have no expression, and in which their wish for national unification forced them to vote for annexation to Piedmont. 'Instead of a free vote by the flower of our best citizens, it has been decided to consult that of the multitude, ignorant and easily influenced';[4] and yet, 'if we are given simply the alternative of Francesco II or Victor Emanuel, there cannot be much doubt about our choice'.[5]

This was precisely Mazzini's position. Mazzini had recognized since the beginning of October that 'the great majority of the country has spoken now clearly enough that monarchy will be chosen as the way to unity; and there is nothing bad in bowing to the national will, save to try gently to modify and transform it'.[6] He would have preferred the continuance of dictatorial rule until the unification of Italy was

---

[1] 18 November (AMB, b. 30)
[2] 25 October, Goodwin to Russell (F.O. 165/134).
[3] 17 October, *L' Unità Italiana* (Genoa).
[4] 19 October, *Il Pungolo* (Naples), letter by Ricciardi.
[5] 22 October, *L' Indipendente* (Naples).
[6] *c.* 6 October, Mazzini to Emilie Venturi (*Epistolario*, vol. XLI, p. 136).

26-2

complete; and once this course had been rejected, he would still have preferred an assembly to a plebiscite, or would have welcomed both together if necessary. The simple plebiscite by itself he disliked. A blind vote without prior discussion was open to great abuse. It had, for example, been the method used by Napoleon to legitimize his *coup d'état*. The very fact that a different method was chosen from that used in Tuscany and Emilia was as much as to say that citizens of southern Italy were inferior to those of the centre, and it would thus offend their dignity. It would also suppress any free expression of views in the south on whether annexation should be immediate or conditional. There was no logic in barring an assembly in the south, when at the same time the deputies at Turin had been able to debate at length in *their* assembly whether and on what terms to accept this annexation. Mazzini made his protest, but he then advised everyone to vote, and to vote 'yes', so as to obtain an enormous majority for submission to Victor Emanuel. He even told the republicans, or those of them who were not specifically bound by public pledges, that they must campaign actively for the monarchy.[1]

The radicals were more or less reconciled to defeat. They had tried their hardest to force a revolutionary policy on Piedmont, and had succeeded better than all but the most sanguine among them could have hoped. They now realized that surrender was their wisest and most patriotic course, and after 15 October they gradually split up or returned into exile. It was as well for Italy that they did so, for if the revolutionary government had not surrendered over the plebiscite issue, Farini was intending to march in to Naples against them,[2] and this would irreparably have turned Left against Right, south against north. Cattaneo returned to Lombardy even before the vote was held, inveighing against 'the king of Turin' for having imposed centralization on a country which, far more than most others, was adapted to federalism. Bertani and Mauro Macchi, when they voted in parliament for Cavour's law of annexation, had been secretly praying that Crispi would somehow still avert or postpone its application; but then Crispi had been defeated by Pallavicino, and had left his post in Garibaldi's government. After

[1] 19 October, *Il Popolo d' Italia* (Naples), quoted in Mazzini, *Scritti politici*, ed. naz., vol. XXIII, pp. 278–80.

[2] 12 October, Farini to Cavour (*CC Lib. del Mezz.* vol. III, p. 93).

this it was difficult for the extreme Left to rediscover a distinctive and practical opposition policy. There was some hope that Crispi and Mordini would manage to spend their last days of office setting aside a large sum of money for the 'party of action'.[1] The radicals badly needed money, for they had exhausted their resources over the Sicilian expedition, and wanted to restock so that their journals could be revived and their election fund refurbished. As soon as Bertani saw his olive branch scorned by the deputies in parliament, he had become hard and unyielding once more, and soon was again suggesting that Garibaldi should retire to Sicily and keep his army intact there for some new venture.[2] He sometimes wondered whether Garibaldi, Mazzini and Cattaneo could not somehow be persuaded to see eye to eye, and in this way perhaps Italian politics could be brought to life again.[3] In the meantime there was no denying that Cavour had momentarily recovered his popularity by the invasion of central Italy, and the opposition would therefore have to wait until he came to debate the difficult problems of internal reorganization before they could hope to detach part of his majority and encompass his defeat.[4]

Garibaldi remained the chief hope of the 'party of action'. For nearly three weeks after the plebiscite he continued to rule in Naples and Sicily, until the king could arrive and the certified results of the vote could be formally presented. The dictator's actions continued to prove that he was no would-be Caesar. He did not try to make political capital out of the grievances of the south or of his volunteer army. He confirmed the moderates in office, and did what he could to see that the king took over a working administration. If he fell short on this last task it was due in part to his own incapacity for administration, in part to his concentration upon the war effort, but perhaps even more to the way he was being called upon to surrender his power. Pallavicino's victory over Crispi deprived his government of its most energetic man, and the political defeat of the radicals took away much of the original

---

[1] 30 September, Bertani to Mordini (ACP, b. 135); 4 October, Asproni from Turin to Crispi (ACP, f. 138; not given in the published version of Crispi's *Memoirs*).

[2] 25 October, Bertani to Garibaldi (copy in ABCM).

[3] 24 March 1861, Bertani to Garibaldi (ACM, no. 1512).

[4] 15 October, *Il Pungolo* (Naples), report from Turin dated 12 October.

excitement and enthusiasm which had attended his movement. As the vision of a march on Rome faded away, so the volunteers realized that they had little left to fight for; and as morale cracked, so desertions multiplied. Such a scratch army as this was no good for defence, but had only been successful when it had a goal and a triumphant sense of mission. Neapolitans knew that Victor Emanuel was coming soon with a different programme, and this was the most important factor in bringing governmental activity to a standstill. Many people did not want to be compromised in the eyes of Cavour by gratuitously serving the dictator. And the result was a virtual interregnum. Since there were three separate governments ruling in different parts of the *regno*, the populace was just waiting for one to overcome the others and restore the land to peace and normality.

In these three weeks anarchy spread contagiously, and early signs of a Bourbon counter-revolution began to appear in every province from Calabria to the Abruzzi. Garibaldi was waiting to submit his powers to the king, but unfortunately the king had to delay his arrival. The Piedmontese did not want it to be thought that the plebiscite had been influenced by the presence of northern bayonets. They were anxious not to occupy too much Neapolitan territory before the attested results of the vote had proved their right to annex the south. For this reason, and even more because General Fanti did not want to inflate Garibaldi's prestige any further, the seven thousand Piedmontese soldiers at Naples were not yet permitted to aid the volunteers attacking Capua, even when the latter were in trouble.[1] Another reason why the king delayed his arrival was because, on Fanti's advice, he wanted to enter Naples only when he had shown his mettle in some signal feat of arms against the Bourbons.[2] Once he had staked his reputation on this, even Cavour had to agree that it would be undignified to invite comparison with the dictator until he had some success to his credit. Naples was therefore left in a state of uncertainty. The point was eventually reached where this was called deliberate policy, an attempt to show up Garibaldi's regime as a symbol of anarchy.

[1] 17 October, Farini to Cavour (*CC Lib. del Mezz.* vol. III, p. 131); 18 October, Persano to Cavour (*ibid.* p. 137).

[2] 27 October, Farini to Cavour (*ibid.* pp. 207–8); 31 October, Farini to Cavour (*ibid.* p. 239).

Farini, whom Cavour had designated to be the future 'dictator' of Naples, by now knew more or less about the troubles which lay ahead of him. 'The reputation of our government is at stake: if we fail to set up an honest and strong rule at Naples we shall be jeered throughout Europe.'[1] His first impression of the Neapolitans was not flattering, and compared unfavourably with Garibaldi's. As he wrote to tell Cavour, they were barbarians who cared little for liberty: 'the country here is not Italy but Africa, and the bedouin are the flower of civic virtue when compared to these people.'[2] This was not a hopeful commencement to annexation. But the diplomatic difficulties in sight were perhaps even more alarming still. While the king was slowly marching through the Abruzzi, ingratiating himself by the distribution of medals to the local notables and endowments to the churches, Cavour was seriously perturbed between 20 and 30 October by the diplomatic congress of Warsaw, where Austria had hoped to turn Europe against Italy. Another disaster was that, on 26 October, Louis Napoleon put his veto on Persano's naval blockade of Gaeta, and this at once became a serious impediment to the national forces. It was a more hopeful sign when, on the same day, Garibaldi advanced to welcome the king in person and to make arrangements for the transference of power. By the end of the month the danger threatening from Warsaw also turned out to have been more in apprehension than reality. The volunteers and regulars were then allowed to combine in the final assault on Capua; and when this fortress fell on 2 November, the king could at last turn his face towards Naples.

The concluding days of October had inevitably witnessed some intensification of party differences, with all the personal intrigue and jostling for place which Garibaldi found so distasteful, and to which he was so unequal. When he heard that his successor was to be none other than the detested Farini, he had at first made up his mind to leave Naples before the northern troops arrived.[3] But sensibly he gave way to

---

[1] 13 October, Farini to Guglianetti (*ibid.* p. 102).

[2] 17 October, Farini to Cavour (*ibid.* pp. 131–2); 27 October, Farini to Cavour (*ibid.* pp. 207–8); cf. 29 October, Garibaldi to Victor Emanuel, where he describes the Neapolitans as intelligent, docile and self-sacrificing, and full of good will (*ibid.* p. 224).

[3] 21 October, Mancini to Cavour (*ibid.* pp. 160–1).

entreaties that his own popularity should not be dissociated from the new regime in this difficult moment of transition. The general's popularity was still enormous among the common people.[1] At the special instance of the king, the dictator therefore entered the city in the same carriage with Victor Emanuel himself. On 8 November he officially handed over his power. His last request of the king was to be allowed to stay on in the south as viceroy with ample powers instead of Farini, using his influence there to tide over the difficult period of unification; but the king said he must first consult with Farini, and of course the proposal was then turned down as quite incompatible with the triumph of liberal-conservatism.[2] All they could offer him were things that he did not want and which he refused, money, titles, a castle, and even a private steamer for his own use. Farini boasted that, in the course of these delicate exchanges, he personally had never once spoken to Garibaldi, nor even so much as looked him in the face.[3] The whole situation was a little unreal; and what should have been a triumphant climax to six months' valiant effort turned out to be an anti-climax, slightly sour and graceless.

The time had come for Garibaldi to leave southern Italy. If he was sorry about anything, it was chiefly that he had not been able to bestow Rome as well as Naples and Sicily upon his sovereign. He was also, and forgivably, a little sorry for himself. As he sadly remarked to the Piedmontese admiral, 'this is what happens, Persano, they just treat men like oranges, pressing out the juice to the last drop, and throwing the peel away into a corner'.[4] The king offered to make him a full general, but he answered that he had not come to Sicily to make his career, and the notice of his appointment was crumpled up and thrown out of the window. There was still other work for him to do with the volunteers. He had given his promise not to retire into respectable idleness until Italy was a great nation,[5] and was determined that there should be no more than a temporary hiatus in the revolution. Mazzini tells how he

[1] 4 November, E. Maison, *Journal d'un volontaire de Garibaldi*, 1861, p. 193.

[2] E. Della Rocca, *Autobiografia di un veterano*, vol. II, 1898, pp. 96–7.

[3] 14 November, Farini to Cavour (*CC Lib. del Mezz.* vol. III, p. 324).

[4] 8 November, Persano, *Diario 1860–1*, part IV, p. 119.

[5] 29 September, Garibaldi's speech at Caserta (*Edizione nazionale degli scritti di Garibaldi*, vol. IV, p. 310).

went to see the retiring dictator before he departed, and how they discussed whether there was any means of overthrowing Cavour during the winter months and then proceeding to the redemption of Venice.[1] On one point Garibaldi felt certain, that he ought to retain his freedom of action for another military campaign in the spring of 1861, and his farewell proclamation to the volunteers accordingly warned them to be ready again at any moment.[2] Frequent private and public references to another movement in preparation for March 1861 suggest that he may have mentioned this date to the king and not been discouraged. The national revolution was everything to him, domestic politics in themselves were nothing—this was where he chiefly differed from the politicians of Turin. As he said, 'it does not matter to me if the prime minister be called Cavour or Cattaneo (though far better the second), so long as on 1 March 1861 Victor Emanuel shall be found at the head of five hundred thousand soldiers'.[3]

When on 9 November Garibaldi quietly left with his bag of seedcorn for the lonely island of Caprera, the moment had come when Cavour could set about curing the last symptoms of 'the Garibaldian disease'. The calling of parliament had already effected a cure in the north. It was obvious that the south would need a longer time to forget and recover. Cavour had the option of killing by kindness, that is to say of neutralizing opposition by winning over the radicals and autonomists he had just outplayed. But instead he decided that Garibaldi had to be reduced by all possible means to life-size, so that the legend of his success and his benevolence should be forgotten. Hoping to smooth over the transition, the *Giornale Officiale* kept silence on Garibaldi's departure for several days. In another unfortunate display of bad manners, the king had called the volunteers out for a special inspection but then omitted to turn up himself. Farini expressly forbad the singing of Garibaldi's hymn, and when he came to assume officially the position of viceroy, he too made no mention of his predecessor. It was all of a piece that the city of Turin, when it summoned citizens to celebrate the fall of Capua, did not think fit to refer to such a dangerous

[1] 8 November, Mazzini to Caroline Stansfeld (*Epistolario*, vol. XLI, pp. 184–5).
[2] G. Bandi, *I mille*, 1903, p. 339.
[3] 28 November, Garibaldi from Caprera (*Edizione nazionale degli scritti di Garibaldi*, vol. IV, p. 337).

and despicable character;[1] nor did the parliamentary deputation mention his name when they carried their official congratulations to Naples and Sicily on the revolution just completed.[2] In sum this amounted to more than mere bad manners, it was calculated policy. Garibaldi had shown himself at his best when he went into retirement, and his successors appeared gauche and clumsy in comparison.

[1]   6 November, *Il Diritto* (Turin), pointing out that this was noticeably different from the practice at Milan.

[2]   Ed. De Vecchi, *Le carte di Giovanni Lanza*, vol. II, pp. 175–7.

CHAPTER XXVII

CAVOUR'S GOVERNMENT IN THE SOUTH: NOVEMBER–DECEMBER

Despite many forebodings in the south, Cavour convinced himself that compromise would now be undignified, unnecessary and even unwise. Michele Amari's council of state made a report on the special needs and interests of Sicily, and the report was signed by twenty-three respectable and even prominent people; but its suggestions could by no means be accepted, for it was assumed that they threatened to question the whole system of centralized monarchy. Cavour was too busy to have enough time left over for affairs in Sicily, and in any case the absence of the king and some of the ministers in southern Italy for nearly three months meant that no new departure in policy could easily be considered. The prime minister had to concern himself far more with the opposition of those who championed 'little Piedmont' than with those who wanted a 'little Sicily'; and for domestic consumption in Turin he therefore had to gild the merger of Piedmont into greater Italy by stressing that it was just another annexation in the 'artichoke' tradition of Piedmontese aggrandizement. Another difficulty was that any special concession to the south might upset the process of levelling out between one region and another, and so might damage the delicate plant of nationalism before it was strong enough to fend for itself. Safer far to graft the new provinces on to the old, imposing on them common institutions and so far as possible a common way of life which had already been found to be both tough and broadly acceptable. The only alternative would have been to allow a constituent assembly to recast the very fundamentals of the state; and this would be dangerous, and possibly also impracticable. It had to be 'annexation' and not 'fusion', for this first word signified that Italy was no new creation, but a development and projection of that virile subalpine kingdom which had contributed much the largest share to the national cause.[1] As a demonstration of this, although the existence

[1] 27 September, *La Perseveranza*, answering *Il Nazionale* of Naples.

of a kingdom of Italy could now be proclaimed, Victor Emanuel was declared to be not the *first* but still the *second* of that name. The new parliament was to rank eighth and not first in the official calendar. Cavour had formally stated that he would accept only unconditional annexation, and he consistently maintained that the plebiscite gave him the unqualified submission which he had required. Notwithstanding all the hopes of Sicilians and the hints given earlier from the north, Piedmont was in fact going to impose her institutions; just as if, despite the modified formula of the plebiscite, it was really an 'annexation', and as if the revolution of Sicily had been all along a 'conquest'. Cavour could at least argue in self-justification that some intelligent Sicilians preferred this.

Possibly this was the only policy which in the circumstances could have succeeded at all. It was not only that Piedmont had sacrificed her men and money most liberally for the common cause, but she was also, of all the five main states in Italy the one with the hardiest political life and traditions; and this must in any case have given her a dominant part to play. What could be objected to was less the fact of her hegemony than its manner, and in particular the ostentatious insistence that the south was a backward and primitive region which would have to be 'piedmontized' for its own good. A prevalent assumption in Turin now made out that Naples was rotten 'jusqu'à la moelle des os',[1] and was the worst country in Europe for 'weakness, vice and filth'.[2] Nature was said to have endowed the south liberally as a Garden of Eden, but only to have these natural endowments squandered by a feckless and irresponsible population. This was an astonishing misconception, and a highly dangerous one. People could in all seriousness speak of how 'with our strength, our greater courage, our superior intelligence and morality, with our experience and character, we shall be able to govern and to tame' the south.[3] Even if there was some truth in this basic assumption, it was not always very tactfully expressed, and its authors were often blinded by this self-satisfaction to a correct view

[1] 30 November, Cavour's words quoted by Hudson to Russell (RP G.D. 22/66).

[2] December, diary of General Solaroli at Naples with the king (*CC Lib. del Mezz.* vol. v).

[3] 6 November, Pantaleoni from Rome to Cavour (*CC La Questione Romana*, vol. i, p. 70).

of other things. Furthermore, if the south was after all so backward, why then was it not accorded special laws and specially kind and liberal consideration?

One example of this lack of tact may be found in the letters of the minister of justice at Turin. They show that he knew nothing of southern law codes—one thing upon which Neapolitans especially prided themselves—and yet he had already secured in October a cabinet decision that Piedmontese laws should as a matter of principle be introduced at once. There was no idea even of waiting until parliament could meet and debate such a measure. On the contrary, it ·was intentionally calculated to present the deputies with a *fait accompli*, so as to escape unwelcome discussion and not to waste parliamentary time on trivialities. There was little appreciation that it might be better to graft with care, and not to try and impose new growth too radically on old stock. There was no suggestion even of holding an inquest by experts to see what could or should be done, and how best to set about it. The one doubt of the minister of justice was whether the south was sufficiently advanced for the introduction of juries:[1] he thought probably not. In other words, the south had the worst of both worlds. She was going to be despised and resented as a depressed area, but without receiving the specially favourable attention which she needed and had been promised, without being cushioned against the impact of a new free-trade world in the north, without being allowed special laws and institutions which might have been more suitable to her experience and capabilities.

Such 'piedmontization', as it was already being called with derogatory implication, may have been in substance legitimate;[2] but it was too suddenly and too universally introduced, it ignored the human element, overstressing symmetry and rounded edges, and assuming that society could easily be taken apart and put together again. By a piece of political sentimentalism, these important geographic, economic and moral disparities were sometimes treated as non-existent, though it was upon them that this self-conscious superiority had first been based, People were torn up by the roots, and then it was wondered why they

[1] 30 October, Cassinis from Turin to Mancini (Archivio Mancini MRR).
[2] B. Croce, *Pagine Sparse*, vol. II, 1943, p. 110; G. Racioppi, *Storia dei moti di Basilicata e delle provincie contermini nel 1860*, 1910, p. 321.

wilted in the glorious release which liberal Piedmont was meant to be bringing them. This was a policy which seemed to grow up empirically and almost by accident. In fact it arose naturally from the attitude of mind with which northerners approached the 'Augean stable', as d'Azeglio called the south; and it contributed its share to the unbalance which has affected Italian life ever since.

Cavour was wont to call the radicals doctrinaire and revolutionary, but they were not so doctrinaire as this, nor so revolutionary. His chief article of attack against his political enemies was precisely that upon which his own system turned out to be most vulnerable. Mazzini knew more than Cavour about the south, and had a better opinion of southerners. He knew that they were ill-educated and inevitably un-practised in honest self-government, but he acted on the assumption that their instincts were good and that they had at least something to teach the rest of Italy. The federalists, too, were not after all so very unpractical by comparison. One of Cattaneo's favourite themes, and one which bolstered his belief in regional devolution, was that any change of law or custom was wrong if made just for the sake of uniformity or administrative convenience; such a change would break with tradition and thereby inflict a wound which would not heal. Cattaneo believed that Italy could not help but be many societies as well as one society. Local differences had been so deeply embedded in Italian life since the Middle Ages, that in 1860 even the volunteer units from neighbouring towns like Florence, Pisa and Leghorn were on occasion at odds through municipal jealousies;[1] and the feeling of Sicily against Naples had overridden all class barriers and political divisions to make one of the most fundamental motives in the national revolution. Cattaneo accepted such provincial feelings and tried to make the best of them. Cavour's government rather tried to pretend that they did not exist, or at least that they could be suppressed and then ignored with impunity. But, so treated, they were only driven into subversive channels.

Many susceptibilities were offended by the insensitive and high-handed treatment which was sometimes allotted to the rest of Italy by the Piedmontese. Some people—and not only Tuscans—were, for instance, convinced that Florence would make a better capital of Italy

[1] 16 August, police report (BR ASF, b. P, f. A).

than Turin, whether on political, strategic, historical or cultural grounds.[1] Piedmont was perhaps the least Italian among Italian provinces, her dialect was remote from classical Italian, members of her ruling classes (including both Cavour and the king) still spoke French or *patois* for preference, and her history was transalpine as much as cisalpine. Some southerners thought that there were 'invincible arguments' for having the capital city at Naples, since this was far the largest city in the peninsula and strategically much better placed than Turin.[2] Each of the main regions of the peninsula had its own local patriotism, and not least Piedmont itself. By the end of October Ricasoli was feeling that only the speedy acquisition of Rome would make Italy a nation; for 'otherwise the scandalous Piedmontese bureaucracy will impel us to another revolution to get rid of a yoke which I find more antipathetic than the Austrian. They will not believe that we want to be Italians and have an Italian soul rather than be automatons on their model.'[3] It is astonishing that so much ill will as this should have been so quickly generated, especially as Ricasoli was next in importance after Cavour himself inside the moderate-conservative party. Again, when Cavour anticipated the plebiscite by issuing decrees for 'those provinces not yet annexed', Sicilians pointed out very pertinently that this was gratuitous regional arrogance, and that the form of vote said nothing of annexation and nothing of Piedmont or Sardinia, but only of union with Italy. 'So which are these provinces "not yet annexed"? Does he mean the Romagna, or Venice, or even Piedmont itself?...His decree is in fact premature and illegal, and is bound to offend people; it represents the action not of a friendly government, but of a party out at all costs to overthrow another.'[4]

The clash of interest between north and south was seen clearly when Professor Amari, who earlier in the year had been persuaded by Cavour that Sicily would receive regional self-government, approached the prime minister for his bond. 'Regional councils are indispensable for the conduct of local affairs', said Amari, and 'it would be a mistake to

[1] M. d'Azeglio, *Questioni urgenti*, 1861; Palmerston and Prince Napoleon also advised this.

[2] E. Cenni, *Napoli e l' Italia: considerazioni*, pp. 92 ff.

[3] 28 October, Ricasoli to Silvestrelli (*Carteggio di Ricasoli*, ed. Nobili and Camerani).

[4] 1 November, *L' Unità Italiana* (Palermo).

think that local "self-government" was not useful and even necessary for Italians.'[1] But an unexpectedly discouraging reply came to this appeal. 'Cavour could not allow that Sicily should have any elective and deliberative council.'[2] Here was an unexpected change of temper. One interesting point about it is that Cavour had only just received confirmation from one of his own cabinet colleagues that 'autonomism' was the prevailing sentiment in both Sicily and Naples.[3] It may be, that is to say, that he now thought his earlier intentions were probably too dangerous to carry out. Whatever the reason for it, a similar change in the same direction is noticeable in *L'Opinione*, the paper in which Cavour's private views were usually seen. In September this paper had been writing about the special need of Sicily for regional autonomy. But by December, when the plebiscite had been fought and won, it was calling decentralization just a temporary expedient: 'we are admirers of the strong, unifying system of France, even though we do not think, it would be possible to introduce this in Italy all at once. Our provincial traditions are too strong for us to cancel them in the space of a few months.'[4]

For all their protests, the statesmen of northern Italy do seem to have found much to admire in French administrative practice, and history was to show that in practice their policy was to compel the south into their centralized system. Hints continued to be dropped that, when passions had cooled and present problems had been settled, it might become possible to introduce 'a real regional self-government';[5] yet Cavour's mature wish, it appears, was not for as much regional

---

[1] 19 December, Professor Amari to Count Amari (*Carteggio di Amari*, ed. d'Ancona, vol. II, p. 144).

[2] 16 December, Count Amari to Professor Amari (*ibid.* p. 141).

[3] 9 December, Cassinis from Palermo to Cavour (*CC Lib. del Mezz.* vol. IV).

[4] 13 December, *L'Opinione*; for the link between this paper and Cavour see L. Chiala, *Giacomo Dina e l'opera sua nelle vicende del risorgimento italiano*, especially vol. I, 1896, p. 321.

[5] 15 January 1861, Cavour to Montezemolo: 'we are in favour of decentralization; our political ideas do not allow that a capital city should tyrannize over the provinces; nor will we tolerate a bureaucracy that subdues every part of the realm to an artificial centre, and against which both our national traditions and our geographic conformation would be in conflict. I hope that when quiet times return...we shall be able to concede a real regional *self-government*' (Bollea, *Una silloge di lettere*, pp. 423–4).

devolution as was consistent with unity, but rather for as much centralization as he could possibly achieve over the inherent municipalism or *campanilismo* of the Italian people. He believed in a strong Italy. Cabinet policy continued to be to impose as much as possible of Piedmontese laws on the south before parliament could meet and question the process;[1] and when Amari protested that this was illegal, the bald answer was shamelessly given in public that 'the action of the government must not be judged by the rigid criterion of what was legal, only by what was expedient in the circumstances'.[2] When parliament met and Ferrari rose to put forward his scheme for a radical reorganization of the state by large concessions of local autonomy, he was three times called to order on the grounds that 'the integrity of the kingdom of Italy cannot be discussed'.[3] This particular issue had already been settled out of court, and without even hearing what the defendant had to say.

The process of 'piedmontization' was in the long run to do much good as well as harm in the south, for Piedmont had much to teach other provinces in the way of honest administration. But the new government was overconscious of this fact, and did not also realize that it might have something to learn. The dominant class in the south was one of landowners, tenacious of privilege and tradition, who were quick to resent this narrow, unsympathetic, unimaginative bureaucracy clamped down on them, with its rigid rules of behaviour, and inability to adapt itself to a new *milieu* with a different culture and different values. Such as they were, the benefits of the new system were slow to sink downwards, whereas its weak points were obvious at once.

It would enlarge too much the scope of this work to discuss in any detail the years of emergency government in the south after November 1860, with all the various political experiments and expedients which were tried in turn to help assimilate the south into the northern system. Many reputations were ruined in the process, thousand of lives were lost, a large-scale, cruelly-fought and protracted civil war had to be endured, harsh and illiberal laws had to be applied; and it was all only

---

[1] 30 January 1861, Cassinis, minister of justice, to Mancini (Archivio Mancini MRR).
[2] 5 April 1861, Amari and Cassinis, *Atti Parlamentari*.
[3] 4 April 1861, *Atti Parlamentari*.

partially successful, because Naples and Sicily still obstinately continued in many of their own ways, and any gains had to be set off against the growth of bitter feelings between north and south. The development of a 'southern question' in Italy is a history all of its own. But the first few months of Cavour's government constitute an important chapter in the story, as well as providing an illuminating epilogue to the history of Garibaldi's dictatorship. Many of the arguments used against Garibaldi's 'incompetence' and 'tyranny' are put into a better perspective when viewed alongside the later conduct of his very critics. For those same critics proved to be equally incompetent and even more tyrannical when they came to tackle the same problems, though they were far cleverer men than he, and had far greater resources, as well as having the benefit of his own earlier experience to guide them. Some additional light is also thrown by this epilogue upon the plebiscite itself, on its significance, on the motives behind the affirmative vote, and on the whole issue of whether a plebiscite was so much more suitable than an assembly. Not many days went by after 21 October 1860 before the ninety-nine per cent majority for 'annexation' began to look very dubious.

Luigi Carlo Farini, whom the king took to Naples with him as his viceroy, did not last in office as long as Garibaldi had done, and his period of government was inglorious as it was brief. Like other northerners, he came full of confidence that he knew the answers better than Garibaldi and Crispi; but after only a few hours of personal acquaintance with southern problems he began to fear that this would be the tomb of his political reputation.[1] He arrived with no set policy, and was overtaken by disaster before he had really decided what he intended to do. At first he gave out hopefully that his government would be one of concord, but when it came to deeds he showed that his set policy was precisely the reverse. The most influential, and apparently the most popular, man in Naples was Liborio Romano[2] a *camorrista* who successfully managed to serve Francesco, Garibaldi and Cavour in turn; and Romano squarely blamed the returned exiles for having given Farini the wrong advice. In their stay at Turin and

---

[1] 10 November, Farini to Cassinis (CF).

[2] In the elections of February 1861, Liborio Romano was elected in eight colleges, and no one else was elected in more than three, Cavour included.

Florence between 1848 and 1860, these southerners had learned to despise their less fortunate brethren who had stayed at home. Now they were back again at Naples with Farini, and 'modestly believed that there was nothing good here except themselves, and held our provinces to be ungovernable, degraded and immoral'.[1] They also had a particular grudge against the Garibaldians which they were determined to repay, for Garibaldi had first succeeded at Naples where they had failed, and then had managed to govern without resorting to their help as much as they would have liked. Unfortunately, these frustrated and embittered men were those upon whom Cavour chiefly relied for advice, and they soon filled all the important departmental posts in Farini's government.

The manner in which Garibaldi's last days in Naples had been so spoiled by a sense of neglect and ingratitude gave the worst possible start to the new viceroy. Cavour protested he was sorry for this, but, if he spoke true, he must have realized too late the dangerous consequences of his own policy. He had received numbers of warnings, both from his own friends in the south and also from leading statesmen in other countries, that he must prevent Garibaldi appearing as a victim. But in practice he found it impossible simultaneously to depreciate Garibaldianism and to pacify Garibaldi. On this dilemma his policy came to grief. Nor did he even try very hard to resolve it. For he had made up his mind in advance that it would be impolitic if not impossible to make the least compromise in substance. The first day of the new regime in Naples revealed to Elliot that there was 'serious dissatisfaction among some classes' at the treatment given to the dictator, for which the 'Ministers cannot be acquitted of want of consideration and generosity'.[2] Cavour's lack of generosity or understanding in this matter comes out particularly in small points from his private correspondence, for example in his innuendo about the volunteers who had been eager only to hold exalted rank and skulk behind the lines in the gay society of Naples.[3] What seemed an unnecessarily rigid scrutiny was now applied to those volunteer officers who wanted to transfer or return to the regular army; only about a quarter were admitted, after long delay. Survivors of the original Thousand fared

[1] Ed. G. Romano, *Memorie politiche di Liborio Romano*, 1873, pp. 97–8.
[2] 9 November, Elliot to Russell (F.O. 70/321/625).
[3] 26 October, Cavour telegram to Persano (*CC Lib. del Mezz.* vol. III, p. 190).

better, and sixteen of them eventually became regular generals; but for most of the others, the impression was all too common that they were undesirables, who had joined Garibaldi for their own private amusement, and whose very existence constituted a sign of disrespect to General Fanti and his colleagues. On the other hand, the former Bourbonist officers, since they came from a regular army even if a defeated one, were sometimes taken on more readily, and had their promotions confirmed even when these had been won in fighting against the Garibaldians. There was a widespread sense of disgust even among the conservatives when the traitor Nunziante at once became a general in the Sardinian army.[1]

Another point of ungenerosity which did not go unnoticed was that Pallavicino had a high order bestowed on him by the king, while Mordini, who had been a prodictator for longer, and was in exactly the same position except that he was not a marquis and had been more loyal to the dictator's wishes, was offered none. Garibaldi wrote to expostulate with Pallavicino, saying that he had thought him above accepting such a reward in these circumstances. Mordini then tried to smooth over the slight by saying that he personally did not want any decoration. But foreign newspapers, notably *The Times* and the *Débats*, seized on this and other signs of political discrimination and ingratitude to impugn the government. Even Pallavicino had to protest to Cavour that none of his own recommendations for public recognition were acted upon by Farini. Garibaldi's ministers had been moderate enough, and Farini's neglect of them was now taken—as was certainly intended —to be a deliberate discourtesy. Small wonder if the Garibaldians, many of whom had sacrificed everything for Italy, became a focus of discontent in the *regno*.

One particular source of embarrassment was the inability to explain why Cavour was not accompanying the king to Naples and Palermo, for the two had gone together to Milan and Florence and the other regional capitals on similar occasions in the past. Legend has it that Cavour's absence was due to 'an exquisite sense of delicacy towards the dictator';[2] but it may be doubted if his views in reality were either so simple or so considerate. For a while he had debated whether he ought

---

[1] 28 November, La Farina from Naples to Cavour (*CC Lib. del Mezz.* vol. III, p. 396).
[2] I. Nazari-Micheli, *Cavour e Garibaldi nel 1860*, 1911, p. 187.

to go and see at first hand the facts on which to base a policy for the south. Perhaps if he had gone he might have realized the need to modify his attitude in detail. Upon consideration, however, he began to fear that he could not increase his reputation at Naples, but only lose it with nothing to gain thereby, and this would be a disaster for himself as well as for the country.[1] He gave two other excuses to Lady Holland when she pleaded with him to come and see things for himself: first, the dangers of the diplomatic situation; and second, the fact that the Garibaldians at Naples had an 'absurd antipathy' towards him.[2] But these were hardly satisfactory as explanations, because by the beginning of November both France and Britain had assured Piedmont against an Austrian invasion, and Garibaldi had already intimated that he would rather hand over his command to Cavour than to Farini.[3] More plausible than these semi-public explanations is the remarkable excuse which Cavour gave privately to Farini on 9 November:

the king does not like me, and is jealous; he puts up with me as a minister, but is glad when I am not at his side. Also La Rosa [the king's mistress] is at Naples, and my arrival there would irritate her.... As the representative of the monarchical principle I am ready to sacrifice for the king my life and everything I own; but as a man I ask of him but one favour, to remain as far away from his person as possible.[4]

This was a statement which carries some conviction with it, for seldom is one more sure of having Cavour's genuine thoughts than when he was writing in private to a close friend with a letter that could not have been intended to leak out into general currency. It is the more interesting to note that Farini in reply quite discounted this particular argument, and repeated an urgent request that Cavour should come south himself. In the next few days the prime minister had confirmation severally from Farini, Montezemolo, La Farina, Cordova, Mancini and his own minister of justice Cassinis, that his presence at Naples was 'absolutely necessary' for the successful solution of the southern question; and all of these men had the advantage over him of basing

[1] 14 December, Cavour to Cassinis (*Lettere di Cavour*, ed. Chiala, vol. IV, pp. 122–3).
[2] *c.* 4 November, Cavour to Lady Holland at Naples (*ibid.* vol. VI, p. 642).
[3] 21 October, Mancini to Cavour (*CC Lib. del Mezz.* vol. III, pp. 160–1).
[4] 9 November, Cavour to Farini (*ibid.* p. 302).

their advice on first-hand evidence about conditions at Naples and the king's state of mind.[1] All his most trusted correspondents in Naples were thus at one in giving him the same advice. But Cavour remained adamant in the face of these petitions. He gives the impression of being nonplussed, of having no solution to offer the south for the moment except the unpopular one of repression, and hence of preferring to stay at home to preserve his reputation for the public good. Because of this he never broadened his experience by travelling to the centre or south to see for himself the new Italy which he had done so much to create; and the result was that no long-term policy for the south had been worked out by the time of his death. In two hours' conversation with Lacaita, 'Cavour acknowledged that he knows the people, the country, the laws, etc. of England much better than he does those of Naples, and had therefore to rely on the information given by the exiles'.[2] Worse still, his presence in Turin, while the king was in Naples and Sicily, created a dangerous duality of government. Cavour said he had foreseen this; and he also said that he had known before Victor Emanuel left Turin that it was a great mistake to let the king go off at all.[3] These were surprising admissions to make. Past precedents showed clearly that Victor Emanuel was almost bound to adopt a distinct policy of his own, and in practice Cavour was hardly going to be able to make his own wishes prevail even by repeated threats of resignation. In one case power was divorced from responsibility, in the other it was divorced from a knowledge of the relevant facts; and the combination of the two was most regrettable in this critical hour of Italian history.

Victor Emanuel and Farini were thus allowed to go and lose their reputations instead. Even before they could arrive in Naples the general impression was growing that the results of the plebiscite were untrustworthy, and hence that both the basis and the justification for their power were insecurely founded. Among people who had personally

---

[1] 14 November, Farini to Cavour (*ibid.* p. 321); 13 November, Montezemolo to Cavour (*ibid.* p. 318); 13 November, La Farina to Cavour (*ibid.* p. 320); 14 November, Mancini to Cavour (*ibid.* pp. 330–1); 20 November, Cassinis to Cavour (*ibid.* pp. 349–54); 23 November, Cordova to Cavour (*ibid.* p. 372).

[2] 8 December, diary of Lacaita (*An Italian Englishman*, ed. C. Lacaita, p. 157).

[3] 16 December, Cavour to Cassinis (*CC Lib. del Mezz.* vol. IV); 23 December (*ibid.*); 23 December, Cavour to Farini (*ibid.*).

observed the proceedings at Naples, there were some who had never been deceived. Admiral Mundy noted that 'under regulations such as those I must chronicle my opinion that a plebiscite by universal suffrage cannot be received as a correct representation of the real feeling of a nation'.[1] Elliot, who did not underestimate the immediate wish for annexation, still thought that 'the vote has been the most ridiculous farce imaginable, and there was never even a pretence of confining it to those who were qualified, people of all countries and all ages and both sexes having had no difficulty in recording their voice'.[2] A third British citizen who witnessed the voting was the public orator of Cambridge University, W. G. Clark, and he said much the same: 'Cavour made a flaw in his claim by resting it on a successful repetition of that French juggling imposture which is as discreditable to statesmen as the miracle of San Gennaro is to priests.'[3] As a device it had served well enough its primary ·purpose: it had given Louis Napoleon to imagine that a unitary state was the will of the people, and therefore could not be gainsaid without peril. But in the process it had also deceived Cavour into adopting a more high-handed attitude than the situation warranted or than he could properly afford. The king, on the other hand, quickly learnt the true state of affairs from what he saw on the spot. Victor Emanuel 'had thought to come at the call of the whole population', and was disillusioned to discover that 'he is here as a conqueror'. By 6 November what he had seen of the provinces had changed his mind about the significance of the plebiscite. 'His Majesty seemed perfectly aware of the little value it deserves as an evidence of the deliberate wishes of the Nation.'[4] Here was another reason for the two leading representatives of united Italy—monarch and minister— falling out of step with each other.

The king's government certainly came into a bad inheritance. As Farini put it, 'I had to take over the legacy of Garibaldi, that is to say many debts, no money in the exchequer, thirty or forty thousand undisciplined soldiers, and some of the provinces in sedition'.[5] But it

---

[1] 22 October, diary of Mundy (*H.M.S. Hannibal at Palermo and Naples*, p. 258).

[2] 30 October, Elliot to Russell (RP G.D. 22/85).

[3] W. G. Clark, 'Naples and Garibaldi', in F. Galton, *Vacation tourists in 1860*, 1861, p. 65.   [4] 6 November, Elliot to Russell (F.O. 70/321/627).

[5] 29 December, Farini to Cavour (*CC Lib. del Mezz.* vol. IV).

made matters worse that Farini arrived without the least idea of what he was going to do. In the same way as he had left Turin without knowing what attitude he should maintain towards the Bourbons, so he had not even settled with Cavour what powers his viceregal government should possess on arrival at Naples.[1] One is reminded of the way La Farina was sent to Sicily in June, with no very clearly defined policy to carry out, and yet with sufficient powers to tie the hands of the home government and do a lot of mischief. The citizenry had been led to expect sudden and important provisions from Farini, but days now went by without a single enactment of any sort, and it soon emerged clearly that the new government had no panacea. A week had not gone by before there were cries in the street of 'Down with Victor Emanuel, we want Garibaldi', even of '*Viva* Mazzini' and '*Viva* Francesco'. Farini sadly concluded that 'annexation must have been approved by this people not out of warmth of national feeling, but in fear of a Bourbon return and of *Garibaldismo*'.[2] By 14 November he was begging Cavour to replace him with a new governor. Many of the sentiments which had successively weakened people's allegiance to Francesco and Garibaldi were at work once more against Victor Emanuel. The same social revolution which at one point had contributed so much to Garibaldi's original success was breaking out again, this time against the national movement and in the name of the Pope and the Bourbons. As pious Catholics, many elements in the population secretly or openly resented the new secular government which had declared war on the Pope. The rule of Victor Emanuel was to prove more rapacious and before long also more efficient than the old, and it was to be disliked for its efficiency as well as its rapacity by the peasants who formed the enormous majority of the people. From the point of view of the peasants, the landlord class was now more than ever in control; and hence the social counter-revolution represented by the dissolution of the monasteries and enclosure of common lands was to receive official encouragement to an extent that had never been known under the *ancien régime*. The trend of the times was already apparent. By 16 November Farini reported that the beginnings of a Bourbon counter-revolution were perceptible in each of the fifteen provinces,

[1] 3 November, Farini telegram to Cavour (*ibid.* vol. III, p. 273).
[2] 14 November, Farini to Minghetti (*ibid.* p. 328).

and this rebellion was always intimately connected with a peasants' revolt against the well-to-do classes.[1]

It was not surprising that the new regime had enemies; what really surprised people was that it had so few friends. Cordova and La Farina, after their first fortnight in Naples, had to tell Cavour that there was 'a most absolute indifference about the new order of things'; 'a constitutional unitarian party does not exist here'.[2] The ninety-nine per cent majority had dissolved like the morning mist. Cavour had assumed that Garibaldi was despised, and also that Neapolitans would be won over by the glitter, the honour, and the gaiety of the royal court. But he was wrong. With the replacement of Garibaldi by the king, enthusiasm fast ebbed away.[3] The *Re Galantuomo* found that the word *galantuomo* had a specially discreditable meaning in the rural districts of the south, where it was used to describe a landlord who was all too often the local tyrant; and the king now seemed to many people just another bullying overlord who squeezed the country dry for his own entertainment. Three days after his entry into Naples it was reported that 'Victor Emanuel's reception...has not been in the least enthusiastic, though the whole town was anxious for his arrival.'[4] A few days later, George Russell wrote from Naples to his uncle Lord John that there was 'very strong feeling' for the exiled Bourbon king among the lower classes. Victor Emanuel 'is not liked, Cavour is distrusted...Re Galantuomo (a sad misnomer) does nothing to correct this state of things. He cannot succeed in ingratiating himself—at least he does not try to do so.'[5]

The king certainly does seem to have behaved badly. He showed far less attention to the Neapolitans who crowded to see the *panache* of

[1] 16 November, Farini to Cavour (*ibid.* pp. 340–1); and also report of October (*ibid.* p. 81).

[2] 23 November, Cordova from Naples to Cavour (*ibid.* pp. 371–2); 28 November, La Farina from Naples to Cavour (*ibid.* p. 396).

[3] Marc Monnier, *Notizie storiche sul brigantaggio*, 1862, p. 39.

[4] 12 November, Elliot to Russell (RP G.D. 22/85).

[5] November, George Russell to Lord John Russell (RP G.D. 22/73). He went on: 'the Army are unpopular and take no pains to make themselves agreeable to the National Guard or to the people. I suspect that the Government will yet find that they have made a great mistake in disbanding 20,000 Garibaldians, and that they may soon be in want of the help they would have given them.'

majesty, than to his mistress and her children who had accompanied him on his march from Ancona. Whereas Garibaldi and the Bourbon monarchs had moved about freely and naturally among the people, Victor Emanuel thought it was expected of him to be splendid and dignified, and so secured the reputation of being proud and remote. His private opinion of the Neapolitans was that they were 'canaille',[1] an opinion which he no doubt embroidered freely in his special brand of unregal language. Mercifully his coarser remarks would have been unintelligible to most people for being in his own peculiar vulgar tongue. He only intended to stay in the south for form's sake, until the fall of Messina and Gaeta had testified to his valour and enhanced his renown. Meanwhile, he went coursing in his new hunting estates almost every day, only appearing in the city for an occasional half-hour. As one shopkeeper told George Russell, 'if he can find better shooting than we can give him he will soon be off'. The British consul, Bonham, wrote: 'during the stay His Majesty has made in Naples he has become extremely unpopular, indeed against the Piedmontese in general there prevails a strong feeling of dislike caused no doubt by the overbearing manner in which they treat the Neapolitans'.[2] Before very long Lacaita had to conclude that 'the sooner the king goes away the better';[3] and Cavour was again informed that 'the friends of annexation are in a very small minority. You must not be deceived by the results of the recent plebiscite, which were due to the general abomination of the perjured dynasty, the aversion to Mazzinianism...and in some part to intimidation.'[4]

From the various reports which came in, Cavour eventually made up his mind that the king had 'lost his prestige' and should return home at once, since his presence at Naples 'made all government impossible'. In the first place there was this swift waning of the king's reputation with the Neapolitans, in the second there was the deviation of his policy from that of the cabinet. Whereas Cavour had laid down a plan of 'no compromise', the king had been so impressed with Garibaldi's loyal resignation that he pledged his word to show gratitude and justice to

[1] 9 December, Victor Emanuel to Cavour (*CC Cavour-Nigra*, vol. IV, p. 287).
[2] 27 December, Bonham to Russell (F.O. 70/322/69).
[3] 22 December, Lacaita to Russell (RP G.D. 22/85).
[4] *c.* 27 December, Lacaita to Cavour (C. Lacaita, *An Italian Englishman*, p. 159).

all who had aided the making of Italy.[1] As a first step, 'le Roi...en se sentant fort de l'amour de tout le peuple Italien et de l'autorité que lui a donné, il croyait devoir effacer tout souvenir des anciennes factions et divisions libérales en amnistiant le peu de condamnés politiques'.[2] But this would have included the dreaded Mazzini himself, and the cabinet at Turin urgently and unanimously sent word back that such an amnesty could not be permitted. There was a second sign of weakening when the king first met Mordini; for though Victor Emanuel had intended to be severe, this 'Mazzinian firebrand' turned out to be a far milder and more sensible man than he had expected, and Mordini in fact was given permission to go back and rule in Sicily for another three weeks until the royal party could reach Palermo. Cavour was amazed, and sent a brusque reminder that the king was a constitutional monarch who should not act like this on his own authority; at all costs the sovereign had to keep out of 'the impure hands of Mordini'. As a third cause of dispute, the king more than once publicly reproached General Fanti for the lack of generosity shown by the army to the volunteers.[3] Here again Victor Emanuel probably showed more common sense than his advisers; but the conflict of policy thus revealed, though it was implicit in Cavour's original pronouncements, was intolerable. Cavour again, and this time Fanti as well, threatened to resign if the king insisted on showing leniency to the Garibaldians. 'For the love of God', wrote Cavour, 'do not make any more concessions to the party of Crispi and Garibaldi, or else government will become impossible in Sicily.'[4]

Farini's counterpart in Sicily was the Marquis di Montezemolo, a Piedmontese noble who had married a Russian princess. He was chosen for this job because La Farina had told Cavour that Sicily, being so thoroughly aristocratic, wanted a change from the vulgar lawyers and soldiers of fortune who had lately lain so heavily on Palermo society. Montezemolo—so Cavour from a comfortable distance assured the

[1] 31 October, Victor Emanuel to Garibaldi (*CC Lib. del Mezz.* vol. III, p. 240).

[2] 12 November, Farini to Minghetti (*ibid.* pp. 315–16).

[3] 12 November, Farini to Cavour (*ibid.* p. 316); 25 November, Cassinis to Cavour (*ibid.* p. 378).

[4] 25 November, Cavour telegram to Farini (*ibid.* p. 376); 29 November, Cavour to Cassinis (*ibid.* p. 399).

king early in November—was eagerly awaited in Sicily 'as a Messiah'. But after his arrival at the beginning of December he proved to be only little less of a failure than Farini on the mainland. As formerly governor of Nice at the time of its cession, his appointment to Sicily was read as yet another deliberate insult to Garibaldi; and the fact that Cordova and La Farina were nominated his two chief assistants to take over from Mordini is proof that injury and insult were intended. These appointments by Cavour were no casual oversight of a busy man. He was warned that they were unwise.[1] Cordova had himself protested that Garibaldi would take such nominations amiss, but the protest was overruled.[2] The king, too, was 'furious' at having to be accompanied by La Farina on his official visit to Sicily; but again Cavour, judging matters from afar, stood quite firmly upon his dignity, and threatened to resign if there was the least concession on this point.[3] It was important for Cavour to have the 'annexationists' in charge when the time came, to 'make the elections' in the New Year, and he did not stop to think that he might be acting to defeat his own purpose. Before those elections could ever be held, Cordova and La Farina had been forced out of power by a convincing demonstration of public opinion, with the national guard almost at open blows with the police. Such tactless appointments only convinced the radicals and autonomists that official statements about concord and compromise were but empty words.[4] Amari was a friend of Cordova and La Farina, but he referred to their selection at this critical time as 'des imprudences impardonables'. When the king arrived at Palermo, he found that the country was far more settled and better ordered than La Farina had ever allowed Cavour to believe.[5] But then a few weeks of the new regime sufficed, just as at Naples, to arouse the old antagonisms and to quench much of the enthusiasm for unity which Garibaldi had aroused; and by the end

[1] 2 November, Lanza (Speaker of the Lower House) to Castelli (*Le carte di Lanza*, ed. de Vecchi, vol. II, p. 179).

[2] Ed. V. Cordova, *Filippo Cordova...Discorsi...Scritti...Ricordi*, 1889, vol. I, pp. 109–10.

[3] 25 November, Cavour to Cassinis (*CC Lib. del Mezz.* vol. III, p. 375); 26 November, Cavour to Cassinis (*ibid.* p. 386).

[4] 15 December, Mordini to Garibaldi (AMB).

[5] 9 December, Victor Emanuel to Cavour (*CC Cavour-Nigra*, vol. IV, p. 287); 7 December, Victor Emanuel telegram to Cavour (*Lib. del Mezz.* vol. IV).

of the year it was apparent that Sicily was repenting of annexation.[1] This was in part due simply to ignorance, tactlessness and lack of imagination. The wrong people were selected for the job, and they set about their work the wrong way. At root it was also a simple failure of generosity, and this was a commodity which would have cost little.

Of course there was great depression in ministerial circles at Turin over these unforeseen difficulties. The northern press had taken for granted that annexation would solve all problems in the south, and was now thoroughly perplexed. Cavour tried to pass off on the inquisitive young Baron Holstein an impression that all was well;[2] but he really knew that the situation was very serious indeed. His immediate reaction when he heard of southern resistance was to outline a policy of 'thorough'. He had omitted to work out any constructive programme before Farini set out for Naples; and now it was too late, because this early appearance of public discontent compelled him to use the method of repression. He had to insist once more with the king that there should be no compromise at all. It was 'absolutely necessary' that Piedmontese laws should be introduced at once, without waiting for parliament; and if the local advisory panel of Neapolitans objected to this, then the panel should be dissolved forthwith. He explained that the grenadiers were there to help enforce this plan if necessary. Cavour's intention was quite clear, and did not admit of any discussion: it was 'to impose unity on the most corrupt and weak part of Italy'; and there should be no hesitation in using force for this if necessary.[3] There was no reason why Farini should allow the existence of a free press.[4] Opposition could not be tolerated, for the national cause itself was at stake.[5]

It is not a mere question of a ministerial crisis, but of saving the country from a tremendous catastrophe. If, when parliament opens, they can say

[1] 2 January 1861, Montezemolo to Cavour (*Lib. del Mezz.* vol. IV); 4 January 1861, Cordova to Cavour (*ibid.*).

[2] 8 December, Cavour to Lanza (*Lettere di Cavour*, ed. Chiala, vol. IV, p. 111).

[3] 14 December, Cavour to Victor Emanuel (*CC Cavour-Nigra*, vol. IV, pp. 292–3, heavily mutilated in Chiala's version); 16 December, Cavour to Farini (*Lib. del Mezz.* vol. IV).

[4] 15 December, Minghetti (minister for internal affairs) to Farini (*Lib. del Mezz.* vol. IV).

[5] 18 December, Cavour to Victor Emanuel (*Cavour-Nigra*, vol. IV, p. 294).

that Garibaldi governed southern Italy better than we, then we shall be ruined...; and this may bring about the collapse of the moderate party, and leave Italy sliding down the slope towards revolution.[1]

Once again he repeated that force must be used at the least sign of disorder; and he added that northerners must be brought in to administer the south, however much the local inhabitants complained. 'The government had to destroy Garibaldi's prestige.'[2] If Neapolitans now did not want unification, then unification must be imposed on them; and 'better a civil war than an irreparable catastrophe'.[3] A terrifying prospect was thus opened up.

Goaded by these injunctions, Farini made some effort to speak sharply to the king. He even permitted himself what he called the 'gross illegality' of deporting a number of people to the islands. He was appalled to find that there were hardly any liberals at all throughout the south, and 'there were less than a hundred believers in national unity among seven million inhabitants'.[4] Cavour criticized Farini for making concessions to the autonomist party, just as the king was criticized for making concessions to the Garibaldians. At Turin the other ministers in the cabinet were unanimous that he 'should not give way one inch', and they could not even see that there was any difficulty about this.[5] But Farini found that things looked more difficult from close at hand than from the blurred and distant prospect of five hundred miles away. He and Montezemolo had the full resources of Piedmont behind them, soldiers, police, money, the best brains in Italy, the king with all his authority and prestige—all the advantages in fact which Garibaldi had not possessed—and yet the situation became positively worse in December. Soon there was not a single accusation once made against Garibaldi which was not being levelled at the government of Cavour. Exactly the same complaints were made about disorder, about the appointment of bad administrators, about persecution of opposition leaders, and about rushing through controversial legislation so as to

[1] 23 December, Cavour to Farini (A. Colombo, *La missione di G. B. Cassinis nelle provincie meridionali*, 1911, p. 54).

[2] 8 December, Lanza to Cavour (*Le carte di Lanza*, ed. de Vecchi, vol. II, p. 184).

[3] 14 December, Cavour to Farini (*Lib. del Mezz.* vol. IV).

[4] 12 December, Farini to Minghetti (*ibid.*).

[5] 18 December, Cavour to Devincenzi (*ibid.*).

avoid proper debate. On top of everything else, about 10 December
Farini became seriously ill; but this only made worse a situation that was
already very bad.

By the turn of the year Naples was in a sorry situation. Brigandage
was assuming 'grave proportions' in the Abruzzi;[1] there were frequent
risings with the cry of '*Viva* Francesco II';[2] 'passive opposition' was
growing up everywhere against the system of government by *émigrés*.[3]
The state of public confidence was shown by the fact that government
bonds, which had stood at 112 when Garibaldi arrived, were at 77
by the middle of December and still falling.[4] Some of the liberal-
conservatives at last realized that they might have been slightly wrong
in their estimation of Garibaldi, and that a government which succeeded
his would be inevitably unpopular.[5] Cavour had some hopes that the
king would regain his prestige in the storming of Gaeta. This last-
remaining major Bourbon fortress had been calculated to fall a few
days after the regular troops arrived to take over from the incompetent
Garibaldians, but the calculation proved to be insecurely based. Three
more months were needed before the town surrendered, and the
humiliation of this reverse turned the regular army generals even more
against the volunteers. Before Gaeta eventually surrendered, the king
had had to return home for the opening of parliament.

Domestic disagreements only became worse in the absence of a
national victory which could rally Right and Left in a common act of

[1] 29 December, Valerio telegram to Cavour (*ibid.*).

[2] 10 January 1861, Spaventa to Nigra (*ibid.*).

[3] 14 January 1861, Arrivabene to Nigra (*ibid.*).

[4] *c.* 16 December 1860, Mancini to Cavour (*ibid.*).

[5] 22 December, Lacaita to Russell: 'the appointment of Farini was a great blunder.
He is utterly unfit for the task he has to perform, and is hated by everybody except
a small circle round him....The aristocracy, powerless to build, but powerful to
spread disaffection and disorder, especially in the provinces where they still own most
of the lands, are disgusted to a degree that a small country doctor, as they call Farini,
should be at the head of the government....The Ministers, who ought to have taken
care that the laws should have their execution and have postponed any *radical* changes
till after the meeting of a parliament and the fall of Gaeta, are on the contrary dis-
playing a feverish activity to model everything on the Piedmontese pattern....The
annexationist party diminishes every day, and the Muratist party is making gigantic
strides....The Mazzinian party is also gaining strength....The liberal party, disgusted
with the men in authority, do not come forward to restore order' (RP G.D. 22/85).

rejoicing. It was thus particularly tragic that the Bourbons retained their foothold on Neapolitan soil under French protection; and the radicals were thereby enabled to pour scorn on Cavour's French alliance as something that did not even have the virtue of being realistic. Lord John Russell hoped that Italy would proceed at once to the incorporation of Venice and Rome;[1] and had this been possible the monarchy might well have recovered some of the lost ground, and perhaps would have been able once more to bridge the gap between moderates and radicals. Until quite recently, even Cavour had been hoping that Garibaldi could be harnessed to a Venetian enterprise in the following spring. But now the general was regarded as a dangerous man, whose popularity might overtop that of the king. Moreover, as Naples was turning out to be as much a liability as an asset, it would be asking for trouble if any big new venture were undertaken in foreign policy.

Another problem for the government was that recent events had given the parliamentary opposition new life. By the end of November, Brofferio was boasting that people were beginning to doubt the infallibility of Cavour, and that his overthrow might soon become possible.[2] Pallavicino commented that 'Cavour is reaping what he has himself sown'.[3] For a moment the 'party of action' really did think that there was some chance of unseating the prime minister. Cattaneo rejoiced at the 'enormous diminution' of his 'artificial popularity';[4] and Cairoli was glad to find that people, 'if not cured, were at least convalescent from the Cavourian disease'.[5]

---

[1] 8 December, draft memorandum by Russell for the cabinet: 'in view of these dangers, H.M.'s Government see no prospect of a permanent solution except in the relinquishment by Austria of her rule in Venice' (RP G.D. 22/27); the Queen, when she saw this, 'was astonished', it was 'objectionable' (*ibid.*); on the 11th she wrote to chide her Foreign Minister: 'if *we* are a *little determined* with this *really bad* unscrupulous Sardinian Government and show them that we will *not encourage* or countenance *further piratical* and filibustering proceedings, they will desist, the Queen doubts not' (RP G.D. 22/14); on 14 February, Russell sent E. d'Azeglio congratulations on the fall of Gaeta, and added: 'I trust the entry of the Piedmontese army into Rome will not be delayed beyond this spring or summer' (*CC Ing.* vol. II, part II, p. 188).

[2] 25 November, Brofferio from Turin to ? (MRR).

[3] 25 November, Pallavicino to Caranti (*Le Memorie*, vol. III, p. 655).

[4] 15 December, Cattaneo to Albert Robinson (Archivio Cattaneo MRM).

[5] 11 January 1861, B. Cairoli (the future prime minister) to Bellazzi (MRR).

But the target of their attacks was meanwhile quietly confident that these present difficulties would melt away as soon as the first parliament of all Italy could be opened. This was Cavour's particular brand of utopianism, as admirable, often fully as effective, but sometimes quite as escapist and possibly misleading as Garibaldi's trust in the king, or Mazzini's faith in 'Dio e popolo'. Cavour may have misunderstood Sicily and Naples, but he knew his own strength at Turin; if he was never properly at home in a revolution, he had at least been bred to a skill in parliamentary government. One of the finest statements of his liberalism is dated 29 December:

Pour ma part je n'ai nulle confiance dans les dictatures et surtout dans les dictatures civiles. Je crois qu'on peut faire avec un Parlement bien des choses qui seraient impossibles au pouvoir absolu. Une expérience de treize années m'a convaincu qu'un ministère honnête et énergique, qui n'a rien à redouter des révélations de la tribune, et qui n'est pas d'humeur à se laisser intimider par la violence des partis, a tout à gagner des luttes parlementaires. Je ne me suis jamais senti faible que lorsque les Chambres étaient fermées. D'ailleurs je ne pourrais trahir mon origine, renier les principes de toute ma vie. Je suis fils de la liberté, c'est à elle que je dois tout ce que je suis. S'il fallait mettre un voile sur sa statue, ce ne serait pas à moi à le faire. Si l'on parvenait à persuader aux Italiens qu'il leur faut un dictateur, ils choisiraient Garibaldi et pas moi. Et ils auraient raison.

La route parlementaire est plus longue, mais elle est plus sûre. Les élections de Naples et de Sicile ne m'effrayent pas. On assure qu'elles seront mauvaises: soit. Les mazziniens sont moins à craindre à la Chambre que dans les clubs.... L'atmosphère calme, pesante même, de Turin les calmera....La majorité de la nation est monarchique, l'armée est pure de toute teinte garibaldienne, la capitale est ultra-conservatrice. Si avec ces éléments nous ne nous tirions pas d'affaire, nous serions de grands imbéciles.[1]

[1] 29 December, Cavour to Comtesse de Circourt (*CC Ing.* vol. II, part II, pp. 284–5).

CHAPTER XXVIII

CONCLUSION

The government was going to recover much of its lost ground in the first months of 1861, when by hook and crook the ministerial party won a convincing success in the parliamentary elections. But although Cavour had relied heavily on a victory in parliament, this meeting of a new legislature was not automatically going to bring about the magical results he had expected. Soon afterwards, early in June 1861, Cavour died, still a comparatively young man and at the height of his powers. In the feverish activity of his last months he could never turn his attention properly to the southern question, and when he died he had still not found the time to consider in detail what other policy except a negative repression would serve to integrate these provinces into the old kingdom of Sardinia.

The unhappy state of the south was thus described by a former prime minister of Piedmont, Massimo d'Azeglio, in August 1861:

at Naples we overthrew a sovereign in order to set up a government based on universal suffrage. And yet we apparently need sixty battalions to hold the people down, and it seems that even this number is not enough....

Suffrage or no suffrage, there is no need of battalions of troops this side of the River Tronto, only beyond it. The only conclusion is that there must have been some error in the plebiscite, and we must accordingly change our ideas and our practical policy. We must ask the Neapolitans once again whether or not they do want us there.[1]

Confirmation of this terrible position came in the same month from Diomede Pantaleoni, sent specially by the government to report on affairs in the south:

A unitarian party does not exist at Naples. I would dare to assert that there are not twenty individuals who want national unity, and these are émigrés, or else people who have government posts. The revolution came about because of middle-class hatred against the Bourbons, and because of the

---

[1] 2 August 1861, d'Azeglio to Matteucci (*Massimo d'Azeglio: scritti e discorsi politici*, ed. de Rubris, vol. III, 1938, pp. 399–400).

admiration for Garibaldi.... Many people do not even know who Victor Emanuel is. It was Garibaldi who liberated them, and Garibaldi was a unitarian and proclaimed Victor Emanuel as king. You would have to be mad to think that the people want to be ruled from Turin, or that they are reconciled to the destruction of their former system of local government.[1]

Pantaleoni reported that communications between Naples and the provinces were as often as not completely severed, that conscription could not be worked, that the strongest party in existence without doubt wanted a return of the Bourbons, and that the country could be held down only by force. This was the extremity of disillusion; but it was only the beginning of a four years' civil war.

The situation was not much better in Sicily. As soon as Italy's attention was taken up with the war for Venice, another Sicilian revolution was to break out; another provisional government was set up in Palermo, and it had to be suppressed by an expeditionary army from the north. The high hopes in which people had voted for annexation were being sadly disappointed. In the long run time was going to heal many of these wounds, and national unity in time brought with it material as well as ideological compensations; but the sense of disappointment remained. One Sicilian sorrowfully recalled how, at the time, 'the affirmative vote meant to the great majority the inauguration of an age of economic and social prosperity: no one then imagined it could conceal a new slavery'.[2] Another repented long afterwards that in 1860 he had been so contemptuous of regional autonomy: 'if only we had managed to behave otherwise, we should certainly be happier now.... Forty years have gone by since our annexation, and in almost nothing are we better off, even though they have sucked the very best blood from the veins of Sicily.'[3] Such disgruntled opinions as these may have been immoderate and unfair; but it is not so easy to say that they were unrepresentative or altogether unfounded.

[1] 21 August 1861, Pantaleoni from Naples to Minghetti (quoted by F. Della Peruta, 'Contributo alla storia della questione meridionale', *Società*, vol. VI, no. 1, March 1950).

[2] L. Natoli, *Rivendicazioni attraverso le rivoluzioni siciliane del 1848–60*, 1927, p. 208.

[3] R. Silvo di Pietraganzili, *Il Piemonte e la Sicilia dal 1850 al 1860*, 1903, vol. II, p. 347.

People are generally agreed that the worry of southern Italy, and of Garibaldi's angry, wounding remarks in parliament, were among the contingent causes of Cavour's death. But he died at the very highest point of his success, a few weeks after the existence of a kingdom of Italy had been officially proclaimed and parliament had given him another overwhelming vote of confidence. The heroic age of the *risorgimento* was just ending, and his own name was not to be associated with the prosaic years to come.

By Cavour's own confession the methods he had employed were often irregular. Not for nothing did he acknowledge his debt to Machiavelli as a master of statecraft. His adaptability and tactical resource had proved quite astounding. He had been flexible enough to realize that Mazzini's concept of national unity was more practicable than he had once thought, and he had then outbidden the radicals in his zeal, and outplayed them at their own game of revolution. At the very moment when he seemed most helpless between France on one side and the advancing army of Italian volunteers on the other, he had with exquisite tact threatened Napoleon with Garibaldi, and Garibaldi with Napoleon; so doing, he had neutralized both of them, and had himself intervened as a *tertius gaudens* to inherit the Papal States from one and the whole of southern Italy from the other. He was not content with this. At the very same moment he was sending arms to Hungary, in case he needed a revolution there, either to check an Austrian invasion or to help win Venice.[1] He was even considering the preliminary moves for annexing Trieste, knowing that 'we must sow so that our children may reap'.[2]

All this was a fine example of resourceful opportunism. Armed at all points, most fertile in expedient, he seized and concentrated on every weakness in his opponents: on Garibaldi's *faible* for Victor Emanuel, on

[1] 3 December, Cavour to Count Groppello (*CC Cavour-Nigra*, vol. IV, p. 282); this shows that, at a time when Cialdini was lamenting the lack of equipment in the south, Cavour sent arms to the Danube, hoping to smuggle them into Hungary; when they were captured, he denied all knowledge of them, and tried to put the blame on Garibaldi. The British government knew that Cavour had sent the guns, and was only confirmed by this and by Cavour's denial into thinking him untrustworthy. See Solaroli's note, *Rassegna Storica del Risorgimento*, 1934, p. 1201.

[2] 30 October, Cavour to Valerio (*Lettere di Cavour*, ed. Chiala, vol. IV, pp. 78–9). But for his realistic appreciation of the Slav and German interests in Trieste, see Cavour's letter to Valerio of 28 December (*ibid.* p. 139).

Rattazzi's ambition for power, on the prevalent dread of revolution, on British suspicion of France, and on the fact that Napoleon could neither join with Britain nor oppose her. These were all exploited to good effect. In his treatment of the radicals he knew that they would sacrifice themselves and pay any cost so that Italy became a unified nation. With the conservatives he had to tread more delicately, for his cession to France of their stronghold in Savoy had been a bitter blow. This was no doubt one reason why another *connubio* with the parliamentary Left could only have weakened him.[1] He could rely on the grudging support of the radicals as soon as he accepted their nationalist programme; but he had to win the conservatives at the price of a breach with Garibaldi, by ending the revolution and extending their power throughout the length and breadth of Italy.

Cavour's success had much that was paradoxical about it. Somehow he managed to persuade people to back a revolution on the excuse that this was the way to prevent revolution. He and the whole moderate party had first to swallow the unpalatable doctrines of universal suffrage and popular sovereignty which they abhorred. He found himself justifying a monarchy established 'by will of the people', and the right of rebellion against a regularly constituted government. In the process he had brought good Catholics to the point where they cheerfully sang Te Deums for the invasion of the Papal States. Liberals had likewise been softened until they thought nothing of harsh repression of the opposition press, and countenancing arbitrary arrest without trial.[2] Southerners, who had rebelled in great part because they wanted to be rid of the excessive centralization of government in the city of Naples,[3] had to accept and like an even greater dependence upon

---

[1] 31 October, Cavour to Audinot (MRR 61/66/1).

[2] 5 October, Zambianchi's protest from prison to the governor of Genoa against Cavour's sham boast about Piedmontese liberal institutions (Archivio di Stato, Genoa, *Pratiche Gabinetto* 192); on 8 November he protested again to Minghetti that he had received better treatment than this even in Patagonia and the Papal States, for there you were at least given reasons for your imprisonment (see MSS Minghetti, Bologna); when Farini was asked about this case, he answered that no trial would be necessary, since all the world knew Zambianchi was guilty (see Lilla Lipparini, *Minghetti*, vol. 1, 1942, p. 355).

[3] E.g. even Massari, the most 'Cavourian' of southern deputies, agreed about this; 2 April 1861, Massari in parliament, *Atti Parlamentari.*

remoter Turin. Not least in difficulty, the king had to be in appearance a constitutional king, that is to say he had to do what Cavour wanted, at the same time as he went on thinking himself the real master in charge.[1]

On close inspection Cavour and Garibaldi become—probably like most people—at once greater and lesser than first appearances had suggested; and it was in their least generous and least perceptive side, namely their hostile attitude to each other, that they found one of the mainsprings of action with which to create a unitary state. Upon the tension between these two the fate of Italy for a time depended. If Garibaldi renounced caution and set out for Sicily, a decisive consideration with him was his fury at Cavour's sale of Nice, and his conviction that the government could not be stimulated to remedial action except under the stress of imminent danger. When, later on, he sailed across the Straits to Naples, this was partly so that he might defy the French in Rome, and so overturn the Napoleonic alliance upon which Cavour relied. If Cavour then invaded the Marches, this was because he was frightened that the revolution would reach Rome and even penetrate his own kingdom of Sardinia. In January 1861, Cavour apparently still considered the 'struggle against Garibaldianism' to be his main task.[2]

The two men were temperamentally as well as politically antipathetic. To see how deep a rift lay between them, and how ineffective were the attempts to bridge it, one must reach behind the sentimental legends of later official history. Some people have professed to see no evidence at all that Cavour 'was either hostile, or uncertain, or treacherous in his actions towards the revolutionary forces under Garibaldi', and to find no support for the theory 'that he was ready to make use of them first and then throw them on one side'.[3] The contention of this present book has been almost precisely the opposite. Cavour was sometimes treacherous, often uncertain, and always more or less hostile to Gari-

[1] The king had written an illuminating letter to Prince Napoleon on 14 April 1859, which Luzio published in the *Corriere della Sera* for 17 March 1931: 'Cavour has lost here in the opinion of serious and enlightened people, because of his *fureurs momentanées*, and because of his unlimited trust in people who do not deserve his confidence.... Luckily, I am the master here. I am a king who governs in fact as well as in name.'

[2] 13 January 1861, Cavour to Poerio (*CC Lib. del Mezz.* vol. IV).

[3] I. Nazari-Micheli, *Cavour e Garibaldi nel 1860*, 1911, p. 194.

baldi; and indeed one can almost say that he was *necessarily* all of these things. The rift between them, it is true, was deliberately widened by arrogant diehards on both sides, chief among them La Farina and Bertani, who had too little charity and vision to know what they were doing. It was also exploited by Rattazzi's party at Turin, who used it as an argument for saying that Cavour must resign; and this forced Cavour into opposing Garibaldi the more relentlessly as an enemy of parliamentary government. But fundamentally it represented just the natural division between Left and Right, between rashness and caution, radicalism and conservatism, between the method of the sword and the method of diplomacy. One side believed in all or nothing, while the other saw the value of circumlocution and gradualism. Yet both were necessary for the making of Italy.

Cavour was too clever and too practical a man to be very consistent in his attitude towards the revolution. He had begun by looking on Garibaldi's expedition as reckless folly, doomed to failure like that of the Bandiera brothers several years before. Then he became frightened that it would succeed too well, that it would spoil his own scheme of gradual expansion by Piedmont under the benevolent protection of Napoleonic France. There were some moments when he was afraid that Garibaldi was a puppet of the republicans; others when he feared that the radical leader was representing dictatorial against parliamentary government; at other moments his was just an aristocratic contempt for an uneducated man, for a vulgar soldier who was too big for his boots and with whom one could not carry on ordinary relations as with a responsible adult.[1] Sometimes Garibaldi was to be feared as someone who might betray the monarchy, at other times as someone who was too good a monarchist to be a good parliamentarian, someone to whom the monarchy might owe too much. At all times, however, Cavour was superbly self-confident that he himself was the only man to be trusted with affairs of state. Neither Garibaldi, nor any other person in Italy, Ricasoli and the king included, should in his view have the power of independent initiative, or else disaster would follow.

Not even the events of 1860 were to shake this self-confidence; indeed they only increased it. For four months Cavour had had to submit to a succession of failures, first in not being able to stop Garibaldi

[1] 27 October, Cavour to Mancini (*CC Lib. del Mezz.* vol. III, p. 207).

leaving for Sicily, then in not being able to annex the island after the fall of Palermo, then in La Farina and Depretis failing to tame Garibaldi and prevent him crossing the straits to reach Naples as a conqueror. Up to this point Cavour had played a much less important and much less happy part than is often thought in the movement which conquered half Italy from the Bourbons. He had done more to hinder than to help, basing himself on a bad miscalculation about the political forces at work and the readiness of Italy for nationhood. But finally he had managed to reassert his influence triumphantly over events. He had successfully arrested Garibaldi's advance on Rome, and had ensured the triumph of liberal and centralized monarchy over all the other radical and federalist alternatives put forward by his opponents.

The contribution of the radicals to Italian unification cannot usefully be measured against Cavour's. In his more magnanimous moments Cavour had the perception to see that the radicals were invaluable, even though he had been compelled to discard them like orange peel—to use Garibaldi's expression. The failure of Cavour's party to win or even to start a revolution in either Palermo or Naples is the best indication of what Italy owed to the revolutionaries. Cavour was wont to look upon them as unpractical ideologues; but the real ideologues were rather the moderate liberals in Sicily and Naples who talked and did little but await the issue of events; not the perhaps extravagant thinkers who acted and bore the burden and heat of the day's labour. The moderates could not easily forgive their own failure to rise and deliver themselves, and this did not make them take any more kindly to being liberated by people they called 'thieves' and 'assassins'.[1] But one must remember that the very word 'moderate' was often claimed merely for propaganda purposes by people who were bigots in their moderation, and who were sometimes a match for any extremists in violence of language. They are often better described as 'conservatives'. They were trimmers, sometimes for worthy, sometimes for unworthy motives, people who lacked strong views and clearness of aim, people who for the most part lacked drive, fire and audacity. Italy owed them a great deal, but not everything.

[1] 3 November 1861, V. Imbriani to Emma Herwegh (*Felice Orsini e Emma Herwegh*, ed. Luzio, 1937, pp. 117–21).

It was Garibaldi, Crispi and Bertani who took on themselves the principal risk and responsibility of failure over this revolution in the south. These radical enthusiasts would have been mercilessly killed had they failed, and as mercilessly condemned by Italians and by history. As events turned out, it was their misfortune to be blamed even for their success. Cavour was always quite ready to disown them, and indeed he even expected to do so; and they knew as much and were content. Looking ahead to Aspromonte and Mentana one can see what might easily have happened in 1860. Cavour's successors twice allowed or incited Garibaldi to risk his life and the future of Italy, but subsequently had to order their troops to fire upon and wound him, to arrest him and his men, and then to cover him with the obloquy of failure. This was what Garibaldi knowingly risked again and again. If he had been ambitious for himself, his conduct would not have been so admirable; but he was in everything unostentatious, not least in his graceful surrender of office in November; and when in April 1861 Musolino proposed in parliament to make him a gift from the nation, this proposal had to be withdrawn at Garibaldi's own wish. If he had not dutifully obeyed the king, this too would have made him lack something of greatness. But he was as loyal in obedience as he was resolute in command. There were many of the trappings of vulgar dictatorship about him; and yet one must not leave out of account how he impressed men of intellect as well as of action with his claims to be considered a liberal and essentially a good man.

Garibaldi's chief service to his country in 1860 was as a fighter. He still remains probably the greatest Italian general of modern times. He had a fine instinct for strategy, and a better grasp on most elements of the art of war than his critics have often allowed. The regular generals derided his contempt for passwords and uniforms and punitive discipline; but when all is said and done, it needed very remarkable teamwork and leadership to raise and provide for forty thousand soldiers,[1] and his great enthusiasm and will-to-win brought Italy her finest military victories of the whole *risorgimento*.

As a civil governor Garibaldi suffered from being unintelligent, inexperienced and prone to take bad advice; but when he really turned

[1] At least one close spectator refused to believe the legend that Garibaldi was a bad organizer (Gustav Rasch, *Garibaldi e Napoli nel 1860*, ed. Emery, 1938, p. 107).

his attention to a point, one cannot help being impressed with what Marc Monnier called his 'rare bon sens qui lui tient lieu de science et d'art politique'.[1] As an administrator he does not compare so very unfavourably with Farini, who had far greater experience, far greater resources, and no military distractions to take away his attention. Despite the arrogant conviction of the moderates that they were the only repository of political wisdom and skill, it seems that Sicily was more anarchical after Montezemolo than after Mordini. In May 1860 the good sense and right political instincts of Garibaldi had served Italy better than the wiles of Cavour. In June and afterwards it was his resistance to Cavour's policy of immediate annexation which made possible the acquisition of central and southern Italy. And finally, looking back in the light of later events, it is not so clear now as it was to Cavour that annexation was better obtained by plebiscite alone without the aid of a consultative assembly.

Garibaldi had an instinctive understanding of some southern problems, an understanding which often escaped observers in the north. Unlike the Piedmontese conservatives, for instance, he had the good sense to see that Mazzini presented no danger to law and order in Naples, except perhaps in so far as the 'moderates' might stir up popular riots against him. Garibaldi understood both Mazzini and the south better than Cavour ever did, for the same reason that he had much more knowledge of and sympathy with the common people. Instead of assuming that southerners were idle and corrupt, and instead of trying to impose a cut-and-dried system upon them, he had worked by appealing to their good nature; and this had evoked a far more positive response than greeted his more technically efficient successors. What he gave them was enthusiasm, faith in a cause, and a fine example of self-sacrifice and courage. These were the very qualities which Mazzini all along had said were necessary for making Italians conscious of their strength, for making them politically conscious and politically responsible. Mazzini's chief objection to the Cavourian system was that it did not start by teaching the nation an awareness of its nationhood, and did not go on to persuade the common people that they ought to co-operate in building their own nation. The party of Cavour was in

[1] 10 September, Marc Monnier, *Garibaldi: histoire de la conquête des deux Siciles*, pp. 302–3; 15 September, p. 312.

general ignorant and frightened of the common people, and preferred to impose its will with the aid of diplomacy, rather than to rouse this sleeping giant and give it ideas above its station.

Once again here was evidence of the sheer practicality of the radical idealists. By comparison, the stolid opposition of southern peasants in 1861 was to show the essential unpracticality of the hard-headed men who worked more by calculation and 'interest'. In comparing the liberal with the radical method, one must first remember that diplomacy exacted a price, Savoy and Nice in exchange for Tuscany; and as a second point, that the radicals in southern Italy had proved the common people to be a superb initiating force. In the eyes of the populace Garibaldi was a hero who brought out the best in them. He stood for all that seemed good in the *risorgimento*, all that was heroic, romantic, honest, and 'popular' in the sense of 'of the people'; while Cavour, for all his skill and success, stood for many of its worst aspects, for what was matter-of-fact, for duplicity, lack of generosity, for shady bargains with Louis Napoleon, and all that was double-faced and deceitful. Early in 1861 some of the deputies had to conclude that Garibaldi would not have been so bad after all as a royal viceroy in the south; and though historians have usually ridiculed Garibaldi's offer to take this post, he could hardly have done much worse than Farini and most of his many successors. At least there would probably have been a more friendly and enthusiastic spirit in Naples and Sicily. People would not so easily have been able to say afterwards that the great majority of Italian citizens were quite detached from, and uninterested in, the movement for national independence.[1]

The plebiscites in the south rounded off the process by which a kingdom of four or five millions in population became one of twenty-two millions. The radical Crispi could fairly claim that 'what you call our "faction" has shed its blood for the cause of national unity and presented half Italy to the house of Savoy'.[2] Crispi himself had a great future to look forward to in the new kingdom of Italy; but Garibaldi and Mazzini now found that their work was mostly done. Garibaldi returned to his bees and his beans on the island of Caprera, Mazzini

[1] E.g. Benito Mussolini, in his speech of July 1943 to the Fascist Grand Council, quoted by himself in his booklet *Il tempo del bastone e della carota*, 1944, p. 18.
[2] 7 September 1860, Crispi to Correnti (ACP, f. 135).

sadly went back into exile at London. In February 1861 Mazzini wrote a memorandum in English for the British foreign minister, protesting against Cavour's 'rancour against all other parties and men, and innate antagonism to popular interference and all that he calls *revolutionary*'.[1] It was bitter for this visionary to see that materialism had succeeded to idealism. He had thought to evoke the soul of Italy, he said, but all he now found before him was its corpse. And yet Mazzini's faith in the future remained as clear and confident as ever. 'Our nationality is not a thing merely of square miles but of ideas and principles. And as soon as Italy will learn that she may proceed in her work with the whole of her forces and shielded from Bonapartist interference, she will desert the policy of Cavour for a better and more dignified one.' This was the faith which, in one very real sense, removed mountains. The combination of square miles and idealistic principles together made up a force which was unbeatable.

Meanwhile, the only consolation left to the radicals was perhaps to say 'I told you so'. Long after the event, Jessie White Mario, who had been one of Garibaldi's entourage in Sicily and Naples, wrote that

to the violent, hurried annexation of the southern provinces was due all the series of disorders and the unhappiness which ensued. If only these provinces had been administered sensibly and kindly by persons sympathetic to the people, as Tuscany was for example, there would have been none of that boycotting of conscription in Sicily, nor the brigandage which raged in the Napoletano.[2]

This was only part of the truth, but it was an important part; and the storm of recrimination between moderates and extremists on this point was to remain a constant theme of Italian politics.

[1] 19 February 1861, Mazzini to Russell (RP G.D. 22/73).
[2] J. W. Mario, *In memoria di Giovanni Nicotera*, 1894, p. 49.

INDEX

[NOTE: The letter *q* appended to a page-number indicates that the page contains a quotation from the person who is the subject of the entry; but this is limited to a few of the leading persons and their more significant statements.]

29-2